EARLY MODERN ENGLAND 1485–1714

To our parents, with gratitude and love:

Lillian Aguirre Bucholz
in memory of Robert Edward Bucholz

Cornelia Buck Key
H. Newton Key

EARLY MODERN ENGLAND 1485–1714

A NARRATIVE HISTORY

ROBERT BUCHOLZ AND NEWTON KEY

Blackwell Publishing

BLACKWELL PUBLISHING
350 Main Street, Malden, MA 02148-5020, USA
9600 Garsington Road, Oxford, OX4 2DQ, UK
550 Swanston Street, Carlton, Victoria 3053, Australia

First published 2004 by Blackwell Publishing Ltd
5   2007

Library of Congress Cataloging-in-Publication Data

Bucholz, R. O., 1958–
Early modern England, 1485–1714: a narrative history / Robert Bucholz and
Newton Key.
p. cm.
Includes bibliographical references and index.
ISBN 0–631–21392–9 (alk. paper) — ISBN 0–631–21393–7 (pbk : alk. paper)
1. Great Britain – History – Stuarts, 1603–1714.
2. Great Britain – History – Tudors, 1485–1603.
3. England – Civilization. I. Key, Newton. II. Title.

DA300.B83 2003

942.05—dc21   2002156117

ISBN-13: 978-0-631-21392-5 (alk.paper)
ISBN-13: 978-0-631-21393-2 (pbk : alk. paper)

A catalogue record for this title is available from the British Library.

Set in 10/12.5 pt Sabon
by Kolam Information Services Pvt. Ltd, Pondicherry, India
Printed and bound in Singapore
by Markono Print Media Pte Ltd

For further information on Blackwell Publishing, visit our website:
www.blackwellpublishing.com

Contents

List of Plates   vii

List of Maps   ix

Preface   x

Acknowledgments   xiii

Conventions and Abbreviations   xiv

Introduction: England and its People, ca. 1485   1

1   Establishing the Henrician Regime, 1485–1525   31

2   (Dis-)Establishing the Henrician Church, 1525–1536   63

3   Reformations and Counter-Reformations, 1536–1558   88

4   The Elizabethan Settlement and its Challenges, 1558–1585   112

5   The Elizabethan Triumph and Unsettlement, 1585–1603   133

6   Merrie Olde England?, ca. 1603   152

7   The Early Stuarts and the Three Kingdoms, 1603–1642   201

8   Civil War, Revolution, and the Search for Stability,
    1642–1660   238

9   Restoration and Revolution, 1660–1689   265

10 War and Politics, 1689–1714   302

Conclusion: Augustan Polity, Society, and Culture, ca. 1714   340

Notes	377
Glossary	390
Select Bibliography	399
Appendix: Genealogies	411
1 *The Yorkists and Lancastrians*	412
2 *The Tudors and Stuarts*	413
3 *The Stuarts and Hanoverians*	414
Index	415

Plates

1   Diagram of an English manor   18
2   *Henry VII*, painted terracotta bust, by Pietro Torrigiano   42
3   *Henry VIII*, after Hans Holbein the Younger   53
4   Diagram of the interior of a church before and after the
    Reformation   71
5   *Mary I*, by Moro   105
6   J. Foxe, *Acts and Monuments* title-page, 1641 edition   109
7   *Elizabeth I* (The Ditchley Portrait), by Marcus Gheeraerts
    the Younger, ca. 1592   113
8   First Encounter Between the English and Spanish Fleets,
    from J. Pine, *The Tapestry Hangings of the House of Lords
    Representing the Several Engagements Between the English
    and Spanish Fleets*, 1739   136
9   Hatfield House, south prospect, by Thomas Sadler, 1700   160
10 Tudor farmhouse at Ystradfaelog, Llanwnnog,
    Montgomeryshire (photo and groundplan)   167
11 Visscher's panorama of London, 1616 (detail)   187
12 A view of Westminster, by Hollar   188
13 *James I*, by van Somer   207
14 *George Villiers, 1st Duke of Buckingham*, by William Larkin   215
15 *Charles I*, by Van Dyck   219
16 The execution of Charles I   250
17 *Oliver Cromwell*, by Robert Walker, 1649   259
18 The entrance of Charles II at the Restoration, 1660   263

19   *Charles II as Patron of the Royal Society*, by Laroon   271

20   *James II*, by unknown artist   289

21   *Mary of Modena in Childbed*, Italian engraving   293

22   *Presentation of the Crown to William III and Mary II*,
     by R. de Hooge after C. Allard   297

23   *Queen Anne*, by Edmund Lilly   318

24   The battle of Blenheim   326

25   Fighting in a coffee-house after the trial of Dr. Sacheverell   332

26   Castle Howard, engraving   352

Maps

1 The British Isles (physical) today   2
2 The counties of England and Wales before 1972   7
3 Towns and trade   16
4 The Wars of the Roses, 1455–85   34
5 Southern England and western France during the later
   Middle Ages   35
6 Europe ca. 1560   60
7 Early modern Ireland   83
8 Spanish possessions in Europe and the Americas   127
9 War in Europe, 1585–1604   138
10 Early modern London   186
11 The Bishops' Wars and Civil Wars, 1637–60   242
12 Western Europe in the age of Louis XIV   279
13 The War of the Spanish Succession, 1702–14   324
14 The Atlantic world after the Treaty of Utrecht, 1713   335

Preface

The authors of this book recall, quite vividly, their first exposure to English history. If you are like us, you first came to this subject because contemporary elite and popular culture are full of references to it. Perhaps your imagination has been captured by a classic play or novel set in the English past (*Richard III, A Man for All Seasons, Journal of the Plague Year, Lorna Doone*), or by some Hollywood epic which uses English history as its frame (*Braveheart, Elizabeth, Shakespeare in Love, Restoration, The Patriot*). Perhaps you have traveled in England, or can trace your roots to an English family tree (or to ancestors whose relationship to the English was less than happy). Perhaps you have sensed – rightly – that poets and playwrights, Hollwood and tour books have not given you the whole story. Perhaps you want to know more.

In writing this book, we have tried to recall what we knew and what we did not know about England when we first began to study it as undergraduates. We have also tried to use what we have learned over the years from teaching its history to (mostly) our fellow North Americans in a variety of institutions – Ivy League and extension; state and private; secular and sectarian. Thus, we have tried to explain concepts that might be quite familiar to a native of England, and have become familiar to us, but which may, at first, make little sense to you. To help you make your way through early modern England we have begun with a description of the country as it existed in 1485, and included several maps of it and its neighbors. We have highlighted arcane contemporary words and historical terminology in bold on their first use, and tried to explain their meaning in a Glossary. We urge you to use these as you would use maps and language phrase books to negotiate any foreign land. When we introduce for the first time a native of early modern England, we give his or her birth and death dates, where known. In the case of kings and queens, we give the years they reigned. We do this because knowing when someone came of age (or, if he was a Tudor politician, whether or not he managed to survive Henry VIII!) should give you a better idea of what events and ideas might have shaped his or her motivations, decisions, and destiny. Thinking about historical characters as real people faced with real choices, fighting real battles, and living through real events should help you to make sense of the connections we make below and, we hope, to see other connections and distinctions on your own.

The following text is, for the most part, a narrative, with analytical chapters at strategic points to present information from those subfields (geography, topography, social, economic, and cultural history) in which many of the most recent advances have been made, but for which a narrative is inappropriate. That narrative largely tells a story of English politics, the relations between rulers and ruled, in the Tudor period (1485–1603, chapters 1–5) and the Stuart period (1603–1714, chapters 7–10). Chapter 1 includes a brief narrative of the immediate background to the accession of the Tudors in 1485, the Conclusion, a few pages on the aftermath of Stuart rule from 1714. The authors believe, and hope to demonstrate, that the political developments of the Tudor–Stuart period have meaning and relevance to all inhabitants of the modern world, but especially to Americans. They also believe that a narrative of those developments provides a coherent and convenient device for student learning and recollection. Finally, because we also think that the economic, social, cultural, religious, and intellectual lives of English men and women are just as important a part of their story as the politics of the period, we will remind you frequently that the history of England is not simply the story of the English monarchy, or its relations with Parliament. It is also the story of every man, woman or child who lived, loved, fought, and died in England during the period covered by this book. Therefore, we will stop the narrative to encounter those lives at three points: ca. 1485 (Introduction), 1603 (chapter 6), and 1714 (Conclusion).

In order to provide a text which is both reader-friendly and interesting, we have tried to deliver it in prose which is clear and, where the material lends itself, not entirely lacking in drama or humor (with what success you, the readers, will judge). In particular, we have tried to provide accurate but compelling accounts of the great "set pieces" of the period; quotations which will stand the test of memory; and examples which enliven as well as inform while avoiding as much as possible the sort of jargon and minutiae that can sometimes put off otherwise enthusiastic readers. Again, this is all part of a conscious pedagogical strategy born of our experience in the classroom.

That experience has also caused us to realize the importance of "doing history": of students and readers discovering the richness of early modern England for themselves through contemporary sources; making their own arguments about the past based on interpreting those sources; and, thus, becoming historians (if only for a semester). For that reason, we have also assembled and written a companion to this book entitled *Early Modern England, 1485–1714: Sources and Debates* (also published by Blackwell). The preface to that book indicates how its specific chapters relate to chapters in this one.

A word about our title and focus. One might ask why we called our book *Early Modern England*, rather than *Early Modern Britain*? After all, one of the most useful recent trends in history has been to remind us that at least four distinct peoples share the British Isles and that the English "story" cannot be told in isolation from those of the Irish, the Scots, and the Welsh. (Not to mention continental Europeans, North Americans, Africans, and, toward the end of the story, Asians as well.) We agree. For that reason the text contains significant sections on English involvement with each of the Celtic peoples (as well as some discussion of England's relationship to the other groups noted above) in the early modern period, all of which are vital for our overall argument. But we believe that it is the English story that will be of most relevance to Americans at the beginning of the twenty-first century. We believe this, in part, because it was most relevant to who Americans were at the beginning of their *own* story, in the seventeenth and eighteenth centuries. We would argue, further, that English notions of right and proper behavior, rights and responsibilities, remain central to national discourse in both Canada and the United States today. Important as have been the cultural inheritance of Ireland, Scotland, and Wales to Americans, the impetus for the inhabitants of each of these countries to cross the Atlantic was always English, albeit often oppressive. Moreover, brutal and exploitative as *actual* English behavior has often been toward these peoples, the *ideals* of representative government, rule of law, freedom of the press, religious toleration, even a measure of social mobility, meritocracy, and gender equality which some early modern English men and women fought for and which the nation as a whole slowly (and often partially) came to embrace, are arguably the most important legacy to us of any European culture.

Finally, as in our own classes, we look forward to your feedback. What (if anything!) did you enjoy? What made no sense? Where did we go on too long? Where did we tell you too little? Please feel free to let us know at earlymodernengland@yahoo.com. In the meantime, there is an old, wry saying about the experience of living in interesting times. As you will soon see, the men and women of early modern England lived in *very* interesting times. As a result, exploring their experience may sometimes be arduous, but we anticipate that it will never be dull.

Robert Bucholz

Newton Key

Acknowledgments

No one writes a work of synthesis without contracting a great debt to the many scholars who have labored on monographs and other works. The authors are no exception; our bibliography and notes point to some of the many historians who have become our reliable friends in print if not necessarily in person. We would also like to acknowledge with thanks our own teachers (particularly Dan Baugh, the late G. V. Bennett, Colin Brooks, P. G. M. Dickson, Clive Holmes, Michael MacDonald, Alan Macfarlane, the late Frederick Marcham, and David Underdown), our colleagues, and our students (whose questions over the years have spurred us to a greater clarity than we would have achieved on our own). A special debt is owed to the anonymous readers for the press, whose care to save us from our own errors is much appreciated – even in the few cases where we have chosen to persist in them. For advice, assistance, and comment on specific points, we would like to thank Fr. Robert Bireley, S. J., Mary Boyd, Carolyn Edie, Gary DeKrey, David Dennis, Alan Gitelson, Michael Graham, Mark Fissel, Jo Hays, Caroline Hibbard, Theodore Karamanski, Kathleen Manning, Eileen McMahon, Gerry McDonald, Marci Millar, Paul Monod, Philip Morgan, Matthew Peebles, James Rosenheim, Barbara Rosenwein, James Sack, Joe Ward, Patrick Woodland, Mike Young, Melinda Zook, and the members of H-Albion. We are grateful for the support, advice, and efficiency of Tessa Harvey, Brigitte Lee, Angela Cohen, and all the staff at Blackwell. Our immediate family members have been particularly patient and accommodating. We would especially like to thank Laurie Bucholz for keeping this marriage (not Bob and Laurie but Bob and Newton) together. For this, and much more besides, we thank them all.

Conventions and Abbreviations

Currency	Though we refer mainly to pounds and shillings in the text, English currency included guineas (one pound and one shilling) and pennies (12 pence made one shilling). One pound (£) = 20 shillings (s.) = 240 pence (d.).
Dates	Throughout the early modern period the English were still using the Julian calendar, which was 10–11 days behind the more accurate Gregorian calendar in use on the continent from 1582. The British would not adopt the Gregorian calendar until the middle of the eighteenth century. Further, the year began on March 25. We give dates according to the Julian calendar, but assume the year to begin on January 1.
	Where possible, we provide the birth and death dates of individuals mentioned in the text. In the case of monarchs, we also provide regnal dates for their first mention *as monarchs*.
BCE	Before the common era.
CE	Common era.
JP	Justice of the peace (see Glossary).
MP	Member of Parliament, usually members of the House of Commons.

Introduction: England and its People, ca. 1485

Long before the events described in this book, long before there was an English people, the ground upon which they would live had taken shape. Its terrain would mold them, as they would mold it. Therefore, to understand the people of early modern England and their experience, it is first necessary to get to know the geographical, topographical, and material reality of their world. Geography is, to a great extent, Destiny.

This Sceptered Isle

The first thing that most non-British people think that they know about England is that it is an island. Unfortunately, this is not strictly true. England is, rather, the southern and eastern portion of a group of islands (an archipelago) in the North Sea known as the British Isles (see map 1). Though the whole of the archipelago would be ruled from London by the end of the period covered by this book, and though the terms "Great Britain" and "British" have, at times, been applied to that whole, it should never be forgotten that this geographical area is home to four distinct peoples, with their own individual national histories and customs: the English, the Irish, the Scots, and the Welsh.[1] This book will concentrate on the experience of the first of these peoples; however, because that experience intertwines with that of the other three, the following pages address their histories as well.

While the English may share their island, they have always defined themselves as an "island people." That fact is crucial to understanding them, for an "island people" are bound to embrace an "island mentality." One place to begin to understand what this means is with a famous passage by England's greatest poet, William Shakespeare (1564–1616):

> This royal throne of kings, this sceptr'd isle,
> This earth of majesty, this seat of Mars,

Map 1 *The British Isles (physical) today.*

This other Eden, demi-paradise:
This fortress built by Nature for herself
Against infection and the hand of war;
This happy breed of men, this little world,
This precious stone set in the silver sea,
Which serves it in the office of a wall,
Or as a moat defensive to a house,
Against the envy of less happier lands:
This blessed plot, this earth, this realm, this England. (*Richard II* 2.1)

John of Gaunt's dying speech from *The Tragedy of King Richard II* is justly famous, for it says a great deal about how the English view their land. The most obvious point to make about these words (apart from their overt patriotism) is that they portray the water surrounding the British Isles as a barrier. Specifically, England is separated from the mainland of Europe (and France, in particular) by the English Channel, a branch of the North Sea which is about 26 miles wide at its narrowest (see map 1). This is the "moat defensive" which "serves it [England] in the office of a wall."

The Channel has, indeed, served England as a moat against foreign invaders on a number of occasions in its history. As we shall see in chapter 5, in 1588 it prevented invasion by the armies of Philip II, who were to have been transported by the Spanish Armada. In 1805, after the period of time covered by this book, it would block a similar attempt by the armies of Napoleon Bonaparte. And in 1940, within the living memory of some readers, it would frustrate "Operation Sea-Lion," Hitler's plan for invasion and occupation by the forces of Nazi Germany. Thus, the English Channel and Great Britain's island status have been crucial to the preservation of England (and, later, Britain) as a sovereign country, with its own distinct traditions of government and social customs.

Less tangibly, the English have often believed that the English Channel shielded them from continental ways and ideas. One of the most obvious facts about the English is that they are not the French or the Dutch. Their political, social, and cultural institutions developed along different lines from those of their continental neighbors. This has sometimes led the English to believe that they are set apart from those neighbors, a "little world," protected by their watery moat from "infection and the hand of war." To believe that one is set apart, that one's situation is unlike others, is very close to believing that one is unique. This is, in turn, just one step away from believing that one is somehow superior to others, "the envy of less happier lands." Perhaps as a result of this feeling, English governments have sometimes acted, first toward the other inhabitants of the British Isles, and later toward the subjects of a worldwide British Empire, as if "God was an Englishman" and that the remaining inhabitants of the planet had been given by Him to be conquered, exploited, even enslaved, by His chosen people. But, for the most part, the "island mentality" is not so much hostile or aggressive as it is indifferent, or mildly condescending, toward Europe. Hence a famous, if apocryphal, nineteenth-century headline: "Fog in Channel; Continent Cut Off."

But in fact, most of the time, there is no fog in the Channel and England and the continent are not cut off from each other. This brings us to the other side of the watery coin: the "island mentality" is, to a great extent, a sham, for the English Channel has acted as much as a highway or a bridge to Europe as a barrier. For most of human history, before the invention of the airplane or the automobile, the easiest and safest way to get from place to place was by water. It is true that the Channel, and England's control of it, prevented the invasions of 1588, 1805, and 1940. But England faced many other invasions in its history, most of which the Channel *facilitated*. In fact, the early modern English people and the early modern English State were products of successful migrations, indeed invasions, by the Celts from 800 to 200 BCE (before the common era), the Romans in the first century CE (during the common era), the Angles, Saxons, and Jutes in the fifth and sixth centuries, the Danes in the ninth and tenth centuries, the Normans in 1066, and, within the time frame of this book, the Dutch in 1688.

Since all of these people decided to settle in England, the notion of English uniqueness must be qualified by the realization that they were and are like contemporary Americans, a mixture of many different ethnic groups and cultures: those noted above and, more recently, Irish, West Indians, Indians, Pakistanis, and others. The people, the culture, even the language of England are the products of a melting pot. Take, for example, the English language. Today, one will occasionally hear commentators complain of the infusion of new words and phrases, slang or sloppiness of speech emanating from the United States, Canada, Australia, New Zealand, or even parts of Britain itself which are distant in space and attitude from Oxford or London. In their view, these emanations corrupt the "purity" of the Queen's English. The trouble with this view is that the Queen's English was never pure. It is, rather, a mongrel born of and enriched by Celtic, Latin, Anglo-Saxon, Danish, French, and Dutch influences. Moreover, even within England itself (and certainly within the British Isles), it has always been spoken with a wide variety of regional accents, vocabulary, and syntax. In short, the English language has never been set in stone. Rather, it was, and is, a living, evolving construct.

Migrations and invasions are not the only way in which new cultural influences have come to England. Because the British Isles are surrounded by water and water serves as a highway as well as a moat, it was probably inevitable that, in order to defend their country and buy and sell their goods, the English would become seafarers. (Obviously, many of them had to be seafarers to get there in the first place.) This implies a naval tradition in order to protect the islands: one of the themes of this book will be the growth of English naval power. But it also implies a tradition of peaceful overseas trade and the domestic industries that go with it (shipbuilding, carpentry, and cartography, for example). By 1714 the English would be the greatest shipbuilding and trading nation on earth.

The resulting wealth would, in turn, lead to military and naval dominance overseas and industrial growth at home. By the end of the era covered by this book, Great Britain (the State created when England and Scotland united in 1707) would be the most powerful nation in Europe; it would rule an extensive overseas empire; and it would possess the economic base to launch the industrial revolution. Another theme of this book is how England rose from being a puny and relatively poor little country in the fifteenth century to the dominant kingdom in the world's most powerful nation, Great Britain, on the verge of superpower status, in the eighteenth. In the nineteenth century, long after the period covered by this book, that combination of military, naval, and industrial might would make Britain the center of an empire that would cover one-fifth of the globe and rule one-quarter of its people. The legacy of that empire is still ever-present and controversial for the descendants of those who ruled it and those who were ruled by it. So a very great deal came of England's being part of an island.

As this implies, if the "island people" have had a profound impact upon many other peoples, so has contact with those peoples and cultures had a profound influence upon them. English people share with Americans the conviction that "imported" often means "better," whether the item in question is French wine, German automobiles, or Italian art. Indeed, it could be argued that part of the friction that existed between England and France for so much of the period covered by this book was born, on the English side, not of blind hatred or haughty disdain, but of a sometimes sneaking admiration, even envy, for the achievements of French culture.

This Seat of Mars – and Less Happier Lands

Up to this point, we have generally referred to "England," not Britain. Non-Britons sometimes use the terms "English" and "British" interchangeably, but, as indicated above, that is inaccurate – and quite insulting to the four distinct cultures which inhabit the British Isles. These cultures, though dominated from London during most of the last few hundred years, are geographically, ethnically, and culturally distinct.

England, to the south and east, is by far the most populous, the wealthiest and the most powerful country, politically and militarily, in the British Isles. We will explore England's internal geography and topography later in this introduction. For now, the important thing to remember is that it is the part of the British Isles closest to Europe, and was, therefore, the region most easily invaded and colonized. As indicated previously, the land that would come to be known as England was, like the rest of the British Isles, settled by Celtic peoples who came over in many waves prior to about 200 BCE.[2] After this point England's experience differs from that of Scotland to the north, Wales to the west, or Ireland further west across the Irish Sea (see map 1). Because of England's proximity to Europe and relatively mild terrain, it experienced repeated invasions and migrations – by the Romans, by the Angles, Saxons, and Jutes, by the Danes, and by the Norman French. As a result, England developed along a different track from the other lands of the British Isles, for each of these movements brought a new way of organizing society and government, a new language and culture, and, eventually, the assimilation of a new people and their ways.

Specifically, partly in response to the threat of invasion, the people of south-eastern Britain (i.e., England) experienced increasing centralization. During the Anglo-Saxon period (410–1066 CE), a series of strong kings of the dynasty of Wessex (most notably Alfred the Great, who ruled from 871 to 899) established their control over the whole of "Angle-land." In order to do this, and in particular to repel a series of Viking invasions in the ninth and tenth centuries, they had to develop an efficient military and a reliable system of taxation to support it – or to buy off the invaders when they did not choose to fight. Readers of *Beowulf* know that Anglo-Saxon tribal kings had always relied upon small bands of noblemen (eventually called *"thegns"*), associated with their households, for their military force. Alfred, who came to rule not a tribe but a nation, needed a bigger, more national force. Thus, he established an efficient militia or *"fyrd,"* made up of the civilian male population serving in rotation, as well as a strong navy. To pay for their supply on campaign, Alfred's successors developed an efficient land tax, called the *"heregeld."*

Anglo-Saxon kings also sought to create institutions which would enhance their control of England in times of peace. Thus, by 1066, they had established a capital at Winchester and divided the country into about 40 counties or shires (see map 2). Each shire had a "shire reeve" or **sheriff**, who acted on the king's orders to collect the *heregeld* or raise the *fyrd*. He received those orders via royal messages called "writs," which were sent out by the king's chancellor and other secretaries, called clerks, working out of an office later called the Chancery. The yield from taxes was sent to the king's Treasury, known as the Chamber because, at first, the king actually kept this money in his bedchamber. After the Norman Conquest of 1066, William the Conqueror and his successors moved the capital to London, but otherwise embraced this administrative system and improved it. All of these developments tended to make England a more centralized and unified country, and to make the king's authority more efficient and secure.

Nothing like this took place in Scotland, Ireland, or Wales. Being farther away from continental Europe, more mountainous and difficult of access, these regions did not experience large-scale invasions or migrations until much later. Subsequent migratory groups, especially the Normans, launched periodic attempts at individual settlement or invasion, but there was little mass displacement of population, settling down, or intermarriage before about 1150. These lands were therefore not subjected to the cultural clashes and transformations experienced by medieval England. They remained Celtic in culture and, to a great extent, language well into the Middle Ages.

Nor did these countries experience the rise of strong centralized kingship as did England. Once again, their harsher climates, poorer soils, and rougher topography (craggy, boggy, forested) worked against the growth of a central court city, large urban administrative centers, nucleated villages, or easy communication. Rather, people lived in isolated settlements, far from each other. This made it difficult for even a strong ruler to gain the cooperation or loyalty of his subjects. During the Middle Ages there arose a king of Scotland, a high-king of Ireland, and a prince of (Northern) Wales, but most people's loyalty went to their individual tribe or, later,

Map 2 *The counties of England and Wales before 1972.*

their clan. A clan was a political and social unit whose members claimed to be descended from a common ancestor; in practice, many had no blood relationship to each other. Rather, most clansmen were simply the tenants of its chief. Like an extended family, the clan provided sustenance, protection, and a sense of belonging, sometimes over very long distances, in return for loyalty and, especially, military service. This system left no room for a powerful sovereign or overarching "national" institutions. Sometimes, rival clans fought over broad issues such as the Crown of Scotland or the principality of Wales, but more often they clashed over local dominance, land, cattle, or women.

As a result, when the medieval English began to move aggressively into the Celtic lands, there were no strong unifying power or national institutions to stop them. Indeed, some clans found it convenient to collaborate with the English Crown, in order to gain a powerful ally against other clans in local disputes. This disunity and disorganization, combined with the greater wealth and superior organization of the English, eventually enabled them to dominate the whole archipelago – though never easily. For example, after a century of warfare, the principality of Wales was united to England under King Edward I (1239–1307; reigned 1272–1307) by the Statute of Rhuddlan in 1284. In future, there would be a prince of Wales, but he would be the eldest son of the king of England. English criminal law was imposed, though the Welsh were allowed to retain their civil law until the early sixteenth century. The English established government centers at Caernarvon and Carmarthen, divided outlying parts of Wales into shires (see map 2), and filled high government offices with Englishmen. To maintain their authority, late medieval English kings relied on English settlers who displaced the native population from the fertile valley areas to the rugged uplands, as well as powerful nobles who lived along the Anglo-Welsh border and the south coast. This borderland area was known as the Welsh Marches (presumably because of the constant need for marching troops to patrol them) and these nobles came to be known as Marcher lords. Later, under the early Tudors (1485–1547), the Marcher lordships were abolished, the full structure of English counties and sheriffs was imposed, and, after the Reformation, a Protestant Church of Wales was established (see chapter 2). But the Welsh retained their language and many of their cultural traditions. Southern Wales, closest to England, is the most populous and wealthiest part of the country – at the beginning of our period because of its rich farmland, at the end because of its rich coal deposits. Northern Wales is more remote, less populated, less well integrated into the English political and economic system. Today, Wales remains part of the United Kingdom of Great Britain and Northern Ireland and is ruled largely from London. But, since 1998, it has had a separate assembly to decide upon policy and administer some internal affairs.

Scotland resisted absorption by England all through the high medieval (1066–1485) and Tudor (1485–1603) periods despite a smaller population, a poorer economy, and a weaker monarchy.[3] That monarchy had theoretically united the country toward the beginning of the eleventh century. But it had done so, in part, by seeking English help, won through marriage alliances and the assumption of feudal obligations. Moreover, the clans, especially in Scotland's rugged northern Highlands, often paid little attention to the king's wishes and sometimes allied with the English ruler against him. Disputes over royal marriages, the Scottish king's subordinate feudal status, and the clashes of aggressive nobles on both sides of the border often led to wider conflict. In 1295 John de Balliol (ca. 1250–1313; reigned 1292–6) renounced his allegiance to Edward I and launched what became a series of wars for control of the northern kingdom. King Edward defeated the Scots at Dunbar in 1296 and crushed another rebellion led by Sir William Wallace (a.k.a. "Braveheart"; 1272?–1305) in 1303, but the struggle was revived by Robert the Bruce (1274–1329; reigned 1306–29). Bruce's resounding victory over the English at the battle of Bannockburn in 1314 paved the way for the reestablishment of Scottish independence under a Scottish king, a fact which was recognized by the Treaty of Edinburgh of 1328.

The next three centuries saw repeated English attempts to reverse the results of Bannockburn, as well as Scottish attempts to interfere in English politics. As we shall see, the Tudor kings of England sought to control Scotland, sometimes through conquest, sometimes through diplomatic marriage (see chapters 1–4). They did so because they were tempted by Scotland's relative poverty and small population; because they wanted to pacify the 110-mile Anglo-Scottish border; because traitors to the English king could always find refuge with the Scots; and because a hostile Scotland could be used by another power, namely, France, to invade England. Franco-Scottish friendship was so longstanding that it became known as the "Auld Alliance." Finally, in 1603, the Tudor dynasty died out and the king of Scotland, James VI (1566–1625; reigned 1567–1625), became king of England, where he was known as James I and ruled from 1603 to 1625. (For his distant family relationship to the Tudors, see genealogies 2–3, pp. 413–14.) But the enmity between the two countries remained, in part because after the Reformation they embraced different religious traditions. The English became Anglicans; the Scots, Presbyterians; and the two differed vehemently as to proper Church government and liturgy. The two countries would continue to be governed by separate institutions until the **Act of Union of 1707** united England (and Wales) and Scotland in the kingdom of Great Britain. The union was controversial in the eighteenth century and remains so today: many Scots saw its economic benefits, but resented the loss of initiative to London. As of this writing, Scotland remains part of the United Kingdom, but for some years there has been a movement urging devolution (i.e., independent government). As a concession to this desire, the Scotland Act of 1998 established a Scottish executive and a Parliament with tax-raising powers. However, the northern kingdom will continue to elect members to the Westminster Parliament as well.

In all this history, the relationship of Ireland to England and to Great Britain as a whole is the one that is most complicated and fraught with bitterness and tragedy – with profound consequences for the whole Atlantic world. Briefly, beginning in the Norman period, the population of Celtic or Gaelic Ireland was very gradually colonized and partly subdued by a small minority of English adventurers. Some Irish clans allied with the English newcomers, others opposed them. In any case, these new Anglo-Irish nobles soon became the dominant power in Ireland. They supposedly acknowledged the English king as feudal overlord, but, in reality, there was little to restrain their local control. To the English across the Irish Sea, the independent Anglo-Irish looked very Irish; to the native Irish (Gaelic) population, they were the English oppressors.

Theoretically, that Gaelic population was relegated to second-class status: according to the Statutes of Kilkenny of 1366, the native Irish were forbidden to marry the English, excluded from serving in cathedral or collegiate churches, and even prohibited from speaking the Gaelic language if living among English settlers. (This was meant as much to preserve the Englishness of the Anglo-Irish as to quash the Irishness of the natives.) Within areas of English rule, the native Irish were excluded from the protections of the common law and membership in mercantile or craft guilds. But in reality, this harsh overlordship did not extend very far. By the time this book opens in 1485, the authority of the English monarchy in Ireland had been contracting; since the early fourteenth century it controlled only a small part of eastern Ireland around the city of Dublin, known as the **Pale**. To be beyond it was to be in an area dominated by feuding Anglo-Irish nobles, such as the Butlers, earls of Ormond, and the Fitzgeralds, earls of Kildare, and Gaelic clansmen. English monarchs vacillated among delegating authority to these great families; playing them off against each other; or trying to break them and rule directly. This, plus Tudor attempts to push the Protestant Reformation on a predominantly Catholic population, produced a series of rebellions which reached their climax in the 1590s. They were put down by the English, but at great cost in terms of lives and resentment. After 1608, the English Crown attempted to strengthen its control by displacing the Gaelic population of the northern counties (Ulster) with Scots Presbyterians. This forced plantation increased native Irish resentment while introducing yet a third interest group into this volatile mix. The result was more rebellions and English reprisals under Oliver Cromwell and William III.

The details of these events will be examined below. Their long-term result was the gradual reduction of the Catholic Irish to a state of servitude and economic misery under the domination of Protestant landowners in the eighteenth and nineteenth centuries. London, perhaps sensing that these landowners were acting not unlike the Anglo-Irish earlier, attempted to increase its control with the Act of Union, which, in 1801, absorbed Ireland into the United Kingdom of Great Britain and Ireland. Another century of English dominance and, in the eyes of many natives, misrule (for example, the British failure to support the Irish people adequately during the potato famine of 1846–51), culminated in the Irish Rebellion of 1916. In 1921 the 26 counties of southern Ireland achieved semi-independent dominion status as the Irish Free State, and, in 1949, full independence as the Republic of Ireland. The six predominantly Protestant counties to the north (in the region known as Ulster) continue, as of the date of this writing, to be ruled from London in what is known, officially, as the United Kingdom of Great Britain and Northern Ireland. However, a sizeable and growing Catholic minority in Ulster, until recent years treated in law as inferiors to the

Protestant majority, has long chafed under British rule. Many Northern Irish Catholics, known as Republicans, support withdrawal from the United Kingdom and absorption into the Republic of Ireland. These demands have been staunchly resisted by the Protestant majority, or Unionists, who wish to remain part of Britain. In the late 1960s these tensions boiled over into violence, known as "the Troubles," which, in its most extreme form, has been undertaken by paramilitary and terrorist groups, such as the Irish Republican Army (IRA) on the Republican side or the Ulster Defence Force (UDF) on the Unionist side. In recent years the British Crown and the Irish Republic have worked together to persuade representatives of both sides to accept governance by an independent legislature under the terms of a compromise known as the Good Friday Accords (1998). The basic question of Ulster's ultimate political allegiance persists, however, as does the tragic legacy of Anglo-Irish hatred.

Thus, the problem of central control vs. local autonomy, of London's authority in all three kingdoms, will persist throughout the period of time covered by this book, and beyond. Today, it remains to be seen whether the English dominance of the archipelago achieved by 1714 will continue or whether Wales, Scotland, and Northern Ireland will go their separate ways as has the Republic of Ireland. The Catholic minority in Ulster apart, many inhabitants of these parts of Britain still feel a resentment at the sense of being second-class citizens. Old prejudices across ethnic lines die hard. Moreover, in the 1980s the fiscal policies of Margaret Thatcher's government did little to assist these regions, while reminding them of how economically dependent they were on England. More recently, the formation of a European Union has opened the prospect that Ireland, Scotland, and even Wales might be able to stand on their own feet economically within such a Union. This has led to revived calls for devolution for Scotland and Wales, in addition to the already rancorous debates about the ultimate possession of the six counties of Northern Ireland. As we have seen, the Blair government has responded by granting increased measures of self-government to Scotland, Wales, and Northern Ireland – with varying degrees of success.

This England

What of England itself? What is it like, physically; and how has its geography and topography influenced its history? In some ways, the regional tensions and issues of control noted above between England and the Celtic lands exist in microcosm in England, between the fertile and economically powerful southeast and the outlying parts of the country to the north and west.

For the purposes of this discussion, southeastern England includes London and what are now called the Home Counties (Middlesex, which includes London, and, clockwise, Hertfordshire, Essex, Kent, Surrey, Berkshire, and Buckinghamshire), as well as, a bit farther out, Bedfordshire to the north, Sussex and Hampshire to the south, and possibly as far northeast as Oxfordshire (see map 2). This part of the country is relatively flat or is characterized (on the South coast) by gently rolling "downs." It is the most fertile part of England because of its rich, deep soil, its milder weather, and its longer growing season. Moreover, it is blessed with many placidly flowing rivers which, in our period, allowed for easy transportation. Add the fact that it also contains London, the largest city in the British Isles, and it will be clear why the southeast has always tended to be the wealthiest and most populous part of the country. This, combined with the fact that it was the ancestral homeland of the Wessex kings who united England, as well as its proximity to Europe, naturally made it the seat of the nation's capital (first Winchester, then London). Altogether, these features made it the cultural center of the country as well. One major theme of this book is how this part of the country attempted to assert control over the rest. That attempt was successful to the extent that, when non-Britons think of England, they usually imagine a southeastern landscape; when they conjure an English accent, they tend to think of one from the Home Counties.

The outlying regions of England comprise (moving clockwise from an eight or nine o'clock position) the West Country, the Midlands and Welsh Marches, the North, and East Anglia. The West Country comprises the counties of Cornwall, Devonshire, Dorsetshire, Gloucestershire, Somersetshire, and Wiltshire. This area, like the South, is fertile, though Cornwall is quite rugged and portions of Devon and Dorset are famous for their moors, large expanses of wild, uncultivated ground. This part of England never became heavily industrialized or highly urbanized. In fact, it is so remote from London that in 1485, as this book begins, many natives of Cornwall still spoke a separate Gaelic language.

The Midlands,[4] the Welsh Marches,[5] and the North[6] are geographically, topographically, and temperamentally a bit like the Celtic lands. That is, their remoteness from London's influence and their rugged terrain meant that they were, during our period, less populous, less wealthy, and less well integrated with the center. Even after the Marcher lordships were abolished by the Tudors, English counties on the border like Herefordshire maintained a rump of Welsh-speaking parishes through the early modern period. The North, especially, tends to be characterized by highland terrain: the farmland tends to be less fertile, its soils thinner, its weather wetter, its growing season shorter. This area is better fitted to sheep and cattle farming than to growing arable crops, resulting in smaller settlements and farms than in the South. Like the frontiers of Ireland and portions of Wales, the North was dominated in the late Middle Ages by a few great – and very aggressive – noble families, in particular the Percies, earls of Northumberland, and the Nevilles, earls of Westmorland. Because of the recurrent violence on the Scots border, these noble houses maintained extensive patronage networks, or "affinities," which could be transformed quickly into large armies. Great magnates often used these forces against each other, or against the English king, in order to secure even more land and power. The rivalries among these mighty families, the ambitions of their chiefs, the "outlaw" nature of the Anglo-Scottish frontier, and the pervasive feeling that the North was often ignored at court rendered this part of the country a frequent source of instability early in our period. As in Ireland and the Welsh Marches, the English Crown often found that it had little choice but to rely on these great families to keep the peace in this far-flung part of its dominions.

After the period of time covered by this book, the ruggedness of the Midlands and North turned out, temporarily, to be an advantage. During the first industrial revolution (roughly 1760 to about 1850), their downward rushing rivers, combined with rich coal deposits, provided perfect locations for the earliest large factories. This led to the expansion of moderately sized towns into the great cities of Birmingham, Manchester, Leeds, Bradford, and Sheffield. Even then, the money generated by these factories (and many of those who grew rich from it) tended to head south, toward London. In more recent decades, the collapse of heavy industry in Britain has turned much of the North, in particular, into a rustbelt with high unemployment.

Finally, remote as the crow flies but better connected to London through coastal navigation are the counties of Cambridgeshire, Huntingdonshire, Norfolk, and Suffolk, which comprise the region known as East Anglia (map 2). This part of England tends to be flat and barren, often fen (or swamp) land and subject to cold winds from the North Sea. Yet, beginning in the sixteenth century, Norfolk and Suffolk's sheep walks experienced an agricultural revolution and Suffolk in particular became rich on the wool trade. Nevertheless, all of these outlying areas have certain characteristics in common: their remoteness, their relative freedom from London's influence and control, and, for most of the period, their relative lack of wealth (apart from East Anglia). These factors help to explain why, during the period 1485 to 1714, these parts of England would often prove most ready to rebel against the political power of the king or the economic power of the ruling elite.

As indicated above, the North and Northern Wales tend to be the most mountainous parts of Britain. The Pennine Range, in particular, runs like a backbone down the spine of the North and Midlands (map 1). But even this range hardly compares to the Rockies or the Alps, English mountains tending to be very tall hills. Indeed, the highest mountain in England and Wales, Mount Snowdon, rises only 3,500 feet. The hilly terrain of the North did have economic consequences, as we have seen, and it could make military operations more difficult, but, by and large, mountains were not important in English history.

Rivers, on the other hand, were important in English history. The most obvious example of this is the Thames, the great river in southeastern England which flows into the North Sea (map 1). The Thames served as the highway for nearly every one of England's migrant groups to penetrate into its heartland. Usually, they settled along its banks – another reason why the southeast is the most populous part of England. Later, the Thames, along with other major rivers (the Severn to the west; the Mersey, the Great Ouse, Humber, Trent, Tyne, and Tees to the north: map 1), served as principal highways and trade routes. Eventually, just after the period covered by this book, they would be linked in a great national canal system. Though there was also a system of roads emanating from London (first laid down by the Romans), water transportation (around the coast or, internally, via the river system) remained the cheapest and safest way to travel or to ship goods.

But if we were to somehow manage a "field-trip" to England in 1485, the natural feature which would probably strike us most forcefully, especially in comparison to England over five centuries later, would be the forests. Early modern England was covered with trees. Most forests were owned by the Crown; indeed, what defined a forest to contemporaries was not so much the presence of trees but the jurisdiction of forest law. In theory, this law preserved the forests for the purposes of providing the king with the pleasures of the hunt and the game it yielded for his table. In reality, these laws were not everywhere strictly enforced. As a result, people who lived in the forest developed a distinct culture and economic system: living in small hamlets, surviving by dairy farming, mining, and poaching the king's game. Trees were, in fact, the most important natural resource in England, for a great deal that we make with steel or plastic or rubber today was made of wood in 1485. Ships, houses, wagons, furniture – all were fashioned out of England's forests. As the population, and thus demand for timber as building material and fuel, grew during the early modern period, the forests thinned out dramatically.

Iron and the raw materials necessary to make it, such as tin and coal, also abounded in England in 1485, but they were not yet important. That is, they were too expensive to mine and too difficult to fashion at the start of our period to have much economic significance. Far more important was the wood noted above – and sheep. Sheep provided wool, which was, in 1485, virtually the only commodity made in England that was demanded highly abroad, in Europe. Nearly every part of the country engaged in sheep farming, but it was especially important in the hillier and remoter areas such as the West Country, the western portion (or West Riding) of Yorkshire, and East Anglia.

Finally, before leaving the question of the physical environment of England, we must mention the climate. A standing joke, in England and elsewhere, is that English weather is awful. But weather is really a matter of perspective. If one is used to the weather of Spain or California, English weather is very disappointing. But if one comes from Murmansk or Chicago, the English climate is really quite mild. Thanks to the moderating influence of the Gulf Stream, England rarely gets very hot or cold.[7] This mildness, combined with frequent, but not torrential, rainfall, means that England is highly suitable for certain crops, especially heavy grains like wheat or barley. This advantage was of the utmost importance, for on the weather depended the harvest and on the harvest depended everything else. Too much sun and the crops withered. Too much rain and they rotted. Too many crops and prices fell, and so did the incomes and purchasing power of farmers. Too few crops and food prices rose, possibly out of the range of the poorest members of society. Too little food and multitudes sickened or starved. The land and its produce do indeed mold the people, for good or for ill.

It is now time to examine the people who were shaped by, and who in turn shaped, the land we have been describing. What were the people of England like in 1485? What mattered to them? How did they explain their world and organize their society? How did they make a living? How would these things change after 1485?

This Happy Breed

If, somehow, we could be transported back to England in the year 1485, we would probably be amazed at how relatively unspoilt and green it all was. The first thing that would strike us about its inhabitants (and the most obvious explanation for our first observation) would probably be how few there were. England (including Wales) in 1485 had only about 2.2 million people (as compared to about 50 million today). In fact, its population had once been much larger, at least 4 to 5 and perhaps as many as 6 million people at the end of the thirteenth century. But in 1348–9 the Black Death – almost certainly bubonic plague – had swept into England, probably carried in the saliva of fleas which were carried by rats which were carried by ships which brought trade from Europe. The Black Death, so named for the swollen black patches it left on the skin, was intensely virulent: if one contracted it, the odds of survival were only one in four. For most victims, a painful death occurred within a matter of days. The result was to reduce the population by nearly one-half by the end of the fourteenth century. It continued to dwindle for most of the fifteenth, in part because the plague would return again and again, albeit with diminishing virulence, until the last major outbreak in 1665.

When the plague did not rage, medieval and early modern English men and women were still prey to all sorts of bacterial and viral infections which have been eradicated or neutralized in our own time. This was partly because they lacked modern antibiotics, partly because they lacked any sense of the connection between hygiene and disease. When the harvest was good, the diet of the average peasant was fairly healthy, consisting of bread, pea soup, cheese, occasional meat, and ale; however, perhaps one harvest in four was poor, one in six so poor as to produce famine. Though deaths from starvation itself were rare (perhaps confined to remote areas of subsistence agriculture in the North), historians have been able to prove a correlation between bad harvest years and those with a higher incidence of epidemic disease, probably a result of malnutrition. Even in temperate years, clothing and housing were, as we shall see, barely adequate to keep one warm and dry. Even where housing was adequate it was made of cheap plaster framed in wood and, thus, prone to collapse or fire. Few knew how to swim, so drowning in England's many rivers was common. And there was always the violence of wars and border raids. As a result of these harsh realities, the average life expectancy of a late medieval or early modern English person was about 35 years. This does not mean, of course, that there were no old people, but it does mean that they were far more rare in this society than in our own. On the other end of life's span, infant mortality ran at about 20 percent in the first year; another 10 percent of children would die before age 10. It is therefore not surprising that England's population only began to grow again in the 1470s or 1480s.

Of England's 2.2 million people in 1485, less than 10 percent lived in cities. Of these, London was by far the largest (see map 3). It was at once the capital, the

Map 3 *Towns and trade.*

legal center, and the primary seaport for trade with Europe. But, at about 50,000 inhabitants, it was less than half the size of modern-day Peoria, Illinois, or roughly equal to Terre Haute, Indiana, or Carson City, Nevada. In 1485 its governmental and cultural influence on the rest of the country was fairly minimal. Both London's population and its influence were to grow immensely, however, during the early modern period. By 1714 London would be the largest city in Europe, with over half a million inhabitants. It would also be the wealthiest city in the world, the hub of a vast empire, an immense emporium for goods and services, and the unchallenged center of government and setter of cultural trends for the British Isles.

The next largest cities – Norwich in East Anglia, Bristol to the west (a seaport off the Severn), Coventry in the south Midlands, and York in the North – had no more than 10,000 people apiece in 1485. Below them came major county towns like Dorchester or Stafford and cathedral cities like Lincoln or Salisbury with a few thousand inhabitants apiece (map 3). In general, the fifteenth century had been a difficult time for such middling-sized cities. There were many reasons for this: a general economic crisis in Europe during the second half of the fifteenth century, the disruption of trade that took place as a result of the Hundred Years' War and the Wars of the Roses (see chapter 1), and, in particular, the decline of the wool trade. Specifically, the demand for raw wool from England fell throughout the fifteenth century. But that for finished wool cloth rose. Cities that got in on the latter trade, like Exeter, Salisbury, and Totnes, did well. Those that did not, such as Coventry, Gloucester, Shrewsbury, and York, saw their wealth and populations decline. As the period wore on, London came to dominate more and more of the international trade in cloth, which hurt lesser port cities.

Below this level, there were numerous market towns ranging in population from a few hundred to one thousand. Abingdon, then in Berkshire, and Richmond in Yorkshire are good examples. Such towns served relatively small rural areas, perhaps 6 to 12 miles in radius. Here, farmers would bring surplus grain or carded wool to sell to merchants who would see to its wider distribution. Such towns were not very urban: they consisted of only a few streets, a market square, and the surrounding land, which most townsmen farmed to supplement their income from trade. On market days and some holy days their population and importance would swell. Otherwise we would barely recognize them as towns.

Most English men and women lived in the countryside – not in cities or even towns, but in settlements of, perhaps, 50 to 300 people. Let us imagine that, in our quest to know the English people in 1485, we have undertaken to meet them in their natural habitat, the English village. Admittedly, villages would be few and far between in this still underpopulated country, especially in the North, West Country, and East Anglia, where most people lived in more isolated settlements. If we sought out the greatest concentration of people, in the southeast, we would notice, first, a steeple, probably Norman in style, indicating a church (see plate 1). Indeed, the only buildings of note, probably the only ones built of stone, would be this church, a grain mill, and, perhaps, the manor house of the local gentleman or lord. The church reminds us of the centrality of religion and parish life to the

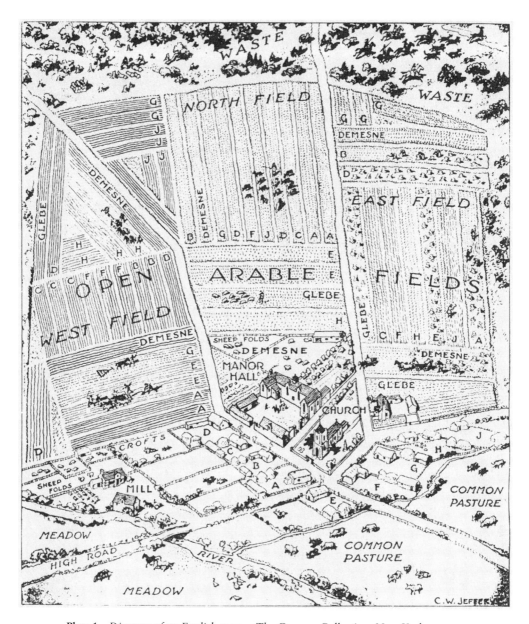

Plate 1 *Diagram of an English manor. The Granger Collection, New York.*

villagers in 1485; the mill reminds us of the importance of agriculture; and the manor house, that the social hierarchy was based very largely on who owned land and who did not.

The church's denomination would be what we would today call Roman Catholic, for England had not yet experienced the Reformation, nor were any other faiths officially tolerated.[8] If we were to watch, unobserved, for a week or a month, we would see that the church was frequented, not only on Sunday morning, or even on holidays, but on weekdays as well. For the church was not only the religious center of the village but its social center. Christenings, weddings, and funerals – that is, every important rite of passage in life – were commemorated here. Villagers also centered their celebrations of holidays ("holy days") at the church. By the late medieval period some 40 such holidays interrupted the work week. On Sundays and "holy days," all gathered at the church to hear mass (in Latin) and a homily (in English), during which congregants not only received spiritual instruction but also heard from the priest all the "official" news which the king and the landlord wanted them to know. (It is worth remembering that in 1485 there were no newspapers, no radio, no television. The monarch's **proclamations** were printed, but often in the hundreds or, at most, in the several thousands, hardly enough to blanket some 9,000-plus parishes. In any case, the vast majority of the rural population was illiterate. The Sunday sermon was, apart from the occasional traveler, the only source of outside news.) After mass, there was likely to be a festival in or about the churchyard or the village commons. At one species of festival, the "church ale," villagers ate, drank, played sports like camp ball or stoolball (forerunners of football/soccer and cricket), chatted up members of the opposite sex, and shared the unofficial news purveyed in village rumor and gossip.

After the excitement of the day, the villagers would return to their homes. At the end of the Middle Ages these were, more likely than not, one- and two-room huts or shacks, made of "wattle and daub" – essentially, mud, animal manure, straw – anything that would hold together.[9] They had one wooden door and few windows – for windows let in the cold. These would be covered by thin horn or greased paper. If we were to enter one of these hovels, it would take our eyes some time to adjust to the darkness, because of the lack of windows and the presence, in the center of the beaten mud floor, of a smoking hearth. This would be the family's main source of heat and implement for cooking. Its smoke was vented through a hole in the thatched roof. Looking about the room, there might be a few pots and pans, some tools, a candle holder with some candles, a chest, a table and a few stools, and some articles of clothing. Bags of flock or straw served as mattresses. The entire family lived in these one or two damp, drafty rooms with very little privacy from each other and, often, but a thin wall to separate them from their livestock. These would consist of perhaps a cow, certainly a sheep. The milk, cheese, wool, and, very occasionally, meat they provided would be crucial to keep the family fed and solvent, especially during bad times. Conversely, the death of the family's animals could spell economic disaster, so it was as important to shelter them as it was to house the family itself.

Prior to the period of time covered by this book, during the Middle Ages, these villagers would likely have been serfs, that is, unfree laborers who received land from their landlord in exchange for work on his estate. But, in an ironic twist, the Black Death which had been so destructive of human life had broken the chains of serfdom for those humans who had survived. That is, the dramatic fall in population which followed the epidemic had led to a labor shortage at the end of the fourteenth century. The peasants who were left alive, sensing their advantage, began to demand their freedom from serfdom and their pay in wages. So few peasants remained to do the work of the **manor** that, if their landlord refused to make concessions, they could always leave him for a master who would do so. At first, medieval landlords resisted. But in the end, the law of supply and demand, which no one in the Middle Ages understood, worked as inexorably for people as it does for products: peasants were able to commute their serfdom into freedom, their work into wages, to be partly paid back to the landlord in rent. By 1485 most villagers were free tenant farmers; that is, they rented from a great landlord who owned the manor upon which the village was built. The villagers, unlike serfs, were able to leave this relationship if they wished. This forced landlords to try to keep their old tenants or attract new ones by increasing wages and lowering rents: since the time of the Black Death laborers' wages had doubled from two pence a day to four, while rents in some areas had fallen from the beginning of the century by as much as one-third.

If we had chosen to visit a small hamlet in the rugged North or a fenland (swamp) settlement in East Anglia, the local people might make their living through pastoral (i.e., sheep or dairy) farming; spinning wool, flax or hemp; quarrying; and, of course, poaching in the king's woods. Those on the coasts survived on fishing and trade. But most villagers in the southeast relied on arable (i.e., crop) farming. Surrounding the village would be a plot of common land, where the animals of the village could be grazed; and individual strips of land, which were farmed by each tenant (see plate 1). Late medieval farmers and estate managers knew about soil depletion and the need for crop rotation, so these strips would be grouped in three different fields. At any given time, one would hold a fall crop, such as wheat; a second would hold a spring crop, such as oats or barley; and a third would lie fallow. The big tasks of medieval farming – plowing, sowing, and harvesting – would be organized communally, which means that the whole village, including its women and children, participated. Work was performed sun-up to sun-down, which meant longer hours in summer, shorter hours in harsher conditions in winter. When not aiding their husbands and fathers in the fields, women cooked, sewed, and fetched water. Older children helped by looking after the family's smaller children and animals. As we have seen, milk and wool could be sold for a little extra income. Another way to make extra money was to turn one's dwelling into a "public house," or "pub," by brewing ale.

Perhaps in the center of the manor; perhaps on a hill overlooking the village; perhaps many miles away on another of the landlord's estates, would be his manor house. He might have been a great nobleman or a gentleman. He might have owned many manors or just this one estate. He might have lived on the manor or at a great distance. What is certain is that his ownership of the manor gave him great power over the villagers. First, the landlord owned most of the land in the neighborhood, apart from that of a few small freeholders. This provided him with a vast income from harvesting crops grown upon it, from mining minerals within it, and, above all, from collecting rents from the tenants who inhabited it. The landlord was also likely to own the best – and often the only – mill for grinding grain and oven for baking it. This provided another means to extract money from his tenants. Control of the land also gave him control of the local church, for he probably named the clergyman who preached there, a prerogative known as the right of **advowson**. He had the further right to call on the services of his tenants in time of war. His power in the land might lead the king to name him a local sheriff or **justice of the peace (JP)**. This meant that he was not only the king's representative to his tenants but their judge and jury for many offenses as well. His local importance might, paradoxically, require him to spend time away from his estates, in London. If he was a peer, he sat in the upper house of Parliament, the House of Lords. If he was a particularly wealthy gentleman he might be selected by his fellow landowners to sit in the lower house, the House of Commons. One of the few sets of records allowing us insight into a landowning family during the fifteenth century, *The Paston Letters*, shows how little time the Paston men actually spent in the country (in this case, Norfolk), and how much more of it they spent in London.[10]

Admittedly, the same forces which had improved the lot of their tenants were compromising the wealth and power of the landed orders at the end of the Middle Ages. The decline in population had led to reduced demand for the food grown on their land. This produced a fall in prices which cut into their profits. Those profits were further compromised by the high wages that landlords now had to pay to keep their tenants from leaving for another estate. As a result, landowners increasingly abandoned **demesne** farming (that is, relying for profit on the sale of the crops grown on that portion of the estate not being rented out) in favor of renting all their land to peasants, who would pay a cash rent. These rents, not the food grown on the land, eventually became the chief source of profit to great landowners. But, as we have seen, the low population also forced landlords to keep their rents low, once again to avoid losing their tenants. So, some landowners went further, abandoning crop farming entirely in favor of sheep farming, which was far less labor-intensive and more predictable, since it was less dependent on the weather. This process, called **enclosure** from the need to erect fences across otherwise open farmland in order to restrain sheep, was highly controversial precisely *because* it was less labor-intensive. In theory, the tenants who had previously farmed the land would be thrown off of it, thus losing both their jobs and their homes. As a result, the Church preached against enclosure, Parliament legislated against it, and socially conscious writers, most notably Sir Thomas More (1478–1535) in *Utopia*, complained that whole villages were being depopulated because of the needs of the sheep and the greed of their owners. Historians now question how many peasants were actually thrown off the land, since it had already been depopulated by the Black Death. In any case, neither legislation nor propaganda was effective in stopping enclosure when a landlord had a mind to do it and in some areas, such as the rich, arable Midlands, extensive enclosure in the sixteenth century did lead to real social problems.

It should be obvious that, despite their declining economic situation, it was far better to be a landlord than a tenant. Even in the midst of recession, land was the key to wealth and power. Because of it, the landlord need do no manual labor himself – indeed, freedom from work is one contemporary definition of gentility. This left him the time and the leisure to judge and to govern. Contemporaries believed that land was the only form of property which automatically gave him the right to do so, since, unlike gold, it could not be transported elsewhere. If you remember one thing about early modern England during the period covered by this book, it should be that the people who mattered – in 1485, in 1714, and beyond – owned land. They owned all those little villages which housed most of the population of England. To some extent, despite the decline of actual serfdom, they "owned" – or at least dominated – the lives of all the people who lived in those villages.

One more social fact. The group at the top, the landowners who possessed most of the wealth and power in the nation, formed a very small percentage of its population: about one-half of 1 percent. This fact raises a rather obvious question: why did the remaining 99.5 percent put up with this inequality? Why did they allow this small minority to have such a preponderance of wealth and power over their lives? To answer that question, we must turn away from the material world inhabited by the English people. We must now examine their mental universe.

The Mental World of the English People, ca. 1485

In 1485, virtually all English men and women were Roman Catholics. All were taught and, so far as we can tell, nearly all believed, that God had created the universe, ordered it, and was active in its daily workings. In other words, the world was a physical manifestation of God's will. It followed that however the world was, was how the world was supposed to be. In 1485 educated English men and women had many ways of describing how the world was supposed to be, most of them metaphorical. One of their favorite metaphors was that of the body politic. That is, when English men and women thought of their nation, they often conceived of it as a human body. The king was the head; the aristocracy the arms and shoulders; the tenant farmers and poor the legs and feet, etc. But there was no place for God and the other creatures of the universe in this scheme.

A more comprehensive metaphor was the one which later came to be known as the Great Chain of Being.[11] That is, when contemporary English men and women thought of the inhabitants of the universe, they thought of a hierarchy that looked something like this:

Being	Physical dwelling place
God	Everywhere
Angels	Heavens (includes, in descending order, stars, planets, sun, moon)
Man	Earth (the center of the universe)
Animals	Earth (but closer to the ground)
Plants	Earth (closer still)
Stones	Earth (the ground itself)

It should be obvious that those at the top of this hierarchy were closer to God than those at the bottom. This was held to be physically true, for in the days before people accepted the Copernican (sun-centered) cosmos, it was thought that God dwelt everywhere, but most often in the heavens. Thus, church steeples aspired upwards. Man dwelt upright on the earth, at the center of the universe, between the angels and the beasts, and so in the very middle of the Chain. Within the earth was the molten core of Hell, where the damned dwelt as far away from God as possible.

Apart from God, who was thought to be indivisible, each of the ranks in the Chain was further subdivided into smaller hierarchies. Medieval theologians did not just think of angels, for example, in an undifferentiated mass. Rather, they divided these celestial beings into nine ranks, from seraphim and cherubim down to mere angels. Animals, too, could be arranged into a hierarchy: was not the lion the king of the beasts? Was not the eagle a nobler bird than the sparrow? The whale a greater animal than the codfish? Plants, too, could be ranked (compare the mighty oak with the lowly fern), as could stones (diamonds vs. granite, for example). And so, with man:

King
Nobles
Gentlemen
Yeomen
Husbandmen
Cottagers
Laborers

The king was, of course, the ruler of the kingdom, the fount of justice and honor, God's lieutenant on earth – and the owner of 5 percent of the land. His office and person will be addressed further in subsequent chapters. Just below him in the Great Chain of Being, ready (theoretically, anyway) to assist him in his rule, were the 50 or 60 families who, in 1485, made up the English nobility. This rank, like all links in the Chain, may be further subdivided into:

Dukes
Marquesses
Earls
Viscounts
Barons

Each of these titles had been granted by the king, and was inheritable by the eldest son of its current holder when the latter died. That is, at the demise of John Talbot, third earl of Shrewsbury (b. 1448), in June of 1473, he was immediately succeeded by his eldest son, George Talbot, as fourth earl of Shrewsbury (1468–1538). At *his* death in July 1538 he was succeeded by his eldest surviving son, Francis Talbot, as fifth earl (1500–60), and so on. Female heirs were ignored, even when older than males. This was because the nobility had originated as the band of loyal warriors around an Anglo-Saxon monarch. Titles, and the lands which often went with them, had been granted in reward for, but also in anticipation of, military service. Despite (or because of) the example of Joan of Arc, contemporary attitudes toward men and women could not conceive of a military role for the latter. Nobility entitled the holder to sit in the House of Lords. Noble titles were, moreover, generally accompanied by grants of high office and, as indicated, landed estates. As a result, these 50–60 families owned perhaps 5 to 10 percent of the land in England and commanded incomes ranging from £3,500 for the greatest landowners, the dukes of York, down to as little as £60 for the relatively poor Lords Clinton. Such great wealth, extensive landholdings, and military commitments implied large affinities (or retinues), including: estate managers, chaplains, servants, tenants, political allies, and hangers-on. Many of these retainers were housed in formidable castles which acted as mini-courts and centers of power in the locality, often in the king's service, sometimes not.

Many of the superior officers in a noble household would be gentlemen or their ladies. In theory, the gentry consisted of knights, identified by the title "Sir" before their names; esquires, identified by an "esq." after their names; and a new group of large landowners who could bear heraldic coats of arms and who increasingly appended the designation "gent." to their names. These totaled about 3,000 people and owned between 25 to 30 percent of the land in England in 1485. The greatest knights held multiple estates and could claim incomes of £100 or more – surpassing some of the peerage. A lesser knight or esquire might make £40 to £100 a year, while a lesser gentleman with a single manor made £20 to £40 a year. Such an income provided a comfortable existence supported by a dozen or so servants. As we have seen, contemporaries believed that only those with the landed wealth to live such a life had the time or the right to have a say in running the country. An act of 1445 enshrined this belief by stipulating that only those with annual incomes over £40 could sit in the House of Commons. The members of this social rank also oversaw day-to-day local government for the king, serving as sheriffs, JPs, and commissioners of array (responsible for raising the militia) for their localities.

In theory, the right to vote for members of the House of Commons was limited by a **statute** of 1430 to those who owned land worth 40 shillings, or £2 a year (for an explanation of pounds, shillings, and pence, see Conventions and Abbreviations). This pretty much defined the lower limit of admission to the next rank in the Chain, the yeomen. Yeomen, were, thus, slightly less wealthy landowners than gentlemen, but still substantial farmers with secure tenure of their land. They might hold several farms at once and usually employed servants, but they were also active in the labor of the farm themselves. They were considered the backbone of county society, serving on juries and the militia. Husbandmen might own or rent one large tract, cottagers a small one. Both might employ a few laborers on a seasonal basis to assist them with planting or the harvest. Laborers thus often lacked a permanent home or work situation. These last three groups formed the bulk of village society, described above.

Theoretically, every person in England could be placed, exactly, within the Chain. For example, individual ducal families could be ranked by order of creation. That is, if one family had received its dukedom from the king before another family, it outranked that family and would line up nearer the sovereign in ceremonial processions, preceded by other, more recent ducal families, who followed families of marquesses, who followed earls, who followed viscounts, etc., all in strict order of creation. And, of course, within every family, noble or common, there was a ranking:

Father
Mother
Male children, eldest to youngest
Female children, eldest to youngest

As this indicates, the Chain implied a hierarchy of genders as well as of classes: traditional theology dating back to Aristotle defined "the female" as "a misbegotten male."[12] In chapter 6 we will examine the roles and relationships of early modern men and women in a variety of settings. In the meantime, it should be understood that under both the Chain and English common law, a woman's status was a direct extension of that of the male to whom she was most closely related: if a woman's father was of gentle status, she was gentle too. Upon marriage she took the status of her husband. If he died and she remarried, then she assumed her new husband's rank. A widow who remained in that status was an anomaly in a society which did not know what to do with a woman who was independent of male control.

An even more important feature of the Chain was that the top rank in every subdivision was analogous to the top rank of every other subdivision – and of the Chain itself. That is, the father in the family, the king in the kingdom (and, of course, the professor in the classroom!) were analogous to God in the universe. They represented him, they wielded his authority, they were the unquestioned heads of their respective links and spheres of activity within the Chain.

Clearly, English people in 1485 were obsessed with order. Their fondest desire was, apparently, to account for every speck of matter in the universe and place it in a hierarchy. Equally, their greatest fear was that order would break down. It should be understood that this was a Chain, not a ladder. No one could move up or down, for that would imply imperfection in God's plan. A fern cannot become an oak; a codfish cannot become a whale; a mother cannot be a father; nor should a husbandman try to become a peer – and, of course, no one could aspire to be king but the divinely appointed, anointed, and acknowledged heir of the previous king. To rise or fall in this society was to rebel against the Chain, against order – and, thus, against God.

Indeed, for any creature to attack its superiors in the Chain – for example, for a son to strike a father or for a subject to compass rebellion against the king – was tantamount to Lucifer's infamous revolt against his Creator. To do so was to disrupt the delicate balance of the universe, as, a century later, Shakespeare has one of his characters imply in *Troilus and Cressida*:

The heavens themselves, the planets, and this centre,
Observe degree, priority, and place,
Insisture, course, proportion, season, form,
Office and custom, in all line of order: ...
... but when the planets,
In evil mixture, to disorder wander,
What plagues, and what portents, what mutiny,
What raging of the sea, shaking of earth,
Commotion in the winds, frights, changes, horrors,
Divert and crack, rend and deracinate
The unity and married calm of states
Quite from their fixture!

Shakespeare refers here to the common contemporary belief in astrology, the notion that changes in the heavenly bodies can affect order upon earth. In the next few lines, he moves from the celestial level to the earthly:

O! when degree is shak'd,
Which is the ladder to all high designs,
The enterprise is sick. How could communities,
Degrees in schools and brotherhoods in cities,
Peaceful commerce from dividable shores,
The primogenitive and due of birth,
Prerogative of age, crowns, sceptres, laurels,
But by degree, stand in authentic place?
Take but degree away, untune that string,
And, hark, what discord follows!

What discord?

... the bounded waters
should lift their bosoms higher than the shores
And make a sop of all this solid globe:
Strength should be the lord of imbecility,
And the rude son should strike his father dead.
Force should be right; or, rather, right and wrong
Between whose endless jar justice resides –
Should lose their names and so should justice too. (*Troilus and Cressida* 1.3)

Clearly, this system was designed to maintain order at all costs. Which means that it was intended to keep the upper one-half of 1 percent of the population on top and the remaining 99.5 percent subordinate to them. To return to our earlier question: why did the lower 99.5 percent buy it? Why did they not rebel against its constraints? One explanation for this is that the Great Chain of Being was taught, sometimes overtly, usually implicitly, from every pulpit in the land. Having had it hammered home to them on a weekly basis since childhood, having grown up being told that it was God's plan, few early modern English men and women were willing to question it. After all, it explained their universe; and, as

Shakespeare argues, the alternative might be disastrous. Indeed, imagine what such a person would think of our world. Would he or she not find it crowded, noisy, violent, disordered, chaotic? Would he or she not find plenty of confirmation of Shakespeare's prediction of anarchy and misery?

Another explanation for the widespread acceptance of the Great Chain of Being was that in theory, and, often, in practice, the potential harshness of this system was mitigated by two conjoined beliefs: paternalism and deference. Paternalism, or, as it was usually known in the Middle Ages, good lordship, was the notion, instilled in great and humble alike, that those at the upper end of the human Chain had a moral responsibility to care for and protect those below them. After all, if a father was like God, God was also like a loving father. If the anointed king or the landed nobleman or the father of a family were God-like, then they not only bore God's power, they also bore his responsibility to look after those of his creatures over whom they ruled. Just as God and the angels were thought to watch, paternally, over and assist His children, so privileged men were expected to watch, paternally, over those without privilege. Thus, the king had a responsibility to protect his subjects; to rule them justly and to keep their burdens of taxation and service reasonable. Thus, the landlord may have had immense economic and legal power over his tenants, but he also had the responsibility to protect them from enemies; to give them fair justice; and to look after them in times of economic hardship. If he was a great man, with an office at court, he was expected to provide subordinate offices for his followers. On holidays, he was expected to open his house to them in a show of hospitality and, at all times, he was expected to redress their grievances. In reality, the degree of paternalism exercised by landlords varied according to the conscience of the individual aristocrat, but the expectation in society was very high. A good king, a good lord was, like God, a good father.

In return, those at the lower ranks of the Chain were expected, like children, to pay obedience, allegiance, and respect – deference – to those above them. All humanity owed these things to God; all subjects, to the king; all tenants, to their landlord; all members of a household, to its head. The people of England paid their debt to God by attending services on Sundays and holidays; by paying annates and tithes (that is, a tenth of their income) to the Church; and by obeying God's law as expressed in the Ten Commandments and the laws of the Church (canon law). The Church even had its own ecclesiastical courts to prosecute those who failed in their obligations by blaspheming, getting drunk, fornicating, committing adultery, or failing to pay their debts. The king's subjects, similarly, paid their debt to him by acting respectfully in his presence (by standing while he sat and by removing their hats while he remained "covered"), by paying their taxes, and by obeying his law (which also had its series of courts). The tenant tendered his respects to his landlord by paying his rents, by giving military service when demanded, and by gestures such as tipping his cap or bowing (if a man), or curtseying (if a woman), or giving the wall to *any* person of superior rank in the Chain. Giving the wall meant that if one was approached by a social superior while walking along a pavement at the side of a street, one stepped into the street to allow that person to pass. If we recall that this was an age before underground sewers and that the streets were full of trash, mud, and the excrement of man and beast, it should be obvious just how powerful a force the Great Chain of Being and its call for deference really were! Finally, the members of a household – whether related by blood or, in the case of a large, extended household, ties of employment and interest – were expected to show the same deference to its head as they would do to God or king in the wider world.

So, in the universe of late fifteenth-century English men and women, God was in his heaven; the king sat on his throne; the landlord lived in his manor house; and everybody else knew exactly where they stood – and stand they would, out of respect for their betters. No one could have had any doubt about the rights and responsibilities of his or her position. Or could they? When contemporaries write about hierarchy or paternalism and deference they always sound anxious, as if the whole, delicate system were under threat. The reason for their anxious tone is that this system *was* under threat – by reality. Life is never neat and fifteenth-century life refused to fit tidily into the little boxes designed for it by the Great Chain of Being. One reason for this is that the Chain stood for permanency, and yet fifteenth-century English men and women were experiencing social and economic changes which would persist to the end of the period covered by this book. For example, the nobility were supposed to comprise the oldest and most distinguished families in England, having earned their titles in military service to the king. But by the end of the Middle Ages, such titles were increasingly won through peaceful service to, or simple friendship with, the monarch. This led to a great deal of resentment toward "upstarts," "courtiers," and "favorites." Moreover, noble status, far from being permanent, could be taken away on proof of high treason or an act of **attainder** by Parliament which, in effect, voted the same thing without the formality of a trial. This happened with some frequency at the end of the Middle Ages. More commonly, great families simply died out for lack of an heir. It has been estimated that something like one-quarter of all noble families vanished every 25 years. Therefore, the "ancient nobility of England" was constantly changing, continually replenishing itself.

The rank from which "new" noble families were drawn was that of the gentry. Here, too, there was a great deal of change and ambiguity, for throughout the late medieval and early modern period it was never precisely clear just who was a gentleman and who was not. A nobleman could at least point to a royal document, called a patent, in which his title and the terms of its inheritance were spelt out. Theoretically, a knight could be identified by the act of having been knighted by the king – but some claimed the honor who had never met the king. As for esquires and gentlemen, they were supposed to register for coats of arms with the Office of Heralds. But not every gentle family did so. Others defined gentleness by an ancient pedigree. But pedigrees could be faked. As we have seen, gentle status was also thought to require the ownership of land providing a certain income. But what about a poor gentleman who, because of the recession of the late fifteenth century, had lost most of his land? Did his gentle status cease? What of a prosperous yeoman who began to amass land, as many did in the second quarter of the sixteenth century? When could he claim to be gentle? Most commentators thought that it took three generations of landed prosperity to justify appending the designation "gent." to the family name. But this is very close to saying that the only requirement to being a gentleman was the ability to call oneself gentle without anyone laughing. So much for the unchanging, God-ordained hierarchy.

Moreover, the categories set up by the Chain were increasingly inadequate to describe the variety of ranks and occupations in late medieval and early modern England. Those categories were either military or rural; they defined individuals by their relationship to land. But, as we have seen, not all English men and women lived on the land or in the country. Increasingly after 1500, English people migrated to the cities, London especially, where they could pursue greater economic opportunity. Between 1520 and 1720 the percentage of urban dwellers in England and Wales would double, to about 20 percent. London's population would rise from about 50,000 in 1485 to 700,000 by 1750.

The growth of cities and the economic opportunities which encouraged that growth posed many problems for the Great Chain of Being. First, this was a system which depended upon people knowing each other, which was easy enough in the village. But once people began moving to cities they no longer experienced personal connections with all of their neighbors. Once in the city they could lose themselves in the anonymity which cities characteristically bestow – and claim a status to which they were not born. Moreover, cities had their own hierarchy which did not fit into that of the Great Chain. Major cities had mayors (in London, a lord mayor), a council of aldermen, and citizens, not nobles, gentry, and yeomen. This urban hierarchy gave fits to those who wrote about status and rank: where did one place the mayor of Bristol in the Chain? Did he rank with a gentleman? Worse, remember that most people came to the city to make money, that is, to *rise* in wealth. Some did; many others fell. But the Chain was based on birth and could accommodate neither change nor wealth measured in anything but land. It had no place for the rich merchant, the moderately prosperous attorney, or the struggling tailor. Normally, no one would have said that a merchant should outrank a gentleman, but what if that merchant made hundreds of pounds a year, the gentleman only a few score? Nor would anyone have said that one could change one's rank; but what if one grew rich, or poor?

The question of where the urban hierarchy fit in the Chain was not the only such problem facing its adherents. The Roman Catholic Church had its own hierarchy:

Pope
Archbishops
Bishops
Priests
Brothers
Sisters
Laity

The pope was held by Catholics to be the vicar of Christ and he and his subordinates to represent God's will on earth. The problem with this hierarchy was its relationship to the secular, human one. That is, if the pope was the vicar of Christ and the king was God's lieutenant on earth, who was higher in the Chain? What if they disagreed? Where did archbishops and bishops fit amongst nobles and gentry? In practice, kings and popes generally cooperated with each other and, in so doing, sustained the Chain. But when they disagreed, the repercussions were enormous. In previous centuries, the pope and the king of England had clashed over the respective jurisdictions of royal and ecclesiastical courts, over the collection of annates, and over which of them could select bishops (the Investiture Controversy). Though the papacy had won some important concessions in these controversies, its prestige had taken a dramatic plunge in the fourteenth century. This happened, first, when the papal court moved to Avignon in France, an event known as the Babylonian Captivity, which lasted from 1309 to 1377. English kings viewed the Avignon papacy as a mere tool of the French monarchy. Things only got worse between 1378 and 1417 when two popes, one Italian and one French, reigned in competition with each other during what came to be known as the Great Schism. The English Crown responded by approving legislation limiting the power of the pope to name clergymen to English benefices (the Statutes of Provisors, 1351, 1390), forbidding English subjects from appealing their cases to foreign courts, including the papal court at Rome, and blocking bulls of excommunication from entering England (**Statutes of Praemunire**, 1353, 1365, 1393). At about the same time, they also encouraged the questioning of papal authority by tolerating the existence of a group of heterodox Catholics called the **Lollards**. It was little wonder that at the beginning of the fifteenth century Pope Martin V (1368–1431; reigned 1417–31) commented: "it is not the pope but the king of England who governs the church in his dominions."[13] Still, the Church remained a powerful and wealthy organization in late medieval England, with thousands of parishes and clergy, its own system of courts and access to the ears, minds, and, it was assumed, souls of every man, woman, and child in the realm. But the possibility always remained that royal authority and clerical authority might once more come into conflict. The resultant religious tensions will be another major theme of this book.

But in 1485 the most immediate challenge to the certainties of the Great Chain of Being came from the political arena. If papal authority could be questioned, so could royal authority. As this book opens, the English monarchy had just experienced the worst nightmare imaginable to those who embraced the Chain: a civil war in which the very person and authority of God's lieutenant, the king, was up for contention. It is now necessary to examine this challenge to the Great Chain of Being; and the achievement of Henry VII, his supporters, and successors in meeting it.

CHAPTER ONE

Establishing the Henrician Regime, 1485–1525

On August 22, 1485 rebel forces led by Henry Tudor, earl of Richmond (1457–1509), defeated a royal army under King Richard III (1452–85; reigned 1483–5) at the battle of Bosworth Field, Leicestershire (see map 4). As any student of Shakespeare knows, Richard was killed. His crown, which was said to have rolled under a hawthorn bush, was retrieved and offered to his opponent, who wasted no time in proclaiming himself King Henry VII (reigned 1485–1509). According to tradition, the former earl of Richmond thus put a stop to decades of political instability and founded the Tudor dynasty, which would rule England for over a century.

As told in Shakespeare's *Tragedy of King Richard III*, Henry's victory and the rise of the Tudors has an air of inevitability about it. But Shakespeare wrote a century after these events, during the reign of Henry's granddaughter, Queen Elizabeth (1533–1603; reigned 1558–1603). Naturally, his hindsight was 20×20 and calculated to flatter the ruling house under which he lived. No one alive in 1485, not even Henry, could have felt so certain about his family's prospects. During the previous hundred years three different royal houses had ruled England. Each had claimed an increasingly disputed succession and each had fallen with the murder of its king and head. Each line had descendants still living in 1485, some of whom had better claims to the throne than Henry did. Recent history suggested that each of these rival claimants would find support among the nobility, so why should anyone bet on the Tudors? In short, there was little reason to think that the days of bloodshed and turbulence were over.

And yet, though he would face many challenges, King Henry VII would not be overthrown. Rather, he would rule England for nearly 25 years and die in his bed, safe in the knowledge that his son, also named Henry, would succeed to a more or less united, loyal, and peaceful realm supported by a full Treasury. The story of how Henry VII met these challenges and established his dynasty will be told in this chapter. But first, in order to understand the size of those challenges and the magnitude of his achievement, it is necessary to review briefly the dynastic crisis known, romantically but inaccurately, as the Wars of the Roses.[1]

The Wars of the Roses, 1455–1485

It might be argued that all of the trouble began over a century earlier because of a simple biological fact: King Edward III (1312–77; reigned 1327–77) had six sons (see genealogy 1, p. 412). Royal heirs were normally a cause for celebration in medieval England, but so many heirs implied an army of grandchildren and later descendants – each of whom possessed royal blood and, therefore, a claim to the throne. Still, this might not have mattered if two of those grandchildren, an earlier Richard and an earlier Henry, had not clashed over royal policy. In 1399, Henry Bolingbroke, duke of Lancaster (1366–1413), protesting the royal confiscation of his ancestral lands, rebelled against his cousin and anointed king, Richard II (1367–1400; reigned 1377–99), deposed him, and assumed the Crown as King Henry IV (1399–1413). In so doing, he established the Lancastrian dynasty on the English throne – but broke the Great Chain of Being. Looking back with hindsight, Shakespeare and many of his contemporaries thought that this was the moment that set England on the course – or curse – of political instability. In *The Tragedy of King Richard II*, he has the bishop of Carlisle predict the consequences of Henry Bolingbroke's usurpation as follows:

> And if you crown him, let me prophesy,
> The blood of English shall manure the ground,
> And future ages groan for this foul act . . . ;
> O if you raise this house against this house,
> It will the woefullest division prove,
> That ever fell upon this cursèd earth.
> Prevent it, resist it, let it not be so,
> Lest child, child's children, cry against you – woe! (*Richard II* 4.1)

Shakespeare, writing long after these events, knew that the prediction would come true. The speech is therefore not so much an accurate exposition of what was generally thought at the time of Richard's dethronement as it is a reflection of how English men and women came to feel about that event under the Tudors.

But many historians would argue that, despite his dubious rise to the top, Henry IV was remarkably successful in establishing himself and his line, suppressing nearly all opposition by the middle of his reign. His son, Henry V (1387–1422; reigned 1413–22), did even better, for he won military glory and an overseas empire (while distracting his barons away from his line's doubtful legitimacy) by renewing a longstanding conflict with France known as the Hundred Years' War (1337–1453). Specifically, after defeating a much larger French force in 1415 at the battle of Agincourt (see map 5), Henry was recognized by the French king, Charles VI (1368–1422; reigned 1380–1422) as the heir to the French throne as well, despite the existence of Charles's son, also named Charles (1403–61). In fact, central and southern France remained loyal to the *dauphin* (the French Crown prince), which led Henry to prepare another campaign for

1421. It was on this campaign, while besieging the city of Mieux, that Henry V contracted dysentery and died.

The untimely death of Henry V was, for many historians, the real starting point for the disasters to come, for, combined with the almost simultaneous demise of Charles VI, it brought to the English and French thrones an infant of just nine months: Henry VI (1421–71; reigned 1422–61, 1470–1). Given his youth, it was inevitable that the early years of the new king's reign would be dominated by his nobility and, in particular, his relatives. But, in fact, this Henry's age was to make little difference to the quality of his rule or lives of his subjects. Even after declaring himself of age in 1437, he proved to be a meek, pious, well-intentioned but weak-minded nonentity. Eventually, he went insane. Even before he did so, he was dominated by family and courtiers, in particular his great uncles of the Beaufort family, dukes of Somerset; and from 1444 his wife, Margaret of Anjou (1430–82). They were famous for aggrandizing power and wealth, for running a corrupt and incompetent administration, and for losing France. In 1436, Paris fell back into French hands. By 1450 the French had driven the English out of Normandy. By 1453, what had once been an English overseas empire on the continent was reduced to the solitary Channel port of Calais (map 5). The French had won the Hundred Years' War. The loser was to be Henry VI and the house of Lancaster.

Put another way, the Hundred Years' War is important in French history because it produced a unified France under a single acknowledged king. Its outcome is important in English history because it destabilized the English monarchy and economy, discredited the house of Lancaster, and divided the English nobility. The result was the Wars of the Roses. Remember that the Lancastrians had come to the Crown not through lawful descent, but through force of arms. Now their military skills had proved inadequate. Moreover, the wars against France had been very expensive and ruinous to trade. In 1450 the Crown's debts were £372,000 and its income but £36,000 a year, a steep decline from an annual revenue of £120,000 in the reign of Richard II. The House of Commons refused to increase taxes, knowing that they would go either to a losing war effort or to line Beaufort pockets. Since royal revenue was not keeping up with expenditure, the king could only pay for military affairs by borrowing large sums at exorbitant rates of interest. As one critic said of Henry VI in 1450: "[his] law is lost, his merchandise is lost; his commons are destroyed. The sea is lost; France is lost; himself is made so poor that he may not pay for his meat or drink; he oweth more and [is] greater in debt than ever was King in England."[2] The problems of royal control, finance, and foreign policy would haunt all the princes portrayed in this book, but perhaps none so disastrously as Henry VI.

Given an incompetent king, a corrupt and inefficient government, a failed war effort, and a wrecked economy, it was inevitable that the nobility would begin to question Lancastrian rule. The most prominent of these critics was Richard, duke of York (1411–60). York was a direct descendant of Edward III through his fifth son, Edmund, duke of York (1342–1402). Through his mother, Anne Mortimer (d. 1412), he inherited the blood of Edward's third son, Lionel, duke of Clarence

Map 4 *The Wars of the Roses, 1455–85.*

The following labels appear on the map:

Norham
Wark
Hedgeley Moor ✕
Bamburgh
Dunstanburgh
Alnwick
Warkworth

NORTH SEA

N

Hexham ✕
Newcastle
Carlisle
Lumley
Brancepeth
Raby
Appleby
Skelton
Barnard Castle
Richmond
Bolton
Masham
Middleham
Sheriff Hutton
Lancaster
Knaresborough
York
Spofforth
Cawood
Towton Moor ✕
Wressell
Wakefield ✕
Pontefract
Sandal
Conisborough
Tickhill
Liverpool

IRISH SEA

Rhuddlan
Beaumaris
Conway
Chester
Denbigh
Ruthin
Harlech

Henry VII defeats
Lambert Simnel's rebellion
Bolingbroke
Stokefield ✕
Newark
Tattershall
Newcastle-
under-Lyme
Belvoir
Blore Heath ✕
Tutbury
Castle Rising

Bosworth Field ✕
Fotheringhay
Caister
Stokesay
Wingfield
Ludlow
Kenilworth
Framlingham
Mortimer's Cross ✕
Ludford Bridge ✕
Northampton ✕✕
Warwick
Tewkesbury ✕
Edward IV restored 1471–83
Pleshey
Grosmont
Skenfrith
St. David's
White Castle
Gloucester
Edgcott ✕
Milford Haven
Kidwelly
Raglan
St. Albans ✕✕
Haverfordwest
Abergavenny
Usk
Barnet ✕
Pembroke
Swansea
Berkeley
Manorbier
Caerphilly
Wallingford
London
Ogmore
Cardiff
Windsor
Farnham
Reigate
Leeds
Dover
Tiverton
Portchester
Arundel
Steyning
Herstmonceux
Okehampton
Bramber
Pevensey
Compton
Carisbrooke
Corfe

English Channel

✕ Battle

Ravenspur

100 miles
160 km

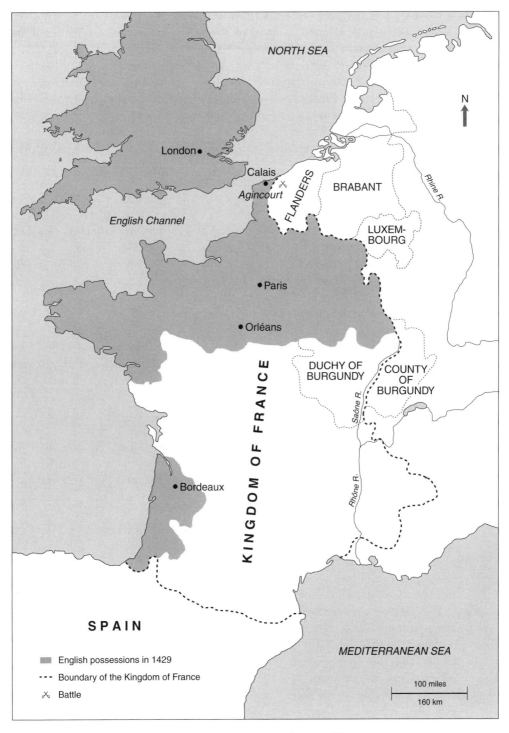

Map 5 *Southern England and western France during the later Middle Ages.*

(1338–68), and the claim of the Mortimer family (see genealogy 1). Thus, he could make nearly as good a claim to the throne as its present, Lancastrian, occupant, who was descended from Edward's fourth son, John of Gaunt (1340–99). Moreover, the duke of York was the greatest landowner in England, which provided him with immense wealth and made him head of the largest affinity in the realm. Finally, he was allied by marriage to the powerful Neville family. None of this is to say that York easily or quickly formed a design to seize the throne. Rather, he began the reign as a loyal servant of the Crown who, like many nobles, found himself frozen out of royal favor by the Beauforts. When, in the 1450s, Henry VI began to decline into madness, the court into corruption, and the country into economic depression, York and his followers began to challenge Queen Margaret and Edmund Beaufort, duke of Somerset (ca. 1406–55) for office, influence, and power at court. That fight turned violent in 1455 when the duke of York and the Nevilles raised their affinities, defeated, and killed Somerset at the battle of St. Albans, Hertfordshire (see map 4). After St. Albans, York was named lord protector of England, but the Beaufort faction was by no means finished. Both sides bided their time, maneuvered for advantage, and prepared for further hostilities: the Wars of the Roses had begun.

They resumed in the fall of 1459, and lasted for two years. At first, the Lancastrians had the upper hand, winning the battle of Ludford Bridge, Shropshire, in October (map 4). They followed up on their victory by attainting and so ruining a number of Yorkist peers. But in June of 1460 Richard Neville, earl of Warwick (1428–71), the commander of the Calais garrison, returned to England and helped turn the tide against the Lancastrians. The next month, the Yorkists defeated the king's forces at Northampton, Northamptonshire, and Richard, duke of York, formally laid claim to the Crown. However, in December, Richard's army was defeated at Wakefield, Yorkshire (map 4), and he was killed. His son, Edward (1442–83), now became duke of York. At this point the Lancastrians had the advantage again, and Queen Margaret marched on London. However, the city, perhaps angry at the state of trade, certainly alarmed at stories of the rapacity of her army, closed its gates to her. Rather, on March 4, 1461, the citizens of London and members of the nobility acclaimed the duke of York as King Edward IV. That claim was finally made good at the end of the month in a seven-hour mêlée during a blinding snowstorm at Towton Moor, Yorkshire (map 4). At the end of it, the Lancastrian army lay defeated and Edward returned to London in triumph. The reign of King Edward IV (1461–83) had begun.

The Yorkists won not because Edward's claim to the throne was stronger than Henry's, but because Henry was a weak and unsuccessful king. The country's leading citizens were sick of defeat abroad, expensive and corrupt government at home, and the vindictiveness of Lancastrian measures against the Yorkists. Nevertheless, King Edward faced massive obstacles if he was to rehabilitate the image of the English monarchy. First, Lancastrian incompetence, cruelty, and greed had besmirched not only that line's reputation, but the very office of sovereign itself. Moreover, by losing the French lands, driving the Crown into debt, and using Parliament to pursue political vendettas, they had weakened the monarchy constitutionally. Worse, the confusion of the previous decade over rival claims to the throne had also weakened the principle of hereditary succession. Finally, it should be remembered that the Yorkists had profited from the fact that for over a decade great noble affinities had made war on the king and on each other with near impunity. It might not be so easy to get them out of the habit. Some, such as Warwick (who was being called "kingmaker"), might feel that the new king owed them much more than lands and favor.

Fortunately for the new regime, Edward IV was, on balance, a good choice to restore the prestige of monarchy and to establish the new line. Unlike Henry VI, who was often criticized for his shabby appearance, Edward had a commanding presence: tall, handsome, approachable, stylish in his dress. These qualities may seem superficial, but they should not be underestimated. The first requirement of a king – and of any head of State – was that he look and act like one. Edward, moreover, loved to participate in elaborate processions, and he encouraged a brilliant and entertaining court. But his high living had a darker side. He could be lazy and was something of a playboy. The former meant that he often relied on his brother, Richard, duke of Gloucester (1452–85), or his confidant, William, Lord Hastings (ca. 1430–83), to get things done. His attraction to beautiful women may explain his marriage in 1464 to the otherwise obscure Elizabeth Woodville (ca. 1436–92). The marriage was highly controversial in Yorkist circles because it wrecked Warwick's negotiations for a diplomatic marriage with a French princess. Moreover, Edward's attempt to raise the Woodvilles' prestige by showering them with favor did nothing for his relations with other nobles, like Warwick, who had longer and more distinguished records of Yorkist allegiance.

These cracks in the Yorkist affinity were all the more alarming because the Lancastrian threat remained. The late king, Henry, was very much at large until 1465, when he was captured and imprisoned in the Tower of London. His queen, Margaret, remained free in Scotland and had powerful allies in France where their son, the young Prince Edward (1453–71), was being sheltered. And there remained many Lancastrian noblemen, in Wales and the North especially, for whom the Wars of the Roses were not over. In 1469 Warwick, joined by the king's other brother, George, duke of Clarence (1449–78), rebelled. In the fall of 1470 they went further, joining with Queen Margaret and King Louis XI (1423–83; reigned 1461–83) of France to liberate and reinstate Henry VI. King Edward was forced to flee to the Netherlands, but he returned in the following year and, supported once again by the fickle Clarence, defeated and slew Warwick on Easter Sunday (April 14) at the battle of Barnet in Hertfordshire (see map 4). Two weeks later the Yorkist forces defeated and killed Henry's son, Prince Edward, at Tewkesbury in Gloucestershire. A few weeks after that, it was announced that the recently recaptured Henry had died "of pure displeasure and melancholy." It is, of course, much more likely that he was murdered in the Tower on or about May 21, 1471.

The ever-present threat of Lancastrian revival obscured the fact that Edward's reign had many solid achievements. Most historians credit him with restoring the power and prestige of the Crown and Henry VII would copy or extend many of his policies. First, he revived the health of the royal finances by adding his estates as duke of York, by confiscating the estates of his enemies (including the vast Duchy of Lancaster), by reviving old feudal laws which allowed him to resume lands at the deaths of their owners, and, during the second half of his reign at least, by refusing to give lands away to favorites and courtiers as the Lancastrians had done. Edward also increased his yield from Customs, first, by supervising the collectors more closely and, second, by pursuing peace with France, which promoted the recovery of international trade. As a result, he rarely had to ask Parliament for funds. This, in turn, weakened Parliament's leverage over the king.

Edward IV not only restored the government's finances; he took measures to restore its reputation for efficiency, fairness, and honesty, as well. While it is true that he concentrated power in the hands of a few great peers (Warwick, Gloucester, Hastings), below this level he appointed men to sensitive positions who were neither barons nor favorites but professionals and members of the gentry who could get the task done. His council included knights, gentlemen, judges, and attorneys, not just landed magnates. These types of individuals had two advantages over his more prominent subjects. First, none of them was so wealthy or powerful as to pose a challenge to his rule. Second, they gave the council practical expertise in the raising and prudent spending of money.

When old institutions could not be revitalized, Edward and his advisers invented new ones. For example, he encouraged the council to meet as a court of law in a room at Westminster Palace known for its ceiling decoration as the Star Chamber. The court of **Star Chamber** was more efficient than other courts because it did not have years of tradition – or many privileges for the accused – to get in the way of swift deliberation. This reminds us that increased royal power often came at the expense of individual rights. Edward also created a Council of the Marches to manage royal lands (and, later, to enforce law and order) in that sometimes rebellious region. He used his personal secretary, who became an embryonic secretary of State, and his servants in the royal household to enact policy when the officers he inherited from the Lancastrians in the official government chain of command proved recalcitrant or disloyal. These measures increased the power and efficiency of the Crown and reduced that of his "over-mighty" noble subjects. They also revived the popularity of the monarchy by restoring peace and good government.

Unfortunately, Edward still had much work to do when his health began to fail, it was said because of his penchant for high living, in the early 1480s. He died, worn out before his time, at the age of 40 on April 9, 1483. This brought to the throne his son, a boy of 12, who ascended as Edward V (1470–83?; reigned 1483). Like all boy-kings, his realm was to be administered for him by a regency council dominated by his uncles, among whom there was, unfortunately, no love lost. This was to have disastrous consequences. The most prominent of these royal relatives was the late king's surviving brother, Richard, duke of Gloucester.[3] Gloucester realized at the outset that the position of the house of York was precarious and that all of the hard-won gains of the last reign were jeopardized by the king's youth. How could a 12-year-old boy preserve his throne and line against future Lancastrian rebellions? Moreover, Gloucester's own position as head of the regency council was threatened by Edward's other uncles from the Woodville side of the family. That is, he saw two threats: one external, to Yorkist rule, from the Lancastrian house and nobility; the other internal, to him, from the late king's in-laws.

Gloucester solved his in-law problem first. At the late king's death, Edward, prince of Wales, was living with Anthony, Earl Rivers (1442–83), one of his Woodville uncles in Wales; Gloucester was holding down the North. As the news of Edward IV's demise penetrated into the countryside, young Edward, accompanied by Rivers, began to move east toward London to claim his kingdom. Gloucester began to move south, along the way striking an alliance with Henry Stafford, duke of Buckingham (1455–83). Buckingham was one of the wealthiest and most powerful landowners in England and he was yet another descendant of Edward III. This party intercepted the king near Stony Stratford, Northamptonshire, on April 30 and had Rivers arrested on a charge of plotting against Gloucester. Thus Gloucester neutralized the Woodvilles and secured sole control of the new king. On May 4 Edward, Gloucester, and Buckingham entered London to the cheers of its populace. The council, dominated by Gloucester's allies, accepted his charge of a Woodville plot and declared him protector of the realm.

But none of these dramatic actions did anything to solve the duke of Gloucester's Lancastrian problem – or to satisfy his own ambitions. Historians will never know Gloucester's precise motives for the actions he took next – though common sense suggests that they speak for themselves. In June 1483, he struck. At a council sitting on June 13 to plan Edward's coronation, he had the old king's lord chamberlain and adviser, Lord Hastings, arrested and beheaded without trial. With Hastings out of the way, Gloucester's allies were able to suggest that Edward IV, famous for his sexual escapades, had promised to marry another woman before his marriage to Elizabeth Woodville. This assertion, if true, would invalidate the Woodville marriage, render King Edward V and his younger brother, Richard, duke of York (1472–83?), illegitimate, and leave the duke of Gloucester the true Yorkist heir to the throne. Parliament, acting on this suggestion – and possibly fearing the consequences of rule by a small boy – declared the late king's marriage invalid. The duke of Gloucester was crowned King Richard III on July 6, 1483.

This still left the problem of the two royal nephews, Edward and Richard, currently housed in the Tower of London. Defenders of Richard like to point out that the Tower was, in those days, a royal palace as well as a royal prison. But recent research indicates that it was almost never used as the former. As July faded into August, the two princes were seen less and less playing in the Tower grounds and, finally, they were no longer seen at all. This led historians for many years to claim that Richard had the two boys murdered, as portrayed in Thomas More's *History of Richard III* and Shakespeare's play which was based on it. During renovations in 1674, two skeletons were found under a staircase which were assumed to be those of Edward and Richard and so were given royal burial.

Forensic examination of the remains in 1933 suggested that their respective physical development was consistent with the ages of the two princes in 1483. While none of this *proves* Richard's guilt, he remains the most likely suspect. Still, alternative suspects have been suggested, such as the ambitious duke of Buckingham. As a result, the question of who murdered the little princes in the Tower remains one of the great murder mysteries in English history,[4] and will almost certainly never be solved. In fact, there may not have been a murder at all. Contemporary chroniclers report that Prince Edward was ill of fever in July 1483. It is quite possible that the two young men, living in the damp confines of the Tower, succumbed to natural causes. This would explain the new king's failure to address their situation publicly or produce their persons for display.

In fact, it does not matter who – or what – killed the princes. Contemporaries assumed that Richard did it. Whatever his responsibility or motivation, his ruthless ascent to the throne divided the Yorkist affinity and left a bad taste in the mouths of his subjects. He spent the remainder of his reign seeking to prove that he really wasn't such a bad guy after all. In fact, Richard III was not the hunchbacked monster portrayed in subsequent Tudor propaganda. He had proven himself able and courageous during the Wars of the Roses. He was intelligent and cultured and prudent enough to continue his brother's policies. The legislation passed by his Parliaments was enlightened and favorable to trade and the economy. Even his physical problems were exaggerated by the Tudors: he seems to have had one shoulder slightly higher than the other, no more.

But the bloody opening of Richard's reign besmirched the Yorkist cause while the flimsiness of his claim encouraged others to try for his throne. In late 1483 he put down a revolt by his erstwhile ally, Buckingham. The duke paid for his gamble, as did most would-be kings in this period, with his head. In the summer of 1485, Richard faced another revolt, this time by a Welsh nobleman with only the most tenuous of Lancastrian claims, Henry Tudor, earl of Richmond. His father was Edmund Tudor, earl of Richmond (ca. 1430–56), a powerful Welsh landowner and the son of Katherine of Valois (1401–37), Henry V's widow, by her *second* husband, Owen Tudor (d. 1461), who was not of royal blood at all. His mother was Margaret Beaufort (1443–1509), a direct, but female, descendant of Edward III's fourth son, John of Gaunt, duke of Lancaster, by his *mistress*, Katherine Swynford (1350–1403; see genealogy 2, p. 413). This provided a claim, but it was weaker than Richard III's; nor, indeed, was it much stronger than that of about half-a-dozen other English peers. Nevertheless, when the Lancastrian cause collapsed in 1471, Richmond had been forced into continental exile. There, he bided his time and attempted to shore up support among the Lancastrian nobility.

In August 1485 he returned, landing with perhaps 2,000 supporters at Milford Haven in Wales. Important noble families flocked to his side, not so much out of loyalty to him as dissatisfaction with a ruthless and usurper king. As we noted at the beginning of this chapter, the rival armies met at Bosworth Field, Leicestershire, on August 22. Richard found out just how weak his support was when, soon after the opening of battle, the powerful Stanley family and their followers deserted for Richmond's side. Indeed, it was actually a party of Stanley retainers who killed the king after he had been unhorsed in a brave but desperate charge of Henry's bodyguard. The sun of the house of York had set. The day belonged to the house of Richmond – or, as historians refer to it, the house of Tudor.

Establishing the Tudor State

By 1485, England had experienced civil war for well over three decades, and an uncertain succession for almost a century. The new king's prospects could not have seemed promising. He was only 28 years old. He had no affinity, no important friends, no experience of government. He had not even run his own estates, having spent his youth on the run, first in Brittany and then, from 1484, in France. Moreover, there remained in play a clutch of Yorkist pretenders to the throne, some with better claims than Henry. There was, for example, John de la Pole, earl of Lincoln (ca. 1462–87), the nephew of both Edward IV and Richard III and the latter's designated heir. There was also Edward, earl of Warwick (1475–99), and his sister Margaret, countess of Salisbury (1473–1541), the children of the duke of Clarence. Later, Henry, marquis of Exeter (1498–1539), a grandson of Edward IV, would become a factor. Finally, for the romantically inclined, it should not be forgotten that the bodies of Edward V and his brother, Richard, duke of York, had never been found. This would give rise to the fifteenth-century equivalent of "Elvis-sightings" and therefore the possibility that an impostor could play on the nostalgic credulity of the populace. That possibility was enhanced by enemies abroad: Margaret, duchess of Burgundy (1446–1503), sister of Edward IV and Richard III, could provide a continental base of operations and sanctuary well out of Henry's reach. As we will see, the French, the Scots, the Irish, even the Holy Roman Emperor might find it in their interests to dislodge Henry or destabilize his regime. After all, the rulers of Brittany and France had done as much for Henry against the Yorkists; just like rebellious barons, they might not find it easy to break the habit.

But the Wars of the Roses did end. Henry VII did establish his authority, and his dynasty as well: the Tudors would rule England for well over a century, effectively and, for the most part, unchallenged. How did he – and they – do it? Before we can answer that question, it is necessary to understand what sort of man he was. His image (see plate 2) provides some clues. Henry Tudor was shrewd, tight-lipped, suspicious, and intensely practical. Like many late medieval rulers, he anticipated the sort of prince described in Machiavelli's book of that name: ruthless, capable of sharp practice and even cruelty if necessary. The result would have pleased the author of *The Prince*, for in the words of one contemporary: "The King is feared rather than loved."[5] But where cruelty was not necessary, Henry VII was content to let sleeping dogs lie. That is, while he forgot nothing, he did not hold grudges or engage in personal vendettas.

This practical side of Henry's character led earlier historians to identify him as a more or less "modern" personality and, indeed, his behavior can sometimes remind one of a twenty-first century CEO. But Henry was born in the fifteenth

Plate 2 Henry VII, *painted terracotta bust, by Pietro Torrigiano. © The Board of Trustees of the Victoria and Albert Museum.*

century and many of his habits were purely medieval. He was a loyal son of the Church who burned **heretics**, heard multiple daily masses, and spent £20,000 building the glorious chapel in Westminster Abbey which bears his name and enshrines his body, as well as those of many of his descendants. A firm believer in **Purgatory**, and perhaps out of concern for what all that practicality and cruelty might have done to the state of his soul, he left money at his death to pay for the celebration of 10,000 masses.

Finally, there is one further aspect of Henry's personality which may be interpreted as either medieval or modern or, perhaps, both at once: his love of ceremony. Like Edward IV, Henry VII believed that a king must be seen to be magnificent, even god-like. He participated in elaborate processions and commissioned works of art to show himself and his regime in the best possible light. There is also evidence that he encouraged artists and writers to besmirch the memory of Richard III and the Yorkists as much as possible. This even extended to having paintings of the late king altered to increase the size of his hunchback's hump! No modern politician was better at going negative.

The new king demonstrated his hard-headedness and practicality in the steps he took immediately after seizing the throne. The first thing Henry did upon his triumphant arrival in London was to get himself crowned, on October 30. Only then, on November 7, did he assemble a Parliament. Thus, rather than ask its members to declare him king (as Henry Bolingbroke had done), he simply informed them of the already accomplished fact. He then had them ruin the most powerful Yorkist peers via attainder, but he left those of lesser power and wealth alone. In fact, Henry VII continued to employ mid-level Yorkists and former servants of the Yorkists in his administration. That is, he destroyed those who had the potential to challenge his rule, while offering his protection and favor to those who were not a threat. This accomplished three purposes. First, it caused many former Yorkists at this level to switch sides to the new king. Second, it deprived possible Yorkist pretenders to the throne of a rank-and-file. Third, it ensured that the new administration would continue to function with the smooth precision of its Yorkist predecessor, because it would largely be the same administration. Later, in 1495, he would sign into law the *De facto* Act, which exempted from prosecution anyone acting on the orders of an English king. The idea was to reassure old Yorkists that he had no intention of pursuing them further for past actions, while encouraging the loyalty of his own followers as well by promising indemnity from the resentment of some future ruler.

Henry's willingness to embrace those associated with the past regime received its ultimate expression in his choice of a consort. Five months after Bosworth Field, in fulfillment of a promise he had made in 1483, he married the Princess Elizabeth (1465–1503), daughter of Edward IV, elder sister of the two princes who had died in the Tower – and therefore the niece of Henry's mortal enemy, Richard III. At this late date, it is impossible to judge the feelings that may have existed between Henry and Elizabeth. Every indication is that their marriage became a solid one, producing eight children (though only three survived their parents). But its beginning seems to have been a matter of pure calculation: on the one hand, it was the clearest indication yet that Henry intended to bury the hatchet with the Yorkists. On the other hand, by waiting five months after his accession, the new king also made clear that his Crown was in no way contingent on a Yorkist alliance. Above all, this union resulted in the mingling of Yorkist, Lancastrian, and Tudor blood. In September 1486, Queen Elizabeth gave birth to a son. Even the choice of name for the new prince was calculated: Arthur (1486–1502). The name was, of course, symbolic of English (and Welsh) unity and seemed to pledge that the monarchy would return to its former greatness.

Finally, in the spring of 1486, Henry made a progress through the North, the most "Yorkist" of his dominions. His purpose was, first, to show himself to his people in full kingly magnificence; but also to demonstrate that he was backed by a large and powerful entourage. Just in case anyone missed the point, that entourage arrested the earl of Warwick, one of the most prominent Yorkist claimants to the throne.

These were shrewd measures, but they did not prevent Yorkist uprisings entirely. Since most Yorkist claimants were either too young, too dead, or safely deposited in the Tower, these attempts tended to involve "pretenders to the throne," i.e., impostors. In 1487 a boy named Lambert Simnel (ca. 1475–1525), the son of a baker, was passed off by the Yorkists as the imprisoned Warwick. On May 5 Simnel, accompanied by the earl of Lincoln (a real Yorkist claimant) and 2,000 German mercenary troops supplied by Margaret of Burgundy, landed in Ireland, where Yorkist support was strong. There, Gerald Fitzgerald, earl of Kildare (ca. 1456–1513), the lord deputy and most prominent Anglo-Irish landowner in the island, recognized Simnel as king. On June 4 his forces, augmented by Irish troops, landed in Lancashire and marched south on the capital. Perhaps because the country was weary of war, perhaps because of early signs of Henry's effectiveness, the rebels gained little support. A royal army met and defeated them at East Stoke, outside Newark, Nottinghamshire. Conveniently for Henry, Lincoln died in battle. As for Simnel, Henry made him a servant in the royal kitchens: the first Tudor was not without mercy or a sense of humor.

These qualities would be tested a few years later by another adolescent impostor, Perkin Warbeck (ca. 1474–99). Warbeck, the son of a Flemish government official, was, apparently, a remarkably well-dressed young man. In 1491 the inhabitants of Cork, Ireland, mistook him for the long-dead Richard, duke of York. (Henry later remarked with exasperation: "My lords of Ireland, you will crown apes at last."[6]) No one in England seems to have believed that Warbeck was Richard, but the Yorkists nevertheless seized the opportunity of presenting him as such. Margaret of Burgundy coached him on how to act and the rulers of France, Scotland, and the Holy Roman Empire went along with the charade for political reasons of their own. In fact, he even managed to marry into the Scottish royal house and use Scotland as a base from which to attack Henry. But successive invasions of England were beaten off in 1495, 1496, and 1497. In the last case, Warbeck joined a preexisting rebellion in Cornwall against high taxes. But he landed after the initial uprising had been suppressed and, even though some 3,000 Cornishmen joined his cause, he was soon captured. Like Simnel, he was spared at first but, after evidence emerged – or was fabricated – that he had been plotting yet another revolt with the real earl of Warwick, both were executed in 1499. This represents the last serious challenge to Henry's regime. By the 1490s, if not earlier, English men and women were heartily sick of civil wars and would-be kings and had decided to settle for the sovereign they had.

Nevertheless, these incidents convinced Henry of the dangers of isolation. It was not enough to overawe, satisfy, or neutralize his own subjects; he needed friends abroad. After all, he had used France as a base from which to launch his own rebellion against Richard III and his enemies had found support in Burgundy, France, Scotland, and the Holy Roman Empire. Henry began by trying to win over the king of France, Charles VIII (1470–98; reigned 1483–98), but the latter was not interested. Henry responded in 1489 by throwing his support to the rebellious nobles of Brittany, claiming the throne of France for himself, and, in 1492, launching an invasion from Calais. This got the French king's attention. The result was the Treaty of Étaples, by which Henry agreed to withdraw in return for a subsidy of £5,000 for 15 years.[7] Similarly, from 1493 to 1496, Henry used trade embargos against Burgundy and the Holy Roman Empire to persuade them to withdraw their support for Perkin Warbeck. Next, Henry set out to secure his northern flank. King James IV of Scotland (1473–1513; reigned 1488–1513) had provided Warbeck with valuable support and an easy route into England. Henry won him over by offering a diplomatic marriage with his daughter, Margaret (1489–1541). A treaty was signed in 1499 and the marriage took place in 1503. While it would not prevent future antagonism with the Scots, it did link the two royal houses. This would lead to a Stuart accession in England after the death of the last Tudor in 1603.

But Henry's greatest diplomatic coup was his alliance with Spain. In the 1480s Spain's situation was not unlike that of England: after a period of division and weakness, it had just been united under the rule of Ferdinand of Aragon (1452–1516; reigned 1479–1516) and Isabella of Castile (1451–1504; reigned 1479–1504). This new dynasty needed friends too, especially against its powerful northern neighbor, France. So, in 1489, England and Spain signed the Treaty of Medina del Campo, by which Henry promised (1) military support against France and (2) his son, Arthur, in marriage to Ferdinand and Isabella's daughter, Catherine of Aragon (1485–1536). Since the two royal children were well under-age, the marriage did not take place until November 1501. It did so amidst weeks of festivals, feasts, tournaments, and dancing. Well might the Tudors have been in a celebratory mood, for by 1501 Spain had acquired a great empire, thanks to the explorations of Columbus (1451–1506) and others. Henry's courtship of this up-and-coming country looked to be a fabulous success.

Unfortunately, Arthur died five months after his marriage. This jeopardized the Spanish alliance, the cornerstone of Henry's foreign policy. Fortunately, or so it seemed at the time, King Henry had another son, also named Henry (1491–1547), whom he offered to Catherine. But Ferdinand, a cagey negotiator, demanded the return of Catherine's dowry. Spain was now a major power and might hope for a more advantageous match; moreover, the Tudors, down to their last heir in the male line, did not look like such a good investment as they had done a decade earlier. The death of Queen Elizabeth early in 1503 further weakened Tudor prospects. But if Ferdinand was a hard bargainer, so was Henry VII. He stopped payment of Catherine's allowance of £1,200 a year and stripped her of her household. Now a widower himself, he began to negotiate with various other European powers for an alternative, not only for his son but for himself. In the end, Henry's own death in April 1509 settled the issue. At the urging of his council, the new king, Henry VIII (reigned 1509–47), decided to go ahead with the marriage to Catherine. After a papal dispensation allowing Henry to marry his brother's widow, the most fateful wedding in English history took place in June 1509. Thus, by the end of Henry VII's reign, it appeared that England was surrounded by, if not friends, then, at least, relatives. Henry VII's successful foreign policy, combined with his cultivation of good relations with the Church, ensured that, at the accession of his son, the new dynasty would have no great external enemies. What about its internal situation?

At this point, it might be wise to say something about the structure of English government at the end of the fifteenth century. At its center was, of course, the king, "the life, the head, and the authoritie of all thinges that be doone in the realm of England."[8] In some sense, the whole kingdom was his property. Clearly, a strong king set the agenda for his government. As a result, it is often popularly assumed that a medieval or early modern king's word was law, that what he said "went," and that there was little room for disagreement. This assumption is probably based upon bad historical films and our modern experience of living under powerful, omnipresent governments, with their multiple departments, vast military and naval forces, and "high-tech" methods of surveillance and coercion. English royal government during the early modern period was not, in fact, like that. It was small: perhaps 1,500 officials in Henry VII's reign. It was also, as we have seen, poor: early modern kings were almost invariably in debt and had to ask Parliament's permission to raise taxes. In part because it was so small and poor, in part because no one expected much from it, the responsibilities of early modern government were much fewer than those of its modern equivalent. There was no standing army, no Federal Bureau of Investigation, no Internal Revenue Service or national postal service, no Medicare or federal loans for deserving students. So what features did it have in common with modern government?

Like modern rulers, the king needed advice. This was provided by a council which consisted, before Henry VII's reign, mostly of important landowners and department heads, the majority of whom were peers or bishops. Because so many wanted the honor of counseling the king, this body was often vast and unwieldy. As a result, late medieval and early modern sovereigns tended to rely upon a trusted inner circle of about 10 to 20 such councilors. By the middle of the sixteenth century the Tudors would institutionalize this smaller, more effective group as the "Privy Council." Even before this development, the council dealt with a wide variety of matters: the administration of royal lands, taxation and justice in the localities, the arbitration of disputes between powerful men, diplomacy, and the defense of the realm. As we have seen, the council was also beginning to serve as a legal tribunal when it met as the court of Star Chamber. This court dealt with such matters as riot, conspiracy, forgery, defamation, and perjury. Royal decisions which had emerged from debate in council were later framed as Orders in Council, in part to demonstrate that the king had consulted with the most prominent people in the realm.

The council was considered part of the king's court or household. The household provided for simple domestic needs: food and drink, tableware, linen, fuel, etc. for the king, his family, those of his servants who lived at court, and guests. At the English court these functions were fulfilled by a department known as the Household Below Stairs, presided over by a great officer called the lord steward. But a court was far more than a domestic establishment. It was the epicenter of national political, social, and cultural life as well as the great stage upon which the theater of monarchy was acted. It was in the splendid halls and corridors of the king's palace that political business, influence, and intrigue were carried on;

the socially prominent (and those ambitious to be so) amused themselves and just "hung out"; the leading authors, artists, and musicians sought patronage and set the trends of fashion; and the sovereign staged splendid processions, feasts, and entertainments designed to remind his guests, foreign and domestic, that he was God's lieutenant on earth. The Chamber, presided over by the lord chamberlain, oversaw the court's ceremonial and artistic life. It employed numerous gentlemen, drawn from every part of the realm, whose job was to give their attendance in the court's public rooms, especially the Hall (where the king's courtiers and officers were fed) and the Presence Chamber (where he could be seen on his throne). Because everybody who thought themselves anybody flocked to these rooms seeking the sovereign's attention and favor, late medieval kings found that they had little privacy. As a result, in the 1490s Henry VII created a new room and set of officials beyond the Presence Chamber called the Privy Chamber, to which he could retreat in search of peace, relative solitude, and, perhaps, greater safety from assassination. Unfortunately, the admiring throng pursued him and his successors even here. To provide additional security, as well as to increase the magnificence of his court, Henry also created a royal bodyguard, the Yeomen of the Guard.

Early in the Middle Ages most of the king's business had been conducted by household servants acting in his name on an ad hoc basis. That is, the king's treasure was stored in chests in his Chamber. His weaponry and munitions for war were purchased by the department which normally supplied his furniture, the Great Wardrobe. If he wished to make diplomatic contact with another ruler, he sent an officer of his court. While this occasionally still happened, by the end of the fifteenth century many of these functions had "gone out of court." That is, they were performed by separate departments with their own heads and chains of command according to fixed procedures. Among these offices was the Chancery, originally the king's writing office. Here, the lord chancellor, often a bishop, kept the Great Seal of England, which was affixed to important documents such as acts of Parliament and grants of land. But by 1485, the lord chancellor's primary function was to preside over the court of Chancery, which administered equity jurisdiction where the common law (see below) was inadequate or in which a strict application of its rules would lead to a miscarriage of justice. That is, the court of Chancery existed to correct injustice stemming from the strict application of the law. No wonder the lord chancellor was called "the keeper of the king's conscience." The clerical functions of the Chancery had been taken over by the office of the Privy Seal, which was a less elaborate royal seal attached to grants of offices and pensions. The Privy Seal office, staffed mostly by clerks, was the clearing house for general government business.

The office which housed and accounted for the king's money was the Exchequer, presided over by the lord treasurer. This office combined the functions of a private banker, tax-collecting agency, accountancy firm, and a law court to oversee taxation disputes. It received its name from the checkered cloth, like a checkerboard, upon which, during the Middle Ages, amounts of money received were marked by counters – necessary because many sheriffs, responsible for receiving and submitting taxation, were illiterate. By the late fifteenth century the procedures of the Exchequer were becoming stultified, full of pointless tradition and red tape. As a result, it took years to pass an account and it was virtually impossible for the king to know at any given time how much money he had. In response, Edward IV and Henry VII began to turn back to their household officers, in particular the treasurer of the Chamber, to handle their finances. By the early 1490s the Chamber was receiving over 90 percent of the king's revenue and its treasurer was the most important financial officer in the kingdom. This was a less public system of government finance, but it gave these late fifteenth-century monarchs greater flexibility and more control than that afforded by the "official" government departments.

In addition to the courts of Chancery and Exchequer, there were in London common law courts of King's Bench and Common Pleas, the former for cases, both civil and criminal, in which the Crown was involved, the latter for civil suits, especially those involving property, contract or debt, between subjects. Common law was the body of law that had evolved out of judicial precedent and custom, as opposed to statute law, which was written in acts passed by Parliament and approved by the king. As we have seen, Parliament consisted of the House of Lords and the House of Commons. Every male peer had the right to sit in the Lords, as did bishops and, before the Dissolution of the Monasteries in the 1530s, abbots of great monasteries. This provided an upper house of perhaps 100–110 members. The House of Commons may sound, from its title, more representative of the English people. There were two members or MPs (the term only applies to those in the lower house) for every county (called knights of the shire) as well as usually two members for (in theory) every major city and town (called boroughs), yielding about 300 members in 1500.[9] But the list of boroughs so represented would be more or less frozen at the end of the Tudor period: that meant that some towns which grew subsequently into major cities thereafter might have no MP, while parliamentary constituencies which declined to few or no inhabitants retained theirs, leaving their landlords with the power to simply name their members. For example, the original site of the old city of Salisbury, called Old Sarum, was by 1500 a nearly vacant hilltop, but it still had the right to name two MPs to the Commons. As a result, its owner simply appointed those members, who, presumably, followed his orders. Such a member was said to be in his patron's pocket – hence the term "pocket borough."

As noted in the Introduction, any male owning land worth 40 shillings (£2) annually could vote for his county's knights of the shire. In most boroughs, the vote was restricted to an inside group of civic leaders or those who lived in a certain part of town. These restrictions varied from constituency to constituency; overall, a bit less than 3 percent of English and Welsh males, perhaps 30,000 people, had a vote. As a result, most members of the lower house were not so much elected as *selected* by a dominant local landowner, or a few leading townsmen. The MPs themselves tended to be prominent members of the classes who selected them: great landowners, wealthy merchants or, in a few cases, leading attorneys or professional men. Thus, "election" to Parliament was usually a sign of local social status, not a career move. As a result, *both* houses of Parliament tended to represent the views of the upper class, not the common man or woman.

Parliament's very existence was entirely at the sovereign's will. That is, only he could call a parliamentary election, summon the Parliament to meet, prorogue it (suspend its meeting until needed again), or dissolve it (send the members home and call for a new election). Indeed, many historians refer to Parliaments, not the singular, for the entire early modern period, in order to emphasize that there was no continued existence except at the monarch's whim. Given that Parliaments had the right to petition the sovereign for redress of grievance and to impeach (try) his ministers for misconduct; and that, in the fifteenth century, they had often criticized those ministers (and, by implication, the monarch himself) for their conduct of foreign policy, corruption, incompetence, or courtly extravagance, one might wonder why a late medieval or early modern ruler would ever call a Parliament? One reason was that kings were notoriously short of money and by the fourteenth century the monarch could impose a new tax only after parliamentary approval. Moreover, if he was pursuing a controversial policy, such as a war or a trade embargo, he might find such approval useful to show that the nation had been consulted. Still, Parliaments met only intermittently, averaging only 24 days a year under the Yorkists, 18 days a year under Henry VII. After 1495, Henry called but two Parliaments, which sat for an average of just eight days a year. When Parliaments did meet, they articulated royal policies and raised grievances in the form of petitions for legislation. Whichever house originated a petition debated it. If approved by a vote, it was then engrossed as a bill. Each bill had to undergo two readings, each one also subject to debate and vote, before it could be sent to the other house to repeat the process of engrossment, readings, debates, and votes. If a bill was approved at each of these steps it was said to have passed and was then submitted to the sovereign, who could attach his seal to it, by which it became an act of Parliament (a law or statute); or veto it, in which case it was lost at least until the next session.

A law passed had to be enforced. In the country at large, the king employed up to 40 administers of Crown lands and up to 90 Customs officials to collect his revenues; as well as a series of traveling **assize** judges to provide royal justice in felony cases, biannually, to the shire court of each county. Since the king did not otherwise have bureaucrats "on the ground" to enforce his will or a standing army to coerce obedience, he had to rely on the cooperation of his most important subjects for everything else. We have already seen that in frontier areas, such as the Welsh Marches, the Anglo-Scottish border or the Irish Pale, late medieval kings depended on powerful local magnates and their affinities to enforce order. Even in less remote areas they called on great nobles to keep a watch on their counties, a relationship which would, by the mid-sixteenth century, evolve into the office of **lord lieutenant** of the shire. Such magnates also held numerous other local posts: as constables of royal castles, keepers of royal forests, stewards of royal manors. These positions paid well, in both money and prestige, for very little work, and were therefore eagerly sought by ambitious noblemen.

Supporting these locally significant nobles were the gentry, whose members might serve as sheriffs or justices of the peace (JPs). The sheriff collected taxes, impaneled juries for shire courts, and, early in the period, raised the militia. He was unpaid and the position, though honorific, was also onerous – not least because he was liable in law for taxes which he had failed to collect. In addition, most counties had scores of JPs. These local gentlemen acted as judges in legal and economic disputes, four times a year at meetings of the shire court called quarter sessions, and, on a more ad hoc basis as needed, at petty sessions. In the cities the king relied on the **corporation** – the mayor and aldermen – whose power he had granted by means of the borough charter. In all these cases, since he could not afford to provide a salary, he depended on the good will of those he asked to serve. That good will might not be forthcoming if the monarch's request was thought to be unreasonable by the local official or his neighbors. This explains why the king of England did not always get his way.

Henry VII adopted and improved the structure of government that he inherited from the Yorkists; he did not radically alter it. Nevertheless, he made English government a more efficient and effective instrument on the king's behalf. He did this by reviving three old principles of medieval kingship, long forgotten by the Lancastrians and only briefly revived by the Yorkists:

> The king must be strong.
> The king must govern with consent.
> The king must live of his own.

First, the king must be strong. Henry had, of course, demonstrated his strength by virtue of defeating Richard III and later usurpers in battle. Away from the battlefield, he was a vigorous and hardworking king. As indicated above, he often bypassed normal channels (such as the Exchequer), running government personally out of his household. He could innovate, as when he used the court of Star Chamber to prosecute rebellion. Above all, he sought to keep the nobility, of whom he was exceedingly wary, in check. Unlike Henry VI, he was very sparing in distributing titles, honors, and lands to his nobles. Unlike Edward IV, he avoided over-reliance on a few mighty peers like a Warwick or a Gloucester. Rather, he revived a different Edwardian strategy by encouraging Parliament to pass a Statute Against Liveries in 1487, renewed and amplified in 1504. These laws outlawed unauthorized private armies of the nobility (whose uniforms were referred to as liveries). He also used attainder, the threat of attainder, or his power to forgive an attainder as a way of keeping over-mighty subjects on probation and off balance. As the reign wore on, he increasingly imposed on offending nobles exorbitant recognizances or bonds to pay huge sums of money (sometimes in the thousands of pounds). These would not necessarily be collected; rather, they would be kept on file as a noble pledge – and a royal threat – against future rebellious behavior. By the time of the king's death in 1509, some three-quarters of the peerage were, or had been, laboring under an attainder, recognizance, or some other financial penalty. According to one of his closest advisers, Edmund

Dudley (1462–1510), the king wished "to have many persons in his danger at his pleasure."[10] This led contemporaries to accuse Henry of greed and vindictiveness. But it is difficult to argue with the results of his policies: the restoration of royal authority and political order, the elimination of effective aristocratic opposition and violence, and the firm establishment of the new dynasty.

If Henry was strong, he nevertheless sought advice and support for his policies, though not necessarily from his nobility. As the Statutes Against Liveries suggest, Henry was careful to secure parliamentary support of controversial measures. He was also careful to follow Edward IV's precedent of summoning a large council of 20 to 30. He did this, first, so that no one would dominate but himself; and, second, in order to include gentlemen, merchants, and attorneys. His closest advisers tended to be lawyers of gentry background, like the aforementioned Dudley, Sir Reginald Bray (fl. 1472–1503), or Sir Richard Empson (d. 1510). This had two effects. First, such men were not sufficiently powerful in themselves to pose a challenge to the king's rule. Second, they could offer practical advice on the economy, the law, and other matters. Along the same lines, Henry VII tended to increase the power of his JPs against that of the more socially prominent (but not always honest or efficient) magnates and sheriffs. In particular, he authorized them to seek out unlawful retainers and to investigate complaints of extortion by government officials. Finally, Henry's revival of court ceremonies and entertainments indicates that he understood the value of propaganda in securing an appearance of consent and approval for royal policies. This is not to imply that he had to deal with a free press (it did not exist), public opinion polls, or public opinion itself in the modern sense. Rather, in this context, consent meant that people were reasonably satisfied with his rule and unlikely to seek out or support an alternative.

One reason for that satisfaction was Henry VII's financial probity. Theoretically, the king owned so much property and received so much money out of land rentals and Customs duties that he should have been able to live "of his own." That is, his "ordinary" revenue should have been sufficient for him to run his household, pay the salaries of his government officials, and pursue domestic policy without having to call a Parliament to vote him any "extraordinary" revenue in new taxes. Such extraordinary revenue was only to be raised in emergencies, such as a state of rebellion or war. Unfortunately the previous century, with its recurrent rebellions and wars, had often seemed like one long emergency. The Lancastrians, in particular, had asked Parliament for frequent tax increases to pay for the Hundred Years' War and their part in the Wars of the Roses. Moreover, the Crown lands and Customs revenue had been so devastated by these wars and so poorly administered by corrupt officials that those monarchs had to ask for parliamentary funds just to keep their domestic establishments running. As a result, the English taxpayer and his representatives in Parliament were growing increasingly hostile to new taxes, as in the case of the Cornish rebellion.

Henry VII was shrewd enough to see that this had to stop. He sought to live almost entirely on his ordinary revenue by carefully exploiting its four sources.

First, he increased the amount of Crown lands. As king he inherited both the Lancastrian and Yorkist estates, and he brought Tudor lands with him. Rather than dispense these to his nobility as previous kings had done, his Parliaments passed five acts of resumption *revoking* previous grants of royal land. He also pursued feudal escheats, that is, lands which were supposed to be forfeit to the Crown on the deaths of their holders. Finally, his aggressive policy of seeking acts of attainder against his principal enemies brought yet more land into his hands. By 1504, the clear yield from Crown lands (that is, the profits from rents and the sale of crops and minerals) had risen from about £29,000 a year to £42,000 a year.

An equally important component of the ordinary revenue was the yield from Customs duties on wool and other commodities. This, too, had fallen during the previous century, largely because the wars had wrecked trade. Henry rectified the problem by embracing a mostly peaceful foreign policy, as we have seen. This sent the Customs yield from £33,000 a year to over £41,000 a year. Third, Henry pursued more aggressively dues and fines owed to the Crown as its feudal right, including fees on inheritances, **wardships**, and the marriage of underage or widowed royal tenants. The annual yield from these sources rose from a mere £343 in 1491 to £6,000 in 1507. Fourth, his more efficient administration exploited legal fines and fees. Finally, Henry VII, like Edward IV, was not above investing in trading voyages, accepting a pension from the French king, or extorting loans and "benevolences" from his subjects without their permission. As a result of these policies, Henry VII's total revenue rose to about £113,000 a year, the vast majority of it raised from ordinary sources, by 1502. Consequently, he rarely had to call Parliament during the last years of his reign.

Henry VII died in 1509, leaving his successor a full Treasury, an efficient government, a stable regime and – despite the grumbling of a subdued nobility – a loyal nation. While he was neither beloved nor even popular, he commanded the respect and fear of his subjects. The first Tudor king had succeeded in establishing his dynasty. Unfortunately, he left that achievement in the hands of his 17-year-old heir – Henry VIII.

Young King Hal

If ever a king has captured the imagination of the general public, both during his reign and right up to our own day, it is Henry VIII. It is very largely his image, "cocksure and truculent, astride one of Holbein's canvases" (see plate 3), which we conjure when we think of a king.[11] For those who grew up in the twentieth century, it is difficult to separate the image in our mind's eye from that created by film actors like Charles Laughton, Robert Shaw, Richard Burton, Keith Michel – even Benny Hill: that of a vain and corpulent lecher, eating, whoring, and executing his way through marriage after marriage, ministry after ministry. Like most popular historical orthodoxies, this one contains a grain of truth – not least in its conveyance of Henry's "larger than life" personality. But it contains much

Plate 3   Henry VIII, *after Hans Holbein the Younger. Board of the National Museums and Galleries on Merseyside (Walker Art Gallery).*

distortion as well. The worst result of the uncritical reception of that distorted image is that it reduces perhaps the single most important watershed in English history – the Reformation – to the by-product of a single man's foibles and appetites. This may be an acceptable interpretation for the movies but, as we shall see, the truth is far more subtle, more complicated, and more interesting.

In fact, Henry's contemporaries were almost universally impressed with him, especially toward the beginning of his reign. And why not? He had many good qualities. He was, first, handsome and athletic, a skilled horseman who loved tilting, falconry, wrestling, and dancing. But Henry was more than a royal jock. He had a mind as agile as his body. Like Plato's philosopher-king, Henry had studied mathematics as well as Greek, Latin, French, Italian, and Spanish. He corresponded with Erasmus (ca. 1466–1536) and befriended Sir Thomas More, two of the greatest philosophers of their day. Indeed, his court was a hotbed of humanist scholarship. The king himself wrote a theological treatise, *Assertio Septem Sacramentorum*, attacking the new reformist ideas of Martin Luther (1483–1546). In reward for this piece of scholarship, the pope named Henry *Defensor Fidei* ("Defender of the Faith") in 1521. Henry was also artistic and, in particular, musical. He sang, played the lute, the organ, and the virginals (a primitive harpsichord) and composed masses, songs, and anthems. He patronized professional artists and musicians, providing employment for the likes of the portraitist Hans Holbein (1497–1543), the composer Thomas Tallis (ca. 1505–85), and the polymath singer, actor, composer, and playwright William Cornyshe (ca. 1465–1523).

Finally, Henry VIII could be generous to friends, charming to acquaintances, and attractively flamboyant in the presence of his subjects. During the first half of his reign, especially, the court sponsored an endless round of jousting, tilting, **mumming**, dancing, wrestling, revels, and pageants for New Year's Day, Epiphany, **Shrovetide**, the return of the king at the end of the summer, and Christmas-time. Unlike his father, who merely presided, Henry VIII participated actively in these events. His court was a movable feast, progressing in an annual circuit around London among the half-dozen larger palaces and the numerous smaller houses which he owned. Henry did this because the 300–400 people comprising his household entourage soon overwhelmed the primitive waste disposal facilities of any given house; because he felt the need to show himself and the splendor of his court to as many of his subjects as possible; and finally because he was notoriously restless and hankered after new sights and sounds. After the careful sobriety of Henry VII's last years, the English people were, perhaps, ready for a little "flash," a little festivity, and, if they lived in the Home Counties, a great deal more contact with their ruler. Henry VIII was just the man to give it to them.

But underneath the new king's charming and exuberant exterior beat a heart which was every bit as cold and calculating, if not as cautious, as that of his predecessor. Henry VIII was emotional, brooding, impulsive, greedy, utterly self-centered, and unshakeably sure of himself. Admittedly, these are all, perhaps, understandable characteristics in a king. But this king seems to have felt no loyalty to any particular set of policy goals or persons. He sacked advisers, favorites, ministers, wives as it pleased him. On the second day of the reign he imprisoned, and would eventually execute, two of his father's most loyal, effective, and therefore unpopular tax collectors, Edmund Dudley and Sir Richard Empson. This was a popular move, especially with aristocrats oppressed by his father's financial exactions. But it was also needlessly cruel, arbitrary, and utterly disloyal to two faithful Crown servants. It was meant to be a break with the past but, in fact, it set a precedent for the future: Henry VIII would seek the judicial murder of two queens, three cardinals, numerous peers and clergymen, and nearly every principal minister who ever served him. His last would-be victim, Thomas Howard, duke of Norfolk (1473–1554), was languishing in the Tower of London, awaiting his beheading the very next day, when Henry himself died, thus canceling the warrant, on January 28, 1547. Finally, where Henry VII had remained loyal to Queen Elizabeth, Henry VIII pursued several extra-marital affairs and fathered at least one illegitimate child. This not only affected his marital relations; it muddied future lines of succession.

But in 1509 these dark events were mostly in the future and Henry's good qualities to the fore. The new king and queen got along well, not least because she gave him his freedom. He spent most of his time "hanging out with the boys," i.e., his courtiers. He turned the Privy Chamber into a kind of gentleman's club whose members spent their days and nights hunting, gaming, drinking, and occasionally whoring. This led one observer to remark in 1515 that the new king "is a youngling, who cares for nothing but girls and hunting and wastes his father's patrimony."[12] All of which raises the question: "But who was running the country?"

The Great Cardinal

At first, Henry VIII was content to let his father's old advisers govern from the council – the unfortunate Empson and Dudley excepted. But as they began to die off or retire, a new minister came to dominate: Thomas Wolsey, soon to be cardinal and archbishop of York (ca. 1473–1530). Wolsey had started from humble beginnings: he was reputedly the son of a butcher from Ipswich, Suffolk. But he had managed to go to Oxford on a poor boy's scholarship and his intelligence and capacity eventually landed him a place as a chaplain, first to the archbishop of Canterbury, then to Henry VII. He began the new reign as royal almoner, charged with distributing the king's charity. Henry soon recognized that his organizational abilities fitted him for something more ambitious. Wolsey managed Henry's campaigns in France in 1512–14 (see below) so successfully that the king rewarded him with an archbishopric in 1514. The pope bestowed a cardinal's hat in the following year. Cardinal Wolsey was energetic, competent, and shrewd, yet one of the most hated men ever to hold high office in England. Why should this be so?

As a churchman, Wolsey was, first of all, a notorious pluralist; that is, he usually held several ecclesiastical positions at once. Thanks to the king's favor he was named dean of Lincoln in 1509, bishop of Lincoln then archbishop of

York in 1514, cardinal in 1515, abbot of St. Albans and bishop of Bath in 1518. In 1524 he exchanged the bishopric of Bath for the wealthier see of Durham; in 1529 he gave up Durham for the even more lucrative bishopric of Winchester – all of which he held simultaneously with that of York. Finally, from 1518 Wolsey was the pope's personal representative, or **legate** *á latere*, in England. This accumulation of high Church offices meant, first of all, that Wolsey had a vast income. Bishoprics and abbacies had extensive estates attached to them, the money from which was at Wolsey's disposal. Moreover, he was willing to sell subordinate Church offices, a practice condemned officially by the Church as simony. At the height of his power his income was something like £35,000 a year. This was a colossal sum. To put it in perspective, one must realize that his nearest noble rival made, perhaps, £8,000 a year and that the king himself had just over £100,000 per year in revenue with which to run his entire government! Wolsey loved to display his wealth: he ate well, dressed magnificently, processed through the streets of London pompously, and built two great palaces, York Place in London and Hampton Court up the Thames Valley, which outshone anything in the king's possession. Wolsey was also a generous benefactor, founding Cardinal College, Oxford, which was the largest and most lavishly funded academic establishment in England. Admittedly, as a cardinal, Wolsey was a prince of the Church: that is, he was expected to live in great state. His wealth and ostentatious display would not have been considered unusual in Renaissance Italy. But they *were* unusual in Renaissance England, and, for many observers, they did not sit well with Wolsey's priestly status or humble origins.

Perhaps even more astonishing – and infuriating – than the Great Cardinal's immense wealth was his neglect of pastoral duty and aggrandizement of place and power. Wolsey clearly could not be simultaneously resident in each of his sees, or personally serve the needs of their flocks, for they were widely scattered about the country and none of them was close to his usual place of residence, York Place in London. This offended churchmen who wanted reform. Nor could reformers have been pleased that Wolsey found positions within the Church for his own children – fathered, of course, out of wedlock and in violation of his priestly vows of celibacy. By holding so many positions in the Church, he and his offspring kept other able men out of them. Above all, as papal legate, Wolsey virtually ran the Church of England. He felt little need to consult the pope, the king, or his fellow bishops. This ended up weakening the English Church on the eve of the Reformation by reducing both its contact with Rome and the size and experience of its leadership.

Wolsey monopolized civil as well as ecclesiastical office. He was, first, from 1515, lord chancellor of England, which made him the Crown's chief legal officer and the keeper of the Great Seal. This meant that the most important documents issued by the government, such as treaties, grants of land, and acts of Parliament, could only be sealed with his cooperation. Since Wolsey's nominees also served as lord (keeper of the) Privy Seal and the king's private secretaries, virtually no document carrying royal authority could be issued without the cardinal knowing about it and, presumably, approving it. In other words, the king and his ministers,

both major and minor, had to consult Wolsey before any policy could be undertaken, grant made or official installed. While the final decision on any matter of
importance was always Henry's, the king's delegation of day-to-day routine and
patronage decisions to the cardinal meant that those decisions were, often,
foregone conclusions.

By aggrandizing so much influence with the king, Wolsey virtually destroyed
the significance of the council as a source of advice. On the other hand, he
increased the council's significance as an administrative and judicial body. He
asked it to investigate the problems of illegal retaining, profiteering in the grain
trade, enclosure, and vagrancy – thus provoking more aristocratic resentment
from those who profited from the first three. As lord chancellor, Wolsey presided
over the courts of Chancery and Star Chamber. In fact, he was a fair and hardworking judge. He prided himself on rendering impartial justice to the poor, even
against the king's own officials, and harangued the council on the need to enforce
justice equitably. But this, too, earned him no appreciation among the rich in a
society that was designed for *their* benefit. Still, litigants flocked to his courts for
cases involving property, contract, perjury, libel, and forgery instead of to the
court of Common Pleas or the ecclesiastical courts, which normally had jurisdiction in such matters. So officers of the latter courts resented the loss of jurisdiction
and fees. Eventually, the cardinal's courts were overwhelmed with the amount of
judicial business they attracted, forcing him to create a new tribunal rooted in the
council called the court of Requests.

Since most government officials were allowed to charge a fee for each piece
of business that passed through their hands, Wolsey's engrossment of office
was another source of his wealth. Though an impartial judge, the cardinal was
thought to be a corrupt administrator, taking bribes, and selling civil as well as
Church offices. In any case, his control of so many government offices and
departments implied vast patronage opportunities. As lord chancellor and the
king's chief minister, Wolsey had the right to appoint over half of the officers of
the royal government. So if you wanted such an office, a pension, a favor – any
of the goodies the Crown had to offer – you were best advised to go to York Place
or Hampton Court, not to Richmond or Westminster Palace, and see the Great
Cardinal first. To fail to do so, to offend the cardinal, was virtually to seal the
doom of one's career. As a result, both God's Church and the king's government
were full of Wolsey's nominees. This meant that he had a vast army of clients and
retainers working for him and his interests all through the ecclesiastical and civil
administration of England. No wonder John Skelton (1460–1529) jibed:

> The kynges courte
> Shulde have the excellence;
> But Hampton Court
> Hath the preemynence!

It will be recalled that Henry VII had been careful to limit the authority of his
most important subjects and to ensure that *he* was the center of power, patronage,

and attention. His son, preoccupied with youthful pleasure, was content to let Wolsey run things. This caused many of Henry VIII's subjects to assume that Wolsey was all powerful, and that his power was unassailable. And so they spent their time at York Place cultivating the cardinal, rather than at Westminster Palace cultivating the king. It is possible that Henry VIII actually encouraged these misconceptions: by allowing the cardinal to seem all powerful, by leaving him with the dirty work of running the country and restraining the nobility, he saved himself not only the tedium of doing so, but also the blame. By attacking retaining, enclosure, and price-gouging on grain or providing justice for the poor, Wolsey offended the landed nobility and gentry. By attracting so much business to the courts over which he presided, he attacked the interests of the common and canon lawyers. And by dominating and exploiting the Church as he did, he alienated his fellow clergymen. As a result, for all his apparent power and wealth, the cardinal's only friend was the king. Presumably, Henry always knew this. He also knew what many of his courtiers, and perhaps Wolsey himself, may have forgotten: that he was still the king, and the Great Cardinal was powerful only so long as (1) Henry remained lazy and (2) the cardinal retained his confidence. During the first two decades of the reign, Wolsey did so primarily through his conduct of war and diplomacy.

War and Diplomacy

For the first 20 years of the reign, neither Henry VIII nor Cardinal Wolsey seem to have been terribly interested in domestic policy. Rather, both concentrated on earning for England a larger place in European affairs. Henry VII had been content to make friends abroad, occasionally rattle the saber against potential enemies, but, for the most part, stay home. That may have been the less interesting course of action, but it was safer and cheaper. His son had different ideas. Why?

First, it must be recalled that, ever since the Norman Conquest, the "continental option" had been attractive to English rulers. That is to say that many English kings had sought adventure, glory, and a distraction from domestic disunity by pursuing continental ambitions. The English had, often in their past history, controlled territory in France. But since the Hundred Years' War, that territory had shrunk to the port of Calais. Revival of England's continental empire was naturally, nostalgically, attractive. Moreover, it could be argued that English involvement on the continent was natural for a European people.

More specifically, Henry VIII – young, dashing, athletic, and a fan of a previous "King Hal" (Henry V) – wanted to earn his own measure of glory in military adventure. In addition, as the reign of Henry V seemed to demonstrate, such adventure would fulfill the ambitions and distract the attention of an aristocracy which had been oppressed and demoralized by his father's policies. Henry VIII seems to have sympathized, canceling over 45 recognizances during the first year of his reign. A chivalrous crusade against an ancient enemy such as France or

Scotland might, if successful, go even farther to placate the grumbling nobility. Playing at tournaments with his nobles was not enough to fulfill this ambition. This latter-day King Hal needed a real war.

This is where the Great Cardinal came in. It will be recalled that Wolsey first came to royal attention by arranging and supplying Henry's early military campaigns. He knew that, in order to maintain the king's confidence, he would have to continue to fulfill royal desires by making Henry a major player in Europe, either through logistical support in war or through his diplomatic efforts. But there may have been more to Wolsey's military and diplomatic machinations than his desire to be the king's good servant. Many contemporaries believed that the Great Cardinal had ambitions to be the first English pope since the twelfth century, though this is now discounted by historians.[13] According to this theory, Wolsey could earn the support necessary to fulfill his goal by becoming the arbiter of Europe.

Unfortunately, these ambitions were simply unrealistic. England was, at the beginning of the sixteenth century, a comparatively poor and militarily weak State, a relative midget hoping to tip the balance between two giants: a unified and wealthy France and the Holy Roman Empire, which comprised most of central Europe. After 1519, the emperor would also rule Spain and the Spanish Empire (see map 6). Even if England had been wealthier and better mobilized, it was far away from the main theater of conflict between these two powers, for they were bickering over control of Italy. England might be a useful auxiliary partner to one side or the other; it was hardly likely to tip the balance or gain much land or glory for itself.

The result was a series of wars between France and the Empire in which England involved itself despite having little business or hope of gain. Those wars and the brief intervals of peace that punctuated them took place in four phases. The first phase, during which Henry and Wolsey's chances of success were brightest, lasted from 1511 to 1514. The king was young, his Treasury full, and his confidence in his almoner great. All the other great powers were currently under the sway of old, cautious rulers of Henry VII's generation: Louis XII (1462–1515; reigned 1498–1515) in France; Maximilian I (1459–1519; reigned 1493–1519) in the Empire; and his nominal ally, Ferdinand in Spain. In 1511 Henry VIII joined with Spain, Venice, and the Swiss to form the Holy League, the purpose of which was to aid the pope in keeping the French out of Italy. The following year, Henry dispatched an army of 10,000 men to northwest Spain, but the cagey Ferdinand eventually made a separate peace with France. The English troops, left in the lurch by their allies, poorly supplied from England, reduced to starvation and mutiny, gradually slunk home without permission. In 1513 the emperor joined the Holy League and contributed 2,000 men. Henry offered 23,000 soldiers in return for the pope's secretly naming him king of France. In response, the French pressured the Scottish king, James IV, to invade England. Henry's force landed at Calais, marched south, captured the city of Tournai, and won a few skirmishes. This, combined with the crushing defeat of the Scottish army and death of James IV at Flodden, enabled Wolsey to engineer a favorable

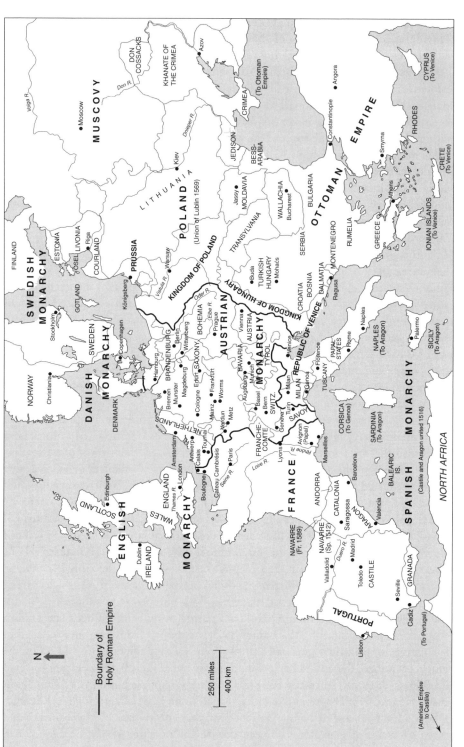

Map 6 *Europe ca. 1560.*

peace the following year. The aged Louis XII married Henry's sister Mary Tudor (1496–1533), paid him a subsidy, and allowed the English to keep the territory they had captured. This was the high-water mark of English success on the continent for almost two centuries and it coincided with the elimination of the Scottish threat for a generation.[14] But Tournai was of dubious value (which one can appreciate by locating it on the map), yet purchased at great cost: Henry spent £650,000 on the 1513 campaigns alone, or six times his annual revenue! Thus, he had wiped out his father's financial nest-egg at one stroke. From this point on, Wolsey would have to raise money the old-fashioned way: through parliamentary votes or the solicitation of loans. Unfortunately, his unpopularity and inability to make domestic allies hindered these efforts. What little money was raised in future would often be spent foolishly on Swiss and Imperial mercenaries who failed to act.

Over the next five years (1515–20), the European situation changed dramatically. First, in 1515 Louis XII died and was succeeded by Francis I (1494–1547; reigned 1515–47). Francis was, like Henry, young, handsome, energetic, and ambitious for glory. In other words, the English king now had a personal rival who was backed by a much wealthier country than England. Francis immediately displayed his aggressiveness by refusing Henry's request that he marry the widowed Princess Mary, and by supporting a Scottish rebellion against Henry's other sister, Margaret, who was now regent there. Wolsey attempted to preserve the peace – and render himself the arbiter of Europe – with a series of summits and agreements which culminated in the Treaty of London of 1518 and the Field of the Cloth of Gold in 1520. The former was a general European treaty involving all of the major powers and 20 lesser States in a promise to act collectively to preserve the peace. The latter was a summit between Henry and Francis, held on the border between English and French territory on the continent. It involved magnificent pageantry and pomp, fountains running with wine, tournaments, pledges of friendship, and even a wrestling match between the two kings – which, ominously, Francis won.

The peace would not last. In 1519 the Holy Roman Emperor, Maximilian I, died. He was succeeded by his grandson, Charles V (1500–58; reigned 1519–56). Because his other grandfather had been Ferdinand of Spain, the fortunate Charles ruled over most of central Europe, the Spanish Empire (where he was known as Charles I), Burgundy, the Netherlands, and Naples. France immediately began to feel threatened with encirclement. On the surface, this seemed to be good news for England, but, in reality, this emperor had even less reason to be concerned about English interests.

England's relative powerlessness became clear between 1521 and 1525. In 1521 Henry allied with Charles V against France; subsequently, he hoped to cement the relationship by marrying his daughter, Mary (1516–58), to the emperor. Over the course of the next four years, an English army landed in France, burnt a few villages, threatened to march on Paris, ran out of money, and went home. The emperor's war was more successful: in 1525 his army crushed the French and captured Francis at the battle of Pavia in Italy. Henry saw this as his great opportunity. His plan was for Wolsey to raise some quick cash, secure the emperor's assistance by finalizing the marriage to Mary, invade France and seize Francis's throne. But Wolsey's tax plan, misnamed the "Amicable Grant," yielded revolts, not money, and was eventually withdrawn.[15] Since Henry's cupboard was now bare, he could not provide a dowry for Mary, which deflated her attractions in Charles's eyes. Instead, the emperor married Isabella of Portugal (1503–39). This enraged the English king, but he was powerless to act.

Between 1525 and 1528 a diplomatic revolution took place. Henry and Wolsey, stung by Charles's indifference, extended feelers toward France. Eventually, they joined the League of Cognac against their former ally, Charles V. In fact, Henry soon had two gripes against Charles. First, he was disgusted at the emperor's continued disregard for English interests. Second, in the spring of 1527 Imperial forces sacked Rome and captured the pope. This was disastrous for Henry because he wanted something from the pope that the emperor did not want him to have: a divorce from Catherine of Aragon, who just happened to be Charles's aunt.

The next chapter will concentrate on the reasons for the king's desire and the implications of the pope's denial. In the meantime, Henry and Wolsey's continental adventures had produced four results, none of which was particularly fortunate for England. First, they had drained the English Treasury. Second, they had increased parliamentary and popular resentment of high taxes and the Great Cardinal who had levied them. Third, they had discredited Wolsey with the king. Finally and above all, they had proved that England was, in the first quarter of the sixteenth century, a second-rate power. The issues of royal finance, the role of Parliament, who would advise the king, and England's role in Europe would persist to the end of the period covered by this book. More immediately, their current disposition would have a profound effect upon the central problem of Henry VIII's reign, a problem which contemporaries called, euphemistically, the King's Great Matter.

CHAPTER TWO

(Dis-)Establishing the Henrician Church, 1525–1536

Sometime in the mid-1520s King Henry VIII began to contemplate an end to his marriage. Those reflections would lead, eventually, not only to his divorce and remarriage, but to the severance of his realm and people from their allegiance to the Roman Catholic Church. The break with Rome would, in turn, lead to a reformation in religion and a revolution in the relationship of the Tudor State to the men and women over whom it ruled. No wonder that "the King's Great Matter" has often been portrayed by conventional wisdom as one of those historical situations in which a major turning point, affecting the lives of millions of people, hinged on the obsessions of a single man. But the situation was more complicated than that.

The King's Great Matter

The problem which Henry wanted to solve was, on one level, simple, personal, and, up to a point, private. It was not, primarily, that he was attracted to another woman or that he was frustrated sexually. From the earliest days of his marriage he had been able to pursue such attractions and fulfill such cravings without much interference from his wife. Rather, his dissatisfaction centered around her status as his legal consort and her tragic obstetrical history. In 1516, after seven years of marriage, Queen Catherine gave birth to a daughter, Mary, the union's only offspring. The ensuing years saw a succession of miscarriages and stillbirths. By 1525, Catherine was 40 years old and had not been pregnant for seven years. Because of poor diet, early modern women tended to experience menopause earlier than women do today, so it was unlikely that she would ever conceive again. Barring her death and his remarriage, the eminently macho King Hal would have no son. Still, despite Henry's dubious fidelity, the marriage had, until this point, been happy. Why should the failure to produce a male child have compromised that happiness now?

The first and most obvious reason for Henry's concern was the succession. As he approached middle age, it became increasingly apparent that he would be succeeded at his death by Princess Mary, a woman. Knowing, as we do today, the achievements of the women who later sat on the English throne, it is difficult to understand Henry's anxiety, which soon reached a point of obsession. But from the point of view of the early sixteenth century – a view based on the Great Chain of Being and England's previous history – the notion of a female sovereign was alarming. First, it violated the fundamental tenets of the Chain: if God was male and the king his representative on earth, how could a woman represent Him or wield His power? If God had placed man at the head of the State, the Church, and the family, what would be the consequences for the Chain, *for Order itself*, in yielding that position to a woman?

More to the immediate point, the one precedent for female rule, the brief "reign" of Queen Matilda (lived 1102–67) in 1141, was universally agreed to have been an unhappy one.[1] This patriarchal interpretation of English history became all the more urgent given England's recent (pre-1485) history of civil war. Henry VIII and his subjects had been reared on the stories of the Wars of the Roses. They had been taught to believe that without a strong (read adult male) presence on the throne of England, the Wars of the Roses could break out again, not least because a number of Yorkist claimants still lived.[2] Henry's fears may help to explain why, in 1525, he named his illegitimate son, Henry Fitzroy (ca. 1519–36),[3] duke of Richmond and heaped offices upon him. Henry may have considered declaring Richmond his heir. But if Henry's subjects might quibble over Mary's gender, they could just as easily come to blows over Richmond's dubious legitimacy.

The fate of Henry's kingdom was not the only consideration weighing on his mind. There was that of his immortal soul as well. It will be recalled that Queen Catherine had been previously married to Henry's brother, Arthur. That marriage ended soon after it had begun when Arthur died in 1502. Henry, something of an amateur theologian, knew of that passage in the Bible, Leviticus 20: 21, which forbids a man to marry his brother's wife. On the other hand, he also knew of Deuteronomy 25: 5, which urges precisely such a union in the case of the first husband's/brother's death. Because of this seeming contradiction, it had been necessary to secure a dispensation from Pope Julius II (1443–1513; reigned 1503–13) in 1504 in order to allow Henry and Catherine to marry in 1509. By the mid-1520s, Henry VIII was beginning to have doubts about the dispensation's efficacy and, thus, about his marriage's validity. After all, if he and Catherine were God's chosen, if their marriage was consistent with the divine will, why had the Supreme Being not blessed it with male children? Were not Catherine's miscarriages and stillbirths a sign of heavenly displeasure? Indeed, contemporary theology would have bolstered Henry's doubts, for any kind of obstetrical accident or malformation at birth tended to be interpreted as a sign of God's punishment or curse.

Only when we grasp the fact that Henry had weightier things on his mind than the demands of the royal libido can we understand the role of Anne Boleyn (1507–36) in the break with Rome: she was the catalyst, not the cause. In 1525 Anne was the 19-year-old daughter of Sir Thomas Boleyn (1477–1539), a diplomat and courtier. She had accompanied her father on an embassy to France and had picked up valuable "polish" at the French court as a lady in waiting to the queen. While Anne was not considered among the most beautiful women of the court, she did have pretty dark eyes and a mind which was bright, vivacious, and highly cultured. These stood in sharp contrast to the sober-sided Catholic respectability of the middle-aged Catherine. The king had first encountered Anne while carrying on an affair with her elder sister, Mary, but by 1526 he had transferred his affections to the younger woman.

There is a popular tradition that it was Anne's ambition to be queen that planted the seeds of Henry's divorce. According to this view, the king was only interested in a love affair. It was Anne who made it clear that she would only sleep with him if she were made his queen. This is a seductive image: the middle-aged and slightly paunchy monarch begging this slip of a girl for a tumble, she imperiously refusing him, the gleam of a crown in her eye. The trouble with this image is that it ignores Henry's other problems. Regardless of his feelings for Anne or her ambitions, these were, by 1527 at least, already moving the king toward his drastic solution. What he needed was not a mistress but a new queen, a legal consort, young enough and strong enough to bear him a legitimate male heir. Thus, irrespective of Henry's or Anne's amorous inclinations, to achieve his goal, he needed a divorce.[4]

To achieve the divorce, Henry turned, as usual, to Cardinal Wolsey. Wolsey was supposed to be the king's faithful servant and a big man with Rome. Moreover, his recent failure to secure funding (the Amicable Grant) for another French campaign had left the cardinal in desperate need of a big success on the king's behalf. This should have concentrated his mind wonderfully on the King's Great Matter. In fact, the divorce negotiations would demonstrate just how light was England's weight and how puny was Wolsey's pull with the great continental powers. The divorce would be his downfall.

But nobody knew this in 1527. On the surface, the King's Great Matter seemed eminently solvable. Contrary to popular belief, the Roman Catholic Church was perfectly willing to annul an inconvenient marriage if the participants were sufficiently important and the diplomatic situation sufficiently pressing. In 1514, after Henry VIII became disillusioned with his Imperial alliance, the pope annulled the prior betrothal of his sister, Mary, to the future Charles V in order to enable her to marry Louis XII of France. After Louis died in 1515, Mary wed Charles Brandon, duke of Suffolk (ca. 1484–1545), who required the annulment of *two* previous marriages in order to be eligible to contract this one.[5] And finally, in 1527, the pope had granted the divorce of Henry's other sister, Margaret, queen dowager of Scotland, from Archibald Douglas, earl of Angus (ca. 1489–1557), which enabled her to marry Henry Stewart, later Lord Methven (ca. 1495–ca. 1551). Both of the last two cases had involved the agreement of the very pope from whom Henry wanted his annulment, Clement VII (1478–1534; reigned 1523–34). So, Henry and Wolsey had every reason to think that dynastic and diplomatic necessity would prevail once more when, in May 1527, the Great Cardinal, acting as papal representative, convened a secret court in London for the purpose of invalidating the king's marriage.

At this point, however, two problems arose, one theological, one diplomatic. The theological problem concerned the king's argument for annulment. In asserting that Leviticus 20: 21 rendered his marriage invalid, he had to argue that the pope's dispensation of 1504 was invalid as well. It was one thing for Clement VII to agree that a marriage was invalid because canon law or the proper Church procedures had not been followed. It was quite another – and much more damaging to his authority – to argue that a previous pope had erred in interpreting that law or in following those procedures. What sitting pope would agree to that?

The diplomatic impediment to the divorce arose out of the long-term struggle between France and the Holy Roman Empire over Italy. At the end of May 1527, the armies of the Empire sacked Rome and, in June, took the pope prisoner. It will be remembered that the emperor was Charles V, the grandson of Ferdinand and Isabella and, therefore, the nephew of Catherine of Aragon. Now that Pope Clement was Charles's "guest," he was unlikely to grant a request that was so insulting to his host's aunt, even if that request came from the king of England. After all, Charles V was not only the pope's jailer; he was far more powerful and important in European affairs than Henry.

The tide seemed to turn in 1528. The French went on the offensive, and this seemed to lessen the pressure on the pope. He made a show of cooperating with Henry by granting Wolsey the right to hear the case for divorce and pronounce judgment. But the cardinal was to share these tasks with a hand-picked papal representative sent from Rome, Lorenzo, Cardinal Campeggio (1472?–1539). In fact, Campeggio had been given secret orders to delay the trial and prevent it from coming to a verdict. In reality, the pope wanted to wash his hands of the whole embarrassing affair, privately advising Henry to divorce Catherine without permission. Henry, convinced of the justice of his cause, obsessed with the proper forms and the state of his soul, refused.

Campeggio did his part by delaying the trial until May 1529. This gave Catherine and her advisers time to prepare a case. To the delight of a cheering crowd outside Blackfriars Hall, the queen appeared at the trial and, in her finest hour, demanded to be heard. First, she questioned the right of the court to examine her marriage. She was a royal person and so above the law. (That is, if the law is the king's, how could the law judge a royal person?) Then she denied that she and Arthur had ever had sexual relations. Thus, her first marriage had never been consummated.[6] In canon law, this rendered her marriage to *Arthur* invalid, leaving her perfectly free to wed Henry. Finally, she demanded the right to appeal her case directly to Rome. These arguments seem to have caught Henry and Wolsey off guard. Worse, in July Campeggio argued that the court had to follow the calendar of the papal court and so adjourn for the hot Italian summer – despite the fact that it was meeting on the banks of the Thames! In fact, it would never meet again. That summer, Charles V went back on the offensive in northern Italy. This, combined with Catherine's arguments, gave the pope sufficient reason to recall the case to Rome where, Henry was sure, no divorce would ever be granted.

Frustrated, Henry turned on Wolsey. He began by charging the cardinal with violating the Statute of Praemunire, the old medieval law that forbade acknowledging another loyalty beyond that of the king (i.e., the pope; see Introduction). Then he stripped the cardinal of all of his civil offices and property. Wolsey, lucky not to face execution, resolved to take up his rarely visited see (archbishopric) of York. But he moved slowly away from the seat of power, hoping that the king would forgive him. Nor could he resist negotiating with agents of France, Spain, the papacy, even the queen in an attempt to engineer his return. His many enemies at court accused him of plotting against the king, who indicted him for treason. In November 1530, while on his way back to London for trial, he fell ill and died at Leicester Abbey. While lying on his deathbed, he is supposed to have lamented: "If I had served God as diligently as I have done the King, he would not have given me over in my grey hairs."[7]

Wolsey's fall surprised many. They had assumed that he was the real power in England. But Henry was no cipher. The Great Cardinal had remained dominant only so long as he accomplished the king's business. Once he ceased to be useful, he was doomed. His many other liabilities – pride, greed, corruption, unpopularity – meant only that when he fell he was unlamented. The significance to aspiring royal servants, ministers, or favorites was clear. The significance for England and its place in the world was also clear. Henry VIII, for all his swagger, was not a major player in Europe, and England, out on the fringes of Christendom, was not a major power. Finally, note that what had started in the marriage bed as a private matter between husband and wife had become intertwined with high politics, international diplomacy, religious doctrine, even Italian weather. Clearly, the King's Great Matter went far beyond the obsessions of just one man. That would become even clearer as it moved into its next phase.

The Attack on the Church

The period from 1529 to 1532 is usually seen as one of drift, without a real policy on the part of Henry VIII. But that does not mean that it was one of inactivity. Rather, these years saw three great court factions vie for the king's ear and, in a manner of speaking, his soul as well. The first, known as the Aragonese faction, consisted of those who supported and advised the queen. They included the Spanish diplomats based at court, Bishops John Fisher (1459–1535) and Cuthbert Tunstall (1474–1559), and Wolsey's replacement as lord chancellor, Sir Thomas More. A lawyer, a scholar, and a devout Catholic, More refused to involve himself publicly in the divorce, concentrating instead on prosecuting heretics and clearing out the backlog of business that Wolsey had left in the law courts. Privately, he did what he could to shore up the queen's support in council and Parliament. Ranged against him were those who supported Henry's desire to be rid of his first wife and Anne Boleyn's ambition to be queen. These included members of the Boleyn family, clergymen who inclined toward Church reform such as Thomas Cranmer (1489–1556), and a shadowy former servant of Wolsey's named Thomas Cromwell (ca. 1485–1540). Holding the balance between these two groups was a faction of conservative noblemen led by Thomas Howard, duke of Norfolk, Thomas, Lord Darcy (1467–1537), and Stephen Gardiner, bishop of Winchester (ca. 1483–1555). Their inclination was toward religious conservatism and against the divorce, but their habit was to do the king's bidding. Eventually, for most of these men, habit won out over inclination. Increasingly, they began to press Catherine to accept the king's terms: a divorce, a pension, and the title princess dowager. She stubbornly refused.

While the factional battle raged at court, the king tried to persuade the pope of the justice of his cause by soliciting the opinions of leading university theologians, but these great minds could not agree. In 1529 Henry VIII opened another, more threatening front. He called a Parliament, the first in five years. While much of its business involved the raising of money, the king also made it clear that he would entertain petitions of grievance about the Church. The Mercer's Company of London dutifully offered a series of articles complaining about clerical abuses, which resulted in legislation. To understand the Church's vulnerability to such attacks, it is necessary for us to conduct our own inquiry into the condition of the Roman Catholic Church in England.

Unfortunately, historians have been unable to agree on the state of Catholicism in England on the eve of the Reformation. For many years, it was assumed that the Church was corrupt, ineffective, and out of touch with the great mass of the English people, who were often ignorant of its doctrines and resentful of the high-handed and sometimes hypocritical ways of its clergy. According to this view, most memorably articulated by A. G. Dickens and updated by Diarmaid MacCulloch, many, if not most, English men and women desperately wanted the Reformation.[8] But more recently, J. J. Scarisbrick, Christopher Haigh, Eamon Duffy, and others have argued that the Church was both less corrupt and more effective than this picture suggests. English men and women knew and embraced the doctrines and practices of their faith far more enthusiastically than the old historical orthodoxy would admit. Thus, the Reformation was not a grassroots movement sought by the faithful, but a dictated solution, imposed from above. In the words of Christopher Haigh, "[i]t was the break with Rome which was to cause the decline of Catholicism, not the decline of Catholicism which led to the break with Rome."[9] Can we sort this out?

Let us begin with some basic facts. In 1529 Roman Catholicism was the official religion of the English State. This meant two things. First, the Church was ever-present in the life of the kingdom and its people. It supplied them with their explanation of the universe and of their own trials and tribulations. It defined or marked the stages of their lives in baptism, marriage, and burial. Their holidays were the 37 major Church holy days. Their weekly day of rest, the Sabbath, was largely spent attending services and social events at the parish church. Their education took place in its schools. Their disputes over adultery, fornication, drunkenness, blasphemy, inheritance, and debt were tried in its courts; indeed, a number of these offenses were only illegal because they were thought to be an affront to God or his Church. Churchwardens monitored notorious adulterers, brawlers, drunkards, breakers of the peace, and absentees from Sunday services. Church-affiliated guilds and livery companies regulated the economic life of towns. Monasteries, convents, and Church-run hospitals distributed charity. The Church owned nearly a quarter of the land in England, which meant that for many peasants and workers the Church was not only their chief source of spiritual wisdom and comfort, but also their landlord, employer, and neighbor. Finally, their primary source of news of the world outside their villages and towns was the priest. And, as we have seen, everyone was expected to attend mass on Sunday.

Second, the Catholic Church was the only legal religion in England. To be a member of any other faith, to offer an alternative interpretation of Christianity, to criticize the dogma or practice or even the personnel of the Roman Catholic Church was to risk indictment for heresy and, possibly, execution via burning at the stake. Thus, if anyone was unhappy about his or her faith or clergyman, they were not likely to express their opinions publicly, or to leave evidence for later historians. The evidence which *does* exist demonstrates strong social and material support for the Church and popular participation in many activities, some of them optional. The English people not only attended mass on Sundays and holy days, but they also observed numerous elaborate calendar rituals and plays. They went on pilgrimage to holy places and saints' shrines, especially that of Thomas à Becket at Canterbury. They joined fraternities and guilds (in effect, clubs) dedicated to particular saints or beliefs and they bought catechisms and devotional books in great numbers. They contributed massively to an explosion of church building and decoration in the fifteenth and early sixteenth centuries, producing such beautiful structures as St. Mary Redcliffe, Bristol, or St. Peter Mancroft, Norwich. The wealthy and the less wealthy endowed or enriched scores of colleges, hospitals, monasteries, convents, **chantries**, and shrines, often with posthumous bequests. In this way, too, the Church was everywhere. This evidence of popular support, combined with the relative lack of evidence for disagreement with Church teaching, has led Haigh, Duffy, and others to argue that, despite significant exceptions, most English men and women in 1529 were orthodox and did not want to see major changes in their faith.

But even if this is true, and despite the popularity of religious clubs, devotional exercises, and books among a literate minority, this does not mean that all or even most English men and women had a very clear idea of what the doctrines of that faith actually were. People may have joined clubs for their social and economic benefits. Books may have been owned but not read or fully grasped. As with many believers today, most people's faith seems to have been simple and none-too-consistent. There is evidence of plenty of ignorance of Catholic doctrine among lay people, especially in remote areas.

This was inevitable given the relative passivity of the laity, the unavailability of the Bible, the low rate of literacy, and the scarcity of priests in such areas. First, lay members of the English Catholic Church were not invited to participate actively in the central rituals or the promulgation of their faith. The mass was said in Latin and heard from the back of the church, through a rood screen (see plate 4). Communion was required of the faithful only three times a year, confession but once. Nor could most devout Catholics avail themselves of the consolation of Scripture, for there was no English translation of the Bible readily available in pre-Reformation England. The Church's official version of the Bible, the Vulgate, was a Latin translation from the end of the fourth century. This served to keep Scripture under the watchful eye of a select few clergymen and scholars. Most churchmen would have considered the reading of the Bible by the laity to have been dangerous. Even if an English translation had been readily available, not all could have read it, for literacy, though growing (see chapter 6), was still largely the preserve of the upper and middle ranks of the population. This meant that while religious books sold well, few ordinary people could have read or understood them. Finally, while estimates for the number of clergy in England vary widely, ranging from 20,000 to 60,000, those numbers were not spread evenly or in the same proportions as the general population across the country. In poorer, rural areas especially, there was, and had been for a long time, a shortage of priests, especially educated priests. In Canterbury diocese toward the end of the fifteenth century, only about one-fifth of the priests were university graduates; in Surrey, one-tenth. That, in turn, meant that many parishes were not being served adequately; their parishioners were not being ministered to or taught Catholic doctrine accurately. All of these factors must have made Reformation easier to swallow: it is difficult to notice or object to changes when one lacks a clear understanding of what is being changed.

In response to these failings, humanist authors such as More, John Colet (ca. 1467–1519), Simon Fish (d. 1531), and William Tyndale (ca. 1494?–1536), influenced by the satirical and scholarly writings of Erasmus, began to argue for reform of the practice, if not the doctrine, of the English Church. They were concerned, first, not only with the lack of priests, but its consequences: pluralism and absenteeism. As we have seen, Cardinal Wolsey was a great pluralist, probably out of greed. But for most clergymen, holding multiple livings was necessary, first, because there were so few priests to go around; and, second, because country parishes often paid so poorly (frequently less than £10 a year) that a priest might have to hold down several just to make ends meet. Because it was impossible for a clergyman holding plural livings to say mass in more than one place at once, he almost necessarily became an absentee; that is, some parishes simply were not served on Sundays. One way of getting around this problem was to hire curates, or deputy priests. But these men were often poorly educated and therefore unable to perform the many tasks demanded of a pastor. The inevitable result was the ignorance or indifference of the laity.

The poverty of most clergy contrasted infamously with the worldly wealth of the Church. Once again Cardinal Wolsey provides the most extreme example of

1 Priest
2 Alb
3 Rood Screen
4 Chasuble
5 Server
6 Rushes strewn on floor
7 Cross and statue of St John on right and Virgin Mary on left
8 Hanging tabernacle (pyx)
9 Sanctuary lamps
10 Statue of the Virgin
11 Wall painting
12 Missal
13 Reredos
14 Altar
15 Chalice
16 Surplice

POST-REFORMATION

1 Minister
2 Royal coat-of-arms
3 Plain glass in window
4 Pulpit for preaching
5 Surplice
6 "Eagle" lectern
7 Wall tablets
8 Table
9 Book of Common Prayer at north end of table. The minister now stands there at communion service
10 White linen cloth
11 Ordinary bread
12 Scarf of black silk
13 Flagon for wine

Plate 4 *Diagram of the interior of a church before and after the Reformation. Reproduced from S. Doran and C. Durston,* Princes, Pastors and People: The Church and Religion in England, 1529–1689 *(London, 1991) by permission of Taylor and Francis Ltd.*

this, but most bishops were able to live like princes. The diocese of Winchester yielded £3,580 a year and 10 others were worth over £1,000. The 21 English and Welsh bishops held around 177 palaces and houses in 1535. While there was, perhaps, nothing inherently wrong in this, it did not sit well in a religion that preached the blessedness of poverty and the acceptance of one's earthly lot. Worse, materialism seemed to be accompanied by corruption. Corruption is a catch-all word that can mean many things. Some priests were accused of greed, charging excessive fees for performance of services, such as burial of the dead and the probate of wills. Others were accused of violating their vows of celibacy or of drinking too much. Admittedly, these are human failings, not the actions of fiends or monsters. Moreover, it should be understood that, given the limited number of professions open to younger sons and daughters at the beginning of the early modern period, becoming a clergyman or woman was, for many, a practical career choice, not a calling. But it was only natural for the laity to resent clerical failings all the more given the priesthood's responsibility to preach moral recti- tude and set a good example. How widespread were these abuses? The vast majority of priests were probably overworked, underpaid, yet conscientious ministers to their flocks. And the educational and ethical standards of the clergy were improving at the beginning of the sixteenth century. But a few "bad apples" can spoil the reputation of many; in early modern England some Catholics began to worry that much of the barrel was rotten. Again, it is difficult to measure the prevalence of this anticlericalism. But the danger attached to any form of criticism of the Church suggests that these complaints should be taken seriously.

One group, in particular, mounted a coherent critique of the Church. In 1517, Martin Luther, a German monk and theology professor, began to write against its structure, practice, and doctrine. He and other reformers, dismayed at what they saw as the growing corruption of the Church and its distance from ordinary people, sought to go back to basics. They emphasized the importance of Scrip- ture, arguing that the Bible was the only sure guide to God's will and that anything not found in its pages – such as the power of the papacy, the doctrine of Purgatory, the selling of indulgences (see chapter 3) – was unnecessary, even detrimental to Christian belief. Luther also argued that faith alone justified salvation, as opposed to the Catholic idea that salvation was to be earned through a combination of faith and good works. And, of course, he decried the clerical abuses noted above. We will explore Luther's ideas further in the next chapter. For now, it is important to understand that he was excommunicated from the Roman Catholic Church in 1520; that Henry VIII had rejected his ideas in print; and that Lutheran heretics seem to have been generally unpopular in England. Nevertheless, Luther's ideas had a small but growing following in cities, at the universities (especially Cambridge), and, most ominously for the Roman Catholic Church in England, in the court circle forming around Anne Boleyn.

The Henrician Catholic Church had one more set of difficulties, rarely men- tioned or apparently understood at the time. Because Cardinal Wolsey had so aggrandized power to himself, his fall caused a dangerous vacuum at the top of the Church's hierarchy. First, Wolsey had weakened papal authority by rarely consulting Rome. Many bishops were Henry's or Wolsey's nominees. That proved, inadvertently, that the pope was not so very necessary to run the English Church. It could be done quite effectively from England by an Englishman. Further, because Wolsey had so monopolized Church offices, other able men had been kept out of positions of authority. Since it took some time to fill these places, this further contributed to the lack of strong leadership after his fall. Finally, Wolsey's habit of acting without consulting others meant that there was no tradition of corporate deliberation and solidarity among the Church leadership. This left them weak, demoralized, and without a field general just as they were about to face their greatest enemy.

Thomas Cromwell and the Royal Supremacy

Henry VIII's next great minister, Thomas Cromwell, was born at Putney, a suburb of London, just as Henry VII was establishing the Tudor regime. Like Wolsey, he was of humble birth, the son of a clothworker and tavern-keeper. Clearly, early Tudor government offered opportunities for ambitious and able young men irrespective of social status. In fact, unlike Wolsey, Cromwell had no formal education. Rather, he spent his youth traveling on the continent, sometimes as a soldier, sometimes as a merchant, sometimes as a secretary or clerk. During this sojourn he picked up a smattering of legal education which would prove significant. Soon after his return to London in 1514, he entered Wolsey's household, eventually becoming the cardinal's legal secretary. He came to the king's attention during the Parliament which met in 1529.

Henry VIII called the Parliament of 1529 to put pressure on the pope. But the noble lords and honorable gentlemen who sat in Parliament were not so much concerned with the pope or even the King's Great Matter as they were with "bread and butter" issues, such as corruption in the Church, excessive fines, and pluralism. And so, they passed laws regulating mortuary and probate fees, and attacking plural livings. In the meantime, Henry decided in December 1530 to charge the whole English clergy with praemunire. They submitted and he pardoned them after payment of a fine of just over £118,000. Ominously, in the prologue to the document of submission, Henry insisted upon being referred to as the "sole protector and supreme head of the English church and clergy." The Convocation of churchmen which agreed to the fine qualified this assertion with the phrase "as far as Christ's law allows." Thus Henry had already claimed dominance – albeit a qualified and ambiguous dominance – over the Church in England. Admittedly, none of this was indicative of a long-term plan and, given Henry's advancing age and barely suppressed libido, time was running out. But the king had noticed Cromwell's enthusiasm and competence as a member of Parliament and began, in 1530, to take him into his counsels.

In fact, Thomas Cromwell and the Boleyn faction did have a plan: if the current head of the English Church (the pope) would not grant the king a divorce, then the king would have to take that position himself, in deed as well as word. This was, of course, a simple but radical idea. While kings had sometimes sought to limit papal power in England, the idea of eliminating it entirely had never been seriously contemplated. Cromwell realized, shrewdly, that such a step had to be taken gradually and with the appearance of parliamentary support. That way, Henry could claim to have broken with the pope and assumed control of the Church only reluctantly and at the insistence of his subjects. But how could Parliament be persuaded to support even a gradual move in this direction? By exploiting their anticlericalism.

Cromwell began the attack early in 1532 by introducing legislation suspending the payment of annates (i.e., fees, also known as First Fruits and Tenths, paid by newly appointed bishops) to Rome and giving the archbishop of Canterbury the power to consecrate bishops and priests. Though approved by Parliament, Henry withheld his confirmation to await the pope's reaction. When this did not produce the desired effect, Cromwell took a gamble. In March 1532, speaking without royal permission, he urged the House of Commons to draw up a list of clerical abuses in need of reform. The Commons Supplication Against the Ordinaries charged the clergy with making laws binding the English people without parliamentary permission, in violation of the royal **prerogative** and English law. Less spectacularly, it also attacked delays in Church courts and the harshness of recent proceedings against heretics. This document was then sent to Convocation, the official body representing the clergy, for an answer. In fact, no satisfactory answer was possible: either the clergy admitted the abuses, thus vindicating its enemies, or denied them, thus appearing to be uncooperative. At first, Convocation chose the latter course. This infuriated Henry, who remarked, angrily, that the clergy "be but half our subjects, yea, and scarce our subjects."[10] Finally, on May 15, 1532, Convocation replied with the "Submission of the Clergy," which gave Henry what he wanted. He was now, in effect, the head of the Church in England in the same way that he was head of State. As with Parliament, only he could call a Convocation; as with parliamentary statutes, only he could approve its legislation. Subsequent acts of Parliament would merely spell this out.

Not everyone fully appreciated the implications of these events. But Sir Thomas More did. He resigned the chancellorship the next day. Cromwell, whose official position was king's secretary, was now Henry's undisputed first minister. As we have seen, he was a brilliant parliamentary tactician, as well as an able debater and a tireless worker. John Foxe summed up Cromwell's other virtues as "pregnant in wit ..., in judgment discreet, in tongue eloquent, in service faithful, in stomach courageous, in his pen active."[11] As we shall see, these qualities would enable him to dominate the political scene for the rest of the 1530s and secure for the king not only his divorce, but a great deal more besides.

With the English clergy brought to heel, things began to move quickly. Toward the end of 1532, Anne became pregnant. In January 1533 Thomas Cranmer, the king's choice as the next archbishop of Canterbury, secretly married the two lovers. (Since Henry believed his first marriage to be invalid, this would not have constituted bigamy in his eyes.) In the spring of 1533 Cromwell opened the parliamentary front once again – and this time decisively – with the **Act in**

Restraint of Appeals. This statute forbade appeals of ecclesiastical cases (like Catherine's) to foreign jurisdictions (like Rome). That is, it stated explicitly that the king's justice was the highest justice to which an English subject could appeal; there was no further recourse beyond England. Cromwell justified this in the act's preamble, which stated:

this realm of England is an empire, and so hath been accepted in the world, governed by one supreme head and king having the dignity and royal estate of the imperial crown of the same. (24 Henry VIII, c. 12)

Put simply, the medieval concept of dual loyalty to a separate king as head of the State and pope as head of the Church was over. The king was to be regarded as the head of all. No other loyalty was to interfere with that primary one. These words and the act which they introduce can be viewed as the capstone of Henry VII's attempt to unify the English people under Tudor rule. As we shall see, some historians have argued that it laid the foundation for the English State's later assumption of power in other areas, such as law enforcement, social welfare, and education.

Of more immediate point, the Act in Restraint of Appeals marks a clear break with Rome: since no other authority but the monarch was to have power over or be appealed to by English subjects, the pope's authority in England was a dead letter. As a result, the Vatican could do nothing to prevent Henry's long-sought-after divorce. In May 1533 Cranmer heard the divorce case and, predictably, pronounced the marriage of Henry VIII and Catherine of Aragon to be null and void. In June, he set the crown on Queen Anne at Westminster. In September, Anne gave birth – to a daughter, named Elizabeth. The king did not conceal his disappointment.

Still, the new queen and the new heir necessitated a new Act of Succession. This statute declared Mary illegitimate and reserved the succession to the Crown to the heirs of Anne's body. Further, it was now treason to deny this new order of succession "in writing, print, deed or act." That is, mere words could be punished by death. Eventually, all adult males were required to swear agreement to the new disposition. In 1534 Parliament spelled out what was already true in practice by passing the Act of Supremacy, which made the king "the only supreme head in earth of the Church of England" (26 Henry VIII, c. 1). A further Act in Restraint of Annates diverted the payment of First Fruits and Tenths to the king's coffers – at substantially higher rates of collection. Additional legislation regulated the prosecution of heretics, gave the selection of bishops to the Crown, and legalized the questioning of the pope's authority. Finally, a new Treason Act was passed, declaring it a capital crime to speak against the succession, the king's title (including his headship of the Church of England), or to call the king or queen a heretic, schismatic, tyrant, infidel, or usurper. Clearly, somebody anticipated trouble!

In 1534 Cromwell was named the king's vice-gerent in ecclesiastical affairs, that is, his deputy as head of the Church. As such, he licensed preachers and saw that the oaths were sworn. In April 1535 he issued a circular letter to the bishops, nobility, and JPs ordering the imprisonment of clergy who preached against the Royal Supremacy. He subsequently ordered the erasure of the pope's name from mass books, the despoiling of shrines, and, more positively, the placement of the Bible, translated into English, in parish churches. He also commissioned a preaching campaign, as well as English-language tracts and Latin treatises to promote the Royal Supremacy at home and abroad. Finally, in 1536, Parliament passed an Act Extinguishing the Authority of the Bishop of Rome and, for reasons only partly religious, began to legislate the Dissolution of Monasteries and Convents in England and the confiscation of their lands by the Crown.

Reaction

These actions were revolutionary, for they changed the fundamental constitution not just of Church and State, but of society itself. This raises some obvious questions. Did Henry and Cromwell get away with it and, if so, how? How did the king's subjects react? Overall, most seem not to have reacted at all. For example, the majority of people who were asked to swear the oath to the new succession did so. Why? The answer probably varied according to the oath-taker's rank. At court, most of the great nobles probably swore the oath because they were afraid: afraid of the king's wrath, afraid of losing their offices, their pensions, their titles, their lands, and perhaps even their lives. If this does explain their actions, then it is yet more evidence that Henry VII and his son had succeeded in winning the fear and respect of their mightiest subjects. Additionally, the nobility and gentry at court and in the countryside may have gone along with the oath because they agreed with the king's need for a male heir and feared another civil war as much as he did. Eventually, these groups would be further won over to the Reformation by the opportunity to acquire Church lands confiscated in the Dissolution of the Monasteries (see below).

As for the parish clergy, they seem to have been genuinely divided. Most went along with Cromwell's orders, some undoubtedly seeing the acts of the early 1530s as part of yet another struggle between monarch and pope and hardly worth risking one's position and life. Yet there is plenty of evidence of dissident priests refusing to cooperate. Some went so far as to preach against these measures. City-dwellers and townsmen, the group most receptive to Luther's ideas, may have embraced the new succession as the price to be paid for Church reform. Many people of lesser rank were not asked to take the oath and so had no choice to make as yet. But when males in this group *were* asked to swear, most did so. Perhaps Cromwell's preaching and pamphlet campaign worked. Perhaps, if Catherine and Mary were popular, Henry was even more so – or more feared. Perhaps, given the relatively low level of theological consciousness among the laity, many English men and women simply did not understand what was at stake.

This is not to say that no one understood the grave implications of the king's actions. At the higher echelons of society, it is true, only a few had the courage to oppose Henry. Among the upper clergy only Bishop Fisher, who had defended Catherine at her trial, refused to take the oath. Among laymen, some northern peers grumbled, but did nothing. The most prominent refuser was Sir Thomas More. After resigning the chancellorship in May 1532, More attempted to live quietly on his estate at Chelsea, out of the king's eye. Both More and Fisher were perfectly willing to agree to the new succession as a matter of political and dynastic expediency. But they could not, as good sons of the Church, deny the legitimacy of the first marriage; that would be to deny the validity of the papal dispensation of 1504. Henry knew this, and that even their silent criticism damaged his claim to have followed the national will. Eventually, both men were imprisoned and tried on the charge of having violated the new Treason Act by speaking against the new order of succession. At his trial, More, in particular, mounted a dazzling defense, but both he and Fisher were convicted on perjured testimony and executed in the summer of 1535. In fact, the judicial murder of More and Fisher was a propaganda disaster for Henry, especially abroad. More's dying words were a ringing declaration against the notion of unitary sovereignty and for some sort of separation of Church and State: "I die," More stated, "[t]he King's good servant, but God's first."[12] The question of whether it was appropriate to dissent from a State Church or whether royal policy could be criticized at all would be raised again and again in the two centuries following Henry's Reformation.

Nor were More and Fisher the king's only victims. A number of Carthusian monks who could not accept the new regime were tortured and executed. Elizabeth Barton (1506?–34), the maid of Kent, a poor woman who claimed to see visions of Henry's just punishment, was executed by act of attainder. But the king's most revealing actions were reserved for a popular movement which arose in the autumn of 1536, called the **Pilgrimage of Grace**. The Pilgrimage of Grace was a series of risings which began in Lincolnshire on October 1 and which, encouraged by local clergymen, spread to Cumberland, Durham, Lancashire, Northumberland, Westmorland, and Yorkshire by the following spring. The most important of these disturbances was led by a Yorkshire gentleman, Robert Aske (d. 1537), who seized much of the northeast with a force of some 30,000 men.

On the surface, the Pilgrimage of Grace appears to have been a popular reaction to the king's divorce and religious policies. For example, the pilgrims wore badges depicting the Five Wounds of Christ and marched behind religious banners. Aske's council at Pontefract, in Yorkshire, issued a series of demands including the end of heretical innovations, the recognition of the pope's authority and Mary's place in the succession, and the dismissal of Cromwell. This has led some historians to argue that the Pilgrimage of Grace was, as its popular title implies, a religious revolt in defense of the old Church. But the middle 1530s saw not only the break with Rome, but also an outbreak of plague, flooding, and several poor harvests. The rebels also called for fair rents, a halt to enclosures, and repeal of the Statute of Uses, an unpopular piece of land law which interfered with prevailing inheritance customs. This has led other historians to argue that the Pilgrimage was more of a reaction to economic and social problems; that its religious demands were window dressing; and, therefore, that there was no widespread hostility in the North to either reformation or the king's divorce and remarriage. The rebels' demand for the dismissal of Thomas Cromwell is consistent with both interpretations.

Whatever the motivation for their demands, the rebels seem to have thought that the recent, hated innovations in religion and land law were really Cromwell's ideas and that, surely, when good King Henry heard their demands, he would dismiss his evil advisers, take pity upon his people, and redress their grievances. The king's initial failure to crush the Pilgrimage must have added fuel to this comforting delusion. In fact, he sent the duke of Norfolk, the leading conservative Catholic peer and president of the Council of the North, with a small force to do just that. But when Norfolk met the rebels at Doncaster Bridge in Yorkshire in late October 1536, he found himself hopelessly outnumbered. As a result, the duke agreed to present their demands to the king and also promised, on his master's behalf, a free Parliament to address their grievances. Upon Norfolk's return, the king angrily repudiated these concessions. He then waited until there was a new series of outbreaks in early 1537. These he put down, ruthlessly, in the spring, executing Aske and about 180 of the rebels.

The course and resolution of the Pilgrimage of Grace provide a few clear lessons. First, as we have seen before, Tudor rule was ruthless and unscrupulous. To forget that was to invite the gravest peril. Second, neither the Catholic nobles nor the general populace in the rest of the country – the prosperous South, the remote regions of East Anglia and the West Country – rose up to defend the pope, Queen Catherine, Princess Mary, or the old religion. They were apparently willing to accept a royal divorce, a royal remarriage, a new royal succession, and a royal head of the English Church. This suggests that they were, by and large, satisfied with Tudor rule. Third, from now on, religious controversies would be intimately bound up with political, social, and economic issues. Aske and his peasant supporters understood that relationship. So, as we shall see, did Thomas Cromwell.

A Tudor Revolution?

In 1953, the historian G. R. Elton published an influential and controversial book entitled *The Tudor Revolution in Government*.[13] Elton argued that the gentlemen and peasants who embarked on the Pilgrimage of Grace were onto something when they failed to separate religious from political and economic issues. While they may have been mistaken in letting the king off the hook, they were more than half right in seeing Thomas Cromwell as the engineer of a new and very different world. Elton argued that in the 1530s, Cromwell, with the king's blessing, undertook to increase the power of the monarchy, and therefore of the State, in many aspects of English life. In order to do this, he launched a series of reforms designed to reduce the ad hoc, household aspects of royal government in favor of efficient departments with national responsibilities run according to bureaucratic routine. The result was, in Elton's view, the creation of the first modern nation-state and the rise of a new, efficient bureaucracy to run it. While Elton's interpretation has never been universally accepted by historians, his theory remains a convenient prism through which to explore the unique development of the Tudor constitution.

According to Elton, the key to the Tudor Revolution was the relatively new and rather modern notion that sovereignty (the ultimate power in the State) and, therefore, the loyalty of its subjects should reside in and with one person and office: that of the king. Parliament had said as much in the preamble to the Act in Restraint of Appeals of 1533 when it called England "an empire...governed by one supreme head and king." In this context, the word "empire" does not mean a vast expanse of territory. Rather, it here derives from the Roman concept of *imperium*: the power to give commands and have them obeyed without fear of contradiction. What this meant to Henry, Cromwell, and their contemporaries was that the king owed obedience to God alone. No one else could judge or command or contradict the monarch in England. Clearly, therefore, his subjects had no room for countervailing loyalties to the pope, the Church, the local landlord, county, or town, as in the old, feudal system. Except for the Roman pontiff, who was now a virtual non-person in England, all were subordinate to and therefore answerable to the king. According to Elton, this crucial piece of legislation went far to articulate the idea of the modern nation-state, with impermeable borders and allegiance to one sovereign power.[14]

But note that this sentiment was articulated in an act of Parliament, one of a series of statutes by which Henry VIII assumed control of the Church. Thus, if England was an empire ruled by a supreme head and king, that king was, nevertheless, not absolute. Elton would argue that the Tudor monarchy was, in some sense, a constitutional one. As Henry VIII himself once said: "we at no time stand so highly in our estate royal, as in the time of parliament."[15] This does not mean that Henry intended to share his imperial sovereignty; both he and Cromwell regarded Parliament as a tool. So why would a man of Henry's imperious nature have said such a thing? Why would a loyal servant such as Cromwell have embraced it? Perhaps because both men realized that, in pursuing radical solutions to the king's and the nation's problems, they needed at least the appearance of support, of governing with the kind of consent that Henry VII had commanded, and so many previous Lancastrian and Yorkist rulers had not. In short, Henry and Cromwell needed partners to push through their broad, legislative program.

But in securing Parliament's partnership, Henry and Cromwell had, perhaps inadvertently, increased its role and, therefore, its potential power. Parliament had long before secured the right to approve or disapprove of taxation. After 1529, the king asked this body to legislate not only on religion, but, as we shall see, on a wide variety of social and economic matters. For the moment, Parliament remained the junior partner because the king was such a commanding presence and because Cromwell, unlike Wolsey, was an effective parliamentary manager. But their expansion of Parliament's role would, in future reigns, provide that body with a justification for continuing to discuss these matters whether the monarch liked it or not. Henry and Cromwell had thus laid the seeds for a debate about sovereignty by creating the potential for conflict between a later, weaker, king and his newly empowered and increasingly experienced legislature. Future generations would be forced to play out this conflict at great cost.

In the meantime, Cromwell sought to make Henry's *imperium* effective over his whole empire. To do that, he had to make English government more efficient. To do *that* he had, in his view, to make himself more powerful. Cromwell's official position was king's secretary. His influence with the king allowed him to make this position the most important in Tudor government, superseding Wolsey's old post of lord chancellor. Indeed, Cromwell may fairly be credited with creating the basis for the later office of secretary of State. Professor Elton also gave him the credit for increasing the speed and flexibility of the council by reducing its membership to about 20, plus a clerk. But recent work indicates that this smaller, more effective "Privy Council" was actually created by the king as a counterweight to Cromwell's power.

Cromwell also sought to make the king's finances more efficient – and more responsive to his, Cromwell's, will. In 1537 he asked all the revenue departments to declare their income and expenditure and state the balance available for the king's use; prior to this, the government's accounting procedures were so poor that the monarch almost never knew how much money he had. Cromwell also reduced the jurisdiction of the Exchequer by placing the king's finances into the hands of a series of four courts whose procedures were ostensibly more rational and efficient.[16] What is certain is that they increased the secretary's patronage and control of the royal purse-strings. As master of the king's Jewel House, Cromwell also had effective personal control of Henry's funds via his access to the royal coffers. Thus, the ad hoc nature of household finance was not so much eliminated as placed in Cromwell's hands.

Thomas Cromwell not only sought to make the king's government more responsive at the center; he also tried to make it more effective in the localities by eliminating all authorities and affinities but the sovereign's. Most of the territory ruled by the king of England was remote from London; much of it was virtual borderland (see Introduction). We have seen how the harsher climates and more rugged terrain of the North, West Country, Wales, and Ireland tended to favor smaller and more isolated settlements, which, in turn, implied less integrated economies, extended kin loyalties, and domination by a few nobles or clan chiefs prone to rivalry and violence. Such areas tended to be difficult to control from the center. In fact, there were still some areas in England, called franchises or liberties, in which the king's writ did not run at all because some local aristocrat or bishop had long ago been granted freedom from royal jurisdiction. For example, in the county palatinate of Durham, the sheriff and JPs served in the name of the bishop of Durham, not the king. In the Marches of Wales, courts ruled in the name of the Marcher lords, not the king. Even in those remote areas where the king claimed sovereignty, he often had to rely on a single powerful nobleman both to keep a lid on local violence and to defend the frontier from hostile foreign intruders. Such noblemen tended to be cooperative only when it was in their interest to be so. If that interest dictated otherwise, as in the case of the Nevilles under Henry VI and Edward IV, or the earl of Kildare under Henry VII (see chapter 1), they might just as easily rebel against their master in London. It was Cromwell's goal to tame such areas and their inhabitants, both noble and common.

For example, Cromwell sought to solve the problem of northern violence by displacing the Percies, Nevilles, and Dacres following their dubious performance in the Pilgrimage of Grace, in favor of strengthened institutions. First, he secured an act of Parliament abolishing the county palatinates of Chester and Durham. At about the same time, he pressured the childless Henry Percy, earl of Northumberland (ca. 1502–37), to make the king his heir, eliminating at one blow the power of a leading northern magnate family while enriching the Crown's holdings. Finally, he revived and strengthened the Council of the North to watch over that area and to respond to the frequent skirmishing that occurred along the Scottish border.

Even more than the North, Wales was a patchwork of jurisdictions. Its northern part, the principality of Wales, was, in theory, ruled directly by the prince of that name. But since the title "prince of Wales" was usually taken by the king's son, it was vacant for most of Henry's reign. The south, especially the English frontier known as the Marches, was administered by about 130 powerful, but not always cooperative, Marcher lords. The lawlessness of Wales was due not only to fragmentary jurisdiction but also to long-smoldering hostility between the native, rural Welsh population and English settlers in urban areas. Nor did it help that Welsh law was relaxed about physical violence and rights of inheritance.[17] In 1536 Cromwell initiated a radical solution: a series of laws abolishing both the principality and the Marcher lordships as governmental authorities, replacing Welsh law and language in the courts with English law and language, and dividing all of Wales into 12 shires with lords lieutenant, JPs, MPs, and circuit courts along English lines. The Welsh Acts of Union also eliminated many distinctions and penalties which had made the Welsh second-class citizens in their own land.

These measures were moderately successful in their immediate objectives. The king's authority was strengthened, but violence (either among English nobles or between them and the Scots) continued in the North. In Wales, such violence subsided and the ruling elite, particularly the gentry of South Wales, began to feel more fully integrated into English government, economy, and society. At the same time, the Welsh gentry and people remained faithful to their culture and language, even if the Marches and southern Wales were bilingual. Perhaps as a result, bitterness at being a colonized people came to be virtually nonexistent among the Welsh of the early modern period. Welsh separatism would only resurface in the twentieth century.

Bitterness has, of course, long characterized relations between the English Crown and Ireland. It will be recalled that Ireland had been colonized by

English settlers since the early Middle Ages. That incursion upon the native Irish, or Gaelic, population had been supported by the Crown and the English king was, technically, overlord of all Ireland. But English power had been in steady decline since about 1300. By 1485, it was restricted to an area around Dublin known as "the Pale." Within this area, a Parliament, largely made up of English landlords, sat; but according to **Poynings's Law of 1494**, it could only debate measures previously approved by the king and council. The rest of Ireland may be divided, first into the so-called "obedient lands" to the south and east of the Pale, ruled by Anglo-Irish nobles descended from the original colonizers; and second, "wild Ireland" to the north and west, which was dominated by rival Gaelic clans, each headed by a great chieftain (see map 7). No English king had any power over the "wild Irish," who were traditionally looked upon as savages by the English population of Ireland. Nor could the king always count on the loyalty of the Anglo-Irish peers, who had embraced Gaelic customs and culture, and even married into the Gaelic clans. Though the obedient lands were divided into shires and theoretically owed their loyalty to the Crown, in practice, the Anglo-Irish peerage tended to behave like the Marcher lords of Wales or the North. That is, they fought for advantage among themselves, sometimes enforcing the king's writ, sometimes making common cause with Gaelic chieftains whom they were, ostensibly, supposed to keep down.

Of these Anglo-Irish peers, the most powerful were the Fitzgeralds, earls of Kildare. Under the Yorkists, successive earls of Kildare had been granted vast estates and given the authority that went along with the title lord deputy of Ireland. It was to them that royal power was delegated – to protect the Pale, to maintain order in the obedient lands, and to pacify wild Ireland, if possible. But, as we saw in the case of the eighth earl's support of Lambert Simnel and flirtation with Perkin Warbeck, the Fitzgeralds proved inconsistently loyal under the Tudors. In 1494 Henry VII removed Kildare from the deputyship in favor of an Englishman, Sir Edward Poynings (1459–1521), who forced the Irish Parliament to assent to the restrictions of Poynings's Law (necessary because the Irish Parliament had supported these pretenders against the House of Tudor) and an army to enforce them. But armies are expensive and unpopular and so, in 1496, the Tudors turned back to Kildare, who remained an uncertainly loyal lord deputy until his death in 1513. His successor as ninth earl and lord deputy, another Gerald Fitzgerald (1487–1534), did not always agree with royal policy, but he continued to maintain a fragile peace in the king's name, building up a vast clientage network through marriage alliances with the Gaelic clans. This rendered him more effective as the king's lieutenant, but it also made him imperious, over-confident, somewhat resented by other, less powerful, Anglo-Irish families – and much harder to control or replace from London.

In 1533 a rival Anglo-Irish family, the Butlers, earls of Ormond, intrigued at court against Kildare's conduct as deputy. The king summoned him to London to answer their complaints, lodging him in the Tower, where he died the next year of natural causes. False rumors that he had been executed led his popular son and heir, "Silken Thomas," Lord Offaly, now tenth earl of Kildare (1513–37), to rise

Map 7 *Early modern Ireland.*

in revolt, declare himself for the pope, and seek aid from both Rome and Charles V. The revolt received support from both the Gaelic chieftains and the Irish clergy, who feared the coming of Reformation. Thus, it became both a war for Irish political independence and a Catholic religious crusade. But the Butlers remained loyal to the king's interests, Dublin held out, and both were relieved by an English army. The new earl of Kildare finally surrendered to the king's forces on a promise that his life would be spared.

But forgiving and rehabilitating the earls of Kildare was inconsistent with Tudor ruthlessness and Cromwell's notion of imperial sovereignty. Instead, as in other borderlands, "aristocratic delegation was replaced by direct rule" from London.[18] Kildare was executed, along with five of his uncles; a new, English-born lord deputy was named; and a garrison was permanently established at Dublin. In 1536 Cromwell engineered an Act of Supremacy for Ireland, making King Henry the head of the Irish Church. In 1541 he assumed the title king of Ireland and began a cultural and political revolution there known as "surrender and regrant," whereby Irish chieftains traded their ancient claims in return for lands and titles bestowed by the English monarch. These policies were consistent with the long-term goal of tightening royal control, but they offended both Anglo-Irish and Gaelic sensibilities. Moreover, the garrison proved ruinously expensive while the Reformation further divided the Gaelic-Irish and Anglo-Irish from the Crown and, later, from Protestant English and Scottish settlers. Since there was no immediate attempt to translate the Bible into Gaelic or to catechize the Irish in the new, reformed faith that Cromwell was pushing in England, most native Irish and many English landlords remained loyal to the pope. This would be another source of bitter disagreement in Tudor Ireland. The pattern for future tragedies had been set: religious friction, mistrust, misunderstanding, violence, rebellion, revenge, and English military occupation would be hallmarks of Anglo-Irish relations for the rest of the Tudor period and, indeed, to the present day. Here, the long-term fruits of Cromwell's revolution would prove bitter indeed.

Closer to home, Thomas Cromwell envisioned a new and wider role for government beyond the mere maintenance of order and unity in politics and religion. That vision did not arise in a vacuum. He was surrounded by a group of humanist writers, later known as the Commonwealthmen, who believed that the proper object of royal government was not to fight wars for the glory of egotistical monarchs but, rather, to improve the commonweal, i.e., the general public welfare. This was a logical extension of the idea of unitary, imperial sovereignty. The Tudors had so expanded the power and competence of royal government that they thought that it could now regulate the economy, distribute charity, and generally promote the well-being of its subjects. These matters had, before the 1530s, been the responsibility of the Church and the guilds that were affiliated with it. Since Henry and Cromwell were weakening the Church even as they took it over, some assumption of responsibility on the part of the government was both necessary and logical. What, specifically, did Cromwell and the Commonwealthmen have in mind?

First, Cromwell and Parliament increased the government's ability to police the economy. They did so by the Statute of Uses of 1536, which regulated the selling and inheritance of land, albeit to improve tax yields for the king.[19] In addition, the Parliaments of the 1530s continued to pass laws restricting enclosure. Above all, the Crown began to assume responsibility for the provision of charity to the poor with the first **Poor Law** in 1536. The problem of poverty, its urgency in the 1530s, and the effects of the new law will be addressed below (see chapter 6). In the meantime, it is enough to note that the new Poor Law authorized local authorities to raise funds to distribute to the deserving poor, i.e., the lame, the sick, the aged, women, and children (those who could not work). The act distinguished these from the undeserving poor or "sturdy beggars" who were physically capable of work but who, it seemed to contemporaries, refused to do it. These were to be whipped, put in the stocks, and otherwise punished to force them out of their idleness. Nineteenth-century historians and economists would view the Poor Law as a classic example of early modern ignorance and hypocrisy. But we now realize that Cromwell and his associates deserve some credit for laying the foundations of a welfare state that was, no matter how partial, capricious, or cruel, ahead of its time.

The governments of Catholic Europe had less need of such expedients because they traditionally left responsibility for poor relief to the churches and monasteries. Up to this point, that had been true in England as well. But in 1536, as the capstone to their revolution, Henry and Cromwell began to dissolve the monasteries and convents. On the surface, the Dissolution of the Monasteries and Convents of 1536–9 would seem to be a religious event, just one more front in the attack on the Catholic Church which the king had launched in 1529. According to Cromwell, the primary reason for dissolving the monasteries was that they were notoriously corrupt. Commissions of inquiry sent out in 1535 did find some evidence of corruption, as well as laziness and a loss of direction among monks and nuns. Also, lay bequests were drying up and recruitment was dwindling. If the commissions' reports are to be believed, this arm of the Church in England really was failing to fulfill its mission.

But the commissions' reports were ultimately irrelevant. Whatever their verdict, Henry and Cromwell had already decided to dissolve the monasteries and convents and confiscate their land, buildings, and wealth: in fact, Parliament drafted a Dissolution Bill for the smaller houses before receiving the commissioners' report. One rationale for attacking the regular orders of the clergy (monks and nuns) had to do with institutional hierarchy. Monks reported to their abbots, who reported to the heads of their orders – whether Benedictine, Cistercian, etc. – who invariably lived in Rome and reported to the Vatican. Obviously, these links had to be broken. But the main motive for dissolution and confiscation was the king's need for money. After all, if royal government was to fulfill all of the new responsibilities which Henry and Cromwell had assumed for it, it would need far deeper pockets. Cromwell's idea was to endow the Crown permanently with the wealth from the monasteries. Their treasures (books, artwork, furniture) would be sold; their land, amounting to 15 percent of the realm, was to be kept to pay for the new, expanded royal government. The 400 smaller monasteries and convents were dissolved in 1536; the 200 larger houses in 1539. Chantries, that is, chapels built and endowed solely for the purpose of saying masses for the souls of the (usually wealthy) dead, would be dissolved in 1547. The process was gradual, possibly because the plan evolved slowly, possibly because it was thought that a divide-and-conquer strategy would be most effective. Indeed, the larger monasteries acquiesced in the attack on their smaller cousins in 1536 in the hope of being spared themselves.

What was the effect of this policy? For the 9,000 or so inhabitants of these institutions and the things they cared about, the news was mostly very bad. Monks were pensioned off. Nuns were told to return to their families, a cruel joke to older religious who may have had no living relations. Priceless artwork was destroyed, precious metalwork melted down, great libraries dispersed, Gothic buildings razed or turned to agricultural use. Church-run hospitals, schools, and charitable institutions were abolished, though in some cases local authorities assumed control and kept them open. At one blow, Henry and Cromwell eradicated a major portion of the Church's wealth, physical presence, and social role. This would make Reformation much easier to accomplish. It would also necessitate the creation of other institutions, such as the Poor Law, to deal with the problems formerly left to religious authorities. Henry also founded six new dioceses with the lands and monies from the dissolved foundations.

But Cromwell's plan to endow the Crown sufficiently to pay for the new role of government – and thereby avoid dependance on Parliament – was only partially and temporarily successful. The Dissolution augmented the king's coffers by about £90,000 a year, which Cromwell might have managed so as to make Henry VIII as self-sufficient as his father had been. But, as we shall see in the next chapter, the secretary was losing his hold on the king in the late 1530s. Moreover, a series of invasion scares in 1538–9 produced a need for quick cash, which was raised by selling monastic lands. By the early 1540s, Cromwell had fallen from power and Henry had fallen back on old habits by starting a costly war with France. Once more in need of funds, he stepped up the sale of the confiscated lands at very reasonable prices. This raised about £66,000 a year from 1539 to 1543, but at the cost of a legacy which might have provided steady future income.

The purchasers of this land were the beneficiaries of a windfall. They were generally professional, gentle, and yeomen families who thereby rose in status and wealth. Thus, Cromwell did achieve something revolutionary by dissolving the monasteries and convents, albeit not the revolution he had planned. What he managed to endow was not the Crown but an expanded English ruling class. Though he unleashed great wealth, the Crown remained poor. This would leave the king beholden to Parliament for funds at a time when, as we have seen, it was growing in power and authority in other matters. This would, in turn, add to the power and confidence of those members of the ruling elite which it represented. Finally, the purchase of monastic lands did one more thing for the ruling elite: it virtually guaranteed that this crucial group of people would not look favorably on a Catholic restoration. The natural desire to hold onto their new land and wealth would, instead, recommend Protestantism.

In the end, these are the most important legacies of Cromwell's – or Elton's – apparent revolution. Since 1953, other historians have pointed out that not all of Cromwell's initiatives were original. Some, such as the use of regional councils to oversee the borderlands, had been pioneered by the Yorkists or by Wolsey. Others, such as his deemphasis of the Exchequer in favor of revenue courts, were reversed subsequently. Still others, such as his measures to suppress Ireland, were simply unsuccessful. Nor is it entirely certain how many of these innovations were part of a master plan and how many were spontaneous reactions to swiftly moving events; or, if there was a plan, which parts of it were Henry's or some other minister's.

In conclusion, if there was a Tudor Revolution in Government, at its heart was contradiction and ambiguity. If its goal was to create an imperial monarchy, answerable to no other power on earth, it succeeded to the extent of eradicating the authority of the pope in England, subordinating the English Church to the king, abolishing franchises and liberties, and breaking down the old aristocratic affinities which had played so important a role in the Wars of the Roses. But, in order to accomplish this, Cromwell also increased the power of Parliament and the wealth of those whom it represented. He also set goals which had more to do with the good of the realm and the welfare of the people than the strengthening of the monarchy. Ironically, this institution, this class, and these goals would serve, eventually, to challenge and permanently weaken the authority of the king. Henry VIII's decision to squander the windfall of the monastic lands only hastened that day. (That is, the problem of finance would exacerbate the problem of sovereignty.) In fact, in fostering national institutions and a bureaucracy which could function independent of the king, it could be argued that Henry, Cromwell, and their colleagues sowed the seeds for a constitutional monarchy in which loyalty would be owed to an abstraction, such as "England" or "the Crown," and in which the actual person of the king would be a mere figurehead whose personal qualities and inclinations were irrelevant. Finally, while Cromwell managed to make the king Supreme Head of the Church of England and while his Dissolution of the Monasteries served to wean a good part of the country away from papal Catholicism, neither of these things ensured religious unanimity in England, or that England's religion would be Protestant. These questions would dominate the final years of Henry's reign, as well as those of his children.

CHAPTER THREE

Reformations and Counter-Reformations, 1536–1558

In the mid-1530s Henry VIII declared himself Supreme Head of the Church of England and appropriated a fair proportion of its wealth. This does not mean that he was a Protestant. In fact, while his religious statements and policies were often ambiguous, on balance they indicate that Henry considered himself to be a good Catholic to the end of his days – albeit one who denied the authority of the pope. A religious conservative, Henry VIII wanted to retain the structure and habits of the old medieval Church, but with himself as its head. His court contained many fellow conservatives, including powerful families such as the Howards and the Poles and Bishops Gardiner and Tunstall, who encouraged him in this stance.

But as the Catholic polemicist Nicholas Harpsfield (1519?–75) wrote, the king was "like to one that would throw down a man headlong from the top of a high tower and bid him stay when he was half way down."[1] That is, once Henry denied papal authority over English religious life, he inevitably, if inadvertently, opened the door to the questioning of other Church teachings. Another faction at court, led by Cromwell, Cranmer, and the circle around Queen Anne, promoted such questioning and Protestant reform in general. They pushed the king in the direction of Church reform, and encouraged the dissemination of new, Protestant ideas and practices. During Henry's last 10 years, these two factions vied for the king's ear, mind, and soul. To possess them was to hold the key to every church door in England, in this reign and into the next.

Henry's apparent vacillation between Catholic and Protestant involved more than his conscience or court politics. It was also wrapped up with his marital situation as well as the European balance of power. Under his successors, this conflict would also be affected by the social and economic tensions England was experiencing by the mid-sixteenth century. In short, throughout the period covered by this chapter, the religious debate was influenced by a complex calculus of political, economic, social, and cultural factors as much as by the personal convictions of the sovereign.

Catholic or Protestant

The fundamental differences between Roman Catholics and Protestants in the middle of the sixteenth century are not quite the same as those of today.[2] As a result, modern adherents to these faiths may not always recognize their own beliefs in the following descriptions. Moreover, since late medieval Roman Catholicism allowed for some latitude in belief and practice, and since Protestantism was not, nor ever has been, a single, organized faith, but was, rather, a movement embracing a variety of individual confessions, the following table and discussion necessarily oversimplify. That is, they present ideal types or archetypes of what early modern Catholics and Protestants actually believed and did. It is important to remember that, in practice, each tradition was a "big tent," often more ambiguous, more nuanced, and more diverse than is possible to explain here. Nevertheless, we would maintain that the battle lines between these two forms of Christianity were drawn, in sixteenth-century England at any rate, more or less as follows:

	Catholic	**Protestant**
Source of Divine Truth:	Scripture + tradition + authority	Scripture alone
Structure:	Hierarchical	Limited or no hierarchy
Clergy:	Semi-sacred priest	Minister
Ritual:	Sacramental and efficacious	Few sacraments; symbolic
Salvation:	Faith + good works (free will)	Faith alone (some predestinarian)

For the purposes of this discussion, the fundamental difference between Roman Catholicism and Protestantism lies in where each finds religious truth, that is, God's wish and will for good Christians. For Catholics, God's will was to be found, first, in the Bible. But the Bible is a complicated document, obscure to some readers and seemingly contradictory in places. In any case, for most of the Middle Ages, few Europeans could read. Books of any kind, including Bibles, were rare and expensive because, prior to the invention of the printing press in the mid-fifteenth century, they had to be copied out by hand. Therefore, the Roman Catholic Church reserved to itself the right and responsibility to interpret the Bible for the faithful. Holy Scripture was to be studied and expounded by religious professionals: the pope, bishops, and priests of the Church who were thought to have a special mandate from God to do so. In theory, priests studied Scripture and Church doctrine rigorously. At their ordination they became consecrated, even semi-sacred beings. Such an important and complicated work as the Bible was to be reserved to their stewardship and kept out of the un-schooled hands of amateurs – that is, the laity. Therefore, the Church kept the Bible in Latin and refused to allow the dissemination of vernacular translations, at least in England.

Moreover, the Roman Catholic Church argued that the Bible was not the only source of God's truth; it was also to be found in the traditions and decisions of the Church itself, which elaborated upon and extrapolated from Scripture. That is, if God's Church had held a belief or performed a ritual for the past thousand years, it obviously accorded with God's will, whether it appeared in Scripture or not. In addition, the Church hierarchy (i.e., the pope, sometimes but not always in conjunction with Church councils made up of cardinals and bishops) frequently made decisions about religious doctrine or practices. According to the Catholic Church, these pronouncements, too, represented God's will. Roman Catholics believed (as they still do) that this hierarchy could be traced in an unbroken line back to St. Peter, whom they believe(d) to have been chosen by Jesus Christ to be the first pope. The Church took literally and seriously Jesus's injunction to St. Peter:

thou art Peter; and upon this rock I will build my church, and the gates of hell shall not prevail against it. And I will give to thee the keys of the kingdom of heaven. And whatsoever thou shalt bind upon earth, it shall be bound also in heaven: and whatsoever thou shalt loose on earth, it shall be loosed also in heaven. (Matthew 16: 18–19, Douai-Rheims translation)

Church leaders tended to interpret this passage to mean that the laity were to obey them without question.

The earliest Protestant reformers, beginning with Martin Luther, rejected this extensive mandate for the Church hierarchy. As a young priest, Luther had journeyed to Rome and been appalled at the materialism and corruption which he had witnessed among high-ranking churchmen. He also found himself at odds with positions and practices sanctioned by the Church hierarchy but nowhere to be found in Scripture (for example, the practice of granting indulgences, ex-plained below). He and most subsequent Protestant reformers came to the con-clusion that only the Word (that is, the Bible and its painstaking elaboration in sermons and liturgy) could be trusted to reveal God's truth. Beliefs and practices not found in Scripture were not divinely authorized. From this radical but supremely simple position flowed most of the Protestant critique of Catholicism. First, it implied that the Bible should be translated, printed, and put into every Christian's hands, not locked away. (Growing literacy among Europeans and the advent of the printing press made this possible.) Second, it implied that there was no need for a hierarchy of semi-divine priests to interpret God's will. It was all right there in Scripture. Indeed, given the Bible's failure to mention popes, cardinals, and bishops, the Catholic hierarchy had no basis in God's will at all. While Luther envisioned that congregations would still be led by ordained ministers, he no longer saw ordination as creating semi-sacred beings. A truly reformed and scriptural Church implied a "priesthood of all believers"; for a few reformers, congregations would, in effect, be their own priests. Finally, since the Church hierarchy was obviously unscriptural and corrupt, the only hope for reform lay with righteous secular authorities, like the German Protestant princes or even, as English reformers urged, Henry VIII.

A second, crucial element of the Protestant critique of Catholicism concerns the path to salvation. Catholics had long believed that salvation was achieved through two mutually supportive means. First, one had to believe: in God, in the divinity and resurrection of Jesus Christ, and in his Church. But belief was not enough. The faithful had also to engage in certain rituals, called sacraments, which could only be performed by ordained priests. Three of the seven sacraments (baptism, penance, anointing of the sick) led directly to the forgiveness of sins and all (including the remaining four: Eucharist, confirmation, matrimony, and holy orders) endowed the soul with grace. Grace, earned by human beings in this life, was thought to be necessary to achieve salvation in the next. Moreover, the performance of good works, such as giving charity to the poor, contributing to the Church, and living a good life generally, would also increase one's store of grace and, by pleasing God, contribute to one's salvation. Specifically, good works were thought to reduce the amount of time one's soul would have to spend in Purgatory. Needless to say, good Catholics wanted to spend as little time there after their deaths as possible. Here, too, Christ's promise that what was bound "on earth" was bound "in heaven" was significant to Catholics. In the Middle Ages, the Church began to grant indulgences, which forgave specified amounts of purgatorial time in reward for particular good works. Such and such a good work would result in an indulgence which took off so many years of one's posthumous punishment. A good work might include a pilgrimage to a holy place, the performance of a set of devotions, or an act of charity or financial generosity to the Church.

To Luther, this amounted to buying one's way into Heaven. Tortured by his own sense of sin, he concluded that his offenses were so great – that human beings were, on the whole, so sinful and so far removed from God's perfection – that no amount of "good works" could possibly purchase God's forgiveness. The idea that humans could do anything to force God's hand in this, or any matter, was obnoxious to him. Therefore, he concluded, the Church had no power to grant indulgences, or even to claim to forgive sins and dispense grace through the sacraments. No human institution could do this. Therefore, good works, while certainly praiseworthy and clear indications of God's grace, could not *produce* it. They were therefore, ultimately, irrelevant to the soul's salvation. God would make up his own mind without human interference. Faith in Him and faith alone led to redemption. From this, it followed that the whole apparatus of priests, processions, blessings, holy water, and images was, at best, useless and, at worst, idolatrous. It stood in the way of the simple truth that all one had to do – all one could do – to achieve salvation was believe in God, read Scripture, and pray.

One continental Protestant reformer, John Calvin (1509–64), took the idea of the inefficacy of human agency even farther. He argued that, since God knows and wills all things, God knows and wills the future. Therefore, God has already determined the fate of every individual soul; that is, whether that soul is to be saved or damned. Therefore, every person's salvation is predestined and irreversible, since there can be no arguing with God. This idea would lead to much soul-searching on the part of **Calvinist** Protestants hoping to figure out whether they were saved (of the elect) or damned (of the reprobate).

It should be obvious from this discussion why Catholicism, with its emphasis on hierarchy, ritual, and obedience, should have appealed to Henry VIII and to many members of the ruling elite. It should also be obvious why Protestantism, with its European origins and its emphasis on literacy, should have struck root in England among continental travelers, merchants, lawyers, and other literate professionals, usually based in port cities.

Marriage, Succession, and Foreign Policy

In the mid-1530s, the Protestant-leaning circle associated with Thomas Cromwell, Archbishop Cranmer, Queen Anne, and the Boleyn family were ascendant at court. Not surprisingly, given the Boleyns' French connections and Catherine of Aragon's Spanish blood, this group also favored a pro-French, anti-Spanish/Imperial foreign policy. But as early as 1535–6, at the very outset of their ascendancy, the Cromwell–Boleyn–Protestant coalition began to fall apart. First, the French proved to be no more reliable as allies than the emperor had been, leading Cromwell to reopen negotiations with Charles V. Second, Anne's outspoken promotion of religious reform seems to have rankled many at court, including the king. But none of this would have mattered if Queen Anne had borne him a son and heir. In January 1536 she miscarried at 14 weeks of a deformed little boy. Given the theological significance contemporaries attributed to such obstetrical disasters, it must have seemed to the king that this marriage, too, was cursed. Moreover, during the winter of Anne's pregnancy he began to be attracted to one of the queen's ladies in waiting, Jane Seymour (1509–37), who had been put forward by the Aragonese faction, the group of courtiers associated with the former queen.

January 1536 also saw the death of Catherine of Aragon. Although Anne celebrated the demise of her rival by wearing yellow instead of black, this event actually left Cromwell and the king free to move against her without having to worry about a revival of support for his first wife. In April 1536, with Cromwell's approval, a secret committee was appointed to find evidence of adultery against Queen Anne. She was accused, almost certainly unjustly, of five counts of adultery with a variety of young men at court, including her own brother, George, Lord Rochford (b. 1504?). Queenly infidelity was high treason, for it could jeopardize the legitimate succession of the king's heirs. It is impossible to know Henry's role in the matter: was he the author of this scheme or had Anne's many enemies duped him into believing the charges? In any case, he accepted the verdict. As usual when the king wished it, Tudor justice moved with brutal swiftness. On May 15, 1536 Queen Anne was tried and convicted; on the 17th her marriage was declared null and void; and on the 19th she was executed along with the five male "adulterers." None protested their innocence, probably out of a desire to protect their families from further retribution by the king. On May 30 Henry married Jane Seymour. On October 12, 1537 she gave birth to a son, christened Edward (d. 1553). Henry had finally achieved his goal of siring a male heir.

Twelve days later Queen Jane died from complications of the birth, leaving Henry VIII an eligible bachelor for the first time in a quarter-century. Henry's single state presented opportunities to both the king and his chief minister, for the former needed not only a new wife but a new alliance and religious settlement. These three matters would be intertwined. At first, Henry sought to return to his old alliance with the emperor. To do this, he would have to show signs of returning to Rome as well. In fact, his government had already enacted a compromise statement on doctrine called the Ten Articles. This document reaffirmed the importance of good works, as well as of baptism, confession, and transubstantiation. On the other hand, it failed to reassert the necessity of confirmation, matrimony, holy orders, and the anointing of the sick. This was not Catholic enough for Charles V, who did not take the bait for an alliance. Neither, when approached, did Francis I of France. By 1538, the pope, seeing no hope for reconciliation, finally excommunicated Henry VIII. In declaring the king an apostate and a heretic, the Holy See, in effect, absolved good Catholics of their obligation to be loyal to him. Worse, the following year saw a peace treaty between France and the Holy Roman Empire, clearly leaving them in a position to unite against the declared heretic on the throne of England. Henry, fearing invasion, scrambled to strengthen his defenses. He had, over the course of the reign, virtually created the Royal Navy, founding dockyards and building some 40 men-of-war. To this he now added a series of coastal forts. But these would be of little use if he had to face France and the Empire alone.

Realizing this, Secretary Cromwell began to pursue a third way in foreign policy between 1537 and 1540 by sounding out northern German princes, who tended to be Protestants and were often at odds with their nominal superior, the Holy Roman Emperor. There were two elements to his strategy. First, Cromwell promoted Protestantism by dissolving the monasteries and by issuing two sets of Injunctions (in 1536 and 1538, respectively) for regulating individual parish churches. These required that every such church have a copy of the new English translation of the Bible by William Tyndale as revised by Miles Coverdale (1488–1568); that all images and statues be removed; and that the clergy preach and teach their flocks, in English, the "Ten Commandments" and prayers such as the "Our Father" (formerly the "*Pater Noster*"). In addition, the number of holy days was reduced, shrines dismantled, and pilgrimages denounced. Finally, in a move for which social historians have been ever grateful, every parish in England was required to keep a record of its baptisms, marriages, and burials. The

Injunctions and related legislation represented the first tangible break with Roman practice for the vast majority of English churchgoers and they were controversial. Perhaps most significantly, while the king did not oppose them, he did little to indicate support. Henry was taking a wait-and-see attitude to reform.

The second prong of Cromwell's strategy was to arrange a diplomatic marriage for Henry with Anne of Cleves (1515–57), the daughter of a powerful anti-Imperial and anti-papal prince in the west of Germany, the duke of Cleves. In order to interest the king, Cromwell commissioned Hans Holbein, the great portrait painter of the Tudor court, to travel to Germany to paint the potential bride. According to legend, Holbein followed the practice of most court painters: he flattered Anne. When Henry saw the portrait, he professed himself enchanted and signed a treaty in October 1539. But when his bride arrived in January 1540 the king was repulsed, nicknaming her "the Flanders mare." Realizing that more was at stake than his marital happiness, Henry went through with the ceremony. But by July the political and diplomatic situation changed again, as explained below. As a result, Henry was able to divorce Anne on the entirely plausible grounds of non-consummation. He granted her lands and a generous financial settlement and the former couple seem to have maintained a regard for each other for the rest of their lives.

Obviously, Cromwell's failure to work out a successful Protestant marriage and foreign policy left him badly exposed to his enemies in the spring of 1540. Despite his elevation as earl of Essex in April, events were beginning to overtake him. A Catholic party led by Stephen Gardiner, bishop of Winchester, and the Howard family opposed Cromwell. While this group was less numerous in Henry's court and government than Cromwell's followers, they did have the king's ear. This was not least because, as we have seen, Henry was naturally attracted to Catholicism so long as it did not involve the pope. Moreover, in the spring of 1540, Henry fell in love with the 19-year-old Catherine Howard (1520–42), niece of the Catholic duke of Norfolk. While Cromwell ran the king's government in London, Norfolk, Gardiner, and Catherine attended his person at Greenwich. As the first two poisoned Henry's mind against his secretary and principal minister, Catherine won his heart.

Perhaps as a result of this influence, perhaps out of his own conservative convictions, perhaps in hopes of placating the Catholic powers, the king now began to distance himself from Cromwell's reforms. As early as November 1538 he had issued a proclamation condemning **Anabaptists**, clerical marriage, and attacks on Church ceremonies. In May 1539, over Cromwell's objections, he forced his secretary to steer through Parliament the Act of Six Articles, which denounced clerical marriage and upheld the efficacy of all seven sacraments as well as masses for the dead. Finally, to ensure that there would be no pretender in the wings for an invader to place on the throne, the king rounded up and executed every important Yorkist claimant within his obsessive grasp. During the summer of 1540 he went further, divorcing Anne of Cleves, marrying Catherine Howard in secret, and (in June and July) imprisoning, attainting, and then executing

Thomas Cromwell, earl of Essex, on charges of abetting heresy and misusing his authority. In August, the marriage to Queen Catherine was made public. With a Catholic queen sharing the throne, the Catholic faction ascendant at court, the mass defended in the churches, and the architect of the Royal Supremacy dead, the Catholic triumph was complete.

But it was also short-lived, for Henry soon had reason to doubt the loyalty of his Catholic subjects and even his Catholic queen. In the spring of 1541 he put down a number of Catholic plots in the North. That fall, the Privy Council acquired evidence that Catherine Howard had been sexually indiscreet with a series of young men, both before and after her marriage to the king. After some hesitation on Henry's part, Parliament passed a bill of attainder against her on February 7, 1542. Catherine was taken to the Tower on February 10 and beheaded on the 13th. To save himself and what was left of the Catholic party, Norfolk joined in the accusations against his niece.

In the summer of 1541 France and the Empire once again resumed hostilities, thus ending all fears of invasion, and relieving the pressure on Henry to appear more "Catholic." Both sides courted the English king, who eventually joined his old ally, the emperor. His first move was to invade France's ally, Scotland, in the fall of 1542. This campaign resulted in a crushing victory over the Scots at Solway Marsh in November. The Scottish king, James V, died, seemingly of pure dejection, within the month. He was succeeded by his infant daughter, Mary, known to history as "Queen of Scots" (1542–87; reigned 1542–67). Henry, negotiating from strength, forced her diplomats to promise that she would marry the 5-year-old Prince Edward in July 1543. But after Henry went further and attempted to reassert feudal sovereignty over the northern kingdom, a pro-French, pro-Catholic Scottish government under David, Cardinal Beaton (1494–1546), repudiated the treaty and resumed the "Auld Alliance." In response, Henry dispatched another invasion force, placing it under the command of the late Queen Jane's brother, Edward Seymour, earl of Hertford (ca. 1506–52). This enterprise would cost over £1,000,000 on the English side, much life on both sides, and the last shreds of good will which might have led to a peaceful union of the two kingdoms.

In the meantime, the king began his last French campaign, in July 1544. By this time Henry VIII was ill and prematurely aged, suffering from obesity, gout, dropsy, and, just possibly, syphilis. As a consequence, the English Colossus had to be carried about the French countryside on a litter. From this position he commanded a huge army of 48,000 men. This force managed to capture the French port of Boulogne, but at the astronomical cost of £1,300,000. To this should be added another £1,000,000 for the navy and coastal garrisons, and, of course, the above-noted cost of the Scottish campaigns. With Cromwell off the stage, King Henry lacked an effective minister and parliamentary manager to reduce expenses or raise parliamentary taxation. While Parliament cooperated, raising well over £1,000,000 in the 1540s, this was obviously not enough to pay for all his military adventures. So the king resorted to selling vast quantities of monastic lands, extorting **forced loans** and illegal benevolences from his subjects, taking out foreign loans at the rate of 14 percent, and debasing the coinage. These last two expedients, in particular, emptied the Treasury, increased the royal debt (Henry would die owing his foreign creditors over £750,000), and promoted runaway inflation. The king's diplomatic and fiscal irresponsibility undid much of Cromwell's "Tudor Revolution," wrecked royal finances for a hundred years, and weakened the English economy as a whole for at least twenty.

Henry VIII's Last Years

It is often difficult to tell precisely what the declining king had in mind during his last years. Perhaps, in his supreme self-centeredness, he felt betrayed by all those who surrounded him. Certainly he was suspicious of the Protestants for their doctrinal heterodoxy and rejection of hierarchy; and of the Catholics for their loyalty to the pope. It is typical of the hot-tempered king that, in July 1540, two days after executing Cromwell, he had three Catholic priests hanged as traitors and three Protestant preachers burned as heretics in Smithfield, London's meat market, simultaneously. It is equally characteristic that in his last speech to Parliament in December 1545, he – of all people – called for charity and tolerance.

But gradually, the king seems to have realized that some decision had to be made, not so much for himself as for his son. In the end, he appears to have concluded that, whatever his personal feelings about Protestantism, Catholics could not be trusted to maintain their allegiance to the dynasty and its achievements. That is, only Protestants, whether reform-minded theologians or lukewarm gentry who had purchased monastic lands, owed everything to a Tudor succession and had everything to fear from a usurpation or revolution. Subsequent actions by English Catholics confirmed his inclinations. Henry was annoyed when, three times between 1543 and 1545, the Catholic party attempted to pry Cranmer out of his archbishopric by accusing him of heresy. The king was alarmed when, in 1546, Henry Howard, earl of Surrey (b. 1517), son of Norfolk, a descendant of Edward I, and a Catholic, began to include the royal arms in his crest. The king interpreted this as a threat to Prince Edward's succession. He had Surrey executed in January 1547 and condemned his father, Norfolk, to follow. In a final blow to the Catholic party, Bishop Gardiner was stricken from the roll of privy councilors.

Thus, as the reign came to a close, the king increasingly turned for advice to a circle of Protestant politicians led by his former brother-in-law, the earl of Hertford. His Protestant family connections were further strengthened when, in July 1543, he married for the last time. The new queen was a middle-aged widow of mildly reformist sympathies named Catherine Parr, Lady Latimer (1512–48). She knew how to handle, even mother, the aging monarch, and she proved to be a good mother to his three children as well. Finally, in 1547 the king buttressed the Protestant circle around the prince by naming Protestant peers to his regency council and reformist scholars as his tutors.

It is thus with no little irony that Henry VIII died in January 1547, his hand in Cranmer's, convinced that he did so a good Catholic to his God and a good king to his people. These two fond beliefs are open to question. Because he broke with Rome, destroyed the Church's institutional structure, and failed to erect a clear religious system in its place, Henry inadvertently encouraged debate and dissent. New, reformist ideas flooded into port cities, especially London, from Europe. Bible study groups and Protestant cells at the universities proliferated. The country at large was not yet Protestant by 1547. But the old Catholic monopoly on English religious life had been broken. Moreover, Henry's patronage decisions ensured that the next king would go even further.

As for Henry's concern for his people, he did leave them a male heir, albeit a very young and, as it turned out, sickly one. Moreover, his use of Parliament to secure both the religious settlement and new kinds of social and economic legislation served to establish that body as a public venue for religious debate and a powerful tool for the redress of popular grievance – sometimes to the chagrin of his successors. His domestic policies strengthened royal authority and increased State power in other areas, and this led, in many cases, to a safer, more secure realm, including Wales. But his policy toward the other Celtic lands only embittered the Irish and drove the independent kingdom of Scotland back into the arms of France. Worse, his foreign policy adventures had done little to increase English prestige abroad, but everything to wreck royal finances and the national economy at home. The government's inability to pay its bills would eventually weaken the English Crown and impoverish its subjects beyond his wildest imagination. This, too, would lead to an expansion of Parliament's responsibilities. Thus, Henry created or exacerbated a series of problems, including those of sovereignty, royal finance, foreign policy, religion, and central vs. local control, that would plague his successors for decades. In many ways, for good or ill, the story told in the rest of this book is the working out of the ramifications of decisions first made by Henry VIII.

The New King, the Lord Protector, and the Legacy of Henry VIII

In short, when King Henry departed this life for what he hoped was a better one, he left his people a raft of problems, many of his own making. These included a massive government debt, widespread economic distress, religious uncertainty, and hostilities with England's three most proximate neighbors, Scotland, Ireland, and France. Perhaps his only real achievement, the road to which had been paved with these problems, was the peaceful accession of his son, Edward VI (reigned 1547–53). In keeping with the imperious personality of Henry VIII, he actually disposed of his kingdom via his last will and testament.[3] This document bequeathed the throne to, first, Edward. Should the new king die without heirs, Henry's eldest daughter, Mary, would follow; if she should die childless, she would be succeeded by Elizabeth (see genealogy 2, p. 413). It is a measure of Henry's power and prestige that, even in death, his wishes were not seriously questioned despite the facts that they reversed previous legislation delegitimizing the two princesses, and that Edward VI was only 9 years of age when he came to the throne. The example of England's last child-king, Edward V, was just about within living memory and yet, remarkably, no one seems to have challenged the right or the ability of this delicate boy to rule. If the young king lacked his predecessor's physical strength and vigor, he at least possessed the same quick mind and strong will. As a child, the new sovereign proved himself an accomplished scholar in Greek, Latin, and French. He also played the lute and demonstrated an interest in astronomy.

Despite his precocious intelligence, Edward's age dictated that he could not yet rule in his own right. Henry VIII had foreseen the problem and provided a regency council made up of prominent Protestant peers and clergymen. But within days of Edward's accession one of the new king's uncles, the earl of Hertford, persuaded his nephew and the Privy Council to name him lord protector of the realm and duke of Somerset. So, despite the late king's best efforts, the history of the last King Edward had repeated itself in at least one way: a royal uncle had seized effective power over a boy-king and his realm. This is not to say that Somerset (as he will be called henceforth) was another Richard III. Unlike that unfortunate monarch, he wanted to dominate the boy-king, not usurp him. This was obviously a less ruthless and more prudent policy than Richard's, but it would leave him exposed to rivals for the king's ear. Like Richard, Somerset was something of a reformer, issuing some 76 proclamations in just two years. In particular, he was a patron of those writers, known to later generations as Commonwealthmen, who sought social and economic justice. But this sympathy for the poor played badly with the nobility and gentry who exploited them. Moreover, the new lord protector was imperious toward his fellow councilors, bull-headed in maintaining policies that were manifestly unpopular with the ruling class, and "looked down upon by everybody as a dry, sour, opinionated man" according to one foreign observer.[4] He was, in short, a poor politician.

Somerset demonstrated his political ineptitude in the first task he set himself, that of pacifying Scotland. As lord protector he continued Henry VIII's policy of "rough wooing," that is, of pressuring the Scots into marrying their new young Queen Mary to England's new young King Edward – and wreaking havoc upon them if they refused. Upon the latest such refusal he invaded, winning the battle of Pinkie Cleugh (just outside Edinburgh) in September 1547. But it is one thing to defeat an enemy, quite another to subdue him. Because Somerset did not possess enough troops to occupy Scotland, his victory, and the subsequent establishment of English garrisons in the south, only succeeded in further alienating the Scots. In 1548, Mary Queen of Scots fled to France where she eventually married the *dauphin*. Thus, Henry and Somerset had managed to drive two of England's bitterest enemies more deeply into an alliance which would cause great anxiety over the next half-century.

One reason for the failure of Somerset's strong-arm tactics was a growing sense of Scottish nationalism. A second was that Mary Queen of Scots was a Catholic and Edward was an increasingly pronounced Protestant. At least this was the impression created by Somerset's religious policy. Almost immediately upon coming to power, he asked Parliament to repeal the Treason Act, the Act for Burning Heretics, the Six Articles, and all restrictions on printing and reading the Bible. English men and women were now more free to discuss religion and religious alternatives than ever before. Vernacular Bibles and Protestant tracts flooded into England, where they were read and debated avidly, especially at the two universities and among urban professionals and merchants. On a more popular level, there was a rash of image-breaking. This was accelerated with the passage that year of the Chantries Act. This statute denounced the doctrine of Purgatory and the efficacy of prayers for the dead and dissolved and confiscated the property of chantries, almshouses, schools, and hospitals. This further reduced the Church's institutional presence in English lives. By 1549, half of 500 or so pre-Reformation charitable institutions for the poor had been closed. From henceforward, local government and private initiatives directed poor relief, education, and healthcare. The act also abolished the religious guilds, brotherhoods, and fraternities which had provided so many town and village social activities. Even parties, festivals, and wedding receptions would now take place somewhere other than the village church.

These measures were essentially negative: they abolished old restrictions and institutions. Somerset's regime also made positive moves toward Protestantism. In 1548, Archbishop Cranmer produced the first Book of Common Prayer. Cranmer's Prayer Book was a compromise. For example, it retained altars, vestments, private confession, and prayers for the dead. But it denied transubstantiation and increased the role of the laity. Above all, it was written, magnificently, in English. For the first time, all English men and women could worship God in their own language. In 1549 Parliament passed the first **Act of Uniformity**, which ordered parishes to use the Prayer Book. In the same year, priests were allowed to marry; about 1 in 10 did so. Most parts of the country received these changes with little overt resistance. But in the remote west, especially Cornwall, many people resented them. On Whit Monday, June 10 (the Monday after Pentecost, seven weeks after Easter, and the day after the introduction of the new Prayer Book), the villagers of Sampford Courtenay, Devonshire, forced the priest to say a Latin mass. The ensuing rebellion soon spread throughout the West Country, the rebels laying siege to its most populous city, Exeter. Somerset offered a general pardon if the rebels would disband. Instead, they demanded a return to the religious arrangements of Henry VIII's Six Articles, the suppression of the English Bible, and the restoration of the Latin mass and some monasteries. Many resented the loss of hospitals, saints' days, and beloved rituals.

For some West Country rebels, these feelings merged with economic woes. Here, Somerset faced overwhelming problems. First, the population was rising, from perhaps 2.4 million people in 1525 to about 4.5 million by 1600. Normally, demographic growth is good economic news, for a growing labor force usually brings increased demand and, therefore, increased employment and wealth generated by fulfilling that demand. But the mid-sixteenth-century English economy was not flexible enough to adjust quickly to the new, overpopulated reality. Based largely upon agriculture, it could not create enough jobs to guarantee employ-ment for the new mouths to feed. Instead, as wool remained temporarily profit-able, some landowners turned to enclosure, either throwing their peasants off the land or, more commonly, taking pasture land to graze sheep instead of the cattle that provided milk, cheese, and meat. A related economic problem facing Somer-set was Henry VIII's massive debts and recoinage. These developments, plus a series of bad harvests, contributed to a 10 percent annual inflation in food prices between 1540 and 1550. This was a sharp increase by early modern standards. Since wages were not rising at the same rate, the purchasing power of workers declined: for urban construction workers by 40 percent between 1500 and 1560. The high price of food left most people with less money to buy other goods, such as wool cloth. Overseas demand for English wool took up the slack until about 1550, when this, too, declined, because of overproduction and religious persecu-tion in the Netherlands, home of Antwerp, the main English cloth entrepôt (see chapter 6). This stifled the one major industry in England, throwing more people out of work and onto the roads in search of employment. This led, in turn, to widespread anxiety about roving bands of homeless and unemployed people.

The dissolution of the chantries added £610,000 to the government's coffers, but this was only a temporary fix for its chronic financial problems and it offered nothing to the English people. Somerset shared the Commonwealthmen's notion that royal government could improve or protect its subjects' well-being, but it was still more or less untried, apart from a weak Poor Law. Moreover, the protector and his advisers lacked demographic information and had little understanding of how the economy worked. Their diagnosis, expressed here in the report of a government commission, was that England's economic troubles resulted from simple greed, leading to enclosures, on the part of aristocratic landlords.

Towns, villages, and parishes do daily decay in great numbers; houses of husbandry and poor men's habitation be utterly destroyed everywhere, and in no small number; husbandry and tillage, which is the very paunch of the commonwealth, ... greatly abated ... All this groweth through the great dropsy and the insatiable desire of riches of some men, that be so much given to their own private profit, that they pass nothing on to the common-wealth.[5]

The authors' resort to bodily metaphors suggests that they had no more sophisti-cated way of understanding the economy. The government's remedy was to pass taxes on sheep and cloth production in order to encourage labor-intensive arable farming. This had little effect on agriculture and it could only hurt the wool trade. To deal with that problem, Parliament passed legislation to eliminate competition from European Hansard merchants and to tighten the monopoly of the Merchant Adventurers (see chapter 6). This was good news for this privileged club of merchants, but it, too, did little to help the English people.

Some took matters into their own hands. In July 1549 the tenants of Robert **Kett**, a minor Norfolk gentleman who had enclosed his land, rioted. Upon hearing their grievances, Kett, remarkably, concluded that they had a point and joined their cause. He eventually came to lead some 16,000 rebels, capturing the regional capital, Norwich, and producing a petition of 29 demands, which they sent to the lord protector. They sought to reduce rents and entry fines, restrict landlords' rights to pasture their animals on common land, participate more in local government, and reform neglectful or absentee priests. Some rebels went further and demanded an end to private landownership. These objectives were mainly economic. What religious content they had was not inconsistent with Protestant reform – indeed, Kett's rebels gathered outside Norwich under an "Oak of Reformation." In other words, this was not, like the Western Rising, a Catholic rebellion against the new religious reforms. Rather, the Norfolk rebels were challenging the freedom and economic power of landlords, and thus the entire social structure of early modern England.

The characteristic Tudor response was to listen patiently to rebel demands, stall for time, and crush the protestors at the earliest opportunity. But Somerset's government, still preoccupied with the Scottish situation, did not have the resources to overpower either rebellion quickly. Moreover, while he was unsympathetic to the religious position of the Western rebels, he was uncomfortable with religious persecution and had some sympathy for Kett's cause, if not for his methods. As a result, Somerset found himself in an impossible situation: a lord protector who was unwilling or unable to subdue subjects in open rebellion because he thought they might have a point, lacked the will, or did not have the military strength to do so. To act would violate his social and economic principles and plunge the country further into debt. To fail to act would display a weakness heretofore unseen from a Tudor government. Such a leadership vacuum was dangerous, not, as it turned out, because of the rebels, but rather, because it invited a far more ruthless man to step into the breach.

Northumberland and the Protestant Reformation

That man was John Dudley, earl of Warwick (1504–53), son of the faithful servant of Henry VII who was executed by Henry VIII. Like Somerset, Warwick had risen to prominence during the late wars of Henry VIII; in particular, he had helped to create the new Tudor navy. He had been an ally of Somerset's and was, in 1549, a member of Edward VI's Privy Council. While the protector negotiated with the rebels, offering them pardons and redress of their grievances if they would just go home, Warwick plotted with his fellow privy councilors, accusing Somerset of abuse of authority, indecision, and cowardice, implying that he would govern in consultation with them. He also appealed to great landowners who saw Somerset's economic and social policies as attacking their interests. Finally, he sought the help of a group of Catholic peers who hoped to turn back Somerset's Protestant tide. In August 1549, King Edward gave Warwick command of an army, which he used to crush the rebels at Dussindale, Norfolk. In true Tudor fashion, Kett was executed and his remains were hanged in chains outside Norwich Castle as a warning to other potential rebels. At about the same time, a second royal army put down the Western rebellion at Sampford Courtenay in a similarly brutal fashion.

Warwick returned to London, secured the blessing of both king and council on October 10, seized power from Somerset, and imprisoned him in the Tower of London on the 14th. The duke would be released and restored to the Privy Council in the spring of 1550, but he proved unable to cope with being just another adviser in the government of his rival. By October 1551 he was rearrested on a charge of conspiracy against Warwick and returned to the Tower. He was beheaded in January 1552. Warwick inherited Somerset's power, but not his title of lord protector. Instead, he had to settle for being created duke of Northumberland in 1551. Who was this new duke, the effective ruler of England?

According to one contemporary, Northumberland was, not unlike Somerset, "a man truly of a stout and haughty courage, and in war most valiant; but too much raging with ambition."[6] Like Somerset, Northumberland was intelligent, capable, and hardworking. Unlike him, he was willing to work with and through the Privy Council and he launched a number of successful efforts to restrain government expenditure and get the king out of debt. For example, he immediately pursued a peace policy with Scotland and France, launched a reform of the Exchequer, and attempted to restore the strength of the coinage. But Northumberland was much less scrupulous, much less burdened with a social conscience than his rival. As a result, he repealed or left unenforced much of Somerset's social and economic legislation. Northumberland was no social reformer. Rather, his primary goal seems to have been power itself, and his primary interest how to secure and retain it.

It was this last concern which troubled him, for anyone seeking to maintain the supreme political power in England in 1551–2 faced terrible problems. The country was under constant alarm from rumors of plots and uprisings. The economy remained poor, thanks to bad harvests in 1549–51. An epidemic of the sweating sickness, a form of influenza, swept the populace. Nor was Northumberland safe within the confines of the court. His power, like Somerset's, Cromwell's, and Wolsey's before him, depended upon the pleasure and confidence of the king. Now that King Edward was an adolescent, his predilections were beginning to emerge more clearly, the most important of which was his enthusiasm for Protestant reform. Therefore, it would seem obvious that, in order to stay on the king's good side, Northumberland would have to embrace the new faith and promote it in the kingdom. But this had the potential to be long-term political (and personal) suicide if the delicate Edward should die, for the heir apparent to the throne was the staunchly Catholic Princess Mary. Obviously, Northumberland could not please the king that was and the queen that was likely to be.

Northumberland bet on Edward to live. He dropped his Catholic allies in the council and began to cater enthusiastically to the king's Protestant wishes by suppressing all prayer books but the Book of Common Prayer, removing the last remaining Catholic bishops in favor of reformers, and encouraging another wave of image-breaking. In 1552 he commissioned a second, more Protestant, Prayer Book from Cranmer, mandated by a new Act of Uniformity. Instead of attending a sacrificial mass celebrated by a priest at an altar at the east end of the church, the English people were now to worship at a commemorative service presided over by a minister at a communion table placed in the middle (see plate 4, p. 71). Failure to attend Sunday services was now to be punished by imprisonment (for life on a third offense!). Finally, Northumberland also commissioned the Forty-Two Articles of Faith of 1553, a new statement of Church doctrine that embraced justification by faith alone and predestination, eliminated transubstantiation and the mass, and included only two sacraments – baptism and Eucharist.

Northumberland did not pursue these measures out of personal religious conviction. Rather, they were intended to cement his relationship with the boy-king. They also had the effect of enriching Northumberland's followers with the spoils from churches heretofore laden with Catholic images. Nevertheless, their long-term significance for English religion, and therefore English history, was profound. Remember that the English Church had, by the 1550s, been in a state of flux for over 20 years. During that time, the country's Catholic heritage had been steadily worn away. As a result, a new generation was growing up which knew less and less of the old ways. This may help to explain why there was little popular resistance to Northumberland's changes. Those changes were the first comprehensive, positive steps toward replacing those ways with Protestantism. Now, in 1552, for the first time, the official doctrine and forms of worship of the English Church were consistently, uniformly, and recognizably Protestant, even if the English people, overall, were not.

Unfortunately for Northumberland, while his Protestant reforms cemented his relationship with King Edward, Edward's long-term prospects did not look good. In early 1553 he began to experience increasing respiratory difficulties and weakness – almost certainly indications of tuberculosis. Northumberland knew that, having embraced Edward's Protestantism, he had no hope for Mary's favor. Her ascent would see the undoing not only of the duke's religious policy but of the duke himself.

Northumberland's only hope was to divert the succession away from Mary to a Protestant. In the spring of 1553, as Edward took to his death-bed, the duke persuaded the failing king to do as his father had done and will the kingdom to Lady Jane Grey (1537–54), a granddaughter of Henry's much-suffering sister, Mary, duchess of Suffolk (see genealogy 2, p. 413). Lady Jane had much to recommend her in Northumberland's eyes: she was of royal blood, a gifted scholar, and, most importantly, a devoted Protestant. She was also an innocent pawn in his plot. He forced her to marry, against her will, his own son, Guildford (ca. 1536–54), so that future Dudleys would forever wear the crown. Knowing that royal favor was fleeting, remembering the fates of Wolsey, Cromwell, Somerset, and his own father, Northumberland sought through marriage and a new succession to translate that favor into a permanent familial bond and inheritance.

Edward VI died of consumption on July 6, 1553. Lady Jane Grey was immediately proclaimed Queen Jane in London. But there was little apparent enthusiasm for her. Mary, who had fled to Norfolk to seek shelter with the Catholic Howard family, was proclaimed queen at Kenninghall, in that county, on July 9. England now had two "sovereigns." Both sides raised armies and, as in a game of chess, sought to capture their opponent's queen. Mary's army, under Henry Fitzalan, earl of Arundel (ca. 1511–80), reached London before Jane's made it to Norfolk. There, Arundel persuaded the Privy Council to change its mind and, on the 19th, proclaim Mary queen. Soon, the entire metropolis rose for Mary.

In the meantime, Jane's army began to desert on its way north. Northumberland learned of the Privy Council's action at Cambridge. There he tried to desert her himself, throwing his hat in the air for Queen Mary, but to no avail. Arundel arrested Northumberland, Guildford, and Jane and threw them into the Tower. At the end of July Mary entered London in triumph. After years of virtual imprisonment, disgrace, repudiation by her father, and marginalization by her brother, the daughter of Catherine of Aragon was now queen.

Mary I and Marital Diplomacy

The people of England had rallied to Mary (reigned 1553–8; see plate 5)[7] because she was the offspring of Henry VIII and next in line for the throne, not because she was Catholic, or the daughter of Catherine of Aragon, and certainly not because she was a woman. Mary's great tragedy was that she failed to draw the obvious lessons from this. Her Tudor blood was an advantage to be exploited to the full while her Spanish lineage and gender were, at best, neutral factors in the eyes of most of her subjects. As for her Catholicism, it divided her people: some loved it, some hated it. But Mary subordinated her strong Tudor personality to the demands of her religion, her Spanish sympathies, and contemporary expectations of her gender. The result was the only Tudor reign that could truly be called tragic, even pathetic.

And yet, like her father and grandfather, Mary possessed many traits which should have fit her for a successful reign. Like all Tudors, she was intelligent, courageous, dignified, and resilient. These qualities had ensured her survival during her father's and brother's reigns. She was well educated: in addition to her native tongue, she spoke Spanish, French, and Latin and could read Greek and Latin. Nor was she entirely serious: she danced and played the lute. Finally, Mary was not without mercy. Apart from Northumberland, few died for the plot to usurp her throne. Even Lady Jane Grey and Guildford Dudley were allowed, for the time being, to live, albeit as close prisoners in the Tower. Unfortunately, she was at her accession naive in politics and inexperienced in government, having been repudiated by her father and, thus, never groomed to succeed. Without training or experience, she was forced to rely on her conscience and her faith. In the end, she had too much of the one and was too inflexible in the other for her own or her country's good. More specifically, she was half-Spanish and all Catholic and so saw it as her God-given duty to ally her country with the Spanish Empire and to undo the "heresies" of the previous 20 years by restoring the Roman Catholic Church in England at any cost. Both policies would bring misery to her people.

Plate 5 Mary I, *by Moro. Museo del Prado, Madrid.*

The first matter facing the new queen was the very personal but also political one of her own marriage. For most of her sad, lonely life, Mary had been the least eligible maiden in England. Disowned by her father, shunted aside by her brother, she was now, with the latter's death and her accession, suddenly "a catch." In her eyes, God seemed to have unexpectedly, miraculously, given her the chance to reign, to restore Catholicism and to perpetuate it by having an heir. But she would have to move quickly. At her accession in 1553 she was already 37 years old in a time when women commonly experienced menopause much earlier than today.

Most of Mary's advisers and many of her people seem to have wanted her to marry an English peer. But the queen, wanting to solidify England's place in the Catholic and European world, more comfortable with her Spanish heritage than her English roots, chose, instead, her cousin, the son of the Holy Roman Emperor and heir to the Spanish Empire, Philip, king of Naples (1527–98; reigned in Naples from 1554, in Spain from 1556). This choice was immediately opposed by most of the Privy Council and Parliament. More ominously, it seemed to be unpopular with Mary's people as well. In January 1554 Sir Thomas **Wyatt** (1521?–54) led 3,000 men, mostly from Kent, toward London. Their goal was, at the very least, to prevent the Spanish marriage and, possibly, to displace Mary in favor of her younger sister, Elizabeth. Lacking an army of her own, Mary appealed to her subjects' loyalty in an eloquent speech at London's Guildhall, rallied the royal guards, and crushed the rebels. Wyatt and about 90 followers were executed. So were Lady Jane Grey and Guildford Dudley, for their very existence was thought to incite rebellion. Princess Elizabeth also came under suspicion and was lodged in the Tower. But Elizabeth had been studiously careful to avoid overt involvement in the plot or to leave evidence of disloyalty to her sister, and so Mary felt her hands tied. Still, the new queen had demonstrated characteristic Tudor tenacity and ruthlessness in the first major crisis after her accession. In the end, like a good Tudor, she got her own way. The marriage to Philip took place at Winchester Cathedral in July 1554. Her next move, the restoration of Catholicism, would be even more controversial and difficult to accomplish.

Catholic Restoration

The break with Rome had come through parliamentary legislation. The mending, if it was to have any popular support or long-term success, would also require parliamentary cooperation. But the nobles and gentlemen who sat in Parliament had a great deal to lose by such a restoration: all their lovely and profitable monastic lands. In October 1553 that assembly agreed to revoke the religious legislation of the previous reign. Gone were the Prayer Book and Act of Uniformity. But Parliament would do nothing positive to restore Catholicism until they knew what was to become of the monastic lands. In 1554 Reginald, Cardinal Pole (1500–58), an English Catholic exile, returned from the continent to serve as both papal legate and Mary's chief religious adviser. He negotiated an agreement whereby the pope granted a dispensation allowing their present owners to keep the monastic lands. In return, Parliament consented to a reunion with Rome and reenacted the heresy laws in January 1555. Thus the pope's concession on monastic lands allowed Mary to achieve her immediate goal of parliamentary restoration of Roman Catholicism as the State religion of England. But in the long term it was bad news for the prospects of a full Catholic revival. It meant that the dissolved monasteries, convents, almshouses, schools, and hospitals – the most attractive and socially significant side of institutional

Catholicism – would not be restored. Mary encouraged the new founding of such establishments, but a shortage of money and time on the throne limited her success. The institutional presence of the Catholic Church would never recover.

In its absence, all Mary could do was to restore previously deprived Catholic bishops like Gardiner and Tunstall, mandate the restoration of Catholic worship in churches, require her subjects to attend mass on Sunday, and persecute those who refused to comply. In fact, the Marian restoration of Catholicism did achieve some success. Many churches, particularly in remote areas, had failed to embrace Protestant reform, or had stored or buried their rood crosses and screens, statues, and images in anticipation of Catholic revival. Many English men and women returned to the old ways eagerly, or at least without a murmur.

But others did not. Devoted Protestants, or those for whom Catholic practices were new, strange, or threatening, would not cooperate. Mary responded, first, by purging the universities and the clergy of Protestants. She ejected some 2,000 priests for preaching Protestant ideas or, more usually, for taking wives: in many cases, the latter was the only clear, outward sign of Protestantism. Those expelled amounted to about one-quarter of the priesthood, a deficit which Catholic seminaries on the continent could not soon fill. Some of the displaced clergy joined the 800 men and women who fled abroad to Protestant centers such as Frankfurt and Geneva, where they would imbibe reformist ideas at the source and wait for the next reign. For those Protestants – clergy or laymen – who could not leave and would not recant, Mary and Pole had one last remedy: burning at the stake. They began on February 4, 1555 with John Rogers, a translator of the Bible into English. They continued in Oxford with the burning of three prominent Protestant clergymen: Hugh Latimer, bishop of Worcester (ca. 1485–1555), and Nicholas Ridley, bishop of London (ca. 1503–55), in October and Archbishop Cranmer in March 1556. It is said that, as the fires were being lit, Latimer called out:

be of good comfort, Master Ridley, and play the man. We shall this day light such a candle, by God's grace, in England, as I trust shall never be put out.[8]

One did not have to be a clergyman to merit persecution. In under four years Mary's regime burned 237 men and 52 women as heretics. Some of her victims were mere adolescents; the majority came from humble backgrounds. Most of the burnings took place at Smithfield market in London. The fires of Smithfield would prove to be a public relations nightmare for the Catholic side.

Indeed, Mary's burning of nearly three hundred of her subjects for their religious beliefs cannot help but strike the sane modern observer as barbaric. But the operative word in the above sentence is "modern." Mary and her contemporaries thought differently from us. Few would have understood the idea that two individuals could disagree about religion and still be both good people and good subjects. Rather, as we have seen, there was a long tradition in England, and in Europe generally, of believing that one's own religion was the One True

Faith; anyone who held opinions at odds with that faith was a heretic, in league with the Devil, and a profound menace to the salvation of other souls. Any ruler who allowed religious pluralism in his realm was acquiescing in his subjects' eternal damnation and promoting more immediate chaos here on earth: according to the Protestant William Cecil, Lord Burghley (1520–98), "that state co[u]ld never be in safety, where there was tolleration of two religions."[9] Once this is understood, Mary's reasoning becomes clear: she had to cut out the cancer of Protestantism before it spread. To fail to do so would imperil her reign, her religion, and the immortal soul of every man, woman, and child in England. Henry VIII understood this and put Lutherans and others to death. Elizabeth would understand it too, executing about the same number of Catholics as her sister did Protestants. (But she did so reluctantly, mainly for reasons of State, and over a much longer period of time.)

So why do we remember this Tudor as "Bloody Mary"? Because history is written by the victors and Mary's Catholic restoration would not outlive her brief reign. After her death, the story of the Protestant martyrs would be indelibly imprinted in English religious and historical consciousness, mainly through the writings of John Foxe (1516–87). Foxe's *Acts and Monuments*, popularly known as the *Book of Martyrs*, was to be the most popular book in English, after the Bible, for a hundred years. It painted a vivid and lasting picture of martyrs' courage and "the great persecutions [and] horrible troubles, that have been wrought and practiced by the Romish prelates [bishops]"[10] (see plate 6). It thus shaped the black legend of "Bloody Mary" and reinforced the English association of Catholicism with bigotry and cruelty. Take, for example, Foxe's moving relation of the burning of Archbishop Cranmer. Cranmer was given numerous opportunities to recant his Protestantism: Mary really wanted this before his execution, for he had been the point man for much of Edward's reformation. Faced with the prospect of death at the stake, the archbishop wavered, agreeing in six separate documents to the papal supremacy and the truth of Roman Catholic doctrine. But when he was brought to St. Mary's Church on March 21, 1556 to repudiate his Protestantism publicly, he recanted his recantations, saying to the congregation: "[a]nd forasmuch as my hand offended, writing contrary to my heart, my hand shall first be punished there-fore; for, may I come to the fire, it shall be first burned. And as for the pope, I refuse him, as Christ's enemy, and antichrist, with all his false doctrine." Foxe continues:

And when the wood was kindled, and the fire began to burn near him, stretching out his arm, he put his right hand into the flame, which he held so steadfast and immoveable (saving that once with the same hand he wiped his face), that all men might see his hand burned before his body was touched. His body did so abide the burning of the flame with such constancy and steadfastness, that standing always in one place without moving his body, he seemed to move no more than the stake to which he was bound; his eyes were lifted up into heaven, and oftentimes he repeated "this unworthy right hand," so long as his voice would suffer him; and using often the words of Stephen, "Lord Jesus, receive my spirit," in the greatness of the flame he gave up the ghost.[11]

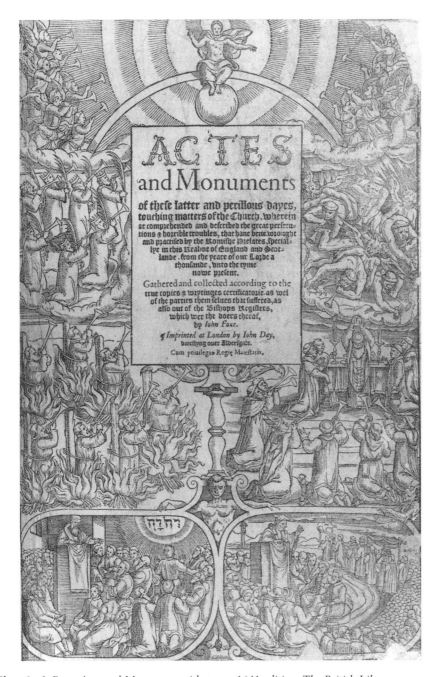

Plate 6 *J. Foxe,* Acts and Monuments *title-page, 1641 edition. The British Library.*

Foxe's vivid accounts of the Protestant martyrs sank deep into the religious, historical, and cultural consciousness of the English people. Given the shortage of Catholic priests, the brevity of Mary's reign, and her succession by the Protestant

Elizabeth, it would be their story which would be remembered. Over the course of the next century, as the English faced Catholic plots at home and invasions from abroad, Foxe's tales of Mary's cruelty would convince his readers that God had chosen them to be an elect Protestant nation, defying the infernal power of the cruel Catholic anti-Christ.

But Foxe would have labored in obscurity if Catholicism had won. It might have done so with time. Mary needed a long reign, a Catholic heir, or a powerful ally to provide military support for her counter-reformation. The dénouement of her tragedy was that she failed in the first and fixed her hopes on Spain for the other two.

Foreign Policy and the Succession

Unfortunately, marriage with Philip proved unhappy for both Mary and her subjects. Mary loved her husband and thought it her duty to submit to him. Philip, on the other hand, seems to have seen the marriage as a purely political and diplomatic affair, viewing his wife as his subordinate and her kingdom as community property. Mary, desperate for an heir, experienced a hysterical pregnancy in the winter of 1554–5. In January 1557 Philip, now king of Spain and looking for something else from his marriage, declared war on France, insisting upon England's support. England, still gripped by economic crisis and lacking a serious military force, was ill-prepared for war. Both Parliament and the Privy Council opposed involvement but Mary, supported by court aristocrats anxious for adventure and ever the dutiful wife, obeyed her husband. In the end, England had nothing to gain and Calais to lose.

The English had once possessed a great empire in France (see map 5, p. 35). By 1557 the last tiny outpost of that empire was the port of Calais. Given Parliament's failure to vote adequate sums of money for the war and Philip's refusal to divert Spanish troops to help his English allies, it was inevitable that Calais would be taken by the French, who launched a successful surprise attack in January 1558. Calais's strategic importance was minimal. But psychologically it was crucial, for it was the last reminder of past English greatness on the continent and of their most heroic monarchs' feats of arms. Its loss was a devastating blow and, for many, a sadly appropriate symbol of Mary's reign, her blind love for her husband, her Spanish ancestry, and her religion. This was not entirely fair, but Mary herself seems to have understood the significance of the event, reportedly saying that, "when I am dead and opened you will find Calais lying in my heart."[12]

Her subjects would not have long to wait. In the summer of 1558 Mary thought herself pregnant again. In reality, she was probably suffering from a uterine tumor and dropsy. As late as early November she still hoped against hope for an heir, but the Privy Council began to prepare for the next reign. They persuaded Mary to acknowledge her sister, Elizabeth, as her successor to ensure that the events of 1553 were not repeated. Princess Elizabeth had, up to this point, lived a shadowy and precarious existence. Like Mary, she had been rejected by her father and resented by her sibling on the throne. She had been the focus of a number of Protestant plots, but she had scrupulously avoided contact with the plotters or any overt act of disloyalty, living quietly, patiently, and hopeful that her time would come. Now, with the smell of death wafting across from Whitehall Palace, Elizabeth began to hold her own court.

Mary died on November 17, 1558. It has been said that her reign was as sterile as she was. Possessing many Tudor virtues, she lacked the most important one of all: a practical flexibility that would have allowed her to respond creatively to the aspirations, anxieties, and quirks of her people. Admittedly, with more time, she might have bent the country to her will as her father had done. But without it, or an heir to continue her policies, they were subject to repudiation by her successor. By 1558 competing religious leaders had given way to competing religious dogmas and now, among the people, competing religious cultures. Over the next century, the clash of these cultures would rock the stability of the English Church and State. Worse, Mary Tudor had confirmed everything that contemporaries feared about female rule. She left her sister a legacy of religious disunity, military defeat, financial exhaustion and economic hardship, even a fatal influenza epidemic that Protestants could blame on the popish regime. There was, finally, the baggage of her gender. Few loyal subjects could have been optimistic about another Tudor queen. They were in for a surprise.

CHAPTER FOUR

The Elizabethan Settlement and its Challenges, 1558–1585

The New Queen

Perhaps no figure in English history has inspired more myth than Queen Elizabeth I (1558–1603).[1] She had many personas: the Virgin Queen, Gloriana, Good Queen Bess to her supporters; the bastard and heretic daughter of the whore, Anne Boleyn, to her detractors. In her day, scores of poets and artists promoted these various images (see plate 7). Afterwards, legions of writers, some scholarly, some popular, as well as filmmakers and playwrights, have sought to relate and explain the achievements of her reign and the mystique she exercised over her people. She herself was well aware of that mystique, cultivating it so effectively that it is almost impossible to pin down the "real" Elizabeth. Still, it is necessary to try, if only because so many of the age's triumphs and failures were intimately bound up with her words and actions.

One place to begin is with her accession on November 17, 1558. According to legend, all England rejoiced wildly, as if anticipating the glories to come. True, few openly grieved Mary's passing. Committed Protestants celebrated, for they had been delivered from the Marian persecutions. Elizabeth's advisers and supporters proclaimed the dawn of a new, more optimistic and glorious age under a queen who would bring harmony and peace. But such predictions must have struck most people as hollow given the situation inherited by the new sovereign. One contemporary summed up that situation as follows:

The Queen poor. The realm exhausted. The nobility poor and decayed. Want of good captains and soldiers. The people out of order. Justice not executed. All things dear. The French King bestriding the realm.[2]

Plate 7 Elizabeth I *(The Ditchley Portrait), by Marcus Gheeraerts the Younger, ca. 1592. National Portrait Gallery, London.*

Indeed, in 1558 England was still embroiled in a disastrous war with France. Calais had been lost and trouble threatened on the Scottish border. The royal Treasury was deep in debt, the coinage debased, trade depressed, the general economy in ruins. An influenza epidemic raged, often fatally. Nor was religion much consolation. The nation lay divided, torn, and almost literally bleeding over how best to worship God. Given contemporary assumptions about the sexes, who could have believed that another woman would have any success in dealing with these problems? Mary's reign had done nothing to disprove the traditional view of female sovereignty. As if to underscore this, in this very year of 1558 a Scottish Protestant preacher named John Knox (ca. 1514–72) published *The First Blast of the Trumpet Against the Monstrous Regiment of Women*, the argument of which should be obvious.[3]

Of course Knox had not figured on the personality or abilities of Elizabeth Tudor. Like her father, Henry VIII, with whom she identified publicly and privately, she was a larger-than-life personality. As with King Hal, this makes it difficult to separate fact from fiction. This much is unarguable. Elizabeth was young when she took the throne: 25 years old. She was also good-looking – an advantage that she was not reluctant to exploit. In addition, the new queen was highly intelligent, witty, hardworking, and well educated. She was fluent in Latin, French, Spanish, Italian, and, of course, English. She wrote poetry and could speak effectively. Elizabeth was also, like her father, something of a scholar: she once translated Boethius's *On the Consolations of Philosophy* into English in less than a month just for her own amusement. She also took after her father in being both musical and athletic. She played the virginals (a primitive keyboard instrument), danced, and hunted with enthusiasm. A final, crucial similarity to Henry VIII was that Elizabeth I was both vain and imperious. Men could flirt with her – indeed, she encouraged them to do so – but they had to be careful not to go too far, for she never forgot her special status as queen.

If even Mary's good qualities proved to be counter-productive, Elizabeth's bad ones were sometimes advantageous. For example, her imperious nature, quick temper, and sharp tongue probably did much to intimidate those who might otherwise have assumed that she was weak because she was a woman. The most common charge leveled against her, also linked to contemporary assumptions about her gender, is that she was indecisive. Thus, Robert Devereaux, earl of Essex (ca. 1566–1601), complained to the French ambassador in 1597 that "they laboured under two things at this Court, delay and inconstancy, which proceeded from the sex of the queen."[4] Indeed, Queen Elizabeth was capable of making her Privy Council and Parliaments wait an agonizingly long time while she made up her mind. In some crucial cases (marriage, what to do about Mary Queen of Scots), it could be argued that she never did so. But it could also be argued that she had been taught by hard experience the dangers of committing herself too early or too definitely. After all, Elizabeth had grown up in a perilous environment in which overt commitment to one side or the other – in politics or religion – often led to disgrace, even death. As queen, she ruled a country which was seemingly at the mercy of bigger, more powerful neighbors. What often struck her subjects (and later male historians) as indecisiveness now looks like prudence, even a mastery of herself and of the situation at hand. In particular she was a virtuoso at playing two sides off against each other, so that they would not turn against her – or England.

Cecil vs. Dudley

We see this prudence and mastery in her handling of her advisers and the factions which grew up around them. Historians have tended to divide her court and Privy Council into two broad groups. The first was led by William Cecil, created Lord Burghley in 1571. Cecil had been trained as a lawyer, was associated with the Commonwealthmen, and had served as secretary to Lord Protector Somerset. He had proved himself an able and industrious administrator and diplomat under Elizabeth's brother and sister. Upon her accession she named him secretary of State and, in 1572, lord treasurer of England. Early in the reign he advocated foreign intervention in support of Protestant causes; but as he grew older and his responsibilities increased, he became, like the queen herself, more prudent and cautious. From about 1570, he tended to favor peace as less dangerous and more frugal than war. Consequently, he saw the need to work with, or at least avoid offending, the Catholic powers of Spain and France. His vast circle tended to attract equally cautious men interested in bureaucratic careers, like Sir Nicholas Bacon (1509–79), Elizabeth's keeper of the Great Seal; Sir Francis Knollys (1514?–96), vice-chamberlain, then treasurer of her household; and Thomas Radcliffe, earl of Sussex (ca. 1526–83), lord president of the North.

Very different was the court circle which assembled around Robert Dudley, from 1564 earl of Leicester (ca. 1532–88). A younger son of the late duke of Northumberland, Dudley was more of a courtier and a soldier than Cecil, so Elizabeth made him her master of the Horse (keeper of her stables and coaches). This was a much more elevated position than it sounds, for it not only paid extremely well but gave Dudley the excuse to attend the queen on horseback when she went outdoors. This was not inconvenient for Elizabeth, for she found Dudley handsome and charming. Where Cecil was sober and careful, surrounded by clerks and accountants, Dudley was fun and exciting and brought with him a circle of soldiers and poets, including the courtly Sir Christopher Hatton (1540–91), who would serve her as lord chancellor and parliamentary "mouthpiece"; and the cunning Sir Francis Walsingham (1532–90), who, as secretary of State from 1573, oversaw her spies and espionage. In general, these men tended to favor an aggressive foreign policy in support of Protestant causes abroad.

Because many of the men in both Cecil's and Dudley's circles also held local offices ranging from lord lieutenant down to JP, theirs were truly national networks of patronage, Elizabethan counterparts to medieval affinities. Usually, these two groups agreed on general aims and, more often than not, on individual strategies to achieve them. Socially, they got along well with each other. But, at times of crisis they tended to divide. Where Cecil and his allies increasingly urged caution, pacifism, and thrift, Dudley and his followers advocated bold military intervention against what they saw as any threat to English interests and the Protestant cause from the Catholic powers. Where Cecil and his circle appealed to the queen's head, Dudley and his group appealed to her heart. The latter attraction led to the reign's first crisis.

Marital Diplomacy I

The first major issue facing the new queen was that of her own single state. Because contemporary society was uncomfortable with the idea of a woman who was not under the control of a man, because the succession was uncertain as long as the queen had no heir, and because England was desperate for friends, most of Elizabeth's subjects assumed that she would, as Mary had done, take a husband as soon as possible. Like Mary, she had had few prospects prior to her accession, but once she assumed the throne she became the most eligible single woman in Europe. There was no shortage of potential bridegrooms, both foreign and domestic, Catholic and Protestant. Among the leaders were the Habsburg Archduke Charles of Styria (1540?–90?), the boy-king Charles IX of France (1550–74; reigned 1560–74), and King Erik XIV of Sweden (1533–77; reigned 1560–68). Closer to home, there was the earl of Arundel and Sir William Pickering (1516–75). Nor was the widower Philip II out of the running. After a decent interval following Mary's death, he too proposed. After all, the last thing he wanted was a breakup of the old Tudor–Habsburg alliance, leaving England free to cultivate a friendship with France. But Elizabeth, characteristically, hesitated. She probably did so for two reasons: she had seen what Mary's loveless and unpopular marriage had done to her sister and her country, and she was attracted to someone else.

That someone was the dashing Lord Robert Dudley. As master of the Horse, he had every opportunity to attend Elizabeth and he often did so, contemporaries observed, alone. When they were not alone, it became clear that the queen had great affection for her "sweet Robin," despite the fact that he was already married to one Amy *née* Robsart, Lady Dudley (b. 1532). Speculation that Lord Robert would find some way out of his first marriage turned to scandal when, in September 1560, Lady Dudley was found dead at the bottom of a flight of stairs in Cumnor Hall, Oxfordshire. Rejected by her husband and suffering from breast cancer, she probably died by accident or, possibly, suicide. But many contemporaries suspected foul play on Dudley's part in order to make himself available to marry the queen. Cecil and his followers in the council argued vehemently against the marriage. Eventually, Elizabeth came to her senses. In 1566 she finally repudiated any notion of marrying Dudley with the comment, "I will have but one mistress, and no master!"[5]

Nevertheless, Lord Robert, who was promoted to be earl of Leicester in 1564, remained a favorite of the queen until his death in 1588; in the meantime, Elizabeth was urged to get herself married again and again. Those urgings came from her Privy Council, from Parliament, and from her people. As we shall see, again like her father, Elizabeth learned to use the possibility of matrimony as a diplomatic trump card or, more crudely, as bait: after all, marriage to the queen of England would be a peaceful and inexpensive way for Spain or France to win that country into an alliance and, perhaps, even back to Catholicism. Throughout the first half of the reign, and especially during foreign policy crises, she entertained a steady stream of French princes and German dukes, all of whom offered undying love – and diplomatic alliance. Unlike her father, however, she knew that marriage was a card that she could play only once. Once played, her freedom of maneuver and, with it, that of her country, would be virtually eliminated. Instead, she preferred to play potential suitors against each other in a brilliant game of amorous, albeit duplicitous, diplomacy.

In the end, Elizabeth never played the marriage card. Instead, she made a virtue of her single state. By the 1580s she would embrace the image of a "Virgin Queen," wedded not to some foreign prince or courtly fop but to her first and greater love, the people of England. In 1599 she would refer to her subjects as "all my husbands, my good people."[6] Remember that, unlike Mary, Elizabeth was born of both an English mother and an English father. Moreover, she seems to have felt real affection for her people. Certainly, she had the common touch, frequently going out amongst them on summer-long cross-country progresses, or being carried in an open chair through the streets of London. At such moments Elizabeth played to the crowd. As the Spanish ambassador noted in 1568, she "ordered her carriage . . . to be taken where the crowd seemed thickest, and stood up and thanked the people."[7]

Back at court, she encouraged artists, poets, and playwrights – for example, Edmund Spenser (1552?–99) in his *Faerie Queene* (1596) – to celebrate her as Diana, Belphoebe, Astraea, or Gloriana, not only the bride of her people but a sort of benevolent goddess to them as well. Indeed, in a country which had largely given up the Catholic devotion to the Virgin Mary, the Virgin Queen came to represent a Protestant alternative: a softer, gentler, more feminine face of power. Above all, the image of Gloriana allowed Elizabeth to portray herself as above faction, an impartial symbol of love and veneration for the entire country. But this image developed slowly and came to fruition only in the 1580s. In the meantime, she had to rely on other means to compose disagreements between Cecil and Dudley and between Catholics and Protestants.

The Religious Settlement

As we have seen, English men and women were divided about religion in 1558. They looked anxiously to the new queen and her advisers to settle these difficulties. Whatever solution they chose would have tremendous implications beyond the walls of England's churches. For many, perhaps most, people in England, Roman Catholicism was too closely associated with Mary's cruelty and a domineering Spanish Empire to be acceptable. But the embrace of full-blown Protestantism would jeopardize Spain's friendship; would invite the hostile attentions of the other great Catholic power, France; and would prove equally unacceptable to many of the queen's more conservative subjects. In the first years of her reign, Queen Elizabeth and her advisers had to walk a tightrope in the area of religion.

Fortunately, the new queen's personality fitted her well to walk that tightrope. Unlike Edward or Mary, she had not yet publicly committed to one religious point of view or the other. Rather, as princess she had been careful to keep her own religious devotions secret. With hindsight, it is pretty clear that she considered herself a Protestant in theology but loved hierarchy and ritual in a way that seems Catholic. Above all, she was, by contemporary standards, practical, tolerant, and even somewhat secular. For example, unlike those of her three predecessors, her Privy Council contained few churchmen. More importantly, Queen Elizabeth, "not liking to make windows into men's hearts and secret thoughts," was not particularly concerned that every English man and woman accept fully the doctrines and practices of one perfectly consistent religion.[8] Though inclined to Protestantism herself, what she wanted above all was her subjects' obedience and loyalty. To ensure these, she needed a religious settlement which most people could mostly accept. To do that, she would have to find a compromise between her Protestant beliefs and Catholic structures and practices.

That compromise was found, but not without a struggle. When the queen and her advisers proposed an Act of Supremacy undoing Mary's restoration of papal power in the spring of 1559, the Catholic bishops in the House of Lords opposed and almost defeated it. In the end, they had to be neutralized by detention in the Tower, with the result that no churchman voted for the Supremacy. Even then, passage was only secured by making a concession to conservatives: the act named Elizabeth Supreme Governor of the Church, not Supreme Head as Henry VIII and Edward VI had been. It further required the clergy and government officials to swear an oath of allegiance to the Supreme Governor, but, in a second accommodation to religious conservatives, it placed no such obligation on the laity. This was a concession to Elizabeth as much as it was to Catholics, for she wanted to avoid anything which forced her people to choose between their queen and their beliefs. Second, and only after much in-fighting, Parliament passed another Act of Uniformity which required all of the queen's subjects to attend church on Sundays and holy days. Services were to follow a revised version of the second Book of Common Prayer first introduced by Northumberland under Edward VI. In 1563, Parliament passed a new Treason Act making it a capital crime to express support for papal jurisdiction or (in another attempt to ease pressure on Catholics) to *twice* refuse to swear the Oath of Allegiance. Finally, that same year produced a new statement of doctrine, the Thirty-Nine Articles of Faith. These, too, were essentially Protestant, even Calvinist. They embraced justification by faith and predestination and denounced Catholic beliefs such as Purgatory and the sacrificial nature of the mass. The religious conservatives in Parliament, however, were able to include a revision in the Prayer Book which allowed some room for belief in transubstantiation. They also preserved the wearing of colorful vestments by the clergyman and, perhaps most importantly, the old Church's hierarchical structure, including bishops.

So the Church of England as established in 1559 was a compromise: Protestant privy councilors and those sympathetic to reformation got their way on doctrine; religious conservatives got theirs, apart from the actual texts of the Book of Common Prayer, on ceremony and hierarchy. Put more simply, the genius of the Church of England was – and is – that it thinks Protestant, but looks Catholic. This juxtaposition was, in fact, perfectly designed to win over the vast majority of the English people. Protestants loved the Word as contained in Scripture. For many of them, the new Church doctrine outlined in the Thirty-Nine Articles was sufficiently consistent with the Word to be acceptable. Catholics loved ritual and the sense of paternalistic community provided by a hierarchical framework. For many of them, the new Church rituals and structure as laid out in the Book of Common Prayer and the above legislation were close enough to those of the old, despite the abandonment of Latin for English, to not be offensive. Others were probably tired of religious controversy and violence by the 1560s. Finally, the generally low level of religious literacy and enthusiasm that some historians have detected in the late sixteenth century may also have contributed to the widespread acceptance of – or acquiescence in – the new settlement. Many people may not have understood or cared.

Admittedly, there are no surviving census records for early modern England in which its inhabitants checked off their religious beliefs. Nevertheless, it seems reasonable to assert that, by the 1580s, the vast majority of the population had accommodated itself without much difficulty to the Church of England as established in 1559–63. But there were two groups, one nominally within the Church, one outside of it, which had grave difficulties with the new settlement. As we shall see, their discontents and the tensions generated by and between them would dominate not only the religious history of England, but its political and social history as well, for well over a century.

The Puritan Challenge

Though a compromise, the religious settlement of 1559–63 was, by and large, one that leaned in a Protestant direction: after all, there were no pope, no mass, no monasteries, no Purgatory or indulgences. But that is not to say that committed Protestants were entirely happy with the new dispensation. Marian exiles, in particular, chafed at its accommodations with Catholicism. The Marian exiles were staunch Protestants who had fled to the continent during Mary's reign to preserve their faith and their lives. These men and women had nearly lost everything for Protestantism and they cherished the memory of the martyrs who had, in fact, lost everything. They spent Mary's reign studying, translating, and listening to continental preachers – imbibing the latest Protestant thought at the very well-springs of the Reformation. At Mary's death, the exiles returned to England expecting to establish a "godly" settlement of Church and State, by which they meant one consistent with their interpretation of Scripture. They could only agree to the settlement of 1559–63 as a temporary half-measure. In their view, the serious business of godly reformation should continue, purging or purifying the English Church of the last vestiges of Catholic practice. By the 1570s their opponents were beginning to label anyone so inclined a "**Puritan**."

Unfortunately, the term "Puritan" is highly controversial. While many contemporaries may have thought that they knew a Puritan when they saw one, the fact is that there never was a specific religious organization with a uniform code of beliefs called "Puritanism." Because the beliefs of those labeled Puritans varied from individual to individual and over time and place, some historians have abandoned the term in favor of "reforming Christians" or "the more enthusiastic sort of Protestants" or something similar. For simplicity's sake, and because the term did have a meaning, however imprecise, to contemporaries, we will continue to use it.

Puritans did not want to form a Church separate from the Church of England. Rather, they sought to reform that Church from within, to make it less Catholic and more Protestant, less of "a mingle-mangle" of the two faiths. Specifically, and perhaps the one goal to which all those labeled Puritan would agree, they wanted their Church to conform to Biblical beliefs and practices. Anything not found in Scripture was to be abandoned. Indeed, the more extreme Puritans sought to eliminate any distinction between Church and State, applying Biblical law and practice to every aspect of English government and society: thus in 1563 one former Marian exile urged the House of Commons to make adultery and Sabbath-breaking capital offenses! But most of the controversies between Puritans and mainstream churchmen took place over religious doctrine, government, and ritual.

The first area of disagreement came over the seemingly innocuous matter of what the clergyman should wear at Sunday services. Puritans associated colorful vestments with Catholic practice, fearing that they distracted the congregation from the Word of God. Therefore, they sought to eliminate elaborate vestments in favor of plain black dress. In 1563, Convocation considered a petition to abolish the compulsory wearing of the surplice, as well as the use of the organ in Church services, the sign of the cross, and the remaining holy days. In 1565, the queen, provocatively and perhaps unwisely, issued an unequivocal defense of ornate vestments and demanded that the bishops enforce their use by suspending clergy who refused. This created a new target for Puritan reformers. In 1570 Thomas Cartwright (1535–1603), a Cambridge divinity professor, presented a series of lectures criticizing the Church of England and, especially, the bishops' role in it. The queen responded by having Cartwright removed from his professorship. A pamphlet war ensued: some clergymen defended Cartwright, others attacked him. Some of Cartwright's defenders argued that the Church should not be organized hierarchically but, rather, that each congregation should be directed by a "presbyter" of teaching elders (ministers) and ruling elders (laymen). Superior guidance for these congregations would be supplied by representative councils or synods (at the lowest level, a regional presbytery, at the highest level, a general assembly). This was, in fact, the model of Church government being gradually adopted in parts of Scotland from the 1560s. It was also a logical extension of Protestant theology. If the Bible is the only reliable source of the Word of God, and if that Word "shines clear in its own light" (i.e., is unequivocal in meaning and accessible to all), who needs bishops? Who needs a hierarchical structure to tell Christians what to think and do?

The answer was clear to religious and political conservatives: the queen, that's who! After all, if the Supreme Governor of the Church of England were to concede that individual congregations or synods were free to determine their own religious beliefs and practices, would not religious disunity and chaos ensue? Worse, if she conceded such religious freedom as governor, would she not have to concede similar political freedom as sovereign? If the people can make up their minds about Scripture without supervision, why could they not make up their minds about the Magna Carta and all of the other proclamations and laws which governed the secular world? In fact, most Puritans were not political or social radicals. But the queen and many others could not help but be alarmed at their attempts to reform religion through Parliament, their apparent reluctance to obey royal religious injunctions, and by their outright claim to Scriptural authority. Their defiance seemed to attack the very hierarchical principle which lay at the heart of the English polity – the Great Chain of Being.

In 1576 Queen Elizabeth ordered her archbishop of Canterbury, Edmund Grindal (1519?–83), to suppress **"prophesyings,"** meetings of clergymen, usually in large market towns, to hear and discuss a set of sermons on a specific Biblical text. But Grindal was himself a Marian exile and had some sympathy with these meetings. Therefore he refused to enforce the queen's order. Elizabeth reacted by suspending him from his clerical duties. Archbishops of Canterbury served for life, however, so the queen and the Church remained deadlocked on this issue until Grindal's death in 1583. Elizabeth then wasted no time in replacing him with an avowed anti-Puritan, John Whitgift (ca. 1530–1604). Using a royal tribunal called the court of High Commission, Archbishop Whitgift persecuted those who refused to conform to the practices of the Church of England, ejecting nonconforming clergy from their livings.

Whitgift's persecutions worked: they maintained the integrity of the settlement of 1559–63, and most people conformed to it. But they also drove some Puritans out of the Church. By 1580 a clergyman named Robert Browne (ca. 1550–1633) had established an independent congregation in Norwich. The following year he and his separatist or Brownist community fled to the Netherlands. In 1593 the government executed three separatist writers and ideologues, leading more Puritans to follow the Brownists overseas. In the early seventeenth century, some would leave for America. But most Puritans stayed in the Church. Those who sat in Parliament agitated for Church reform and complained unceasingly about the continued existence of the other religious minority in England: Roman Catholics.

The Catholic Threat

One further reason for Queen Elizabeth to reject the Puritan program was that she wanted to establish a Church which would be acceptable to religious conservatives, including Roman Catholics. It was imperative that she and her government find ways to please, or at least not offend, Catholics. This was true at home, so that they would not rebel; and abroad, so that the Spanish and French would not attack England on their behalf. In fact, she succeeded, at least partially, on both fronts, for over a decade. Most Catholics did conform in some way to the Church of England. The pope probably facilitated this process inadvertently when, in 1566, he decreed that good Catholics could not attend public Church of England services at the parish church to satisfy the Act of Uniformity and then attend private Roman Catholic services in their homes to satisfy their consciences. In effect, he forced Catholics to make a choice. Most chose the national Church and, therefore, ceased to be Catholics in the eyes of Rome. Still, many of these never quite gave up on the habits and rituals of the old faith. Moreover, a small and declining minority, anywhere from 1 to 5 percent of England's population (but a higher proportion of the landed aristocracy), remained practicing, but therefore secret, Roman Catholics. However, even these die-hards sought to live quietly amongst their Protestant neighbors, hoping that neither the pope nor Parliament would ever force them to choose between their English loyalty to the queen and their Catholic loyalty to the pope.

Their desire to be left alone was naive. The papacy was not about to simply concede England to Protestantism. In 1559 the pope refused to sign onto the Treaty of Cateau-Cambrésis, which made peace among England, Spain, and France and recognized Elizabeth as queen. Still, he hoped that she might see the light and return England to (in his view) the One True Faith. Should this hope be dashed and she overtly repudiate or even persecute Catholicism, he held out the threat that he might depose her by declaring her a heretic, absolve her Catholic subjects of their allegiance to her, and encourage them to rise up and the Catholic powers, France and Spain, to attack. This was one more reason for the queen to see Puritan reform as dangerous: too vigorous a pursuit of Protestantism might arouse the anger of Rome and the Catholic powers. It also explains her appearance of interest in a Catholic diplomatic marriage. Since, for most of the first half of the reign, Elizabeth's navy was in decay, her army nonexistent, and her finances a mess, she had no choice but to walk the tightrope of religious moderation, suppress Puritan reform, and keep the lines of communication open to Spain, France, and her Catholic subjects. As long as she could hold out even the remote possibility of a return to Rome, the pope and the Catholic powers would stay their hand.

England and Scotland

Unfortunately for Elizabeth and her fellow high-wire artists, the stormy international situation would eventually blow them over to one side or the other. The problems began at England's northern doorstep. England's relationship with Scotland had long been difficult, but was especially so of late: after the Tudors' failed attempt to force a dynastic marriage between Edward VI and Mary Queen of Scots, the latter had fled to France and married Francis II, its eventual king (1544–60; reigned 1559–60). This united England's nearest enemy (Scotland) with its bitterest and wealthiest enemy (France). But in 1560 Francis II died, leaving Mary free to return to her native land in the following year. What was the disposition of her people in 1561?

Scotland had always been poorer, less centralized, and less stable than England. This goes far to explain why the Catholic Mary could return to her realm in 1561 and find that many Scottish lairds (landowners) who controlled key Lowland regions had embraced the Protestant faith. Without a strong centralized monarchy to suppress Protestantism, it had filtered into the country in the mid-sixteenth century. Mary Queen of Scots' mother and her regent in Scotland, Mary of Guise (1515–60), responded by persecuting Protestant heretics. In 1557 a group of powerful Scottish nobles and lairds retaliated by making a pact or covenant to support a Protestant "Congregation of God." The signers of this pact, the Lords of the Congregation, united for numerous reasons: some hoped to benefit by claiming Church wealth, some desired to keep their political autonomy, some feared for their religion, and all resented French interference. In 1559 they rebelled against their absent queen, seized Church lands, abolished papal authority and the mass, and established a very rudimentary **Presbyterian** form of Church government. The French, fearing loss of the "Auld Alliance" with Scotland, sent troops, establishing a garrison near Edinburgh. The rebellious Lords of the Congregation appealed desperately to Elizabeth, as a fellow Protestant, to send English troops to rescue them.

The problem posed to Elizabeth by this request should be obvious. On the one hand, to support the Scottish Protestants would be to encourage rebellion against a fellow monarch – and therefore against the Great Chain of Being. It would also signal to the pope and the rulers of Spain and France that her religious sympathies were truly anti-Catholic. Finally, if such support failed, the Scots and their French allies might retaliate by invading England. On the other hand, committed Protestants in the Privy Council and Marian exiles in Parliament argued that rebel success would drive the French from Scotland and reduce tensions between the two nations. They reminded Elizabeth that failure to act would not only weaken international Protestantism, it might also leave a strengthened Catholic regime tied to France on England's northern border. Worse, so long as Elizabeth lacked an heir, her cousin, Mary Queen of Scots, was next in line for the English throne (see genealogy 2, p. 413). Under these circumstances, the last thing Elizabeth wanted to do was to strengthen Mary's position.

After weighing all the options, the queen decided to intervene on the side of the Protestant rebels. She sent, first, money and, later, what few troops and ships she had available. This support sustained the rebels until the death of Mary of Guise in June 1560 weakened the Catholic side. The result, signed in July, was the Treaty of Edinburgh. Mary Queen of Scots recognized Elizabeth's title to the English throne; Scotland enacted religious toleration; and a council, evenly divided between Calvinist Protestants and Catholics, governed that country. Mary's government was to be more or less run by James Stewart, earl of Moray (ca. 1531–70), the queen's Protestant half-brother. Since Protestants now controlled the wealthier parts of Scotland, the Reformation proceeded apace. Still, it would take until 1578 to establish a true Scottish Presbyterian Church, or Kirk. In the meantime, Scotland remained difficult to rule, filled with warring clans led by powerful nobles, many of them Calvinist and anti-monarchical. What sort of woman inherited this situation in 1561?

Hollywood and historical romances have struggled mightily to turn Mary Queen of Scots into a dashing and heroic figure, a Catholic counterpart to her cousin, Elizabeth. Certainly, her contemporaries found her beautiful, courtly, and clever. But where Elizabeth was cautious, Mary was impulsive. Where Elizabeth was shrewd, Mary was duplicitous. Where Elizabeth identified with her subjects' hopes, anxieties, and prejudices, Mary ignored her people's increasingly Protestant sympathies. And, finally, where Elizabeth overcame contemporary prejudice about her gender by acting like a man without ever submitting herself to one, Mary repeatedly placed herself in the care of men who were, in the end, unworthy of her. That is, unlike Elizabeth, she mishandled her marriage options, with disastrous effect for herself, her kingdom, and her cause.

In 1565 Mary ended her widowhood by marrying a Scottish nobleman, Henry Stewart, Lord Darnley (1545–67). Because Darnley was descended from Henry VII's daughter, Margaret, the marriage strengthened Mary's claim to succeed Elizabeth – a fact which did not recommend the match to the English queen. Nor did it prove happy for Mary. Darnley turned out to be a vain, self-centered, and hot-headed youth. In 1566, just one year after their marriage, he accused Mary of having an affair with her Italian secretary, David Riccio (1533–66). In March, Darnley and a faction of anti-Catholic nobles stormed the queen's chambers at Holyrood Palace, seized Riccio, and murdered him virtually in Mary's presence. Whether Mary and Riccio were innocent or guilty, this was surely no way for the Scottish royal family to behave.

The soap opera of Mary's reign turned even more bizarre in 1567. In that year a Scottish nobleman, James Hepburn, earl of Bothwell (ca. 1535–78), having won Mary's favor, engineered Darnley's murder (February 9) and "kidnapped" the queen (April 21). Letters were subsequently discovered indicating that Mary had encouraged Bothwell and fled with him willingly. While historians remain dubious about the authenticity of the "Casket Letters," Mary implicated herself by marrying Bothwell on May 15. Appalled at this behavior, her Calvinist subjects rebelled and deposed her in favor of her infant son, the offspring of her marriage with Darnley, Prince James (1566–1625). Mary and Bothwell met the rebel forces at Carberry Hill, southeast of Edinburgh, on June 15. But while the two sides parlayed, her army deserted. The next month she abdicated in favor of her son, who thus became King James VI of Scotland (reigned 1567–1625). In May 1568 Mary made one final bid to regain her throne, but her army was soundly defeated on the 13th at the battle of Langside. Abandoned and discredited, the former Queen of Scots had no choice but to flee south and beg asylum from her enemy, Elizabeth.

Once again, a demand from Scotland posed a dilemma for the English queen. On the one hand, Mary was a kinswoman and a fellow monarch, unjustly deposed by her subjects. On the other hand, she was a Roman Catholic and, because of her Tudor blood and Elizabeth's childlessness, the next heir to the English throne. Elizabeth remembered full well the destabilizing role that she, as princess and heir, had inadvertently played under Mary Tudor. As she said, "I know the inconstancy of the people of England, how they ever mislike the present government and have their eyes fixed upon that person that is next to succeed."[9] It was inevitable that Mary Queen of Scots would play the same role under Queen Elizabeth – with two added twists. First, if the religious and diplomatic situation of England deteriorated, plots in her favor might well receive the support of the pope and the Catholic powers. Second, Mary might not be so discreet as Elizabeth had been: given her impulsive nature, there was every reason to believe that she, too, would give active support to any scheme to put her on the English throne. In the end, one of these two women would have to go. The catalyst for that choice would come from Spain.

England and Spain

The situation of the great Catholic powers was more complicated, with regard to England, than might at first appear. For most of the sixteenth century, France had been England's most consistent and dangerous enemy. Just as English kings had tried to use their base at Calais to aggrandize French territory, so the French had used their Scottish allies to threaten English sovereignty. But by 1568 Scotland was more or less under the control of a Protestant government at peace with England; while France was about to enter a long period of religious and political instability. First, a series of sickly, weak boy-kings of the Valois family ascended the throne, to be controlled, fitfully, by their mother, the Catholic queen regent Catherine de' Medici (1519–89). As the Valois line dwindled to a weak conclusion under Henry III (1551–89; reigned 1574–89), two other families emerged to challenge for power in France, the Catholic Guises and the Protestant Bourbons. Although France remained a Catholic country, there was an important Calvinist-Protestant minority, especially in the south and among the merchant classes, called the Huguenots. Catholics and Protestants fought not only over who should succeed to the French throne after Henry III, but also over whether Huguenot Protestantism should be tolerated at all. That struggle took a dramatic and violent turn on August 24, 1572, St. Bartholomew's Day, when Catherine de' Medici ordered a surprise massacre of Protestants in Paris. This event affected England in two ways. First, it left France even more bitterly divided than before on the questions of the succession and religious toleration. The ensuing civil conflicts, called the Wars of Religion, eliminated the French threat to England for a generation. Second, the St. Bartholomew's Day Massacre provided yet more evidence, in English eyes, of Catholic treachery and cruelty.

Spain was another matter. Thanks to the Habsburg–Tudor alliance that dated back to Henry VII and Ferdinand and Isabella, England and Spain had generally been partners in earlier sixteenth-century conflicts. The Anglo-Spanish alliance, renewed by Mary, survived even the more-or-less Protestant religious settlement of 1559: so long as France remained strong and aggressive, Spain relied on England to help protect its Netherlands possessions. But as the French began to decline into disunity and Spanish power grew in the 1560s, cracks began to appear in the edifice of Anglo-Spanish friendship.

England and Spain divided in part because of the very wealth and power that otherwise made the Spanish such attractive allies. Thanks to the Habsburg genius for advantageous marriages, the discoveries of Columbus, and the conquests of men like Cortez (1485–1547) and Pizarro (1470?–1541), Philip II ruled an empire that included not only Spain but most of Southern Italy, the Netherlands, and all of Central and South America, apart from Portuguese Brazil (see map 8). That empire supplied the Spanish government with vast wealth, mostly in the form of Mexican and Peruvian silver, mined by Native American and (increasingly) African slaves, and transported across the Atlantic in biannual treasure fleets. That wealth paid for the greatest army in Europe. Elizabeth's government worried that, given Philip's devout Catholicism, he might, sooner or later, be tempted to use these resources to take advantage of the presence of Mary Queen of Scots in England. Philip's government worried that, given the wealth and vulnerability of his empire, English mariners might, sooner or later, be tempted into piracy.

In fact, every European power looked greedily upon the Spanish Empire and its monopoly of trade. But it was English sailors who actually took steps to break into it. One way to do that was to acquire and sell African captives to Spanish landowners in the New World, who would employ them in slave labor. In 1568 Spanish vessels attacked a "peaceful" English slaving fleet commanded by John Hawkins (1532–95) – and secretly authorized by Queen Elizabeth – at San Juan de Ulúa in the Caribbean. Only two English ships escaped: Hawkins's and one commanded by a young mariner named Francis Drake (ca. 1540–96). Allowing Drake to escape was a big mistake, for he would forever after harbor a deep hatred against the Catholic Spaniards who vanquished his comrades. That hatred was fanned by stories that captured English Protestants were brutally mistreated by the Spanish Inquisition, which often sentenced them to hellish conditions as oarsmen in the galleys of the Spanish Mediterranean fleet. (The poetic justice that those conditions were just deserts for the atrocities committed on their African slave cargoes was, of course, lost on the English.)

As we shall see, Elizabeth responded to the incident of 1568 by confiscating Spanish ships which blew into English ports and by turning a blind eye to the piracy of men like Hawkins, Drake, and Sir Martin Frobisher (ca. 1535–94). She even granted them privateering commissions which, in effect, allowed them to make their own personal war on Spanish shipping. Sometimes she invested in their voyages, as did Leicester, Walsingham, and other important courtiers. In 1573 Drake daringly raided the isthmus of Panama, netting a cargo worth the phenomenal sum of £20,000.[10] In the period 1577–80 he grew even bolder,

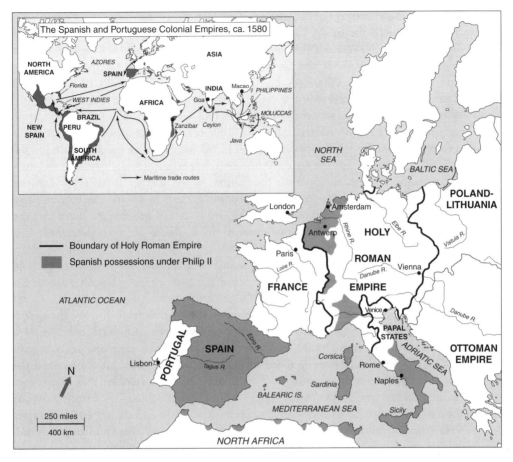

Map 8 *Spanish possessions in Europe and the Americas.*

sailing his ship, the *Golden Hind*, across the south Atlantic to the east coast of South America, through the Straits of Magellan, up the west coast as far north as California, across the Pacific, around the Cape of Good Hope, and back north to England – plundering Spanish shipping and reading to his crew from Foxe's *Book of Martyrs* all along the way. They became only the second expedition (Ferdinand Magellan, 1480–1521, had commanded the first) and the first Englishmen to circumnavigate the globe. Not that Drake could be sure of a hero's welcome: upon his arrival at Plymouth in September 1580, he is said to have asked local fishermen if the queen still lived. He knew that if Elizabeth had died and Mary Queen of Scots had succeeded her while he was away, his adventure would have been viewed as piracy and his life and treasure forfeit. But the queen did still live. That spring she knighted him on the deck of the *Golden Hind* – and claimed a percentage of his treasure (he handed over at least £264,000). Of course she did this more or less in secret. Publicly, she denounced the depredations of her sailors.

Philip knew better, but, in the interest of peace (and the distant hope that Elizabeth might die or declare herself a Catholic), he decided that Spain could afford to absorb these occasional English pinpricks. The second area of conflict between the two nations was far more serious: Spain's empire in the Netherlands (see map 9, p. 138). Charles V had given the Netherlands to Philip, his son, in 1554; two years later Philip ascended the throne of Spain. Despite Spanish-Catholic rule, much of the Low Countries had been attracted to Calvinist Protestantism. In 1566 a group of Dutch and Flemish noblemen, both Catholic and Protestant, led by William of Orange (1533–84, also known as "William the Silent"), formed a league to oppose Spanish influence and, in particular, any future imposition of the Spanish Inquisition on the Netherlands. The following year, Philip attempted to do just that, sending Fernando Alvarez de Toledo, duke of Alva (1508–83), and 20,000 troops to ensure order. Instead, the arrival of the Inquisition backed by the occupying army incited a revolt against Spanish rule which would drag on for decades.

Once again, Elizabeth faced a dilemma. Should she support Philip as her ally and fellow monarch and, in so doing, allow the Dutch rebels to wither away? Or should she support her fellow Protestants, at the risk of undermining the Great Chain of Being, disrupting trade, and inviting war with Spain? Toward the end of 1568 she was pushed to a decision after bad weather and privateers forced a Spanish fleet carrying £85,000 in gold bullion for Alva to take shelter in English ports. The Spanish, assuming that Elizabeth would seize the bullion, arrested the English merchants trading in the Netherlands and impounded *their* ships and goods. This, combined with the news of the attack on Hawkins's fleet, gave the queen an excuse to fulfill Spanish expectations by confiscating the bullion in retaliation. It should be obvious that rising levels of distrust and duplicity between the two powers were destroying their alliance, despite the absence of overt acts of war. Henceforward, the queen secretly supplied the rebels with money and offered a safe haven in English ports to Dutch privateers, known as "the sea-beggars." In public, she condemned the revolt. Philip was not fooled. In response, he closed the port of Antwerp, England's main cloth entrepôt in Europe, for five years. He did not want war any more than Elizabeth did, but events seemed to be moving in that direction. In any case, the presence of a Catholic minority and, from 1568, a Catholic heir in England meant that two could play at Elizabeth's game: Philip II began to wage a secret war of his own.

Plots and Counter-Plots

In the late 1560s, the pope began to encourage a revival of Catholicism in England. As we have seen, the Roman Catholic Church had responded slowly to the Reformation. That response, sometimes referred to as the Counter-Reformation, was formulated at the Council of Trent, which met, off and on, from 1545 to 1563 in Trent, Italy. This assemblage of churchmen had pursued a thorough inquiry into Catholic dogma and practice. In the end, it rejected most of Luther's doctrinal and structural criticisms of Catholicism. It reaffirmed the efficacy of the seven sacraments and good works, transubstantiation, Purgatory, even the granting of indulgences. Organizationally, it reasserted the authority of the pope and bishops and the sanctity and celibacy of the priesthood. On the other hand, the council tacitly conceded Luther's point about corrupt churchmen. It called for reforms of pluralism, absenteeism, and in the education and behavior of priests. The establishment of the Society of Jesus, or Jesuits, in 1540 is yet another sign of the Church's desire to reinvent itself. This order of priests, supremely well educated and organized according to military discipline by a former soldier, Ignatius of Loyola (1491–1556), was well equipped to engage in theological controversy, preaching, and pastoral and missionary work in order to combat what Catholics saw as Protestant heresy. And they targeted England.

By the 1560s, the small group of Catholic priests who refused to conform to the new religious settlement in England was dying out – and so was Roman Catholicism. In 1568 Fr. William Allen, a Catholic exile (1532–94), sought to remedy the shortage of priests by founding a seminary for the training of English Catholic clergy at Douai, France. In 1579 the Jesuits founded another such seminary at Rome. From the mid-1570s a steady stream of seminary priests began to filter back into England and Wales. In 1580, Allen arranged the first Jesuit mission to England in the persons of Edmund Campion (1540–81) and Robert Parsons (1546–1610). Their avowed purpose was to maintain the preaching and teaching of Catholic doctrine in order to preserve the English Catholic minority in its faith, not to convert Protestants, nor to foment rebellion against Elizabeth. But the actual record of these early missionary efforts is ambiguous. In the 1560s and 1570s the largest concentrations of Catholics in England were to be found in the remote North country and Welsh Marches, often among fairly isolated and humble communities. Yet, the seminary priests concentrated their activities in the southeast, ministering to aristocratic Catholic families who could provide a chapel and, if needed, a place to hide. They seem to have believed that the only hope for a Catholic restoration lay with the powerful and wealthy gentry of the South, not the peasants of the North and West. This may help to explain, first, why Catholicism continued to die out among the general populace and, second, why these religious missionaries soon found themselves embroiled in plots against the throne.

It was probably inevitable, given the queen's apparent sympathy for Protestantism, her Scottish cousin's presence in England, the Jesuits' courage and zeal, and Spain's wealth, power, and sense of grievance, that some Catholics, including, eventually, the pope, would call for violent action, even a Holy Crusade against Elizabeth. In 1568 Thomas Howard, fourth duke of Norfolk (1536–72), a nominal Protestant but the leader of the most powerful Catholic family in England, devised a plot to wed Mary,[11] purge Cecil and other Protestants from the council, and dictate terms to the queen. His scheme had the support of a number of disgruntled northern Catholic peers whose local power had been reduced by Elizabeth, most prominently Thomas Percy, earl of Northumberland (1528–72), and Charles Neville, earl of Westmorland (1543–1601). More surprisingly, some avid Protestants, including the earl of Leicester, also promoted the plot, in its early stages at least, hoping to break Cecil's hold on power. At the crucial moment, late in 1569, Norfolk lost his nerve and failed to go through with the plan. But when the court summoned Northumberland and Westmorland to explain themselves, they concluded that they had already passed the point of no return. They raised their affinities, marched south, entered Durham Cathedral (November 14), ripped the English Bible into pieces, and celebrated Latin mass before large crowds. They then continued south, bearing the banner of the Five Wounds of Christ last seen in the Pilgrimage of Grace, with 3,800 foot and 1,600 horse. But the Catholic nobility of Yorkshire and Lancashire, whether out of loyalty to the queen, a lack of direction from Rome, fear, or inertia, refused to join them and the farmers who made up the rebel army began to drift home. In the end, the duke of Norfolk was seized and imprisoned in the Tower. The earls of Northumberland and Westmorland fled to Scotland. Westmorland eventually made it to the continent, but the Scots handed Northumberland to the English early in 1570, who executed him along with about 450 of their followers. This was virtually the last popular Catholic rebellion in English history.

One alleged reason for the failure of the **Northern Rebellion** of 1569–70 was Rome's ambiguous stance toward the queen. Too late to aid the revolt, in February 1570 Pope Pius V (1504–72; reigned 1566–72) issued the bull *Regnans in Excelsis*, excommunicating Elizabeth, absolving her subjects of allegiance to her, and calling for her deposition in favor of Mary Queen of Scots. This move was, in fact, a blunder. The bull put Catholics in the terrible position of having to choose their faith and pope over their State and queen. Most, even priests, tacitly chose Elizabeth by refusing to take up arms against her. Nevertheless, to Protestants, the papal bull of 1570 was one more sign of an international Catholic conspiracy against England, its queen, and Church.

Their fears received additional confirmation in the following year. In 1571 Robert **Ridolfi** (1531–1612), a Florentine banker and Catholic agent, secured the endorsement of Pope Pius, Philip II, Mary Queen of Scots, and the imprisoned duke of Norfolk for another plot against the queen. The king of Spain, however, refused to send troops until English Catholics actually rebelled; those Catholics who might have acted would not do so until they saw Spanish troops. In the meantime, Sir Francis Walsingham had infiltrated the Catholic movement with spies. This enabled the government to uncover the plot, arrest the conspirators, and execute Norfolk in 1572.

These events had no effect on who wore the crown, but they did produce two other developments. First, they solidified anti-Catholic feeling in England. After 1569 all JPs were made to swear an Oath of Supremacy. In 1571 Parliament, over the queen's objections, revived the old Henrician treason statutes, making it a capital crime to call the queen a schismatic or a heretic, to question her title to the throne, or to promote in speech, writing, or deed her death or removal. Another act made it treason to distribute, receive, or possess papal documents. In 1581, following the arrival of the first Jesuits, an act was passed against recusancy (absence from church). Such absence now cost the offender £20 per month. This was an impossible sum for cottagers and artisans earning, at best, a pound a month; these fines were meant to cripple the Catholic elite. It also became illegal to convert anyone from his or her allegiance to the Church of England, or to allow oneself to be so converted. Finally, in 1585, Parliament made it treason to be a Catholic priest in England and otherwise tightened the existing treason laws in order to further secure the queen's safety. These measures drove the Catholic missionary movement and the community it was supposed to sustain even further underground. The queen liked to say that she prosecuted Catholics for their subversive political activities, not their religious beliefs, but Jesuits attacked this distinction as hypocrisy. It is true that, in practice, the government persecuted few Catholic lay people for breaking the law against recusancy. But in the last two decades of the reign Elizabeth's regime executed roughly 120 priests and 60 lay Catholics for treason. By starving Catholics of priests and proscribing missionary activity, the government was slowly eradicating Roman Catholicism in England. By 1603, only about 35,000 Catholics remained in the kingdom.

Marital Diplomacy II

The plots against Elizabeth almost certainly convinced both her and Philip that a war between their two nations was all but inevitable. But not yet. Throughout the 1570s one group in council, led by the earl of Leicester and Secretary Walsingham, advocated aggressive support for the Dutch rebels as part of a Protestant crusade against Philip II. But Secretary Cecil (Lord Burghley from 1571 and lord treasurer from 1572), Lord Sussex, and their supporters persuaded the queen that England was simply not ready, either financially or militarily, for war against the most powerful empire on earth. Rather, they urged her to negotiate and, if possible, to avoid an expensive and bloody conflict; if impossible, to buy time to build up England's first line of defense against invasion, the Royal Navy.

Elizabeth pursued these suggestions on two fronts. First, she toned down her support for the Protestant rebels in the Netherlands and became more secretive about her encouragement of privateers like Drake. Second, the Virgin Queen spent the 1570s and early 1580s pursuing a series of negotiations for a diplomatic marriage. The most serious of these involved François, duke of Alençon and Anjou (1554–84), brother to Henry III of France, who visited England in 1579 and 1581–2. Evidence suggests that, for a time in 1579, the queen was in love – if not, perhaps, with Alençon (she called the pock-marked prince her "ape" and her "frog," but these seem to have been terms of endearment), then with the idea of marriage. Perhaps she realized that this was her last chance at domestic bliss. Whatever her feelings, Elizabeth wanted to convince the Catholic powers that war might be unnecessary. Why invade when she and her realm might be conquered peacefully, with love?

The queen's double game worked remarkably well for a time. But by the mid-1580s it was clear that a Catholic marriage was unpopular not only with her council but with her people as well. Moreover, the continued weakness and division in France would have rendered such a union of limited diplomatic usefulness to England as she faced growing Spanish power. In 1580 Spain annexed Portugal, thus adding Brazil and much of the Far East to her already immense holdings. In the summer of 1584 a Catholic fanatic assassinated William of Orange and the Dutch revolt came close to collapse. Over the course of the next year, town after town fell to the Spanish army, now commanded by the veteran Alexander de Farnese, duke of Parma (1545–92). It was now or never: Elizabeth had to decide whether or not to prop up the Protestant revolt on a grand and public scale. For once, driven by events to a decision, she struck boldly, sending 6,000–7,000 troops to the Spanish Netherlands under the command of her beloved Leicester.

This, Philip could only regard as an act of war. The ensuing conflict, fought against the superpower of the age, would be the greatest challenge faced by the Tudor State. In the first half of Elizabeth's reign, her regime had tried to settle religion as well as England's place on the international stage. Now, in the second half, that settlement would be threatened by the mightiest empire on the planet. The Tudor State would rise to the challenge, but at the cost of the internal stability that the queen and her advisers had fought so hard to achieve.

CHAPTER FIVE

The Elizabethan Triumph and Unsettlement, 1585–1603

In December 1585, the earl of Leicester landed in the Netherlands to lead English troops in support of the Dutch rebellion against Spain. In response, Philip II began to plan the invasion of England. The English assumed that his goal was to place Mary Queen of Scots on the throne, restore Roman Catholicism as the State religion, and bring England back into the Spanish sphere of influence. In fact, he would have been content simply to force the English to enact a toleration of Catholicism and withdraw from the Netherlands. His plan was to assemble a vast Armada of 130 war and merchant ships which would ferry Parma's army across the Channel. It would take three years to fund, build, and assemble this fleet, the largest ocean-going navy yet seen on the face of the earth. The fate of everything that the Tudors had worked for hinged on its defeat.

As Philip assembled his Armada in the mid-1580s, all that stood between it and victory was the Royal Navy. The Royal Navy had more or less been founded by Henry VIII, who had delighted in spending royal treasure on its ships and dockyards. He also established a Navy Board under a lord high admiral which supervised the building, outfitting, manning, and provisioning of ships. After a period of dormancy under Edward VI and Mary, the navy had been revived by Elizabeth. Though Charles, Lord Howard of Effingham (1536–1624), was lord high admiral, its brain was Hawkins; its heart, Drake. Together, they had designed a new generation of English warship: longer, faster, more maneuverable, and more heavily gunned than their Spanish counterparts. By 1588 the queen had but 35 of these, although she could requisition additional merchant ships.

During the previous three years, the Royal Navy had done what it could to even the odds. In 1585 Drake had captured and burned the Spanish port of Vigo. Two years later he attacked Cadiz harbor, where the Armada was assembling, and destroyed 30 ships. This delayed the invasion for a crucial year, because Spain needed both to repair and replace those ships and to raise additional loans to do so. In fact, worse than the physical and financial damage to the Spanish fleet was the hit taken by Spanish prestige when Drake "singed the King of Spain's beard."

What about Mary?

Elizabeth's government braced for invasion in another way: by taking care of its most dangerous guest, Mary Queen of Scots. As the living, Catholic alternative to the Protestant queen, Mary had long been the focus of plots against the latter. In the mid-1580s Mary herself began to correspond with the agents of various European powers and potential conspirators. Even though Secretary Walsingham intercepted and read her letters, he and the Privy Council knew that they needed more evidence to convince Elizabeth to get rid of her cousin. In mid-1586 yet another plot, organized by a former page to Mary named Anthony **Babington** (1561–86), gave them their opportunity. As with previous plots, Babington sought to rally native Roman Catholics to support a Spanish invasion which would place Mary on the throne. But there was a new twist which would have dire consequences for one of the two rival queens: Elizabeth was to be assassinated. Walsingham learned about the plot through his spy system, but he took his time in suppressing it because he wanted to know Mary's reaction. Eventually, the Scottish queen gave her approval; the letter in which she did so would seal her fate. With the incriminating letter in hand, the Privy Council persuaded Elizabeth to try Mary in the fall of 1586; the ensuing trial convicted Mary of violating the 1585 legislation to secure the queen's person. Still, even with unequivocal proof that her cousin had authorized her death, Elizabeth hesitated. She signed an execution warrant, then left it in the hands of her other secretary of State, William Davison (ca. 1541–1608), with no clear instruction that it be sent.

There followed one of the most remarkable episodes in English history. Davison held the object that Elizabeth's loyal advisers had so long coveted – Mary's death warrant – but without clear royal permission to use it. He summoned his fellow councilors together and they decided to waste no time. They agreed to back Davison as he sent the warrant up to Fotheringhay Castle, Northamptonshire, where Mary resided under house arrest. Within hours, on February 8, 1587, she was beheaded. The news made Elizabeth furious. She gave Mary a full state funeral; Davison was sacked, fined, and sent to the Tower. But Elizabeth's sincerity is questionable, for in 1589 he was released, his fine remitted, and his secretary's salary paid until his death in 1608. Was Elizabeth's anger toward Davison and her council dissimulated to placate Scottish, French, and Spanish opinion? Even more intriguingly, what was Elizabeth's motivation in signing the death warrant, but refusing to send it, in the first place? A Machiavellian manipulation of her advisers in order to deflect blame from herself? The recourse of a perennially hesitant mind, always reluctant to commit irrevocably to one policy or another? Or, perhaps, the tortured maneuvers of a soul torn about a deed which was at once abominable and necessary?

The Spanish Armada

The execution of Mary Queen of Scots removed one immediate danger to Elizabeth's rule, but it precipitated another, for it gave the final impetus for Philip II to unleash the Armada. The fleet which sailed in the spring of 1588 consisted of about 130 ships manned by 7,000 sailors, carrying 17,000 soldiers dispatched from Spain. A further 17,000 troops were to be picked up in the Netherlands and ferried across the Channel. But, despite its awesome size, there were problems with *El Invencible* (the Invincible). Those problems began at the top with its commander, Alonso Pérez de Guzmán, duke of Medina-Sidonia (1550–1615). Medina-Sidonia's selection had more to do with his distinguished pedigree, upstanding character, and courtly manners than with any merit or experience as a naval commander – for Medina-Sidonia had nearly no experience at sea! Still, he worked hard to round up and supply his fleet.

The second problem facing the Armada was the composition of the fleet itself. It must be understood that this force was less a battle fleet than a convoy, sailing in a great crescent formation, the naval vessels on the outside to protect the transports (converted merchant ships) on the inside (see plate 8). Therefore, if the fleet wanted to stay together, it could sail only as fast as the slowest merchant vessel – a tortuously slow 8 knots (about 9 miles per hour). Moreover, the warships themselves were ill-fitted for protecting a convoy. They carried few of the heaviest cannon, capable of sinking English ships at long range (less than one-fifth the number their English counterparts had). Rather, the Spanish planned to sail up to the English fleet, grapple, board, and capture their opponents' vessels. The only problem with this plan was that it required the cooperation of the Royal Navy: because the English ships were generally faster, it was up to them whether they sailed close to the Spanish or stood off at a distance and pounded the Armada with cannon-fire.

Medina-Sidonia tried to bring these problems to the Spanish king's attention. But Philip was confident that they would not matter. A person of deep Catholic faith, the king was certain that God would favor the Armada as a means to punish the English for their Protestant heresy and restore them and the Dutch to what was, in Philip's eyes, the One True Faith. After all, he had secured from Pope Sixtus V (1521–90; reigned 1585–90) a papal blessing. Admittedly, this was given somewhat reluctantly: Sixtus privately admired Elizabeth and had grave doubts about invasion as a means to reconvert the English. Nevertheless, as the fleet departed, its greatest ships named for saints and members of the Holy Family (*Santa Ana, San Martín de Portugal, Nuestra Señora del Rosario*), Philip and his Spanish subjects could not conceive that this crusade could fail. The English were naturally just as certain of God's support. But, while the queen, her advisers, and naval commanders certainly prayed for and expected divine assistance, they had not neglected more practical remedies, forging a small but battleworthy Royal Navy. Even the names of their ships bespoke confidence, self-reliance, and tenacity: *Victory, Triumph, Revenge, Ark Royal.*

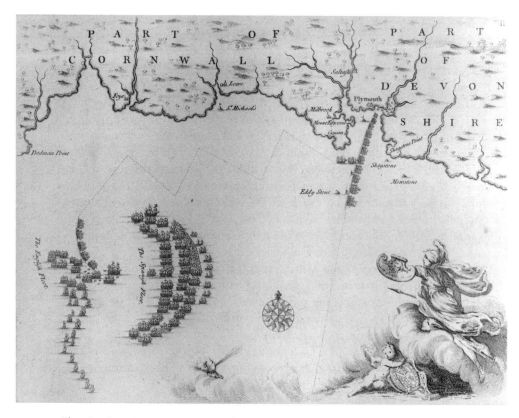

Plate 8 *First Encounter Between the English and Spanish Fleets, from J. Pine,* The Tapestry Hangings of the House of Lords Representing the Several Engagements Between the English and Spanish Fleets, *1739. The British Library.*

On land, the English were far less well prepared. Elizabeth had no real standing army. Rather, the forces she sent to the Netherlands, and, later, France and Ireland, were ad hoc affairs. For home defense, there was only her palace guard and the militia. The latter consisted of a nucleus of about 26,000 men called the trained bands, whose members received equipment and military instruction 10 days a year. They were supported by a wider corps of about 200,000 largely untrained civilians, armed with their own muskets and pikes. The whole levy was organized by county, each county's contingent under the command of its lord lieutenant, an office made permanent in 1585. If the Armada landed, this rag-tag assemblage of yokels would be England's last defense against the greatest, most battle-hardened army in Europe. Nevertheless, they were apparently ready to serve and Elizabeth, in a brilliant act of queenly solidarity with her people, went down to join them at their assembly point at Tilbury, Essex, in July. Here, she gave a speech which famously illustrates her courage, her common touch, her ability to play off her own gender and the memory of her father, and her care to identify herself, in her subjects' eyes, with England:

My loving people, We have been persuaded by some that are careful of our safety, to take heed how we commit our selves to armed multitudes, for fear of treachery.... Let tyrants fear, I have always so behaved myself that, under God, I have placed my chiefest strength and safeguard in the loyal hearts and good-will of my subjects.... I know I have the body but of a weak and feeble woman; but I have the heart and stomach of a king, and of a king of England too, and think foul scorn that Parma or Spain, or any prince of Europe, should dare to invade the borders of my realm; to which rather than any dishonor shall grow by me, I myself will take up arms, I myself will be your general, judge, and rewarder of every one of your virtues in the field.[1]

Still, England's best hope lay with the Royal Navy.

The English sighted the Armada off the southern coast on July 19, 1588 (see map 9). Immediately, they lit coastal bonfires to raise the alarm. The fleets met two days later. As expected, the English ships were faster and more maneuverable than their Spanish opponents. This meant that they could stand off from the Spanish fleet and pound it with gunfire at long range (about 300 yards). The Spaniards were too slow to close with and board the English vessels, leaving their onboard troops useless. Still, the Armada suffered little serious damage and the crescent held until they made port on the 27th.

Philip planned for the Spanish fleet to pull into the Dutch port of Flushing, where Parma's army would embark. But the Dutch rebels had done their part by taking Flushing, which forced the Armada to pull into Calais. On the night of the 28th the English floated fireships (old vessels filled with combustibles and set on fire) into Calais. Given a favorable wind, the result was devastating: only a few Spanish ships actually ignited, but the rest cut their cables and made for sea. There, out of formation, they ran into the guns of the Royal Navy. Superior English firepower took its toll, sinking Spanish ships one by one. Having been broken up, the Armada was now a spent force.

Medina-Sidonia knew that the invasion attempt was now over. His only thought was to shepherd as many of his ships as possible safely home to Spain. Unfortunately, the Channel was now firmly in English control. So the unfortunate duke ordered his fleet to sail in the opposite direction, around northern Scotland, then down Ireland's western coast, into the Atlantic, and home to Spain (map 9). Along the route, violent gales battered the remnants of his fleet; seeing God's hand in this, the English would dub these storms "the Protestant wind." Provisions ran low and numerous Spanish ships foundered on the Irish coast when they tried to put in for supplies. In the end, between 5,000 and 15,000 men perished; as for their ships, about half of the 130 vessels which had made up the Armada made it back to Spain. Spanish might was not broken; the empire was too immense for that. But the Tudor State had faced its greatest crisis and survived.

The defeat of the Spanish Armada boosted English confidence and morale. It was, in English eyes, yet another example of God's providential deliverance, as in 1558. More specifically, it fueled an increasingly popular, Foxeian view that England was a chosen nation, fighting a Biblical struggle against the anti-Christ, represented by international Catholicism. According to this view, the English

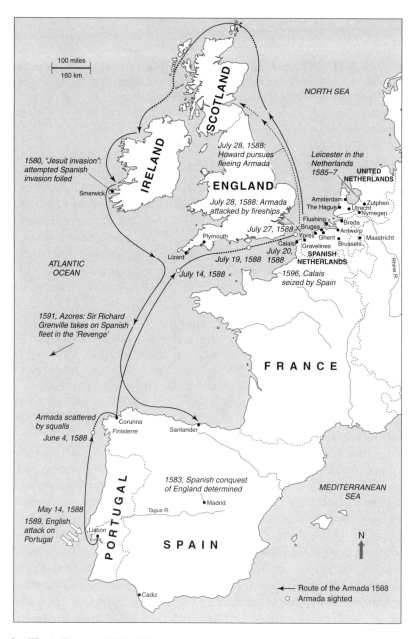

Map 9   *War in Europe, 1585–1604.*

people might suffer great trials, but their triumph was assured, for God was, in his sympathies, Protestant and English. Thus, the commemorative medal struck by Elizabeth's government bore the inscription "*Afflavit Deus et dissipati sunt*": God blew and they were scattered.

The War at Sea and on the Continent

In fact, 1588 marks only an early stage in a very long struggle. The war with Spain would rage beyond the deaths of Philip or Burghley or even Elizabeth herself, coming to an end only in 1604. The loss of the Armada only increased Spanish resolve and the war would expand to new fronts. The struggle with Spain might even be said to be the first world war, in that it was fought on three continents (Europe and the Americas) and two oceans (the Atlantic and, just barely, the Pacific). Far more than Henry VIII's summer military junkets (or those of the Hundred Years' War), the war with Spain would strain England's administrative and financial infrastructure to the limit. Vast armies would have to be raised, equipped, ferried to overseas destinations, and supplied. The Royal Navy would have to be expanded, maintained, crewed, and supplied sufficiently to enable it to perform complex operations at sometimes thousands of miles distance. The Elizabethan State showed the strain, the Elizabethan taxpayer complained; and the end result was, often, far less glorious than the Armada win.

Perhaps one reason for these ambiguous results is that neither Elizabeth nor her Privy Council ever resolved on a master plan for winning the war. One group of councilors and administrators, led by Burghley and his son, Sir Robert Cecil (1563–1612), argued for a limited defensive war against Philip's armies in the Netherlands and, later, in France. The other group, comprising mostly soldiers and courtiers led by Leicester's stepson and political heir, Robert Devereaux, earl of Essex, wanted to pour England's resources into a vigorous offensive war on land and sea. This would have the twin virtues of starving Philip of the silver fleets which paid his armies while enriching the very privateers, soldiers, and courtiers promoting this strategy. Characteristically, Elizabeth decided not to decide. That is, she pursued both strategies at once – supporting neither adequately. Rather, the queen, ever miserly with precious royal resources, ever reluctant to call Parliament, tried to fight the war on the cheap. Instead of raising taxes to mount overseas expeditions, she often had them financed by groups of courtier-adventurers who naturally treated such adventures as financial opportunities. Since the investors often demanded the right to command the expeditions which they had paid for, they ended up fighting their own private war, not the queen's.

For example, as early as 1589 Sir Francis Drake persuaded the queen to take the war to Philip II by mounting a massive (140 ships, 23,000 men) search and destroy mission aimed at surviving Armada remnants. When these had been sunk, the Royal Navy, supported by marines, was to foment rebellion in Portugal, then take an Atlantic base such as the Azores, from which Spanish shipping from the New World could be attacked. Once at sea, however, Drake and his fellow investors had a change of heart. They seem to have engaged no Spanish warships; instead, they landed at the Spanish port of Corunna and ransacked it, their troops getting thoroughly drunk in the process. From here they sailed to Lisbon, where an amphibious assault with naval support from Drake was botched and the siege abandoned. By the time this flotilla landed in the Azores, they had lost so many troops to disease that they could not even maintain this small Atlantic foothold. This episode cost £100,000 and the lives of 11,000 soldiers and sailors. Similar such adventures, with similar results, were mounted in 1595, 1596, and 1597. Hawkins and Drake died on such an expedition, a characteristically bold, but ultimately foolhardy, attempt to capture Panama in 1595–6. The naval war did see some dashing successes by individual independent contractors (privateers). But none of these hampered Philip's ability to wage war.

On land, England's war machine creaked on in the Netherlands under Leicester's command. Unfortunately, the English recruiting and supply systems were inadequate. Between 1585 and 1603 the Crown conscripted some 90,000 men, amounting to 11–12 percent of the male population aged 16–39 of England and Wales. But the muster masters who went out into society to "recruit" – really draft – able-bodied males chose from among the dregs of society: landless laborers, vagrants, criminals. In 1600, the Privy Council complained of Welsh recruits: "it would seem they were picked so as to disburden the counties of so many idle, vagrant and loose persons rather than for their ability and aptness to do service."[2] Once mustered, individual companies were placed under the command of a captain, whose responsibility it was to pay, clothe, feed, and equip his troops out of a lump sum dispersed out of the Exchequer. It was up to him to determine the quality of goods and how much he wanted to pay to the Ordnance Office which supplied them. There was a great temptation for him to keep costs low by ordering inferior food and equipment, and pocketing the rest. This may help to explain why so many of Elizabeth's courtiers hankered to go on military adventures. It also explains why morale was low, desertion frequent, and disease rife among Her Majesty's forces. Inadequate diet and clothing combined with poor sanitation led to illnesses such as typhoid fever and dysentery which killed many more soldiers than did enemy blades or bullets.

Moreover, Leicester turned out to be a poor general. He returned to England in 1588 a broken man; nominally in charge of the queen's troops during the Armada campaign, he died that fall. Nevertheless, despite his failure to achieve victory on the battlefield, the queen's help had given the rebels the military resources and the time to hold off Parma, to regroup, and to develop their own military tradition under a much more effective general, Prince Maurice of Nassau (1567–1625). By 1590 the Dutch had seized the initiative and the English were the auxiliaries. During the next decade the allies took key towns, such as Breda (see map 9). After Parma died in action in 1592, the Spanish were on the defensive. By the decade's end, the Dutch no longer needed England's financial support and they began to repay their debt.

This was fortunate, because the English Crown had, in 1589, made yet another commitment on the continent. In that year a crazed Dominican monk assassinated the Huguenot-leaning Henry III of France, and Henry of Bourbon, a Protestant, succeeded to the throne as Henry IV (1553–1610; reigned 1589–1610). The Catholic League, backed by Philip II, immediately renewed the civil wars of religion that had long plagued France. The new king, besieged on all sides, asked Elizabeth for help. For once, she did not hesitate. She knew that a Catholic victory in France would doom the Netherlands and might well lead to another attempted invasion of England. In September she sent 4,000 men, who immediately helped Henry secure Normandy. She sent two more contingents in 1591. None of these later expeditions succeeded and all saw heavy casualties from disease. But, as in the Netherlands, they bought the French king time. Henry solidified his position by converting to Roman Catholicism. This calculated maneuver (the king was said to have muttered "Paris is well worth a Mass") split the Catholic side by giving them much of what they wanted (a Catholic monarch), while preserving a toleration for Huguenots. Henry made peace with the last remnants of the Catholic League in 1596 and with Spain at the Treaty of Verviens in 1598. That same year the toleration for French Protestants was made official by the Edict of Nantes.

The War(s) in Ireland

Notwithstanding success on the Dutch and French fronts, the war with Spain dragged on and expanded. The most important such expansion occurred in 1594 when the northern Irish province of Ulster rebelled against Tudor overlordship and drew much of the island into a vicious war (in Irish history labeled the Nine Years' War). As will be recalled, the Tudors ruled very little of Ireland directly, but both the Anglo-Irish aristocracy and the Gaelic (or "wild") Irish heads of clans were supposed to acknowledge the English monarch's overlordship, especially after Henry VIII proclaimed himself king of Ireland and began the policy of "surrender and regrant" (see chapter 2) in the 1540s. But Gaelic unrest in 1546–7 convinced Henry VIII and Somerset to abandon surrender and regrant for an entirely military solution by expanding the garrison. Even so, the number of troops was never large enough to subdue the island. As a result, in areas where the Irish refused to cooperate, the English government began to sponsor plantations: that is, confiscating the lands of Gaelic chieftains and redistributing them to Protestant English (and later Scottish) landlords (soon to be known as the "New English"). The Gaelic landlords and, to a degree, the Gaelic peasantry itself were thrown off the land. The English created such plantations in Leix-Offaly in 1556, Down in 1570, Antrim in 1572–3, and Munster in 1584 (see map 7, p. 83). For the rest of Ireland, they introduced English shires (but no JPs), English law, English courts, and, with less success, English religion.

While these interlocking policies extended English rule to every part of the island except Ulster by 1590, that rule was only nominal. The truth was that most Gaelic Irish clansmen who surrendered and were regranted their lands felt little loyalty to the Crown. Even the Anglo-Irish (henceforward known as the "Old English") came to resent the "New English" interlopers, corrupt English officials, and the high taxes necessary to pay them and the English garrison troops. Above all, the plantations caused tremendous hardship and lasting bitterness among those whose land was taken away, and most plantations failed in economic terms. These policies created numerous Old English and Gaelic victims who were – or thought themselves to be – innocent. Both groups disliked the frequent martial law declarations and suspensions of the Irish Parliament. Both remained staunchly Catholic, not least because there was no Gaelic New Testament until 1603 and few Protestant preachers willing to proselytize in a land which the English considered a wild frontier. As a result, official attempts to impose Protestantism only added to Irish resentment of the English presence. Finally, the rivalries among powerful Old English and Gaelic families such as the Geraldines (earls of Desmond and Kildare), the Butlers (earls of Ormond), and the O'Neills (earls of Tyrone) continued. When the government in London showed favor to one side, it increased disaffection in the other.

Under Elizabeth, English policy and Irish resentments spawned a series of localized rebellions – of the Butlers in the 1560s; of the O'Briens, Fitzgeralds, and some Butlers (and thus much of the south and west) in 1568–73; of the earls of Desmond and Lord Baltinglass in Munster and the Pale in 1579–83; of Connaught in 1589; and of Ulster in 1594. These uprisings usually began either as local feuds between rival nobles or clans, or as protests against some particular government policy or official. They were not nationalistic wars for Irish liberation or for the reestablishment of the Roman Catholic Church. Ethnicity and parochialism divided Ireland too much for such concepts to have had much appeal. The Old English and the Gaelic Irish may have been Catholic, but they did not see each other as countrymen; clans of one region had little to do with those of another. And so, while the last of these rebellions certainly made England's war against Spain more difficult, they were not, at first, part of that war.

Perhaps because these rebellions involved longstanding local hatreds and elements of blood-feud, the Crown and its Irish allies suppressed them with increasing severity, sanctioning massacres of defeated men, women, and children, the burning of crops, and other atrocities. Edmund Spenser described the results of such policies as follows:

from the woods people came creeping forth upon their hands, for their legs could not bear them. They looked like anatomies of death, they spake like ghosts crying out of their graves, they did eat of the dead carrions.... In short space there were none almost left and a most populous and beautiful country suddenly left void of man or beast.[3]

Not surprisingly, with each suppression, both the Old English and Gaelic Irish grew even more embittered toward the government in London, the lord deputy in Dublin, the New English, and the Protestant religion which many of them brought. Ireland, always incendiary, was fast becoming a powder keg.

By the time war with Spain began in 1585, Hugh O'Neill, earl of Tyrone (1540?–1616), known as the Great O'Neill, the most powerful clan leader in Ulster, felt himself and his position particularly isolated and threatened by the Dublin government. Fearful of an English attack, Tyrone struck first, seizing Enniskillen in the west and Blackwater Fort in the east (map 7) in the winter of 1594–5. Knowing full well that he was in a fight for his life against a relatively wealthy and well-organized State, Tyrone sought the assistance of Old English Catholics, the pope, and the Spanish king by appealing to anti-English and anti-Protestant sentiment. But the Old English remained aloof, suspecting that he intended to establish Gaelic domination. The Spanish eventually mounted an expedition in 1596, but another "Protestant wind" destroyed it. They tried again in 1597 and 1599; but each time bad weather intervened decisively.

Still, England's forces were already overextended in the Netherlands and France, so Elizabeth and her Privy Council sought at first to negotiate. Tyrone demanded much: full pardons for the rebels, *de facto* religious toleration, and recognition of an autonomous Ulster under O'Neill control. Rebel victories in 1598 made the English situation critical. The queen responded by dispatching an army of 16,000 men and 1,300 horse under the command of her favorite, the earl of Essex. As Leicester's stepson, Essex had inherited not only the former's standing with the queen, but also his vast clientage network. Like Leicester, he was brave and chivalrous. But he was also impulsive, prideful, and, worse – again like his stepfather – a poor general. Essex landed in the spring of 1599. Rather than take the war to Tyrone's stronghold in the north, he wasted about £300,000 in five months marching aimlessly around the south of Ireland. In September he agreed to peace talks with Tyrone which were technically treasonous and in which the latter outmaneuvered him. Finally, when it became clear that Essex had botched the campaign, he left his army in Ireland and returned to London, without orders, in order to defend his reputation against whisperings at court. Tyrone took this opportunity to march south and burn the lands of English loyalists. The queen took the same opportunity to replace Essex in February 1600 with a much more effective soldier, Charles Blount, Lord Mountjoy (1563–1606). Mountjoy eventually succeeded in suppressing the rebellion, but not before one last Spanish invasion attempt. In 1601 Philip III (1578–1621; reigned 1598–1621) sent about 3,400 crack troops to seize the southern port of Kinsale (map 7, p. 83). In fact, this force was too small to help Tyrone; instead, it increased his obligations. By laying siege to Kinsale, Mountjoy drew Tyrone out from his northern stronghold and routed the Irish relief forces on Christmas Eve, 1601. The Spanish surrendered a week later. Mountjoy accepted the earl's submission on March 30, 1603, ending this Nine Years' War just days after Elizabeth's death.

Much treasure and many lives had been lost in bitter guerilla warfare in the bogs of Ireland. The campaign had cost £2 million and left Ulster devastated, Munster and Cork depopulated, trade ruined, and famine stalking the land. As one of Mountjoy's lieutenants, Sir Arthur Chichester (fl. 1599–1619), wrote: "we have killed, burnt and spoiled all along the lough [Lough Neagh, the largest lake in Ulster]. . . . We spare none of what quality or sex soever, and it had bred much terror in the people."[4] That terror would be visited again and again on the inhabitants of Ireland. Mountjoy's ruthless "pacification" was successful in its own terms, but its legacy of sorrow and bitterness further divided Irish from English and Irish from Irish.

In 1607 the cream of the Irish nobility, led by Tyrone and Rory O'Donnell, earl of Tyrconnell (1575–1608), absconded to Europe. "The flight of the earls" left their poor tenants to face the consequences. The following year, the English government began to confiscate both Gaelic and Old English land in Ulster, turning out landlords and tenants and replacing them with new, Protestant owners. These new plantations were, initially, a bust, economically. But they served their political, social, and religious purpose. They transformed Ulster from a stronghold of Gaelic and Catholic resistance to a society dominated by English Protestants and Scottish Presbyterians. These groups make up the majority of the population of Northern Ireland to the present day. By 1640, some 40,000 Scots and another 10,000–20,000 English had arrived in Ireland, displacing many Catholic Irish men and women. Admittedly, in 1640 Catholics still owned 60 percent of Irish land; it was not until the later plantations and displacements under Oliver Cromwell and William III that they would become a tiny minority of landowners. Still, the changes which followed the Elizabethan wars in Ireland intensified the bitterness of the Gaelic and Old English populations. That bitterness would erupt into violence during the 1640s and beyond.

Crises of the 1590s

World war with Spain and rebellions in Ireland stretched the capabilities and resources of the Elizabethan State to their limit. But they did not lead to major reforms. The structure of Elizabeth's government was more or less what it had been under her grandfather, apart from the modifications introduced by Thomas Cromwell. Elizabethan government expanded in size and scope in only two areas: local government and the military. We shall examine the apparatus of local government in detail in the next chapter. We have already noted the expansion of the Royal Navy and militia, and the raising of large, ad hoc forces to prosecute the war in Ireland and on the continent. The cost of all this fell squarely on the English royal Treasury and it was immense: a total of about £4,500,000 or about £240,000 a year over 19 years (1585–1604), with Ireland accounting for half. Fortunately, Lord Treasurer Burghley managed to increase the annual revenue from about £160,000 at mid-century to nearly £300,000 by its end. He did so by extreme frugality, exploiting feudal dues, and selling off Crown lands. But these were only short-term solutions and each had major drawbacks. For example, as the court grew more frugal, it left ambitious peers and commoners disgruntled. The exploitation of feudal dues did nothing for the queen's popularity. The sale of Crown lands obviously weakened the monarchy's long-term financial health. In any case, despite Burghley's ingenuity, total government expenditure still exceeded total revenue (including the proceeds from land sales and borrowing) by about £100,000 per year. Clearly, the queen would have to find additional sources of funds. She would have to turn to Parliament.

Elizabeth did not particularly like Parliaments. While Parliament had met 28 times in the 30 years before her ascent in 1558, it met only eight times in the 25 years thereafter. There was nothing unusual or sinister about this: Parliaments were seen as signs of crisis and usually resulted in increased taxes. Once the war began, however, she summoned Parliaments in 1585, 1586, 1587, 1589, 1593, 1597–8, and 1601. These meetings had two results. First, Elizabeth's later Parliaments approved a series of taxes which more or less paid for the war. Between 1589 and 1601 that body voted about £1,100,000 in taxes. As a result, the war was funded and, at her death in 1603, Elizabeth's government debt was only £365,254. This was a considerable deficit, but far less than it would have been without parliamentary assistance. In contrast, Philip II went bankrupt three times.

The second set of effects produced by frequent meetings was to give the members of Parliament more opportunities to raise uncomfortable issues, to develop expertise on them, and even to begin to feel a degree of corporate solidarity with each other. Admittedly, they spent most of their time passing laws about local affairs (for example, whether a bridge could be built in Staffordshire, or the market regulated at Salisbury) and usually cooperated fully when asked by the Crown to provide support, financial or otherwise, for its domestic and foreign policy. As for corporate solidarity, 62 percent of Elizabethan MPs sat in only one Parliament. But the rest were called together more than once and some repeatedly so. As a result, a small cadre of seasoned MPs began occasionally, and perhaps not entirely consciously, to reassert the ancient notion that Parliament existed not only to give financial assistance to the monarch but to redress the grievances of the subject.

Like any self-respecting Tudor monarch, Queen Elizabeth was not pleased with her Parliaments' occasional aggressiveness and self-appointed role as defenders of the commonweal. Early in the reign she grew to resent the attempts of religious MPs, such as Job Throckmorton (ca. 1545–1601) or Paul and Peter Wentworth (1533–93 and 1524–96, respectively), to meddle with areas she considered her responsibility, such as Church reform, her marriage and foreign policy. She repeatedly rejected the idea that the honorable members had any right to debate "matters of state," specifically religion, war and diplomacy, her marriage, or the succession – the last looming larger as the queen's marital prospects faded with age. Often, it was her privy councilors, especially the trusted Burghley, who, working behind the scenes, actually orchestrated the raising of these issues in an attempt to push her into focusing or making a decision on some matter over which she had stalled in council. But most of the time these offensives only managed to arouse the queen's characteristic Tudor imperiousness. For example, as early as 1563, a group of MPs met before the opening of the session to plan action on the issues of the queen's marriage and the succession of the Crown. The queen reacted by sending their leaders to the Tower. Subsequent attempts to raise these and similar issues by Peter Wentworth, in 1587, 1593, and 1596, would lead to similar royal reaction.[5] In fact, Wentworth died in the Tower in 1596, causing later historians to see him as something of a martyr for free speech or, at least, for free and open parliamentary debate. Here too, religious, political, and even constitutional matters were inseparable in early modern England.

The queen could not put the whole of a Parliament in the Tower. Generally, Burghley or, after his death in 1598, his son, Sir Robert Cecil, were sufficiently persuasive to convince Parliament to fork over the money and behave. If this failed, the queen could deflect the peers and honorable members from these issues by alternating Tudor imperiousness with Tudor charm. In particular, she tended to hector the House of Lords, which had fallen to about 60 noblemen and bishops at this time. But in dealing with the 462 members of the House of Commons, she more often relied on persuasion. That is, with her Commons, she played her trump card: the aura of sanctity, courage, affection, and popularity which was at the heart of her image as "Gloriana."

A perfect example of the Commons' growing sense of grievance and Elizabeth's skill in manipulating their feelings occurred near the end of the reign, in 1601. By 1601, the Elizabethan taxpayer was heartily sick of the war, the constant state of emergency, the incessant calls for money. Add to this the strain of militia musters and recruitment of soldiers for duty overseas, the queen's exploitation of feudal dues, and the practice of purveyance, by which the royal household had the right to commandeer a specified amount of food from each county to feed the court. To make matters worse, the economy was in crisis in the 1580s and 1590s. The Dutch revolt and wars of religion had played havoc with the wool trade and, in the mid-1590s, the country experienced a succession of disastrous harvests. Wheat prices more than doubled and famine hit the North and West Country. Newcastle-upon-Tyne reported "sundry starving and dying in our streets and in the fields for lack of bread."[6] Mortality increased and the death rate rose by half. As we shall see in chapter 6, these crises were part of larger trends caused by rapid population growth resulting in price inflation, wage stagnation, and unemployment. It was, perhaps, little wonder that Elizabeth's last Parliament met in 1601 in a surly, disrespectful mood.

Though Parliament had attempted to deal with economic and social distress by passing new Poor Laws in 1598 and 1601, the big issue around which the above-noted surliness converged was that of royal monopolies. Because the queen had so little money with which to reward favorites and friends, she had taken to granting them monopolies on the sale of commercial goods. Instead of pensions or gifts, she bestowed on individual courtiers the privilege to sell all the nails in England, or all the soap, etc. For example, she granted the courtier and adventurer Sir Walter Ralegh (1552?–1618) monopolies on tin, playing cards, and the licensing of taverns. This did not mean that the courtier in question suddenly became a merchant. Rather, it meant that he could claim a cut of the profits from any merchant selling the commodity in question, who, naturally, passed the added costs onto the consumer. Whatever the benefit of monopolies to a government strapped for cash and for the small minority of products needing protection in lieu of patent law, they hurt consumers. To give just two examples, starch prices trebled after the licensing of a monopoly on that product; salt prices increased 11 times! In effect, monopolies were taxes that had never been voted by Parliament. They were also seen as violating the paternalistic principle implied in the Great Chain of Being. By 1601, they had been granted for so many goods, both luxuries and necessities, that when a list of monopolies was read out in Parliament, William Hakewill (1574–1655), MP, asked sarcastically, "Is not bread there?"[7]

Parliament had tried to deal with the issue in 1559, 1571, and 1576, but had achieved little. In 1598 the queen had promised to do something about monopolies, but afterwards granted more. When Parliament met in order to fund the war in 1601, it found Westminster Palace surrounded by angry crowds, demanding action. The Commons responded with a bill to outlaw the hated practice. The queen, aware of the anger behind the measure and anxious to avoid a statutory limitation of the royal prerogative, responded with honeyed persuasion instead of bluster. On November 30, she summoned the Commons to an audience. To fully understand what happened next, it has to be recalled that Elizabeth had now been queen for over 40 years, as long as most of the honorable members could remember. By 1601, she had aged considerably, and showed that age in her pale complexion, her excessive use of makeup, her need to use a wig (her own hair had fallen out), and her decayed teeth. And yet, she still insisted upon cultivating the aura of Gloriana, still dressed magnificently, still affected the regal bearing of a Tudor. And thus, when she spoke, it must have seemed to those who listened, kneeling, as if a goddess, at once familiar and yet from another world and time, had opened her mouth.

The queen began by thanking her Parliament for its work that session and by assuring its members that:

there is no prince that loves his subjects better, or whose love can countervail our love. There is no jewel, be it of never so rich a price, which I set before this jewel; I mean your love.... And, though God hath raised me high, yet this I count the glory of my crown, that I have reigned with your loves.

Having reminded them that they loved her, she assured the members that she loved them back:

Therefore, I have cause to wish nothing more than to content the subject, and that is a duty which I owe. Neither do I desire to live longer days than I may see your prosperity; and that is my only desire.... My heart was never set on any worldly goods, but only for my subjects' good.

At this point, she asked her Commons to rise and then thanked them for informing her that monopolies were causing her subjects pain,

For, had I not received a knowledge from you, I might have fallen into the lapse of an error, only for lack of true information.... That my grants should be grievous to my people and oppressions privileged under colour of our patents, our kingly dignity shall not suffer it. Yea, when I heard it I could give no rest unto my thoughts until I had reformed it.

And then the old queen began a philosophical discourse on monarchy:

I know the title of a King is a glorious title; but assure yourself that the shining glory of princely authority hath not so dazzled the eyes of our understanding but that we well know and remember that we also are to yield an account of our actions before the great Judge. To be a King and wear a crown is a thing more glorious to them that see it, than it is pleasant to them that bear it.

She then came to the emotional crux of her speech, reminding her hearers of Tilbury and 1588, when God

made me His instrument to maintain His truth and glory, and to defend this Kingdom . . . from peril, dishonour, tyranny and oppression. There will never Queen sit in my seat with more zeal to my country, care for my subjects, and that will sooner with willingness venture her life for your good and safety, than myself. For it is my desire to live nor reign no longer than my life and reign shall be for your good. And though you have had and may have many princes more mighty and wise sitting in this seat, yet you never had, nor shall have any that will be more careful and loving.

She then concluded by asking of her privy councilors who sat in Parliament that "before these gentlemen go into their countries, you bring them all to kiss my hand."[8]

It was a masterful performance. There can hardly have been anyone unmoved at the sight of the queen, probably addressing Parliament for the last time, reminding them of the dangers and glories which they had shared together, and of the love which she had reserved for her subjects, rather than share it with any man. One suspects that many in her audience were so overwhelmed with emotion that they failed to notice that she had made only another oblique promise to do something about monopolies. Rather than encourage a new law, her dismissal of Parliament had killed it for at least another session. Admittedly, she did repeal 12 monopolies shortly thereafter. But she did so of her own will, not because she was forced into it by parliamentary statute. The honorable members had shown that they could apply pressure to the monarch and get a reaction, possibly even a modification of policy. But the Crown's right to grant monopolies remained intact. On balance, the queen had won – again.

But she could not avoid all such controversy indefinitely. By the 1590s, Elizabeth was an old and often difficult woman. She was also, increasingly, a lonely one, for many of the councilors and courtiers who had served and entertained her for decades began to die off: Leicester in 1588, Walsingham in 1590, Hatton in 1591. Burghley remained, as influential with the queen and dominant in council as ever, but even he was run down by illness. New favorites arose such as the aforementioned Essex and Ralegh. The dashing Ralegh rose to be the captain of the queen's guard, but was never appointed to the Privy Council, which remained the keystone of late Tudor government. The council did more than deliberate and advise; it oversaw revenue collection and expenditure; it named commissioners, lords lieutenant, and JPs, and issued Books of Orders for their conduct; and it sat as a court of law in Star Chamber. Unlike some of her predecessors, who saw the council as almost a representative body, to be filled with every important administrator, magnate, and clergyman in the realm, Elizabeth kept hers to a small cadre of trusted personal advisers – almost a cabinet – of between 11 and 13 members toward the end of the reign.

During the 1590s, the old division in council between administrators and courtier-soldiers intensified. The former were led by Burghley until his death in 1598 and thereafter by his son, Sir Robert Cecil, who had been added to the Privy Council in August 1591. Like his father, Cecil was an assiduous administrator with a following among the queen's servants. Like his father, he was opposed by a faction of courtier-adventurers. This faction was led by Essex, who struck many as a reincarnation of Leicester. He had inherited both the Dudley clientage network and his old household office, serving Elizabeth as master of her Horse. Like Leicester, Essex was courtly and warlike, having served with distinction in the Netherlands and captured Cadiz in 1596. Much less successfully, he had led a failed expedition to the Azores in 1597 and the disastrous Irish campaign of 1599. Like Leicester, he patronized artists and writers and had a following among those courtiers who thought the queen too frugal and too prudent. In a final similarity with his stepfather, Essex attracted the sovereign's affections. Elizabeth enjoyed a flirtatious relationship with the earl despite his married state, and he undoubtedly made her feel young again. But unlike her previous love affair, this was a May–December romance: while Essex was in his thirties, Elizabeth was in her sixties. Moreover, Essex was conceited and overbearing, qualities which created many enemies for him at court, in particular the quieter Cecil.

The two men and their followers clashed over policy and patronage. The Cecils still favored supporting the Dutch and the French as auxiliaries, largely because it was cheap and relatively free from risk. From 1598, the Cecil faction even began to urge a negotiated settlement with Spain. Essex wanted a more aggressive amphibious strategy, largely to give him and his friends a chance to enhance their glory. As for patronage, throughout the medieval and early Tudor period, one way a great man proved he was great was by finding government jobs for his clients. Few offices required special skills or formal qualifications and there were no competitive entrance examinations; rather, nearly all places were filled on the basis of family connection or clientage. Unfortunately for Essex, most of the government's patronage had been sewn up long before by the Cecil faction and, despite the war, central government did not expand much. At the end of Elizabeth's reign there were perhaps just 2,500 officials of the central government, of which about half, 1,200, held posts suitable for a gentleman. Moreover, Elizabeth was frugal: she held her household expenses down to just £40,000 a year by avoiding expansion of the court and, in sharp contrast to her father, building no new palaces. (The paucity of glittering prizes did not stop the competition at court: even in the last decade of the aging queen's life, hopeful courtiers vied for her attention by wearing gaudy hose and even dyeing their hair green!) Elizabeth also wanted to keep her court apolitical. Finally, because she was a woman, women filled the jobs which brought their holders into the closest contact with her, those of her personal attendants (such as the ladies of the Privy

Chamber and maids of honor). This served to close off such opportunities to politically ambitious males.

As the reign wound to a close and the succession question loomed ever larger, the rivalry between the Cecil and Essex factions grew more intense: each one wanted to be in power when the next monarch ascended the throne. Because the Cecil faction dominated patronage and since Elizabeth refused to adopt a more aggressive war policy, Essex became profoundly frustrated. Things came to a head in a Privy Council debate on Irish strategy in July 1598. After a heated verbal exchange, Essex rose and turned his back on the queen – an act of profound disrespect to any sovereign. Elizabeth ordered him to return, struck him across the face, and told him "Go and be hanged." For Essex, a proud nobleman, to receive such treatment from a woman, even a queen, was too much. The earl clasped the hilt of his sword, saying that Elizabeth had done him "an intolerable wrong." The implied threat of physical retaliation now bordered on treason. At this point other councilors restrained Essex. Naturally, he was immediately thereafter banned from court.[9]

This left the earl in an impossible position: how could the leader of a great faction, the patron of a vast clientage network, continue to be so if he did not have access to the royal ear? In October 1598 he apologized to Elizabeth and in the following March he was given command of the queen's forces in Ireland. While Essex undoubtedly saw this as a last chance to prove his courage and military abilities, it actually played to Cecil's advantage by removing his rival from court. As we have seen, Essex blew his chance, botching the Irish campaign, abandoning his forces, and returning to England without permission. The first anyone knew of this at court was when he burst into the queen's Privy Chamber on the morning of September 28, 1599 in order to plead his case in private. She reacted by charging him in Star Chamber with abandoning his command and entering into dishonorable negotiations with Tyrone. After a private hearing in June 1600 he was stripped of his offices except his mastership of the Horse, and confined to his London residence, Essex House. Even worse, that fall the queen refused to renew the earl's valuable monopoly on the importation of sweet wines. This was a devastating blow because Essex's noble generosity and high living had left him deeply in debt.

At this point the favorite began to plot rebellion. Counting on his popular following among the London populace, Essex claimed that he intended to free the queen from the clutches of Sir Robert Cecil; others thought that he aimed at the Crown himself. Whatever his aims, the scheme was utterly mad. He began his revolt on the morning of February 8, 1601 by marching on the heart of London. Few joined this foolhardy enterprise. Fleeing to Essex House, he surrendered by the end of the day, was tried and executed by the end of the month. Essex's career, particularly its end, demonstrated a great truth about the later Tudor State: noble power was no longer to be found in vast landholdings or feudal affinities but in royal favor and one's standing at court. In other words, England under the Tudors had become a relatively united and centralized State under a powerful personal sovereign. This becomes even more clear as one examines the last great crisis of the reign: the choice over the queen's successor.

In the months following Essex's abortive rebellion, the succession question loomed ever larger. Elizabeth, remembering her own position under Mary and deeply afraid of death, basically refused to address the issue. Being childless, she obviously represented the end of the Tudor line, but she adamantly opposed the idea of publicly naming an heir, both because that heir might begin to supplant her while alive and because to do so would be to admit that she would, in fact, die. Privately, she seemed to agree tacitly that the next logical heir to the English throne was James VI, the Stuart king of Scotland and the son of her late cousin Mary (see genealogies 2–3, pp. 413–14). King James, for his part, cultivated those who advised the queen, especially Sir Robert Cecil. Together, they worked out an agreement whereby James would make no attempt to seize or claim the throne until after the queen's death. In return, Cecil would ensure James's smooth succession – and, in the process, his own power in the next reign.

Queen Elizabeth died at Richmond Palace on March 24, 1603. Immediately, Secretary Cecil had James VI proclaimed as King James I of England, founding the Stuart line. The reign of the Tudors in England was over. It is a tribute to the Tudor achievement in government that the transition to the new king and royal house was handled smoothly and peacefully in the middle of a war, economic crisis, and much national anxiety. That smoothness and peace contrast sharply with the uncertainty and violence that had brought the first Tudor to the throne over a century before. Henry VII and his descendants had calmed the disorder that had brought them to power, tamed the nobility and the Church, and, in the process, forged a nation that was English and Protestant, ruled by a strong centralized monarchy, well able to defend itself against foreign enemies. In short, England was far more stable and secure in 1603 than it had been in 1485 or even 1558. Still, as we shall see in chapter 6, the English people remained very much at the mercy of such unpredictable natural and human phenomena as the weather, disease, population growth, and their economic and social consequences. Moreover, the Tudor achievement in government had ignored, marginalized, or oppressed many who lived under Tudor dominion, both English and non-English, particularly on the borderlands of the North and Ireland. As we shall see in chapter 7, the resulting tensions would do much to unsettle the Stuart century.

CHAPTER SIX

Merrie Olde England?, ca. 1603

Had Mary Queen of Scots, Philip II, and the pope succeeded in their designs on England, its political and religious history would have been very different. But short of full-scale invasion and occupation, Reformation or Counter-Reformation, most of the dramatic events chronicled in previous chapters either had little effect on the daily lives of most people, or they worked their implications slowly, in conjunction with much broader, less obvious long-term trends. What were those trends at the end of Tudor rule? How had the economic, social, and cultural lives of English men and women changed in the century or so after Henry VII's victory at Bosworth Field? Had the Great Chain of Being weathered the twistings and turnings to which it was subject over the long Tudor century? Below, it will be argued that the Chain had, by and large, survived, but its links were weakening at key points.

Population Expansion and Economic Crisis

Our inquiry must begin with a single, fundamental fact which drove much of English social and economic history during this period: between 1525 and 1600 the population of England and Wales rose from about 2.4 million souls to 4.5 million. It continued to rise thereafter to over 5.5 million by 1660. This growth was not steady: there were slowdowns and setbacks due to plague epidemics in 1546–7, 1550–2, 1554–5, 1563, 1578–9, 1582, 1584–5, 1589–93, 1597, 1603–4, 1610, and 1625; the "sweating sickness" or influenza in 1551 and 1555–60; and bad harvests in 1519–21, 1527–9, 1544–5, 1549–51, 1554–6, 1586–8, 1594–7, 1622–3, the 1630s and late 1640s. Epidemics especially endangered young people who had no previous resistance to the disease then raging. Poor harvest years rarely resulted in outright starvation, but as supplies dwindled food became more expensive and so less available to the poorer classes. This, too, resulted in lowered resistance to disease and increased mortality. Such crises produced temporary halts in population growth in the 1550s, 1590s, and 1620s. But the overall story was one of demographic expansion.

This growth had far-reaching consequences for national social and economic life. Landowners, especially those with extensive holdings, did well. More people meant more demand for the food grown on their land and, therefore, higher food prices. In fact, prices rose for a number of reasons: royal recoinages in 1526–7 and 1544–5 devalued English currency, and Spanish bullion flooding into Europe from the New World may have done the same thing. But the most important factor was the growing number of mouths to feed. Because England's ability to respond by clearing more land, draining fens, and improving agricultural efficiency was limited, the food supply failed to keep up, especially after a bad harvest. As a result, grain prices rose in England nearly 400 percent between 1500 and 1610. More people also meant that landlords could exact higher rents from tenants and pay lower wages to workers (often one and the same), since anyone who refused to put up with these changes could be replaced easily. In fact, some rents increased tenfold from 1510 to 1642. For big landowners this meant greater profit margins and, sometimes, greater holdings. Many independent small farmers and tenants, unable to keep up, went into debt and, eventually, sold out. A great landowner could thus acquire more land fairly cheaply, allowing him to rationalize and consolidate his holdings, a process called engrossment. England's demographic expansion at the end of the sixteenth and beginning of the seventeenth centuries thus led to a near Golden Age for the landed aristocracy.[1] The rich were, indeed, getting richer.

And the poor were getting poorer. The demographic expansion and associated inflation of prices and rents between 1550 and 1650 was a slow-going disaster for husbandmen whose holdings were so small that they had no surplus crops to sell and whose incomes, therefore, had to be supplemented by wage-work on a great landlord's land; or for cottagers who owned no land, bought all their food, rented their houses from such a landlord, and whose main source of livelihood came from such wages – that is, for the vast majority of the English population. Increasingly, too many workers competed for too few jobs on farms or in towns; too many renters for too few cottages; too many mouths for too little food. Admittedly, the average annual rate of inflation of prices was low by modern standards, less than 2 percent a year. But most workers' wages had been set in the late Middle Ages and were not rising at all. This led to a catastrophic decline in real wages, which led, in turn, to the breakdown of old economic and social relationships. Husbandmen might find that a series of bad harvest years could force them, first, to go into debt, and then to sell their land and become cottagers. Cottagers, faced with ever-declining real wages, might "break" (i.e., "go broke") entirely, join the ranks of the landless laborers, migrate, or seek the relief of the Poor Law.

Many went to London or other cities, hoping to obtain work no longer available in the countryside. They often failed to do so, not least because England's one major industry, the wool trade, stagnated at the end of the sixteenth and beginning of the seventeenth centuries. Migrants unable to find jobs were generally regarded as vagrants and potential criminals – masterless men and women who had dropped out of the Chain. Parliament passed several Poor Laws to relieve those unable to work and to punish or deter able-bodied people from leaving their homes and hitting the roads. After 1580, an increasing number of such individuals crossed the Atlantic to seek land in the British colonies of the New World. Most of the poorest traveled as indentured servants or, from the mid-seventeenth century, as convicts whose sentences had been commuted to transportation (in effect, banishment) overseas. The population expansion and the struggle for resources and livelihood that it implied will be the fundamental theme, affecting all the others, throughout this chapter.

The Social Order

How did the Tudor–Stuart social order weather these changes? As we have seen, the Great Chain of Being hinged upon the notion of a semi-permanent "estate" or "degree" to which each English woman or man was assigned by God at birth. But the changes described above made such permanence elusive. For example, the number of noble families in England rose from as low as 36 at the end of the Wars of the Roses to about 60 in 1600, and then to over 130 by the 1640s. The nobility's increasing thickness on the ground may actually have hurt its prestige: after all, the more such families there were, the less special each one became. James I exacerbated the problem by selling noble titles. This violated the idea that the oldest families had a right to their status because of birth. These changes, combined with the sheer expense of maintaining a noble lifestyle and the growing importance of the gentry, have led some historians, most notably Lawrence Stone, to argue that the titled aristocracy was in economic and political decline by the end of the Tudor period.[2] But members of the higher nobility still made thousands of pounds a year in rents alone. They still dominated the Privy Council and the great offices of the court. In the localities, as we have seen, the Tudors sought to lessen their dependence on great noble families, like the Percys, Nevilles, and Fitzgeralds, and outlawed their affinities. But they still relied on titled lords lieutenant to maintain order, raise the militia, and enforce Orders in Council in each county. Given their continued status, wealth, and power, Stone's view is clearly an exaggeration; it might be better to say that while the English nobility maintained its privileged position, other social groups were catching up.

Just as some historians have posited a decline of the nobility, so, for many years, there was a debate about the rise of the gentry, an idea first proposed by R. H. Tawney.[3] That debate was never conclusively settled, for two reasons. First, the term "gentleman," never very precise, was being redefined during our period. This was partly due to the influx of new men who had bought monastic lands or risen through government service. James I added to the confusion by creating a new title, that of "baronet" (to come after the noble ranks, but before knights and esquires), which he also sold. Moreover, contemporaries began to see education and professional activity as compatible with gentility. This left William Harrison

(1534–93) to offer the more or less circular definition that anyone who "can live ydlely [idly] and without manuell labour, and thereto is able and will beare the port, charge, and countenance of a gentleman ... shall be ... reputed for a gentleman."[4] A second problem with the notion of a rising gentry class is that gentry fortunes varied from family to family, region to region, and generation to generation. Still, it is clear that the overall number of gentle families *was* rising during this period and that the proportion of land in the hands of those with middling estates was rising too. According to Stone, between 1500 and 1640 the number of baronets and knights in England rose from about 500 to 1,400; of esquires from 800 to 3,000; and of plain gentlemen from 5,000 to 15,000, for a total of nearly 20,000 gentlemen by the middle of the seventeenth century.[5] If we assume (conservatively) four persons per family, this still comes to less than 2 percent of the total population of England and Wales. Nevertheless, recent estimates suggest that this tiny fraction of late Tudor and early Stuart England amassed between one-third and one-half of its land.

That is not to say that land stayed in the same aristocratic hands for very long. Because of a high rate of infertility, many noble and gentry families died out, making plenty of land available for purchase. The land market grew even more active and profitable thanks to the Dissolution of the Monasteries and Elizabeth's alienation of Crown estates. In addition, there is growing evidence that peers and gentlemen began, during this period, to diversify by investing in their mineral rights, or in schemes to drain fens, or in trading voyages. Still, the incomes of individual gentlemen varied considerably: a landed knight with extensive landholdings might make from £1,000 to £4,000 a year, a substantial "county" gentleman with multiple estates, £500 to £2,000. Gentlemen with one small estate, often referred to as lesser or "parish" gentry, might make far less, some struggling even to reach £100.

Below the privileged 2 percent, contemporary writers had the greatest admiration and affection for those "commoners" they called "yeomen." The greatest of these, perhaps 10,000 families in 1600, might equal or surpass the parish gentry in wealth. The 80,000 or so lesser yeomen families made anywhere from £40 to £50 a year. Generally, they owned or leased as freeholders at least 50 acres of land and could vote for their county's parliamentary representative because their landed income far exceeded the 40 shilling (£2) requirement. (See the Introduction; in fact, inflation was increasing the numbers of men who so qualified.) Though about 8 percent of the total population of England and Wales, their share of the land was rising from about 20 percent in the fifteenth century to as much as 25 percent in 1600. Unlike gentlemen, most yeomen worked their own land; unlike most husbandmen, they had farmhands and domestic servants to assist them. Their wills indicate that, increasingly in the sixteenth century, they slept on feather beds, they ate well, and sent their sons to good **grammar schools**. Such education, combined with continued economic success, might gentrify the family over a generation.

Below this level came husbandmen and cottagers. The former generally rented up to 30 acres apiece on a variety of tenures less secure than freehold. Such holdings might yield, on average, around £15 a year and, therefore, a vote; but that income could fall to dangerous levels in times of dearth. According to a statute of 1589, all cottages were supposed to have four acres attached, but, in practice, most cottagers had little or no land and no help from servants. Even for those with a small parcel of land, it probably yielded only a few pounds a year. As it required about £12 a year to support a small family in the later Elizabethan period, this latter group, in particular, had to find supplemental sources of income. Men could bring in about £10 a year in wages by taking on additional work on someone else's land. Women might engage in wool-spinning at home. But since both real wages and the wool industry were stagnating or declining, these people had their hands full just maintaining solvency. During the bad years of the mid-1550s, mid-1590s, and early 1620s, it was common for members of this group to go into debt, lose their land or house, and have to go on the poor rate or take to the roads in search of work. According to parish registers, one-half to two-thirds of any given village were no longer resident there 10 years later. Most moved to another village, or to a town where they populated an alternative social chain (see below). A few went to America; the rest swelled the ranks of the itinerant poor.

Elite Private Life

What was life like for the subjects of Elizabeth I or James I? How did it differ from the lives of their late medieval ancestors? How did it vary from rank to rank, place to place? In recent years, historians have grown increasingly interested in the nature of what might be called "private life." They have begun to examine those aspects of living with which every human being is concerned, sooner or later or day to day: birth, childhood, and education; courtship (what we would call "dating"), marriage, sexuality, and the relations between the genders; work and play; material culture (housing, clothing, and possessions); nutrition and disease; aging and death. These subjects are not only fascinating in themselves, they also help us to understand England's political and economic history. For example, early modern political theorists often looked to the contemporary patriarchal relationship between husband and wife to explain that between monarch and subject; therefore it behooves us to know more about what early modern marriages were like. As in political history, these subjects have given rise to their own controversies. How big were families? Did parents love their children? Did they rear them more harshly than we do today? Did they arrange their children's marriages? Could young people marry for love? Did men oppress women? Were people more religious than we are today? Harder working? Less materialistic? How did they deal with their own mortality? The answers to these questions varied from rank to rank but also, less dramatically, from family to family.

The differences between privileged and common life began at birth. Despite humanist and Protestant arguments against the practice, a noble or gentry family was likely to place its newborn child in the hands of a "wet nurse": probably a family servant or a tenant who had just given birth to her own child and was, therefore, lactating. She would provide the sustenance and much of the care for the newborn aristocrat for the first few months. Why? First, by freeing an upper-class mother from nursing, this practice enabled her to sooner resume her duties as a wife, hostess, and, often, manager of a great estate. Paramount among those duties was providing more heirs. A second reason for putting elite children to wet nurse was that their mother was far more likely to become pregnant again if she were not nursing. Unfortunately, the practice may have increased the mortality and compromised the health of these children. There may also have been psychological implications to the relative lack of physical contact between elite children and their parents, though this point remains controversial among historians.

The physical and psychological distance between elite parents and children implied above continued as the child grew. Children of the landed elite had separate rooms and, often, servants to look after them. These included nurses, nannies, and tutors, some of whom in the sixteenth century exposed their charges to the new humanist ideas. Their parents were often away in London attending the court, serving in government, sitting in Parliament, or sampling the delights of the metropolis. At around 10 years of age, a male child would be sent out to a local endowed grammar school or an expensive and exclusive **"public" school** such as Eton or Winchester. There, a young nobleman or gentleman studied English, possibly some Greek, but, above all, the classics of Latin history and literature. This exposed him to the international language of the time, as well as to the experiences and attitudes of the Roman patriciate – perfect models for future governors of England and its empire. Increasingly, a privileged adolescent might go up to one of the two universities, Oxford or Cambridge, followed by a stint at one of the four Inns of Court, or common law schools, in London. Most such scholars, particularly elder sons who were heirs to landed estates, were not expected to take a degree or even to study very hard. Rather, these institutions acted as "finishing schools" where the future leaders of the country picked up a smattering of polish, learning, and law, meeting and "networking" with those with whom they would be running it. After 1625 it became fashionable to complete such finishing and networking by making "the Grand Tour" of continental Europe in the company of one's tutor, who acted as both guide and chaperone. Only then was the young aristocrat ready for his debut at court, which, if successful, might lead to office, more lands, and a suitable marriage.

Thanks to the practice of primogeniture, *only* the eldest surviving son of a great family was guaranteed an estate and, therefore, a prominent role in government and local landed society. A younger son was expected to work harder; though provided with a "portion" out of the family holdings, this was more of a stake than a maintenance. Thomas Wilson compared the portion afforded younger sons to "that which the catt left on the malt heape."[6] As a result, younger sons of the aristocracy tended to head for professional careers, often according to the following pattern: "the second or third son for the law, the next for the Church and the youngest for trade."[7] After the mid-seventeenth century, military and naval careers offered additional opportunities to rise. Success, if it came, might enable a younger son to purchase his own estate and found a new branch of the family.

During the sixteenth century, the Tudors and some of their courtiers embraced the new humanist learning for both men and women. Thus, an upper-class woman might receive a very fine liberal education at home – witness the examples of Princesses Mary and Elizabeth or Lady Jane Grey. But she was more likely to be taught by her mother how to preside over the domestic arrangements of a great estate. This was because the chief goal of her young life was to marry and marry well. To assist her in this and to provide a stake for the resultant young couple she, too, would be accorded a portion out of the family estate as a dowry; and she, too, might go to court. The most socially prominent young women became maids of honor attending the queen. At court, the round of parties, masques, and balls provided an opportunity for young people – and their parents – to make suitable matches.

So what did "suitable" mean in this context? People, then and now, tend to marry within their social group. A landowning family with a title or a crest could not risk its children throwing away the family legacy on someone of inferior birth and estate. True, a marriage just beyond one's status, say, between the son of an impoverished aristocratic family and the wealthy heiress of a merchant, was not unheard of. In such a case, each family got something (wealth for the former, status for the latter). Such matches became more common as the London merchant and professional community grew in wealth and status. But a love-match with no advantage of birth or wealth – say, between a nobleman and his seamstress or a gentlewoman and her footman – was a non-starter, to be frustrated by an aristocratic family at all costs. After all, land exchanged at the marriage of an heir, principally the provision of a dowry by the bride's parents, was usually the most important business deal struck by any given family in a generation, and so parents, friends, and community tendered plenty of advice and exerted immense pressure. Another reason for family involvement in elite marriage decisions was that aristocratic children, with no need to worry about finances, tended to marry fairly young, in their late teens or in their early twenties, at a time of life when parental advice was, theoretically, decisive.[8] But this does not mean that young people at this level were often forced to marry people whom they disliked for the sake of a land deal. While parents often proposed a match, young people generally had veto power over anyone they found really unsuitable.

Still, because social and economic suitability was more important than love in the arrangement of most aristocratic marriages, it has often been assumed that noble and gentle marriages were loveless. Certainly, aristocratic marriage projected a formal image. Husbands and wives addressed each other in public as "Sir" and "Madam" and often lived their lives separately: the wife at the family seat, the husband in London or, perhaps, abroad on a diplomatic or military mission. This encouraged a double standard by which aristocratic men engaged in extra-marital affairs while their wives were denied the opportunity to do so. Aristocratic society was much less tolerant of female infidelity because it was so important to maintain the purity of the family bloodline. But it is also true that many aristocrats and their families did take compatibility, if not necessarily passion, into account when assenting to a match. Furthermore, letters and diaries suggest that many elite spouses came to have sincere affection for their partners in life and experienced genuine grief at separation or death. In 1584 Robert Sidney married Barbara Gamage, a Welsh heiress, without having met her, as a result of negotiations between the two families at court. And yet, over the course of a lifetime of military service abroad, he wrote letters giving every indication of real love, addressing her playfully as "Sweet wench" and "Sweetheart." Thomas More's suggestion in *Utopia* that prospective brides and grooms should have an opportunity to view each other "stark naked" indicates that the English elite were interested in more than the shape of the family tree.

After marriage, most Elizabethan and Jacobean aristocrats spent the bulk of their lives in the countryside. There, they managed their estates, oversaw the administration of justice, presided over important festivals and social events, and attended the local church. Some historians, aware of the networks of political, social, and family connection which centered on these families and estates, noting that contemporaries used the word "country" to mean their "county" or "locality," have posited the existence of "county communities" whose leaders governed together, socialized together, and married their children to each other. In fact, as we shall see, great noble and gentry families increasingly based their lives in London as well as their estates and, thus, often married and socialized across county lines. But most middling and lesser gentry did, indeed, tend to think and act as if their principal county of residence was the world, its center, their country house.

We wrote "country house," not castle, because the late sixteenth and early seventeenth centuries were a great age for tearing down castles. This was largely due to the Tudor suppression of great noble affinities and the rise of siege artillery which could knock down any castle wall. Between 1575 and 1625, outmoded and drafty castles were being replaced by large, airy country houses surrounded by extensive gardens and parks. The greatest of these, such as Sir John Thynne's Longleat in Wiltshire or Sir Robert Cecil's Hatfield in Hertfordshire, were known as prodigy houses (see plate 9). These houses tended to reflect two contrasting goals of aristocratic life: the longstanding desire to project to the outside world an image of status, wealth, and power; and a new concern for privacy. Their ground plans were often in the shape of an E or an H (see diagram), with a hall in the center or on one wing for dining and ceremonial occasions, and private apartments on the other. The former would allow the family to entertain lavishly other county community members; the latter would allow their daily lives to take place in private. The days when most great landowners dined in their great hall surrounded by servants and retainers were gone. Indeed, an important early modern architectural and social development was the rise of the "withdrawing room," or, as it came to be called, the drawing room, to which the family could retreat from the prying gaze of guests, servants, and tenants. These two areas and their functions would be connected by a long gallery full of paintings of the family's ancestors, a display of lineage to those privileged to be invited inside. For the rest of the world, there was the building's magnificent, if not necessarily welcoming, façade behind high walls and impressive gates.

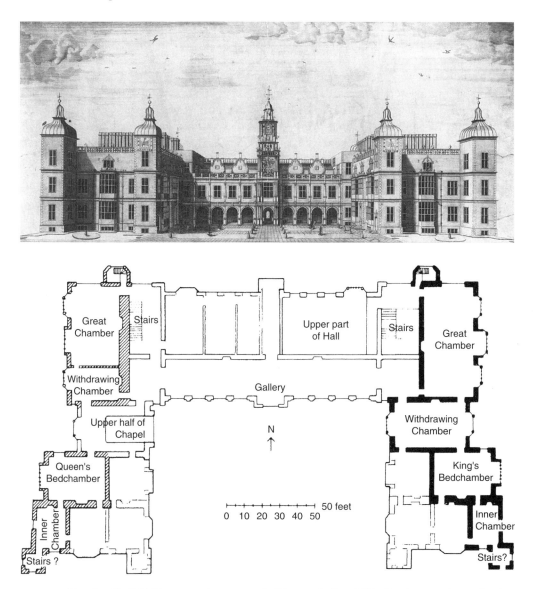

Plate 9 *Hatfield House, south prospect, by Thomas Sadler, 1700. The diagram shows the plan of the first floor. Courtesy of the Marquess of Salisbury.*

These houses thus provided both public space and private space. The former allowed them to be great political and social centers. Here, the local aristocracy gathered to select MPs or plan the implementation – or thwarting – of some royal policy. Here, great families were supposed to provide hospitality at key times of the year, such as Christmas, inviting the whole community, down to its lowest ranks, into their houses for feasting and revelry. Queen Elizabeth often imposed upon the hospitality of her most prominent subjects by turning up at their estates with her entire courtly entourage while on summer progresses through southern England. This mark of royal favor was highly prized, but it could also be ruinous: the earl of Leicester once spent £6,000 to entertain the queen and her court at Kenilworth Castle, Warwickshire!

At least the man who paid the piper did not have to play the tune: that's what servants were for. A great nobleman's household might comprise over 100, a middling gentleman's, at least 20. During the sixteenth century a great peer employed gentlemen ushers to open doors, valets and ladies' maids to assist his or his spouse's daily toilet, chambermaids to clean his house, tutors to instruct his children, cooks for his kitchen, servers for his hall, footmen and grooms to perform menial tasks about his stables, and, of course, an army of grounds keepers, laborers, and tenants to farm his estate. Supervising all of these would be a majordomo or steward, who was, himself, a gentleman of some education and ability. As the seventeenth century wore on, aristocrats would find less need for all this attendance and would reduce the size of their domestic establishments accordingly.

Large establishments of servants freed the landed classes from manual labor. Early modern society geared the activities of the vast majority of people toward providing pleasant and fulfilling lives for a very small minority who did not work and who were proud of never having to do so. This freedom from work (or, more accurately, from manual labor) and the deemphasis of their military role allowed the aristocracy to concentrate upon other things: their duties as government officials, MPs, lords lieutenant, JPs, or sheriffs; the round of hospitality noted above; the traditional activities for men of hunting and hawking, for women of sewing and playing music; the making of lawsuits (a form of aristocratic conflict, usually over land, which, along with the highly ritualized individual duel, replaced the old-style blood-feud between families); and scholarship. By 1550, illiteracy was virtually unknown among the elite and the Tudor and Jacobean periods saw both upper-class men and women, many educated in the humanist tradition, devote themselves to scholarship, poetry, and art. The English gentleman excelled particularly at the literary arts: Sir Thomas More wrote *Utopia* (1516) and a *History of Richard III* (first English edition 1543); Sir Thomas Wyatt developed the sonnet; Sir Philip Sidney (1554–86) wrote *Arcadia* (1593); Sir Walter Ralegh, a history of the world (1614); and Sir Francis Bacon, Viscount St. Albans (1561–1626), laid important ground for the development of the scientific method in his *Advancement of Learning* (1605) and *New Atlantis* (1626), and for letters in his *Essays* (1597 and 1625). These men combined private learning with public duty: both More and Bacon were lord chancellors and Wyatt, Sidney, and Ralegh were courtier-soldiers.

One reason for this cultural activity, as well as the above-noted decline in numbers of servants, was that nobles and great gentlemen were increasingly forsaking their country homes for the delights of London and the court. A small but growing minority rejected local society entirely, living at court as permanent employees of the government or the royal household – or hanging about in the hope of landing such employment. Others were amphibious: at home both in their provincial estates and the metropolis. By the Jacobean period there developed a London "season" from the late fall to early spring, during which the landed aristocracy resided in the capital, attending plays, balls, and parties, and keeping an eye on economically desirable marriage prospects for their children. Several technological developments allowed for easier and more frequent contact with the court and capital. In particular, the invention of the coach with box springs meant that an aristocrat could transport his entire family to the city in relative comfort, in a matter of a few hours or days, rather than the many days or weeks that it had taken on horseback. There was a concurrent improvement in the safety and quality of the roads – although any gentleman whose coach was overtaken by highwaymen or became mired in late spring mud would dispute this. For those who could not make it to the metropolis, an increasingly efficient postal service from at least the mid-seventeenth century enabled them to receive news and stay connected via correspondence with those who were there.

The increasing resort of aristocrats to the metropolis and the court contributed to the gradual domestication and nationalization of the English landed elite. That is, by the end of the sixteenth century the Tudors had done much to transform the English nobility and gentry from a feudal military cohort of limited local horizons and parochial ambitions into a service aristocracy whose primary responsibilities and interests were governmental, social, and cultural, whose loyalties were paid to the sovereign, and whose tastes were increasingly cosmopolitan. These changes would continue under the Stuarts, rendering the landed elite partners of the monarch instead of rivals – at least most of the time.

Commoners' Private Life

How different were the private lives of those who served or rented from the landed elite, those who, traditionally, had "neither voice nor authoritie in the common wealthe"?[9] As we have indicated, those differences appeared, first, in the nature of the family into which one was born. Non-elite families tended to be smaller, more self-contained and "nuclear" than those of the upper ranks of society. There were many reasons for this. People of all ranks did not, in general, live long enough for there to be simultaneously living grandparents, parents, and children. At the lower ranks, this was exacerbated by the fact that ordinary men and women tended to marry much later than their superiors, in their mid-to-late twenties for men, their early-to-mid-twenties for women. They did so because of financial considerations: a non-elite male was expected to be able to support his wife and family. Even if their parents and grandparents were living, the common expectation was that they would set up separate households. It might take years of hard work to reach this point. Since menopause tended, during the early modern period, to come in a woman's mid-thirties or early forties, this limited her childbearing years and so the number of her children. Breastfeeding, a common practice at this rank, had some contraceptive effect. Yet another, more tragic, limitation on family size came from very high rates of infant mortality at the end of the sixteenth century: one in eight children died within the first year of life and fully one-quarter of those born never reached age 10. A final reason for small, nuclear families was that, as indicated above, people in the lower orders often had to move about in search of work, cutting contact with extended family. Therefore, for the great mass of the people, families were small, say four to five people.

In fact, despite the high rate of infant mortality, the relatively short life expectancy of adults (about 38 years)[10] must have meant that children formed a higher proportion of the general population (perhaps 40 percent) than they do in highly developed countries today. That is, children were everywhere. What was early modern childhood like at this level of society? A relative lack of evidence on this question, much of it subject to conflicting interpretations, has led to a vigorous academic debate. There were some contemporary guidebooks, but, like modern books on how to raise children, they may reflect more wishful thinking than actual practice. Surviving diaries and letters of ordinary people are sparse and often terse. In particular, parental reactions to the deaths of children were often, by twenty-first-century standards, short and unemotional. Thus, the preacher Ralph Josselin (1617–83) wrote of his infant son, Ralph, who died at 10 days old, that he "was the youngest, & our affections not so wonted unto it."[11] This has led historian Lawrence Stone to argue that, because the loss of a child was so common, parents may have reserved themselves, emotionally, from their children during the first few years of life. Stone and others, noting the formal and utilitarian nature of children's dress, the relative lack of toys, and the contemporary emphasis in children's literature on moral conduct instead of entertainment, have argued that early modern children were generally ignored, disciplined severely, or treated like miniature adults or pets. But other historians, such as Ralph Houlbrooke, Linda Pollock, and Keith Wrightson, have argued that few words may hide deep emotion.[12] In fact, there is a fair amount of evidence to support the marquess of Winchester's contention that "the love of the mother is so strong, though the child be dead and laid in the grave, yet always she hath him quick in her heart."[13]

There is even more evidence that, in life, non-elite parents did love and, to some extent, indulge their children. Unlike upper-class children, these tended to be nursed, sometimes for as long as three years, and reared, at least until early adolescence, by their own parents. This physical proximity may, possibly, have encouraged a psychological closeness lacking among the landed elite. Non-elite parents made toys for their children and seem to have worried constantly about their futures. They attempted to ensure those futures by educating them at home or in a parish or "petty" school. The sixteenth century saw a boom in the foundation and endowment of such schools. They were usually run by the local clergy, who taught reading, writing, and some arithmetic in English. The endowment allowed poor boys to attend and also, very occasionally, some girls as well. However, young children could not always be spared for schooling because they were required to help their parents with agricultural work. As a result, by about 1600, only about a quarter of the male population of England could write their names. The figure for women was but 8 percent. A higher proportion could probably read simple passages from ballads and elementary religious texts.

Children of yeomen or tradesmen might attend school until mid-adolescence; those of husbandmen or cottagers probably left school at about 7 or 8 to begin working full time on the family farm. Most adolescents then experienced a period of service outside of the family: this was true for 80 percent of boys and 50 percent of girls in early modern England. If they could afford it, the family might try to launch a son on a career by purchasing an apprenticeship with a town or city tradesman. In such a case, the young man went off around the age of 14 to live with the merchant, who would teach him his trade. This relationship lasted seven years and, for that period of time, the boy was a part of the merchant's household and family. As such, he could not marry and was subject to his master's discipline. Young girls were also frequently "put out" to other families in the village as servants. Even a family with few girls might still "farm them out" and take in someone else's offspring. The idea seems to have been that future wives and mothers would learn best how to run households from someone other than their own mothers.

Unlike their upper-class contemporaries, ordinary people often chose their marriage partners more or less on their own, without much initial parental direction. The reason for this freedom is simple: young people below the level of the elite had little property to lose. That does not mean that material circumstances were irrelevant at this rank. As we have seen, its young folk customarily delayed marriage until the economic circumstances were right. Surviving testimony indicates that young women looked for men who had a reasonable prospect of making a living; while young men sought women who would be good household managers. Once a choice had been made, parental approval would customarily be sought, though denial might not be decisive. Alternatively, the families or the village community might act to prevent a marriage which had no hope of producing a stable household. Quite naturally, the village community did not want to be stuck supporting an improvident family on the poor rate.

How did young people of the lower orders meet? They often met at church or in the fields while performing daily chores about the farm. The custom of placing young people out to apprenticeship or service in other families also facilitated social contact – and diminished parental control. There seems to have been some common recognition that young people needed privacy and time alone to determine their feelings for one another. Once these were determined, however, things moved swiftly: canon law dictated that when a promise to marry had been made (a public, oral declaration in the present tense), the marriage was valid, albeit irregular, until it could be confirmed by a ceremony in church. Even a promise in future tense was considered binding. Despite the Church's preaching to the contrary, this led to the common convention that it was acceptable for an affianced couple to engage in physical relations before the marriage ceremony took place. It is clear from parish registers that something like 20 percent of the brides in early modern England went to the altar pregnant.[14] But this does not mean that sexual promiscuity was tolerated, that promises to marry were often made solely to initiate sexual relationships, or that the latter were entered into lightly. We know this because Tudor and early Stuart illegitimacy rates were astonishingly low, perhaps 2 to 3 percent of births. That is, once a promise to marry had been exchanged, the marriage did, usually, take place. A couple who failed to carry out their promise and conceived a child anyway stood a good chance of becoming pariahs in the village, which would be expected to support the child.

What was married life like for most ordinary people? Preachers and authors of guidebooks tried to set an ideal that can be traced to St. Paul, in particular 1 Corinthians 7 and Ephesians 5. Following Paul, the husband/father was to be the head of the household and, thus, of his wife. In keeping with the Great Chain of Being, William Gouge's (1575–1653) *Domesticall Duties* (1622) argued that "he is the highest in the family, and has authority over all, ... he is a king in his own home." But Scripture and contemporary guidebooks also urged mutual respect and love. Neither the violence of spousal beatings nor the double standard resorted to by the upper classes was defended from the pulpit or advocated from the printing press. On the other hand, wives were expected to put up with nearly any ill treatment that was short of actual physical violence: "She never ... saw Mr. Becke use any cruelty," a servant deposed in a 1565 Church court case, "but that any woman might well bear at her husband's hands."[15] Divorce was almost impossible – it required an act of Parliament. Formal separation was nearly so – it required the agreement of an ecclesiastical court (Mary Becke was seeking the same in the case just mentioned). Both were well beyond the resources of all but wealthy married couples.

So much for the ideal and the official; what of real-life marriages? Contemporary legal records, personal diaries, and letters indicate a full range of marriages, from happy to miserable. There is some evidence to suggest that the marriages of ordinary people were closer than those of their social superiors, with more mutual consultation and shared decision making. After all, non-elite husbands and wives had to work very closely together to keep their families solvent. Thus Edward Newby of Durham declared in his will of 1659 "that what estate he had, he together with his wife Jane had got it by their industry."[16] Wives might assist their husbands by tending vital farm animals, spinning wool, and going out to the fields to weed, make hay, or bring in the harvest.

Nevertheless, some marriages did fail. Since divorce was virtually impossible for people at this rank, the community tolerated informal separation. Sometimes, husbands left wives altogether. More often, marriages ended because of death. In fact, the high and often sudden mortality of early modern society probably broke up as many marriages prematurely as divorce does today in the modern Western world. When it did so, rapid remarriage was expected, especially for women. There were several reasons for this. First, a widow might possess property, which enhanced her economic attractiveness but also made her anomalous in a society which thought that all property should be vested in men. Second, a widow was assumed to have sexual experience in an age when women were thought to be the gender most driven by their sexual passions. Failure to marry her off might lead to unwanted competition for other women, both single and married. In other words, this was a society which simply did not know what to do with or where to fit women with money and experience. Widows of urban craftsmen could carry on a deceased husband's trade if they were able – we have records of a substantial number of widows continuing as printers – but most women had no legal existence or personal initiative apart from their husbands. Indeed, contemporaries most often defined women only as spinsters, wives, or widows – that is, by the presence or absence of husbands. With the abolition of the convent as an alternative at the Reformation, there remained only remarriage, service of some sort, or such disreputable alternatives as begging, theft, or prostitution.

According to Church of England liturgy and numerous moralists who wrote on the subject, the primary purpose of marriage was neither to exchange property nor to contain sexual energy, let alone to fulfill mutual love. Neither was it to avoid sin nor to provide help and comfort for husband and wife, although these were sanctioned as secondary reasons. Instead, couples were supposed to marry, principally, to have children. According to figures derived from a sample of parish registers, about one-third of all married couples bore a child within the first year of marriage; two-thirds to four-fifths did so within two years. Childbearing was dangerous for both mother and child, especially past the age of 35. In an age which lacked effective painkillers, surgery, or antibiotics, death from excessive bleeding or sepsis was rightly feared – note the fate of Henry VIII's third wife, Queen Jane (Seymour) – but not as common as one might think. This fear, along with poor diet and early menopause, may help to explain a noticeable drop-off in fertility among married women around age 35: despite the opposition of the Church, there is some evidence of the employment of primitive contraceptive techniques (*coitus interruptus*), devices (animal skin condoms, potions), and folk-remedy abortifacients. Whether popular or effective, these practices suggest that some early modern people were interested in limiting the size of their families or the length of their childbearing years.

What were the living and working conditions of ordinary people at the end of the sixteenth century?[17] Despite the destructive effects of inflation, most people were living lives of greater material comfort than had their ancestors at the end of the fifteenth century. First, beginning in southern England and sweeping westward and northward, there was a "Great Rebuilding" of the houses in which people lived during the sixteenth century. Slowly, starting in an area known as the Weald in Kent, one- and two-room huts were being replaced by more substantial dwellings designed to last more than one generation. Lesser gentry, yeomen, and substantial husbandmen, in particular, began to build multi-roomed houses of timber frame with an infill of plaster, wattle, or, for the most prosperous, brick (see plate 10). Stronger, thicker materials meant that walls could be punctuated with windows, letting in more light. Typically, at the center of this "Wealden" house would be a hall with a hearth in the middle whose smoke floated through a hole in the roof. At the far end was a cross passage with service and storage rooms beyond; at the other end was a parlor. Bedchambers occupied an upper story above each wing (see diagram). Sometime in the sixteenth century, Kentish

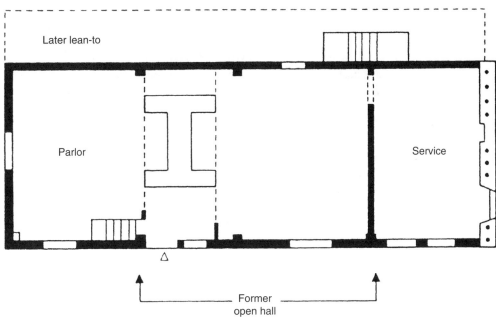

Later lean-to

Parlor

Service

Former
open hall

Plate 10 *Tudor farmhouse at Ystradfaelog, Llanwnnog, Montgomeryshire (photo and ground-plan). Crown copyright: Royal Commission on the Ancient and Historical Monuments of Wales.*

yeomen families began to put a ceiling over the hall and add more rooms above with separate fireplaces and chimneys. Thus, a substantial farmhouse might have 12 rooms. A poor cottager would still have to be content with one or two, but they were increasingly made of stone or wood and he and his family, too, could warm themselves at a real fireplace with a chimney. Even humble farmers slept on beds with mattresses and laid their heads on pillows, as opposed to the bare rushes on dirt floors of earlier days. Yeomen abandoned their wooden trenchers, plates, and spoons for tin, pewter, even, in the best houses, a bit of silver. Diet consisted, for the well off, of meat and fish, wheaten bread, a variety of dairy products, beer, and wine. Most days, the lower orders consumed simple rye bread, cheese, milk, and beer. Hence the importance of parish feasts, which provided rare opportunities for humble men, women, and children to indulge themselves.

Even during good times, no one could depend on a long and healthy life. Early modern people lacked a basic understanding of hygiene, nutrition, and disease, were prone to sudden accident, and survived at the mercy of the elements. We have already noted the frequent and utterly baffling (to them) recurrences of plague, influenza, typhoid fever, cholera, whooping cough, not to mention innumerable undifferentiated fevers, fluxes, agues, and afflictions like "griping of the guts." Simple infections – a cut on the leg, a sore in the mouth, the bacterial stew associated with childbirth – could prove fatal in days. Others might live for years with debilitating conditions: arthritis and rheumatism, bad or missing teeth, lameness due to rickets or badly set bones. Only the wealthy could afford doctors. This was just as well given the contemporary state of medical knowledge, which was still based on humoral theory and classical precedent. Early modern medicine was iffy on diagnosis: it knew when you had plague; but diagnoses like "griping of the guts" are more graphic than scientific. And it was utterly hopeless on cure, often violating the Hippocratic doctrine "Do no harm" with treatments involving leeches, blisters, plasters, purgatives, and horrendous surgeries minus anesthetics or antibiotics. If the doctor, apothecary, or surgeon did not finish you off, an accident might suffice. Children frequently drowned in rivers, ponds, and wells. Animals could gore, crush, or maim. Since dwellings were made of wood and thatch, fire was an ever-present danger, especially in cities, where flimsy buildings were packed within old medieval walls.

When it came, death, like life, was experienced differently according to one's social rank. The family of a great Elizabethan nobleman who died usually mounted a heraldic funeral. This was an elaborate affair, organized by the royal Office of Heralds, in which the many banners and honors of the deceased would be put on display. The idea was not so much to console the family at the loss of an individual as to remind the community of the continued power and importance of the family. But by the 1630s, heraldic funerals fell out of favor as an expensive and "fruitlesse vanitie."[18] Increasingly after 1650, the elite buried their dead privately, at night. Expensive tombs and monuments in parish churches continued to emphasize the status and honor of the lineage well into the seventeenth century, but they too were eventually replaced by simple wall plaques.

The death and burial of an ordinary person was much less elaborate than a heraldic funeral, but here, too, community was important. In the early modern period death generally took place not in a hospital but at home, among one's relatives and friends. Once the moment of death had passed, women of the family or village prepared the corpse. Prior to the Reformation, mourners engaged in a pre-funeral vigil, called a wake, followed by the funeral and prayers for the deceased – for days, months, and years on end – all in the hope of reducing his or her time in Purgatory. The Church of England abolished much of this ritual when it repudiated the doctrine of Purgatory, but funerals remained elaborate communal affairs in which the deceased was expected to leave monetary bequests to the community and gifts, both large and small, such as gloves and rings, to those who attended. In return, one's neighbors were expected to turn out, even the very poor, who might receive gloves or a suit of clothes for the occasion. The ceremonies concluded with a feast which served as a sign of the healing of the community. Over the course of the seventeenth century, even these rituals and acts of charity gave way to less public funerals in which the nuclear family concentrated on its own grief.

Given the vast differences in experience, traditions, lifestyle – and deathstyle – between the upper and lower classes, it is perhaps no wonder that some historians have focused more on those differences than on the attitudes and institutions which united English men and women into one nation and culture. Some have argued that the hierarchical principle in English society was so strong, the lives and attitudes of aristocratic English men and women so different from the great mass of ordinary people, that there were really two cultures in England. Those two cultures, separated at the Reformation, were growing farther apart in the seventeenth century as upper-class men and women grew richer, better educated, more urban, more cosmopolitan – and increasingly withdrawn from those below them in the Chain who did the work to sustain their privileged lives. What institutions and attitudes linked the various segments of the Chain into something which we can, still, meaningfully call England?

Religion

For most early modern English men and women, religion was, undoubtedly, the chief institutional and intellectual bulwark against disorder and social strife, their primary source of explanation and solace for the uncertainties of life, and the foundation of their code of moral conduct. After the Reformation, the Protestant religion did much to define who the English were *vis-à-vis* their Catholic – and often hostile – neighbors. Some historians believe that this identity as a crusading Protestant nation, a chosen people under attack by infidels, was the primary influence in the creation of English nationalism and that sense of English uniqueness referred to in the Introduction of this book. How were these ideas instilled in the populace?

As we have seen, every English subject was expected to attend the local parish church on Sunday – from 1549 under pain of law. At church, loyal subjects were asked to pray for the royal family against its enemies. There, they heard sermon after sermon defending the Reformation, delineating Catholic error, and justifying civil and clerical authority, arguing that they came from God and that to question or disobey them was a grave sin. The church layout represented this theology physically. Although the Edwardian attacks on "superstitious" images had laid waste to thousands of rood crosses, statues, and stained-glass windows, the church walls still displayed memorials to the most important members of the congregation. Indeed, the Elizabethan and early Stuart period was the great age for constructing gentry family tombs and monuments. Moreover, living congregants still arranged themselves according to the prevailing social hierarchy, with local aristocrats sitting in special pews at the front, followed in decreasing social rank by the other members of the congregation. A century later, Richard Gough could write a top to bottom history of his village by going through the pews of its church from front to back.[19] In theory, and on a more personal level, the Church also provided most English men and women with the foundation for their understanding of life and the course of world events, as well as an arena for every important rite of passage through their lives: one's birth, in baptism; one's progress to adulthood, in confirmation; one's marriage; the births of one's children at their baptisms; and one's death at one's funeral. Church feasts and festivals undoubtedly furnished highlights and happy memories; while the Church's ceremonies and teachings about death and the afterlife offered the one consoling note in an uncertain world.

It is therefore not a little ironical that for most of the century and a half after 1536, religion was often a source of controversy, if not disorder and violence, for many English men and women. Die-hard Catholic recusants stayed away from the parish church entirely, thus calling their political loyalty into question. Would-be Puritan reformers attended the Church of England but objected to many of its practices, such as the sign of the cross at baptism; the churching of women (i.e., the ritualistic thanksgiving to God for their safe deliverance and reacceptance into the community) after childbirth; the throwing of grain at a wedding, or, as we shall see, any special remembrance of Christmas. Such occasions tend to be stressful in any case; imagine the level of tension aroused when an individual Puritan conscience clashed with local tradition, the convictions of the clergyman, or the instructions of the bishop, possibly leading to the unwanted attention of his consistory court or that of High Commission.

Adding to the stress on the local clergyman was the fact that after the numerous purges and deprivations of the Reformation, Counter-Reformation, and Elizabethan settlement, there were only about 8,000 pastors left to serve the 9,000 or so parishes in England. Obviously, absenteeism and pluralism would continue to be a problem at a time when the various royal dissolutions and raids on Church property had reduced the Church's wealth. While this undoubtedly compromised the affluence of the bishops, it was the rural clergy who had the most trouble making ends meet. In 1535 one-half of all incumbents made less than £10 a year, one-third less than £5, often because their tithes had been impropriated (that is, appropriated) by a lay patron. This placed them on the level of the humblest cottager. On a more positive note, the clergy was becoming better educated in the sixteenth century: in Canterbury diocese the proportion of clergy with university degrees rose from 18 percent in 1571 to 60 percent by 1603; even in the poor diocese of Lichfield the percentage rose from 14 in 1584 to 24 in 1603. At the same time, the fact that post-Reformation pastors were no longer viewed as semi-divine, consecrated beings, but could marry and have children, may have given them greater insight into the daily problems of their flocks.

This does not mean that they were necessarily more effective at instilling belief into those flocks. There is plenty of evidence from the late Elizabethan period that, despite the law, Church attendance was poor and the general level of knowledge about religious doctrine low. Puritan clergy and laity, in particular, complained about the number of people who neglected Sunday services for work or the pleasures of the alehouse, gambling, morris-dancing, bear-baiting, hunting, archery, or football. The great divine Richard Baxter (1615–91) recalled the Sunday experience in his boyhood Shropshire:

In the village where I lived the reader [curate] read the Common Prayer briefly, and the rest of the day even till dark night almost, except eating-time, was spent in dancing under a maypole and a great tree not far from my father's door, where all the town did meet together.... So that we could not read the Scripture in our family without the great disturbance of the tabor [drum] and pipe and noise in the street.... [W]hen I heard them call my father Puritan it did much to cure me and alienate me from them; for I considered that my father's exercise of reading the Scripture was better than theirs.[20]

Puritans, fearing that most people saw the Sabbath as an excuse to engage in such activities, sought to outlaw or regulate them on Sundays and, sometimes, altogether. As we shall see in the case of alehouses, they often failed. Since many gentlemen and civic authorities were Puritan, a significant segment of the ruling elite became enemies to a wide range of popular activities, and, so, further distanced from ordinary people. Instead, they constructed an alternative, Puritan, culture.

Even those who did make it to church on Sunday and heard the message of the preacher may not have done so willingly or attentively. One clergyman complained that "Some sleep from the beginning to the end ... as if the sabbath were made only to recover the sleep they have lost in the week." Nor was waking congregational behavior as decorous as it is today. For example, in Dorchester in the 1630s Church officials complained of Henry Greene, who was charged with "laughing and talking and walking up and down" during services. This was, perhaps, not so bad as the physical blows or exchanges of "lousy rogue" and "lousy bastard" which passed among teenage boys during long sermons.[21] Even those who listened quietly may not have emerged with a coherent understanding of their faith. Evidence indicates that late sixteenth- and early seventeenth-century religion was poorly understood by its lay believers. The Church's message probably contributed to a greater tendency among the English to accept the social order than to challenge it. But it was apparently not enough, by itself, to keep them always toeing the line. That message had to be reinforced by contemporary notions of paternalism and deference.

Paternalism and Deference

The "grease" that was supposed to lubricate the links in the Great Chain of Being was the set of symbiotic attitudes called paternalism and deference. As we have seen, an aristocratic landlord was expected, like a good father (hence "paternalism"), to look after his tenants and the ordinary people in his locality as he would his children. In return, the common man or woman was expected, in the words of the Prayer Book, "to ordre myselfe lowlye and revernetlye to al my betters"[22] (see Introduction). It is difficult for people reared with our modern emphasis on individual self-fulfillment to understand the seemingly universal acceptance of paternalist/deferential ideas and forms of behavior at the end of the sixteenth and beginning of the seventeenth centuries. In fact, they may not have been embraced sincerely or wholeheartedly even then. Marxist historians have argued that paternalism was merely a screen for the depredations of a greedy ruling class. That is, in reality aristocrats exploited aggressively their power over the lower orders and, in return, gave only a small portion of their time, attention, and income back in legal or charitable endeavor. Paternalism did not aim to ease the lives of the less fortunate but simply to fool them into putting up with their lot. The impulse for sincere paternalism was, in any case, ebbing among the upper classes, first because the Tudors weakened notions of "good lordship" and local allegiances between the aristocracy and their subordinates; second, because the economic situation at the end of the sixteenth century encouraged a more capitalistic (read ruthless) exploitation of land, rents, and tenants; and, third, because the Reformation rejected the spiritual efficacy of good works. We have already noted that at the end of the Tudor period the landed classes were getting richer while many of their tenants were stagnating economically or growing poorer. As the former spent more time abroad or in London, they spent less time on their estates, close to their tenants. Hence, contemporary complaints about the decline of aristocratic hospitality and modern arguments that the upper class was distancing itself – physically and emotionally – from the lower orders. When they were at home, seventeenth-century aristocratic landlords increasingly erected high walls and wrought iron gates around those homes, ostensibly to contain wildlife in ornamental deer parks, but also to keep out "the rabble." For their part, the rabble may have acted deferentially in public, but there is evidence of grumbling and questioning in private, as in the case of the Norfolk parish clerk who, in the wake of Kett's rebellion, supposedly opined "[t]here are to[o] many gentylman in Englande by fyve hundred."[23]

The Marxist interpretation is not entirely fair, in that it judges a former time by our own standards. The upper classes may have been out for themselves, but there is plenty of evidence that they believed, possibly naively, that they were also helping their fellow subjects. When aristocrats endowed a school or treated their tenants at Christmas, they may have been trying, subconsciously, to buy off their inferiors or alleviate their guilt, but the vast majority were not sufficiently critical of the general economic and social situation to realize that they were attempting to solve problems of their own making and far too vast to be cured by a few bequests. Moreover, because society promoted the idea of paternalistic responsibility, peasants could sometimes use it to exact concessions from their betters, as we shall see in the case of riots. In any case, it could be argued that society was held together not so much by "vertical" bonds of loyalty to one's social superiors and inferiors as by the glue of common interest that existed "horizontally" among kin and neighbors of more or less the same rank.

Kinship and Neighborliness

At first glance, there is very little evidence that extended kin cared for or had much use for each other in early modern England below the ranks of the elite. Below this social level, geographical mobility tore kinship ties asunder. But that also meant that if one left one's village to go to a provincial city, to London or to the colonies, one might very well have been preceded there by a relative. One might legitimately ask an uncle or a cousin for help in finding a first job or, perhaps, for financial assistance. Indeed, for early modern people the word "cousin" was applied elastically to any relation, no matter how distant – often in expectation of some benefit. But even this contact tended to be fortuitous and temporary. Once established in a new location, or if one decided to stay at home in the first place, one's chief source of help would be one's neighbors.

There were no guidebooks, no written rules on how to be a good neighbor. Rather, neighborliness was a set of attitudes, shared but unspoken, which dictated certain behaviors that enabled people in the early modern village to deal collectively with hardship and to get along with each other. A villager could call on his neighbors to loan money or tools or to watch his home or goods if he had to leave town. At moments of crisis or celebration – giving birth, a wedding, illness, or death – neighbors helped out by preparing meals. Indeed, one's coming into and one's leaving from the world occurred in the company of neighbors. When a woman began to "lie in" for childbirth, there was no obstetrician to call; the local midwife and other neighborly women assisted her. When a villager died, these same women cleaned and dressed his or her corpse. In the early modern period, neighborliness – a sense of communal sharing and mutual responsibility – knit the community together in a web of personal credit and debt, filling in for a lack of institutions, such as banks, hospitals, mortuaries, and insurance companies, which perform similar services in the modern world.

Neighborliness could also stifle and hurt. It employed peer pressure and, sometimes, the law to enforce community standards and curb objectionable behavior. That is, a good neighbor was never (or not often) loudly drunk or blasphemous, quarrelsome, litigious, abusive, violent – or even too different. If a neighbor were guilty of such transgressions, he or she could be pressured to desist or punished in a number of ways. A husband or wife who beat his or her spouse or was a notorious adulterer might be treated to "rough music," that is, the banging of pots and pans outside his or her window; or the offending couple might be burnt in effigy or run out of town on a rail (a skimmington) either figuratively or – in really serious cases – in person. Another way of applying peer pressure was public ridicule. Thus, mocking rumors and rhymes might circulate the village:

> Woe to thee, Michael Robins,
> That ever thou wert born,
> For Blancute makes thee cuckold,
> And thou must wear the horn.
> He fetches the nurse
> To give the child suck,
> That he may have time,
> Thy wife for to fuck.[24]

Only when such informal pressure failed did good neighbors resort to the institutions of local government or the Church. A reputed scold might be ducked in the local millpond before being brought to the attention of the local JP. Property disputes and minor punch-ups might be taken to the local clergyman before resorting to the manorial, hundred, or borough court. A notorious blasphemer might be brought up on charges before a Church court by his or her parish priest or neighbors. In very serious cases, a ne'er-do-well or ill-liver might be excommunicated by such a court – that is, forbidden to take communion in church. This meant that the individual was literally out of communion and so out of community with his or her fellow villagers, a situation which could imperil not only one's social or economic well-being but one's very soul. This should remind us that early modern society did not draw great distinctions between moral and legal codes, spiritual and civil transgressions.

Still, a major tenet of neighborliness was that one did not complain to the civil or ecclesiastical authorities lightly. Rather, one did so only if one's neighbor's behavior was chronic or heinous. Good neighbors worked things out. Put another way, neighborliness not only kept village society together; it, perhaps more immediately and effectively than religion or deference, was the real first line of defense against disorder. It was important for the justices and priests who administered the common or Church law to remember where their jurisdiction ended and to keep their noses out of people's business as much as they could – hence the widespread unpopularity of Puritan kill-joys bent on reform. Thus, neighborliness encouraged cooperation not just among members of the lower orders, but between the orders as well. How did it deal with the very lowest order in society, the poor?

Poverty and Charity

The medieval worldview embraced the poor; the early modern worldview did not. That is, medieval Catholics looked upon the poor not only with pity, but also with a certain amount of approval, even affection. Unfortunate in this world, they were virtually guaranteed salvation in the next. Moreover, they provided opportunities for good Catholics to perform soul-saving works on their behalf, by giving alms, contributing to monasteries and hospitals, etc. Perhaps another reason for medieval acceptance of the problem of the poor was that the number of poor people seemed to be manageable for late medieval society, probably because the Black Death had left a labor shortage in its wake.

But by 1600, rising unemployment caused by the increase in population, growing numbers of people who had lost or been thrown off their land, high prices and stagnant wages were creating ever greater numbers of poor people. It has been estimated that at the end of the Tudor period, depending on the current state of the economy, something like 10 to 20 percent of the general population could not meet their expenses out of their income. By the end of the sixteenth century, about a third of the town population was itinerant; the same percentage of the country population resorted to begging. Overall, some 20,000–40,000 people in England were in a state of near-perpetual migration. The migrant poor included seasonally employed laborers, the unemployed, demobilized soldiers, beggars, the lame and sick, and criminals. Contemporaries had a great deal of trouble distinguishing these various categories of poor people from each other, not least because any poor individual might fall into one or the other category at any given time. For example, laborers who hired themselves out to work in the fields or on building projects during spring, summer, and fall often became unemployed in winter. This might lead to vagrancy, begging, illness, even theft as they tried to feed their families.

Contemporaries tended to react to the poor, especially the roving poor, with hostility and fear. Because the modern study of economics was unknown, they did not understand that the poor might not have had much choice in the matter. Most people seem to have assumed that, apart from the lame, the sick, children, or the elderly, poor people might find jobs easily if only they were willing to look for them and to work at them. The first Poor Law of 1536 thus distinguished between the "deserving" or "impotent" poor (i.e., those unable to work as noted above, for which relief was to be supplied by voluntary subscriptions) and the "undeserving" poor, popularly known as "sturdy beggars," who were able-bodied but, apparently, refused to work. That refusal suggested that they were lazy and, probably, up to no good – shiftless, masterless persons who had opted out of the Great Chain of Being. According to popular myth, they went about the country in roving bands, robbing, assaulting, and, in general, intimidating honest, respectable folk. Therefore, the proper governmental and social response to the poverty of sturdy beggars was punishment.

As early as 1495, Parliament ordered beggars placed in the stocks for three days, whipped, and then sent back to their home parishes.[25] The Vagrancy Act of 1547 ordered that anyone leaving his or her home parish or refusing to work be branded with a "V" for vagrant and enslaved for two years. This law was unenforceable and soon repealed, but previous legislation still mandated whipping masterless men and women until bloody. In 1572 Parliament ordered vagrants to be whipped and bored through the right ear as a punishment for a first offense, condemned as a felon for a second offense unless taken into service, and hanged for a third. Many communities refused to enforce such harsh punishments, but not all: between 1572 and 1575 the Middlesex JPs branded 44 vagrants, put eight in service, and hanged five! The death penalty for vagrants was only abolished in 1593.

Fortunately, as we have seen, there was a countervailing tendency in dealing with the "deserving" poor. First, despite the Dissolution of the Monasteries and the Protestant deemphasis of good works, private charity continued unabated in the later Tudor and Jacobean periods, as evidenced by the number of schools and hospitals endowed in this period. Second, many local communities, including London, launched charity schemes of their own: by the end of the century, many towns had almshouses. Finally, the parliamentary acts of 1563 and 1572 made the support of the "deserving" poor compulsory by a local tax on parishioners which came to be known as the poor rates. These were to be administered by local JPs assisted by churchwardens who collected them and overseers of the poor who distributed them. The funds subsequently distributed were known as "outdoor relief": that is, poor parishioners could receive relief and stay in their own houses.

Many contemporaries objected to such handouts. They felt that poor people should repay the community with their own labor. And so the act of 1572 authorized parishes to put the homeless poor, including sturdy beggars, into workhouses ("indoor relief") where they were required to spin wool, hemp, and flax or work iron to sell for the parish. In the workhouse, families were broken up, husbands separated from wives, parents from children. The latter were often put into apprenticeships. The goal of this institution was threefold: first, to give the poor a usable skill; second, to get them to pay for their own relief; and, third, to make the experience of going to the workhouse so unpleasant that no one would want to resort to it. Thus, the system's ultimate objective was to reduce the tax burden which the poor represented. This strategy never produced the desired effects; the number of poor people and the expense of relieving them continued to rise. The famines of the 1590s resulted in further parliamentary statutes of 1598 and 1601 which enabled parishes to erect dwellings for the homeless, provide schooling, or purchase apprenticeships for poor or orphaned children. Finally, the Act of Settlement of 1662 allowed overseers of the poor to ship them back to the parishes of their birth.

The Poor Law's combination of carrots and sticks was often cruel and always inefficient. Some parish officials did everything they could to drive the poor away, using the Act of Settlement as an excuse to reduce their tax rolls. Others were more lax, even welcoming and generous, to the unfortunate. But even their generosity could not eradicate poverty. Some historians think that private charity was far more abundant and effective during this period than any of the government's various stratagems. Still, the English Poor Law was one of the first attempts to provide government relief since Roman times. Its recognition that the nation as a whole had a responsibility to care for its least fortunate members, and that local government should be the State-mandated vehicle for that care, was remarkably advanced for its time, far ahead of anything on the continent. Hypocritical, inconsistent, and inadequate as the Poor Law may seem to modern eyes, it probably did help to tide people over during a crisis. Its existence may even help to explain why, despite real famine in the 1590s and 1620s, England did not experience widespread popular rebellion as did, say, France during the same period. This appearance of paternalism, neighborliness, fairness, and generosity by the haves in English society may have alleviated the misery, or at least forestalled the questioning, of the have-nots.

Law and (Dis)order

What happened in this society when religion, paternalism, deference, and neighborliness broke down? Much of the history of crime remains speculative because contemporary records simply do not allow for modern-style crime statistics, and many offenses went unrecorded in any case.[26] The crimes perpetrated by, or inflicted upon, early modern English men and women may be divided, for the sake of convenience, into four types: violence against persons, theft or destruction of property, moral offenses, and riot. To judge from surviving court records and the anecdotal testimony of natives and foreigners, premeditated murder and assault in families were fairly rare. So were rape and infanticide, but this may be an illusion created by the failure to report such transgressions. Rather, most bloodshed in early modern England seems to have been spontaneous, centered around or inspired by drinking and gambling. Aristocrats always went out armed with swords, while working men often bore knives or tools. This, plus a contemporary assumption that dueling or fisticuffs were appropriate ways to settle points of honor or reputation, undoubtedly contributed to impromptu violence.

Still, contemporaries seem to have been far more worried about theft. During a period when the rich were getting richer and the poor poorer, we should not be surprised to learn that three-quarters of assize court prosecutions involved property crimes, that the vast majority of the accused were poor, or that their number rose in times of dearth. In theory, early modern society treated thieves especially harshly. In 1600 theft of goods above the value of one shilling was a felony, punishable by death, and the number of other forms of theft or property damage punishable by death was rising all the time.[27] Not all thieves went to the gallows, however. First, if there were no fatalities, the victim had the choice of whether or not to report the crime. Good neighbors tried to work things out without resorting to the law. If the victim did "raise the hue and cry" or complain to the local constable or JP, the latter could investigate, interrogate witnesses, and make out a warrant for arrest. Since there was no police force and the office of constable was a part-time one, apprehension was uncertain, for the accused could flee easily to another locale. If the constable managed to apprehend the accused, he was brought before the JP. Since there was no such thing as a district attorney, the victim now had a choice as to whether or not to prosecute and under what statute to do so. The victim or the justice might also undervalue the goods stolen so as to avoid the possibility of capital punishment. If both agreed, then the suspect was "bound over" (held) and an indictment drawn up. Then a grand jury, composed of minor but respectable gentry and yeomen, met to determine whether the case went forward or the indictment thrown out. If the latter, the accused went free; if the former, the case was tried at the assizes. The assizes were meetings held twice a year in which two assize judges, royal appointees, arrived at a large market town on their regular circuit to preside over felony cases. The case was tried by attorneys before a regular or "petty" jury, who passed judgment of innocence or guilt. It was up to the assize judges to pass sentence of mercy or death.

At trial, the cards seem to have been stacked against the accused: for example, he or she could only call witnesses at the judge's discretion. Still, a fortunate defendant might yet escape punishment at many points. Jurors might reduce the value of the goods lost so as to prevent capital punishment; a pregnant woman could "plead her belly," postponing it, possibly indefinitely. Some felons escaped via benefit of clergy. This was an ancient custom dating back to the Middle Ages, during which clergy could not be punished by civil courts. To prove that one was a cleric, one was asked to read, for during the Middle Ages only clerics could do so. Literacy was increasing by the sixteenth century, but this loophole remained on the books, so that anyone who could read Psalm 51 – popularly known as the "neck verse" – literally saved his or her neck![28] At trial, a jury might, of course, acquit the accused on the evidence, or even their own feelings of neighborliness: according to one contemporary, "most comonly the simple cuntryman and woman ... are of opynyon that they wold not procure a mans death for all the goods yn the world."[29] In the end, between 20 and 40 percent of those arraigned for felonies in one three-county sample were found not guilty. Even for the remainder, all hope was not lost. Mercy might be bestowed by the judge at sentencing: only about 20–30 percent of those convicted above were sentenced to death. Or the king might, often at the judge's recommendation, issue a pardon at any point before a sentence of death was carried out: about 10 percent so sentenced were so reprieved. Nevertheless, Tudor England executed about 800 people annually.

As this implies, discretion, community feeling, and an awareness of individual circumstances were part of how the law was carried out: victims prosecuted, JPs indicted, and juries convicted as much on the reputation and circumstances of the accused as they did on the evidence. We see this in the case of those laws designed to regulate personal morality and enforce community standards of behavior. The number of such laws multiplied rapidly between 1550 and 1650, in part because of pressure from Puritans, in part because of growing upper-class anxiety over disorder generally. They included the Act of Uniformity and those against recusancy, drunkenness, sexual license and illegitimacy, illegal begging and vagrancy, and unlicensed alehouses. A series of lower courts enforced these laws: quarter sessions (meeting four times a year) and petty sessions, presided over by JPs; borough courts in towns, manorial courts in the country, and archdeacon's and other ecclesiastical courts for moral offenses.

Cooperation with these laws was not always easy to obtain. Take the regulation of alehouses.[30] The ease of brewing ale was (and is) such that almost anyone could open their house as a "pub." A government survey of 1577 found some 15,000 alehouses; by the 1630s that number had doubled. One further reason for this was that alehouses grew increasingly important as community centers after the Reformation. That is, when the newly reformed churches withdrew from hosting wakes, wedding receptions, church ales, and other social events, the alehouses stepped in, with one difference. Whereas the whole community might gather at the church for such events, the local elite would not, generally, enter an alehouse. Alehouses were associated not only with drinking, but also with other, even more dubious activities such as music-making, dancing, gambling, and, in some cases, prostitution and the fencing of goods, not to mention the violence and disorder that always accompanied such pursuits. Consequently, critics viewed the alehouse as the enemy of family life and church attendance. Thus Christopher Hudson opined in 1631: "Alehouses are the nests of Satan where the owls of impiety lurk and where all evil is hatched."[31]

Little wonder that the ruling elite sought to regulate alehouses. From the reign of Edward VI on, the government required such establishments to be licensed by the local JP. This initiative was largely unsuccessful: a survey of 40 townships in Worcestershire in the 1630s reveals the existence of 81 licensed alehouses, and 52 unlicensed. Things were much worse in Lancashire by 1647, where the 83 licensed alehouses were outnumbered by the 143 unlicensed houses. Obviously, in an age without a police force, it was impossible for the local country gentleman to look into every cottage which opened its door to the thirsty. The constables responsible for closing down unregulated alehouses confronted two conflicting concepts of order – the elite's concern for regulation and authority and their fellow villagers' concern for consensus and neighborliness – not to mention some angry drinkers! On a deeper level, the example of alehouses reveals the limits of royal and aristocratic authority: if the community as a whole rejected a law, that law was virtually unenforceable. Ordinary men and women may have been deferential, but only up to a point.

Perhaps the most notorious form of social deviance addressed by the law concerned witchcraft. Contrary to popular belief, witchcraft accusations were not very common during the Middle Ages and it was not until 1542 that a statute against the practice was even passed.[32] Historians have long wondered why there was a sudden rash of witchcraft accusations and prosecutions in England between about 1560 and 1640. Their interest stems from the hope that the phenomenon may tell us something new about the nature of the Reformation, the relationship of men and women, and the character of the village community which produced these accusations. Numerous explanations have been offered. Some see the trend as in some way having been inspired by the rise of the Puritans, though it has been demonstrated that Puritans were no more afraid of witches than other Christians. Others have seen the increase of witchcraft prosecutions as a means of asserting male supremacy over women, since men were almost never accused. It may or may not be a significant counter-argument that at least half the witnesses and accusers were other women. A variant feminist argument contends that women used witchcraft accusations to compete with other women in disputes over reputation and the control of female social space.

Perhaps the most suggestive explanation for the rise of witchcraft accusations was offered by Keith Thomas in *Religion and the Decline of Magic*.[33] Thomas's argument operates on many levels. At the simplest level, he noted that medieval (Catholic) religion had provided consolation for the ever-present disasters and high death rate in pre-modern England, while that of the Reformation did not. In particular, Catholicism offered remedies in the form of prayers and rituals which, according to Catholic belief, were efficacious. That is, if one prayed to St. Margaret, the patron saint of childbirth, one would be safely delivered; if one prayed to St. Oswald, associated in some places with shepherding, one's flock would be protected; and if one thought that one had been bewitched, one could ask the priest for an exorcism. The Reformation continued to emphasize Satan's great power, but it abolished the beliefs and practices which had been used to fight him, leaving early modern English people feeling alone and helpless in the face of misfortune. No wonder that they feared the evil magic of witches and found it a persuasive explanation for misfortune.

But this does not explain why the accused witch was usually female, old, poor, widowed or single, and well known to her accuser. Typically, a poorer, older woman would approach a neighbor for assistance, especially so after the Reformation when the economy began to slump and monasteries and other institutions which had looked after such individuals were largely abolished. Such a beggar, if turned away, might mutter a curse which, given the precarious nature of early modern life, might seem, later, to have come true – hence the subsequent accusation. Thomas's argument places the focus on the better-off *accuser*, whose new self-interested worldview rubbed up against an older notion of community, creating guilt and, at times, recourse to accusation and the law. Historians have not taken Thomas's theory as the last word on the subject. But it does serve to remind us of the power of religious belief to explain the unexplainable; the potential of national economic trends to affect individual lives; the precarious place of women in the local community; and the narrowness and cruelty of which the village neighborhood was capable.

Finally, the village community could transgress the law *en masse*. The most obvious way in which this happened was in revolt or riot. Popular revolt – as opposed to the rebellions led by aristocrats detailed in previous chapters – was a much less serious problem for the later Tudors and early Stuarts than it had been for their predecessors. Much more common during this period were individual riots. Riots may be divided (albeit not exclusively) according to motivation: those, usually based in London, directed against some ethnic or national group; "calendar" riots associated with particular festivals and times of year; demonstrations by unpaid or demobilized soldiers or sailors; and, finally, food or enclosure riots. The first were the result of the xenophobia and anti-Catholicism for which the English were famous during the later sixteenth and early seventeenth centuries. Often, a group of apprentices would attack a foreign merchant or the entourage of a continental ambassador. For example, on July 13, 1618 a crowd of some 4,000 to 5,000 people besieged the Spanish ambassador's house in London after one of his servants accidentally knocked over a child in Chancery Lane. In the end, they were persuaded by the authorities to disperse, but similar incidents sometimes ended in violence and bloodshed.

A second common excuse for riot was a festival gone out of hand. The most famous example of this is the riots which traditionally occurred in London on Shrove Tuesday. From the late Elizabethan period into the 1670s young men, usually apprentices, attacked the brothels and playhouses concentrated in London's suburbs. These riots were large, sometimes involving hundreds, even thousands, of persons. They were also highly ritualized: the rioters were very specific in their targets and behavior, destroying property but not, generally, assaulting persons. Other, smaller, demonstrations might occur during or immediately after wartime when soldiers or sailors might assault government officials, demanding their pay.

Food or enclosure riots generally happened in times of high food prices, when the community's well-being was thought to be jeopardized: examples occurred in Gloucester in 1586, Kent, Somerset, and Sussex in 1596–7, in London throughout the 1590s, and throughout southern England in 1630–1. They often began with women, who were, of course, especially concerned with the business of putting food on the table. They were directed against middlemen such as grain sellers, corn factors, and millers. However, unlike the ethnic riots mentioned above, these demonstrations were usually non-violent, involving theatrical or ritualized gestures and symbols rather than bloodshed: marching, burnings in effigy, rough music, pulling down fences. Clearly, these activities were meant to grab the attention of the ruling elite, inform them of a grievance, and remind them of their paternalistic duties. They were not meant to unhinge the prevailing social order: in fact, enclosure rioters sometimes carried copies of royal proclamations against that hated practice and they often petitioned the local lord or JP for redress. Still, the implied threat of mob violence must always have been apparent to such authority figures. Perhaps because they were outnumbered; perhaps because there was no standing army and the militia was an ineffective tool against its own neighbors; perhaps because, as good paternalists, they often saw the rioters' point of view, they frequently punished the gouging merchants or even, very occasionally, the enclosing landlord. The rioters themselves were rarely punished severely. In this case, the village community asserted itself against the local elite or its subordinate allies and, sometimes, in the short term, won.

This may seem surprising given the Tudor reputation for savage reprisals against rebels and traitors. But rebellion and treason threatened the fabric of the national political order. Local bread and enclosure riots did not. Rather, they may have reinforced that fabric by reasserting the role of the king and the ruling elite to guide the economy. The inhabitants of early modern England – both elite and non-elite – seem to have known when to apply violence and when not to do so; generally, it was a last resort. Rioting was a necessary safety valve which the upper classes were careful and wise not to try to shut off completely. By not doing so, by, instead, redressing the immediate grievances of the rioters, the ruling class enhanced their reputation as paternal rulers and protectors, and so encouraged deference.

What of those who fell out of the Chain or left their villages because of poverty or a lack of opportunity? Were there no alternatives to the pastoral "paradise" outlined above for those who could not succeed or would not conform? Of course there were; for starters, one could go to town.

Cities, Towns, and Internal Trade

In 1600, as in the Middle Ages, cities and towns represented freedom, an alternative social order, and economic opportunity. As we have seen, one alternative to the Poor Law was to take to the roads, which helps to explain why the percentage of English men and women living in cities and towns was on the rise. It has been estimated that by 1550 some 10 percent of English and Welsh people lived in cities of 2,000 or more inhabitants. For our purposes, urban England may be divided into market and county towns, provincial capitals, and London. Salisbury in Wiltshire, Dorchester in Dorset, and Rye in Sussex were good examples of market or county towns. A market town might have about 1,000 people; the county town, seat of the shire or diocese, perhaps several thousand people. But both would swell during a fair, after harvest time, or, in the case of a county town, during the assizes. There were only a few provincial capitals in England: York in the North, Norwich in East Anglia, and Bristol in the West Country. Such cities held between 10,000 and 13,000 people ca. 1600 and had complex economies. They might trade with London or even be involved in international trade. All such towns were connected to the countryside: yeomen and husbandmen brought their grain to sell, minor nobles and gentry came to command the local garrison or to attend meetings of the assize courts and quarter sessions, their sons to attend schools. Thus, these urban centers were closely linked to the rural social Chain, even if they were not part of it.

The reason they were not fully integrated into the traditional Chain of social ranks was that they had long before developed their own hierarchies, based not on birth or land but on mercantile and professional wealth. Since wealth fluctuates and may desert one family as it attaches itself to another, there was more economic, social, and even political mobility in town than in the countryside. At least that's what people thought. Most people knew the myth about Dick Whittington (d. 1423), a poor but industrious apprentice boy who is supposed to have risen to be lord mayor of London through sheer dint of hard work. When later historians examined the facts, it turned out that Whittington was, indeed, lord mayor of London for three terms, but that, far from being poor, he had come from a Gloucester landowning family. Perhaps the point is that cities were *thought* to be wide open centers of opportunity. In reality most were, like the county community, dominated by an oligarchy.

In most towns, the corporation headed that oligarchy. The corporation consisted of the mayor and the town's council or court of aldermen. These officials administered civic government, enforced order, and, generally, made the law. In the sixteenth and early seventeenth centuries, they gave orders to keep the streets lit and clear of refuse, to contain the plague, and to facilitate poor relief. If the town sent representatives to Parliament, the corporation members were frequently the only townsmen who had a vote. In general, they comprised the oldest and wealthiest mercantile families in a town and their rule was self-perpetuating. They alone could appoint to vacancies on the aldermanic council and they were careful to name members of their own families. To further secure their privileged position, they often intermarried and, increasingly in the sixteenth century, sought royal charters enshrining their privileges. They also did their best to maintain good political and social relations with the local aristocracy while trying, at the same time, to preserve their town's independence of it.

Just below the mayor and aldermen in the hierarchy of town government were the guilds or (as they were called in London) livery companies. At the end of the sixteenth century, each small town generally had one guild consisting of all of its merchants and craftsmen. In a big town there would be guilds or companies for each trade or craft. The guild was a sort of combination of Better Business Bureau, trade association for standards and practices, lobbying group, Rotary Club, and trade union all wrapped up into one. It set prices, wages, and standards of workmanship on locally made products. Guilds also founded schools and hospitals for members and their children and they tended to look after widows of deceased guildsmen. As in the Middle Ages, one had to be a member of the local guild (a "freeman," i.e., "free of the guild") in order to set up a shop and pursue trade. Unfortunately, getting into one could be difficult. Guilds were often accused of using high entry fines and strict (or arbitrary) standards of workmanship to keep membership low and, therefore, profits raked in by their members high. Moreover, in most towns, only guild members were considered citizens, though in some towns this encompassed most of the male population. This body of freemen elected a host of lesser officers which kept the town running and in some big towns they, not just the corporation, voted for the MPs. As the sixteenth century wore on, the guild, full of small merchants and tradesmen, often found its economic and political interests at odds with those of the big merchants in the town's corporation, not least because of the widening gap in wealth between the two groups. Moreover, the constant traffic of migrants made it more difficult for the guild to maintain its control of trade. Increasing numbers of merchants sought to avoid guild control by setting up their shops just outside the town's walls and, therefore, the guild's jurisdiction.

Despite in-migration from the countryside, most big towns went through a period of decline or stagnation in the sixteenth century. There were many reasons for this: the Dissolution of the Monasteries (which did away with much business), the increasing decentralization of wool manufacture into provincial market towns and villages (which hurt larger regional centers like Norwich), and the rise of London as the country's chief port. In 1520 London was already far and away the greatest city in England with perhaps 60,000 people. By 1600 it had grown to about 200,000 people and by the end of the seventeenth century it would reach over half a million.[34] This was twice the rate of growth being experienced in the rest of the country. No wonder that James I worried that "with time England will only be London and the whole country be left waste."[35] In fact, while London's phenomenal expansion offended believers in the Great Chain such as King James, it served as a demographic safety valve, absorbing people from the countryside who could find little hope elsewhere. At a higher social level, London provided opportunities for younger sons and apprentices to make their fortunes, while the landed elite could come to court and sample the delights of the capital's cultural and intellectual life.

In fact, London's growth could not have been due to the reproduction of its own population, for early modern London's death rate was higher than its birth rate: out of every 1,000 people, 35 would be born each year, but 40 would die.[36] The reasons for this are not difficult to understand. The metropolis was crowded and full of disease and crime (with an average life expectancy of only 25–30 years); there was a shortage of female immigrants; and apprentices, who comprised a high proportion of London's population, were forbidden to marry. Thus, in order to grow at the rate noted above, between 6,000 and 8,000 new people had to come to London every year. Put another way, it would appear that about one-sixth of all English people lived in London at some time in their lives.

According to historian E. A. Wrigley, these facts had a profound effect on England as a whole. First, the massive city had to be fed. As a result, English farms were forced to improve production rates and grain merchants to improve distribution. In the years following 1600 a true market economy developed and England's transportation system improved via the dredging of rivers and better roads, carriages, wagons, and carrying services. The English shipping industry likewise expanded to service not only foreign trade but also the crucial coastal trade that supplied London with fish and coal. By 1700 sophisticated credit facilities, a penny post, and newspapers would arise, in part to facilitate trade and communication between capital and countryside.

In the meantime, the experience of London must have had profound social, cultural, and psychological effects on all of its immigrants. Imagine having grown up in the countryside in a small and relatively quiet village, with its own calendar and traditions. Everyone knew everyone else. Now imagine arriving in London to find more people crowded into one place than you had ever experienced in your life. The sights, the noise, the smells would have been nearly overwhelming. Many complained of London's stink and filth. In 1606 Thomas Dekker (ca. 1570–1632) was more concerned with noise and crowding:

In every street, carts and coaches make such a thundering as if the world ran upon wheels: at every corner, men, women, and children meet in such shoals, that posts are set up of purpose to strengthen the houses, lest with jostling one another they should shoulder them down. Besides, hammers are beating in one place, tubs hooping in another, pots clinking in a third, water tankards running at tilt in a fourth.[37]

Unlike your experience in the narrow world of the village, you would encounter individuals from every part of England, with different accents and, perhaps, different religious and social traditions from yours. Your own customs would soon be left behind as irrelevant. Where, in the village, the sun and agricultural seasons (spring for planting, fall for harvest) determined time, now your day ran according to your master's watch; your job as a servant or a tradesman being carried on irrespective of the season. Disease and sudden death would have been even more prevalent than in the village. This, plus changing economic opportunities, meant that your business relationships and friendships would be made and broken far more quickly, far more casually, and far more often than in the village. While the city provided economic opportunity, it might also be a very lonely place for someone used to close, paternalistic village life. But if you had found the village community stifling, with its lack of privacy and enforcement of communal norms by your neighbors through rough music, skimmingtons, gossip, etc., you might revel in the freedom and anonymity to be found in the city.

London was at once the capital, court, legal center, chief port, and entertainment center for the entire country. During the early modern period it set the tone for English fashion as never before or since. In many ways, London was really two cities joined by a river (see map 10): London proper (i.e., within the walls) and Westminster, city and court. First, let us examine the river. The River Thames was the reason for London's existence in the first place. As with the English Channel and the seas around the British Isles, the Thames was a highway, connecting the southern interior of England with the Channel, those seas, and the continent. London sat at a crossroads: the last point on the river wide enough for big ships to dock; the first point narrow enough for land traffic to cross. This made London an intersection between traffic north–south and east–west. London Bridge (see plate 11) had linked the north and south banks of the Thames since the twelfth century. In fact, London mostly developed on its northern bank; to the south, outside of the jurisdiction of the city fathers, was the suburb of Southwark. Here flourished theaters such as the Rose and the Globe, bear-gardens (for bear- and bull-baiting), and taverns. In short, if you wanted an exciting – or a dangerous – time in London, you headed across the bridge.

But for most Londoners, the crucial connection was between London in the east and Westminster in the west. Since the road between London and Westminster, known as the Strand, was still not entirely (or reliably) paved in the sixteenth and early seventeenth centuries, the river continued to be London's chief east–west link via the watermen and their barges, which operated as water-taxis for its inhabitants. It was also its chief source of wealth, for the river below London Bridge and to the east was full of docks, and ships, lighters, and barges waiting to

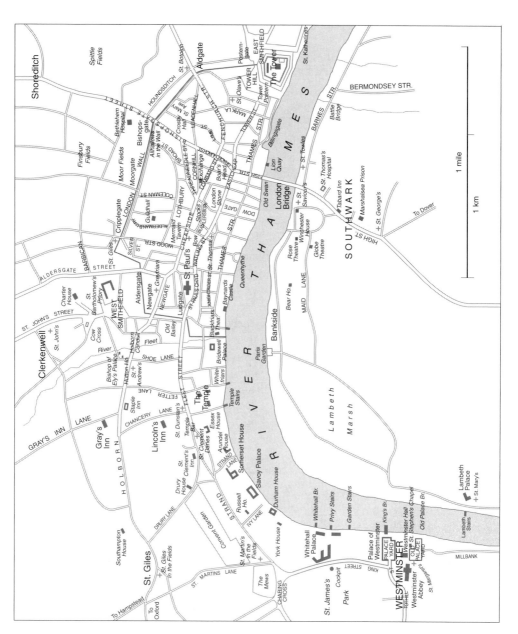

Map 10 *Early modern London.*

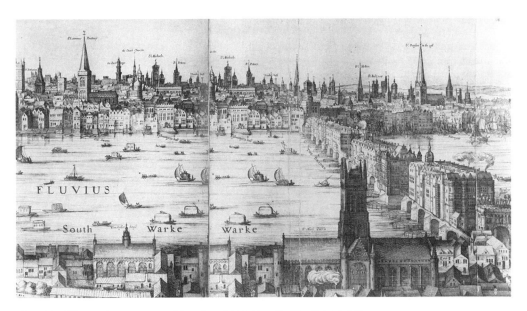

Plate 11 *Visscher's panorama of London, 1616 (detail). The British Library.*

use them. These brought immense profits into the oldest part of London, later known as "the City" (map 10). "The City" is modern shorthand for the financial district which still sits within the square mile bounded by the old Roman city walls. Here, ca. 1600, might be found the Guildhall, London's city hall, where its lord mayor and 25 aldermen met to govern the metropolis; numerous smaller halls which housed the livery companies associated with each trade; and the Royal Exchange, built by Sir Thomas Gresham (1519?–79) in 1566–7, where merchants met to strike deals. The merchants who struck those deals helped make London England's greatest concentration of wealth. Loans from the London corporation and merchant community were crucial to the government, especially in times of crisis. That, combined with the prestige of its civic government and its great population, made the city a vital ally or a dangerous enemy to any royal regime.

The city skyline was dominated by the spires of 96 parish churches and, towering over even them, old St. Paul's Cathedral. The other landmark recognizable to all Londoners was the Tower of London, at once a former royal palace, a fortress that dominated the river approaches to the city, and a royal prison for political prisoners of the highest rank. Here, the Tudors' most prominent victims had met their ends. Apart from these great buildings, London within the walls was a maze of narrow medieval alleys and courts dominated by multi-story ramshackle wood and plaster buildings, their eaves projecting into the street. Many had been thrown up hurriedly to deal with its population explosion and were none too safe. These narrow lanes and rickety buildings, lacking modern sewer facilities or street lighting, help to explain why London was such a dangerous place and, more particularly, why its death rate was so high. Such overcrowded conditions bred crime, disease, and fire.

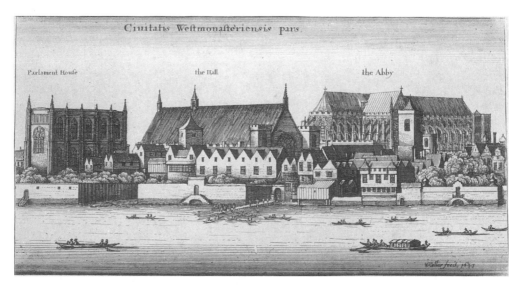

Plate 12 *A view of Westminster, by Hollar. Palace of Westminster Collection.*

No wonder the royal family had long since abandoned the Tower and the city within the walls to move west, upriver and upwind, to the network of palaces around Westminster (map 10). Unlike neighboring London, Westminster was not an independent city with its own charter and government but a royal borough and the seat of royal government. At Westminster might be found a complex of buildings which formed the nation's administrative heart (see plate 12). First, there was Westminster Abbey, where English monarchs were crowned and, prior to 1820, buried. Close by was Westminster Hall, originally a part of Westminster Palace but in 1600 the site of the courts of King's Bench, Common Pleas, and Chancery. The law courts drew the elite to London, for the complications of land inheritance and purchase caused frequent litigation. Another such drawing card was Westminster Palace, located on the river, which was the site of the Houses of Parliament. This ancient structure was donated by Henry VIII to Parliament when he acquired Whitehall, just a few yards away, in 1529. The building was never adequate, either as a royal palace or the site of a legislature. It was to burn down in 1834 and be replaced by the present, far more splendid, Palace of Westminster. But the most significant attraction to London for the upper classes was the court at Whitehall. This massive, disorganized series of buildings, consisting of well over 1,000 rooms, had been built for Cardinal Wolsey as York Place. Henry VIII confiscated and renamed it in 1529. Henceforth, Whitehall was where the great offices of Tudor and early Stuart government, such as the Privy Council and Exchequer, met; indeed, to this day the word "Whitehall" is synonymous with government in Britain. This was where the king or queen attended the Privy Council; appeared in the Presence Chamber; and presided over elaborate balls, plays, masques, or State dinners. This was where the monarch's chief ministers and foreign ambassadors might be found and conversed with, privately if necessary. This was where the latest play or poem or fashion or invention often made its first appearance. Most intriguingly, this was the place where the sovereign himself, God's lieutenant on earth, might be approached and begged for favor. Courtiers thronged Whitehall's galleries hoping to be noticed for bravery or beauty or talent or wit. Most failed: court annals are full of the rueful stories of aspiring courtiers who spent the bulk of their youth and fortunes sacrificing their self-respect and good reputations in false flattery and base cringing, all in pursuit of the mirage of royal favor, fame, or fortune. Nevertheless, if one wished to rise in the world or found a great family in 1600, one went to court.

In order to be close to all of this opportunity, the aristocracy increasingly followed the court by moving west. As we have seen, many young gentlemen acquired a smattering of legal knowledge and social polish at the Inns of Court, four law schools (the Middle Temple, Inner Temple, Lincoln's Inn, and Gray's Inn) just west of the city within the walls. Before the Reformation, wealthy bishops had built enormous palaces along the Strand. After the confiscations of the mid-sixteenth century these palaces were awarded to great courtiers, many of whom renovated or rebuilt them. Thus, Protector Somerset built Somerset House and the earl of Essex, Essex House. The Russell family, earls of Bedford, had even bigger plans. They acquired a parcel of former Church land just west of the City and north of the Strand called Covent (i.e., Convent) Garden. In the 1630s they commissioned the architect Inigo Jones (1573–1652) to design accommodation for gentlemen who attended the royal court or the law courts. The result was the first London square, a form of civic design intended to provide airy yet private housing. During the seventeenth century, the ambitious aristocrats who flocked to court, along with rising merchants and professionals, would push even further westward, leading to the building of additional squares throughout what became known as the West End of London.

Foreign Trade, Exploration, and Colonization

London, like most cities, rose or fell on the profits from trade. At the end of the Middle Ages, international trade was dominated by great trading companies, the most famous of which was the Hanseatic League. The Hanseatic League was a union of merchants from Northern Germany who had been given the privilege to trade with certain countries, including England. Such leagues and unions were not investment opportunities; rather, they were like modern trade associations – except that they held a monopoly. As with urban guilds, if one wanted to trade, it was necessary to be a member in good standing. To maintain their monopolies, they might build fleets of warships or lobby governments to keep out interlopers. In 1407 the English began to carve out a piece of the lucrative wool trade in Northern Europe by chartering their own rival to the Hanseatic League, the Merchant Adventurers. In theory, they were a national company, but most Merchant Adventurers were Londoners. This led to London's increasing domination of that trade and the gradual decline of other wool ports, for no English subject could send wool overseas who was not a Merchant Adventurer. Thus, between 1500 and 1600 the Merchant Adventurers and the port of London dominated England's foreign trade in wool, which comprised at least three-quarters of the nation's foreign trade in general. Before 1550 they shipped mainly raw wool to the continent for finishing; after 1550 wool cloth was finished in England itself. This wool was transported from London to some great European port, usually Antwerp, where it was distributed to the continent. The Merchant Adventurers persuaded Parliament to wrest English trading privileges from the Hanseatic League in 1553, then pushed successfully to have the Hanseatic merchants expelled from England altogether in 1598.

As their parliamentary influence implies, the Merchant Adventurers were fabulously wealthy and powerful, the greatest of them rivaling important nobles in these respects. No government could afford to offend or ignore them, for their loans, their ships, and their ability to move goods might come in very handy in time of war. Within the big port cities, especially London, they played a similar political role to the nobility in the countryside; that is, they dominated corporation and city government. For example, between 1550 and 1580 nearly every lord mayor of London was a Merchant Adventurer. These men lived in great multi-story, multi-chimneyed houses, their rooms decorated with molded plaster ceilings, expensive tapestries, and ornate carved furniture, their presses brimming with gold and silver plate, their closets bulging with expensive gowns lined with velvet and fur. And yet, by the end of the Tudor period, their power and privilege was crumbling.

The main reason for this was the increasing stagnation of the wool trade. The wool trade was England's one major industry through the first half of the early modern period; its tentacles reached deep into the countryside, connecting remote villages with market towns and big cities. Shepherds and farm wives raised sheep in all parts of England, but especially in the rugged and forested country of the North, West, and Wales. These sheep were shorn in spring. The wool was carded or combed in the village, then spun into wool thread and woven into wool cloth for sale to big London merchants (i.e., Merchant Adventurers). At the beginning of the sixteenth century, the last two steps in the manufacturing process took place in big towns, but by its end, technological improvements in spinning machines and looms made it possible to farm out even this part of the process to smaller towns and country villages, hence a decline in urban manufacture.

Wool had been a very lucrative commodity through the boom years of the Yorkist and early Tudor periods. But by about 1550 this trade began to experience a century of stagnation or slow growth, punctuated by dramatic slumps in 1551–2, 1562–4, 1571–3, 1586–7, 1614–16, 1621–4, 1641–2, and the 1650s. One reason for the leveling off of wool exports was the political, religious, and military situation of Europe during the period 1550–1650. The Merchant Adventurers' shipments to Antwerp were disrupted by the Wars of Religion, the Dutch revolt, the war against Spain, and, from 1618 to 1648, the Thirty Years' War. As a result, after 1568, Antwerp was often closed to English trade. While the

Merchant Adventurers found other ports in these storms (Emden, Hamburg, Stade), none was as convenient to them or to their customers as Antwerp. In addition, wool prices began to fall at the end of the sixteenth century because the European market was flooded. The inhabitants of the continent had enough heavy English wool. English manufacturers responded to this situation by developing new, lighter, cheaper forms of wool cloth known as the "new draperies." These were moderately successful, leading to some good years at the beginning of the seventeenth century. But the overall foreign demand for wool continued to lessen and its price to fall. During the bad years noted above merchant incomes stagnated, clothworkers lost their jobs, and farm families were unable to supplement their incomes in areas highly dependent on the trade, such as the West Country, Kent, Suffolk, and the north Midlands. Other areas saw regional industries pick up the slack: the mining of tin in Cornwall, lead in Derbyshire and Somerset, and coal around Newcastle and in Nottinghamshire and North Wales; ironmaking in Kent and Sussex; steelworking in and about Sheffield; pottery in Staffordshire; and shipbuilding along the Thames estuary. But none of these undertakings was large enough to have national significance. In early modern England, for good or ill, wool was still king.

The decline of wool was a problem for the country at large and disastrous for the Merchant Adventurers in particular. The Crown, desperate to save the wool industry, began to encourage other companies to find new markets for England's chief commodity. It granted royal charters to the Muscovy Company (1555), the Spanish Company (1577), the Eastland Company (to trade with the Baltic, 1579), the Turkey (later the Levant) Company (1581), the Senegal Adventurers (1588, later the Royal Africa Company), the East India Company (1600), the Virginia Company (1606), and the Massachusetts Bay Company (1629). In most cases these organizations were originally intended to sell wool to the area concerned, but in order to maintain profitability they often found it necessary to export fish, tin, or, when all else failed, gold in return for lucrative commodities like silks, spices, and, later, tea in the case of the Levant and East India Companies; timber and naval stores by the Eastland Company; and, most notoriously, African human beings, sold into slavery in the New World by the Royal Africa Company. The later companies were founded with little expectation of assisting the wool trade: the Virginia Company was interested in gold mining but eventually specialized in tobacco; the Massachusetts Bay Company, animal pelts. These new trades led to the revival of ports other than London, such as Bristol, Exeter, Hull, Newcastle, or Southampton.

All of the above enterprises were royal monopolies. That is, trade remained unfree, channeled by the government for its own purposes and toward its own friends. Often, a group of merchants or courtiers fronting for merchant partners would offer the Crown a tempting cash payment to secure their privileges. The East India Company had the potential to benefit a wider clientele, for it was the first joint-stock company in England. Anyone could buy stock in the company, which mounted its own voyages. Thus, as with all stock companies, profit and loss were *shared*. Still, because the French and the Dutch already had a foothold in the Asian trade, it would be half a century before the East India Company made anybody rich. In any case, not even this venture had much of an effect on the great mass of the unemployed.

This was not the only reason that the English began to look beyond existing products, markets, and routes to those which could be discovered through exploration and established through colonization. English men and women had noticed how Spain, a poor, disunited country with dynastic problems prior to 1492, had, within a generation, become a world power. Tudor monarchs sought a piece of the same action. The discovery of a route to the wealth of the East or to new sources of wealth in the West might solve the Crown's money problems as they had for the Spanish monarchy. Thus, the earliest English explorers and colonists left their homeland to seek out, first, new markets for the flagging wool industry; second, new sources of wealth for the royal Treasury; and, third, new areas of vulnerability for England's enemies, such as Spain.

Unfortunately, England's location and late start meant that English adventurers and merchants would be limited to less desirable routes and colder, less hospitable climates in the northern hemisphere. Put simply, by 1600, all the good colonies were taken. The geographical point is made easily by looking at a map. If you sail due west from "the sceptered isle," you do not bump into China, India, or the tropical paradises of the Caribbean as Columbus did; instead you run into Newfoundland. Thus, in the 1490s, when Europeans dreamed of finding an easy route to the riches of the Orient, Henry VII supported John and Sebastian Cabot (fl. 1461–98 and 1474–1557, respectively) in their search for a *northwest* passage to Asia. In 1553 the Crown sponsored a similar attempt to find a northeast passage around Russia. Both operations were doomed by the pack ice of the North Pole. The English never found a convenient route to the fabled East.

When the English tried to trade in southern waters, either with South America or India, they ended up having to fight the nations which had gotten there first. Hence the raids of Drake, Frobisher, and Hawkins that eventually helped provoke war with Spain. Similarly, in 1623 the Dutch massacred an English trading colony at Amboyna in the Moluccas. From this point on, English East India ships would be armed in preparation for literal trade war. By the late seventeenth century, the English East India Company was fielding whole armies in India and fleets in the Indian Ocean, ready to fight the Dutch, the French, and their allies among the native population in order to force their trade on that population.

Long before this, the English realized that the most effective way to infringe upon the Spanish, Dutch, or French trading position was to establish permanent bases or trading posts of their own in the New World. The earliest such attempts, sponsored by groups of adventurers and courtiers like Sir Walter Ralegh, were all abortive, though they did manage to claim for England a portion of the eastern seaboard which they dubbed "Virginia," after the Virgin Queen. Only in 1607 did a consortium led by Sir Thomas Smith (1558?–1625) succeed in establishing a permanent colony in Virginia at the headwaters of a river which they named the James, after the new king who had ascended in 1603.

But Jamestown did not really get off the ground until after 1610. The colonists discovered that, while Virginia soil contains no gold and is not especially favorable to the growing of English wheat and barley, it will grow tobacco. The habit of taking, or smoking, tobacco was just beginning to be popular in England, despite the prescient opposition of King James. In 1619, the colony discovered an even more sinister road to profit: the importation of African slaves to do the hard work of planting and harvesting the tobacco plant. Thus, within a dozen years of the founding of the first viable English colony in North America, the cruel foundations of the plantation/slave economy had been laid. Tobacco and slaves allowed the colony to survive, but it did not, at first, prosper. By 1635 Jamestown and the surrounding area had a population of 5,000, but it was bankrupt. Eventually, the government stepped in and made Virginia a Crown colony, the first of what would be 13 such colonies on the eastern seaboard of North America.

The English colonies of the New World offered solutions to two additional problems vexing the mother country. First, they provided an alternative to the Poor Law for many who could not make a go of it in England. Second, they offered a refuge for those who could no longer put up with England's religious rules. In 1608 a congregation of Puritan separatists emigrated to Leyden in the Netherlands. In 1620, about 100 from this group returned to England via Plymouth and then embarked on the *Mayflower* for what would become the Plymouth Plantation. This colony, too, had a difficult first winter, but, not least because of good relations with the native population, it survived and grew. The Massachusetts Bay Company, a joint-stock company chartered in 1629, established a much larger settlement around Boston which absorbed the Plymouth community in 1691. Its charter allowed for self-government and its leaders, notably Governor John Winthrop (1588–1649), consciously set out to found a Puritan "New Jerusalem," a "city on a hill" where Scriptural liturgy and morality could be enforced free from the persecution of Church of England clerics like Archbishops Whitgift and Laud (see chapters 5 and 7). While they sought freedom for their own form of religion, they banned other religious groups, as well as traditional Christmas celebrations and other calendar customs. But most Massachusetts Bay colonists came for economic opportunity, not out of religious conviction. Poor people driven out of England by bad harvests and a poor economy, as well as the less poor searching for cheap, plentiful land, chafed under a religious regime that was less tolerant than that of the mother country. In response, a Salem clergyman named Roger Williams (ca. 1603–83) founded a colony at Rhode Island, based upon religious toleration for Protestants. Later, in 1632, George Calvert, Lord Baltimore (ca. 1580–1632), a Catholic, received royal permission to establish Maryland, which eventually enacted toleration for all Christians, including Roman Catholics.

The English colonies of North America proved to be of limited commercial or military significance before, say, 1650. Yet, between 1629 and 1642, about 60,000 English men and women made the dangerous voyage across the Atlantic. Unknowingly, they laid the foundations for a new nation and civilization in North America.

Cultural Life

Before returning to the chronological narrative of English history, it is important to say something about the cultural life of Elizabethan, Jacobean, and Caroline England, for the years 1558 to 1642 saw an efflorescence of culture that was unprecedented in size, scope, and quality in English history. Never before had the English excelled at so many artistic and intellectual pursuits. Why should this have been so? Certainly, the growth of London, the prominence of the court, and the relative freedom and wealth commanded by the ruling elite all created conditions which made art possible. But we cannot explain why these opportunities were taken; even less can we explain why they resulted in the miracles of Shakespeare's *King Lear*, Byrd's masses, Dowland's lute music, Hilliard's miniatures, Jones's Banqueting House, or the King James Bible.

Perhaps the first condition for the creation of art is the existence of an audience, preferably one which is willing to both pay the artist and supply his or her subject matter. Prior to the Reformation, the principal patron for English art was the Church. But the break with Rome was accompanied by the destruction of much existing religious art, the proscription of new images, and the financial decline of that institution. Fortunately for scholarship and the arts, this wealth was deflected into the hands of a royal house and aristocracy willing to spend it on cultural endeavors. Admittedly, the Crown's patronage of writers and artists was usually indirect, especially under the frugal Elizabeth I. That is, apart from the presentation of tournaments, pageants, and processions, especially on her Accession Day (November 17), the queen commissioned few works of art; apart from the musicians of her Chapel Royal, she paid few artists. She was far more likely to give a poet or a painter, most especially the author of a literary product which glorified her, a court office or a lucrative monopoly. Direct patronage in the form of a commission was easier to obtain from a great nobleman, such as the earl of Leicester. Still, the monarch's personality and activities, and those of her entourage, provided subject matter for art and the court was the most important venue for catching the attention of such a patron. That does not mean that all or even most English art was produced at or for the court. But the court was the primary center for the production of culture, and fashions in art or dress either originated or made their debut from Europe there. In the following paragraphs we will touch briefly upon various forms of art, always beginning at court and moving outward to the productions of the city and countryside.

Generally, the most dramatic and expensive peacetime activity in which monarchs engage is building. Henry VIII was a great builder and renovator of royal palaces but his children were too short-lived or too poor to follow his lead. As a result, most of the great buildings put up from 1547 to 1603 were aristocratic, not royal, palaces – the prodigy houses noted earlier in this chapter. Elizabeth's successor, James I, was no more comfortable financially, but he was far more willing to go into debt, and he was more able to do so because of peace with Spain in 1604. He commissioned Inigo Jones to build the Banqueting House at

Whitehall and the Queen's House at Greenwich. Jones had studied the neoclassical designs of the Italian architect Andrea Palladio (1518–80), and so his buildings represented a radical departure from the old Gothic style in vogue until the mid-16th century. Elsewhere, as we have seen, Jones erected the first large-scale housing development, and the prototype of the London square, for the earl of Bedford at Covent Garden. In the countryside, the Reformation put an end to church building in the grand style; rather, as indicated above, this was a great age for the building of country houses.

The Elizabethan was not a great age for English painting. Indeed, the queen probably set portraiture in England back for half a century by her government's careful regulation and censorship of her image to ensure that she always be portrayed as she was early in her reign. In any case, there was, arguably, no portraitist in Elizabethan England of the quality of Hans Holbein to grab her attention. The possible exception to this generalization was the miniaturist Nicholas Hilliard (ca. 1547–1619), who created exquisite portraits of Elizabethan courtiers on a small scale. A few aristocrats, such as Leicester and Essex, engaged in collecting: the former had over 200 pictures including 130 portraits. But it was not until the Jacobean period that the visual arts received really effective royal and aristocratic patronage. This occurred because James I's son, Prince Charles (1600–49), along with a number of aristocrats, began to take an avid interest in the visual arts and, especially, the artists of Europe. In particular, Charles encouraged his father to bring over and patronize Peter Paul Rubens (1577–1640) and Anthony van Dyck (1599–1641). This patronage resulted in masterpieces such as the former's ceiling for the Banqueting House, *The Apotheosis of James I*; and the latter's series of portraits of the royal family. As king, Charles I (1625–49) assembled the greatest art collection in Europe by asking his diplomats and aristocrats on the "Grand Tour" to purchase desirable items. George Villiers, duke of Buckingham (1592–1628; see plate 14, p. 215), Thomas Howard, earl of Arundel (1585–1646), and other courtiers emulated the king by filling their residences with the finest paintings, sculpture, furniture, metalwork, woodwork, porcelain, embroidery, and tapestry hangings the continent had to offer. There were no public art galleries, so the only way to experience such visual splendor was to go to court or visit some nobleman's house. Fortunately, such buildings were at least open to gentle visitors. Indeed, such collecting (as well as elaborate dress) was intended to impress important visitors with the patron's status, wealth, and lineage. Charles I had exquisite taste and loved beautiful things, but when Van Dyck painted him standing with nonchalant dignity surrounded by the royal regalia (see plate 15, p. 219), the two undoubtedly meant to convey a more particular message about monarchy.

That message was, for the most part, aimed at the ruling elite. Most English people were never exposed to such sophisticated art. Still, court styles in art did have an influence beyond Whitehall. For example, the sovereign's Chapel Royal, which included such masters as Thomas Tallis, William Byrd (1543–1623), and Orlando Gibbons (1583–1625), was the premier center for the production of Church music, which was then borrowed by cathedral and Church choirs around the country. The court also produced instrumental dance music for balls and madrigals, lute or keyboard music for quiet hours from the likes of Byrd and John Dowland (ca. 1563–1626), which was often published, and sung or played in aristocratic, gentle, and mercantile households. Toward the end of the reign of Elizabeth I the court began to combine all of the art forms available ca. 1600 in formal choreographed pageants with allegorical or mythological plots, spoken lines, elaborate sets, costumes, and music. These masques, as they came to be known, achieved their greatest sophistication, splendor, and expense under James I and Charles I thanks to the pen of Ben Jonson (1572–1637) and the scenic designs of Inigo Jones. Their intent was usually to glorify the monarch; however, they, too, were restricted to a courtly audience, so it is difficult to argue that they had much propaganda value for any but a small circle of nobles and gentry.

Beyond the court, urban corporations maintained minstrels or waits to perform on ceremonial occasions. Ordinary people sang carols in church, and folk songs and printed ballads in taverns and out-of-doors. The ability to read and sing from ballad sheets reminds us that literacy was rising in late Tudor and early Stuart England. With the increasing number of endowed parish schools, and the printing press, much popular culture was transmitted through cheap, easy-to-read chapbooks and almanacs. But most such culture was traditional and oral: that is, its authorship was unknown and it was transmitted by word of mouth from generation to generation and place to place by roving minstrels, ballad singers, and players who often appeared at fairs and markets. In 1606 one contemporary complained that many people knew more about Robin Hood, a legendary figure since the fourteenth century, than they did the Bible. The popular calendar was full of holidays like Shrove Tuesday (the day before Ash Wednesday), St. Valentine's Day, and May Day which once had religious significance but had now become an excuse to relax and have a good time singing, drinking, playing football, or, on the last of these, dancing around a Maypole. Puritan social reformers scorned such activities, but other members of the elite were not so hostile. Early in the seventeenth century James I even issued the *Book of Sports*, condoning a wide variety of recreations and revels which could be performed on the Sabbath.

The art form for which the Elizabethan and Jacobean age is best known was, arguably, the theater. The first plays in the English language were medieval mystery and mummers' plays, mounted on religious feast days. During the sixteenth century, strolling bands of players presented short secular interludes in private houses. By the time of Elizabeth's accession, full-fledged five-act plays were being mounted by young men at the universities and Inns of Court. The greatest of these university wits was Christopher Marlowe (1564–93), who wrote *Dr. Faustus, Tamburlaine*, and the *History of Edward II*. The queen occasionally attended such productions while on progress or on visits to the Inns for their Christmas revels. She enjoyed these plays so much that she began to encourage their performance at court, establishing the office of Master of the Revels in 1579 to supervise their production. She also gave royal protection to a company of actors, the Queen's Men, as did Leicester and other court peers. This allowed such companies to mount plays for paying audiences.

Such protection was necessary because the law was hostile to roving bands of masterless men: in particular, the Poor Law of 1572 outlawed "common players in interludes & minstrels, not belonging to any baron of this realm" (14 Eliz. 1, c. 5). Actors ran into the stiffest opposition from the civic authorities of London, who disliked the idea of large numbers of ordinary people – their employees – idling away their time watching plays. In fact, large crowds of any sort were thought to be dangerous. This explains why the earliest theaters were built outside of the city walls, beyond Guildhall jurisdiction. The first was the Red Lion, established north of the city in Whitechapel in 1567. In 1576 James Burbage (d. 1597) founded a public playhouse called, appropriately enough, the Theatre in the London suburb of Shoreditch. In 1577 a large open-air public theater entitled the Rose was established in unincorporated Southwark, on the south bank of the Thames. This was followed in 1598 by the Globe. Here, all London could come together in the afternoon to see the latest play. But even here, hierarchy obtained: the wealthy sat in upper boxes, the middling orders below them, and relatively common people in the large open area on the ground level – hence their designation as "groundlings."

As readers of this text will know, one player and writer among the Lord Chamberlain's Men was a young immigrant to London from Stratford-upon-Avon named Shakespeare. No historian, and quite possibly no scholar, can do justice to, let alone explain, the dramatic power, the beauty of language, or the insight into the human condition demonstrated in the plays of William Shakespeare. For over 20 years, among a host of talented authors including Marlowe and Jonson, Shakespeare produced a series of comedies (*Much Ado About Nothing*; *A Midsummer Night's Dream*; *Twelfth Night*; *The Merry Wives of Windsor*), histories (*Richard II*; *Henry IV, Parts 1 and 2*; *Richard III*), and, above all, tragedies (*Hamlet*; *Macbeth*; *King Lear*; *Romeo and Juliet*) that delighted Londoners then and continue to speak to humanity now. It remains for the historian to note that these and similar miracles would not have been possible without, first, the royal protection and patronage which gave Shakespeare and his compatriots their start; second, the courage and ruthlessness of impresarios like Richard Burbage (ca. 1567–1619), who drove their authors and players hard in order to scrape together a profit; third, the rise of a popular audience with some disposable income and an interest in being entertained; and, finally and most miraculously, the development of the English language to a point of sufficient refinement and versatility by the end of the Tudor century that it could be deployed by playwrights to such great effect, and yet still be understandable to people of all social ranks.

Ultimately, the language of Elizabethan, Jacobean, and Caroline England may be its most powerful and lasting cultural achievement, for it was during this period that English became eloquent, expressive, and comprehensible in a wide variety of forms of writing. Historians have offered a number of reasons for this development. First, there was the impetus given to greater directness and refinement of the language by the controversies over the divorce and Reformation. Related to this was the temporary relaxation of censorship under Edward VI and, with it, the increasing use of the printing press. Protestantism was also associated with the growth in schooling and rise in literacy noted above, which fueled a hunger for the books so printed. Where 800 books had been published in the decade 1520–9, that number rose to 3,000 in 1590–1600. Many of these books went to the great libraries of the nobility, gentry, or scholarly community: the mathematician and astrologer John Dee (1527–1608) had a personal library of 4,000 books. But an even greater number seem to have trickled down to the lower levels of society: in the city of Canterbury in the 1560s only 8 percent of household inventories (usually compiled when someone died) listed books. By the 1620s that percentage had risen to 45.

Most of these books are little known today, but some have achieved immortality. We have noted the philosophical and historical works of Bacon, Foxe, and Ralegh, as well as the plays of Marlowe, Jonson, and Shakespeare. In poetry, the English language made possible the works of Sidney noted above, Shakespeare's *Sonnets* (1609), Spenser's *Faerie Queene*, Michael Drayton's (1563–1631) epic poems, and, later, John Donne's (1571–1632) and George Herbert's (1593–1633) metaphysical poetry and the cavalier lyrics of Sir John Suckling (1609–41) and Abraham Cowley (1618–67). In geography, Richard Hakluyt (1552?–1616) wrote the *Principal Navigations, Voyages and Discoveries of the English Nation* (1589, 1598–1600) to tell the story of early English exploration, while William Camden (1551–1623) described the homeland in *Britannia* (1586, trans. into English 1610). English history was recorded in Raphael Holinshed's (ca. 1520–ca. 1580) *Chronicles* (1577) and Camden's *Annales* (1615, trans. 1635). In theology, Richard Hooker (1554–1600) provided the first thoroughgoing rationale for the Church of England in his *Laws of Ecclesiastical Polity* (many volumes published between 1593 and 1682). In a lighter and more popular vein, there was the satire of Thomas Nashe (1567–1601) and the doggerel of the "water poet" (formerly a "cabbie," as it were, on the Thames) John Taylor (1580?–ca. 1653).

But if one had to sum up the Elizabethan and Jacobean achievement in language and, indeed, in culture generally, one might best turn to a work commenced at the behest of the Crown which became the most widely read and influential book in the English-speaking world: the Authorized Version of the Bible. It was commissioned by King James I in 1604 and labored over by a panel of 54 scholars for seven years. The King James version was, in fact, heavily dependent on the scholarship of previous English translations – that of Coverdale and Tyndale, the Geneva Bible, the Bishops' Bible, etc. Whatever the source of its scholarship or theology, its language has captured the imagination of all users of English to the present day, from its opening "In the beginning..." Consider these passages from Isaiah foretelling the coming of a savior, later set by George Frideric Handel (1685–1759) in his great oratorio, *Messiah*:

Comfort ye, comfort ye My people, saith your God, Speak ye comfortably to Jerusalem, and cry unto her, that her warfare is accomplished, that her iniquity is pardoned.... The voice of him that crieth in the wilderness; prepare ye the way of the Lord; make straight in the desert a highway for our God. Every valley shall be exalted, and every mountain and hill made low; the crooked and the rough places plain. And the glory of the Lord shall be revealed.... The people that walked in darkness have seen a great light; and they that dwell in the land of the shadow of death, upon them hath the light shined. For unto us a child is born, unto us a Son is given, and the government shall be upon His shoulder; and His name shall be called Wonderful, Counsellor, The Mighty God, The Everlasting Father, the Prince of Peace. (Isaiah 40: 1–5; 9: 2, 6)

Modern translations are more accurate to the ancient Hebrew and Greek, but it was language like this which captured the imaginations of contemporary English men and women and convinced them that their struggles against Spain, Catholicism, and the Devil were Biblical, if not apocalyptic. Its cadences and actual phrases still reverberate through our language and literature. Perhaps the most astounding thing about this document is that it was produced by a committee. There could be no more eloquent indication of how the vocabulary and cadences of Shakespeare had permeated the educated classes.

We have ended our extended portrait of later Elizabethan and early Jacobean society with, perhaps, its greatest achievement. But even here, as in so many other aspects of the Tudor inheritance, there was cause for worry as well as self-congratulation. Such an eloquent and powerful language was, like the Bible itself, able to inform, but also to inspire and inflame. The printing press which spread the Word of God and the First Folio of Shakespeare was capable of spreading more revolutionary ideas, such as the notion, embraced by some Puritans, that all who had a Bible were perfectly justified in interpreting it according to their own lights. It was no accident that the government soon reenacted censorship after the Edwardian experiment with a freer press: statutes of 1549 and 1554 forbade the publication of heretical or seditious books. In the 1580s, when fears of Catholic restoration and Puritan sedition were increasing, these prohibitions became capital. In order to enforce them, Star Chamber decreed in 1586 that all printing presses had to be based in London, apart from those of the two universities; that no press could be run that was not licensed by the Stationer's Company; and that no book could be printed unless it had first been perused, then licensed, by a bishop. In 1593 John Penry was executed for his role in publishing a series of Puritan tracts critical of the bishops.

If places like London and the New World were safety valves, they were also sources of new, potentially unsettling perspectives and ideas. For example, experience of the American wilderness would revive in England discussions of natural law, and its relationship to the king's, Parliament's, and the common law. Given the existence of wildly different societies in America, how could the English claim that theirs was the one best way, or that royal power and elite domination, paternalism, and deference were perfectly "natural"? London was itself a thriving example of a capitalistic society, one whose hierarchy was based not on birth but on wealth and hard work and, therefore, it could be argued, on merit. The very idea of mobility, both geographical and social, which London represented was revolutionary and, potentially, corrosive of the Great Chain of Being. Finally, the language of Shakespeare and the King James Bible might be used by King James himself to assert his Divine Right to rule; but it might be used with equal effectiveness to challenge that notion. Clearly, the English polity was full of tensions: local and national, political and geographical, economic and social, religious and cultural. Many of those tensions would come to a head in the next generation, during the first years of Stuart rule.

CHAPTER SEVEN

The Early Stuarts and the Three Kingdoms, 1603–1642

The great triumph of the Tudor State was, arguably, not the defeat of the Spanish Armada in 1588. That was as much a matter of luck as pluck, of poor Spanish planning and bad weather as English prowess. The great triumph of the Tudor State was, rather, the peaceful accession of their successors, the Stuarts, in March 1603. Despite war with Spain, division at home, and an ambiguous and foreign claim, James VI of Scotland was duly and smoothly proclaimed Elizabeth's successor as James I of England.[1] While Edward IV and Henry VII had won their crowns in bloody battle and were forced to rush to London at the head of their armies to make good their titles to the throne, James won *his* through delicate negotiation with the sitting government, specifically Elizabeth's secretary of State, Sir Robert Cecil. As a result, the new sovereign was able to take his time, embarking on a leisurely six-week progress south to his new capital. In the meantime, the Privy Council continued to run the country from London; the lords lieutenant, sheriffs, and JPs continued to run the countryside beyond it; and Cecil's spy system continued to keep watch in between. It is a measure of the stability and competency of late Tudor government that all did so in the king's name, but without the necessity of his actual participation. James finally arrived in London without incident, to cheering crowds, in May 1603. They cheered, in part, because, popular as Queen Elizabeth had once been, over a decade of economic depression, war, and high taxation, presided over by an increasingly miserly and reclusive head of State, had left many of her subjects yearning for something new.

None at the time would have guessed that within two generations, Charles I, the son of the monarch they were cheering so wildly, would process through the streets of London not to acclamation but to stony silence but for the muffled drums of a military guard, not to a crown but to a scaffold, where he would be executed by parliamentary order in the name of those very people who had turned out to greet his father. This event would be the climax of a series of bitter Civil Wars which would rage in England, Scotland, and Ireland for over a decade (1637–51), destroying many of the gains of the Tudor State and dividing these countries more thoroughly than anything known during the Wars of the Roses.

Because historians, blessed with hindsight, know that the British Civil Wars happened, they have had difficulty writing the history of these kingdoms under James I and Charles I with any objectivity: how can one judge their rule on its own merits knowing its disastrous end? For most of the last 400 years the early Stuarts have been seen as directly causing the Civil Wars. In this view, every government policy, parliamentary debate, or local protest was part of a continuous struggle between the king and the forces of autocracy on one side and the people and the forces of liberalism and democracy on the other. This interpretation has been labeled Whig, after a political party which would develop later in the seventeenth century and which was generally associated with limiting monarchical and promoting parliamentary power (see chapter 9). The Whig interpretation was especially popular during the nineteenth century, when liberal ideas and representative institutions seemed to triumph all across Europe and the Americas. British historians could not help but see these developments as rooted in the strife between king and Parliament which culminated in the British Civil Wars.

More recently, during the first half of the twentieth century, Marxist historians saw the Civil Wars as the climax of a struggle between the landowning and the merchant classes which dated back to medieval times. According to Marxist theory, the Civil Wars were the most dramatic stage of a long-drawn-out fight between a feudal aristocracy, trying to retain its hegemony over British society, and a rising class of merchants and professionals, trying to seize that hegemony and remake England, in particular, into a bourgeois society. Toward the beginning of the last century, another group of historians, influenced by the writings of Max Weber, attributed the causes of these wars to primarily religious factors, in particular the rise of an aggressive Puritanism. According to this view, Puritans emphasized rationality, the acquisition of property, and individual conscience – first in religion, but then in civil matters – over obedience to institutions like monarchy. They demanded reform not only of the Church of England but of society itself. Since the Stuart kings were apparent enemies to Puritans and to such reform, they had to go.

The trouble with all of these views is that hindsight is 20×20. More recent historians, examining a wider array of sources with more circumspection, have been careful to guard against a number of their assumptions. First, it does not follow that the Civil Wars were ever inevitable, whether in 1588 or 1603 or even in 1640. A different turn of events, a different royal personality or education for the young Prince Charles, a slowdown of the inflation discussed in chapter 6: all might have led to a different result. Second, no one foresaw or wanted a civil war. Nor should it be assumed that either the king or Parliament consciously strove to increase their respective power at the expense of the other. More recent work has argued that both king and Parliament (and the wider constituencies they represented) in the early Stuart period were striving for mutual agreement and cooperation, not dominance. Third, no group in early Stuart society was homogeneous in its views or united in its aims. It is therefore ridiculous to speak of "Parliament," or "the merchants," or "Puritans" as being monolithic parties made up of individuals who all sought the same thing – let alone fought to dominate their society. Finally, it should not be assumed that most English subjects had long-cherished hopes of overthrowing royal power and establishing some sort of democracy. As we learned in chapter 6, the English people were, by and large, a traditional and deferential lot. The vast majority were content that the king should rule and they should follow. Admittedly, they wanted the king to rule wisely and justly, with respect for the law. But even when Charles I was perceived as failing to do so they would oppose him only gradually and reluctantly – though perhaps a bit less reluctantly than they would have done Queen Elizabeth.

From the 1970s onwards, an influential group of historians has sought to revise the old Whig, Marxist, and Weberian interpretations by arguing that the policies and politics of the early Stuarts should be judged on their own merits, without reference to the Civil Wars. After all, James I and Charles I ruled three kingdoms, successfully, for nearly half a century. These historians, often labeled Revisionists, argue that the Civil Wars were not a product of a long-term conflict between king and Parliament or king and people, let alone aristocrats and merchants or Puritans and more traditional members of the Church of England; that these groups rarely disagreed over basic principles or constitutional ideology; and that for most of the early Stuart period the king and his ruling elite worked in close partnership. Revisionist historians deemphasize the role of Parliaments, pointing out that they met only rarely and always at the pleasure of the monarch. They clashed with the king even more rarely. These historians argue that the only permanent venue in which the king had contact with his subjects and their problems was the court; that this was the great arena for the pursuit of conflict and, more often, the forging of consensus. They also emphasize that James I and Charles I were not merely kings of England but of Scotland and Ireland as well. Indeed, to the extent that the Civil Wars (or "Wars of the Three Kingdoms" as many Revisionists would style these conflicts) *did* have any long-term causes, they can be found in the ramshackle structure of the triple Crown that the Stuarts wore. That is, the early Stuart State(s) was (were) eventually overwhelmed by the difficulties inherent in ruling three different peoples, each with a different majority religion, legal system, social structure, and culture.

As all of this should suggest, if the British Civil Wars are the most dramatic events covered in these pages, their causes are also the most complex and subject to historical argument. Lawrence Stone, author of one of the many books seeking those causes, has compared the search to trying to trace a strand of DNA.[2] Given the number of students of the period who have become entangled in those strands, the authors of this book must separate them out, even if this leads to a certain amount of oversimplification. In our view, the English, Scottish, and Irish Civil Wars did not happen by accident or overnight. They arose out of unanswered questions, tensions, and flaws inherent in the Tudor and early Stuart polity which, despite the desire for consensus and cooperation detected by the Revisionists, became worse as the seventeenth century approached its mid-point.

We see five major areas of uncertainty and tension in the early seventeenth-century English polity.

1   **The Problem of Sovereignty, Law, and Counsel**: What is the king's relationship to the law; is he above it or subordinate to it? Who, primarily, should advise the king: courtiers, councilors, or Parliament? If the last, whose interests does Parliament represent: king or people? Later, what should be the respective, proper roles of king and Parliament? When push comes to shove, who decides on policy?

2   **The Problem of Government Finance and the Economy**: How should the government pay for itself? Does the king have a preemptive right to the property of his subjects? What role should government play in the national economy?

3   **The Problem of War and Foreign Policy**: What is England's proper role in Europe? Should the English taxpayer support a more active role?

4   **The Problem of Religion**: What should be the State religion of England? Should other faith traditions be tolerated? Who makes religious policy: king, Parliament, the bishops, local communities, or a combination of all four? What should be the answers to these questions for Scotland and Ireland?

5   **The Problem of Local Control**: What is the proper relationship between the central government in London and the English localities? What should be the relationship between that government and those of Scotland and Ireland?

It would be going too far to say that these problems "caused" the Civil Wars or that the king and his subjects were always or even frequently very divided over them. We accept the Revisionist argument that, most of the time, early modern English people were looking for peaceful, consensual answers to these problems – to the extent that they dealt actively with them at all. But so long as they remained unresolved, they had the potential to lead to conflict. As we have seen, the Tudors had been adept at papering over, postponing, or winning temporary consensus on them. It is perhaps another, shorter-term "cause" of the British Civil Wars that the Stuarts were neither so skillful nor so lucky. For whatever reason, they sometimes misunderstood the political and religious cultures of each of their three kingdoms in ways that the most successful Tudors had not. As a result, the potential for violent conflict was reached in Scotland in 1637, in Ireland in 1641, and in England in 1642, during the reign of Charles I.

The Problem of Sovereignty, Law, and Counsel

On the surface, there was no problem of sovereignty in early Stuart England: clearly, the sovereign was sovereign. That is, according to the Great Chain of

Being, the king was God's lieutenant on earth and the head of the body politic. The king had long possessed the prerogative to make peace or war, appoint all major government officials, and direct how government monies be spent. His powers had actually increased during the Tudor period, when he became the Supreme Head of the Church of England and, thus, assumed command of his subjects' souls as well as their bodies. But even Henry VIII agreed that his power was at its greatest when it assumed the form of king-in-Parliament. As we have seen, throughout the late medieval and Tudor periods, Parliaments had successfully maintained the right to be partners with the king in the making of law, and, especially, in the levying of taxes, which could be done only with its approval. Under the Tudors royal and parliamentary power had increased simultaneously, as successive rulers turned to Parliaments for religious legislation. This is paradoxical only if one sees these two bodies as being naturally in conflict, which no one did in 1603.

Nevertheless, the king-in-Parliament formula introduced an element of ambiguity and possible tension into the English constitution. Under the early Stuarts, that tension first centered around the king's relationship to the law: was he above the law or subject to it? Put another way, since the king was the fountain of law, could he break the law – his law – with impunity? Late Tudor and early Stuart monarchs tried to get around this difficulty by pledging in their coronation oaths to govern within the law. But what if they broke that promise? What if Parliament, or the people, disagreed with the king's interpretation of the law? Indeed, whose interests was Parliament supposed to serve: king or people? Once again, early Stuart monarchs would insist that those interests were identical. But what if they were not? And if Parliament's ultimate responsibility *was* to the people of England, did this not charge them with the duty, or give them the right, to disagree with the king when he pursued policies which they judged harmful to the good of the realm? Might not such a disagreement raise the deeper issue of who – or what – was the true sovereign power in England?

Few of James's subjects had followed the implications of these questions to their conclusions in 1603. Still, throughout Elizabeth's reign, Parliament had, as we have seen, frequently annoyed the queen by debating – admittedly, often at the behest of her own privy councilors – such sore subjects as religion, foreign policy, her marriage prospects, and the limits of free speech. Sometimes Elizabeth had dealt with this annoyance by the brute exercise of her constitutional rights of veto, dismissal, and prorogation; but more often through the persuasion of her ministers or, in really tight situations, that of her own great personal charm. As we saw in the case of the debate on monopolies, this often served only to postpone resolution of a problem. As a result, she left for her successor a country still grumbling over high taxes, monopolies, purveyance, and wardship, still at war with Spain, and still divided in religion; a revenue inadequate and growing more so due to inflation; courtiers who were increasingly greedy and unsatisfied; and a Parliament which felt competent to raise all these matters with that successor. As a result of this legacy, the broad theoretical questions raised above would grow more pressing in the new reign. What sort of man inherited this situation?

James Stuart, the only son of Elizabeth's old nemeses, Mary Queen of Scots and Lord Darnley, has long had a bad press among English historians. This was, in part, because he possessed an unconventional personality for a king, especially after the forthright authoritarianism of the Tudors. But his relatively easy-going nature resonates better with our own time, which has begun to rehabilitate him. For example, unlike the last two Henries, he was not a military man: in fact, he was once frightened by the guns of a military salute on the Isle of Wight. Rather, he fancied himself a *Rex Pacificus* (peaceful king) who would bring peace and concord not only to the three kingdoms but, as a moderator among his fellow monarchs, to all of Europe. In this, he was ahead of his time. He was also a relatively tolerant man, preferring, like Elizabeth, to let Catholics and Puritans live in peace if they maintained their political loyalty to him. His failure to engage in military adventures against the Catholic powers or to enforce the penal laws against Catholics at home would be controversial with his subjects. In fact, his decision to end the war with Spain in 1604 was precisely what the English economy needed, while his flexibility over religion promoted sectarian peace for 20 years.

Rather than assume the Henrician mantle of a great warrior, the new king was an accomplished scholar, publishing widely on subjects ranging from demonology to tobacco (which he detested) to the art of governing. As this implies, he had considerable intelligence and, like his Tudor cousins, he could be crafty behind the scenes. As his attitude toward Catholics and Puritans implies, he was also flexible and willing to compromise when necessary. Consequently, he proved especially adept at balancing off factions, something which he had learned to do in Scotland. In fact, James had ruled Scotland quite successfully for two decades; this was no mean accomplishment, for the northern kingdom remained riven by opposing noble factions, Catholic, Presbyterian, Highland, Lowland. James's strategy in each of his kingdoms was to negotiate and compromise in private while publicly emphasizing his exalted status as God's lieutenant on earth.

Unfortunately for his image, both then and later, the new king did not look, sound, or act very much like a surrogate for the Supreme Being, especially in his private life. It is not James's fault that he was a rather odd-looking man (see plate 13): skinny legs supported an ungainly body, crowned by a rather ponderous head. That head housed a tongue that was also rather too large for its mouth, causing a pronounced lisp. The lisp exacerbated a stutter and what to English ears was a thick Scots accent. In our politically correct age all of this might be overlooked or even celebrated in the name of diversity. But contemporaries used to the regal bearing of the Tudors and bound by their own prejudices could not help but draw unflattering conclusions. In particular, James's Scottish descent was difficult to stomach for English men and women who had long seen their northern neighbors as rude, impoverished brigands. Some charged that the king had swept down from his poor northern kingdom accompanied by "the hungry Scots": Scottish courtiers who saw England as a vast treasure house to plunder.

The new king's manner also contrasted sharply with that of his Tudor predecessors, sometimes to his disadvantage. Once again, some of his personal traits

Plate 13 James I, *by van Somer. The Royal Collection* © *2002 Her Majesty Queen Elizabeth II.*

were far more damaging then than they would be today. For a king, he could be remarkably informal, even affable. He was not a stickler for ceremony and was good at putting people at ease. This was, in some ways, an advantage, for it meant that his court was welcoming to men and women of all political and religious persuasions. This openness meant that the king always had a pretty good idea of what various sides in a debate were thinking; while each might hope that their view would prevail. On the other hand, the Tudors' success had stemmed, in part, from their ability to keep people off balance and inspire respect and fear. The new king's personality worked against these feelings in several ways. James's affability often manifested itself in excessive drinking, made worse by a poor ability to tolerate its effects. He was also known in later years to have rather dubious personal hygiene. More seriously, and unlike his Tudor predecessors, the new king hated crowds and rarely showed himself to his people outside London. Once, when told that a number of his subjects had gathered to express their loyalty to him, he responded testily and with characteristic earthiness, "God's wounds! I will pull down my breaches and they shall also see my arse."[3] Worse, as the reign wore on he grew increasingly lazy, leaving pressing matters to government ministers with whom he did not always communicate and whom he sometimes undermined. This served to increase faction because on any given issue there always seemed to be hope of changing the king's mind. An athletic man – he introduced the Scottish sport of golf to England – he preferred to spend his time hunting with his favorites at his beloved lodge at Theobalds, Hertfordshire.

And then there is the matter of the favorites themselves. Though James I had married Anne of Denmark (1574–1619) and had several children, his sexuality has long been a matter of debate. He clearly preferred the company of handsome young men. The evidence of his correspondence and contemporary accounts have led some historians to conclude that the king was homosexual or bisexual. In fact, the issue is murky. Contemporaries were rarely, if ever, frank about such attributions because such sexual variety was considered a heinous sin in Church law. They would have been especially reluctant to make such an allegation in the case of a king. Moreover, assumptions about what constitutes heterosexual or homosexual behavior may well have differed in the past. What we *can* say is that his relations with his favorites – Esmé Stuart, duke of Lennox (1542?–83), in Scotland; Robert Carr, earl of Somerset (1587?–1645), and then George Villiers, duke of Buckingham, in England – were, if not overtly sexual, certainly physical. Contemporaries remarked at length on how James hung about their necks, in the words of one scandalized Puritan gentleman, "kissing them after so lascivious a mode in public [as] . . . prompted many to imagine some things done in the tyring house [dressing room] that exceed my expression."[4] Thus, whatever James's sexual preference, his public and private behavior, like his abhorrence of military pursuits and devotion to scholarship, contrasted sharply with Queen Elizabeth's dignified bellicosity and flirtatious interest in the opposite sex. Above all, they did not fit contemporary images of a king, in particular one who claimed to be God's representative on earth.

And claim James did. He had spent most of his career loudly trumpeting the Divine Right of Kings; that is, the notion that, because kings represented and wielded God's power on earth, they had no one to answer to but God. In James's view, kings were clearly above Parliament and the law, though a good ruler might, out of the goodness of his heart, agree to consult the former and abide by the latter. Above all, James argued that no subject had the right to resist a divinely appointed monarch, even if he violated the law or was a manifestly bad king. Only God could remove a king. This rebutted an emerging argument among both Protestant and Catholic theologians that a bad king might be resisted or even overthrown. James had articulated his ideas in two influential works, *The Trew Law of Free Monarchies* (1598) and *Basilikon Doron* (*The King's Gift*, written to edify his sons, 1599). To ensure that no one missed the point, both were reissued in 1603 upon James's accession.

The new king's views and style may be inferred from the following speech to Parliament, delivered in March 1610:

The state of monarchy is the supremest thing upon earth: for Kings are not only God's lieutenants upon earth and sit upon God's throne, but even by God himself they are called gods.... That as to dispute what God may do is blasphemy, ... so is it sedition in subjects to dispute what a King may do in the height of his power.... I will not be content that my power be disputed upon; but I shall ever be willing to make the reason appear of all my doings, and rule my actions according to my laws ... do not meddle with the main points of government: that is my craft: I am now an old King. I must not be taught my office.[5]

Now, in fact, there is nothing really new here: both Henry VIII and Elizabeth I would have agreed heartily with the sentiment. But compare this to Elizabeth's "Golden Speech." She would never have actually *said* this, nor called public or parliamentary attention so baldly to her "absolutist" notions of her office. James had dealt effectively for years with a Scottish Parliament in Edinburgh, but it was a far less powerful or prickly body than its English counterpart. The new king was inexperienced in dealing with a strong legislature; his speeches to the English Parliament show him feeling his way, adapting to the new institution. James was trying to retrofit his Scottish Divine Right to the English king-in-Parliament arrangement which had been advanced by the Tudors. Unfortunately, his pedantry, clumsiness, and inexperience would provoke suspicion and even conflict in his first Parliaments.

When Parliament met on March 19, 1604, both houses, and in particular the House of Commons, were already restive. Many members hoped that the new king would deal with complaints over monopolies, purveyance, and wardship left over from Elizabeth's reign. A few seem to have read up on James's scholarly work and so were on the defensive, fearing that he might wish to rule without Parliament. Their fears seemed justified, for all across Europe strong kings had circumvented, marginalized, or eliminated once powerful legislative bodies: the French Estates General lost its power to delay taxes by the 1580s (and did not meet at all after 1614), and the Aragonese (Spanish) *Cortes* had only very limited powers after 1592. As some MPs were to write later in the session, "[t]he prerogatives of princes may easily and do daily grow; the privileges of the subject are for the most part at an everlasting stand."[6]

In fact, James would soon come to feel that it was *his* prerogative which was being infringed upon. This was because a small group of MPs, led by the jurist Sir Edward Coke (1552–1634), believed that the English constitution, and

Parliament's privileges in particular, derived from the common law, not from the king. Drawing upon the research of a new generation of antiquaries and historians, such as William Camden and John Selden (1584–1654), they argued that the common law dated back from before the Norman Conquest to time immemorial; and that Parliament descended from the Witan, the set of councilors who had advised Anglo-Saxon kings. Parliament and the common law were part of something they called the Ancient Constitution of England – a historical myth rather than a document that anyone could point to – that had been ignored or suppressed by the Normans. In the extreme view, the Norman and Plantagenet kings (1066–1154 and 1154–1399, respectively) had asserted their divinity and trampled on the ancient rights of Parliament and of Englishmen generally – a development referred to as "the Norman yoke." Still, those rights, however obscured by time and tyranny, remained the birthright of every Englishman. According to its adherents, study of the Ancient Constitution would reveal that Parliament was a body independent of the king and, so, ought to be his full partner in government. For a bold few, Parliament predated kings. The implications of this idea for the question of sovereignty should be obvious.

These conflicting interpretations of history and the constitution emerged at the opening of the 1604 Parliament around an election dispute known as Goodwin's case. Briefly, the election of Sir Francis Goodwin (1564–1634) as MP for Buckinghamshire had been thrown out by the court of Chancery on the technical grounds that he was an outlaw because of an unpaid debt. But after hearing Goodwin at the bar of the house, the Commons decided to seat him on the grounds that it, not the law courts, had the right to determine its own membership. James objected to this because it placed the rights of the Commons above those of a royal court of law; he countered by arguing that they "derived all matters of privilege [such as the regulation of their membership] from him and by his grant."[7] The more radical members responded with a document entitled the *Form of Apology and Satisfaction*. In its most famous passage, they assert, respectfully but firmly, that:

[w]e most truly avouch, First, That our privileges and liberties are our rights and due inheritance no less than our very lands and goods. Secondly, That they cannot be withheld from us, denied, or impaired, but with apparent wrong to the whole state of the realm.[8]

That is, Parliament's rights and privileges do not derive from the king. Rather, they exist independently of him and are, instead, inherent in the MPs, as was the ownership of their property and goods. Historically speaking, this was nonsense, but the king was too inexperienced in English law and practice to know that. In any case, this was the first significant use of the language of rights by Parliament, a language which would have tremendous importance not only for their relations with the king but for the future development of representative government in Great Britain and elsewhere, including the United States. The passage then goes on to assert that Parliament speaks not only for its own privileged members but for "the whole state of the realm." Heretofore, the only body capable of making such an assertion had been the king himself. The authors of the *Apology* clearly saw the role of Parliament as being far more extensive than that of a mere advisory body to the sovereign or a mouthpiece for the secret agendas of councilors. In 1621 Coke would make this point more explicitly, claiming, "[w]e serve here for thousands and ten thousands"; another MP would add, "if we lose our privileges, we betray it [our country]."[9]

However, one should not exaggerate the importance of this document or the degree of conflict between king and Parliament at this early stage. The *Form of Apology and Satisfaction* was never presented to the king, who thus never had to respond to it. James, too, chose the path of conciliation, backing down from his initial position and acknowledging Parliament's right to regulate election disputes. For most of his reign, king and Parliament sought a partnership and no one would have suggested seriously that the former should not lead in the dance. Still, the question of sovereignty had now been framed. It would become more pressing as king and Commons clashed over a second long-term problem intimately related to the first: the royal finances.

The Problem of Government Finance

James can hardly be faulted for the inadequate revenue he inherited, nor for reigning during a period of continued rapid inflation, or between two periods of agricultural stagnation, even famine (the mid-1590s and the mid-1620s). Inflation made everything purchased by the Crown – from building materials to tapestries to muskets and uniforms – more expensive. Nor was it James's fault that he had inherited from the Tudors an administration which, despite some growth during the war, was still ramshackle and inefficient. Its employees at the center were so poorly paid that they had to be allowed to engage in practices we would today call corrupt: fee-taking, bribery, sale of office, etc. As a result, the king's servants mostly looked out for themselves, to his ever-increasing cost. In the countryside, he depended on the cooperation of local officials who tended to put their interests and those of their communities – also smarting under the effects of inflation and dearth – above those of the king. This meant, for example, that they often assessed their neighbors' wealth for purposes of taxation ridiculously low and were lackadaisical in collecting even those amounts. Such low valuations kept a degree of local consensus and minimized opposition to the Crown; but they did nothing to relieve the royal finances.

It was not James's fault that his needs were in some ways greater than his predecessor's. Most of his subjects were generally pleased that, after the uncertainty about the succession born of Elizabeth's refusal to marry, James brought with him a wife and children. Unfortunately, each member of the new royal family had to be supported out of the royal revenue, along with their personal – and quite extensive – households. The court of his eldest son, Prince Henry (1594–1612), alone cost £25,000 a year. This was in sharp contrast to the unmarried Virgin Queen, who had come relatively cheap. It was not James's fault that he had inherited from his frugal predecessor a rapacious court, anxious to make up for lost time in the pursuit of riches. Finally, it was not James's fault that, for all her frugality, Queen Elizabeth had bequeathed him a debt of £365,000 – about a year's worth of royal revenue.

If the new king inherited a difficult situation, it is unarguable that he made it worse by spending lavishly on himself, on his friends, and on his courtiers. Up to this point the master of a relatively poor country, with his accession to the English throne the middle-aged James described himself as "like a poor man wandering about forty years in a wilderness and barren soil, and now arrived at the land of promise."[10] He made up for lost time, first, by spending vast amounts on fine buildings, commissioning the Banqueting House at Whitehall and the Queen's House at Greenwich – both intended to be part of much larger projects – from Inigo Jones. He also employed Jones to design the scenery and costumes for the court masques noted in the previous chapter. These elaborate multimedia productions required actors, dancers, and musicians supported behind the scenes by armies of seamstresses and carpenters. All of this contributed to the general costliness of James's English court: the expenses of his Chamber rose by 40 percent over those of Elizabeth, those of his Great Wardrobe (which provided furniture) by nearly 400 percent!

It was also James's tendency, part of his open-hearted nature, to spend money on his favorites. As Sir Robert Cecil said, "[f]or a King not to be bountiful were a fault"[11] (one which many had attributed to Elizabeth), but James shunned this particular failing far too strictly. In just his first four years on the throne he gave out £200,000 in pensions and gifts to courtiers. Much of this largesse went to Scots: by 1610 he had given his countrymen nearly £250,000. As a result, royal expenditure rose from Queen Elizabeth's wartime figure of £300,000 a year to £500,000 a year under King James during a period of peace. The royal debt, which had stood at under £400,000 at the queen's death in 1603, rose to £600,000 by 1608, £900,000 by 1618 – the largest peacetime debt in English history up to that point.

This left the king and his advisers with but two choices: cut expenditure or raise revenue. Both had significant drawbacks. On the one hand, cutting expenditure involved eliminating court and government jobs, pensions, and other features which made the king popular and the court attractive for the ruling elite. As a result, many of those closest to the king did everything in their power to oppose such cost-cutting measures. In other words, the contest between administrators and courtiers fought in the previous reign was to a great extent replicated in this one (with, as we shall see, one crucial difference). On the other hand, raising revenue required parliamentary permission. This was unlikely to be granted in peacetime, for many MPs privately shared one member's view that the money would just end up in courtiers' pockets: "to what purpose is it for us to draw a silver stream out the country into the royal cistern, if it shall daily run out thence by private cocks [taps]?"[12] Moreover, if new taxes *were* granted, Parliament's role in government would inevitably increase. If refused, this would throw the king back onto option one.

Sir Robert Cecil was the first minister to tackle these problems seriously. He had inherited his father's, Lord Burghley's, old administrative connection and was, as we have seen, highly instrumental in James's smooth accession. James rewarded him, first, by continuing him as secretary of State, then creating him earl of Salisbury (1605), and finally promoting him to his father's old office of lord treasurer (1608). Like his father, Salisbury worked hard to enhance the government's revenue and to keep royal expenditure in check. As early as 1608 he launched a reform of the administration of Crown lands and sought to raise the Customs yield by farming out its collection. That is, he sold the right to collect the Customs revenues to a consortium of the highest bidders, who would pay the government a large lump sum and keep whatever profit remained. He was forced to do this, in part, because the royal Customs administration was simply inadequate to do the job itself. To ensure that there was enough revenue to make everybody rich, Salisbury issued a new Book of Rates which added some 1,400 new items to the Customs rolls – without asking parliamentary permission. He could do this because in 1606 the government had won Bate's case, in which John Bate, a London merchant, had sued over a similar "**imposition**" on red currants from Turkey. The court agreed with the government that the impositions were a legitimate part of the prerogative by which the king made foreign policy by regulating foreign trade. But despite this legal victory, Salisbury's retrenchment policy was, in the end, unsuccessful. Because the royal administration was so inadequate, the new survey of Crown lands was never completed. Even so, it became obvious that the Tudors had sold or given away so much land that the potential yield from the remainder was negligible. As for the impositions, they did raise much needed revenue, but at the cost of deep resentment among the merchant community and a growing feeling of distrust between king and Parliament on money issues.

This explains the failure of Salisbury's next initiative, the Great Contract of 1610, in which he proposed that the king voluntarily give up his rights to feudal dues from wardship, knightage, and purveyance in return for permanent, annual taxes yielding £200,000. This was promising, but the deal was wrecked when Parliament upped the ante by demanding the surrender of additional prerogative rights and presenting a list of grievances, headed by the hated impositions. The king dissolved Parliament and the Great Contract was never struck. This left James with few options, none of them pretty. One was to begin to sell titles: in 1611 he created that of baronet, ostensibly to raise cash to suppress yet another rebellion in Ulster. While this at first brought in £1,095 a creation, it also cheapened the social hierarchy, and so weakened the Great Chain. In fact, the subjection of "honor" to market forces led to discounting: by 1622 a baronetcy could be had for just £220. In addition, James, like the Tudors, sold monopolies on goods and services and forced loans from the wealthy. These initiatives kept the government going, but at a price in the Crown's reputation and its subjects' good will.

In the meantime, ambitious courtiers opposed and often thwarted Salisbury's attempts to restrain James's bountiful nature.[13] First, it was the "hungry Scots," led by Robert Carr, earl of Somerset. Though James lavished lands and titles on his favorite, Somerset never sought to translate this into political clout. Rather, he aspired to enhance his new-found social status by marrying the well-connected but notoriously promiscuous Frances Howard (ca. 1593–1632). Unfortunately, she was already married to Robert Devereaux, third earl of Essex (1591–1646). Moreover, Somerset's close friend and mentor, Sir Thomas **Overbury** (1581–1613), opposed the match, threatening to reveal damaging secrets about him. Eventually, a divorce was secured by proving that Essex had been unable to consummate his five-year marriage because of impotence by bewitchment! As for Overbury, he had managed to offend the king on a number of other accounts, and so was safely locked up in the Tower, where he conveniently expired. James blessed the new marriage by his attendance in 1613, only to discover later that the countess had engineered Overbury's poisoning, possibly with Somerset's assistance. Both Somersets were convicted and imprisoned in 1616. Although the king later pardoned them, the damage to the court's reputation and the royal finances had been done. In any case, by the time of his fall, Somerset had already been displaced by a favorite of much greater weight.

In 1614 James I was introduced to a young courtier from a minor gentry family named George Villiers (see plate 14). Villiers had all the qualities required of a favorite: he was handsome, courtly, and an excellent dancer, musician, and horseman. Historians have charged him with vaulting ambition and an absence of scruples, though he possessed some administrative ability. In any case, the king saw something in young Villiers which he liked very much, for he showered him with honors, offices, pensions, and favors. He rose to be a gentleman of the Bedchamber in 1615, master of the Horse and knight of the Garter in 1616; earl of Buckingham in 1617, marquess by the same title in 1618, admiral of England in 1619, and, finally, duke of Buckingham in 1623. The titles were pleasant, the offices lucrative. More importantly, they gave him control over vast amounts of patronage, allowing him to fill the government with his clients. By the 1620s, Buckingham's stranglehold on royal largesse had given him an army of followers comparable to Wolsey's a century previously.

But a more apt comparison might be drawn with Leicester in the previous reign, for Buckingham had James's heart as fully as Elizabeth's "sweet Robin" held hers. However, James was far less discreet than his predecessor, informing his Privy Council in 1617 that "Christ had his John, and I have my George."[14] Moreover, again unlike Elizabeth, James gave into his heart more often than his head. In particular, after Salisbury died, worn out with administrative care, in 1612, there was no one at court powerful enough to restrain the king from showering wealth and power on his favorites. In response, Parliament grew even less willing to finance his pleasures. It should therefore come as no surprise that the next Parliament, called in 1614 to deal with the king's debts, became known as "the Addled Parliament" for its failure to initiate any important legislation. The 1621 Parliament was to prove little more cooperative.

By this time, James's debts stood at over £1 million and City loans were drying up. Without a parliamentary subsidy to stave off his creditors and critics, he cagily turned to one of them, a London merchant named Lionel Cranfield

Plate 14 George Villiers, 1st Duke of Buckingham, *by William Larkin. National Portrait Gallery.*

(1575–1645). Initially supported by Buckingham, Cranfield was named lord treasurer in 1621 and earl of Middlesex in the following year. Middlesex introduced vigorous cost-cutting and almost succeeded in eliminating the king's debts. But his attack on expenditure threatened Buckingham and his considerable following. For a while Middlesex fought back, even trying to promote another young male courtier as a rival to Buckingham. But the latter was too powerful with the king and had too many followers in Parliament. In 1624 a compliant House of Commons impeached Middlesex. The king pardoned him a year later, but he would never again play an important role in government. James continued to spend time and money on his favorite and on his favorite's projects. By 1624, those projects included something more ambitious and expensive than before: a war.

The Problem of Foreign Policy, War, and England's Place in Europe

As we have seen, one of James's first acts as king of England was to negotiate a peace treaty with Spain. For most of the remainder of his reign, he pursued a pacific foreign policy. This was wise, for it kept England out of a series of bitter and bloody European wars fought among the Catholic and Protestant powers. These wars culminated in the Thirty Years' War (1618–48). This conflict pitted Habsburg Spain, the Holy Roman Empire, and their mostly Catholic German allies against Bourbon France, Protestant Denmark and Sweden, and a number of northern German States. The former were, for the most part, Catholic countries, the latter mostly Protestant. (While France was officially Catholic, it had a large number of Protestant Huguenots, thanks to Henry IV's Edict of Toleration of 1598.) So, on one level, the Thirty Years' War was a war of religion. But the fact that Catholic France fought Catholic Spain indicates that it was also a geopolitical war between the two most powerful European nations. Governments spent massively to field vast armies which criss-crossed central Europe, laying waste to the countryside and destroying, directly or indirectly, as much as one-third of the population in some areas. In the end, these wars would devastate the Holy Roman Empire, bankrupt Spain, and convince many contemporary Europeans that religious uniformity could not – and perhaps should not – be won by force of arms.

The Thirty Years' War was one of the great tragedies of early modern history. James showed greater wisdom than his predecessor, Henry VIII, by staying out of this continental quagmire. In fact, one of his long-cherished goals was to engineer a European-wide peace using an old Tudor strategy: diplomatic marriage. The linchpins of James's new European plan would be two royal matches: that of his eldest son, Prince Henry, to a princess of Spain, the principal Catholic power; and that of his daughter, Elizabeth (1596–1662), to Frederick V (1596–1632), the ruler of Rhine-Palatine and one of the Protestant leaders. Through the lineage of the *Rex Pacificus*, the two sides would be brought together in peace. James would be the arbiter of Europe.

It was not to be. The Catholic marriage was scuttled when Henry died of typhoid fever in 1612. The Protestant marriage to Frederick V went off the next year without a hitch. Puritans were thrilled when, in 1618, the rebellious Protestants of Bohemia, in the opening act of the Thirty Years' War, threw off their allegiance to the Catholic Habsburg Holy Roman Emperor and offered their Crown to Frederick. They were ecstatic when he and Elizabeth decided, before consulting the cautious James, to accept that Crown. They were correspondingly alarmed when the emperor decided to fight back; and suitably disappointed when, in the fall of 1620, Bavarian forces allied with the emperor crushed Frederick's Protestant army at the battle of the White Mountain. Frederick and Elizabeth fled their new kingdom after less than a year. Soon a Spanish army also drove them out of their ancestral lands of Rhine-Palatine, making them refugees. This was the chance for which many red-blooded Protestant Englishmen had been waiting. Puritan MPs in particular, fearing the extinction of European Protestantism, saw the Thirty Years' War as an apocalyptic struggle between good (Protestantism) and evil (Catholicism) that England was morally bound to join. They found the court's pacifism, profligacy, and obsession with pleasure disgraceful. In fact, like Henry VIII before them, few had any realistic idea of how much such a war would really cost or of how puny English power really was.

The Parliament called in 1621 to deal with the European crisis met in the midst of a deep economic depression. As a consequence, its members intended to exact a price for their cooperation. Many supported legislation to abolish monopolies, end the impositions, and impeach Lord Chancellor Bacon as an example for taking bribes. James would concede some of this program if the Commons voted funds sufficient to raise an army to restore Frederick to his ancestral lands. But many peers and commoners wanted more: a full-scale naval war against Spain in the spirit of Drake. James and Buckingham opposed this because they still wanted the freedom to contract a Spanish match for the king's surviving son, Prince Charles. In fact, they hoped that the threat of war would compel Spain to pursue the match more eagerly. But talk of such a marriage revived long English memories of the union of "Bloody" Mary and Philip II, the Protestant martyrs, the Armada, and more recent Spanish atrocities in the European war. The king responded to Parliament's obstinacy by falling back on his predecessor's old argument that it had no right to debate foreign policy or how the money it voted should be spent. This once again raised the issue of Parliament's privileges, this time, that of free speech. The Commons replied by registering a written protest which extended the argument of the 1604 *Apology*:

That the liberties, franchises, privileges, and jurisdictions of Parliament are the ancient and undoubted birthright and inheritance of the subjects of England; and that the arduous and urgent affairs concerning the King, State, and defence of the realm and of the Church of England, and the maintenance and making of laws, and redress of mischiefs and grievances which daily happen within this realm, are proper subjects and matter of counsel and debate in Parliament.[15]

Obviously, the problem of foreign policy had collided with those of sovereignty and finance. This prompted James not only to dissolve Parliament but to imprison some of the Commons' leaders and to rip the protest out of the Commons' Journal with his own hand. So much for cooperation between the king and his parliamentary advisers. From henceforward, the tensions between king and Parliament would grow more serious, the stakes higher.

In the winter of 1622–3, over the objections of a hostile populace, Buckingham reopened negotiations for a marriage between Prince Charles and the *infanta* (or Crown princess) of Spain. It is a measure of England's relatively low prestige that the Spanish were not terribly interested in the match, refusing to grant diplomatic credentials or safe conduct passages for Buckingham and the would-be groom. Undeterred, the duke concocted a mad scheme to travel to Spain in disguise. Armed with false beards and calling themselves "Thomas and John Smith," Prince Charles and the favorite actually got to the point of climbing the garden wall of a Spanish royal palace to get a look at his *inamorata*. In the end, the ardent wooers were caught and, after some diplomatic embarrassment, returned to England without their royal marital prize.

This bizarre escapade had three results. First, upon their return to England in 1623 Charles and Buckingham found themselves wildly popular – the first and only time in their lives that they would be so – because they *failed* to contract a Catholic marriage. The citizens of London and other cities, recalling the disastrous marriage of Mary and Philip II, rang bells and lit bonfires in the streets to celebrate this latest example of providential delivery from a Catholic takeover. The second result of the escapade was that Buckingham forged a relationship with James's son and heir apparent – a necessity as the old king was slowing down rapidly by the early 1620s. Thus, when James died in March 1625, Buckingham remained in charge of his son and, therefore, of his son's government.

It was, in fact, nothing new for Charles to be dominated. As a youth he had lived in the shadow of his dynamic and charismatic elder brother, Henry. When Prince Henry died in 1612, people grieved genuinely because he had projected the sort of chivalrous and Protestant bellicosity that many expected of an English king and which James had failed to provide. The son who survived and succeeded in 1625 as King Charles[16] was a very different sort of man. Nevertheless, in some ways he, too, fulfilled kingly expectations rather better than his father had done. Unlike James, Charles looked every inch a Divine Right monarch, despite his relatively short stature (see plate 15). That is, he bore himself with regal dignity and maintained proper courtly etiquette at all times. He was also conventional in his morality, monogamous, and kept a much more respectable court than his father. Highly cultured, he was probably the greatest connoisseur ever to sit on the English throne. Charles sent his diplomats scouring the studios of Europe to fill the palace at Whitehall with the most distinguished collection of artwork of any early modern ruler. It was at his insistence that both Rubens and van Dyck

Plate 15 Charles I, *by Van Dyck. The Royal Collection* © *2002 Her Majesty Queen Elizabeth II.*

came to England and painted for the Stuarts. Van Dyck's portraits of the royal family are one of the great achievements of Western art and kingly propaganda, projecting an image of monarchy serenely confident in its exercise of divinely inspired royal power.

Unfortunately, that image concealed a more ambiguous reality. As with so many rulers before him, the new king's good qualities had a dark side. Charles's sense of royal dignity often struck his subjects as mere aloofness; indeed, it cannot be said that he was ever generous or possessed of a common touch. Perhaps his punctiliousness was a form of compensation for insecurity: over his short stature, his stutter, and his general awkwardness in dealing with people. Unlike his voluble father, Charles was a shy and reticent man who, nevertheless, rarely took advice. He would make a decision or issue an order without consultation and then expect unquestioning obedience, no matter how apparently absurd the request. He felt no need to explain himself to his Parliaments or his people. As a result, his enemies were able to put their own "spin" on his motives. His authoritarianism was the product of an inflexible mind which saw dissent as disloyalty, retreat as a sign of weakness. That is, unlike James, Charles was incapable of compromise or even understanding an opposing point of view. He was, according to one historian, "[a] man of high principle and low intelligence."[17] His court may have been more decorous than his father's, but it was also more narrow. Buckingham was allowed no rival in distributing patronage and politicians out of royal favor received clear signals that they were not welcome. This left the court isolated from opinion in the rest of the country. Charles did not wish to moderate between competing views; he expected compliance and he was perfectly capable of being disingenuous or duplicitous in order to win it. Such an attitude may seem appropriate to an absolute monarch, but not to one who had to work the subtleties of that delicate and sometimes recalcitrant machine known as the English constitution. Even his art collection had a "down" side. Its propaganda value was limited to those members of the elite who went to court; but its cost was borne by every English taxpayer, much to their resentment. It should therefore come as no surprise that the new king's relationship to Parliament and his financial situation would be no happier than those of his father. Moreover, to these areas of tension would now be added the problem of war.

The third result of the Spanish escapade was that Buckingham, smarting at the insult to England's honor – and his own – went over to the war party. The issue came before Parliament in 1624, just before the old king's death. Middlesex argued that England was in no shape to go to war against the most powerful nation on earth. Buckingham and Prince Charles responded by securing his impeachment. Parliament proved equally compliant in voting for war, especially after James conceded that it could establish a commission to monitor how the funds were spent. This was unprecedented. Never before had Parliament interfered in how the king spent money which they had voted. There could be no greater indication of the distrust which existed between that body and the Crown. Even after this concession, Parliament voted far less money than

Buckingham had asked for. As James said just before his death, they provided enough "to make a good beginning of the war. For what the end will be, God knows."[18]

Parliament's distrust seems to have been well placed, for Charles I was no Henry V and Buckingham was no war minister. As had happened so often under Elizabeth, several pointless continental expeditions only served to highlight an inefficient and corrupt royal administration. Soldiers and sailors complained of rotten food and decrepit ships. At one point the Royal Navy was forced to reuse sails which had first seen service against the Armada nearly 40 years earlier. Back at home, the English people complained of high taxes, the imposition of martial law by deputy lieutenants, and of having to billet and feed soldiers in their homes. As the recorder of Taunton opined, "Every man knowes there is no law for this; we know our howses are our castles."[19] Modern historians have sought to absolve Buckingham of at least some of the blame for these disasters; certainly, he never had the funds to fight a proper war. By 1625 the king's military needs exceeded £1 million a year; and yet the Parliament of that year voted only a fifth of that amount.

In fact, contemporaries had no difficulty in assigning blame. In 1626 the Commons called for Buckingham's impeachment. In order to shield his favorite, Charles took two drastic actions. First, he violated Tudor precedent by taking personal responsibility for the miscarriages of the war. Up to this point the king could do no wrong: his ministers always took the blame for policy failures. This step may appear generous today, but it was also dangerous, for it opened to the contemporary mind the possibility that the king might actually be at fault with regard to other problems in the realm. Charles's second step was to dissolve Parliament and imprison those who had led the charge against Buckingham. This forestalled impeachment, but also any additional funding for that year's military and naval campaign. In order to pay for the war, the king imposed another forced loan. The resulting £260,000 helped, but it was not enough. Parliament would have to be called again soon. Worse, when 76 gentlemen refused to pay on the grounds that this was a tax unauthorized by Parliament, Charles had them imprisoned without charge. This prompted five of them to sue for a writ of habeas corpus. In the end, the judges refused to rule on the Five Knights' Case, but the implication that the king had broken the law and abused his authority was clear for all to see. And worse was to come.

Late in 1626, the Buckingham administration bungled into a second, simultaneous war with France over shipping rights, the treatment of the Huguenots, and resentment at the French failure to support the war against Spain. Foolish as some of the Tudors had sometimes been in their choice of enemies, none was ever so reckless as to take on *both* European superpowers at once. This war, too, went badly, culminating in a botched amphibious assault on the Isle of Ré, off La Rochelle, between June and October 1627. As a result, the 1628 Parliament met in an angry mood. In its elections, some of those who had refused to pay the forced loan won seats. Many feared that if they sufficiently funded a royal army it might be deployed not against the Spanish or the French but to suppress English liberties. They took the position that before the Commons voted any money, the king would have to agree to a document called the **Petition of Right**. This piece of legislation went much farther than the *Form of Apology and Satisfaction*. It had four major planks:

1   No man could be compelled to pay a tax not voted by Parliament.
2   No free man could be imprisoned without reason shown (the right of habeas corpus).
3   No soldiers or sailors could be billeted on the population without their consent.
4   No civilian could be subject to martial law.

Charles tried to wriggle out of the agreement in the House of Lords. In the end, however, the war was too pressing, his financial situation too precarious. In order to obtain five new taxes, he agreed to the Petition of Right.[20] As soon as he did so, the Commons once again demanded Buckingham's impeachment. The king once again responded by dissolving Parliament rather than subject his favorite to a trial.

In fact, there were limits to the king's ability to protect Buckingham. That summer, an unpaid and resentful gentleman officer named John Felton (ca. 1595–1628) assassinated the duke while on his way to join the fleet. Felton's knifework horrified the court and he was duly executed. But many ordinary people celebrated his act in bonfires and doggerel verse. This event had two profound effects. First, it served to further alienate Charles from his subjects, and especially from the parliamentary leaders who had, in his view, stirred up resentment toward his friend. Second, it led to the perception, probably false, that the king would now turn for advice to his new wife, Queen Henrietta Maria (1609–69). If true, this was alarming, for Henrietta Maria was a Roman Catholic.

The Problem of Religion

The religious situation of the British Isles as inherited by the early Stuarts was nothing if not complicated. As we have seen, the Church of England was, officially, Protestant but there was much debate as to precisely what that meant. To Puritans, Protestantism meant continued, perhaps even continuous, reformation. Though persecuted under Elizabeth, most Puritans had remained in the Church, and many clergymen, even some bishops, embraced Puritan ideas. That is, they believed in predestination, the necessity of Scriptural justification for both doctrine and practice, and a stern "godly" morality. Indeed, their influence was such that, by 1603, these were mainstream theological views within the Church of England. But some Puritans wanted more. They sought to enhance the material circumstances of the chronically poor parish clergy, but disliked hierarchy (represented for some by the power of the bishops), ceremony, and such activities as sports and dancing on the Sabbath. To more conservative churchmen, including

King James, these activities were perfectly harmless: as we have seen, in 1618 James issued a compendium of allowable Sunday pleasures called the *Book of Sports*. Such conservatives, later known as "high" churchmen, embraced hierarchy and ceremony, leading to Puritan charges that they intended to revive Catholicism.

To alarm Puritans even further, there remained a small but dedicated Catholic minority in England numbering perhaps 40,000. These people were caught in a struggle that was both international and internal: though they followed Rome in religion, most were loyal to the Crown in temporal matters and had given Spain no assistance during the war. By 1603 they had, for the most part, given up the political struggle and wished to be left alone to practice their faith quietly. But, as we have seen, contemporaries could not easily separate religious from political loyalty and anti-Catholic feeling amongst the generality of English men and women had only grown. This was due, in part, to the persistent memory of Bloody Mary, the writings of John Foxe, and the more recent memories of war with Spain. Indeed, some historians argue that anti-Catholicism (or, really, anti-popery as it was usually directed outwards, against the Catholic powers, instead of against one's neighbor), far more than any positive sense of "Englishness," helped the English to define themselves as a nation at the end of the sixteenth century. Consequently, the Elizabethan penal laws against Catholic priests and recusant lay people remained on the statute books; however, as the political activities of the Catholic minority seemed to die down in the 1590s, Elizabeth's government had ceased to enforce them with any regularity, much to the chagrin of radical Puritans.

The situation in the Stuarts' northern kingdom of Scotland would have been more to their liking. While there remained a Catholic minority in the Highlands, it was relatively poor and isolated from political power. The most powerful religious body in Scotland was the Presbyterian Kirk. Run by a general assembly, a sort of council of elders, its power was diffused through a series of regional synods down to individual congregations in the localities. Grudgingly acknowledged by the Stuarts, the Kirk maintained the sort of unadorned liturgy and church decor that Puritans sought for England. While James had reintroduced Scottish bishops, their power and jurisdiction within the Kirk remained weak. In Ireland, by contrast, the majority of the native population was Roman Catholic, as were many of their Old English landlords. The Crown had established a Protestant Church of Ireland, but made little effort to proselytize the native population. Instead, after the wars and rebellions of the sixteenth century, Elizabeth and James had encouraged Protestant immigrants by granting them the land of dispossessed Papists, especially, after the fall of Tyrone, in Catholic Ulster. Irish lands were too poor to attract many English settlers, but they *were* attractive to Scots, and thousands of Presbyterians emigrated to northern Ireland. By 1625 this group controlled much of Ulster and increasing amounts of land in the rest of the island. In summary, none of the three Stuart kingdoms embraced religious unanimity or a toleration free of resentments. How did the Stuart kings deal with this situation?

King James had been reared a Scots Presbyterian, but he had never taken to that faith. He resented its deemphasis of hierarchy and the related notion, put forth by his own tutor, George Buchanan (1506–82), that political power came from the people, who could revoke it from a bad ruler. James found the Church of England, with its emphasis on hierarchy, ritual, and order, far more to his taste. He tended to see Puritans as English Presbyterians, "brainsick and heady preachers," self-righteous, dubiously loyal, naturally anti-authoritarian if not outright rebellious. Still, English Puritans hoped that he would encourage the reforms that had been stifled by Elizabeth. On his way south they presented him with the Millenary Petition, signed by 1,000 ministers, which asked for the abolition of certain traditions such as the making of the sign of the cross at baptism, greater freedom of discretion in the use of vestments, more sermons, and stricter enforcement of the Sabbath. James, ever one to enjoy intellectual debate, called a conference of conservative and Puritan divines at Hampton Court Palace in 1604. At the conference, James promised moderate reform and a new, authorized translation of the Bible, which appeared in 1611. But he also rejected more radical change and made clear that he was a high churchman at heart by declaring "No bishop, no King." In James's eyes, radical Puritan attacks on the ecclesiastical hierarchy (i.e., bishops) were tantamount to attacking the civil hierarchy (i.e., monarchy). He viewed the logical implication of radical Puritan "reform" to be political disorder. After the conclusion of the conference, James underlined the point by authorizing the conservative Archbishop Richard Bancroft (1544–1610) to expel nonconforming clergy from their livings, depriving about 90 men of their congregations. In future, the king would continue to appease moderate Puritans by offering gradual reform and ecclesiastical preferment, leaving radicals isolated. As a result of James's divide-and-conquer strategy, most Puritans did not leave the Jacobean Church; rather, they remained an important proportion of its hierarchy and membership. Tragically, his son would see this not as an achievement but as a problem.

James tried a similar strategy – toleration for moderates, hostility toward extremists – on his Catholic subjects. Like the Puritans, this group hoped for much from the new king in 1603; and their most fervent members, too, were disappointed by the result. Like Elizabeth, James had no stomach for religious persecution if he could count on political loyalty. Prior to his accession he had promised the Catholic Henry Howard, earl of Northampton (1540–1614), privately, that he would not "persecute any that will be quiet and give but an outward obedience to the law."[21] The fact that he immediately began to negotiate a peace with Spain was also a good sign. When James insisted that Protestant British merchants and sailors should not be subject to the Inquisition when trading with Spanish possessions, many expected Spain to demand relaxation of the penal laws against English Catholics in return. But the resulting Treaty of London contained no such provision. Worse, in the aftermath of the Hampton Court Conference the king renewed low-level persecution of Catholics in order to appease Puritan critics in Parliament. Catholic expectations of their new king were dashed.

This helps to explain why in 1605 a group of hot-headed Catholic aristocrats, upset at King James's unwillingness to grant a more explicit toleration, made desperate by Spain's abandonment of their cause, launched the **Gunpowder Plot**. Their plan was to blow up the king and both houses of Parliament when they met in the House of Lords for its State opening on November 5. Remarkably, the plotters simply rented the undercroft below the House of Lords and filled it with barrels of gunpowder. Fortunately, the court was tipped off when one of the conspirators tried to warn a relative, William Parker, Lord Monteagle (1575–1622), who, in turn, approached the Privy Council. On the evening of the 4th a search was made and another conspirator, Guy Fawkes (1570–1606), was caught red-handed in the undercroft with the barrels – only hours before the king's arrival. Here, in the eyes of many English men and women, was yet more proof of Catholic treachery and God's providential care for the Protestant nation. For years afterward, they would "remember, remember, / the fifth of November" with bonfires and church bells. More immediately, the conspirators were tried and executed by February 1606. New penal laws prohibited Catholics from living in or near London, practicing law, or holding office. Finally, Catholics were forced to swear an oath acknowledging the king and denouncing the pope's claim to be able to depose civil rulers.

But James enforced the penal laws only intermittently, usually when he was trying to placate Puritans in the weeks leading up to a Parliament. As for the oath, he hoped that moderate Catholics would swear it, leaving extremists without allies. In fact, this worked, more or less. As a result, while Catholics did not secure official toleration or recognition, they were very largely allowed to live and worship in peace under the early Stuarts. The number of priests rose between 1603 and 1640 from 300 to 750; the number of Catholics from around 40,000 to perhaps 60,000. While this was a victory for tolerance, it did nothing for the Stuarts' contemporary reputation as leaders of a Protestant nation.

Jacobean religious policy in Scotland and Ireland will be discussed below. In England, at least, James had been largely content to let sleeping religious dogs lie. Unfortunately, his son Charles was not so given to compromise. Rather, he was a committed high churchman before there was such a term. What did this mean? Under James there had arisen within the Church a group of clergymen influenced by the Dutch theologian Jacobus Arminius (1560–1609). Arminius modified the Calvinist insistence on predestination by arguing that God's judgment might be influenced by human free will. That is, salvation might be won, in part, by the actions of men and women. This implied a greater emphasis on good works, religious rituals (in particular communion), and the sanctity of the clergy necessary to perform them. This, in turn, implied a stronger role for episcopacy. This theology appealed to religious conservatives, but Puritan critics saw these as Catholic beliefs and practices, short and simple. It did not help that **Arminians** generally regarded the Roman Catholic Church as the "mother" Church of all Christian denominations, albeit one that had gone astray. When the Dutch synod of Dort met in 1618, Church of England representatives voted with the majority to censure Arminius.

Things changed with the accession of King Charles in 1625. The Arminian idea that the clergy were sanctified beings fit nicely with similar notions about kings; in fact, Arminian preachers continually emphasized the sanctity of kings. Not surprisingly, Charles promoted Arminians to positions of power within the Church of England. Their leader, William Laud (1573–1645), became bishop of London in 1628 and archbishop of Canterbury in 1633. Puritan and even moderate Calvinist Church members grew alarmed, and in February 1629 a committee of the House of Commons condemned the "pernicious spreading of the Arminian faction."[22] Charles and Archbishop Laud responded that it was the Calvinists who were out of the mainstream and insisted on conformity and liturgical uniformity as Elizabeth had done. In doing so, they wrecked the spirit of religious compromise that had obtained under James. Their first major initiative was to order all communion tables to be moved back to the eastern ends of churches, thus giving them the orientation of Catholic altars. They also enforced the wearing of vestments, banned the preaching of unlicensed (usually Puritan) preachers, and attacked landowners who had impropriated (i.e., confiscated) tithes at the Reformation. Laud and his fellow Arminians regarded these orders as a return to the "beauty of holiness" of the Church, but most others saw them as dangerous innovations or Romish revivals. Unpopular, they were enforced by more frequent **visitations** by bishops and archbishops and the persecution of nonconforming clergy and lay critics in the courts of Star Chamber and High Commission.

These policies had two unforeseen results. First, they revived feelings of anticlericalism. Landowners felt that the attempt to claim back impropriate tithes violated their property rights. Puritans felt that their Church was turning against them and the Reformation which had given it birth. Overall, neither the changes in the fabric of English churches, nor the increasingly overbearing presence of Arminian clergymen, nor the persecutions of Puritans sat well with the English people. The most famous expression of this discomfort came in 1637 when William Prynne (1600–69), John Bastwick (1593–1654), and Henry Burton (1578–1648) were condemned in Star Chamber for writings critical of the bishops. Their punishment was not as brutal as Bloody Mary had imposed: they were to have their ears cropped. But on the day, a great crowd cheered them to the place of punishment; subsequently, in a show of support, many spectators dipped their handkerchiefs into the "martyrs'" blood. As this implies, the second unforeseen result of Laud's policies was that people began to draw parallels with the last Catholic reign. Staunch Protestants – and not only Puritans – thought that Arminianism looked a great deal like Catholicism. In their eyes, these persecutions were signs that Charles wanted to bring England back to Rome. But their most compelling piece of evidence for this charge lay much closer to the king: his Catholic wife.

Arguably, Buckingham's most momentous legacy had been that, after failing to engineer a Spanish marriage, he had negotiated a French one. In 1625 Charles wed the daughter of Henry IV, Henrietta Maria. In Buckingham's defense, it must be said that the marriage made a great deal of diplomatic sense: England needed powerful friends, especially as she took on Spain (though, as we have seen, the duke managed to squander that advantage in a remarkably short time by declaring war on France as well). Moreover, the marriage was, after an initial period of coolness, a very happy one which produced six children. But it was never popular. From the first, Charles's subjects disliked what they could only see as a "popish" marriage and feared that Henrietta Maria would poison his mind against Protestantism. Worse, as a princess of France and queen of England, she was entitled to maintain a court which included Catholic servants. Worse still, the treaty of marriage stipulated that she be able to worship according to the dictates of her faith. This meant a Catholic chapel staffed by Catholic clergy in the heart of the English court. Worst of all, what about the religious training of the children? This was a very good question, for in granting a dispensation to marry the "heretic" king of England, the pope had secretly advised the new queen that she was obligated to rear her children as Roman Catholics. Consequently, she regarded herself as the means by which both the king and his kingdom would eventually be returned to the One True Faith.

Today, in our tolerant and ecumenical age, it is difficult to conjure up much understanding of the religious anxieties of Charles's subjects. But if one compares the English fear of international Catholicism with the mid-twentieth-century American fear of international communism, then the picture becomes a little clearer. It was as if, during the most dangerous period in the Cold War, the first lady of the United States, Mamie Eisenhower or Jacqueline Kennedy, were a publicly acknowledged card-carrying member of the Communist Party. In fact, Protestant England's situation was much worse. Not only did the king's spouse have his ear, not only had she filled his court with her fellow sympathizers, she was paving the way for a future Catholic takeover by ensuring that the hereditary succession would bring her presumably Catholic children to the throne. Charles's tolerance for the growing number of "Papists" at court, combined with his avid persecution of Puritans – who may have been extreme, but were at least Protestants – led to the darker charge that he was a secret Catholic himself.

In fact, the charge was false. King Charles was a Church of England Protestant, as was his archbishop of Canterbury. The former insisted that his children should be raised as Protestants; the latter refused the pope's offer of a cardinal's hat. If the king was married to a Catholic, it was because that match made the most sense given the international diplomatic situation. If he was soft on Catholics it was because he saw them as a relatively small, loyal, and, ultimately, harmless minority. If he was hard on Puritans it was because he saw the implications of their thought to be revolutionary and dangerous. These reasons all made a great deal of sense – to the king and his court circle. Unfortunately, that circle was smaller and more narrow than his father's had been. Moreover, neither Charles nor his courtiers made any significant attempt to justify themselves to his subjects beyond Whitehall through a propaganda campaign. As a result, the weighty straw of religion was added to the pile of long-term issues breaking the back of consensus upon which the English State depended.

This became clear in the Parliament of 1628–9. Once again, the king needed money to fight the war. Once again, his plea came in the middle of a depression, this time in the textile trade. With Buckingham removed, at least one major issue of contention between king and Commons had been eliminated. However, after furious debate, the lower house voted to assist merchants who refused to pay the impositions; and to condemn the Arminian clergy. At this point, the king decided that enough was enough. On March 2, the Speaker of the House of Commons announced an adjournment, which many interpreted as the first step toward dissolution. In response, one of the most outspoken members, Sir John Eliot (1592–1632), rose to offer a series of resolutions. The Speaker attempted to cut him off by rising from his chair, which would end debate. At this point, two of Eliot's colleagues forced the Speaker back into it, one of them, Denzil Holles (1599–1680), exclaiming: "zounds, you shall sit as long as the House pleases!" As the king's sergeant-at-arms pounded on the door with his mace, the house passed three resolutions: that any subject paying the impositions, that anyone counseling their collection, and that anyone intending innovation in religion was "a capital enemy to the kingdom and commonwealth." This language, stark as it was, hid an even grimmer reality: the monarch himself had initiated all of these measures. Obviously, the relationship between king and Parliament, as well as the financial, military, and religious situations, had reached a crisis point. Their resolution would come well beyond the walls of Parliament or even of London, in the localities of England, Scotland, and Ireland.

The Personal Rule and the Problem of Local Authority

It should come as little surprise that after the dramatic events of 1629, King Charles chose to not call Parliament again for 11 years. There is some question as to whether this was, at first, a conscious resolution to rule without Parliament or one which grew over time as the king found that he got away with it. Certainly, he must have concluded that the honorable peers and gentlemen were more of a hindrance than a help. They had proved not only uncooperative but challenging to his authority as sovereign and unhelpful to his management of his financial situation, the war, and his "reform" of England's complicated religious situation. There was no reason for the king to wish to hear from them again. Nor was there, in his mind, any obligation to do so. Before examining Parliament's point of view, it is necessary to probe more deeply the king's attempt to return the English constitution to its pristine, pre-parliamentary state, an enterprise that lasted 11 years and that has come to be known as the "Personal Rule."[23]

The chief difficulty facing Charles in attempting to rule without Parliament was the very reason he had been forced to call it in the first place: he needed money. He needed money to run his court, to pay for his art collection, and, above all, to fight his wars with France and Spain. How could the king possibly meet his financial obligations without parliamentary taxation? As Salisbury had reminded his father, there were only two choices: cut expenses or raise revenue. Remarkably, Charles did both. First, he authorized his lord treasurer, Richard, Lord Weston (1577–1635; from 1633 earl of Portland), to launch a thorough reform of court and government, to match Laud's reform of the Church and the activities of Thomas Wentworth, earl of Strafford (1593–1641), in Ireland (see below) – in fact, the policy came to be known as "Thorough." It called for the elimination of useless offices (sinecures) and of fees in favor of established salaries. The Privy Council established standing committees for Ireland, the militia, and trade. The performance of masques and the purchase of artwork were both curtailed. More importantly, the king sued for peace with both France and Spain. This allowed him to disband the bulk of his military forces, which were far more expensive than his paintings.

One might assume that the king's frugality and pursuit of peace would be popular with the political elite. But some former MPs were angry that the Protestant crusade against Spain and France had been called off; others worried that a frugal monarch with a more efficient administration would use it to encroach on his subjects' liberties. They found grounds for these fears in Charles's measures to raise revenue. First, in violation of Parliament's resolution of 1629, he raised the Customs rates unilaterally once again – more impositions. Next, following an Elizabethan precedent, he sold monopolies and farmed out other government services to anyone who could offer quick cash. More positively from a Puritan point of view, his government collected recusancy fines more assiduously. Finally, he had his officials search medieval statute and precedent books for any law recorded therein which might enable him to squeeze a few more shillings out of his subjects. Thus, the government revived old fees and fines associated with refusing a summons to be knighted, enclosure, hunting and building in royal forests, and the inheritance of widows and wards. In each case, violation of the law or use of a royal "service" resulted in a fee to the Crown. Most notoriously of all, in order to pay for the navy (which Charles wanted to keep in a state of readiness as a bargaining tool with France and Spain), he extended an old tax called **Ship Money** from payment by few coastal towns and maritime counties to the whole nation.

These policies just about solved the king's financial problems, at least for a while. Assisted by a boom in foreign trade which increased Customs yields, Weston managed to get the revenue up to between £900,000 and £1 million. As a result, the royal debt became manageable by 1638. Unfortunately, but perhaps predictably, if the king felt that Parliament had violated the constitution by interfering in his right to govern, many aristocrats now began to conclude that the Personal Rule violated the constitution by infringing on the notion that an Englishman's property was his own and that no king had the right to confiscate it without his (parliamentary) permission. In 1636, a wealthy landowner named John Hampden (1594–1643) instigated a test case at law by refusing to pay his Ship Money assessment (all of £1) on the grounds that it was a non-parliamentary tax. While the king argued that he had a right to suspend the law, and so collect the tax, during a state of emergency (the so-called **suspending power**), Hampden countered that there was no current state of emergency to justify its collection. The king responded by taking him to court. In the end, Charles won the Ship Money case, but just barely: although the panel of 12 judges was hand-picked by the Crown, five decided for Hampden. Moreover, one of the judges deciding for the majority foolishly claimed that the king could command all of his subjects' property if he wished. No landowner could support that. While Hampden lost his legal case and paid the tax, he had won a moral victory. By the end of the 1630s his example, combined with an agricultural depression, was encouraging others to withhold their payments of royal taxes and forced loans. Ship Money assessments returned 96 percent of the amount demanded in 1636, but only 89 percent in 1637, 39 percent in 1638, and just 20 percent in 1639.

The tax strike signified bigger problems for the Stuart regime than a mere lack of money. At this point, it should be remembered that Charles did not, like his French counterpart Louis XIII (1601–43; reigned 1610–43), have a vast, efficient, and well-paid bureaucracy to run his government, collect his taxes, or keep the peace, generally, in the localities. Instead, he relied on the loyalty and good will of unpaid aristocrats and gentry, who served as his lords lieutenant, JPs, and sheriffs. In the 1630s, that sense of mutual interest began to break down. Increasingly, the landed elite began to resent the growing interference of the Privy Council and bishops in local life; and they began to refuse not only to pay taxes themselves but to collect them from their friends and neighbors. Order was beginning to break down in the shires of England.

By 1640, the king was in a precarious position. While he had cut expenditure significantly, the growing tax strike meant that his court and administration were living on the tightest of budgets. Any increase in expenditure, any crisis, would cause the king to fall into spiraling debt and – probably – to have to call a Parliament. Worse, if he should face such a crisis, he would have to deal with the accumulated resentment of his subjects, the victims of "Thorough," who had seen the Church and government increase their presence in their lives and their costs to their pocketbooks. As the decade of Personal Rule came to a close, the king precipitated such a crisis by mishandling a combination of old problems – money, war, and religion – which originated among his own people, the Scots.

The Crisis of Scotland

As we have seen, in 1603 King James VI of Scotland became James I of England. He continued to rule both countries separately, like a modern chairman of two boards. That is, the king governed England through his court and administration in London according to English constitutional arrangements and law; while he governed his northern kingdom through that in Edinburgh according to Scottish custom and law. The Scots resented this cumbersome arrangement: since the sovereign resided permanently in London, all decisions were actually made there, very likely according to the advice of English courtiers. James tried to mollify this resentment and ease the tensions between the two kingdoms. Early in his reign he began to style himself king of Great Britain, France, and Ireland; redesigned the coinage; ordered the use of a union flag (similar to that in use today) by all ships at sea; and proposed a Treaty of Union between the two nations as part of his general plan for peace at home and abroad. But, after heated debate, the English Parliament roundly rejected the treaty. These debates exposed the ancient animosity between the two countries as English MPs pushed the envelope of parliamentary free speech. One, referring to Scotland's troubled political history, declared that "[t]hey have not suffered above two Kings to die in their Beds, these two hundred Years," while another opined that a union between England and Scotland would be like that between a judge and his prisoner.[24] In short, the English saw the Scots as impoverished savages. For their part, the Scots continued to feel like second-class citizens in the new constitutional arrangements.

Neither James nor his son did much else to alleviate that feeling. Each visited his northern kingdom but once more, James in 1617, Charles in 1633. Still, James managed to keep the Scottish nobility in check; pacify the Highlands and borderlands; and even persuade the Kirk to recognize the authority, albeit limited, of a revived Scottish episcopacy. His ultimate goal was to neutralize the most radical Presbyterians and bring the Kirk into line with the Church of England. But he was smart enough to realize that this process could only happen incrementally, with a maximum of friendly persuasion and subtle intrigue and a minimum of brute royal force. Once again, his son was not so shrewd. Charles expected obedience and conformity from his Scottish subjects as surely as he did from his English ones – even in that most troubled area of seventeenth-century life, religion. After all, good subjects should worship as the king worshipped. In 1637, just when he least needed trouble, without consulting the Scottish Privy Council or Parliament, the king decreed that a version of the English Book of Common Prayer, revised by the Scottish bishops in a Laudian direction, should be used in the churches of his northern kingdom.

Perhaps Charles thought he could get away with this because Scotland was, as we have seen, notoriously divided – into Highlanders and Lowlanders, urban dwellers and farmers, lairds and clergy. But on this issue he managed to unite nearly the whole country. As with English Puritans, so with Scottish Presbyterians, the promotion of an Arminian-style high Church liturgy in Scotland smacked of a movement back to Rome. At the debut of the new rite in St. Giles's Cathedral, Edinburgh, on July 23, 1637, a group of maidservants shouted down the minister with cries of "[t]he mass is entered amongst us." One woman hurled a stool at the bishop of Edinburgh, who barely escaped bodily harm in the ensuing riot. This was not the sort of decorous ritual and meek submission that Charles and Laud had in mind. More seriously, in February 1638, representatives of nearly every important constituency in Scotland (excluding Catholics) signed the **National Covenant** to oppose the king's religious policies, binding themselves to remain united to each other and to uphold true religion against Laudian innovation. Specifically, the Covenant stated that only the Scottish Parliament and the general assembly of the Presbyterian Church had the right to make religious policy for Scotland. Later that year, the Covenanters abolished the power of the Scottish bishops and declared episcopacy incompatible with the Kirk.

This, Charles could only regard as an act of rebellion. During the winter of 1638–9, he called on his English lords lieutenant and other local leaders to raise an army to fight what would come to be called the First Bishops' War. The Scots Covenanters replied by raising an army of their own. The king's forces were hastily assembled, poorly trained, and starved for funds. But their biggest problem was morale. Charles was counting on the traditional English hatred of the Scots to inspire his forces; in fact, the gentlemen and their tenant farmers who made them up were reluctant to leave their native land to attack fellow Protestants in order to enforce royal policies they found oppressive. In other words, however much they may have hated the Scots, they hated Laud, "Thorough," and the policies of the Personal Rule more. Indeed, some Puritan nobles and former MPs were beginning to pull for the Scots; the most committed went so far as to begin secret negotiations with them. As the royal army marched north, it began to desert, more or less drifting away without firing a shot. By contrast, the Scottish army, inspired by religious fervor, remained in being following the inconclusive truce initiated by the Treaty of Berwick of June 1639.

By April 1640 the king was effectively bankrupt and facing a rebel army within his northern kingdom. He had little choice but to call a Parliament. Naturally, when it met for the first time in 11 years, that body had no intention of voting money for another army before its grievances could be heard. After all, the king was likely to take the money, raise the army, defeat the Scots, and then turn it on his unruly English subjects. When Charles realized that this Parliament was not going to cooperate, he dissolved it in disgust, giving rise to the nickname it has borne among historians ever since: the Short Parliament.

During the summer of 1640, order, already under strain, began to disintegrate all over England. The tax strike was now widespread; the City of London refused to advance the king money; there was isolated rioting; and the Scots continued to march south. Charles called upon the Irish Parliament for assistance so that he could resume hostilities in what would be called the Second Bishops' War. But that August the Covenanters defeated a throw-together royal force under the king's new chief military adviser, the earl of Strafford, at Newburn, Northumberland (see map 11, p. 242). This allowed the Scots to occupy the counties of Durham and Northumberland, an arrangement confirmed by the Treaty of Ripon in October. According to the treaty, the king had to pay the Scots forces £850 a day until a more permanent settlement could be reached. Worse, there was no royal army between them and London. Now Charles had no choice. He had to call a Parliament and let it sit.

The Long Parliament

That summer, for the first time in English history, parliamentary elections were actually contested all over the country. Heretofore, the vast majority of MPs had been selected in friendly but closed-door meetings of like-minded local nobles and gentry doing the king's will, or in public but amiable acclamations of recognized provincial leaders. Now, for the first time in many constituencies, there were real elections because there was a real choice between candidates who more or less favored royal policy and those who did not. The former might not have approved of all the king's actions, but he was still king, God's lieutenant on earth. They thought it necessary for the defense of the realm and incumbent upon their duty as good Christians to vote him the money for an army and trust that, out of the good will thus generated, he would listen to reason afterwards. Their opponents also recognized the king as king, but for the past 11 years they had been compiling a list of grievances against his government in Church and State. They intended to use Parliament's power of the purse, the threat of Scottish invasion, and his need for an army (the problem of war and foreign policy) to force the king to change his domestic policies and, perhaps, even agree to limitations on his power. More specifically, they campaigned on a platform of safeguarding the position of Parliament within the constitution (the problem of sovereignty), the property of all Englishmen (the problem of finance), and the Church of England as a Protestant establishment (the problem of religion). Thus, all of the long-term tensions of the English polity came to a head in the localities (the problem of local control) during the election of that summer and fall of 1640.

Overwhelmingly, the king's critics won these contests. Seemingly the entire political nation, with the exception of a few die-hard loyalists and slavish courtiers, agreed on what was wrong with the country and, for the first time, it was royal policy. What would eventually come to be called the **Long Parliament** first met in November 1640. Unlike previous Parliaments, it was not to be dominated by privy councilors and officeholders. Rather, a group of leaders emerged whose reputations had been forged in previous disagreements with King Charles: in the Lords, the earls of Bedford (1593–1641) and Essex and William, Viscount Saye and Sele (1582–1662); in the Commons, John Hampden, Denzil Holles, Oliver St. John (ca. 1598–1673), and, above all, John Pym (ca. 1584–1643). Indeed, one of their first acts was to cut off the king from more conservative advice by having Strafford arrested. Their long-term goal was to limit the power of the king to do what he had done in the 1630s. The result was a sweeping program of legislation confronting each of the five areas of tension described in this chapter.

For example, one of their earliest bills addressed the sovereignty problem head on by stating that they were not to be prorogued nor dissolved but by their own consent. Charles's agreement to this act ensured their permanency during the headlong race to reform. Along the same lines, they passed the Triennial Act, which required the king to summon Parliament at least once every three years. Second, they addressed the financial problem by prohibiting impositions, monopolies, Ship Money, distraint of knighthood, and the revival of the Forest Laws – that is, the whole financial program of the Personal Rule. As a corollary, they reaffirmed the illegality of taxation without parliamentary permission. Next, Parliament turned to the vexed matter of religion by eliminating the ecclesiastical courts and the apparatus of censorship which had so profoundly intruded upon the private lives of English men and women. Parliament also abolished the prerogative legal tribunals by which the royal or episcopal will had been enforced: gone were the courts of Star Chamber, High Commission, Requests, and the Councils of Wales and the North. Finally, the House of Commons impeached Strafford on charges of high treason – the first such parliamentary charges against a royal official of this rank since the Wars of the Roses. Strafford mounted an effective legal defense and his fellow peers were reluctant to convict him. So the Commons fell back on another old procedure to secure his death: a vote of attainder. (Later, in 1644, they would use the same expedient to condemn Laud.) Each of these measures reduced or interfered with the royal prerogative or changed the current structure of Church or State. Thus, each had deep implications for the issue of sovereignty, as well as the more specific issues which they respectively addressed. Indeed, England, for a few brief months in 1641, might even be considered a constitutional monarchy.

Of course, none of these measures, including the attainder of Strafford, could become law without the royal assent. After some hesitation, Charles gave it in every case. He felt that he had no choice, because he still needed the cooperation of Parliament in order, first, to pay the Scottish army and, eventually, to pay for an English army to fight them! As for the Scots themselves, they would wait and see. At some point in the early 1640s their goal became not simply to defend Presbyterianism in Scotland; it was to strike a bargain, perhaps with the king, perhaps with the parliamentary leadership, to impose Presbyterianism on England. As for Parliament, there was, in fact, little prospect of it voting the king funding for an army, for there was no trust between its leaders and the man who sat on the throne. Many members feared that, once voted, a royal army might be turned upon them, used to imprison those leaders and repeal their legislation.

In fact, their fears were well grounded, for this is precisely what the king, the queen, and his advisers at court had in mind. Charles, in particular, believed not only that Parliament's actions were sinful in themselves because they attacked the Great Chain of Being and his Divine Right; but that to cooperate with them would have been sinful as well. Instead, he pretended to go along, bided his time, and waited for an opening. Ironically, that opening came precisely because Pym and his supporters could not trust the king. This became obvious in May 1641 when it was learned that Charles had encouraged his army officers to rescue Strafford from the Tower in what came to be known as the Army Plot. The parliamentary leadership responded by rushing the earl to execution on May 12. As Essex so ruthlessly put it, "stone dead hath no fellow."[25] Simultaneously, Pym secretly encouraged the Scots to stand fast, so that the king would continue to keep Parliament in being. So long as Charles was forced to do so, the parliamentary leaders could promote more and more radical legislation to reduce his power. Unfortunately for the parliamentarians, this strategy had a built-in flaw: the more radical Pym's proposed legislation became, the less acceptable it was to moderates and conservatives in Parliament. These men might not have been happy with the king's past policies, but they still wanted him to rule. With every measure pushing the envelope of the constitution, the majority supporting it shrank while those who felt that Pym was going too far increased. Few would have sided with Charles in 1640; perhaps half the political nation did so by 1642. This became clear in the summer and fall of 1641, when Pym proposed a series of radical measures culminating in the Grand Remonstrance.

The Grand Remonstrance was a long list of grievances against the king ranging over the past 16 years. It concluded with two radical demands. The first was that the king should name as his ministers only men approved by Parliament. The second was that he should call a synod for a general reform of the Church of England. Many in the ruling elite thought that this was going too far. The first demand would establish a right of parliamentary oversight on royal appointments that is a standard feature of many constitutional governments today. But to contemporaries it was tantamount to eliminating the king's ability to choose his own servants – an intolerable position for a monarch who was supposed to rule as well as reign. Worse, the second demand was widely taken as an attack not only on the bishops but also on the Book of Common Prayer and, thus, traditional forms of worship. Many country gentlemen loved their Prayer Book and opposed Puritan innovations in religion as staunchly as they had opposed Laud's. Moreover, while they may have had little love for the bishops, they still associated episcopal authority with royal authority and order. Both were clearly suffering in the summer of 1641 as political, religious, and economic demonstrations became more common in London and the countryside. When Sir Edward Dering (1598–1644), a former anti-court MP, read with horror reports of mob icono-clasm in his home county of Kent, he spoke against the Remonstrance, noting: "I did not dream that we should remonstrate downward, tell stories to the people and talk of the King as of a third person."[26] Debate on the Remonstrance was spirited – swords were drawn in the House of Commons – and lasted late into the night of November 22–3. In the end, the Grand Remonstrance passed, but narrowly: 159 votes to 148. The losing 148 would form the nucleus of a Royalist bloc. Pym's coalition had broken down as its more conservative element gravi-tated back toward the king. The next issue to arise in Parliament would indicate just how real these divisions were. It also promised to determine whether the king would weather the crisis and repudiate Pym's legislative program or continue down the road toward constitutional monarchy. As before, the balance was to be tipped from one of Charles's other kingdoms.

The Crisis of Ireland

During the fall of 1641, as debate over the Grand Remonstrance raged in England, Ireland was, once again, gripped by rebellion. This action was revenge for 30 years of English and Scots Presbyterian arrogance, exploitation, and religious persecution. It should be recalled that, following the last major rebellion in Ireland and the flight of the earls in 1607, the government in London had returned to the expedient of plantation: the forcible eviction of native Gaelic and even "Old English" Catholic landowners and tenant farmers and their replacement by Scots Presbyterian (or "New English") immigrants. The practice was carried through especially harshly in Ulster, the ancestral home of the O'Neills. Many Irish landowners and peasants were forcibly removed from their lands and the protection of their clans to the rocky and infertile western shore of the island. Those who remained became virtual serfs, paying exorbitant rents to often absentee Protestant landlords. Their new neighbors on the confiscated lands, immigrant Scots Presbyterians, had nothing but disdain for their religion and culture. By the accession of Charles I, the New English Protestants dominated the Irish government and Parliament; yet the vast majority of the population remained Catholic, either in the form of the remaining Old English landlords or Gaelic Irish peasants.

Throughout the early Stuart period the Crown maintained its power and a degree of law and order, as in Scotland, by playing each of these groups off against the other two. The most skillful and ruthless such player had been Charles's last lord deputy, Strafford, who had come to Ireland as Sir Thomas Wentworth in 1633. He had secured the cooperation of the Irish Parliament, leading to full treasuries and a powerful army, by promising the Old English to consider easing the penal laws against Catholics while at the same time promising the New English that he would enforce them! In fact, his failure to keep these promises combined with his ruthless continuation of plantation and his dedication to "Thorough" had eventually made him as hated a figure in Ireland as Laud was in England and Scotland. Nor did it help Strafford's popularity that he had enriched himself along the way. He had united Ireland, but only in opposition to himself.

After Strafford returned to England to advise Charles in 1640, these groups went their separate ways. The New English had more in common with the Scottish Covenanters and Pym's forces in the English Parliament than with the rest of the Irish. Gaelic Irish clan leaders began to plot rebellion in Ulster. They hoped that a weakened king might be forced to make concessions, including toleration for the Catholic Church. In the fall of 1641, the O'Neills of Ulster rose. As the Catholic Gaelic peasantry began to settle scores, the rebellion careened out of control. Some 3–4,000 Protestant settlers were slaughtered outright. Others were stripped naked and forced to flee along the roads, a symbolic reminder, perhaps, that they had arrived in the plantations with nothing and would be forced to leave the same way. Symbolism aside, this was nothing short of a death sentence in a cold, wet winter: perhaps twice as many died of starvation and exposure. The Old English, repulsed by the bloodshed but fearing a Covenanter settlement in Ireland if they did not fight, and convinced that the Catholic side was actually the loyal one, joined the clan leaders in the Confederation of Kilkenny in 1642.

The Irish Rebellion confirmed everything that English Protestants believed about Irish Catholics. By the time news of the rebellion reached London, the number of Protestant dead had been inflated to 150,000. Popular pamphlets described Catholic atrocities in lurid detail – "no quarter is given, no faith kept, all houses burnt and demolished, man, wife and child put to the sword."[27] Well into the eighteenth century, annual memorial sermons would recount this sectarian horror. More immediately, London was in an uproar. There was much sympathy for the murdered settlers; but also much fear that the Catholic Irish, no doubt assisted by the continental Catholic powers and the native English Catholic population, were about to invade, reestablish their religion, and put nonconforming Protestants to the sword. Worse, the Irish rebels claimed to be acting in the name of the king and had a forged document to prove his support. It was in this atmosphere that the Grand Remonstrance was proposed, debated, and passed.

Obviously, another army was necessary to pacify Ireland. It was equally obvious that neither side in English politics trusted the other to command that army. In December 1641, the House of Commons introduced and passed a Militia Bill entrusting command to a lord general to be named by Parliament. At the same time, a group of Puritan merchants seized control of the civic government in London, closing off City funds to the king and putting its well-equipped trained bands at the service of Parliament. Charles could only regard these measures as an attempt to strip him of the last shreds of his prerogative: after all, even the most biased devotee of the Ancient Constitution would agree that the king's most basic function had always been to lead the military. On January 4, 1642, he responded with force. On that day he strode into the House of Commons accompanied by courtiers and royal guards, their swords drawn, in order to arrest Pym and four other parliamentary leaders. But the five MPs had got wind of their imminent arrest and fled, leaving Charles looking rather foolish in the short run. In the long run, it was clear that there could be no peace, let alone cooperation, between king and Parliament. Nor did he feel safe in the Puritan-controlled metropolis. In February he put the queen on a ship bound for the continent and then fled with the court to York.

By this stage, military action of some kind between king and Parliament was inevitable. That is not to say that anyone wanted war. Centuries of belief in the Great Chain of Being and monarchy were difficult to break. But now, with rebellion in Scotland and Ireland fueling military solutions in England, no one knew how to make peace. Each side armed itself, either in reaction to the violence abroad or out of fear of violence at home. Each could only view the other's posture of "self-defense" as threatening war. In March, Parliament, fearing a popish plot, passed a Militia Ordinance and, acting on it without royal consent, seized all the garrisons it could and began to raise troops. In June, the king began to do the same, presenting local leaders with a difficult choice – whose order to obey? Finally, on August 22, 1642, King Charles raised the royal standard – tantamount to a declaration of hostilities – at Nottingham. The English Civil War had begun.

CHAPTER EIGHT

Civil War, Revolution, and the Search for Stability, 1642–1660

At first glance, twenty-first-century Americans should be well disposed to understand Britain's mid-seventeenth-century crisis. Their own Civil War exposed them to fighting that pit brother against brother, as well as the long-lasting resentments and lingering disputes inherent in such a conflict. But Americans might be surprised by how little the British Civil Wars are remembered officially today in Britain. Compare Gettysburg, littered with monuments to the combatants of both sides, victors and vanquished, survivors and fallen, to the absence of so much as a marker for most English battlesites of the 1640s before the nineteenth century, and the misplacement of both the nineteenth- and twentieth-century obelisks for the battle of Naseby! For Britain has never embraced the revolutionary actions that resulted from its Civil Wars. Margaret Thatcher even claimed, during bicentenary festivities for the French Revolution in 1989, that Britain was great precisely because it had never *had* a revolution. If British attitudes to the events of the 1640s and 1650s are conflicted and ambiguous, it may be because, unlike the American Civil Wars, there was no clear "right" side for politically correct moderns to embrace. Rather, most participants, whether Royalists or Parliamentarians, soldiers or clergymen, were attempting to uphold some version of the established order. Nearly all claimed that they were defending traditional values and the core of the English constitution in Church and State. They just could not agree on what those values and core were.

When the Long Parliament met in 1640, the political nation – nobility, gentry, and urban oligarchs – had been almost unanimous in their desire to undo the policies of the personal rule. But over the course of the next two years, as the parliamentary leadership grew more radical in pursuit of that goal, a remarkable transformation took place. In the months following the king's departure from London, some 236 MPs followed him, leaving 302 in the capital. What separated these two groups? While both agreed that Charles had gone too far in the 1630s, the former felt that Pym and his supporters had gone even farther in the opposite direction, and thus become the greater danger to the English constitution in Church and State. Put simply, this group of MPs worried less about royal tyranny and popery than they did about civil disorder and anarchy. They were unwilling to sanction a fundamental readjustment of the constitution in order to enhance Parliament's power at the expense of the king's. Nor did they want to see godly reformation of the Church if it meant tampering with beloved ceremonies and repudiating uniformity and discipline. They would go to war to defend a traditional order which they knew to be flawed but which, in their view, still represented the best interests of themselves and the nation. During the ensuing conflict, these men would come to be known as Royalists or **Cavaliers**.[1]

Even among their opponents, there were very few in 1642 who wanted to depose the king and establish a republic. Most believed that they, too, fought for the proper balance of the English constitution and some went so far as to say that they opposed the king in order to defend him from malevolent advisers who were manipulating him into popery and tyranny. In any case, most on this side were committed so fully to the gains made by the Long Parliament, believed so fully in the existence of a Catholic plot to subvert their religion and liberty, and distrusted Charles so completely, that they saw their only recourse in taking up arms against him. This group of MPs would come to be known as the Parliamentarians or **Roundheads**.[2]

Still, it takes more than 538 people to make a war. Most English men and women were reluctant to take a stand, let alone fight. Ordinary people often failed to see this as their feud: "what is the cause to me if my goods be lost?" was the sentiment of many.[3] Others tried to opt out on principle. In at least 11 counties by 1645 lesser gentry and yeomen, armed with clubs and farming implements, formed anti-war groups to stop troops and tax assessors from both sides despoiling their county. Generals from both sides found themselves having to parley with these "Clubmen": "[t]hey conceive themselves able to keepe of[f] both the Parliament's forces and the Kings alsoe from contribution and quarter in their County. That is their vaine hope."[4] In fact, many were eventually forced to abandon that hope and choose a side. When that moment came, on what bases did the English people choose?

This was a civil war, not a war between states nor a class war. It therefore was – and is – difficult to predict who would support which side. Certainly, more peers and clergy supported the Royalists, but these groups were insignificant proportions of the total population. In any case, there were Parliamentarian peers and clergy as well. The gentry split almost evenly, with over half avoiding choosing either side openly. London merchants and lawyers probably opted more for Parliament than the king, but their bread and butter lay in London, and so material interest probably influenced their decision. Artisans in the many clothworking towns also sided with Parliament. But probably as many town councils supported the king as supported his opponents. At the lowest level, historians used to assume a lack of choice: tenants would simply do what they were told by their landlords in support of one side or the other. But recent research suggests that ordinary people at the parish level knew what the war was about and followed the political, military, and religious changes closely. Thus, both sides could call on unfeigned support up and down the social scale. Geographically, the king's strength lay to the West and the North, Parliament's to the East and South, but this had as much to do with the location of their respective headquarters as anything else. Theologically, those with "godly" or Puritan religious values became Parliamentarians, whereas Laudians and those loyal to the conservative liturgy became Royalists. Catholics may have sympathized with the king, but most, understandably, sought to stay well out of the fighting. Overall, then, religious belief had the greatest perceptible influence on which side one chose, but since we have no religious census for the 1640s, we must still be cautious.

Nevertheless, it should be obvious from this analysis that, whatever the motivations behind these choices, however heterogeneous the two sides, one of them had all the long-term material advantages. By controlling the southeast, Parliament had access to the wealthiest and most populous part of the country. This gave it the larger tax base and recruitment pool for its armies. More particularly, in seizing control of London, Parliament possessed the nation's greatest port, its administrative and financial nerve center, and the metropolis's substantial trained bands. This would make it easier to collect taxes, solicit loans, raise armies, and keep them supplied. Moreover, in controlling the ports, the navy, and that part of England closest to Europe, Parliament was able to block the king from receiving aid from other European monarchies, all of whom paid lip service to his cause but, in the end, little more. The only question was whether the parliamentary side could survive long enough for these factors to come into play. This was uncertain because, as in the American Civil War two centuries later, while most of the nation's fiscal, industrial, and naval capacity was on one side, most of its experienced military talent fought on the other. That is, at first, the best soldiers were the king's. So, in one sense, the First English Civil War was a race to see if Royalist military experience could win the day before parliamentary fiscal and demographic might proved overwhelming.

Rebellion, 1642–1646

It should therefore come as no surprise that the first campaign, in the fall of 1642, began well for the king. The earl of Essex, who led the parliamentary army, had allowed the Royalists to get between him and London when both armies met and fought the first set-piece battle at Edgehill, in north Oxfordshire, on October 23 (see map 11, p. 242). The king's nephew, Prince Rupert of the Rhine (1619–82), leading a wing of the Royalist cavalry, smashed through the parliamentary horse and pursued them for miles. By the time his men and their worn-out horses returned to the battle, however, the parliamentary infantry had stood firm at the push of pike in the center and both sides retired. The battle was, therefore, technically a draw, but it left the Royalists controlling the west Midlands, with a clear path to

London. The king's army set off for the capital; only a massed defense by soldiers and the London trained bands halted Rupert's troops just west of the city at Turnham Green. Subsequently, Charles retired to winter at Oxford, which would be his headquarters for the duration of the war.

Edgehill showed that there would be no quick fix to this war. Both sides had to prepare for the long haul along a broad front. Yet, traditional English military organization, the militia, was temporary and local. When, for example, Norfolk first raised money and troops for Parliament, one gentleman specified they were "for the defence of the county, not to be sent out."[5] The farmers and tradesmen who made up the county militia tended to grumble and desert if they fought too far from home. Parliament dealt with this by reorganizing county-based armies into regional ones: the Eastern Association, comprised of East Anglia and surrounding counties, was one of the strongest. But no one region was exclusively loyal to one side or the other. Even Kent, solidly controlled by Parliament, experienced localized Royalist uprisings. Clearly, localism, the lack of a sense of national purpose, would hamper both sides.

Further, paying and outfitting vast armies required massive organization. Here, Parliament proved the most innovative, thanks to the realistic leadership of John Pym. In order to man the parliamentary armies, he convinced Parliament to agree to the forced impressment of soldiers. In order to supply and pay them he secured parliamentary approval for the sequestration (i.e., confiscation) of land owned by Royalists, compulsory weekly (later monthly) county assessments, and a new tax called the **Excise** (today, we would call it a sales tax) on those necessary and popular commodities ale, beer, cider, perry, and tobacco. Ultimately, these measures would mock earlier concerns about Charles's illegal taxation. As one Lancashire man noted, parliamentary assessment was "illegal, and the Earle of Strafford lost his life for the like act."[6] Parliament's Excise commissioners had unlimited search powers, which had been one of the great complaints against the early Stuart monopolists. Perhaps unsurprisingly, Charles was more inclined to operate within the confines of traditional institutions – transferring Chancery, Exchequer, and the court of Wards to Oxford – and local assessments. But as these broke down, his field officers resorted to free quarter and plunder. Counting the costs of this war is impossible. Who records pillaging? But a single example gives some idea of the scale: Kent's *yearly* payment for Ship Money in the 1630s barely equaled that county's *monthly* payment to Parliament in 1645–6. England's tax burden, as a proportion of the gross national product, was probably heavier in the 1640s than it had ever been or would be until the world wars of the twentieth century.

Despite Parliament's financial superiority, the campaigning season of 1643 saw Royalist victories in the North, west Midlands, and southwest, in particular the capture of the port of Bristol. This made it easier for the king to maintain communications with, and eventually employ, troops from Ireland. That year, he ordered the Royalist commander there, James Butler, marquess of Ormond (1610–88), to come to terms with the Catholic Confederates of Kilkenny for the purpose of raising troops for England. Parliamentary seizure and publication in

Map 11 *The Bishops' Wars and Civil Wars, 1637–60.*

1645 of the king's private correspondence on this matter – in which he promised the Catholics not only religious toleration but that their bishops could sit in the Irish House of Lords – would further discredit him with his Protestant subjects.

But Parliament, too, sought outside reinforcements from a Celtic kingdom. Early in 1643, Pym, dying of cancer, engineered the **Solemn League and Covenant** with the Scots, whose army was the most battle-hardened in the British Isles. The Covenanters put a high price on their friendship: £30,000 a month (here, Parliament's new taxation was crucial) and a parliamentary commitment to establish a strict Presbyterian settlement on England. In the end, the religious settlement worked out by the Westminster Assembly of (largely Presbyterian) Divines pleased few. But the military settlement worked: early in 1644 the Scottish Covenanters marched south in support of Parliament, threatening the king's control of the North. Rupert rushed to relieve the Royalists at York and, late in the day on July 2, 1644, met the parliamentary forces, which included the Scots and armies from Yorkshire and the Eastern Association. The battle of Marston Moor (see map 11) was the bloodiest of the entire war.[7] The turning point came when the Eastern Association cavalry, led by a little-known gentleman from Huntingdonshire named Oliver Cromwell (1599–1658), charged and routed Rupert's flank. In the center, the Scots infantry stood firm and, when Cromwell turned his horses back to help them, the battle turned to a rout. Some 4,000 Cavaliers were killed. As Cromwell noted, "God made them as stubble to our swords."[8]

Marston Moor was a shattering blow to the Royalists, but not the decisive victory for the Parliamentarians that it could have been. This was because there seemed to be no consistent war strategy and precious little military competence on the parliamentary side. In 1644, for example, Essex was lured into Devon and Cornwall only to be surrounded on a tiny peninsula, from which he and his staff managed to escape by boat, leaving their infantry and artillery to surrender. In the face of such disasters, the parliamentary coalition began to fall out over war aims. For example, Cromwell attacked the Eastern Association commander, Edward Montagu, earl of Manchester (1602–71), for failing to pursue energetically the king's troops in several indecisive battles in the Midlands. Manchester's response indicates the ambivalence on the parliamentary side: "if we beat the King ninety and nine times yet he is King still, and so will his posterity be after him, but if the King beat us once we shall be all hanged, and our posterity made slaves." Cromwell, who often saw things with crystal clarity, replied, "My Lord, if this be so, why did we take up arms at first? This is against fighting ever hereafter; if so, let us make peace, be it never so base."[9] Their exchange exemplifies the emerging struggle among the Parliamentarians between a peace party and a war party, between those who fought in order to get the king back to the bargaining table, and those who fought to defeat the king, and then bargain. The former tended to be moderate Puritans who were attracted to the order and discipline of a Presbyterian religious settlement. At great risk of oversimplification, therefore, the peace group, led by Essex in the Lords and Denzil Holles in the Commons, will be referred to as parliamentary **Presbyterians**. Ranged against them was a group of MPs who fought the war with greater enthusiasm and who increasingly favored a more radical religious agenda which would leave individual congregations free, or independent, to make their own decisions about governance and ritual within a loose national Church. This group, led by Saye and Sele in the

Lords and Oliver St. John in the Commons, will be referred to as parliamentary **Independents**.

While the Scottish option temporarily solved Parliament's military difficulties, it proved ruinously expensive, not to mention offensive to Independents who had no intention of trading religious oppression by Laudian bishops for that by an English version of the Kirk. A fresh start was necessary. In the spring of 1645, Parliament passed a Self-Denying Ordinance, which ordered that all current peers and MPs surrender their military commands. This neatly excluded such under-achievers as Essex and Manchester, though at least one exception was made for Cromwell, the most successful general. At the same time, it was proposed to "new model" the army, i.e., reorganize Parliament's various county and regional units into one centralized force, with unified command and promotion through the ranks, without regard to social standing, birth, or connection. In other words, Parliament was abandoning the traditional militia model – county-wide musters of farmers, serving locally, under the command of their landlords – upon which most previous English armies had been based. This army's soldiers would be full-time, well paid, and ready to march anywhere – within England, at least. Their captain-general, Sir Thomas Fairfax (1612–71), and their general of horse, Cromwell, were men of proven ability.

The New Model Army demonstrated its mettle at Naseby, in Northampton-shire, on June 14, 1645, by defeating a more experienced Royalist force in the last decisive battle of the war (see map 11). Cromwell commanded the right wing of cavalry, his son-in-law, Henry Ireton (1611–51), the left, and Fairfax the infantry in the center. Rupert's Royalist cavalry pushed through Ireton's horse only to meet heavy resistance at the baggage train. The infantry at the center was evenly matched. But when Cromwell's forces charged down the flank, they over-whelmed, first, the Royalist cavalry on his wing, and then the infantry in the center: 4,500 Royalist officers and soldiers surrendered. It was only a matter of time until Charles's last western strongholds fell. The first English Civil War ended within a year. Before turning to its aftermath, it is important to note the impact of the war itself. In four years of continuous fighting (in fact, hostilities would persist throughout the British Isles off and on through 1651), about one in eight adult males had seen combat; perhaps one in three bore arms for some part of the war. Over 180,000 people were killed, some 3.6 percent of the population – a higher proportion of Englishmen killed than in any other war, including World War I.

Revolution, 1646–1649

One might think that, with the war won by Parliament, the issues which had provoked it could now be settled. But how? After all, the consequences of Naseby were unprecedented in early modern England: a rightful and undisputed king had been defeated militarily by a rebellious army which sought not to depose him but to limit his power. Previously, during the Wars of the Roses, the struggle had been between rival claimants to royal power – one king vs. another. But in 1646 there was only one king and everyone agreed on who he was. The question was now, what to do with him? Would he agree to a compromise with Parliament limiting his prerogative? And, if not, what then? Recall Manchester's fear that if he "beat us once we shall all be hanged." Even if Charles was disposed to be conciliatory, there was a deeper constitutional problem to be addressed. How could the king accept limitations to make him behave as his subjects wanted and still be king? There were few precedents or models in the early modern world for a compromise: that is, a constitutional monarchy. In their absence, few people wanted to confront the real question left over from the First Civil War: "king or no king?" Because they were unable to confront this question, the interested parties began to negotiate.

Before turning to the negotiations themselves, it must be understood that the interested parties were not confined to king and Parliament. They included the Scots Covenanters, Irish Confederates, and the European powers who considered sending aid to both sides at various points. Parliament itself continued to be divided between the Presbyterian "peace party," who feared disorder and so wanted an agreement with Charles at any price, and the Independent "war party," who had sought his abject defeat in order to pursue religious reform and preserve the new constitutional framework erected in 1641. And finally, there was the instrument of victory itself, the chief consumer of the government's revenue and the greatest concentration of ordinary people on either side, the army. No wonder that Sir Jacob Astley (recently created Lord Astley; 1579–1652), one of the last important Royalist officers to surrender, supposedly said to the victorious parliamentary forces, "[y]ou have now done your work, boys, and may go to play, unless you will fall out amongst yourselves."[10] The large number of groups with a stake in these negotiations meant, on the one hand, that the king could play various sides off against one another. Having lost the war, he might still win the peace. On the other hand, he might become the prize, like the king in a colossal game of chess.

For the next two years Charles negotiated with each of these interest groups, sometimes simultaneously, often repeatedly. But he never did so sincerely. As in his dealings with the Long Parliament in 1640–2, he played for time and, perhaps, a continental, Scottish, or Irish army. He never had any intention of giving up one iota of the prerogative. Rather, he felt that he had already given up too much in signing Strafford's death warrant and that his recent military defeats were a punishment from God for his earlier compromises. So, once again, he prevaricated, dissembled, and, when push came to shove, refused to budge. He knew full well that this course might be personally fatal; his goal was to preserve the monarchy for his children and successors. As he told Prince Rupert just prior to surrender in 1646:

I confess that, speaking as a mere soldier or statesman, there is no probability but of my ruin; yet, as a Christian, I must tell you that God will not suffer rebels and traitors to prosper, nor this cause to be overthrown; and whatever personal punishment it shall please him to inflict on me, must not make me repine, much less give over this quarrel; . . . Indeed I cannot flatter myself with expectation of good success more than this, to end my days with honour and a good conscience.[11]

For the king, honor and a good conscience had meant sneaking out of besieged Oxford in disguise and riding to surrender himself to the Scots outside Newark, Nottinghamshire, in May 1646 because he thought they might offer him the most lenient terms. He was correct, but when he balked at giving up episcopacy the Scots gave him up to Parliament in January 1647 for £400,000. For a few months Holles's Presbyterians controlled both Parliament and the king. Their only problem was the army and the swingeing taxes it consumed. Despite the soldiers' obvious service to the parliamentary cause, the conservative Presbyterian majority in Parliament did not know what to do with them now that the war was over. The soldiers were demanding their back pay (about £600,000) and an Act of Indemnity, that is, a law absolving them of responsibility for acts committed in wartime. No Parliamentarian soldier wanted to return home to, say, the formerly Royalist Cheshire and be brought up on charges of commandeering horses or food from Royalist gentry who might happen to still be serving as JPs. In fact, many Presbyterian MPs were more worried about the disorder, both potential and real, that such a large, experienced force of relatively common soldiers trained in violence could bring to the countryside. Since the army was said to be full of religious zealots, they also feared that the soldiers wanted to turn their victory into revolution by breaking down the existing religious, social, and political order.

In 1647 Parliament decided to deal with the issue by disbanding as much of the army as it could without pay, and sending the rest to pacify Ireland. Understandably, the soldiers took a dim view of being sent off to die in Irish bogs before their pay and indemnity were resolved. The resulting crisis ended up politicizing them. Unpaid and unloved by their parliamentary masters, the soldiers began to listen to radical notions of independence in religion, equality in society, and even a degree of democracy in government. Their leaders came to see the only hope of getting justice for their men in having a say in the negotiations to settle the State. Regiments each selected an "agitator," a sort of union shop steward, to represent them – an example of democracy in action. In June the army declared that it was no "mere mercenary army" fighting for pay but was, rather, dedicated "to the defence of our own and the people's just rights and liberties," and that they would not disband until their grievances were settled.[12] In other words, the army and the army alone (not Parliament) truly represented the national interest – and would now decide where the revolution stopped. To emphasize the point, a group of subordinate officers seized the king and deposited him at army headquarters. In August, the army entered London, forced out Holles and other Presbyterians, and began to negotiate with the king on the basis of a document entitled the *Heads of the Proposals*. It proposed that a bicameral Parliament be elected every two years; that Parliament control the army and navy and nominate all royal ministers; and that all Protestant churches be tolerated in England under a non-coercive episcopacy. This document, if enacted, would have been the first written constitution in English history. Instead, as usual, the king prevaricated, then refused it outright.

At this point the army itself divided. The generals and most officers, known as the Grandees, sought to maintain military discipline and gentry control of the localities. The rank-and-file, led by their agitators and a small group of political activists known as the **Levellers**, sought a fundamental change in how England was ruled. For starters, they demanded near universal manhood suffrage, liberty of conscience, and the abolition of the king and the House of Lords. They also advocated reform of the legal system, urging that it be written in simple English, that punishments fit crimes, speedy trials by juries, and equality under the law. Finally, they wanted a welfare State for widows and orphans of soldiers. The Levellers put their case to the Grandees in a series of debates at Putney Church, just outside London, at the end of October 1647. The Putney Debates focused on a proposed Leveller constitution, *The Agreement of the People* (1647), and, specifically, its suggestion that the franchise be enlarged. Though many spoke, Ireton best advanced the Grandee position, arguing that they had fought the king to restore the Ancient Constitution, not to change it. Therefore, the time-honored requirement of 40 shillings (£2) of land for would-be voters in county elections should remain. He maintained that the franchise should always reside in those with "a permanent fixed interest in this kingdom," that is, in "the persons in whom all land lies, and in those corporations in whom all trading lies." We have seen this argument before, though Ireton's admission of those "in whom all trading lies" was a progressive concession to the growing wealth and ambitions of the mercantile community. In response, Colonel Thomas Rainsborough (d. 1648) set forth the Leveller position that "the poorest he that is in England has a life to live as the greatest he." His corollary was "that every man that is to live under a government ought first by his own consent to put himself under that government."[13] Here, with eloquent simplicity, the common man demanded to be part of the political process irrespective of birth or wealth. Rainsborough's rationale, based not on civil law (Ancient Constitution) nor God's law (the Bible) but on natural law (Reason), was a new and dangerous concept that seemed to undermine the hierarchical principle heretofore at the heart of English life. Later in the century it would receive an even clearer and more decisive exposition by John Locke and others. In the end, though the army left Putney with nothing really decided, the Debates remain a monument to the political consciousness of ordinary people, and, more immediately, reveal the army discussing the future with little or no thought about the king.

Soon after Putney, the king fled once again, this time to Newport on the Isle of Wight. This put him no closer to safety: though he might look across the English Channel to France, Cromwell's cousin governed the island. After more negotiation, Parliament gave up in despair and, in January 1648, voted to make no more addresses to the king. The Scots, however, had continued to parley and, in December 1647, a group of conservative Covenanters signed an "Engagement" with Charles. In return for an army, he promised to establish Presbyterianism in England for three years. This led to a Second Civil War, comprising a series of

Royalist revolts in the South, in Wales, and in Scotland. Unfortunately for the rebels, these revolts were not simultaneous, and Fairfax and Cromwell were able to mop up the English and Welsh outbreaks before marching north to subdue the Engagers. Any moderation shown toward the enemy during the First Civil War evaporated as Cromwell and his men now saw the Royalists as flaunting the evident "Providences of God" revealed in the outcome of the earlier conflict. Many prisoners were summarily executed, and, ominously, soldiers began referring to "Charles Stuart, that man of blood." It was becoming clear that there would be no peace in England while the king lived.

The Presbyterian MPs, however, reached quite a different conclusion from the Second Civil War. Surely, now, Charles would be ready to negotiate. On the morning of December 5, 1648, Parliament voted 129–83 to resume discussions with the king. This outraged the army. The next morning, December 6, Colonel Thomas Pride (d. 1658) positioned his men outside the House of Commons, refused entrance to those who had voted for treating with the king, arrested some 45 of the Presbyterian leaders, and secluded another 186. A further 86 members protested this coup, which became known as **Pride's Purge**, by withdrawing. Although many of these later drifted back, this still left only about 200 MPs, about half the original, to make up a reduced House of Commons. Soon, the few remaining Lords ceased to attend their house. The resulting rump of a Parliament no longer represented even the original supporters of the parliamentary cause, let alone the entire kingdom.

But the **Rump** knew what it had to do. In January, it set up a High Court of Justice to try the king on a charge of high treason. This statement is, on the face of it, a logical absurdity. Allegiance in a monarchy is always paid to the person of the king. How could Charles have been guilty of treason against himself? They got around this problem by alleging that the king had violated not statute law or even common law but a more fundamental principle, part of the Ancient Constitution, as expressed in his coronation oath. The legislation establishing the court read as follows:

Whereas it is notorious that Charles Stuart, the now King of England..., hath had a wicked design totally to subvert the ancient and fundamental laws and liberties of this nation, and in their place to introduce an arbitrary and tyrannical government, and that...he hath prosecuted it with fire and sword, levied and maintained a cruel war in the land against the Parliament and kingdom, whereby the country hath been miserably wasted, the public treasure exhausted, trade decayed, thousands of people murdered, and infinite other mischiefs committed.[14]

Put simply, the king was charged with committing treason against the English people and Ancient Constitution. This was, of course, a revolutionary idea. At its heart was a notion relatively new to early modern Europe: that the king had a responsibility not only to God but to the people over whom he ruled. Even more revolutionary was the idea that, should he fail in that responsibility, he could be tried by the representatives of the people and, if found wanting, removed from his office. These ideas and their implications would have earth-shattering effects not only in England but abroad over the next century and a half.

In the meantime, King Charles could not, of course, agree. When the trial convened in Westminster Hall on January 20, 1649, he questioned the court's jurisdiction. After all, the law, in a monarchy, is always the king's law; the courts are his courts. How, therefore, could any court put the king on trial?

I would know by what authority – I mean lawful – there are many unlawful authorities in the world – thieves and robbers by the highways – but I would know by what authority I was brought from thence and carried from place to place, and I know not what. And when I know what lawful authority, I shall answer. Remember, I am your King – your lawful King.[15]

Refusing to recognize the court's authority, he also refused to plead. For the next several days he stood or sat, impassively and disdainfully but with great dignity, as the prosecution sought to make its case. The spectacle must have been impressive: the largest medieval hall in England packed to the rafters with spectators. At its south end, on several tiers of red velvet benches, underneath not the royal arms but those of England, sat the commissioners: assorted army officers, MPs, and gentlemen, presided over by a heretofore obscure judge, John Bradshaw (1602–59). Before them sat an array of lawyers and clerks, all in black. At the north end and in the upper galleries, crowds of spectators, held back by wooden rails and soldiers in their red coats. On the other side of a hastily constructed wooden partition, in a makeshift dock in the middle of the hall, sat the magnetic object of all eyes, a solitary figure in black, but for the brilliant blue and silver of the Star and Garter – the king. Given his refusal to plead, the verdict was a foregone conclusion. King Charles was found guilty of high crimes and misdemeanors against the people of England. On January 27 he was condemned to death by beheading. At this point he demanded to speak, but Parliament refused permission. Then, 59 commissioners signed the most notorious death warrant in English history.

The night before his execution, the king burned his papers and saw his youngest children for the last time.[16] The next morning, January 30, 1649, he rose and, after asking about the weather outside, put on an extra shirt for the walk across St. James's Park to the scaffold: ever concerned with the dignity of his appearance, Charles did not want to create an impression of fear by shivering. Then he was escorted by armed guard through the park to the Banqueting House at Whitehall – one of those expensive building projects of his father's which had alienated the English taxpayer. One wonders what he thought as he walked through the hall under its magnificent ceiling – a depiction of his father's apotheosis in heaven by Peter Paul Rubens – and thus the sort of expensive art project which had proved controversial in his own ill-fated reign. At the end of his walk was an open window facing west; outside it a scaffold draped in black, at the center of which was the block (see plate 16). Beyond and below stood a crowd of ordinary Londoners, held back by soldiers. The king emerged into the gray light of the January day and asked to speak, but, dogged by his weak voice and bad luck to the last, he was inaudible. He then turned to his archbishop of Canterbury, William Juxon (1552–1663), and remarked that the executioner sent him "from a corruptible to an incorruptible crown."[17] Turning back to the block, he knelt down, said a brief prayer, and, in a signal worked out with the henchman beforehand, stretched out his hands. The axe fell and, as was customary, the executioner raised the late king's dismembered head for all to see.[18] It is said that at this sight, which normally elicited cheers, the crowd uttered a deep groan.

And well they might, for the events of that January day would have grave consequences for all members of the English polity. For the first time in their history, the English people had judicially and publicly murdered their king. Such an act violated the Great Chain, Divine Right, and a thousand years of sermons and royal propaganda. And this was only the beginning of the demolition of the old world. On March 17, Parliament abolished the kingly office; two days later they abolished the House of Lords. And so, on May 19, 1649, England was declared a commonwealth, that is, a republic.

Plate 16 *The execution of Charles I. Ashmolean Museum, Oxford.*

The Radical Hydra

To the framers of the revolution, the clearing away of so much of the old order must have been exhilarating, opening up new possibilities for reform, even a fundamental reconstruction of English society. But it was also frightening. Remember that according to the doctrine of the Great Chain, none of its links could be broken without incurring God's wrath and political, social, and religious chaos. The problem for the gentry – or that part of it which supported the Rump – was to maintain the rest of the Chain and so prevent that chaos. Put another way, having engineered a revolution which benefited themselves, they now had to ensure that the revolution stopped before other groups began to seek the same benefits. Like Henry VIII throwing a man down from a high tower (see chapter 3), they had to make him stop before he hit the ground.

This would be all the more difficult because in opposing the king, the parliamentary gentry and urban oligarchy had been forced to do something unprecedented: to attract, rather than simply commandeer, the loyalties and assistance of the common people who had fought in the army and elsewhere. They had made the people partners in their revolution and, in the process, taught them how to question and even overthrow authority. That questioning had been accomplished by a relatively free press. Censorship had been abolished, newspapers appeared for the first time, and the number of political and religious pamphlets published each year mushroomed. One surviving collection alone, assembled by the London bookseller George Thomason (d. 1666), holds nearly 23,000 items from 1641 to 1662. Most were traditional and conservative in sentiment: Charles I's last thoughts and meditations, *Eikon Basilike* (1649), was a runaway bestseller. But many were not, and some expressed opinions that had never previously been allowed into print. John Milton (1608–74) celebrated this flowering of ideas in *Areopagitica* (1644), the classic defense of free speech. But social and religious conservatives were aghast. Presbyterian Thomas Edwards's (1599–1647) encyclopedic *Gangraena* (1646) diagnosed these radical ideas as so many sicknesses to the body politic, seducing the people into embracing philosophies and lifestyles and claiming rights heretofore unknown. In fact, it was only natural that ordinary people, having helped to dislodge the top of a centuries-old hierarchical structure, would question why they should have to stay at the bottom. Put simply, the common farmers and artisans who made up the victorious parliamentary armies now wanted a piece of the pie; or, to use a more contemporary metaphor, having unseated one rider, they did not want to hoist another on their backs. This feeling could only have been exacerbated by current economic and social conditions. The harvests of 1649–51 were as bad as those of the 1590s; taxes were higher than they had ever been under Charles I; plague and disease ran rampant, spread, ironically, by the very army which had been formed to protect the people's liberties.

The army spread not only disease but also Leveller ideas about political change. After the king's trial and execution, the possibilities for radical reform seemed especially promising. One leading Leveller, John Lilburne (ca. 1614–57), made a career out of provoking the government by calling for a wider franchise, religious toleration, free speech, law reform, and individual rights, all of which he summarized in one ringing, radical phrase: "the Sovereignty of the People." Was his call heeded? No. In the spring of 1649 the Rump suppressed a second round of army agitation by arresting the Leveller leaders, executing the leading agitators, and buying off the rank-and-file by paying some arrears. Lilburne spent most of the next decade in prison or exile before dying in 1657, convinced that "posterity... shall reap the benefit of our endeavours, what ever shall become of us."[19] In fact, Leveller arguments would take centuries to bear fruit and some remain so radical as to be unrealized today. But the fact that they could be aired at all reveals that the framers of the revolution had opened a Pandora's box of new ideas when they deposed the king. This becomes even clearer if we examine the area of religion.

Here, too, the Long Parliament's abolition of censorship, and with it the temporal power of the English clergy, was crucial. Remember that it was only in the previous hundred years that the English people had been allowed to read the Bible; now, for the first time, they could interpret it from the pulpit and in print without fear of persecution. Admittedly, the increasingly conservative Presbyterian majority in the Rump Parliament made some attempt to enforce Kirk-like religious discipline on England. This failed, in part because they never reestablished adequate mechanisms for persecution or censorship; in part because they were effectively opposed by the parliamentary Independents, who sought toleration for virtually all Protestant beliefs. The Independents, including Cromwell, embraced the revolutionary notion that it was not necessary for everyone to agree on the details of religious belief in order to be good Christians and citizens of the State. Like modern Congregationalists, they found more truth in the spirit, among individuals and small congregations, than in a national Church or the decrees of the Rump or Westminster Assembly. In fact this tendency was a necessary implication of the Protestant, and especially the Puritan, mindset. After all, if all men (and, for some, women) could read the Bible; if God desired a priesthood of all believers; and if all were equal in sin, who could say whose interpretation was right? In September 1650 the Independents in Parliament secured repeal of statutes compelling Sunday attendance at the State parish church.

This new-found freedom of thought, speech, and print resulted in a proliferation of unorthodox interpretations of the Bible and strains of Puritanism. Some had longstanding antecedents; all were controversial. For example, the **Baptists** or "Dippers" could trace their ancestry to the German Anabaptists from a century earlier. They believed that baptism should be delayed until adulthood, when a rational person could make a free choice of his or her beliefs. Reasonable as this may sound, many contemporaries found it outrageous to rear children without baptism into a Christian faith. Moreover, adult baptism implied separation of Church and State, since the former would be limited to true believers. This was the antithesis of the mandatory State Church urged by **Anglicans**, Presbyterians, and even most Independents.

And yet, the Baptists were, in many ways, the most moderate of the sects which came into the sunlight of toleration in the 1640s and 1650s. Related to the Baptists were the Seekers, who sampled church after church in search of truth and, presumably, a final confessional allegiance. More alarming were the **Diggers**, who could find no Biblical authorization for private property and the accumulation of riches. Their leader, Gerrard Winstanley (ca. 1609–ca. 1660), anticipated later socialists by urging the wealthy to give up their property and share it in common with their fellow Christians. One can imagine what the landed gentry or even minor freeholders thought of this! The Diggers attempted to put their beliefs into practice by establishing communes of sorts at St. George's Hill in Surrey and elsewhere, but these collapsed due to the hostility of local landowners and bad weather. Yet another group sought neither political nor economic change but a revolution of the spirit: the **Ranters** believed that, since God was present in all things, and He was, obviously, without sin, sin could not exist. In any case, according to the Ranter Abiezer Coppe (1619–72), "[t]o the pure all things are pure."[20] That is, Ranters emphasized the role of individual conscience in deciding questions of right or wrong. In the words of Laurence Clarkson (1615–67),

[s]in hath its conception only in the imagination.... there is no such act as drunkenness, adultery and theft in God ... What act soever is done by thee in light and love, is light and lovely, though it be that act called adultery ... No matter what Scripture, saints or churches say, if that within thee do not condemn thee, thou shalt not be condemned.[21]

The Ranters, reacting to centuries of tight social control and repression of individuality, reveled in "freedom of the spirit." As might be expected, *all* other groups reacted in horror at the Ranter program, and the "Ranter moment" of 1649 was followed by harsh repression and acts against blasphemy and adultery.

Even more alarming – in part because more numerous – were the **Quakers**. Quakers believed that each person possessed an inner light, the Holy Spirit, or the spirit of Christ. In their view, this inner light was invariably correct and to be obeyed over the dictates of the State, the Church, even Scripture. Moreover, they believed that every person had God's inner light in *equal* measure. "Every person" meant, of course, king and commoner, landlord and tenant, master and apprentice, man and woman. This led Quakers to refuse to acknowledge earthly authorities like the State, the courts, or their social superiors; indeed, they publicly stressed God's impending vengeance on "the great ones of the earth." They manifested their disdain for the prevailing social order by refusing to pay tithes, swear oaths, doff their caps, or bow to those superiors. Moreover, because women possessed God's inner light as amply as men did, they participated fully in Quaker services; some went out into the world to testify, in violation of all contemporary gender norms. Finally, those services themselves scandalized hostile observers, for the inner light compelled Quakers to sing, rant, "quake," and move about in a trance-like state during their ecstatic communion with the deity. Some went farther, going "naked as a sign" or violently shouting down rival preachers (pacifism would only be adopted as a Quaker ideal during the 1660s, after a decade of harsh repression). In 1656, James Nayler (ca. 1617–60), one of the founders of the Quaker movement, reenacted Christ's entry into Jerusalem by riding through the streets of Bristol on an ass. Nayler clearly meant his performance to symbolize Christ's presence in all human beings, but Parliament saw it as "horrid blasphemy" and a sign of growing disorder. They decreed that he be pilloried in London, whipped through the streets of Bristol, his tongue pierced with a hot iron, his forehead branded with a "B" (for blasphemer), and, finally, put to death. Although Cromwell, by then lord protector, would not allow his execution, the savagery of this sentence indicates just how frightened the ruling elite were by the specter of Quakerism.

Nayler's entry into Bristol also suggests a strong millenarian aspect to these movements. That is, many of them, applying Old Testament prophecies and the Book of Revelation to recent, earth-shattering events, had concluded that the thousand-year reign of the anti-Christ was ending, and the beginning of the end of the world was near. One group believed that Lodowick Muggleton (1609–98), a tailor from the West Country who had experienced a series of religious visions, was the last prophet named in Revelation. Muggletonians believed that he had the power to save or damn on the spot, which he did publicly – when not imprisoned for blasphemy – throughout the 1650s. But most radical and frightening of all to conservatives were the Fifth Monarchy Men. This group believed, in common with most people in the seventeenth century, that all legislative power was God's. But the conclusion they drew from this position was that the legal profession should be abolished and all legislation should be Biblical, specifically based on the Mosaic law articulated in the books of Leviticus and Deuteronomy. They argued, on this basis, that moral offenses were as serious as civil ones: for example, they advocated that adultery be punished as a capital crime. Finally, following Daniel 7, they believed that the Bible had foretold five great monarchies. Four had, according to their interpretation, already risen and fallen: those of Babylon, Persia, Greece, and Rome. The fifth would undoubtedly be that of "King Jesus," whose return they thought imminent after the execution of King Charles. They were prepared to hasten this Second Coming by force if necessary. For a brief moment, around 1653, this group had extensive political influence; Fifth Monarchist Major-General Thomas Harrison (1606–60) had the ear of important politicians like Cromwell and wielded vast clerical patronage.

It should be obvious that a free press and religious toleration had, predictably, led to religious diversity or, in contemporary eyes, chaos. It should also be obvious that these religious ideas had political and social implications and that all three, when added together, were the ruling elite's worst nightmare. Where religion had once been one of the principal props of law and order and the status quo, it now seemed to justify, even demand from its followers, civil disobedience and radical change. Suddenly, extreme Puritanism's emphasis on individual conscience, which had so alarmed Queen Elizabeth and her Stuart successors, was beginning to frighten moderate Protestant country gentlemen as well. As a consequence, the idea of a State Church with the power to coerce conformity began to look good to them. In the end, the radical ideas of the Levellers and the sects proved to be too much for the landed gentry and urban oligarchy, who began to pull back from the revolutionary doings of 1649, if they had ever approved of them. Increasingly, they yearned for the kind of political and social stability which they had enjoyed under the monarchy – without the monarchy itself. They would spend more than a decade searching for it.

Commonwealth, Protectorate, and the Search for Stability, 1649–1658

The Commonwealth, or government by the Rump, lasted from 1649 to 1653. In the end, it proved too conservative to please the radicals and too radical to earn the confidence of the ruling class. More specifically, it was too tolerant of the lower orders for the landed gentry; too Presbyterian for the Independent sects; and too tolerant of the sects for the Presbyterians and die-hard Anglicans. Its continued sequestration of Royalist lands raised badly needed cash, but never enough, and at the price of continued disaffection from this quarter. Above all, the new regime never effectively subdued or came to terms with the army. The Rump might have raised its popularity by lowering taxes, but this would have necessitated disbanding the army. But disbandment required payment of the army's arrears, and this would have necessitated a tax increase! Instead, precisely because it lacked broad-based support in the country, the Rump found itself utterly dependent upon the army for its continued existence. No one, not Holles and the Presbyterians in 1647, not the Rump 1649–53, not even Cromwell nor his son 1653–8, would solve this conundrum. The Commonwealth would prove more successful with the Scots Covenanters and Irish Confederates, but at tremendous cost in money, blood, and bitterness.

Once the business of the king's execution had been dispatched, the Rump sought to kill two additional birds with one stone by sending the army overseas to deal with the Irish rebels. While the English were forging their revolution, the Gaelic and Old English Confederates had joined forces with the Royalists under Ormond to seize control of Ireland. Cromwell and the New Model Army landed in August 1649 and began to take the island back town by town, starting just north of Dublin (see map 7, p. 83). Within two months, they put the inhabitants of Drogheda and Wexford to the sword after their defenders refused to surrender. In the first case, they did so on the orders of their general; in the second, they simply ran amok. Cromwell's pronouncement on his slaughtered enemies was characteristically sanctimonious: "I am persuaded that this is a righteous judgement of God upon these barbarous wretches who have imbrued their hands in so much innocent blood."[22] In other words, the massacre of some 3,500 townspeople in 1649 was vengeance for the atrocities visited on New English settlers during the rebellion of 1641. This was fine reasoning, apart from the fact that the 1641 rebels had been Gaelic and Drogheda was Old English; the English never wasted time on the subtleties of the Irish situation! The massacres were also effective acts of terrorism calculated to "prevent the effusion of blood for the future" by convincing the rebels to submit, and several towns capitulated soon thereafter. This was only the beginning: throughout early 1650 the Cromwellian troops practiced a policy of scorched earth in Ireland, burning the crops and evicting natives, leading to the death by starvation and other causes of at least 200,000 and possibly as many as 600,000 in a total population of 2 million. Still, it took three years to subdue the Catholic armies. Once this was accomplished, the government resumed plantation, confiscating land from Catholics and giving it to Protestant soldiers and adventurers. Some 40,000 Catholic landowners and their families were evicted from their land and forced to move to the stony, infertile west of the island. In 1641 Catholics had owned 60 percent of the land in Ireland; by the mid-1660's that percentage had fallen to 20. The result left Ireland firmly in Protestant-Parliamentarian hands, but it also further embittered not only the Gaelic inhabitants of the island but also the formerly loyalist Old English.

Having laid waste to Ireland, Cromwell next dealt with Royalist rebellion in Scotland. In 1649–50, the Scots, horrified at the execution of King Charles, declared for his son, whom they proclaimed Charles II. In return, he repudiated his Church of England upbringing and agreed to the Covenant. Once again, the New Model Army and Cromwell (Fairfax resigned rather than march against his fellow Presbyterians) had to be called upon to remind everyone who had won the Civil Wars. Cromwell's exasperated plea to the Scots – "I beseech you in the bowels of Christ, think it possible you may be mistaken" – shows that he had more time for debate with the Protestant Scots than with the Catholic Irish.[23] On September 3, 1650 he defeated the Covenanter army at Dunbar, in Scotland (see map 11). One year later to the very day he defeated a second invading force made up of Royalists and moderate Presbyterians under Prince Charles himself, at Worcester in England (map 11). These victories finally sealed Parliament's triumph in the Civil Wars and left the Royalist and Scottish forces in disarray for a decade. As for the young "king," he was forced to hide in an oak tree (which would forever after be commemorated in British pub signs as "the Royal Oak"). Eventually, by means of disguise and the covert assistance of a network of mainly Catholic families, Charles made his way to the continent. He would spend the next decade as the impoverished and harried guest of a variety of European rulers. He kept a small, shabby, peripatetic court populated by Royalist exiles and hangers-on who plotted with sympathizers in England to engineer a restoration. These plots were all doomed to failure, partly because there was little will to restore the Stuarts either on the part of the English people or the continental powers, partly because the Commonwealth had infiltrated the Royalist court with spies.

Pacifying Ireland and Scotland should have bolstered the prestige of the Commonwealth. To an extent it did. Some Royalists and Covenanters now resigned themselves to rule by the Rump, taking an oath to be "faithful" to the English government "without a King or House of Lords." This should, in turn, have enabled the Rump to enact the real reforms for which the Independents and the army had fought. As Cromwell, in one of his progressive moods, urged them after Dunbar, "relieve the oppressed, hear the groans of the poor prisoners..., be pleased to reform the abuses of the professions; and if there be any one that makes many poor to make a few rich, that suits not a commonwealth."[24] The Rump made some attempt to do all these things. For example, in 1650–1, it sought to improve the economy by improving trade. It passed the first **Navigation Acts** which forbade foreign powers from trading with England's American colonies and required all such trade to be carried in English merchant ships with crews that were at least 75 percent English. The Rump also pursued reform of the law courts, the Poor Law, the clergy, and the moral character of the nation, passing harsh statutes against adultery, fornication, blasphemy, and swearing. Finally, its administration was more efficient and less corrupt than its Stuart counterpart. In the long run, the Navigation Acts would revolutionize English colonial trade by protecting it from foreign competition while breaking the old system of trading monopolies. But in the short run they led to a trade war with the Dutch which the Commonwealth could ill afford, coming on the heels of the expensive Irish and Scottish campaigns. Lawyers and JPs held up legal and Poor Law reform as these promised to adversely affect their interests; while religious reform proved unpopular and unenforceable – the abolition of Christmas because of its pagan trappings was, unsurprisingly, a non-starter. In the end, the Rump's record left many disillusioned, especially in the army.

By 1653, the Rump was supposedly finally taking steps to dissolve itself and call new elections; but it exasperated many by taking forever to do so and, then, suggesting that there would be no limitations on who could vote, thus opening the way for the return of Royalists to government. Cromwell finally erupted in a blaze of anger, entering the House with soldiers and dissolving the Rump on April 20:

[He] told the House, that they had sat long enough...that some of them were whore-masters...that others of them were drunkards, and some corrupt and unjust men and scandalous to the profession of the gospel, and that it was not fit that they should sit as a parliament any longer.[25]

Perhaps more telling, no one rose up to defend them. As Cromwell later recalled, "[w]hen they were dissolved, there was not so much as the barking of a dog."[26]

The end of the Rump provided the army leadership, most of whom were Independents, with the chance to establish what they had long dreamed of: a true theocracy. That is, they would select many of the next representatives not from the old constituencies of county and borough but largely from Independent congregations. The result was to be an "Assembly of Saints," though it has become more popularly known as the "Barebones Parliament" after Praise-God Barebone (1598?–1679), a well-known London leather-seller and preacher who became a member. As this implies, a number of its members belonged to radical sects, including Baptists and Fifth Monarchy Men, who hoped to usher in God's kingdom on earth. In fact, the Barebones Parliament proved to be a disaster. Many of its members were long on ambitious plans, short on practical political experience. For example, following the lead of the Fifth Monarchy Men, they seriously contemplated replacing English common law with the law of Moses.

While this Parliament passed some enlightened legislation to establish new procedures for the registration of births, marriages, and deaths, probate of wills, the relief of creditors, and the incarceration of lunatics, its members also offended important segments of the country by seeking to abolish or reform the court of Chancery (upsetting the lawyers), lay patronage of Church livings and purchase of tithes (upsetting landowners), and the collection of the Excise and monthly assessments (upsetting the army). Cromwell, who was by now the most powerful man in the country, reacted with disgust, complaining that where before he had to deal with knaves, now he had to deal with fools. The godly reformer in him had initially welcomed the "Saints." But the hard-headed country gentleman realized that government required prudence and practicality as well as religious enthusiasm and godliness. The rest of the ruling elite were coming to agree. In December, Cromwell's supporters in the Assembly engineered their dissolution, fittingly, while the most godly members were attending a prayer meeting!

Who would rule next? On December 12, 1653 an army delegation presented to General Cromwell the only written constitution ever implemented in England, the Instrument of Government. This named Cromwell as executive, giving him the title "lord protector." Who was this man who had begun life "by birth a gentleman, living neither in any considerable height, nor yet in obscurity," and had risen – as he saw it, through God's "dispensations" – to equal any king?[27] Oliver (see plate 17), a distant relative of Henry VIII's minister Thomas Cromwell, was born in 1599 in tiny East Anglian Huntingdonshire. He was educated at Sidney Sussex College, Cambridge, a hotbed of Puritan thought. Still, he would have spent his life as an anonymous country gentleman of godly propensities and middling estate if the war had not uncovered his leadership ability and tactical skill, rocketing him to the center of national affairs. Once it did so, his repeated successes convinced him that God had a special purpose for him. This is not to say that Cromwell was always sure of himself. Over the next decade he would sometimes be torn between the conservative instincts of an English landed gentleman and a Puritan zeal for godly reform in Church and State. However, once his mind was made up, his conviction of being God's instrument became his greatest strength. Ironically, King Charles had, as we have seen, the same certainty of God's favor and purpose. But there was one significant difference between Charles I and Oliver Cromwell: Cromwell had a killer instinct. It was this killer instinct, along with his propensity for seizing the main chance, that enraged his enemies, whether Royalists, the Irish, or even former allies like the Levellers.

Advising Cromwell would be a Council of State, filled by generals and the protector's nominees, which would share control of the government's finances and armed forces. Legislation was to be made by a Parliament elected every three years by those with estates worth over £200 a year. This was a far stiffer property qualification than the old franchise – an indication of just how conservative the ruling class had grown in the four years since the abolition of the monarchy. In fact, if this constitution looks suspiciously like the old one, with Parliament, Privy Council, and "king" in all but name, that was no accident. The only major difference, apart from the franchise, was that this time the ruler's power would

Plate 17   Oliver Cromwell, *by Robert Walker, 1649. National Portrait Gallery, London.*

be backed up by a standing army. It was therefore little wonder that radicals viewed Cromwell's acceptance of the Instrument of Government as a great betrayal; or that most members of the ruling elite – even Royalists – accommodated themselves to it.

Oliver Cromwell ruled as lord protector of England for a little under five years. In many ways, his regime contrasted favorably with that of the early Stuarts. It provided rational, efficient government with a minimum of corruption. It launched a much needed reform of the law and sought to make education more accessible. It pursued a broadly tolerant religious policy which allowed for much individuality of practice among congregations; left adherents of the old Prayer Book and Catholics to live in peace if they would live peacefully; and allowed Jews to return to England for the first time since their official expulsion in 1290.

It pursued an aggressive and largely successful economic and foreign policy. The Navigation Acts provoked trade wars with the Dutch and the Spanish which the Cromwellian regime won in the first instance and fought to a draw in the second. This led, in turn, to the acquisition of more colonies, in particular the soon-to-be-lucrative Jamaica, and laid the foundation for future commercial success. The navy also safeguarded trade in the Mediterranean by attacking the Barbary pirates. Thus, English soldiers, sailors, and merchants finally had their aggressive Protestant foreign policy. Altogether, the Protectorate anticipated or pioneered many later developments which would make England the most progressive major state in Europe by 1714.

But there were costs to such "big-government" successes. First, a more efficient government was bound to be more intrusive. In 1655, after an unsuccessful Royalist rising, Cromwell attempted to ensure local control by dividing the country into 12 military districts, each overseen by a major-general. Not unlike lords lieutenant, the major-generals enforced law and order, the Poor Law, and religious toleration; but they also spied on Royalists and Presbyterians, bullied JPs, and purged corporations of anyone suspected of disloyalty to the regime. In keeping with the Puritan sentiments of most Independents and Cromwell's conviction that God's judgment could only be averted by moral reform, many major-generals also fought drunkenness, blasphemy, swearing, gambling, whoring, and indecent fashions wherever they found them. They also suppressed alehouses, playhouses, Sunday sports, and Christmas celebrations. Needless to say, the Protectorate did not succeed in stamping out any of these practices or institutions, but it did leave a lasting impression nevertheless. The major-generals and their Puritan supporters would long be remembered as prudes, kill-joys, and intruders into local communities, while standing armies generally would be associated with the oppression of English liberties, local autonomy, and even harmless fun.

The Protectorate was also expensive. A more efficient government, policing the nation at home and prosecuting war abroad via a standing army and permanent navy, had to be paid for. The average annual expenditure of the Cromwellian administration was nearly £2 million – far more than that of Elizabeth I, James I, or Charles I at their respective heights. This necessitated, in turn, very high tax rates. Naturally, Cromwell continued the lucrative but unpopular Excise and monthly assessments and even extended the former. His government also sequestered Royalist lands, selling some and forcing proprietors to compound, or pay a high fee to reoccupy, others. None of this did anything for the regime's popularity or the protector's ability to get along with a Parliament full of landowners who had to answer to other landowners back home. As a result, like his royal predecessors, he frequently found it necessary to prorogue or dismiss Parliament.

This should sound familiar. If Oliver Cromwell looks, in retrospect, very much like a king without a crown, his followers would have agreed. In 1657 they sought, via a document entitled *The Humble Petition and Advice*, to rectify the omission by offering him the title of king and the power to appoint both his successor and peers to a House of Lords. Cromwell refused the title but accepted the powers (along with reinstallation as protector complete with purple and ermine robe and a gold scepter). It should be obvious that after nearly 30 years of constitutional experimentation, 10 of them without a king, many in the ruling elite were longing for the old structures of government. This became even clearer after Cromwell's sudden death on September 3, 1658. Like a king, he was given an elaborate State funeral patterned on that of his Stuart predecessors. Like a Crown prince, his eldest son, Richard (1626–1712), was allowed to succeed to the position of lord protector.

The Restoration, 1658–1660

Richard Cromwell inherited three peoples divided in politics and religion and a regime that was both financially exhausted and increasingly unpopular. The nobility and gentry, in particular, resented not only the Protectorate's tax burden but also the usurpation of their former place as the State's representatives in the localities by Puritan nonentities. When not oppressed by the major-generals, they feared the breakdown of social and religious order described in the previous section. In short, the ruling elite had had their fill of godly reformation, whether purveyed by wild-eyed individuals, independent congregations, saintly Parliaments, or oppressive armies. Increasingly, and somewhat myopically, the country – or at least the traditional ruling class – began to long for the good old days under the Stuarts. Only a man of strength and conviction like Oliver Cromwell could have held the nation together and maintained his regime in power under such circumstances.

Unfortunately for that regime, Richard was no Oliver. Richard Cromwell was, in fact, an intelligent, amiable, thoroughly decent man who would soon lose control of events. In the spring of 1659 Parliament attempted to assert its authority over the Council of the Army. This led the army to force another dissolution of Parliament, banish Richard into retirement, and recall the surviving members of the Rump. The Rump, quite naturally, also sought to control the army, which, true to form, sent it packing on October 13, 1659. The diarist John Evelyn (1620–1706) well expressed the general feeling of uncertainty when he wrote:

The Armie now turn'd out the Parliament. . . . We had now no Government in the Nation, all in Confusion; no Magistrate either own'd or pretended, but the souldiers & they not agreed: God Almight[y] have mercy on, & settle us.[28]

In late October, a Committee of Public Safety headed by General Charles Fleetwood (d. 1692) established, in effect, rule by the Grandees. But by Christmas Fleetwood had thrown up his hands and resigned power back to the Rump. At this point, General George Monck (1608–70), the ranking commander in Scotland, began to march south with the only fully paid army in the British Isles. No one knew what he would do but each group – Republican, Royalist, Presbyterian, Independent – seems to have hoped that he would embrace their position.

He reached London in February 1660. After some vacillation, on February 11 he ordered the Rump to call for immediate elections, thereby dissolving itself, with or without the return of the members secluded in 1648. The populace greeted this news with joy – expressed by the roasting of rump steaks in London streets that night. The secluded members returned on February 21 and, on March 16, the full Long Parliament ordered new elections and dissolved itself. Simultaneously, Prince Charles, sensing his moment, issued from the continent the Declaration of Breda in the hope of swaying the election. In it, he promised amnesty to all who had participated in the Civil Wars apart from those to be excepted by Parliament; liberty "to tender consciences" (i.e., freedom of religion), also subject to parliamentary approval; and the recognition of all land sales since 1642. Each of these provisions was designed to allay the fears of former Parliamentarians that a restoration would bring political, religious, or economic revenge. Thus, Charles sought to begin the healing of old wounds and to present himself as a consensus choice who would be fair to all, not just former Royalists.

It worked. The Parliament elected in April 1660, known as the Convention Parliament because no monarch had convened it, was overwhelmingly moderate in composition. That is, it was dominated by Royalists and Presbyterians, the latter of whom now supported the Stuarts as their best hope for the restoration of order and good government. When Parliament met at the end of the month, it issued an invitation for the exiled prince to return as sovereign. It also dispatched a fleet to bring the nation's favorite son home. On May 29, 1660, coincidentally the anniversary of his birth, King Charles II (1660–85) entered London accompanied by Monck, newly created duke of Albemarle and master of the Horse, as well as a host of aristocratic supporters, both old and new. This time, Evelyn wrote far more optimistically, even triumphantly:

This day came in his Majestie, Charles the 2d to London after a sad, & long Exile, and Calamitous Suffering both of the King & Church: being 17 yeares: This was also his Birthday, and with a Triumph of above 20000 horse & foote, brandishing their swords and shouting with unexpressable joy: The wayes straw'd with flowers, the bells ringing, the streetes hung with Tapissry [tapestry], fountaines running with wine: the Major [mayor], Aldermen, and all the Companies in their liver[ie]s, Chaines of Gold, banners; Lords & nobles, Cloth of Silver, gold & vellvet every body clad in, the windos & balconies all set with Ladys, Trumpets, Musick, & myriards [myriads] of people flocking the streetes & was as far as Rochester, so as they were 7 houres in passing the Citty.

As described above and depicted in a contemporary print (see plate 18), it was as if the Great Chain of Being had not only been restored but was laid out in person, horizontally, end to end, from Rochester to London, in all its glory. No wonder that Evelyn, a devout member of the Church of England and a landed gentleman who had lost much during the preceding revolution, wrote, "I stood in the strand, & beheld it, & blessed God."[29] The old order was restored, the clock turned back. The people of England had experienced a long national nightmare, a winter of profound discontent which had reached its nadir on a cold January day in

Plate 18 *The entrance of Charles II at the Restoration, 1660. Mary Evans Picture Library.*

1649. They now awakened in springtime to find themselves in love with their new, young sovereign of the old Stuart line.

Or did they? Could the English really "go home again"? Could either Charles Stuart or the people who now embraced him with open arms ever entirely forget that they had publicly vilified and executed the last Charles Stuart, his father, broken the Great Chain, smashed the old Tudor–Stuart State, tried out several new forms of government, a free press, and religious toleration, and debated unorthodox social and religious systems? Could the English constitution and the people it was meant to govern ever go back to 1603, or 1625, or even 1642? Could they forget the many years when the House of Commons had ruled on its own without king, Lords, or bishops? Put another way, had the Civil Wars and Restoration really done anything to solve the problems of sovereignty, finance, foreign policy, religion, and local control that had led to them? The answers to these questions were uncertain on that brilliant May day in 1660. In fact, they would take most of the next half-century to be resolved.

CHAPTER NINE

Restoration and Revolution, 1660–1689

The Interregnum and Restoration resolved none of the questions over which the British Civil Wars had been fought. Rather, after so many bloody battles, revolutions in government and religion, the deposition and beheading of a king, and an experiment with a republic, in 1660 the English people appear to have opted to go back to square one: the restoration of the constitution in Church and State more or less as they were before the Civil Wars. In fact, the Restoration settlements only *seemed* to turn the clock back. This appearance of *déjà vu* sometimes left contemporaries confused – and, increasingly, bitterly divided – about the meaning of the dramatic events through which they had just lived.

This is not to say that the Civil Wars, their onset and their aftermath, settled nothing. The upheavals of the past three decades had taught the English ruling class three hard lessons. First, while they had not settled the question of sovereignty, it was now established that the English constitution required *both* king and Parliament. Unfortunately, this still left open the question of which was to predominate. For Evelyn and other old Cavaliers, the more specific lesson of these years was clear: kings might err, but they were still semi-sacred beings whose authority was not to be questioned. To kill the king, as the revolutionaries had done in 1649, was to sin against the universal divine order. For the Royalists, the Civil Wars, Revolution, and Interregnum demonstrated clearly the fatal effects of abandoning the Great Chain of Being. Eventually, these beliefs would become the underlying ideology of one of the first political parties, the **Tories**. But for old Roundheads the events of 1629–60 held a different lesson: that Parliament was the true guarantor of English liberties. The 1630s, in particular, had proven that body was and should be an integral and regular part of the English constitution as much as the 1650s had proven the necessity of a king. Some went further to argue that the past quarter-century had taught that kings were not gods but men; a bad king could and should be deposed. This implied the sovereignty of Parliament and, by extension, the people whose interests it, theoretically, represented. Contemporaries with these opinions would eventually come together to form an opposing political party known as the **Whigs**. In other words, the question of sovereignty, and by implication the related questions of finance, foreign policy, and local control, would continue to dominate the political battles of the next half-century, at court, in Parliament, and in the country at large, as they had those of the previous 50 years.

The second lesson taught by the Civil Wars and learned by the ruling class of England was that Puritans could no more be trusted with political and religious authority than could Catholics. From henceforward they, too, would be associated with political and religious extremism: killing the king, republicanism, toleration of outlandish sects, intolerance toward beloved ceremonies and traditions. This does not mean that the Puritans would cease to be an important force in English life, despite their apparent defeat in 1660. On the contrary, it means that religion would continue as an emotive touchstone for English men and women as Puritans fought for their beliefs and practices, increasingly from outside the established Church. Indeed, if the Civil Wars clarified, but failed to solve, the questions of sovereignty, finance, foreign policy, and local control, they rendered that of religion even more complicated and dangerous.

One more thing became clear as a result of these experiences: the vast majority of the English ruling elite had become strongly averse to using violence, or making common cause with the common people, in order to effect constitutional or political change. The past quarter-century had proven that such expedients were just too unpredictable, too dangerous to their own interests. Since the tensions which had led to those expedients were not yet resolved in 1660, this raised the pressing question of how such change was to be effected in future. The Convention Parliament would attempt to solve each of these problems.

The Restoration Settlements, 1660–1665

Given the lack of consensus described above, the Restoration was bound to be a compromise. It did not restore the monarch's powers as they were in 1603 or 1640 but as they had been modified by the Long Parliament in 1641. In many ways, this was good news for the new king, Charles II. First, he was restored to the executive power of government. That is, the king could once again conduct foreign policy as he saw fit. According to the Militia Acts of 1661 and 1662, he, and only he, could call out that body – an issue that had been disputed on the eve of the Civil War. He could appoint what ministers he wanted and he could remove judges at will. He could, moreover, dispense with the law in individual cases and, theoretically, suspend it during national emergencies. Finally, he could summon, prorogue, or dismiss Parliament with much the same freedom as his predecessors had exercised, within the limitations of the Triennial Act. That is, he was merely required to convene it for a brief meeting once every three years.

Realizing that such power would prove hollow if the king were forced to beg constantly for money, the honorable members of the Convention also tried to provide him with the first truly adequate royal revenue since the accession of

Henry VIII. That is, they sought to base Charles II's financial settlement on a reasonable estimate of what royal expenses actually were, not on what they felt like paying in taxes. They restored Crown lands confiscated during the war and granted the Customs for Charles's life, a courtesy denied his father. In order to make up for the abolition of fees of wardship and feudal dues, Parliament also granted the king a continuation of the liquor Excise. The whole package was designed to yield the truly princely annual sum of £1,200,000 – far more than any previous Parliament had granted any previous sovereign. It would appear that, once more, God's lieutenant sat on the throne, now truly master in his own house.

Or was he? Many Convention members were moderate Parliamentarians or Presbyterians, not arch-Royalists. They rejected the most extreme legislation of 1641–2 and deplored the killing of the king in 1649. But they did not regret the tax strike of 1638 or the moderate reform legislation of 1641 or even, necessarily, the taking up of arms in 1642. These men agreed to Charles II's restoration in 1660 because they saw him as the best hope for the reestablishment of order, not because they wanted him to be all powerful. Thus, while they restored the royal power to make peace and war, they failed to vote Charles funds for a fully fledged army, such as Cromwell had commanded. They recalled vividly and ruefully the New Model Army and rule by the major-generals, and they knew that such armies were powerful instruments for royal oppression all over Europe. They feared that a standing army would make the king absolute and, like most members of the English ruling elite, they opposed it vehemently. The New Model Army was paid off, leaving only a few guards regiments to protect the king. Similarly, while Charles II controlled the militia in theory, he still had to raise it the old-fashioned way: by asking the lieutenancy – the lords lieutenant of the counties and their deputies – to call out the troops.

The king's power was also circumscribed in non-military matters. While he could dismiss judges at will, the prerogative courts which had enforced that will under the Tudors and early Stuarts (i.e., those of Star Chamber, High Commission and Requests, as well as the Council of the North), abolished by the Long Parliament in 1641, were not restored in 1660. More importantly, while the new king was voted revenues in 1660 *estimated* to yield £1,200,000, that estimate was not reliable. In fact, the revenues described above averaged less than half that amount in the first two years of the reign. Parliament would respond in 1662 by passing the Hearth Tax – easy to collect by counting chimneys. This and other new taxes did eventually bring the yield up to the promised amount. But even that amount was not itself altogether realistic: it was based upon royal expenditure during the reign of Charles I, a very different time. While taxes eventually yielded £1,200,000, the new king's expenses soon outran this by £200,000–300,000 a year. This was not, as we shall see, Parliament's fault. Nevertheless, it ensured that the new king would, like so many of his predecessors, be chronically short of money. Nor could he, like those predecessors, raise funds from extra-parliamentary taxation, for the Long Parliament's condemnations of the impositions, forced loans, and Ship Money remained on the books. That meant, in turn, that it would be much more difficult to rule without Parliament. In short, the financial settlement papered over, but did not erase, the most basic area of tension in Stuart politics, that of sovereignty and Parliament's constitutional role.

This becomes even clearer if we look at the religious settlement. It will be recalled that, in the Declaration of Breda, Charles II had promised "a liberty to tender consciences" and an indulgence for differing religious opinions. Charles pursued religious toleration partly to reconcile all sides to his regime; partly because he felt indebted to Catholics for saving his life after Worcester and to Presbyterians in the Convention for his Restoration; and partly because he was truly tolerant on matters of faith. Catholicism interested him; even Quakers amused him. Restored as Supreme Governor of the Church of England in 1660, he could nevertheless only accomplish religious change by act of Parliament; that is, with the agreement of the ruling elite.

Unfortunately, the new king had spent too many years away from England to have a good sense of what his most important subjects would put up with. They had experienced a form of religious toleration in the 1650s and had not found it to their taste. Their views on "Papists" remained unchanged and they did not feel much better disposed to the Independent Protestant sects which had preached madness up and down the country for a decade. When conservative members of the Church of England saw a Puritan, they now saw a breaker of the Great Chain of Being; a king-killer; a Leveller, a Digger, a Quaker, or a Fifth Monarchist; a persecutor of conservative clergy and traditional ceremonies; an imposer of high taxes; an instrument of the major-generals – in short, as great and radical a danger to the status quo as any Catholic. This goes far to explain the spontaneous revival of the Church of England in many localities at the Restoration: from May to December 1660, parish after parish forced out Puritan clergy and restored "high" Church ceremonies. In contrast to the sects, the newly resurgent Church of England embraced the restored monarchy and the social hierarchy over which it presided. After 1660 its clergy thundered from their pulpits on the necessities of loyalty, passive obedience, and non-resistance to the sovereign. They began to refer to Charles I as "the Royal Martyr," and, annually on the anniversary of his execution on January 30, they would remind their congregations of the intimate connections between the Puritan sects and the radical politicians who had struck him down. Early in the reign, that association was reinforced by a number of die-hard radical revolts – most "spectacularly" the brief uprising of 35 armed Fifth Monarchists who proclaimed the reign of King Jesus in the middle of London in 1661. No wonder that conservative Protestants increasingly saw themselves as representing the true, or "Anglican," strain of the Church of England.

As a result, the best that Charles II could hope for was comprehension: that is, modifying the structure, doctrine, and liturgy of the restored Church of England to make moderate Puritans, particularly Presbyterians, feel comfortable in a more inclusive national Church. But the Convention of 1660 had no success in passing measures either for toleration or for comprehension before its dissolution in 1661. The new Parliament elected that spring was far more heavily Anglican and Royalist than its predecessor – hence its nickname, the Cavalier Parliament (1661–78). One might think that so Royalist a Parliament would do the king's bidding, but precisely because they were Royalists, for all the reasons noted above, its members could not share Charles's enthusiasm for religious toleration or even comprehension. Rather, between 1661 and 1665 the Cavalier Parliament sought to exclude the sects from public life by passing a sweeping program of anti-Puritan legislation. This set of laws came to be known as the **Clarendon Code** after Edward Hyde, earl of Clarendon (1609–74), the lord chancellor and nominal head of Charles II's government. In fact, "**Cavalier Code**" would be a fairer term, for Clarendon, though a staunch Anglican and political conservative, was no persecutor of Puritans. Instead, it was old Royalists (or their sons) in the Cavalier Parliament who sought not only the full restoration of their beloved Church of England but vengeance on those who had persecuted it during the Interregnum. Almost immediately, the Cavalier Parliament threw down the gauntlet by restoring the temporal and spiritual power of the bishops, the ecclesiastical courts, the Book of Common Prayer, the wearing of vestments, and the right of advowson (i.e., the right of a local squire to handpick the clergy for the churches on his land).

Having thus rejected comprehension, the framers of the Cavalier Code now became punitive. The **Corporation Act of 1661** required municipal officers to renounce the Presbyterian Covenant and to receive the sacrament according to Anglican rites. The Quaker Act of 1662 made it illegal to refuse to plead in court (thus attacking the Quaker aversion to swearing oaths) and proscribed all meetings for worship outside the parish church of groups of five or more. The **Act of Uniformity of 1662**, the central plank of the Code, required all ministers, professors, and schoolmasters to swear oaths repudiating the Covenant and the taking up of arms against the king. It also required the use of the restored Book of Common Prayer for all Church services and each minister was to swear his consent to "all things" in the Prayer Book or face deprivation of his living. In effect, the act created nonconformity by testing for outward conformity of practice. Altogether, this legislation and the more ad hoc purges noted above deprived about 1,760 clergy, over 15 percent of the total in England and Wales, of their livings between 1660 and 1663.

Whatever hopes remained for a tolerant religious settlement were dashed when a short-lived rising against the government, the Yorkshire Plot of October 1663, encouraged Parliament to pass the **Conventicle Act** in 1664. This act, which would be fine-tuned in 1670, ordered huge fines (and exile for the third offense) for those attending nonconformist meetings (i.e., conventicles). JPs could break into houses upon information of a conventicle there. Finally, in 1665 Parliament passed the **Five Mile Act**. It prohibited any nonconformist preacher from coming within 5 miles of his former parish or of an incorporated town unless he took an oath stating that it was unlawful to take arms against the king.

The intended effect of these laws was to squeeze Puritanism out of existence by driving its adherents out of public life and discourse, the clergy, the schools, the cities, and, ultimately, even their own meetings. Puritans thus joined Catholics as officially defined second-class subjects and potential enemies to the constitution. From this point on, they, too, would be subject to crippling fines, imprisonment, transportation to the colonies, having their meetings broken up and their property seized. To offer but one statistic, during the period from 1660 to 1688 some 15,000 Quakers were sent to prison; 450 died there. Even when the authorities left the sects alone, they were subject to periodic mob violence. In effect, the Cavalier Code had split the Protestant majority in England into the acceptable and loyal (Anglican) and the unacceptable and disloyal (Puritan). In fact, from this point it is no longer accurate to refer to "Puritans" at all, for, clearly, they no longer had any hope of "purifying" the Church of England of its more conservative practices. Rather, this group came increasingly, and more accurately, to be referred to as "**Nonconformists**" or "**Dissenters**," names which emphasize that they now formed a community apart from the Anglican majority. Presbyterians would continue to hope for comprehension within a less restrictive national Church, but most Dissenters would focus not on reform of Church and State but on mere survival.

Clearly, the monarch and the Church of England had been restored to their primacy in State and Church. But a careful reading of the Restoration Settlements shows that the monarch's primacy was qualified: for all their protestations of loyalty and submission to the king, the parliamentary aristocracy had reserved a great deal of power to their own hands, not only in Parliament but also in the localities. The new regime revived the lieutenancy and stocked it with Royalists and loyal Presbyterians. They worked with the JPs, using the militia to enforce the new religious settlement and purge corporations of the disloyal. And yet, the return to local control, after the infamous attempt at centralized control under the major-generals, meant that officials in the country could once again enforce *selectively* the many statutes and proclamations coming down from Privy Council, Parliament, or Whitehall – more harshly or more laxly as the local situation dictated. In other words, if the Restoration political settlement was ambiguous for the king, it was an unalloyed triumph for the local nobility and gentry, who were united in a vision of the traditional order that was "propertied, parochial and pre-eminently protestant."[1] Political leaders would ignore this basic fact at their peril. Already, in violation of Charles II's intentions at Breda, the aristocracy had used its power to create winners and losers. The success or failure of the Restoration Settlements would ultimately depend on the new king's ability to ally with those winners and accommodate his policies to their power.

Charles II and the Unraveling of the Restoration Settlements

It is practically impossible to separate the failure of the Restoration Settlements from the personality of King Charles II (see plate 19). In an age of personal monarchy, when all government was His Majesty's Government; when all policy and patronage emanated directly from the king and his court; when all loyalty was owed to the sovereign, royal personality *mattered*. At first, as with nearly all new rulers, only the king's good points shone through. Charles II was highly intelligent. He spoke fluent French and some Italian; he had a particular interest in science, maintaining a laboratory and serving as the founding patron of the Royal Society. He was also witty, affable, and approachable. (He would, in our own day, have made a terrific TV talk show host.) This was in sharp and, for the most part, agreeable contrast to his father, who had been impossibly aloof and formal. The new king was also vigorous, as he proved on the tennis court and in the bedroom: in the words of one historian, he was "unmistakably the 'sport' of his line."[2] More importantly, he was tolerant, flexible, and open to compromise – again, in welcome contrast to his father. Above all, Charles II saw the need for healing after a quarter-century of bitter conflict. At Breda he had promised forgiveness to his enemies, and, in general, he lived up to that promise: fewer

Plate 19 Charles II as Patron of the Royal Society, *by Laroon. Christ's Hospital, Sussex.*

than 40 old rebels and servants of the Commonwealth and Protectorate were left out of the Act of Indemnity and Oblivion (1660). The most serious revenge was reserved for those who had signed Charles I's death warrant and, of these, only 11 were executed. Those unfortunate souls, however, suffered the full fury of the traditional punishments associated with treason: they were hanged, drawn, and quartered, and their boiled remains impaled on the City gates. The new regime even vented its wrath on the dead: the bodies of Oliver Cromwell, Henry Ireton, and John Bradshaw were exhumed and hanged at Tyburn in their shrouds. Afterwards their heads were placed on pikes to look over Westminster Hall – the place of Charles I's trial – as a warning to all potential rebels.[3]

On the other hand, Charles II forgave many surviving Roundheads, reappointing them to the offices they had performed so well for the Commonwealth and Protectorate, rewarding them for their new-found loyalty with titles, pensions, and lands. This eased bitterness on their part and it kept experienced and competent people in government. But it also left many old Royalists, impoverished by their long and faithful service to the Stuarts in defeat and exile, resentful that they were not rewarded more generously. In fact, most Royalist nobility and gentry regained lands lost during the Interregnum, but those further down the social scale suffered more hardship. A fund of £60,000 was established for indigent officers, but it allowed only a pittance each to the many former Cavaliers who applied. No wonder that they joked darkly that the Act of Indemnity and Oblivion meant indemnity for the king's former enemies and oblivion for his friends.

Charles II's willingness to slight old friends for new ones was, in fact, characteristic of the man. As his reign progressed, it became increasingly clear that his loyalty to servants and favorites was undependable; that his intelligence frequently manifested itself as cunning and duplicity; that his charm was often deceptive and self-serving; that his easy-going nature was also lazy and indecisive; and that his flexibility was, in part, the corollary of having no long-term goal or plan. Basically, Charles II was a cynic – and who could blame him? After all, the people who now professed their undying loyalty and affection for him were the very ones who had killed his father. He would never fully understand their prejudices. On his last visit to his dominions in 1651 he had been forced to hide in a tree before sneaking out of the country in disguise. During his exile in the 1640s and 1650s he had been threatened, denounced, promised to, lied to, used, and spied on by them – as well as every government in Europe. Often, he would find that a confidential servant was in the pay of his enemies; or that a fellow monarch had used him as a pawn in some diplomatic game of chess with Cromwell. No wonder that he trusted no one. He never knew when the English, Scots, and Irish would change their minds once more and force him to go "on his travels" again.

So, perhaps understandably, the young but wizened king decided to make hay while the sun shone. Hence his laziness. Hence his apparent lack of a long-term plan, besides survival. Hence his almost obsessive interest in "diversion": having fun and relieving boredom through the pursuit and patronage of art, music, literature, the theater, witty conversation, gambling, drinking, and womanizing. A positive result of these tendencies was that the Restoration court was the greatest center for cultural patronage of its day. It has been credited with introducing England to the comedy of intrigue, the first stage actresses, new French and Italian styles in both sacred and secular music, the man's three-piece suit, periwigs for both men and women, and such delicacies as champagne, tea, and ice cream. The king promoted, if he did not necessarily pay for, the careers of the poets John Dryden (1631–1700) and John Wilmot, earl of Rochester (1647–80); the dramatists George Etherege (ca. 1635–91) and William Wycherley (1640–1716); the painters Sir Peter Lely (1618–80) and Sir Godfrey Kneller (1646–1723); the musicians Henry Purcell (1658?–95) and John Blow (1648–1708); the woodcarver Grinling Gibbons (1648–1720); and the architect Sir Christopher Wren (1632–1723), among many others. This concentration of talent made the Restoration court supremely attractive and entertaining. According to the French ambassador:

There is a ball and a comedy every other day; the rest of the days are spent at play (gambling), either at the Queen's or at the Lady Castlemaine's, where the company does not fail to be treated to a good supper.[4]

The two ladies referred to in the above quote were not insignificant. The first was Charles II's wife, Catherine of Braganza (1638–1705). She was a Portuguese princess (and, therefore, a Catholic) who had brought a huge dowry at their marriage in 1662: the ports of Tangier on the north coast of Africa and Bombay on the west coast of India. It was hoped that the marriage would provide England with both prosperous trading colonies overseas and heirs to the throne at home. It did neither. Tangier proved expensive and disease-ridden and was abandoned in 1683–4. Bombay had more potential, but it would take the East India Company many years to realize it. As for the royal marriage, it proved to be passionless, not least because poor Catherine seems to have been the one woman in the British Isles whom the king was incapable of impregnating.

This brings us to "the other woman" in the quote, Barbara *née* Villiers Palmer, countess of Castlemaine (1641–1709). Castlemaine, later duchess of Cleveland, was only the most prominent of a virtual harem of mistresses whom Charles II maintained at his court. Among the others were the actress Nell Gwyn (1650–87) and the French Catholic aristocrat Louise de Keroualle, duchess of Portsmouth (1649–1734). The king's notorious infidelity (one of his nicknames was "Old Rowley" after his most successful stud-horse) had several important results. First was the birth of 14 acknowledged but illegitimate children. Nearly all were given titles, offices, and estates. A second result of the king's amorous adventures was that they provided opportunities for individual women at court to gain in wealth and status. Charles II was, like his grandfather James I, generous to a fault. His government spent over £60,000 a year at the beginning of the reign just to feed his court; by its end, it was spending £180,000 (one-seventh of the royal revenue) on pensions.

Third, Charles II's openness and love of pleasure led people to assume that the great courtiers, mistresses, and drinking companions with whom he spent his time wielded immense power at his court and exerted comparable influence over him. Thus, when the king took a fancy to pretty, young Frances, "La Belle" Stuart (1647–1702), George Villiers, second duke of Buckingham (1628–87), saw an opportunity to increase his influence through her, forming "a committee...for the getting of Mrs. [Mistress] Stuart for the King."[5] Certainly, royal mistresses and Bedchamber servants could act as gatekeepers to the king, facilitating – or preventing – the access of anyone who wanted to see him. But historians now doubt that they had much power to influence Charles II when it really counted. Whether or not they could do so *in fact*, there is no doubt that their *reputation* for being able to do so, combined with the king's apparent luxury and decadence, disgruntled the taxpayer and lessened respect for the monarchy – thus weakening both his finances and his standing in the localities. But the king's love of pleasure also did much to bring the ruling class back to court, both physically and figuratively, after the upheavals of the Civil War years. In short, tensions and differences of perspective between court and country, center and locality would remain a feature of English political, social, and cultural life.

Finally, the king's inability to produce a legitimate heir had one further significance. It increased the importance of his brother, James, duke of York, as both heir apparent and the father of two little girls who might themselves succeed to the throne eventually: Princess Mary (1662–94) and Princess Anne (1665–1714; see genealogy 3, p. 414). This, too, would have profound consequences for the future.

Problems of Sovereignty, Finance, Religion, and Foreign Policy, 1660–1670

In the meantime, it should be obvious that the king's personality hardly fit him to deal with the great issues left over from his predecessors' reigns. Take sovereignty. Despite the Restoration compromise between those who favored unqualified royal sovereignty and those who favored Parliament's claims to partnership (if not supremacy), Charles II proved to be every inch a Stuart, no more ready to share power with or accommodate his policies to Parliament than his father or grandfather had been. Worse, he had spent much of his exile on the continent, in the shadow of his cousin, the Sun King, Louis XIV (1638–1715; reigned 1643–1715).[6] As their reigns wore on, Louis became the most powerful and successful monarch in Europe, and, therefore, something of a role model for Charles II. The French king ruled absolutely, without the necessity of having to get his policies approved or funded by a parliament. Louis used this power to make France the most powerful and aggressive nation on the continent. As we shall see, this came to alarm contemporary English men and women, not least when the Catholic Louis began to cast his eye over the vast Spanish Empire. But Charles II could not help but envy it all, and there was some suspicion that he would seek to emulate it.

Those fears may have been exaggerated; "absolute rule" was more of an occasional pipedream than an ever-present goal for Charles II. He had neither the resources, personal determination, capacity for hard work, nor sheer ruthlessness to follow through with absolutism that Louis XIV possessed. Nor did he have a first minister who might have supplied the necessary toughness to manage Parliament for him. Instead, the lackadaisical king left government in the hands of Lord Chancellor Clarendon, a principled but old-fashioned man who believed that the Elizabethan methods of Lord Treasurer Burghley would still work in the age of Charles II. He thought that if he could just explain the king's position clearly enough, Parliament would see its reasonableness and vote the necessary funds. As we have seen, such methods had not worked under Charles I and they did not always work now.

Nevertheless, king and Parliament maintained fairly good relations early in the reign. This was, in part, because that body still feared a return of anarchy and disorder more than it did the powers of the Crown. Working from painful memory, the Cavalier Parliament passed the Corporation Act, restored censorship of the press (via the Licensing Act of 1662), and made it a crime to denigrate royal authority, call the king a Catholic, gather more than 20 signatures on a petition or deliver it with a delegation larger than 10. In 1664 Parliament repealed the penalty clauses to the Triennial Act, so that, in effect, the sovereign could now once again rule without Parliament – if he could afford to do so. In 1668 they gave the king greater freedom to dismiss judges with whom he disagreed. And yet, there were certain issues upon which even the Cavalier Parliament would not budge. By the early 1670s these loomed larger and automatic support for royal policy evaporated.

We have already observed that Charles II had money problems. Despite what Parliament saw as a very generous financial package, he was constantly in debt. There were many reasons for this. First, Parliament refused to pay off his or his father's obligations from before the Restoration: as a result, Charles II began his reign over £900,000 in the hole. On the revenue side, a trade depression at the beginning of the reign reduced yield from the Customs and Excise. Soon after, London's commerce was virtually paralyzed as the Great Plague (1665) and then the Great Fire (1666) laid waste to the metropolis. This was to be followed by a disastrous war against the Dutch (see below) which would raise the royal debts to about £2.5 million by the end of the decade. As always, the Crown was left with only two choices: reduce expenditure or raise revenue. The king – or, more accurately, the Treasury – attempted financial retrenchments in 1662–3, 1667–9, and 1676–7, but in every case, pressured by demanding courtiers, he eventually went back to his old spendthrift ways. As for the alternative, Parliament grew increasingly reluctant to raise the king's revenue for two reasons. First, it feared that more money would only find its way to mistresses and favorites. A second – and worse – possibility in its eyes was that the money would be spent to raise an army *à la* Louis XIV or Cromwell, which might be used to reduce the liberties of the subject and impose a new religious policy on the nation.

Charles II's religion was a matter of great anxiety to his subjects. During his formative years he spent more time in the company of his Catholic mother than his Anglican father. After his exile in 1646, much of his young adulthood was spent in Catholic countries and courts. It is clear that he was impressed by the splendor and pomp of Roman Catholic ritual, which, as Henry VIII would have agreed, nicely complemented the splendor and pomp of monarchy. Nor could he have forgotten that, while Anglicans, Puritans, and Presbyterians had all questioned royal authority and some had eventually killed his father, Catholics had either supported the Royalist cause unswervingly or had lived quiet, apolitical lives. He recalled with gratitude that he had been harbored by Catholics after his defeat at Worcester in 1651. What is not clear is how strongly Charles II felt this attraction to Catholicism. The king was never a particularly religious man and he was far too cagey to admit such inclinations publicly, for he knew the strength of anti-Catholic feeling among his subjects. Still, in 1662, as we have seen, he married a Portuguese Catholic princess, thus recreating the fraught religious situation at his father's court. Once again a Catholic Queen of England worshipped in her Catholic chapel at St. James's Palace, ministered to by Catholic priests and monks. Once again Catholics were welcome at court. At least it appeared that the English people did not have to worry about Catholic heirs as it became clear that Charles II and Catherine were unable to produce children. But just as this fact became obvious, so did another one: the king's brother and heir apparent, James, duke of York, was also inclined to "popery." By 1670 he had probably converted secretly to Rome. Even worse, James was a far less subtle man than his brother: by 1673 he was shunning Anglican services.

Religious policy in England was always bound up with foreign policy. At the start of the reign, it appeared to many English men and women that the country had little to fear from its traditional Catholic enemies, the Spanish and the French, because both were exhausted in the aftermath of the Thirty Years' War. Rather, throughout the 1650s and 1660s England's most important economic and military rival was the Dutch Republic, the United Provinces of the Netherlands. The Dutch already possessed a commercial empire in North America and the Indian Ocean. The decay of Spanish power left them fighting with the English over dominance of trade with the New World. This, plus the fact that the United Provinces was a republic and the Dutch Calvinist religion was theologically similar to Puritanism, did nothing to endear them to the new Anglican-Royalist regime. Rather, if one had asked a moderately conservative Englishman in the 1660s where lay the greatest danger to English liberties, he would have said with radical Dissenters at home and the Dutch Republic abroad.

Parliament dealt with the Dutch and their trading empire by renewing the Navigation Acts of 1650–1 in 1660 and passing the Staple Act in 1663. This legislation forbade foreign ships to trade with English colonies and required that certain goods shipped to and from those colonies pass through an English port. Once again, the English and Dutch went to war over this legislation, in 1664–7. The Second Anglo-Dutch war began well in 1664, with the English taking New Amsterdam (renaming it New York). However, after a series of inconclusive naval battles in the Channel in which York, as lord high admiral, distinguished himself, the English laid up their fleet in 1667 in order to save money. This was a fatal mistake. It allowed the Dutch to sail unmolested up the Thames and Medway, burning the docks at Chatham and capturing English shipping, including the flagship of the Royal Navy, the *Royal Charles*.

This humiliating defeat for the new regime eventually led to the fall of Clarendon and the rise of a group of courtier-politicians known as "the Cabal" (that is, a small coterie involved in intrigue). The Cabal were so named from the initials of their last names. Thomas, afterwards Lord, Clifford (1630–73), Henry Bennet, Lord Arlington (1618–85), the duke of Buckingham, Anthony Ashley Cooper, Lord Ashley (1621–83), and John Maitland, duke of Lauderdale (1616–82), are sometimes seen as precursors to the modern cabinet, for each one took on a particular ministry or responsibility: Clifford at the Treasury, Ashley as lord chancellor, etc. In fact, real power still lay with the king, who often withheld information from his ministers and played them off against each other. As this implies, the Cabal did not really operate as a team and felt little loyalty to each other. What they did have in common was a hatred of Clarendon, an inclination toward religious toleration, and a desire to increase royal power as well as their own.

One way to do all of those things was to reform the king's government and retrench its vast expenditure. There was a pressing need for such reform because the Second Dutch War had exposed naval and military inefficiency and corruption, added £1.5 million to the national debt, and depressed trade. This last caused the royal revenue to fall to about £650,000 a year – just over half of its intended yield. The new ministry established a Treasury Commission to centralize financial control in one office (the Treasury), to reform the collection of revenue, and to examine the minutest details of royal expenditure. Their short-term goal was to get the king out of debt; their long-term goal was to increase his power by saving him money and so decreasing his reliance on Parliament. Another way to do this was to gain the diplomatic and financial support of France. All members of the Cabal were sympathetic to Louis XIV (or at least antipathetic to the Netherlands), and at least two of them were sympathetic to Catholicism. These sympathies would lead to the next crisis of Charles II's reign.

The Declaration of Indulgence and the Third Dutch War, 1670–1673

As we have seen, as long as Parliament feared the king's religious sympathies and his desire for an army, it would not give him more money. So long as it did not give more money, the king could never raise an army or permanently dissolve Parliament. And so long as he had to live with Parliament and without an army, he could never significantly expand royal authority, embrace Catholicism, or impose its toleration on his people. For the king and the Cabal, there was only one way out of this impasse: alliance with the wealthiest and most powerful State in Europe, Louis XIV's France. Coincidentally, Louis was looking for allies to support his wildest ambition yet: the annexation of the Spanish Empire. Since the sixteenth century, Spain had possessed a vast expanse of territory that included the southern or Spanish Netherlands (what is today Belgium), Portugal (to 1641), much of Italy, most of Central and South America, and the Philippines (see map 8, p. 127). In the later seventeenth century, Spain was ruled by a sickly and mentally incompetent invalid, Carlos II (1661–1700; reigned 1665–1700). Since Carlos had proven himself incapable of having children, a new royal line would inherit his kingdom and empire when he died. Louis's position, bolstered by his marriage to a Spanish princess, was "Why not Louis?" He signaled his intentions in 1667, when his armies swept into the Spanish Netherlands (see map 12). This was the first step in a master plan to acquire the greatest empire the world had ever seen. The resulting combination of French military power with Spanish wealth would make the Sun King the master of Europe.

Obviously, Louis's dream was Protestant Europe's worst nightmare. In particular, the eventual stadholder of the Netherlands, William of Orange (1650–1702), was adamant in his refusal to allow France to conquer or annex Spain.[7] For the Dutch, Louis's actions in 1667, and later incursions into Franche-Comté, Luxembourg, Lorraine, and Orange in 1679–88, were particularly alarming, for they brought his armies to the very borders of the Republic (map 12). The Dutch were deeply aware that they were the last Protestant State on the continent west of the Rhine. To oppose Louis's aggressive moves, they began to cultivate a Grand Alliance with other such States on Louis's borders to the east. This led to a series of wars in which Louis would, on at least one occasion, come close to wiping the Dutch off the map. Clearly, for Louis XIV, the road to Spain lay, militarily and politically if not geographically, through the Netherlands. Moreover, he wished to expand France's share of trade. No wonder that, as the 1660s drew to a close, many Englishmen began to feel that the real danger to their liberties came not from the Protestant Dutch Republic but from the vast Catholic conspiracy for a seemingly world-encircling monarchy headed by Louis's France. Worse, they worried that a crypto-Catholic regime in London was aiding and abetting that conspiracy. This helps to explain why, in 1668, Parliament agreed, despite the humiliations of the second Anglo-Dutch War, to an alliance with the United Provinces in order to keep Louis XIV at bay.

This, in turn, explains why, when Charles II began to make approaches to the French court through his sister, Henrietta Anne, duchess of Orléans (1644–70), Louis was ready to listen. The result was the Treaty of Dover of 1670. According to the public provisions of this treaty, Charles II's British kingdoms would ally with Louis XIV's France against the Dutch, in return for a payment of £225,000. Thus, each side got what it wanted. Louis detached Britain[8] from its Dutch alliance and acquired the use of the Royal Navy in the bargain. For Charles II, Louis's subsidy meant that he would not have to ask parliamentary permission to raise an army. Freed from Parliament and possessed of an army, the king could pursue a new religious policy. And that was just the public side of the Treaty of Dover. According to a secret provision of the treaty known only to Charles, Arlington, and Clifford, the king was to convert publicly to Roman Catholicism

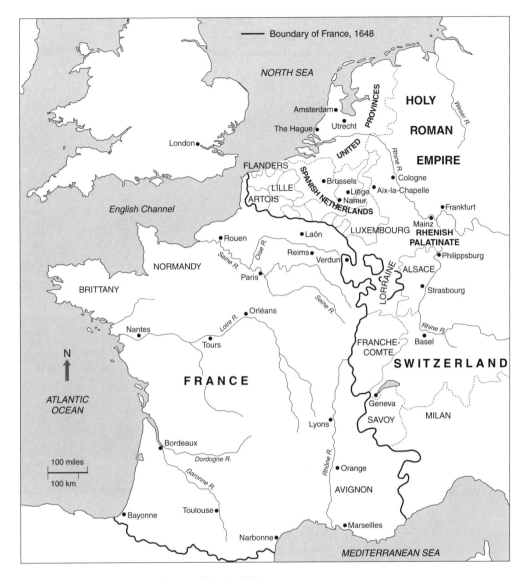

Map 12 *Western Europe in the age of Louis XIV.*

and reconcile his three kingdoms to Rome. In return, Louis would supply an additional £150,000 and French troops should the Protestants in those kingdoms rebel. In other words, the Treaty of Dover was a risky attempt to solve the king's constitutional, financial, religious, and military problems at one bold stroke.

What Charles intended by the secret provisions may never be known. Certainly he never attempted any public reconciliation with Rome. Some historians see the signing as a characteristic piece of duplicity, a promise of anything to get Louis to fork over the money. But Charles had to show some good faith on his side, and, in

1672, he acted. He proclaimed a **Declaration of Indulgence** which suspended penalties against both public Nonconformist and private Catholic worship. The king hoped that Dissenters would be so grateful to have their liberties restored that they would not object to similar liberties being extended to Catholics. In fact, many Dissenters and virtually all Anglicans seem to have felt that this was too high a price to pay. Local response to the 1672 Indulgence was generally negative: in at least one market town officials beat drums to drown out the voice of a Nonconformist preaching in the market place. To provide money for the war, the king also proclaimed the Stop of the Exchequer; that is, he suspended payment to those who had made loans to the government. This freed up funds to outfit the navy, but it also bankrupted a number of great merchant-financiers and ruined the Crown's credit for years to come.

Worse, the Third Dutch War went badly for the English and proved to be far more expensive than Charles or his ministers had anticipated. As a result, in February 1673, he was forced to recall the Cavalier Parliament. It was no more sympathetic to the Declaration of Indulgence than it had been to Charles's previous calls for toleration. It rejected the Indulgence and instead passed the **Test Act**. The Test Act was an extension of the Cavalier Code. It required *all* officeholders to deny transubstantiation and to take communion at least once a year in an Anglican service. Many Dissenting officeholders would accommodate themselves, with some difficulty, to this law by the practice of **occasional conformity** (i.e., taking the sacrament just once a year and then attending their own services the rest of the time). But no good Catholic could ever deny transubstantiation or accept Anglican communion. As a result, the new law "smoked out" many secret Papists in government, including the lord high admiral, James, duke of York, and the lord treasurer, Lord Clifford, when they were forced to resign their places. The revelation of James's Catholicism shocked the nation, raising the specter of a Catholic plot to subvert the constitution at home just as the Stuarts were helping the Bourbons to liquidate the Protestant Dutch and absorb the Spanish Empire abroad. These fears and revelations doomed the French alliance and the Cabal. In order to secure any supply from Parliament at all, the king was forced to make peace with the Dutch in 1674 and to dismiss most of his ministry. This ended Charles II's boldest attempt to solve the problems of sovereignty, religion, foreign policy, and finance.

The Earl of Danby and the Court and Country Blocs, 1673–1678

Thus, popery and the French, not Dissent and the Dutch, reemerged as the English people's greatest nemeses. The king and royal family had also lost credit, for they stood revealed not only as pro-Catholic and pro-French but also as fiscally and militarily incompetent. In order to correct this public relations disaster, the king chose as his new lord treasurer and first minister a conservative Anglican, Sir Thomas Osborne (1631–1712), whom he soon elevated to the title Lord Osborne, and then in 1674, earl of Danby. Danby's first task was to give the government and its policies enough of an Anglican face to defuse fears about Catholicism. He did this, first, by securing the appointment of like-minded Anglican and Royalist gentlemen to offices at both the center and in the localities. Second, he forged an alliance with the bishops to support the Church in general and to persecute Catholics and Dissenters in particular. The period of Danby's ministry saw the strictest enforcement of the Cavalier Code yet: Catholics were fined, Dissenting services were broken up, and repeat offenders imprisoned. Third, he insisted that James's two daughters, Princesses Mary and Anne, be raised as Anglicans and, when old enough, marry Protestants. In 1677 Mary wed William of Orange, stadholder of the Netherlands and Louis XIV's greatest enemy. Six years later, Anne married Prince George of Denmark (1653–1708), who had also distinguished himself as a military leader and a fervent Protestant.

These marriages had both foreign policy and domestic implications. The Dutch marriage, in particular, was the linchpin in a new Protestant alliance against Louis XIV. On the domestic front, both unions did much to allay English fears of James's religion and, in particular, a Catholic succession. After all, James was nearly as old as his brother and, since he was thought to be in less robust health, there was every chance that he would not succeed to the throne. Even if he did succeed, his reign would be short, followed by that of one of his two Anglican daughters and her Protestant spouse. It was true that, in 1673, after the death of his first wife, Anne *née* Hyde, duchess of York (1637–71), he had married another young Catholic princess, Mary Beatrice of Modena (1658–1718). If Mary Beatrice produced a son, that child would take precedence over James's female heirs, Mary and Anne. But as the 1670s progressed into the 1680s this possibility grew remote as the new duchess of York experienced a series of obstetrical mishaps. Therefore, thanks to Danby and the Yorks' bad luck, a Protestant succession seemed assured in the long run, whatever the short term might bring.

Danby's second great task was to restore the regime's financial credit. Though the debts owed before the Stop of the Exchequer were never fully repaid, the new lord treasurer did what he could to cut expenditure and raise revenue. Unfortunately, his attempts to restrain the king's extravagance were not very successful, and they did nothing for his credit with the ravenous army of mistresses and courtiers. Danby was more successful on the revenue side. He continued the Treasury Commission's reforms of the Customs, Excise, and Hearth Tax services.[9] He also got lucky. Because the French and the Dutch continued to fight after England withdrew from the war, their share of trade fell to the English who, being neutral, could do business with both sides. As a result, English commerce boomed and the yield from Customs, in particular, swelled. Unfortunately, the king's spending continued to outrun his income.

The final recourse open to Danby was to try to raise revenue by enlisting the aid of the heretofore reluctant Cavalier Parliament. We have seen how the lord treasurer attempted to change their minds by pursuing the Anglican religious and foreign policies described above. He also sought to appeal to their pride and their pocketbooks by offering court offices, pensions, secret service payments, and favors to peers and MPs, in return for their votes. In short, he sought to build up a "court" bloc in Parliament. Yet, Danby could never bribe enough members to form a majority; nor is it clear that he could count on even a small nucleus of court supporters. He therefore had to rely on his Anglican and reformist policies to convince the remainder.

But there was one group of MPs whom he could never convince. This was made up of old Parliamentarians, many with Roundhead pasts and Dissenting sympathies, who eventually came under the leadership of Lord Ashley, now earl of Shaftesbury. Shaftesbury was one of those nimble politicians who had managed to serve first Cromwell, then Charles II. After the Cabal's fall in 1673 he began to organize an opposition to Danby's government. This opposition criticized court luxury and waste, Danby's bribery of Parliament, the king's sympathy with France and Catholicism, the growing influence of the bishops and Church courts and the resulting persecution of Dissenters. In their view, royal power was increasing alarmingly, to the point where it threatened the political and religious constitution of England. In 1677, Andrew Marvell (1621–78) wrote that "[t]here has now for divers years a design been carried on to change the lawful government of England into an absolute tyranny, and to convert the established Protestant religion into downright Popery."[10] Shaftesbury's group claimed to represent "the country," that is, the true interests and views of the vast majority of the landed aristocracy in the countryside. In fact, because their views were still associated with republicanism and the violence of the Civil Wars, the country group was a minority within the political elite, unable to win majorities in the Cavalier Parliament. They needed a more specific, pressing issue in order to prove that they did, indeed, represent the views of the political nation at large. In August 1678, they got it.

The Popish Plot, Exclusion Crisis, and Loss of Local Control, 1678–1681

Toward the end of the summer of 1678, a defrocked preacher named Titus Oates (1648–1705) approached the government with claims of a Catholic plot to kill Charles II; replace him with his brother James; raise English and Irish Catholics against their Protestant neighbors; and bring over a French army to restore Roman Catholicism. To their credit, no one in authority took this story seriously at first. Oates was not exactly a monument of veracity: starting out as an Anabaptist, he was eventually expelled from the Merchant Tailors' School, two Cambridge colleges, two Anglican livings, the Royal Navy, and, finally, two Jesuit Colleges for a variety of offenses ranging from lying to drunkenness to sodomy! Only after several terrible coincidences did belief in the Popish Plot gain momentum. First, James's former secretary, Edward Coleman (1636–78), was found to have been corresponding secretly with the French court about reestablishing Catholicism. Second, in mid-October the JP who first interrogated Oates, Sir Edmund Berry Godfrey (1621–78), was found dead in a ditch. In fact, the evidence for foul play is ambiguous – Godfrey's death remains one of the great "murder" mysteries in English history. But coming as it did after these other accusations, Godfrey's untimely end seemed to contemporaries yet more evidence of a sinister international Catholic plot. Suddenly, people took Oates's story seriously. Anti-Catholic hysteria flourished. Rumors flew of Catholics secretly arming themselves, of bombs being planted in Protestant churches, of "night riders" – presumably Catholic spies – criss-crossing the country, of French and Spanish troops landing on the coasts. As a result, Catholic houses were searched; Catholics were forbidden the court; London streets were blocked off and the trained bands and militia called out.

In fact, historians now know that Oates's plot was a tissue of lies and that the English Catholic community in 1678 was small – about 1 percent of the population – and more apolitical than ever before. But Charles's subjects could not or would not see this. What they did see was that the Catholic powers, France in particular, were on the march in Europe. They saw popery flourishing at court as never before. Above all, Oates's charges played brilliantly on a long heritage of anti-Catholic fear and suspicion by recalling the Northern and Ridolfi Plots of 1569–72, the Armada of 1588, the Gunpowder Plot of 1605, the Irish Rebellion of 1641, the burning of London (which the government had cynically blamed on Catholics) of 1666, and the machinations of 1670–3. In short, most of the political nation saw the plot as yet one more piece of evidence confirming their worst fears and prejudices. Their response was swift and decisive: prominent Catholics were arrested on charges of high treason and subjected to kangaroo trials in which presiding judges admitted hearsay evidence and ridiculed defense witnesses. Overall, some two dozen people were executed either for complicity in the supposed plot or for officiating as priests, which was prosecuted as a capital crime at this time. Even the queen was accused of trying to poison the king, a charge at which Charles II scoffed. But not every unlikely charge proved false: in the third terrible coincidence of 1678, at the end of the year the arch-Anglican and supposedly anti-French earl of Danby was discovered to have written to Louis asking for money so as to avoid recalling Parliament.

The king tried to save his first minister – impeachment might expose the *real* Popish "plot" of the secret provisions of the Treaty of Dover – by dissolving Parliament. That was a mistake. Now Shaftesbury and his country group not only had their issue – a Catholic plot against Church and State – but also an election with which to take that issue to the voters of England. They ran on a platform of anti-popery, anti-France, and anti-arbitrary and corrupt government. Ultimately, they collapsed those agendas into one: to exclude James, duke of York, from the succession to the throne because he was a Catholic. The next few years have come to be known as the **Exclusion Crisis**, during which three general elections produced three Parliaments. The Exclusion Parliaments would debate whether to alter the hereditary succession (exclusion) or limit the powers of a popish successor. But since these elections were the first in England in almost two decades, they were, in fact, more than a referendum on Exclusion. They put the entire reign on trial. In the course of that trial there emerged two sets of loyalties, based roughly on the country and court groups but coalescing into well-organized, almost modern, political parties: the Whigs and the Tories.

Who were the Whigs? The term "whig" originally meant a Scottish Presbyterian rebel; as this implies, it was bestowed by the party's enemies. In fact, many Whigs could trace themselves or their ancestry back to the Parliamentarian rebels of old, even more to Shaftesbury's country bloc. The Whigs' principal policy initiative, the exclusion of York from the throne by act of Parliament, implied parliamentary sovereignty over that of the king. Consistent with this, they supported limitations on royal power and opposed the establishment of a standing army. In James's place, some proposed the king's eldest and favorite but illegitimate son, James Scott, duke of Monmouth (1649–85). Since his main qualification, besides his dubious lineage, was his Protestantism, it should be obvious that the Whigs were anti-Catholic and, by implication, strongly in favor of Dissenters' rights and a new Church settlement. In power, they would seek to abolish the Cavalier Code as it applied to Dissenters, while enhancing and enforcing its application to Roman Catholics. Since the Catholic menace was international in scope, they were also anti-French. They saw clearly the danger of Louis's overarching ambitions. This, in turn, made them natural supporters of William of Orange and the Dutch. Finally, while many Whigs were country gentlemen, their embrace of Dissenters also made them popular with urban dwellers, particularly merchants.

Shaftesbury and the Whigs cultivated this popularity by using many techniques that we associate with political campaigns today. First, they organized. They founded a number of political dining societies, the most famous of which was London's Green Ribbon Club. At its meetings they planned electoral and parliamentary tactics, propaganda, and street demonstrations. They capitalized on the temporary end of press censorship, producing a torrent of partisan pamphlets and newspapers after the Licensing Act lapsed in 1679. Running through this literature were several radical notions, some of which had not seen their way into print since the Interregnum. Clearly, in arguing that Parliament could alter the succession, the Whigs rejected the divine basis of authority. In its place, they revived the supremacy of the common law, or even the old Leveller notion of "the sovereignty of the people," but with a moderating twist. To most Whig country gentlemen, "the people" did not mean everybody in England but only those who elected and sat in Parliament. However one defined "the people," all government, even in a monarchy, had its origins in their consent. Since that consent was given so that the government could protect the lives, liberty, and property of its citizens, Whigs argued that it could be withdrawn in the event that the ruler failed to provide that protection – as Charles II was, manifestly in their eyes, failing to do. Once consent was withdrawn, the government ceased to have any legitimacy and resistance, even rebellion, was justified.

The Whigs made this case so effectively that they won the first election in a landslide. This presented Charles II with a terrible dilemma. While he found Whig ideas abhorrent, he could not ignore their parliamentary majority and apparent popularity in the country at large. He must have been sorely tempted to embrace Shaftesbury and the Whigs, jettison his brother and wife (neither of whom he much cared for), and agree to the succession of his illegitimate son (whom he clearly loved). This would give him a quiet life in the short term, but end his absolutist dreams in the long term. Instead, like his father in 1640–2, he played for time, hoping that Whig extremism would breed a Royalist reaction. Thus, when in the spring of 1679 the first Exclusion Parliament was about to pass a bill excluding York from the succession in favor of his daughter, Princess Mary, Charles prorogued, then dissolved it.

The elections for the Second Exclusion Parliament, which took place in the late summer of 1679, resulted in another Whig landslide. In response, the king continued his strategy of delay, proroguing it repeatedly until October 1680. Shaftesbury and the Whigs saw this as yet another example of arbitrary Stuart rule. For a year they kept alive popular partisanship by organizing mass "monster" petitions urging Charles to summon Parliament. Instead, he prosecuted journalists supporting Exclusion and Whig petitioning on charges of seditious libel. The Green Ribbon Club also organized pope-burnings on November 5 and 17, the anniversaries of the Gunpowder Plot and Queen Elizabeth's accession, respectively. The Whigs turned these popular celebrations into elaborately stage-managed party rallies, processing through London in 1679, 1680, and 1681. But not everyone joined in the fun. Critics organized addresses from official bodies in "abhorrence" of Whig petitions. These Abhorrers became the first Tories.

Who were the Tories? The term "Tory" was also a slang word first applied by the other side – this time for an Irish cattle thief. Their opponents considered Tories soft on Catholics (hence the Irish connection) because they did not favor excluding James from the throne. Based on Danby's court group, which was in turn full of old Anglican Royalists, the Tories believed fervently in the sovereignty of the Crown. While they conceded the necessity for Parliaments, for them the lesson of the Civil Wars was that, ultimately, the king was the only safeguard for order in England. Because Parliament was subordinate to the king, and because the king was chosen by God through hereditary succession, it could not exclude the next rightful heir, not even if he were a Catholic. As for rebellion, it was a heinous sin against the divine order. Even in the face of a bad ruler (which was not how they saw Charles II), Tories counseled patience, passive obedience, and non-resistance. Therefore, while they would soon become as skilled as the Whigs in appealing to the masses, in theory they deplored doing so. As all this implies, Tories were the party of the Great Chain of Being, embracing hierarchy and ceremony – and, thus, the Anglican Church. They were not pro-Catholic, but they saw a far greater danger from the Dissenters who, they would point out, had actually succeeded in killing the last king, bringing revolution and chaos on England. Thus, they associated religious dissent with political disloyalty and so favored strict implementation of the Cavalier Code to force conformity to the Church of England. In foreign policy, they viewed Louis XIV with some suspicion, but most concluded that he was pursuing initiatives appropriate to any Divine Right monarch. In short, their foreign policy was pro- (or not particularly anti-) French. Toryism was especially popular among courtiers and, of course, the king and royal family. But like Roundheads and Cavaliers of the Civil Wars, there were Whigs and Tories at every social level. Thus, while Shaftesbury and the Whig lords wined and dined Whig London councilmen, Tory lords or even

Charles II provided venison for Tory apprentice feasts. While Whig mobs burned effigies of the pope, Tory mobs burned effigies of "Jack Presbyter."

Whig and Tory ideological battles produced classic works of political theory. The Tories upheld Divine Right monarchy, first printing Sir Robert Filmer's (1588–1653) *Patriarcha, or the Natural Power of Kings Asserted* in 1680. Filmer argued that the king's power derived directly from that bestowed by God on Adam, as the father of the whole human race. A deluge of Tory tracts and sermons reinforced Filmer's arguments for non-resistance to the divinely ap-pointed sovereign. In response, Shaftesbury's protégé, John Locke (1632–1704), wrote his *Two Treatises of Government* to justify the right to resistance in the early 1680s (although not published until 1689–90). Algernon Sidney (1622–83) penned a line-by-line rebuttal of Filmer while fellow Whigs discussed more radical steps against arbitrary rule. For example, proposals circulated for an "Association," a paramilitia to resist any Catholic coup.

When Parliament finally met in October 1680, it refused to grant supply without Exclusion. The Second Exclusion Bill (which would have banned York not only from the succession but from England as well) passed the Commons quickly, only to be rejected by the Lords on November 15, 1680. MPs spoke darkly of conspiracy and civil war seemed to loom. Charles II hastily dissolved Parliament and summoned a new one to meet at Oxford, distant from Whig radicals in London. Once again, despite a Tory challenge, mainly Whigs were returned. The Third Exclusion Parliament, the Oxford Parliament, met on March 21, 1681 and again began to consider the vexed question of Exclusion. But Charles dissolved Parliament a week later, gambling that he could do without them for a while.

Charles's gamble worked because by 1681 public opinion was swinging back toward the Crown and its supporters. First, it became apparent that there was no Catholic plot to kill the king and promote his brother. Second, many landed gentlemen came to be persuaded by the Tory argument that to deny James's right to the throne was akin to denying their right to inherit property. No landowner could enthusiastically stand for such a fracture in the Great Chain. Moreover, the Tories won the propaganda war. The Whig press wilted, as civil prosecutions and the barbs of Tory writers took their toll. In particular, John Dryden's satirical poem *Absalom and Achitophel* compared Charles II to the Biblical King David, and held up the Whigs to merciless ridicule. Shaftesbury, for example, was portrayed as a man "In friendship false, implacable in hate / Resolved to ruin or to rule the state." The Tories were now in a position to have their revenge.

The Tory Revenge and Reestablishment of Local Control, 1681–1685

In 1681, like his father in 1629, Charles II opted to rule without Parliament. As before, the decision was based on electoral realities: so long as the electorate continued to return Whigs to the House of Commons, the king could not work with them. But unlike his father, Charles II anticipated a time when he might have to do so. Therefore, using the power afforded him in the Corporation Act and a legal device called *Quo Warranto*, he began, once more, to tackle the issue of local control by revoking city charters, purging their councils of Whigs and Dissenters and replacing them with loyal Tories. The king also purged the lieutenancy and the county bench to ensure that local control was more firmly in Tory hands. These newly purged town councils and county commissions of the peace renewed the prosecution of Nonconformists instead of Catholics, imprisoning some 1,300 Quakers alone by 1685. Moreover, since in many boroughs the officers of the corporation were the only ones with a vote, and since, everywhere else, local officials had a powerful influence on how votes were cast and counted, the king was also, in effect, packing the next Parliament.

In the meantime, Charles II had to figure out how to do what Charles I had done during the Personal Rule: live without parliamentary funds. Like his father, he immediately began to enhance his revenue while retrenching his expenses. He did the first by secretly accepting a subsidy of £125,000 a year from Louis XIV and by pursuing stricter collection of the Customs, Excise, and other ordinary revenue. Here, he got lucky. The trade boom of the 1670s was about to become a bonanza. A commercial revolution was beginning in Europe which would make English trade with India, its colonies in America, and the continent itself fabulously prosperous. This, in turn, increased the yield from all taxes to nearly £1.4 million a year. With this money, the Crown was able to maintain an army of 9,000 men in England, in addition to forces of a similar magnitude in Scotland and Ireland. As for the royal expenses, for once Charles II stuck to his budget, shutting down the payment of pensions and cutting household expenditure by about half.

If the Exclusion Crisis thus taught the king thrift, it also educated him in the loyalty of Anglican Tories and the value of propaganda. In order to retain that loyalty, Charles behaved himself with regard to religion, making no move toward Catholicism until he was on his deathbed in 1685, when he finally converted. While alive and well, he surrounded himself with loyal Anglicans, whose clergy responded from the pulpit with continued exhortations to passive obedience and non-resistance to the divinely appointed monarch. As for the Whigs, they grew more frustrated, then more desperate, and, finally, more radical. Without Parliament, without elections, they had lost their arena. As Charles's law courts began to prosecute minor Whigs, Shaftesbury lost his nerve and fled to the Netherlands in 1682, dying there in 1683. Most Whigs had already been purged from town councils and county benches of justices when evidence was uncovered in the latter year of radical Whig plans to kidnap and kill the royal brothers Charles and James. Whether this was wild talk or a coherent plan, the Rye House Plot revelations ended all hope for Exclusion and drove radical Whigs underground. Locke hid his papers and followed Shaftesbury abroad, as did Monmouth; Sidney died on the scaffold merely for writing his unpublished "Discourses Concerning Government." Tory ideology, which equated Whig principles with fanaticism, was vindicated. When he died of a stroke on February 6, 1685, Charles II left his successor a prosperous country, a healthy Treasury, a supportive national Church, an opposition Whig party in disarray, a compliant local government firmly in the hands of Tory loyalists, and a Crown that was more popular than it had been since Tudor times. Unfortunately, he left all of these things to his brother, James.

James II and the Attempt at a Catholic Restoration, 1685–1688

James II (1685–8) ascended the thrones of England, Scotland, and Ireland on a wave of Royalist sentiment and good will. He was a Catholic, but the horrors of Cromwell's regime and Shaftesbury's extremism were much more recent than those of Bloody Mary and the Gunpowder Plot. At first, the new king did everything possible to maintain this popularity. His first official act was to promise in Privy Council to respect the constitution, the Church of England, and the property of his subjects. Then, as usual for a new monarch, he summoned a new Parliament. The monarchy's current popularity, as well as Charles II's gerrymandering, helped return Tories in overwhelming numbers. The resulting Tory, Royalist Parliament voted the new king the same taxes as those enjoyed by Charles II. What it perhaps did not realize was that, thanks to the trade boom of the 1680s, those taxes now yielded far more than they had done in the previous reign. James II's ordinary revenue came to about £1,600,000, some £300,000–400,000 a year *more* than Charles II had enjoyed. Moreover, the compliant new Parliament voted James an additional £400,000 annually for the next five to eight years to enable him to put down any rebellions which might arise during this time. In their defense, they were reacting to one at the very moment.

In the summer of 1685, the Whig duke of Monmouth, Charles II's eldest if illegitimate son, abandoned his exile in the Dutch Republic, landed in the West Country, and raised a rebellion against the Catholic monarchy with a rag-tag army of tradesmen and farmers. Against this, thanks to his generous Tory Parliament, James II was able to expand the small army he had inherited from his brother into a much larger and better-equipped force and staff it with loyal, and in some cases, on an emergency basis, Catholic, officers. This force, effectively led by one of the king's favorites, John, Lord Churchill (1650–1722), defeated the rebels at the battle of Sedgemoor, near Bridgwater in Somerset. The rebellion was a short-lived failure, but James's response revealed much about his character and purpose. First, he used the occasion of the rebellion as an excuse to keep his army in being. Second, he dispatched his lord chief justice, George, Lord Jeffreys (1644–89), to deal with the surrendered rebels. Already known as "Hanging Judge Jeffreys" for his treatment of Whigs during the Tory revenge, he presided over a series of savage trials – 1,336 cases in nine days! – forever after known as "the Bloody Assizes." These resulted in the execution of over 300 rebels, most of them poor men and women, by hanging, drawing, and quartering. Their rotting corpses were still being displayed in West Country villages a year later. A further 800 prisoners were transported to the American colonies. This response should have given

James's subjects pause. But, for now, the new king sat secure on his throne, with rebellion defeated, the Whigs cowed, the Tories supreme, Parliament cooperative, the royal Treasury full, the Church loyal, and the people apparently content with, if not necessarily enthusiastic over, their new sovereign. So what went wrong? How did James II manage to blow it all within a little more than three years?

One place to begin to find an answer is in the new king's personality. James II (see plate 20) was neither so clever, nor so subtle as his brother. As we have seen, he was incapable of dissembling the Catholicism that so alarmed his subjects. Instead, from the moment he became king he worshipped openly and ostentatiously, asking Sir Christopher Wren to design an elaborate Catholic chapel at

Plate 20   James II, *by unknown artist. National Portrait Gallery, London.*

Whitehall. As his piety might seem to imply, James II was not as fun-loving as Charles II. It was remarked at the beginning of his reign that he banished from Whitehall all the men and women of pleasure, including (albeit temporarily) his own mistress, Catherine Sedley, countess of Dorchester (1657–1717). In some ways, this sobriety was not such a bad thing. After the scandalous behavior of the "Merry Monarch," the Crown needed to restore its dignity. It also needed to save money. The new king's orderly mind caused him to launch a major "downsizing" of the court, eliminating sinecure offices and much of the fee-taking system. The result was a smaller, more efficient, and thriftier court – but also one which was much less exciting and lucrative – than his brother's had been.

In short, James II may have been an excellent administrator, but he was a terrible politician. A soldier since youth and a Roman Catholic for nearly two decades, he craved order, hierarchy, clear-cut rules of conduct, and obedience to them. He regarded questioning or disagreement from his subordinates, whether in Parliament, the court, or the military, as signs of disloyalty. Consistent with this, he was a lifelong absolutist. In James's view, his father's (Charles I's) only mistake was to make concessions. Above all, James II was convinced of the truth of the Roman Catholic faith and of his moral duty, as king, to bring his people back into the fold – regardless of their individual feelings on the matter. In his defense, it should be understood that James II had no intention of forcing his subjects to convert or recant *à la* Mary I, his predecessor. Rather, he seems to have believed that, if all Christian faiths were put on an equal footing by a toleration, thus creating a free market of ideas and discourse, Catholicism would emerge the clear winner and Catholics would inevitably persuade their heretical Protestant brethren to return. As a result, and somewhat ironically given the rigid nature of James's personality, the pursuit of religious toleration became the major policy initiative of his reign. Here, as in his administrative reforms, this otherwise old-fashioned and conservative man was too far ahead of his times for his own good.

The king began to act on his convictions within six months of his accession. In November 1685 he demonstrated his complete lack of political savvy by announcing to Parliament not only that he intended to keep his army in being, but that he intended to retain its Catholic officers. James's heretofore compliant Parliament balked, demanding their dismissal. The king's immediate reaction was to end the session. His long-term reaction was multi-pronged. First, he began to pack the judiciary to ensure that they would support his interpretation of – some would say his assault on – the laws. As a result, in the test case Godden vs. Hales, the courts upheld the king's ability to dispense with the Test Act in the case of particular individuals. This allowed him to place more Catholics in civil government and the army, not only in England but in Scotland and Ireland as well. Next, James used his prerogative power to suspend the Cavalier Code. That is, in April 1687 he issued another Declaration of Indulgence, in effect granting religious freedom to both Dissenters and Catholics. As in 1672, the king hoped that those on either extreme of the religious divide would make common cause against the Anglican supremacy. As in 1672, he would be disappointed, for, once again, many prominent Dissenters refused to cooperate.

These were piecemeal initiatives. What James really wanted was *repeal* of the laws against Dissenters and Catholics, not a temporary suspension. To secure this, he would need a Parliament of a different color. Taking a page from his brother's notebook, in 1686 he had begun to remodel the corporate governments, and therefore, the electorates, of the towns. He also purged the lieutenancy and county bench. That is, he began to remove Anglican Tories – heretofore his staunchest supporters – from serving as lords lieutenant, JPs, civic officials, even masters of university colleges. This process was stepped up in the fall of 1687, when government agents began to ask JPs, militia officers, and other local officials the notorious "Three Questions": each was asked if he would support repeal of the penal laws and Test Act if elected MP, the election of MPs so disposed, and the Declaration of Indulgence by "living friendly with those of all persuasions." These questions were profoundly uncomfortable for the Tory gentry, for they asked them to choose between loyalty to their king and that to their religion. After much equivocation, only a quarter could give their unqualified assent. Most who gave an answer did so in the negative to the first two questions and a few even denied that they could live friendly with Catholic and Dissenter neighbors. Even time-serving Tories took a dim view of sitting on the bench of justices alongside "fanatics" as they termed Dissenters, with "their avowed King-Killing Principles."[11] And so, James purged thousands of heretofore loyal Anglican Tory JPs and local officials.

The king would have liked to replace them with Catholics, but by 1685 there were so few left, and even fewer willing to offend their neighbors by assuming these positions (many who were appointed never officiated), that this was effectively impossible. As a result, the king filled the lieutenancy and local bench with obscure Dissenters and old Whigs – in fact, just about anybody who might be willing to give him a positive vote on toleration. It is very important to understand what James was doing here. In order to try to secure agreement for a wildly unpopular (with the ruling elite at least) policy, James was disgracing and abandoning his most loyal friends, those who had stood by him during the Exclusion Crisis, the strongly Royalist, Anglican Tory gentry. He was, in effect, dispossessing the ruling class, disinheriting the "natural" leaders of the country by depriving the old landed families of political power which they had held for centuries and which they had come to view not as a privilege but as a right – indeed, as their property. He sought to replace them with a new, untested group who owned little land and embraced religious beliefs which most English men and women found repellent. He was, in short, taking a massive risk by asserting his powers of local control to the full.

Worse, James II expected the leadership of the Church of England to go along with these policies out of Royalist loyalty. Early in the reign he established an Ecclesiastical Commission to regulate the Anglican clergy. He also ordered the bishops to restrain anti-Catholic preaching. When the bishop of London, Henry Compton (1632–1713), refused to do so, the Commission suspended him from his pastoral duties. In the spring of 1688 James added insult to injury by ordering the clergy to read the Declaration of Indulgence from their own pulpits in May and June: in effect, they were being forced to endorse toleration and, thus, the end of their religious monopoly. Several refused; seven bishops, including the archbishop of Canterbury, William Sancroft (1617–93), publicly questioned the royal **dispensing** (and, by implication, suspending) **power** by way of a printed petition. James was furious, calling it a "standard of rebellion," and he sent the seven bishops to the Tower on a charge of seditious libel.[12] This was a great blunder, for it turned the leaders of the Church, figuratively if not actually, into martyrs.

Why did those leaders, their clergy, and the Tory landed families whom they served put up with this for so long? There were two reasons. First, no one wanted another civil war. The English ruling class remembered very well the violence of 1637–60. They had resolved never again to rebel against the king, a resolution strengthened by the constant preaching of Anglican clergymen that all good subjects owed passive obedience to even the most tyrannical monarch. Second, most people expected a short reign. James II was 51 years old at his accession: by the era's standards, a relatively elderly man. Therefore, he would be dead in a few years and safely succeeded by one of his Protestant daughters and her spouse – either Mary and William of Orange, currently living in the Netherlands, or Anne and Prince George of Denmark, who resided at court. Therefore, in 1687–8 as in 1557–8, the unpleasant Catholic experiment seemed destined to be a short one. Better to grumble and put up with it than risk another social and political upheaval as had been experienced within living memory. In short, for the first few years of the reign, the Great Chain as restored in 1660 still held.

It began to break in the late fall of 1687. At that time, the king's young wife, Mary Beatrice, announced that she was expecting a child. Court Catholics viewed the announcement as a miracle and evidence of God's favor for their side. If the child was a boy, James would be assured of an heir whom he could raise as a Catholic. Protestants viewed the announcement with suspicion, since Mary Beatrice had shown no signs of successful childbearing in the previous 15 years of her marriage. Why were Catholics so certain that *this* pregnancy would bear fruit? And how could they be so sure that it was a *boy*, anyway? Protestants immediately began to whisper that the pregnancy was being faked. For her part, Princess Anne went to take the waters at Bath, Somerset, to avoid being present at the birth. She did not want to know.

The queen's pregnancy came to term in the early summer of 1688. James invited all of his loyal courtiers to witness the happy event. In fact, public royal births were not unusual. After all, everyone needed to know that the child being born was, indeed, the legitimate heir. But there was obviously more urgency than usual to James's request. Those Protestant peers who could not find a suitable excuse to be away were summoned to St. James's Palace on June 10, 1688. But at the crucial moment, nearly every Protestant in the room held back or turned away – ostensibly, to give the queen privacy (see plate 21). Their refusal to witness the birth allowed them to claim for years afterwards that it was a fake or that the child was stillborn, and a substitute smuggled up the backstairs in a warming pan. As for the Catholics present, who would believe them when they said that they had witnessed a real birth – of a little boy?

Plate 21 Mary of Modena in Childbed, *Italian engraving. Sutherland Collection, Ashmolean Museum, Oxford.*

The king named his son James Francis Edward (1688–1766) and immediately ordered the ringing of bells and the setting of bonfires for the birth of the prince. But few of his subjects could muster enthusiasm for a Catholic heir whose godfather was the pope; in fact, the acquittal of the seven bishops a few weeks later caused far more public rejoicing. Immediately, the rumor began to spread that the child was not the king's; poor James was forced to the indignity of having to deny this to the Privy Council. Many in the ruling class realized immediately the significance of the birth of a Catholic heir. In fact, three days before, a group of seven aristocrats – the earl of Danby, William Cavendish, earl of Devonshire (1640–1707), Richard, Lord Lumley (1650?–1721), Edward Russell (1653–1727), Charles Talbot, earl of Shrewsbury (1660–1718), Henry Sidney (1641–1704), and Bishop Compton – had gathered together to assess the situation. This group included nearly every shade of contemporary political opinion: three Whigs (Devonshire, Russell, Sidney), but also a Tory peer (Danby), a Scots peer (Lumley), and an Anglican bishop (Compton). Two (Lumley and Shrewsbury) were even converted Catholics. In addition, Sidney had strong connections at court, Lumley with the army, Russell with the navy. In short, James II had managed to offend virtually every segment of the political nation. This group of men, which had been meeting secretly with representatives from the Dutch Republic for over a year, decided to write to William of Orange, urging him to invade England.

The Glorious Revolution, 1688–1689

William had been considering invasion for some time. He had three reasons for accepting the invitation in the early summer of 1688: to protect Mary's rights to the throne; to keep England from turning Catholic and allying with France; and to bring the increasing wealth and power of the British Isles onto the Dutch side in their fight for survival against Louis XIV. It took most of the rest of the summer, and all the financial and personal credit William possessed, to assemble a force consisting of about 21,000 foot, 5,000 horse, at least 300 transports, and 149 warships by the time of its departure on November 1. These ground forces were more than matched by James's English army of, perhaps, 40,000, but it was spread around the three kingdoms. Moreover, James's forces had only drawn blood against frightened townsmen and peasants at Sedgemoor. William's host – largely Dutch, but including mercenaries and exiled English Whigs – was battle-hardened by years of fighting against the French, generally considered to be the best army in Europe.

In other respects – and unlike the Spanish a century before – William got lucky. First, despite the warnings of his advisers, James initially refused to believe that his son-in-law would take arms against him. As a result, he refused French naval help. Second, Louis, trusting James's instincts, decided to launch an invasion of Rhine-Palatine in September (see map 12). This tied up his forces for the fall and winter, making it impossible to take advantage of William's absence by invading the Netherlands instead. Even the weather cooperated with the prince of Orange. In November, the wind shifted, blowing William's ships across the Channel and keeping James's fleet bottled up in the mouth of the Thames. As a result, William of Orange landed unopposed in the southwest of England on November 5, 1688 – the day after his birthday and the anniversary of the failed Catholic Gunpowder Plot of 1605. Thus, not only the weather but also the calendar seemed a good omen for the Protestant side.

On the Catholic side there was a loss of nerve. As soon as James II realized the seriousness of William's preparations, in late September he tried to back-pedal on previous policies, abolishing the Ecclesiastical Commission, restoring the old city charters and their Anglican Tory oligarchies, and promising to call a free Parliament. This did nothing to placate the Tory clergy or gentry or attract Whig townspeople; instead it demoralized Catholics and threw the local government of the nation into confusion. Soon after hearing that William had landed, James developed a massive nosebleed – an obviously psychological reaction. At first glance, the king's panic makes no sense. James had at his immediate disposal

25,000 troops encamped on Salisbury Plain, squarely between William at Exeter and his goal of London. His coffers were full. He had "home-field" advantage. And there had not been a successful invasion of England since the Wars of the Roses. He should have been able to throw William into the sea in a matter of weeks, if not days. But he must have realized that his forces were largely untested and divided in religion and loyalty. Nor could he have been encouraged by his own obvious personal unpopularity. Perhaps he could not forget the tragic history of the Stuarts.

In the meantime, the country hesitated between safety and hope. In particular, the ruling elite seems to have taken a wait-and-see attitude to William's invasion. But as James hesitated to act, his support began to evaporate. The first to go over to William was Edward Hyde, Viscount Cornbury (1661–1723), the king's own nephew. By mid-November, the lords lieutenant who had been asked to raise the militia did so – and then marched it over to the prince of Orange. Thus, at the moment of crisis James II turned out to be vulnerable on the last long-term issue that had cost his father the Crown, that of local control. Ultimately, that control still rested with the landed aristocracy who held estates in the localities. In the course of two successive mornings between November 23 and 25, James awakened to find that his other son-in-law, Prince George, his dearest friend, Lord Churchill, and the head of the most staunchly Royalist family in England, James Butler, second duke of Ormond (1665–1745), had gone over to William. On the 26th he learned that Princess Anne had also fled the court, leading James to lament, "God help me ... my own children have forsaken me."[13]

At this point the king decided that the jig was up. He abandoned his army and hurried back to London by coach. Once there, he put Queen Mary Beatrice and Prince James into a boat for France. On the night of December 11 he threw the Great Seal (required for registering statutes) into the Thames and attempted to make his own escape. He botched even this when he was discovered, disguised as a fisherman, while attempting to board a boat bound for the continent. The king returned briefly to London but, despite the urging of a number of Tory peers, he had no intention of staying. By the same token, William had no desire to see or capture his inconveniently returned father-in-law. So, when James requested to go to Rochester, on the extreme east coast of Kent, there were no objections. The unfortunate monarch took advantage of this location and made his second, successful, escape attempt on December 23. The Restoration Settlement was at an end.

Put another way, the Great Chain of Being had been broken once again within a generation. The ruling elite understood that, in the king's absence, someone had to run the country. Chaos threatened as Londoners attacked Irishmen and burned Catholic property. On December 24, 1688 an assembly of 60 peers asked the prince of Orange to administer the government temporarily, until a new settlement could be worked out. On December 26, 300 former members of the House of Commons, joined by London's civic leaders, agreed. These peers and former MPs called for a second Convention to decide the disposition of the Crown; it met on January 22. The Whigs elected to this Convention came to an early and easy decision. Since they believed in a contractual basis for governmental authority, in the right of revolt against a bad ruler, and in the supreme power of Parliament, they had no trouble asserting that James had broken his contract with the English people and had been deposed. In their view, Parliament had every right, as the people's legitimate representative, to have excluded James from the throne 10 years before, and to grant it to William now. On the other hand, Tories, who had been raised on the doctrines of the Great Chain of Being, the Divine Right of monarchy, passive obedience, and non-resistance, and who had supported the Stuarts through thick and thin with their very lives and fortunes, were appalled. It is true that they had opposed James in religion, and many had supported William's invasion, but in the hope that he would curb his father-in-law's folly, not usurp him. Despite his flight, was not James II still the one true and rightful king? In short, while the Whig position was eminently rational and practical, that of the Tories was romantic and emotional. The latter proposed a number of fictions to enable them to hang on to their beloved notions of hereditary monarchy and Divine Right. First, they suggested that James remain king in name, with William as his regent. But James was unlikely to accept such an empty Crown. Next, they suggested that the Crown be vested in Mary, who was at least a Stuart (and even the rightful heir, *if* one accepted the fantasy that James II's "son" had been smuggled in in a warming pan). To this suggestion, William replied that he had no interest in "being his wife's gentleman usher."[14]

Increasingly, it became clear that William of Orange would take his army and go home, leaving the English to their fate, if they did not offer him the main prize. Finally, after two weeks of heated debate, at the beginning of February Parliament agreed that James II had "abdicated" the throne, and that it was thereby "vacant." On February 13, 1689, in the Banqueting House at Whitehall, site of Charles I's execution, William and Mary were offered the Crown jointly, with administrative control to be vested in the former (see plate 22). They thus became William III (1689–1702) and Mary II (1689–94). At the ceremony, the dual monarchs were also offered a document, the *Declaration of Rights*, which condemned the suspending and dispensing power, royal manipulation of the judiciary, taxation without parliamentary permission, and the continuance of a standing army. It also reaffirmed the subjects' right of petition and the necessity of free elections. Historians have argued ever since as to whether the *Declaration* was a contract; that is, whether the offer of the Crown was conditional on their acceptance of this document. In fact, it does not matter. Clearly, for the first time in English history, Parliament had chosen a king and a queen.

So much for the settlement of the Crown which James had squandered. What about the Church which he had, in contemporary eyes, attacked? Remember that upper-class Englishmen had revolted not because they wanted a different king or constitutional settlement but because the current king, enabled by his vast constitutional powers, was attacking the Protestant ascendancy. More specifically, Anglican Tories revolted because they wanted to preserve the religious status quo, in particular the special position of the Church of England as the State Church – indeed, really the only legal Church – in England. Whig Dissenters had

Plate 22   Presentation of the Crown to William III and Mary II, *by R. de Hooge after C. Allard.*
Mary Evans Picture Library.

been offered a toleration by James II, but many had refused. They had revolted against him because they felt that Catholic emancipation was too high a price to pay for their own freedom. Since the leading Dissenters had thus, by and large, remained loyal to the Protestant ascendancy even in the face of their own immediate interests, and since Dissenter goldsmith bankers and merchants provided William's government with desperately needed financial support immediately after the Revolution, Anglicans were going to have to reward them with concessions. In effect, Dissenters could argue that they had atoned for their extreme and violent behavior during the Civil Wars and Interregnum. Strengthening their argument was the further inconvenient fact that the new king was himself not an Anglican but a Dutch Calvinist – in other words, in an English context, a Dissenter. As a result, in 1689 the Convention Parliament passed the Toleration Act. Henceforward, virtually all Trinitarian Protestant Churches were to be tolerated; most of the penalties of the Cavalier Code were removed.[15] The chief remaining obstacle faced by Dissenters was the Test Act. This was very important psychologically, but, as we have noted, it could be got round by the practice of occasional conformity. That is, all that a Dissenting officeholder had to do was swallow his religious sensibilities once a year by attending and communicating in an Anglican service. Catholics, of course, could do no such thing; they remained subject to extensive penal legislation.

So what does all this mean? Why did contemporaries come to refer to the Revolution of 1688–9 as "Glorious"? Why did subsequent historians see it as one of the most significant events in all of British history? The first question is easily answered. The Revolution was glorious, first, because few Englishmen got hurt: apart from James II's nosebleed, it truly was a Bloodless Revolution (as we shall see, it was quite another story in Ireland, Scotland, or the colonies). Moreover, while all seemed to be in confusion at the time, in retrospect the relatively non-violent and almost orderly course of the Revolution caused it to seem inevitable, even God-ordained. After all, it happened in the magical year of 1688, an exact century after the defeat of the Spanish Armada. As in 1588, a Protestant wind had apparently saved England at the eleventh hour. Furthermore, William's landing took place on November 5, another red letter anniversary of Protestant deliverance, this time from the Gunpowder Plot of 1605. There was, too, the rapidity with which James's Catholic regime collapsed and the fact that it did so without the sort of long-drawn-out social revolution that had, in upper-class eyes, blighted the British Civil Wars at mid-century. This time, the top link of the Great Chain had been broken, yet the subordinate links had held. This time, the ruling class had remained in charge; the lower orders had done what they were told. No Levellers, Ranters, or Fifth Monarchists came out of the woodwork to push their radical utopias. All these things rendered the events of 1688–9 a "Glorious Revolution" in the eyes of its makers.

And yet, the very qualities which made the Revolution of 1688–9 so glorious to its contemporaries might seem to reduce its significance or appeal to later generations, particularly our own. After all, this Revolution was raised in defense of religious intolerance born of anti-Catholic prejudice. It strengthened the contemporary hierarchical system of ranks and orders and it tightened the stranglehold of the landed aristocracy on political and social power. Finally, it did nothing, apparently, for the great mass of the English people. Recent historians of the Revolution have emphasized that the English elite in 1688–9 were "reluctant revolutionaries," hoping, at most, for a counter-revolution, which would halt the transfer of their oligarchical control to Catholics and obscure Dissenters. But the authors of this book would counter that revolutions rarely begin with a complete, forward-looking vision of the future. For example, the English elite of the early 1640s were also "reluctant revolutionaries," but the process they began ended by abolishing the monarchy. We would go farther to argue that 1688–9 represented the final break of early modern England with its medieval past and the irrevocable embrace of its modern future. It did so by resolving most of the questions that the Tudors had left to plague the Stuarts.

First, the Revolution of 1688–9 provided a rational and forward-looking answer to the question of sovereignty. Though contemporaries were reluctant to admit it, and William and his successors would surely have denied it, from henceforward the ultimate sovereign power in England was vested in Parliament. After all, the 1689 Convention had called itself into existence, debated the succession, taken the Crown from James II, ignored his son Prince James, and offered it to William and Mary. Despite Anne's claim to the throne after Mary, Parliament mapped out a succession that would jump to her only if William failed to have children, either with Mary or some future wife. Admittedly, most contemporaries were not comfortable tinkering with the succession. They preferred to act as if Parliament's actions in 1689 were a one-time emergency measure, regrettable and never to be repeated. But, as we shall see, within the next decade Mary would die, William would remain a widower, and Princess Anne would prove unable to bear healthy children of her own. That would force Parliament to consider the succession again. By the Act of Settlement of 1701 it decreed that, after William and Anne, in the event that neither produced an heir, the Crown would go to the Stuarts' nearest Protestant relative. This proved to be a member of the Brunswick family, the electors of Hanover, in Germany. In so decreeing, Parliament skipped over numerous Catholic candidates with better claims, including Prince James. In fact, this legislation barred Catholics from ever sitting on the throne of England. That is, Parliament ignored the laws of hereditary succession, and what had previously been thought of as the will of God, to redraw the succession according to its own liking. As early as 1690 one radical made this implication of the Revolution explicit when, asked to drink the healths of King William and Queen Mary, he hoisted one "to our Sovereign Lord the People for we can make a king and queen when we please."[16]

It should be understood that in 1689 the king still retained both the title of "sovereign" and most of the executive powers restored to him in 1660: for example, those to choose ministers, set policy, and make war and peace. But from 1689 it would remain an unspoken but ever more obvious truth that English monarchs would have to do so in such a way as to please Parliament. This was not only because of the implied threat of deposition, but because, if they were to have any hope of succeeding in those policies, they would need the support of a parliamentary majority to vote the necessary funds. For reasons that will become clearer when we explore the issues of war, foreign policy, and finance, the days when the monarch could dissolve Parliament to avoid unpleasant confrontation or inconvenient legislation, let alone rule entirely without it, were over. Rather, Parliament had to remain in being to keep the government running; and ministers had to be chosen with whom it could work. Thus, 1688–9 marks the shift from a monarch's Parliaments to *Parliament* as a separate, permanent, and, ultimately, dominant institution. The end result would be the modern British monarchy, limited and constitutional.

The Revolution solved another longstanding problem in an enlightened way by embracing the notion of a limited religious toleration. That is, for the first time since the Civil Wars, and now permanently, Parliament enshrined in law the notion that Protestants of different hues could worship in their differing ways and still be good subjects, living together in peace. Admittedly, this was a very limited toleration. Catholics were excluded from it entirely; their toleration lay well over a century in the future. Nor were Dissenters *fully* tolerated, since they were still required to register their meeting houses with the government and keep the doors open during services. Nevertheless, there was something revolutionary and modern in the rejection of the notion that all had to be of one faith to be good English men and women. It would take until the nineteenth century, but religious tensions would gradually ease and thereafter all these groups would be brought fully into English public life. Here, too, the Glorious Revolution was a step toward a modern society, tolerant, diverse, and multi-confessional.

The Revolution also provided new, if provisional, answers to the questions of war and foreign policy as well as money – questions which would be increasingly linked. It should be recalled that William had not invaded to solve the questions of sovereignty or religion. What he wanted was to enlist the wealth of England, Scotland, and Ireland into his crusade against the exorbitant power of Louis XIV. Louis, for his part, could not allow this to happen: first, he wanted to keep the United Provinces isolated and Britain neutral; second, as an absolutist Catholic monarch he could not sit idly by while his cousin James II was overthrown. As a result, a war between France on the one side and Britain and the United Provinces on the other became inevitable in 1688. In fact, that war would be the first of seven colossal conflicts pitting Britain and her allies against France and her allies between 1688 and 1815. These wars would test British resolve, the British economy, and the British political, social, and administrative systems to their utmost. Remember that, up to this point in history, the three British kingdoms had played a small and often inept role in European affairs. France was a much larger and wealthier nation, its population three times that of England and Scotland. Moreover, because both sides had colonial empires, these would be world wars. Obviously, they would answer the longstanding question of Britain's role in Europe and the world.

Just as obviously, they would be very expensive. Therefore, even without the constitutional changes noted above, William III and his successors would have to call Parliament regularly in order to fight them. As a result, Parliament has met every year since 1689 without exception. This would further strengthen parliamentary sovereignty as that body wrested concessions from successive monarchs in return for financial support for these wars. In turn, Parliament's cooperation, the resultant increase in levels of taxation, the development of new techniques for raising money, and the growth of the royal administration necessary to supply the logistical demands of these wars would render the British Crown (if not its wearer) both rich and powerful. Britain would field vast armies and far-flung navies, all coordinated by a massive, but increasingly efficient, bureaucracy and paid for by what would turn out to be the most powerful economy in the world. And so, as a result of the international fallout from the Glorious Revolution of 1688–9 and the need to settle the question of their place in the world, the three kingdoms would settle the question of finance as well. Finally, it should be obvious that the Revolution also settled the issue of local control. Despite the growth of royal bureaucracy, that control would remain, for the next hundred years at least, very much in the hands of the landed aristocracy who had chased one king out of the country and selected another. That said, the passage of the Toleration Act, which benefited primarily urban, Dissenting merchants and financiers, and the crucial role these people would play in the war effort, signals an important social change underlying the political revolution of 1688–9. As we shall see, tensions between this monied interest and the old landed interest would characterize the remainder of the period.

There is perhaps, one more general point to be made about the Revolution of 1688–9. It was, in our view, a profoundly modern event. To say that people can depose their kings; to say that they can choose their rulers and their religion(s) is to embrace rationality, modernity, and a belief in the ability of human beings to solve their problems without divine intervention. It is no coincidence that the age which produced scientists such as Boyle, Halley and Newton, or the first economists, such as William Petty and Gregory King (about whom more below), should have leaped to that embrace. It is true that there was much talk of divine providence from the pulpits in 1689, of a "Protestant Wind" that had saved England. Many of the forward-looking intellectuals named above would have embraced such an interpretation enthusiastically. But, in reality, human beings overthrew God's lieutenant; human beings chose a new king and queen; and those beings were now free to choose among a variety of religious beliefs. In other words, the most profound significance of the Glorious Revolution of 1688–9 is that it broke, finally and forever, the Great Chain of Being. Pieces of the Chain would remain intact for years, and some continue to hold to the present day. But the broad notion of a God-ordained hierarchy in Church, State, and society which could never be challenged or changed was shattered. The next century would see English men and women explore and exploit this new situation. Having broken their chains, they would now begin to flex their muscles.

CHAPTER TEN

War and Politics, 1689–1714

When the "immortal seven" invited William of Orange to invade their country in the summer of 1688, they did so, primarily, to preserve the Protestant ascendancy and the rights of Parliament. Many who supported the ensuing revolution probably did not realize that they were also committing British arms and resources to a full-scale war with France.[1] In fact, the Revolution of 1688–9 made that struggle, known as the Nine Years' War (or, in America, King William's War), inevitable. James II still lived and, unpopular as he may have been with most of his subjects, there remained in all three kingdoms a substantial number of hard-core loyalists. These individuals, soon to be called "**Jacobites**," would work for the overthrow of the Revolution Settlement and the restoration of King James. War was inevitable because their efforts would be supported by France. Louis XIV offered that support, in part because James was a friend and fellow monarch, in part to fulfill his lifelong goal of absorbing the Spanish Empire into the French. To do this, he would have to wreck the Anglo-Dutch alliance and break Dutch power. Conversely, war was necessary on William's part to preserve the Revolution Settlement, the Anglo-Dutch alliance, and the territorial integrity of the United Provinces; and to further *his* lifelong goal of stopping Louis from becoming the master of Europe.

William's major problem, therefore, was to convince the British ruling class and, by extension, the British peoples that his war was *their* war; that they were fighting not only to save the Dutch or the Spanish (hardly popular allies after the conflicts of the past century), but to preserve their own constitution and way of life. He had, in other words, to convince them that James II and Louis XIV still threatened both Parliament and Protestantism. This was an especially hard sell, in part because British arms had such a poor record in continental wars. Moreover, this particular war was likely to prove the most expensive ever fought by the British State, stretching the resources and capabilities of the Crown, as well as Parliament's willingness to pay for them, to their very limits. How well was the new regime fitted to make this case?

William III, Mary II, and the English People

The very name "William and Mary" reminds us from the start that the new regime rested on an unusual and precarious constitutional foundation. The new king was not the rightful heir of the previous monarch; indeed, his predecessor, whom many continued to regard as the real king, still lived. Those willing to act on that opinion became Jacobite conspirators. Others may have had little love for King James personally, and would not lift a finger to help him return, but they could not, in conscience, swear allegiance to the new regime. This group, mainly Tory clergymen, became known as "**nonjurors.**" Finally, while most of William's subjects tacitly acknowledged him as king, there is little evidence that they ever loved him or saw him, as they had seen Henry VIII, James I, or even Charles II, as God on earth or the Father of the Nation. Remember that William's subjects had been preached to for centuries about the hereditary succession and the Great Chain of Being. They had been told repeatedly, especially after the Civil Wars of mid-century, that only the hereditary monarch was the true king and that resistance to him, let alone revolution against him, was a grave sin. This did not dispose them to embrace the Revolution Settlement or revere its chief beneficiary. Admittedly, they had also been told that whoever sat on the throne *currently* was entitled to at least passive obedience as the *de facto* king. Still, William III never felt completely at home among his British subjects, for he could never be completely assured of their heartfelt loyalty.

This is where Mary II came in. Mary was, of course, a real Stuart, the daughter and (if one believed the warming pan myth about Prince James's birth) heir apparent of the last king. Therefore, Tories who felt no love for William felt an instinctive loyalty to her. Early in the reign, when Mary frequently served as regent while William was away on campaign, Tory politicians encouraged her to assert herself against her absent husband and take a more active role in government. While she ruled firmly and ably during these regencies, she refused to be disloyal to William. Apart from Church patronage, she professed to have no interest in politics. Another advantage which Mary brought to the dual monarchy was that she was English-born of English parents and a committed Anglican. She therefore had a great deal more in common with her subjects than her husband did. Moreover, she was pious, charitable, a promoter of the arts, gregarious, fun-loving, and pretty. Her piety is often credited with inspiring an Anglican revival and "reformation of manners" among the English people (see Conclusion); certainly, it did much to restore the prestige of the British monarchy from the depths into which it had fallen under her uncle, Charles II. Her charitable works made her popular with ordinary people. Her love of the arts led to the renovations of Kensington Palace and Hampton Court by England's greatest architect, Sir Christopher Wren; their interior decoration by its greatest carver, Grinling Gibbons; and the commissioning of annual birthday odes celebrating the monarchy from its greatest musician, Henry Purcell. Mary's love of good conversation led her to host frequent receptions. These "drawing rooms" brought the ruling elite to court and helped to attract it to the new regime. Since William III was busy with the war and had neither the time nor the personality for such seeming frivolity, Mary fulfilled a crucial function. No wonder that William remarked before one of his absences, "Though I cannot hit on the right way of pleasing the English, I am confident she will."[2] No wonder that, at her sudden death from smallpox in December 1694, both king and country were plunged into a grief comparable to that felt in our own day over the death of Diana, princess of Wales. William mounted an elaborate State funeral and the crowds outside Whitehall Palace, where Mary lay in state, choked the streets for weeks.

The death of Mary II was all the more lamentable because it left William III alone with his British subjects, most of whom had never really warmed to him. To understand their antipathy, one only has to compare his personality to that of his far more popular, but less ambitious, predecessor, Charles II. Both men were exceptionally intelligent. But where Charles expended his brainpower on scientific speculation and witty repartee, William applied his to the practical details of administration and diplomacy. As this implies, where Charles was lazy and indolent, William was driven and hardworking. Where Charles had no long-term plan, William had one goal: to stop France. Oddly, that obsession was born of a formative experience not all that dissimilar from Charles's. As a young man, William had seen French armies devastate his homeland and overwhelm Protestant State after Protestant State in northern Europe. But where Charles's experiences had left him with a cynical aversion to commitment and a resolve never to "go on his travels" again, William's endowed him with a cause and a bold strategic vision. His cause was to preserve the Dutch Republic and defend the Protestant religion. His vision was that only a Grand Alliance of European States could contain France. By this means, William believed, a European balance of power could – and must – be achieved. The British kingdoms, with their growing wealth and mighty navy, were a crucial weight in that balance. He would do anything to ensure that it remained on the Dutch Protestant side of the fulcrum.

His British subjects, lacking his experience and continental perspective, never really saw it that way. Admittedly, the French were as unpopular as the Dutch, especially among English Dissenters or Scots Presbyterians. But in the experience of most Britons, royal military adventures and foreign wars always meant high taxes, high casualties, and disappointing – sometimes disastrous – results. The British never really saw themselves, as William did, as a major European power, let alone a global one. The English, in particular, clung to the island mentality, the notion of "little England," tenuously attached to the barely tolerated Scots and the loathsome Irish, seeking to have as little as possible to do with the strange and barbaric continent of which they were nominally a part. No wonder that William once remarked, "I see that I am not made for this people, nor they for me."[3]

If the British can be accused of never having made a real effort to understand their new king, it must be said that he returned the favor. Again, in contrast to Charles II's affability and wit, William III was cold and taciturn. Charles may have spent his youth in poverty, but he had picked up the fine manners of European courts. William felt more at home in army camps and could not stand court social occasions. Early in his reign he virtually abandoned Whitehall Palace for more remote and private royal residences at Kensington (on the western outskirts of London) and Hampton Court, Surrey. The official reason was the king's poor health (another contrast to Charles II): the damp and sooty climate of the palace by the Thames was bad for his asthma. But there is little doubt that the change suited his temperament as much as it did his constitution. Though William had highly refined artistic tastes, and loved French fashions in painting and gardening, his rough manners were those of a military man. Though he spoke more than adequate English, his closest friends were Dutch soldiers. Above all, he relied on the advice of his trusted Dutch favorites, Hans William Bentinck, whom he created earl of Portland (1649–1709), and, later in the reign, Arnold Joost van Keppel, whom he created earl of Albemarle (1669–1718). These men were given key positions at court in the king's Bedchamber, Portland as groom of the Stole and keeper of the Privy Purse 1689–1700, and Albemarle as master of the Robes and other Bedchamber offices between 1690 and 1702. As with Somerset's or Buckingham's court posts under James I, these offices gave Portland and Albemarle daily access to the king and, therefore, the opportunity to influence him. These positions also gave them the power to facilitate or prevent the access and influence of others. As a result, many Englishmen felt the same resentment toward William's favored Dutch as their ancestors had directed at James I's "hungry Scots."

William's relative isolation from his British subjects may help to explain his failure to grasp the English party system. One might think that he would be drawn to the Whigs, given their firm support for him and antipathy to James in the Convention Parliament of 1689. But William III associated the Whigs with radicalism. After all, if good Whigs like Locke and Sidney could argue that English subjects had every right to rid themselves of a "bad" king, what was to stop them from doing so again? William was far more attracted to Tory ideology. Tories were natural supporters of royal power and, since many had been in office for over a decade, they had the administrative experience necessary to run a war. While his early administrations included both Whigs and Tories, the latter predominated. What William did not understand was that the Tories were so tied to the notion of Divine Right monarchy that, while they all supported the king, the king many supported and felt real affection for was the deposed James II! Their Anglicanism had led them to oppose James's policies in 1688 and to support William's invasion. But that did not mean that they were comfortable with the idea of his ascending the throne or with his sympathy for Dissenters. William wanted to trust the Tories, but he eventually discovered that many were secret – and some not so secret – Jacobites. This would become apparent after the reign's first real crisis, the Irish campaigns of 1688–91.

The Irish Campaigns, 1688–1691

At the Revolution, James II had fled abroad for the second time, to the court of Louis XIV. Louis soon formulated a plan to restore his friend and cousin to the

Irish throne, which could be used as the base from which to invade England. Ireland must have seemed ripe for the taking to James and Louis, for the Irish had been resisting English rule for centuries. As will be recalled, Ireland was the only one of James's three kingdoms in which the majority of the population was Catholic, yet many Catholic Irish farmers had been deprived of their land during the previous hundred years. This had resulted in periodic rebellions, most notably in 1641, which had led, in turn, to harsh reprisals, savage repression, and more confiscations and plantations under the Commonwealth and Protectorate. The Restoration Irish land settlement allowed most Cromwellian soldiers and adventurers to keep the land they had confiscated, if they paid compensation to the dispossessed former landowners, usually Catholics. This compromise left all sides with some grounds for complaint. The old duke of Ormond nevertheless managed to govern Ireland effectively as lord lieutenant for most of the next two decades, maintaining the power of the New English Protestant minority while treating Catholics relatively mildly. But when James II ascended the throne in 1685 he gave control of the Irish army and, later, the deputy lieutenancy to Richard Talbot, earl of Tyrconnell (1630–91), a Roman Catholic. To the alarm of the New English oligarchy, Tyrconnell used this power to fill the army and magistracy with his fellow Papists. By 1688, half of the Irish army was Catholic. Tyrconnell had also confiscated every borough charter in Ireland, and displaced every Protestant sheriff and numerous judges and JPs. As a consequence, Ireland was the only one of James's three kingdoms which stayed loyal to him in 1688.

James II landed at Kinsale, with French support, in the spring of 1689 (see map 7, p. 83). He immediately convened an Irish, Catholic Parliament to revoke the Restoration land settlement and to pass legislation leading to Catholic emancipation. In other words, James was bent on abolishing the Protestant ascendancy in Ireland. But that does not mean that he had come to free Ireland from *English* control: for example, he balked at repealing Poynings's Law, which subordinated the Irish Parliament to its English counterpart. Nor did he seek primarily to alleviate the suffering of the Irish people. What James wanted in 1689 was their support for his restoration in England. They gave it by joining a hastily scraped together Jacobite army, manned largely by poorly trained tenant farmers. Nevertheless, it caught the Protestant landowning class off-guard. Many retreated to the heavily Protestant northern counties of Ulster, holing up in the garrisons of Londonderry and Enniskillen (map 7). In April, at Londonderry, Protestant apprentices closed the gates on James's forces and waited for relief.

That relief would have to come by sea from England, for James II now controlled the whole of southern and western Ireland. By the time a Williamite relief force arrived on July 30, thousands of Protestant Ulstermen and women had died from starvation and disease. Moreover, the situation of the rest of Protestant Ireland remained desperate, despite the arrival in August of an Anglo-Dutch army under the veteran Protestant commander Frederick Herman, duke of Schomberg (1615–90). Schomberg's army wasted away from disease born of inadequate provisions, heavy rains, and typhus emanating from the bogs of Ireland. Worse, in June of 1690, a combined British and Dutch fleet under Arthur Herbert, earl of

Torrington (1647–1716), was defeated by the French at the battle of Beachy Head, off the southern English coast. For the first time in a generation, the English had lost control of the seas. With the main army away in Ireland, England itself seemed ripe for invasion.

Because William III was forced to spend 1689 establishing the new regime, it was not until the summer of 1690 that he could take personal command of his forces in Ireland. He landed with 35,000 troops, mostly untried Englishmen but also some battle-hardened and loyal Dutch regulars. Given the far inferior quality of James's troops, William had little trouble relieving Ulster and pushing the Catholic forces back to the River Boyne, north of Dublin (see map 7, p. 83). There, on July 1, 1690, the two armies fought a decisive battle in which the Jacobites broke and ran. King James, his nose bleeding again from the stress of yet another disaster, fled Ireland for France. While Jacobite sympathizers in all three kingdoms would continue to work toward his restoration, he would, in fact, never again set foot within the British Isles. Amazingly, James's Irish army would regroup and fight on for another year until it was smashed at Aughrim, Galway, on July 12, 1691.

William's victory in Ireland confirmed the Protestant ascendancy and spelled disaster for the Catholic population. The king himself wanted no reprisals and the Treaty of Limerick of 1691 promised religious toleration. But he needed the Protestant aristocracy to fight his war, and they wanted revenge. Between 1695 and 1727, he and his successors allowed the Protestant landowners to pass a series of laws in both the Irish and English Parliaments, known collectively as the Penal Code, which had the effect of reducing the native Catholic population to a state of utter misery. Catholics were barred from voting, officeholding, practicing law, teaching, attending a university, wearing swords (a mark of gentility), and purchasing both land or any horse worth more than £5. They were, moreover, forbidden from inheriting land from Protestants and from bequeathing it to an eldest son. Rather, they were forced to divide their holdings among *all* their sons, which ensured that no Catholic family could preserve large holdings. During the same period, non-resident English landowners and local Protestant landlords consolidated their positions. As a result, Catholics, amounting to four-fifths of the population of Ireland, were reduced by 1727 to ownership of but one-seventh of its land.

None of this is to say that their English cousins considered Irish Protestant landowners and merchants their equals. The English Parliament tightened its hold on its Irish counterpart by the Declaratory Act (1720). Throughout the period, it sought to restrict Irish trade so as to favor England. For example, an act of 1699 forbade the Irish from exporting woolens except through English ports, where they were loaded with exorbitant tariffs. It is no exaggeration to say that, as this book closes, Ireland was ruled from London with every regard to the interests of the English ruling class, some regard to those of the Protestant Irish ruling class, and no regard at all to those of the native Irish population. As a result, the eighteenth century was to prove, in many ways, the most miserable in Irish history. In 1729 Jonathan Swift offered a startling comment on that misery by making the satirical suggestion, in *A Modest Proposal*, that since the English had apparently sought to liquidate the Irish in any case, they might as well eat their children. Even today, after the establishment of an independent Republic of Ireland in the south, the memory of William's relief of Ulster and victory at the Boyne continues to rankle with Irish Catholics, while it is celebrated, tauntingly, by Ulster Protestants.

The War and the Parties, 1688–1697

For England and Scotland, William's Irish victory provided a moment of relief. The danger of immediate invasion passed and the king returned to his capital in triumph. Still, the domestic political situation looked grim. Remember that after Beachy Head the French navy controlled the Channel and Louis threatened invasion. Worse, William remained unsure about his subjects' loyalty to the new regime, especially his Tory subjects. After all, the very act which had led to the establishment of that regime – the Glorious Revolution – went against everything that Toryism stood for on the relationship between sovereigns and subjects. The Tories in William's government found themselves living a contradiction. They were the party of Divine Right monarchy, yet they served a usurper. They were the party of high Anglicanism, yet the new king was a Calvinist who had brought with him a toleration for Dissenters. They were the party of peaceful isolation and friendship with France, yet they were forced to fight a European war against Louis XIV. They were the party of much of the landed gentry, yet the war forced them into a heavy tax on land.

Is it any wonder that the Tories seemed to be half-hearted about the war and the king for whom it was being fought? Tories in the administration seemed to be uncooperative, corrupt, or suspiciously incompetent when it came to the war. Tories in Parliament tended to favor a "blue-water" strategy in which Britain would use her navy to harass the French Empire overseas while remaining aloof from the European conflict. Tory landowners saw this as a cheap alternative to William's advocacy of expensive land armies and continental entanglements; William saw it as cowardly and defeatist. Worse, by 1692 it became clear that a number of prominent Tory peers, including William's ablest military commander, John Churchill, now earl of Marlborough, had been writing to King James, apologizing for their part in the Revolution of 1688 and, in some cases, offering assistance for a restoration. Most of these letters were probably just insurance policies against the possibility that James might return. Their authors may not have been committed Jacobites willing to risk outright rebellion so much as realists, careful to ensure the favor of whichever side won. Still, King William cannot be blamed for assuming the worst. The most prominent letter writers, including Marlborough, were sent to the Tower and Tories began to be purged from the central government.

In their place, William III began to name Whigs. If the Revolution of 1688–9 and the Nine Years' War tore the Tory party apart with contradiction, they solved many such contradictions for the Whigs. After all, the Whigs had always supported the ideas of parliamentary sovereignty and revolution against a bad king. Whigs, many of whom were Dissenters, embraced the toleration. Whigs had no love for Catholic France and feared Louis's ambitions; they therefore supported with enthusiasm Britain's part in the Grand Alliance and Nine Years' War. Since the Whig party included large numbers of merchants and financiers as well as landowners, they had less cause to grumble over high taxes on land. Indeed, many Whig landowners began to move over to the Tories.

In short, the 1690s and the war which dominated them saw a seismic shift in the roles and composition of the two political parties in England. The Tories' ideological problems with King William, his war, and co-religionists gradually turned them from being a court or government party into an opposition or "country" party of political outsiders. The same factors turned the Whigs, heretofore the radical opposition party, made up of political and religious outcasts, into the party of government – but with one crucial difference. The Tories (and before them their Cavalier and "court" ancestors) had been the party of the Crown because they had believed passionately, even irrationally, in the Great Chain of Being generally, and in the Stuarts as God's lieutenants on earth in particular. During the Civil Wars, many Tory families had suffered, losing loved ones and lands, for those beliefs. They had revered Charles II and even James II, in spite of their faults, not only because they rewarded them with positions at court, but because they were the rightful heirs, the ceremonial fathers of the country. For Tories, there was something magical and heart-stirring in the name of "king," a name which only God, not Parliament, could bestow.

The Whigs, on the other hand, felt no such affection for William III because they had never attached any magic to the title which Parliament had, in fact, bestowed upon him. If Whigs believed passionately in anything, it was in the rights of Parliament and the need to defend Protestantism. Many Whig families had made comparable sacrifices for their beliefs during the Civil Wars and, more recently, during the Tory revenge of 1681–5, but those beliefs were not necessarily Royalist. Their support for the new king was practical, a sort of business proposition. He was a chairman of the board or chief executive officer, not a god or a father. Though the Whigs would work hard on behalf of William's regime, though many would develop some affection for him, they were not above threatening to quit or oppose his government in order to gain political advantage. In particular, Whig majorities, seeking to bolster Parliament's power, sometimes threatened to withhold funds unless the king made concessions, such as a new Triennial Act to force him to call Parliament at least once every three years. Since William III was far more interested in defeating Louis XIV and saving the United Provinces than he was in defending the prerogatives of the Crown, he usually gave in. These concessions did more to overtly reduce royal power than had the Revolution itself. Thus, the political revolution of 1688–9 and the war that followed recast the two parties and, in the long run, further subordinated the British Crown to Parliament.

The Rise of the Whig Junto, 1693–1697

In the short run, however, William III's turn toward the Whigs gave him exactly what he wanted: a government and a Parliament which would support the war. The Whig leaders proved to be exceedingly competent as war ministers. Those leaders comprised five men who, because they formed an effective and cohesive political and administrative team, came to be known as "the **Junto**."[4] The most flamboyant member of the Junto was Thomas Wharton (1648–1715), from 1696 Lord Wharton. He held a lucrative position at court as comptroller of the Household, and he was a brilliant orator, capable of swaying parliamentary opinion. He was also a great landowner. Given the realities of English electoral politics, this meant that he could dictate the representatives of a number of parliamentary constituencies and control their votes in the House of Commons. (He was also a notorious libertine and one of the great swordsmen-duelists of his age.) The Junto's constitutional and legal expert was Sir John Somers (1651–1716), from 1693 lord keeper of the Great Seal, from 1697 Lord Somers and lord chancellor of England. Somers was an attorney who proved to be an excellent draftsman of legislation, including the Bill of Rights of 1689. (He, too, was a bit of a rake and also a great literary patron.) The youngest member of the Junto, Charles Spencer (1674–1722, later to succeed his father as earl of Sunderland), proved to be an important leader in the House of Commons after Wharton and Somers were elevated to the Lords. Spencer also had important connections to the Churchills (he married Anne Churchill [1683–1716], one of Marlborough's daughters) and he would, in the next reign, develop an expertise in foreign policy. Naval affairs were handled by Admiral Edward Russell, from 1694 first lord of the Admiralty and from 1697 earl of Orford. In 1692, Russell won a decisive victory against the French navy at La Hogue, thus restoring Britain's command of the sea and ending the invasion threat. Subsequently, he established a British naval presence in the Mediterranean and launched a reform of the Royal Navy, building new ships and updating dockyards. The former disrupted French trade and led to British dominance in the region for 250 years; the latter provided the infrastructure for overall British naval supremacy for decades.

Russell's victory at La Hogue enabled William to take the war to the French on the continent. This required large armies supported by an extensive logistical network to train, pay, feed, clothe, equip, and transport them. To this must be added the charge of the expanding Royal Navy. The result was the most expensive war in English history to date. The Nine Years' War drove total government expenditure to about £5.5 million a year, three times its average annual peacetime revenue. Failure to raise this sum would doom the British war effort and, perhaps, the Revolution Settlement. In order to pay for each summer's campaign, William had to turn to Parliament. In 1693 that body voted a Land Tax of four shillings in the pound; that is, for every pound's worth of land an owner possessed, he had to pay four shillings (or one-fifth of a pound). Theoretically, this meant that all landowners owed one-fifth of their annual income from land to the government. But William's government never received that level of funding because taxes were assessed and collected by local JPs and other landowners, who were reluctant to assess their neighbors up to the real value of their estates or to collect enthusiastically the taxes so assessed (which came on top of the poor rate, tithes for the Church, etc.). In any case, this tax was never expected to yield more than £2 million a year. As a result, the new regime was falling behind in the arms race with Louis – who, remember, did not have to call a parliament to tax his people.

This brings us to the financial genius of the Junto, Charles Montagu (1661–1715, from 1700 Lord Halifax). Named a lord of the Treasury in 1692 and chancellor of the Exchequer in 1694, Montagu realized that in order to win the war, William's government would need lots of ready cash – quicker and more abundant cash than could be raised by the Land Tax. He saw an alternative source of income in the wealth flowing into the country from the commercial revolution. As will be recalled, the Customs and Excise were already the most profitable taxes in the Crown's portfolio. The Parliaments of the 1690s raised Customs rates as high as 25 percent and extended the Excise to all sorts of new products, including leather, coal, malt (important for brewing), salt, spices, tea, coffee, and wine. But such taxes took as long to collect as the Land Tax; nor did Montagu wish to expand them any further, as that would have the effect of strangling the goose that was laying the golden egg of English commerce. Rather, he wanted to persuade its keepers – large and middling merchants and investors in trading ventures – to loan ready money to the Crown voluntarily. This was a tough proposition because the Crown was a poor risk: recall that, in 1672, Charles II had actually declared a kind of bankruptcy.

Montagu and the Whigs had another idea. In 1693 Parliament authorized the government to solicit a loan of £1 million on the security of a fund fed by the Land, Excise, and other taxes. This marks the establishment of the funded national debt. For the first time, interest on the debt was to be paid out of a specific "pot." This made such loans much more attractive as their repayment seemed much more secure. Montagu went farther by proposing that in future the government make no promise to pay back the *principal* of such loans by any particular date; instead, they would remain outstanding for the course of the war, if not longer. But the government did promise to pay lenders 14 percent *interest* on their loan, out of the fund described above, for life. What this meant was that, if William won the war and the lender lived, he and his family could make their investment many times over. This was so attractive that, as time went on, the government found that it could lower the interest paid and still find takers. Later, the Crown also offered lenders self-liquidating annuities for a number of lives or for 99 years and sold tickets to public lotteries. They also charged corporate bodies like the East India Company and, in the next reign, the South Sea Company vast sums in return for the privilege of being allowed to exist. The greatest example of this fund-raising strategy, and Montagu's crowning inspiration, was the charter for the Bank of England, established in 1694. In return for an immediate loan of £1.2 million, the Bank was allowed to sell stock in itself, receive deposits, make loans, and even print notes against the security of its loan to the government. In future years, the Bank of England would be the Crown's largest single lender, its principal banker, and the manager of the funded national debt which Montagu had initiated under William III.

The fiscal expedients described above were so far reaching that they have been dubbed "the financial revolution" by historians. Their impact was profound. First, in the short term they enabled His Majesty's Government to raise fabulous sums of money very quickly. This, in turn, enabled William to raise and supply his armies in Europe and to maintain his navies across the Atlantic. Admittedly, the one weakness in the Junto system was that there was no great military leader. With Marlborough tainted by Jacobitism, William III acted as his own general and he was generally not thought to have been a very good one. The early years of the war saw a series of catastrophes as the Grand Alliance (consisting of the British, the Dutch Republic, the Holy Roman Emperor [Austria], Spain, Savoy, Brandenburg-Prussia, Hanover, and Bavaria) lost land battle after land battle, fortress after fortress to the armies of Louis XIV. This led to increasing Tory demands for withdrawal from the continent in favor of their preferred "blue-water" strategy, as well as "country" demands for investigations into government misconduct. Nevertheless, thanks to Britain's vast financial and material resources, William's unrelenting determination, and the Junto's sheer competence, the Grand Alliance held and the French began to be worn down. By 1695 the Allies took the key French fort at Namur (see map 12, p. 279). More importantly, Louis, who only had the poor French peasantry to rely on, was running out of money. In 1697, he asked for peace. According to the **Treaty of Ryswick**, the French king agreed to recognize William III as king of England, Scotland, and Ireland and, thus, withdraw his support for King James. He also agreed to restore nearly all the territories he had seized since 1678 and to negotiate a Partition Treaty with William to ensure that when Carlos II of Spain died, no one European power would receive the whole of the Spanish Empire. In short, as Daniel Defoe (ca. 1661–1731) would later recognize, it is "not the longest sword, but the longest purse that conquers."[5] Thanks to the financial revolution, Louis XIV had been stopped; his great dream of a Franco-Spanish Empire was put on hold; and the Revolution Settlement in Church and State, Protestantism in Britain and Europe, and parliamentary sovereignty in England were safe. For the moment, at least.

In the long term, the wealth produced by the financial revolution – what one historian has termed the "sinews of power" – would ensure Britain's growing military domination of Europe in the eighteenth century, and the world in the century after that (see below). A second long-term effect of the financial revolution was that it initiated the funded national debt of Great Britain. The British government was now committed to pay or service that debt for the foreseeable future. Clearly, it would have to collect more taxes and contract more debt, every year, in order to continue to pay the interest on the debt already contracted. In other words, the debt would be self-perpetuating: though it would be greatly paid down during periods of peace, it would never completely go away. In order to secure Parliament's continued approval for contracting and servicing the debt, William III would have to summon it annually, as well as agree to a Commission to examine his government accounts in 1691; to the Triennial Act in 1694; to the reduction of his Dutch guards in 1698; and to provisions reducing the royal prerogative in the Act of Settlement of 1701. The financial revolution thus played a key role in shaping the English constitution – and increasing the power and initiative of Parliament.

And yet, while the war and the financial revolution reduced the *personal* power of the sovereign, it vastly increased that of the Crown, that is, His Majesty's Government. That government now had at its disposal enormous armies and navies and the expanding bureaucracy necessary to oversee and supply them. For example, William's army numbered 76,000 men, almost twice that of James II. It has been estimated that the central administration comprised some 4,000 officials in 1688. By the 1720s it would come to over 12,000, with over 3,000 officers serving the Excise alone. Old departments grew while new ones would be established, such as the Office of Trade and Plantations (to administer Britain's new colonial acquisitions) and new revenue-collecting departments (a Glass Office, Salt Office, Stamp Office, and Leather Office). The Treasury increasingly controlled this vast bureaucracy, and sought to run the government more efficiently and thriftily. In order to weed out old, corrupt practices, it initiated adequate salaries and pension schemes, drew up handbooks of conduct, and calculated statistics to make realistic appraisals of the tasks at hand. As this implies, the late seventeenth and early eighteenth centuries saw a growing sense of professionalism among government workers. Men like William Blathwayt at the War Office (ca. 1649–1717), Samuel Pepys (1633–1703) at the Navy Office, and William Lowndes (1652–1724) at the Treasury were career bureaucrats who remained in office despite shifts of faction and party.[6]

The socioeconomic significance of the financial revolution was that it made investors, usually Whig financiers and government contractors who supplied the war, very wealthy, very fast. In fact, it seemed to create a new class of men, whom contemporaries called "monied men," who made their wealth not from the land or even from the sale of goods but from the exploitation of credit. That is, they seemed to make money out of money (their loans), or paper (government bonds, lottery tickets, and bills of exchange), or out of thin air (credit itself). These new men now played so important a role in government finance that they often served on government commissions, their advice sought by government officials. They thus acquired influence, not only on fiscal policy but on foreign and domestic policy as well. This would prove controversial.

Indeed, this whole business – the vast government bureaucracy necessary to fight the war, the burgeoning national debt which paid for it, the novel and complex system of finance which serviced the debt, the heavy taxes on land which secured the debt, and the growing wealth of non-landed men, financiers, contractors, government officials, and soldiers who profited from it all – jolted contemporaries, Tory landowners in particular. Years later, during the next war against the French, Jonathan Swift would write:

Let any man observe the equipages in this town; he shall find the greater number of those who make a figure to be a species of men quite different from any that were ever known before the Revolution, consisting either of generals or colonels, or of such whose whole fortunes lie in funds and stocks: so that power, which according to the old maxim was used to follow land, is now gone over to money, and the country gentleman is in the condition of a young heir, out of whose estate a scrivener [lawyer] receives half the rents for interest, and has a mortgage on the whole.

Swift's point is that the wars, and the financial revolution and government bureaucracy invented to fight them, threatened the traditional hierarchy based on birth and land. Landowners grew poor because they were paying the Land Tax; while military men (who made huge profits from subcontracts for uniforms, weaponry, and food), government officials (whose jobs depended on the war), and "monied men" (who invested in government loans, funds, and lotteries) became wealthy. Anyone could rise. Nor did it bode well that the average English man or woman found the new financial instruments complicated if not impenetrable: "[t]hrough the contrivance and cunning of stock-jobbers [brokers], there has been brought in such a complication of knavery and cozenage, such a mystery of iniquity, and such an unintelligible jargon of terms to involve it in, as were never known in any other age or country of the world."[7] Anyone who, in modern times, has struggled to understand the workings of junk bonds, derivatives, or the Dow Jones index can probably sympathize. Even worse, in Swift's eyes, was the deliberate contracting of massive debt, to be paid off who knew when? All of this helps to explain the country's apparently curious reaction to the Treaty of Ryswick, a Tory resurgence.

The Tory Resurgence, 1697–1701

The Treaty of Ryswick was a remarkable achievement. Yet Louis XIV's concessions seemed to many Britons to be very small return for all the blood and treasure expended in the enterprise. The British taxpayer felt hard put upon and resented the king's apparent desire to maintain his standing army despite the admittedly fragile peace. Country politicians, mainly Tories, were able to exploit these sentiments. Their leader was an ambitious young MP named Robert Harley (1661–1724), whose father had been a Parliamentarian, an anti-Danby country MP, and an old Exclusion Whig before migrating along with Robert himself and numerous other landowning Whigs to the Tory party in the 1690s. Under Harley's guidance, the Tories began to evolve into a true country party: suspicious of big government, modern finance, foreign entanglements (particularly with the Dutch), standing armies, and war. They claimed, with some justification, to represent the national mood. This, along with Junto overconfidence and disunity, explains why Tories and anti-administration Whigs gained seats in the parliamentary elections of 1698. William lost confidence in his Junto ministers and began to name Tories in their place. Parliament was now so necessary to pay government expenses that the king had no choice but to appoint ministers with whom its majority could work. Here is another indication that the wartime expansion in the size and power of royal government was actually another milestone on the road to parliamentary sovereignty. Over the next three years Parliament would vote to cut the Land Tax in half; reduce the army to 7,000 men; send home the king's Dutch guards; declare illegal and confiscate the gifts of Irish lands that he had bestowed on favorites; and impeach the leading former Whig ministers for their conduct of the war.

Parliament's most notable initiative, however, was the **Act of Settlement of 1701**. This piece of legislation became necessary when Anne's last surviving child – and therefore the last Protestant grandchild of James II – William, duke of Gloucester (1689–1700), died the previous year. Both Tories and Whigs were desperately aware of the fact that, apart from Anne, the only remaining Stuart claimant to the throne was young Prince James, the Catholic son of James II. Even Jacobite Tories, who would otherwise have welcomed the younger James, were afraid of his Catholicism and the hostile popular reaction should he be designated heir apparent. And so, facing political realities, the Tory-leaning Parliament passed legislation which stated that, failing the birth of further heirs from the widowed William and the aging Anne, the Crown would pass at the survivor's death to their nearest Protestant relatives, the descendants of James I's youngest daughter Elizabeth. These were Sophia, electress of the German State of Hanover (1630–1714), and, if she should predecease Anne, her son, Georg Ludwig (1660–1727). In taking this step, Parliament again abandoned the notion of a sacrosanct hereditary succession, for there were dozens of Catholic relatives with better claims than the Hanoverians. The Tories went along with this, but not without adding some provisos, intended as a slap to William, limiting the power of a foreign-born king – hence the statute's official title: "An act for the further limitation of the crown and better securing the rights and liberties of the subject" (12–13 William III, c. 2). For example, the act specified that the king could not make the English fight a war to defend his European holdings or leave the British Isles without parliamentary permission. Both had occurred under William. Henceforward, no foreigner – not even a naturalized one – could hold government office or receive Crown lands. This provision sought to eliminate the power and influence of any future foreign favorite, like Portland or Albemarle. The Act of Settlement also made it illegal for salaried government officials to serve in Parliament after Anne's death. The idea was to eliminate the power of the Crown and the sitting ministry to influence parliamentary votes by bribing MPs with offices, as once Danby and now the Junto were accused of doing. What is perhaps most remarkable about this piece of legislation is that it came from the party that had once been the home of Danby and his court partisans!

The Spanish and English Successions, 1700–1702

In fact, the Tory triumph was short-lived, for so was the peace signed at Ryswick. That peace was shattered by a series of royal deaths which followed that of the duke of Gloucester in 1700. First, at the end of October 1700, Carlos II, the sickly and mentally defective Habsburg ruler of Spain, finally died, heirless. It will be recalled that Louis XIV and William III had worked out a Partition Treaty to divide the Spanish Empire among several competitors, thus preventing its annexation to France. Unfortunately, no one had consulted Carlos. That fall, he may have been near death and barely competent, but he was in no doubt that he alone had the right to dispose of his empire, and he had no wish to see it divided. His will therefore decreed that the whole entity was to be offered, first, to a grandson of Louis XIV, Philippe, duke of Anjou (1683–1746), who had to agree to renounce the throne of France. Should Anjou refuse, then the Spanish Crown was to go to the second son of the Holy Roman Emperor, Charles, archduke of Austria (1685–1740), who was to make the same promise about the Empire.

Imagine Louis's dilemma. Here, on a silver platter, was the prize for which he had so long been striving – to unite French military power with Spanish imperial wealth. The stipulation that his grandson should never be king of France was, in Louis's eyes, a mere formality; something could undoubtedly be worked out. But if Louis accepted, he would break his Partition Treaty with William and, possibly, provoke a second war with the one enemy he had never beaten, the British. Imagine the scene at Versailles on November 6 when, after deliberating with his ministers and marshals, Louis emerged from the Council Chamber with Anjou at his side, proclaiming "Gentlemen, you see here the King of Spain.... Such was the will of Heaven; I have fulfilled it with joy." Louis had decided to gamble. At the proclamation of "His Most Catholic Majesty, Felipe V, King of Spain and its Empire," the Spanish ambassador to Versailles is said to have fallen to his knees, remarking about the mountain border that separated France and Spain: "The Pyrenees have been leveled!"[8]

Louis's gamble seemed to pay off at first. While William wanted to renew the war, his Tory Parliament did not. After all, most of their constituents viewed this development as having no obvious significance for the British Isles, especially if Anjou abided by the terms of the will and renounced the French throne. But Anjou did not renounce his ancestors' throne. Instead, early in 1701, Louis persuaded the French courts to rule that Carlos's will could not affect the French succession. Worse, he also marched into some key fortress towns in the Spanish Netherlands, on the Dutch border. Finally, in a deliberately – and stupidly – provocative move, he announced an embargo against English trade with *both* France and Spain. Louis XIV was acting as if he already ruled both countries and those actions were already detrimental to British trade. This offended even the Tories, who understood well the significance of trade. In June, the Tory Parliament agreed to vote large sums for war and support any alliances that William might make to secure the "liberties of Europe."

War became inevitable in the wake of the next royal death. In September 1701 poor old James II, now living with a small court at the château of St. Germain near Paris, died. On his deathbed, he asked Louis, as a last favor, to recognize his son, Prince James, as the rightful king of England, Scotland, and Ireland. Once again, the French monarch faced a dilemma. On the one hand, recognition of Prince James would surely mean war with Britain, as it would repudiate the recognition of William made at Ryswick. On the other hand, how could he refuse the dying request of his old friend? Once again, Louis consulted with his ministers and marshals. Once again, he announced his decision to the court, this time assembled in James's sickroom at St. Germain: "I come to tell Your Majesty that...I will be to your son what I have been to you, and will acknowledge him as King of England, Scotland, and Ireland."[9] Once again, Louis took the gamble, proclaiming the adolescent prince as James III (of England and Ireland) and VIII (of Scotland). Once again, the assembled courtiers, this time Jacobite exiles, fell to their knees. But no one made any sanguine predictions about draining the English Channel.

As Louis feared, this decision did, indeed, mean war with the British – but not with William. Almost immediately, William ordered British diplomatic representatives to reassemble the Grand Alliance and Crown ministers to begin to plan for war. Then, after a fall and winter of feverish activity, he sought some rest and relaxation. In February 1702, while hunting in Richmond Park, the king's horse stumbled over a molehill and fell, throwing him. For years afterwards, Jacobites would secretly toast "the little gentleman in black velvet" – the mole that built the molehill that tripped the horse that threw the royal rider. William suffered a cracked collar-bone, which soon became infected. William III died on March 8, 1702. But the Grand Alliance he fashioned would live on.

Anne and the Rage of Party

The woman who succeeded William III was acclaimed with rapturous cheering, bells, and bonfires at her accession – but she has not always received a good press since. Queen Anne (1702–14), the youngest surviving Protestant daughter of James II and the last Stuart to sit on the British thrones, was 37 years old at her accession. But a series of 17 pregnancies, none of which had resulted in a surviving child, as well as poor eating habits and the vagaries of contemporary medical care had left her prematurely aged (see plate 23). She had always been a bit plain and she was, by 1702, seriously overweight, nearly lame from gout, and in poor health generally. She was also quiet, shy, and of average intelligence. In short, Queen Anne had none of the star quality of Elizabeth I or even Mary II. But, in its place, Anne had many positive attributes missing from her Stuart predecessors, including a strong fund of common sense, a dedication to the job of being queen, a respect for the post-Revolutionary English constitution, an unshakeable attachment to the Church of England, and an instinctive love for and sense of responsibility to her people, which they reciprocated. Happily married to Prince George, she could not be a "Virgin Queen" to them; instead she embraced the image of their "nursing Mother." During her reign, the promise of the commercial and financial revolutions, the Grand Alliance, and William's

Plate 23 Queen Anne, *by Edmund Lilly. By kind permission of His Grace, the Duke of Marlborough.*

military buildup would pay off in a series of crushing victories over the French, and ultimate triumph in the War of the Spanish Succession. At her death, Britain would be the wealthiest and most powerful State in Europe.

For years, most historians believed that these victories were won in spite of Anne's dull personality, or because she was dominated by more intelligent friends and favorites. It is true that during her long apprenticeship as a young princess she had relied heavily, almost slavishly, on her friend and confidante Sarah Churchill, countess (later duchess) of Marlborough (1660–1744). As queen, Anne made Sarah her groom of the Stole, keeper of the Privy Purse, and mistress of the Robes, three of the most lucrative and powerful court posts. These offices brought the countess into close daily contact with the queen, while giving her the power to regulate such contact with other courtiers and politicians. Given Anne's shyness and supposed lack of intelligence, contemporaries assumed that the countess advised her, among other things, to employ Sarah's husband, the earl (later duke) of Marlborough, as captain-general during the war, and the Churchills' friend Sidney, Lord (later earl of) Godolphin (1645–1712), as lord treasurer of England. Many years after Anne's death, Sarah wrote her *Account of the Conduct of the Dowager Duchess of Marlborough* (1742) in which she claimed to be the real power behind Anne's throne and in which she accused the queen of being weak and easily manipulated. But it is now recognized that Anne chose her advisers as much for their ability as her friendship with them: Marlborough proved to be the reigning military and diplomatic genius of his day and Godolphin one of its greatest administrative and financial minds. To this team, Anne added Robert Harley, its most able politician, to supervise her business in the House of Commons. In other words, Queen Anne may not have been a skillful administrator herself, but she knew how to delegate power wisely. That skill, combined with the other attributes already mentioned, would render her not only the most popular and successful of the Stuarts but, arguably, the most successful ruler portrayed in this book.

Queen Anne needed every one of these qualities because, empowered by the post-Revolutionary constitution, each political party was determined to force her to employ its members, and only its members, in office. As this implies, by 1702 the Whig and Tory parties had matured into effective and cohesive organizations. Virtually every parliamentary politician aligned sooner or later with one or the other and there is plenty of evidence from division lists (of how members of Parliament voted on particular issues) that crossing party lines to vote with the other side rarely occurred. Indeed, the "rage of party" permeated polite society even beyond the walls of the two houses. There were Whig newspapers and periodicals (*The Flying Post* and *The Observator*) and Tory newspapers and periodicals (*The Post Boy* and *The Examiner*); Whig clubs and coffee-houses (the Kit-Cat and White's) and Tory clubs and coffee-houses (The Society of Brothers and Ozinda's); Whig toasts ("to the Immortal Memory of King William") and Tory, even Jacobite, toasts ("To the King across the water," said over one's water glass, to indicate King James); even different sides of the face upon which to wear paper patches (artificial beauty marks) for ladies of Whig or

Tory sympathies! In the countryside Whig and Tory aristocrats competed against each other for seats on the lieutenancy and magistracy, while in the boroughs Whig and Tory oligarchs fought for control of the corporation, of local religious life, and of poor relief. In short, party conflict colored almost every aspect of public, professional, and even recreational life in post-Revolutionary England.

The winners in that conflict would depend on which party could capture royal government. This depended, in turn, on which party could forge a parliamentary majority. Such a majority by one party or the other would force the queen to employ its members in the "big-ticket" offices (lord treasurer, lord chancellor, the two secretaries of State, chancellor of the Exchequer, etc.) or face a Parliament unwilling to support royal policy or, in particular, vote money to fight the war. That is why after 1688, and especially during time of war, the sovereign had to choose ministers who could put together majorities in Parliament. Increasingly, that implied choosing ministers from only one party. Anne, like William before her, was averse to this, thinking it a concession of her freedom of maneuver. As we shall see, she fought to maintain "mixed ministries" containing the best minds of both parties who would come together to push her agenda. The party leaders had a different idea. Their goal was to force the queen to name their party's members to every post in court and government. Then it could force her to pursue its policies.

All of this was dependent, in turn, on which party could garner the most seats in a general (parliamentary) election. After the Revolution, such elections became more common. There were 11 major party contests between 1689 and 1715, more general elections than in any other similar time period before or since. And there were more contested seats than in any period of British history before the twentieth century. This served to increase party tensions, focus party positions, and introduce more and more people to political participation – and into conflict. Though the franchise was still restricted to male property holders worth 40 shillings in the countryside and a hodge-podge of different groups (sometimes the corporation, sometimes particular residents, sometimes the whole town) in cities, this still left more people with a vote in England than anywhere else in Europe. Moreover, thanks to inflation and each party's attempts to increase its voter base through the courts, the number of potential electors was on the rise: from around 200,000 in 1689 to 330,000 or 5.8 percent of the population by 1722. This latter figure represented anywhere from a fifth to a quarter of the adult male population of England.

Admittedly, many of these voters still had little real choice in how they exercised this right. Some constituencies were so fully dominated by one family or political interest that there was no opposing candidate. Even where a genuine choice *was* offered, a landlord or an employer might intimidate ordinary voters into following his lead because there was no secret ballot. On the other hand, many voters were property owners themselves and, so, free agents; moreover, in county elections or those for London's MPs or other large corporations it was more difficult to keep track of or intimidate individual voters – there were simply too many of them. In such cases, a candidate had to mount a genuine campaign.

This implied not only speech-making and other propaganda but also treating voters to free beer, free meals, and, occasionally, more outright forms of bribery – though, again, a really large constituency was almost impossible to bribe. Indeed, treats were often given indiscriminately, not just to voters but to women and commoners who clearly did not meet property-based voting qualifications. All of this made electoral contests increasingly expensive for the candidates. It also meant that, possibly for the first time in English history, the will of the people really mattered: in the words of Geoffrey Holmes, "the English electorate emerged in the 1690s and remained for two decades a force genuinely, if crudely, representative of the will of the politically-conscious classes in the country."[10] Therefore, neither party could afford to ignore popular opinion. After the lapsing of the Licensing Act in 1695, both sides sought to influence that opinion by churning out mountains of political treatises, pamphlets, poems, and broadsides (one-page handbills, often with an illustration). By 1702, Harley had recognized the advantage of employing "some discreet writer on the government's side";[11] two years later he hired Defoe to write *The Review*. Clearly, high politics in the reign of Anne would be about real issues. What were the issues that the "politically conscious classes" cared about? What were the principles that Whigs and Tories fought over?

The issues which dominated Anne's reign and separated the Whigs from the Tories were in many respects the same ones that had racked Stuart England all through the seventeenth century. The Revolution of 1688–9 had offered definite answers to those questions, but it remained to be seen whether and how those answers would be implemented. It will be recalled that the Revolution of 1688–9 and Act of Settlement of 1701 had seemed to establish parliamentary sovereignty. Parliament had chosen the monarch, implying precedence over him or her in the English constitution. Whigs were quite comfortable with this. They had supported the Revolution and would support Parliament's choice of the Hanoverians to succeed Anne without reservation. Indeed, as the reign wore on, some Whigs began to seem indecorously anxious for the queen's demise and replacement. But the Tories were torn about Parliament's choice of the Hanoverians in 1701, as they had been about that of William in 1689. Hanoverian Tories accepted Parliament's right to determine the succession and supported the Protestant heirs with varying degrees of enthusiasm. But Jacobite Tories secretly plotted for Prince James (called by his opponents "the Pretender") to succeed the queen. Anne was officially a Hanoverian, but, like Queen Elizabeth before her, she disliked talking about the succession because, of course, it depended on her death. Perhaps for this reason, Jacobites assumed that she was secretly one of them. Some even hoped to displace Anne while she lived. Indeed, should Louis XIV win the War of the Spanish Succession, he would establish not only Felipe V on the throne of Spain but James III and VIII on those of England, Scotland, and Ireland.

The outcome of the war would also affect the great religious questions that divided the parties. On the most basic level, a French victory would mean the succession of the Catholic Pretender, who could be expected to relaunch his father's program to emancipate Catholics all over the British Isles. But, as we shall see, the war went well, making a Catholic restoration increasingly remote. As a result, the parties fought mainly over the toleration of Dissenters: the Whigs were for it, the Tories against it. That is, the Whigs, who had a strong Dissenting constituency, tried to drum up support for the Dissenting position, and, in particular, repeal of the Test Act, by harping on the old prejudices against Catholics. Tories, on the other hand, thought the chief dangers to the Church were not Catholics but clerical poverty, rational skepticism, and Dissent. They worried about clergymen who could not support themselves; the new scientific knowledge and emphasis on reason which (combined with the end of censorship in 1695) seemed to undermine belief in revealed religion (see Conclusion); and the apparently growing number of Dissenters from the established Church. By 1714 there were, perhaps, 340,000 Dissenters in England, comprising about 6 percent of the population. This may not seem like much of a threat, but their prominence in society far exceeded their actual numbers. Tories knew that many of the new monied men, the leaders of towns, and the Whig party which supported them were Presbyterians, Baptists, Congregationalists, even Quakers, and that the war made them ever richer and more powerful in the State. They knew that these men flouted the Test Act by the practice of occasional conformity. Tories still equated Dissent with republicanism and disorder. They wanted to ban occasional conformity and roll back the toleration. Here, the Tories seemed to have an ally in Anne. In one of her first speeches to Parliament she promised to employ those who "have the truest zeal" for the Church of England.[12] Early in the reign, she supported a bill to outlaw occasional conformity. But as time went on she seems to have realized that she needed her Dissenting subjects too much – to help fight the war in which her nation was involved and her Crown was at stake – to make legislative war upon them.

If the previous issues boiled down to who would win the war, the war boiled down to how much money Britain could throw at it. As we have seen, Tory politicians and the landowners they represented were reluctant to support another war against France. Some were Jacobites and so sympathetic to Louis's aims. Most had little love for the Dutch or German allies of William III's Grand Alliance. Nearly all resented the Land Tax and the way in which it seemed to enrich the monied men, contractors, and military officers, many of whom were upstarts, Dissenters, and Whigs. Hence continued Tory advocacy of a "blue-water" strategy as the least expensive and most consistent with Britain's seafaring tradition. The Whigs, on the other hand, were for taking the war directly to Louis, on the continent, as William had done, by means of an Allied army with a major British component. In short, Whig politicians were enthusiastic about this new war. They agreed with William on the need to stop the Catholic absolutist Louis in order to preserve not only the freedoms of Europe but the freedoms of Englishmen. They saw more clearly than their Tory opponents that defeat would spell an end to the Revolution Settlement, the Protestant succession, the toleration, and the financial and commercial revolutions. For Whigs, the fact that monied men, contractors, and career soldiers were making their fortunes out of the war was only an added incentive to support it. As a result, Queen Anne, temperamentally a Tory, would find herself, like William III, drawn increasingly to Whig politicians to get her war funded and fought.

The War and the Parties, 1702–1710

To recap, the War of the Spanish Succession, sometimes known in North America as Queen Anne's War, was ostensibly fought to determine who sat on the throne of the Spanish Empire: France's candidate, the Bourbon Philippe, duke of Anjou, who called himself Felipe V; or the Alliance candidate, the Habsburg Archduke Charles of Austria, who called himself Carlos III. The war would also determine the balance of power in Europe for at least a generation and possibly a century. Closer to home, its outcome would decide who sat on the British throne, the constitutional and religious makeup of the British Isles, and whether Britain or France would dominate the Mediterranean and Atlantic trades. Befitting a conflict with so much at stake, the War of the Spanish Succession was to be a true world war, fought in the valleys and forests of North America and on the high seas of the Mediterranean and Caribbean, as well as on the plains of Europe. The principal combatants comprised France and Bavaria, on the one side, vs. the Grand Alliance, consisting of Britain, the Dutch Republic, Denmark, most of the Holy Roman Empire (including the States of Austria, Prussia, and Hanover), and, after 1703, Portugal and Savoy, on the other. At first, this Grand Alliance moved cautiously, for Anne's Tory government pursued the campaign at sea while the still awesome reputation of Louis XIV and his armies intimidated Britain's Dutch and German allies on land. In the spring and summer of 1702 Marlborough managed to capture key forts on the Meuse and Rhine rivers (see map 13). But for the remainder of the 1702 and 1703 campaigning seasons the Allied armies did little, while the British taxpayer grumbled.

Finally, late in 1703, the French broke the stalemate – but the Allies were to reap the rewards. Louis XIV and Maximilian II of Bavaria (1662–1726) decided to try to knock the Holy Roman Emperor out of the war by marching on Vienna. In response, Marlborough worked out a brilliant plan with the commander of the Allies' southern armies, Prince Eugene of Savoy (1663–1736), which they put into effect in the summer of 1704. Ignoring the protests of the other Allied commanders, Marlborough's army drove south from Flanders deep into enemy territory. He met Eugene's forces coming up from the south at the end of June, thus splitting the French and Bavarian forces in two. This march was one of the great feats in the annals of military history: 40,000 troops covered some 250 miles in just six weeks. The duke, with Godolphin's financial and logistical support, planned every detail down to having new boots waiting at predetermined intervals along the route for his advancing soldiers. Finally, on August 2, 1704,[13] the Allied forces, totaling 52,000 men, cornered the French and Bavarian army of 60,000 under Marshall Camille de Tallard (1652–1728) between the villages of Blindheim and Hochstedt on the banks of the River Danube (map 13).

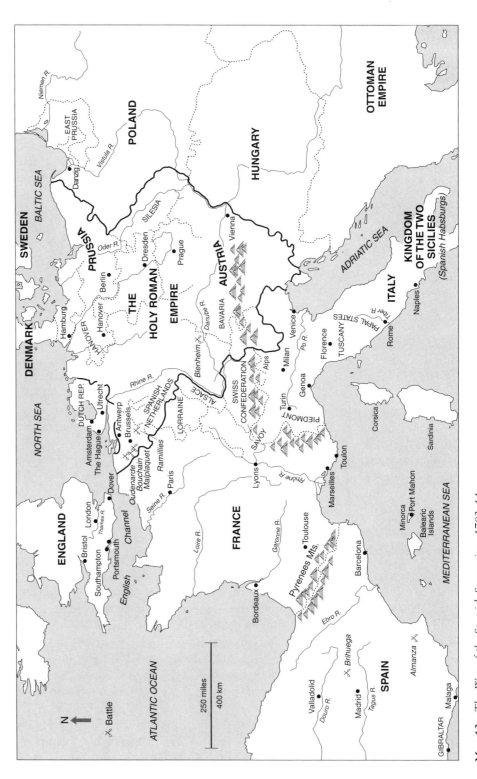

Map 13 *The War of the Spanish Succession, 1702–14.*

Having displayed his brilliance as a strategist in getting to this place, Marlborough now proved himself a consummate tactician. Holding his main forces in reserve, he made a feint to capture the first village. This broke up the French and Bavarian center. In the late afternoon, he committed the bulk of his army, including over 80 cavalry squadrons, against the exhausted enemy troops. For the first time in living memory, the French line broke and its soldiers ran, heading into the river. The battle of Blenheim, as the British called it, had turned into a rout. Thirty thousand French or Bavarian troops were killed or captured; 28 regiments and 18 generals surrendered. At the end of the day, the duke, tired but elated with victory, wrote a dispatch to his wife on the back of a tavern bill which read, in part, "I have not time to say more, but to beg you will give my duty to the Queen, and let her know her army has had a glorious victory."[14]

Indeed, the battle of Blenheim proved to be one of the most decisive victories in European history. In the short term, it saved Austria from French invasion and kept the Holy Roman Empire in the war. At the same time, it knocked Bavaria out of it. This left Louis bereft of allies. He would henceforward have to fight a defensive war. That war would be made more difficult because the flower of the French army had been crushed. It would take years to rebuild its strength. But Blenheim was even more devastating for the French on a psychological level. Remember that Louis XIV had dominated the European scene for 50 years. He had been able to do so in large part because of the French army and its reputation for invincibility. Now, for the first time in decades, that army had not only been defeated; it had broken and run from the field of battle. No wonder that the Sun King forbade the name of the battle to be uttered in the precincts of Versailles. The psychological effect on the British side was just as pronounced. For the first time since Agincourt in 1415, a British army under a British commander had won an unequivocally significant continental victory. (In fact, most Allied troops at Blenheim were not British, but this is how the victory was widely perceived.) Clearly, the financial revolution had paid off: a nation which had repeatedly embarrassed itself in foreign wars could now play with the big boys. Blenheim marked Britain's coming of age as a European – and therefore a world – power.

A grateful queen rewarded Marlborough by granting him the royal manor of Woodstock. Parliament rewarded him by funding the construction of a great palace there called, appropriately enough, "Blenheim." The Emperor rewarded him with the title of prince of the Holy Roman Empire. Far more important than these honors, the British ruling class and the British people finally got behind the war. Thomas Coke, a Tory MP from Derbyshire, wrote in response to Marlborough's bold march: "[t]he country gentlemen, who have so long groaned under the weight of four shillings, in the pound, without hearing of a town taken or any enterprise endeavored, seem every day more cheerfull in this war."[15] This was good news for the Whigs, who did well in the parliamentary elections of 1705 and 1708. The Tories, in their frustration, grew increasingly desperate. In 1704 they offended the queen and nation by attempting to tack a clause banning occasional conformity onto the annual bill for the Land Tax: that is, they would hold funds for the war hostage unless Parliament did their bidding on the religious issue.

Plate 24 *The battle of Blenheim. By kind permission of His Grace, the Duke of Marlborough.*

Failing in this, they insulted Anne in 1705 by moving in Parliament that the Church was in danger under her administration. Failing once again, they infuriated her in the same session by moving that a member of the Hanoverian family be invited over to live in England until the queen died. They did not do this because they were committed Hanoverians. Rather, they sought to put the queen into an embarrassing position. Like Elizabeth before her, Anne naturally saw such a plan as morbid and dangerous to her interests, but how could she refuse without looking like a Jacobite? In the end, all the Tories succeeded in doing was convincing Anne that they were irresponsible and untrustworthy. Even before Blenheim, she had begun to employ more Whigs in her government, and she continued to do so in 1705 and 1706. Gradually, and sometimes against her will, the Junto began to return to power, to prosecute Queen Anne's war as they had done King William's.

The Whig resurrection between 1704 and 1710 had important repercussions both at home and abroad. First, Whig parliamentary majorities guaranteed that the war would continue to be funded liberally. As a result, by 1708 Marlborough, Godolphin, and the government they headed grew ever more dependent on the Whigs. The Whigs' financial generosity combined with Marlborough's brilliant generalship led to a series of victories against the French: at Ramillies in 1706, Oudenarde in 1708, Malplaquet in 1709, and Bouchain in 1711. Nor were Britain's allies idle. In 1706 Prince Eugene swept the French out of Italy (see map 13). In 1703 the Allies opened a second front in Spain itself. At first they succeeded here as well, capturing Gibraltar and defeating the French fleet at Malaga in 1704, then taking Barcelona in 1705 and Madrid in 1706. But the war in Spain overextended the Allies, who were also fighting at sea and in North America as well as in northern Europe. Moreover, the largest portion of the Spanish people, the Castilians, favored Felipe V. As a result, the Allied forces suffered two disastrous defeats, at Almanza in 1707 and Brihuega in 1710. These virtually guaranteed that the Bourbon Felipe, not the Habsburg Charles, would occupy the Spanish throne. Still, this was Louis's only major success; the Grand Alliance stymied him on every other front and in every other war aim. By the end of the decade, Marlborough's victories and the sheer expense of fighting a world war against the British financial juggernaut had just about brought the Sun King to his knees.

At home, the Whig ascendancy at court and in Parliament enabled that party to pass legislation to safeguard the Protestant or Hanoverian succession. In 1706, they responded to the Tory demands for a Hanoverian to live in Britain by securing passage of the **Regency Act**. Instead of subjecting Queen Anne to the discomfort of her successor's presence on site, this legislation established a regency council, to be stocked with staunch pro-Hanoverians, to act as an executive and to ensure a smooth transition on her death. As a further safeguard, Parliament was to remain in session following that event for six months. Thus were the Tories outmaneuvered and the Protestant succession strengthened. Incidentally, this legislation also repealed the provision of the Act of Settlement which forbade government officers from sitting in Parliament: the Whigs knew that they would be the court party under a Hanoverian, and they wanted to ensure that they controlled both the legislature and the spoils of government.

More importantly, in the following year the Whigs pushed through an Act of Union with Scotland. As we have seen, James I's attempts to knit the two countries together a century previously had been thwarted by longstanding hatreds and prejudices between the two peoples. Those hard feelings had, in some ways, only intensified during the Stuart century. It will be recalled that while most English people were Anglicans, the Scots were mainly Presbyterians, with a significant Catholic population in the northern Highlands. Charles I's attempt to force Anglicanism on the Scots in the late 1630s had led to the Civil Wars. Cromwell briefly united the two nations, from 1654 to 1660. But at the Restoration this union was dissolved and the Anglican Church reestablished in the northern kingdom as the Church of Scotland. This led to the persecution of Presbyterians and much overall resentment. Regional and religious tensions were made worse when, in the late 1670s and 1680s, the Stuart regime used Highland troops to subdue risings in the Presbyterian Lowlands.

At the Revolution of 1688–9, the Presbyterian Kirk seized power, the Church of Scotland was disestablished, and the power of the Crown weakened. But there remained other causes of resentment. For example, toward the end of the mostly successful campaign to pacify the Jacobite Highlands, some 40 men, women, and children of the MacDonald clan were senselessly massacred at Glencoe in early 1692. Supported by leading Presbyterians, this atrocity provided one more reason for Highland Scots to hate the London regime. Economics exacerbated that hatred. Scotland remained a poor country at the end of the seventeenth century and King William's war disrupted Scottish trade, especially with France. Worse, the English Navigation Acts continued to treat the Scots as if they were the Dutch or the French. No Scottish merchant could trade with the English colonies but in an English ship and through an English port. When the Company of Scotland attempted to set up its own trading colony in 1698, at Darién on the isthmus of Panama, Spanish and English hostility was so intense that it failed, with the loss of some 2,000 lives and perhaps a quarter of Scotland's monetary capital. This took place in the middle of five disastrous harvests, leading to a real subsistence crisis, between 1695 and 1699. To some, it appeared that the English were attempting to starve their northern neighbors out of existence.

Queen Anne's accession did nothing to ease these resentments. In 1703, the Scottish Parliament passed a series of anti-English laws. The Act Annent Peace and War decreed that, after Anne's death, all foreign policy decisions from London would have to be approved by the Scottish Parliament. The Wine Act and Wool Act allowed for trade with France even during hostilities. Finally, and most alarmingly to the English, the Act of Security stated that in the event of Anne's death, the Scottish Parliament would choose her successor in Scotland. The implied threat was that they would choose the Pretender, Prince James. This meant that, even if the English Acts of Settlement and Regency worked and the Whigs secured the accession of a Hanoverian in England at Anne's death, the Scottish Act of Security might install his Catholic Stuart cousin on his northern border. Given the French support for the Pretender, there was every possibility that the "Auld Alliance" between Scotland and France would be revived and the situation would revert to what it had been under the Tudors, when those monarchs were constantly at war with their northern neighbors. Should the English lose such a war, the gains of Blenheim would be wiped out and the Revolution Settlement of 1688–9 would be undone.

Once the Whigs achieved power in London, they pursued the only clear solution to this dilemma: a union of England and Scotland. This was easier said than done, given English prejudice toward the Scots, Scottish resentment toward the English, and the understandable reluctance of the Scots to lose their national identity and be absorbed by their wealthy neighbor to the south. In the end, that wealth won the day, on two counts. First, the Whigs offered the economic advantages of being let into the English trading system. Henceforward, the English and Scots would trade as part of one British nation, open to all the wealth of the new British Empire. This message worked on Scottish MPs, merchants, and landowners who depended on the cattle trade with their rich neighbors to the south. English wealth assisted in a second, more direct, way: bribery. Scotland itself was to receive "the Equivalent," a one-time payment of £398,085. More quietly, many individual Scots peers and MPs happily took bribes in return for voting their nation and its Parliament out of existence; as one English minister crowed: "We bought them."[16] Still, the Scots did win some real concessions. In the new London-based Parliament of Great Britain, Scotland would be represented by 16 peers, elected from among the total Scottish peerage, and 45 MPs. This was proportionally somewhat lower than Scotland's population vs. that of England (few, other than the Levellers [see chapter 8], even considered proportional representation before the late eighteenth century). But it was much higher than the Scottish contribution to the war merited vs. that of England. Scottish landowners were required to pay only one-fortieth of the Land Tax; their proportion of the Excise was 1:36, yet there was one Scottish MP to every 11.4 from England and Wales. Furthermore, the northern kingdom would retain Scottish law and, of course, the privileged status of the Presbyterian Kirk. As a result, the Act of Union, creating the State of Great Britain, was passed in the spring of 1707; the first Parliament of Great Britain met that fall.

Despite the concessions noted above, many Scotsmen, particularly Tories, were unhappy with the union. England and its capital would dominate the new State of Great Britain politically, socially, and culturally, often treating the Scots as if they were second-class citizens. But most historians would nevertheless argue that the union was good for Scotland. Economically, it laid the groundwork for a tremendous upsurge of prosperity in the eighteenth century. That led, in turn, to a cultural flowering, largely based in the big cities of Edinburgh and Glasgow, which is sometimes called the Scottish Enlightenment. It is difficult to see how this would have happened in an independent Scotland under the control of the Catholic branch of the Stuarts. For England and the Whigs, the Union's major advantage was that it made more certain the Hanoverian succession.

The Act of Union was the high-water mark of Whig success under Queen Anne. As the reign wore on, the Whigs, and their Junto leaders in particular, became increasingly unpopular with Anne and with the country at large. This was due, in part, to their overconfidence and ambition, in part to a shift in the country's mood on some of the major issues which separated the two parties. First among these was the war and its related issue, money. At first, Marlborough's succession of victories over the French had been greeted with universal approbation, the queen and court processing through the streets of London to St. Paul's Cathedral for elaborate services of national thanksgiving. But after a while, the queen and her subjects began to wonder why no victory seemed to be decisive; why the French were never brought to the negotiating table. After the battle of Malplaquet in 1709, which saw the loss of nearly 35,000 men on both sides, she is supposed to have remarked: "When will this bloodshed ever cease?"[17]

In fact, toward the end of the decade, nature gave the Whigs a chance to make peace. The harsh winter of 1708–9 resulted in a terrible harvest, reducing the French peasants who paid Louis's taxes to near starvation. The Sun King's funds ran dry. He was actually forced to melt down the silver furniture at Versailles. Finally, in March 1709, he opened negotiations for peace. It is a measure of his desperation that his diplomats came to the peace conference in the Netherlands willing to concede Spain, Italy, the Indies, fortress towns on the Dutch border, and the Protestant succession. But this was not enough for the Whig diplomats. They made further, incredible demands: not only that Louis's grandson give up his claim to the Spanish throne, but that, if Anjou refused, the French king would forcibly remove him from Madrid with French troops. To this Louis replied that if he was required to make war, he would rather do so against the British than his own children. The peace talks, therefore, collapsed. At this point the Tories began to charge, and many English men and women began to believe, that Marlborough, Godolphin, and the Whigs were intentionally prolonging the war to keep themselves in power and to get rich off of the sale of army commissions, government contracts, lotteries, and the funds. Thus, old country fears of standing armies and resentment of high taxes combined with prejudice against the rise of new men. These charges were probably unfair. Rather than consciously seeking to prolong a profitable war, the Whigs were more likely blinded by their own fears of France and Catholicism. They failed to realize that Louis was effectively finished. They had been so afraid of him for so long that they fought on past the point of reasonableness.

The second issue upon which the Whigs misjudged the mood of the country was religion. Remember that most English men and women were Anglicans, and somewhat distrustful of occasionally conforming Dissenters. In 1709 the Whig government offered shelter and naturalization to the Poor Palatines, a group of German Protestant refugees displaced by the war. This was unpopular, first, because the Poor Palatines were foreigners. British xenophobia was still powerful and there was a widespread feeling among the Tories that their German and Dutch allies were coasting, not doing their part in the war. The poor Palatines were also resented on the grounds that they might take jobs away from English men and women. Finally, they were unpopular because their theology and religious practice were similar to those of the Dissenters.

Worse, in 1710, the Whig government decided to prosecute a prominent Anglican clergyman named Henry Sacheverell (ca. 1674–1724) on a charge of seditious libel. Sacheverell was a high Tory rabble-rouser who had preached on November 5, 1709 – the anniversary of the Gunpowder Plot and William's landing at Torbay – in favor of passive obedience and non-resistance. The sermon, *The Perils of False Brethren in Church and State*, was an implicit attack on the Revolution of 1688–9 and, by extension, the whole course of English history over the last 20 years. Sacheverell went on to decry the Marlborough–Godolphin ministry, Whigs, low Church Anglicans, and occasionally conforming Dissenters as "double-dealing, practical atheists" and "bloodsuckers that had brought our kingdom and government into a consumption."[18] The sermon was printed, reaching 100,000 copies and sparking a partisan religious debate that reached 600 titles on the subject within a year. Sacheverell's words were stupid things to say in public; but to prosecute their author for saying them was even stupider. In December, the Whig government launched a parliamentary show trial of Sacheverell. The government thought that it was defending "Revolution Principles"; but many Anglican Tories saw the trial not as a referendum on the Revolution but as Dissenting Whig persecution of a poor Church of England clergyman. When the indictment was announced on March 1, 1710, ordinary Londoners rioted. They took out their frustrations by tearing down Dissenting meeting houses, many of which had been built and frequented by the new monied men. Clearly, in religion as well as war, the Whigs were pushing their luck.

Finally, the Whigs managed to offend the queen on the issue of sovereignty. Anne had turned to the Whigs as her allies in fighting the war. But she had never really warmed to them, in part because they did not treat her with the traditional reverence for monarchy. As will be recalled, she had sought to govern by appointing the best men of both parties. But the Junto had other ideas. Knowing full well that the queen needed their expertise and parliamentary support to fight the war, they demanded a clean sweep of Tory officeholders. Anne resisted "the five tyrannizing lords," as she called them, for years, continuing to employ moderate Tories like Harley as one of her secretaries of State. In February 1708, after it became clear that Anne and Harley might try to construct a government without the Junto, Marlborough, Godolphin, and the Whig leaders forced the secretary's dismissal by threatening to withdraw their services. This deprived the queen of the one minister who had counterbalanced Junto ambitions. Later in that year Anne's beloved husband, Prince George, died and, with him, some of Anne's stomach for the fight. By late 1709 every Junto lord but Montagu (now Halifax) held office, and there were few or no Tories left in government. The queen seemed a pawn in Whig hands, forced to put up with a ministry she did not like, a war she no longer supported, and attacks on the Church she loved.

Plate 25 *Fighting in a coffee-house after the trial of Dr. Sacheverell.* © *British Museum.*

The Queen's Revenge, 1710

In fact, as the year 1710 dawned, it became clear that Anne had had enough. She began to consult secretly with Harley through the hands of a number of her court attendants, most notably a woman of the Bedchamber named Abigail Masham (1670?–1734). Masham's duties were those of a lady's maid, necessitating close personal attendance on the sovereign. Because of Anne's poor health, Masham was at her side constantly as a virtual nurse. Fortunately for Harley, her sympathies were Tory and she was more than willing to be a go-between.

In the meantime, Anne had grown estranged from her Whig favorites, the Churchills. Her friendship with the duchess had soured because of Sarah's constant pushing of the Whig point of view. Her friendship with the duke had taken a turn for the worse when, in the previous year, she had refused his request to be made captain-general for life. The Churchills blamed these reversals on Masham's influence. Marlborough wrote: "I have deserv'd better than to be made a sacrifice to the unreasonable passion of a bedchamber woman."[19] In January 1710 the Whigs considered moving in Parliament for an address to the queen demanding Masham's removal from court. To Anne, this was the ultimate act of *lèse-majesté*, for it took out of her hands the right to appoint her closest and most personal servants. In order to stop this move, she canvassed peers and MPs of all political persuasions, sometimes "with tears in her eyes."[20] During similar meetings in March, she took the opportunity to indicate that while she agreed with Sacheverell's guilt, she did not want to see him punished harshly. Clearly, the queen was attempting to undermine her own ministry. The monarchy still had enough prestige that many peers and MPs, including some Whigs, did Anne's bidding on both issues: the address to dismiss Masham was never moved and Sacheverell was convicted, but punished lightly.

These victories gave Anne courage. In April she began to fire Whigs, starting with her lord chamberlain, a Junto ally named Henry Grey, marquess of Kent (1671–1740). In June she attacked the Junto directly, removing Sunderland as secretary of State. In August she dismissed Godolphin as lord treasurer. He was succeeded by a Treasury Commission whose most influential member would be Robert Harley. From this point Harley was, in effect, the queen's principal minister, though he would not receive the staff as lord treasurer and the title earl of Oxford until the following May. Harley is often seen as a Tory but this does not mean that he intended a Tory ministry. Throughout the summer of 1710 he worked hard to undermine the Junto while keeping moderate Whigs in the ministry: after all, the point of the queen's actions was not to exchange a Whig ministry for a Tory one but to restore the balance between the two. But party loyalties were too strong. It soon became clear that few Whigs would work with Harley and that he had no hope of presiding successfully over the current Whig-dominated Parliament. And so, in September 1710, the queen dissolved her Parliament. The resulting election was a referendum on the war and Whig fiscal and religious policy. The Tories, running on a platform of peace with France, low taxes, and the defense of the Church of England, won the majority of seats in a landslide. The brief Whig ascendancy under Anne was over.

The Treaty of Utrecht, 1710–1713

Queen Anne, Robert Harley, and their supporters had gone to the country with, first and foremost, a promise of peace. Immediately following the election, Harley began negotiations with the French. The Whig minority in the new Parliament opposed the peace every step of the way, charging that any treaty that allowed the duke of Anjou to remain on the Spanish throne would be a sellout after so many victories and so much blood and treasure expended. It would also betray Britain's allies, since none of them would want to agree to the ensuing treaty. Partly because of Whig resistance and the intrigues of the Allies, the peace took two and a half years to negotiate. It was won only after much shady dealing on both sides. For example, in December 1711, the Whigs betrayed one of their guiding principles by promising the dissident Tory Daniel Finch, earl of Nottingham (1647–1730), that they would vote for a bill against occasional conformity if he would persuade other Tory peers to oppose the peace. Anne countered by creating 12 pro-peace Tory peers to outvote the Whigs. Many contemporaries thought this an unseemly stretching of her prerogative. Even more unseemly was the queen's treatment of Marlborough and the Allies. She dismissed the former in December 1711 after it became clear that his military aggressiveness threatened the peace negotiations. Then she issued "restraining orders" to his replacement, Ormond, so as not to embarrass Louis. Now it was the turn of the Allies to feel that the British were not doing their part, that "perfidious Albion" was selling them out to the French.

On the surface, the **Treaty of Utrecht of 1713** does, indeed, appear to be a sellout. For starters, Britain agreed to Anjou's ascent of the Spanish throne as Felipe V. This was qualified only by a provision which stated that the French and Spanish Crowns could never be united in one holder. The Allies received territory, but not so much as Marlborough's and Eugene's victories would seem to have promised. The Dutch were awarded a series of forts on their southern border to form a barrier against France. According to the later Treaty of Rastadt (1714), the Holy Roman Emperor received significant Spanish territory in Italy as well as what had once been the Spanish Netherlands, thus forming a further buffer between the French and the Dutch. Savoy claimed Sicily. At Utrecht, the British acquired Gibraltar and Minorca in the Mediterranean; Nova Scotia, Newfoundland, and Hudson's Bay in Canada; St. Kitts in the Caribbean (see map 14); and the *Asiento*, an agreement which guaranteed British slave traders the exclusive right to sell human beings to the Spanish Empire for 30 years as well as other trading rights with the Spanish colonies. Finally, the French promised to recognize the Hanoverian succession and withdraw support for the Pretender. The Whigs thought these acquisitions small potatoes after the earth-shaking victories at Blenheim and elsewhere. As for Louis's promises to recognize the

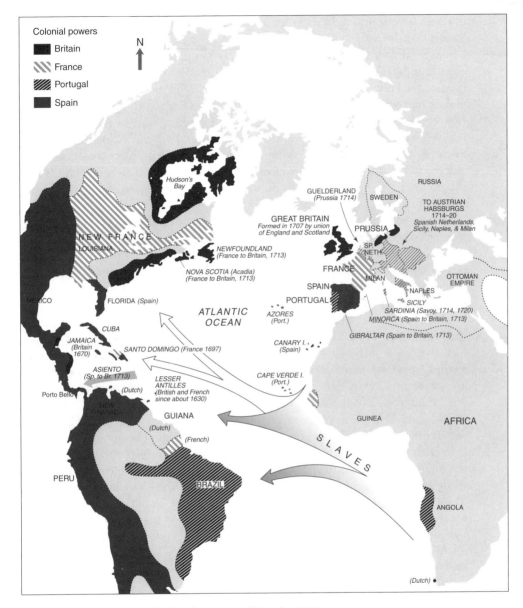

Colonial powers

- Britain
- France
- Portugal
- Spain

N

Hudson's
Bay

RUSSIA

GUELDERLAND
(Prussia 1714)

SWEDEN

TO AUSTRIAN
HABSBURGS
1714–20
*Spanish Netherlands,
Sicily, Naples, & Milan*

GREAT BRITAIN
*Formed in 1707 by union
of England and Scotland*

PRUSSIA

NEW FRANCE

LOUISIANA

SP.
NETH.

NEWFOUNDLAND
(France to Britain, 1713)

FRANCE

MILAN

OTTOMAN
EMPIRE

NOVA SCOTIA (Acadia)
(France to Britain, 1713)

SPAIN

NAPLES

MEXICO

FLORIDA *(Spain)*

ATLANTIC
OCEAN

PORTUGAL

AZORES
(Port.)

SICILY

SARDINIA (Savoy, 1714, 1720)

MINORCA (Spain to Britain, 1713)

GIBRALTAR (Spain to Britain, 1713)

CUBA

CANARY I.
(Spain)

JAMAICA
(Britain
1670)

SANTO DOMINGO (France 1697)

ASIENTO
(Sp. to Br. 1713)

Porto Bello

LESSER
ANTILLES
*(British and French
since about 1630)*

(Dutch)

CAPE VERDE I.
(Port.)

NEW
GRANADA

GUIANA

(Dutch)

(French)

GUINEA

AFRICA

S L A V E S

PERU

BRAZIL

ANGOLA

(Dutch) •

Map 14 *The Atlantic world after the Treaty of Utrecht, 1713.*

Hanoverian succession, withdraw support from the Pretender, and refrain from uniting the French and Spanish Crowns, they knew from hard experience that he had broken similar promises before. In the next reign they would revenge themselves on Oxford and other Tory peace negotiators by impeaching them in the House of Lords.

They should not have done so, for Utrecht was, in fact, a master stroke of British diplomacy. It demonstrated clear-eyed realism about the European situation as it was; and prescience about what it would be in the future. First, the Spanish settlement could not have been otherwise after the Allied defeats at Almanza and Brihuega. The Spanish people wanted "Felipe V." Moreover, the Allied candidate for the Spanish throne, "Carlos III," the Archduke Charles, had become the Holy Roman Emperor in April 1711 upon the death of his brother. To endow him with the Spanish Empire would be to replace an over-mighty French Bourbon State with an over-mighty Austrian Habsburg one. In any case, Oxford realized what the Whigs did not: that it did not matter who sat on the throne of Spain. France was too weak, economically and militarily, after two decades of war to either unite the two Crowns or to profit much from their unity. Nor would the Bourbons be in a position to do much for the Jacobite cause. French power was broken, whether the treaty said so or not.

Moreover, the economic provisions of the treaty would ensure that, during the long period of peace while the French licked their wounds, the British would grow wealthier and more powerful. While Gibraltar may be a tiny rock, whoever possessed it controlled the trade between the Mediterranean and the Atlantic. Nova Scotia and Newfoundland may be bleak and remote, but they were a foothold in Canada, and they offered the rich fishing of the Grand Banks. The acquisition of another island in the West Indies (St. Kitts) meant that, thanks to the Navigation Acts, London would control an even greater share of the most lucrative trade of the eighteenth century – sugar. Finally, the slave trade, a crime against humanity heretofore dominated by the Spanish and Portuguese, would also, from now on, enrich British coffers. (The human implications of that trade will be addressed in the next chapter.) Overall, Utrecht guaranteed that Britain would remain the greatest European trading nation during the eighteenth century, far wealthier and more powerful than any single potential enemy or ally.

In retrospect, the Glorious Revolution and commercial revolution had begotten the financial revolution which had enriched an important segment of the nation while guaranteeing that Britain would stop France in 1697 and defeat her in 1713. Those victories would lead to more colonies which would lead to even more trade. That trade would guarantee, in turn, that when the French were ready to fight again, the British would have even more money at their disposal to plow into the War of the Austrian Succession (1742–8), the Seven Years' War (1756–63), the American Revolutionary War (1775–83), the French Revolutionary Wars (1793–1801), and the Napoleonic Wars (1803–15). Britain would unequivocally lose only one of those conflicts, and, despite that loss, would emerge on the field of Waterloo in 1815 as the unchallenged leader of Europe and the master of a worldwide empire. All this occurred because of parliamentary sovereignty and the vision of individuals such as William III, Anne, Montagu, Marlborough, Godolphin, and Oxford in the 1690s and early 1700s. Samuel Johnson (1709–84) relates an anecdote which sums up the contrasting experiences of Britain and France. At the end of the Nine Years' War, William III had sent Matthew Prior (1664–1721) to France to negotiate a Partition Treaty with Louis XIV. During the embassy, Prior spent a great deal of time at Louis's magnificent Palace of Versailles, which was financed by the same method used to pay for the Sun King's many wars: by taxing the French peasantry. Prior's French hosts, knowing full well that the British monarch could not exploit his people in the same way because of Parliament's power, knowing further that the British monarch had spent all of his money on fighting their master and that he had no palace of the size and magnificence of Versailles, asked Prior what he thought of their master's house. Prior is said to have replied: "The monuments of my Master's actions are to be seen everywhere but in his own house."[21] Admittedly, what Prior did not say was that some of those monuments, such as the Irish Penal Code or the *Asiento*, were cruel and shameful. But for the most part, for the people of England at least, the implications of the Glorious Revolution, the commercial and financial revolutions, and the settlements at Ryswick and Utrecht would lead to national wealth and a more equitable society beyond anything experienced by Louis's subjects.

The Oxford Ministry, 1710–1714

Queen Anne raised Robert Harley, earl of Oxford, to power in order to save her from the "five tyrannizing lords" of the Junto. She expected him to assemble a ministry which would include the best men from both parties. This was consistent with Oxford's own political philosophy of moderation, but it was made difficult by the fact that almost no Whigs supported the peace; and that the elections of 1710 and 1713 were Tory landslides. As a result, those few Whigs who sat in his government were increasingly unreliable in their support; while the Tories, led by Henry St. John, Viscount Bolingbroke (1678–1751), demanded their removal. In short, Oxford walked a tightrope, trying to please the queen by hanging on to Whigs while trying to placate the vast Tory majority in the House of Commons by appointing Tories. As we have seen, he successfully negotiated that tightrope on the issues of peace and war. The issues of religion and the succession would cause him to fall off.

The Tories elected in 1710 and 1713 wanted to strengthen the Church of England and weaken Dissent. Specifically, they wanted to revive the power of the bishops and the Church courts, to establish new Anglican parishes in expanding cities, and to roll back the toleration. This last was a difficult personal issue for Oxford because, though associated with the Tories, his ancestry was Dissenting. Even Anne viewed the Tory program as needlessly divisive. But both realized that such legislation was the price for Tory support of the peace, which was at the top of their agenda. In April 1711 they agreed to the passage of a law to build 50 London churches; in December, more ominously, to one banning occasional conformity. In 1714 Parliament went further still, passing the Schism Act. This piece of legislation forbade Dissenters from teaching or keeping schools. That meant that the Anglican majority could shut down every Dissenting academy in the country, thus preventing Nonconformists from educating their children anywhere but at home. The last two acts were designed to drive them from public life and, eventually, out of existence. Because so many Dissenters were

Whigs, these laws would also serve to reduce Whig electoral power. Not surprisingly, by 1714 virtually every Whig in government office had resigned or been sacked. This left Anne as much a prisoner of the Tories as she had once been of the Whigs.

But the issue which destroyed the queen's confidence in Oxford, and thus the ministry itself, was the succession. Queen Anne had been in poor health for most of her reign, but the question of the succession became especially pressing after the winter of 1713–14, when she came dangerously close to death. As we have seen, Parliament had already named her successor, the head of the House of Hanover, via the Act of Settlement. Following the death of the Electress Sophia in May 1714, the heir designate was Georg Ludwig, elector of Hanover. While Georg had Whig support, the Whigs did not control the Commons. The Tories, who did, were split between those who grudgingly supported the Hanoverian succession and those who secretly hoped for the restoration of the Pretender, Prince James. In order to maintain his majority in the Commons, Oxford had to keep both sides of the Tory party happy, usually by making conflicting promises to each. Moreover, in order to assure his position in the next reign, he negotiated with both men: like Warwick, Northumberland, or Robert Cecil before him, Oxford sought to be a kingmaker.

By 1714, the pressures of maintaining his delicate balancing act began to wear on Oxford. Anne, not one to be trifled with, complained to her cabinet that

he neglected all business, that he was seldom to be understood, that when he did explain himself, she could not depend upon the truth of what he said; that he never came to her at the time she appointed, that he often came drunk, that lastly to crown all he behav'd himself towards her with ill manner indecency & disrespect.[22]

What Anne meant by this last was that in the summer of 1714 she discovered Oxford's double game with the Elector and the Pretender. In an emotional meeting at Kensington Palace on July 27, she demanded the lord treasurer's staff from the earl. That night, Anne was overheard, through the bedchamber door, to be weeping. We will never know the cause: she may have been weeping for her broken friendship with Oxford; she may have been weeping for the end of royal initiative. That is, Anne knew that, within days, she was going to have to hand her government over, either to a Whig, like Marlborough, or to the Tory leader, Viscount Bolingbroke. Either way, she would be entirely in the hands of one political party. Parliamentary sovereignty left her no other course. Her personal wishes as sovereign were now secondary.

In the end, Anne never had to make this choice. On the morning of July 30, while standing in the long gallery at Kensington, she seems to have suffered a stroke, perhaps the result of the tension produced by these events. Immediately upon being notified by the ladies of the Bedchamber in waiting, Whigs, Tories, Hanoverians, Jacobites all flocked to the palace, the succession and, indeed, the constitution itself at stake. The queen's leading advisers consulted among themselves and recommended to the dying sovereign that she name as her lord treasurer Charles Talbot, duke of Shrewsbury, a moderate Whig and one of the "immortal seven" who had signed the invitation to the prince of Orange in 1688. Though popular with Tories, no one doubted that Shrewsbury would use his power to ensure the proclamation and accession of Georg Ludwig. According to one story, as her counselors guided her hand, containing the staff, toward Shrewsbury's, Anne said, "use it for the good of my people."[23] The story is apocryphal; but the good of her people had usually been her guiding principle. Her actions at this moment assured the Hanoverian succession and preserved the post-Revolutionary constitution. There remained one last act: Queen Anne, the last Stuart sovereign of Great Britain and Ireland, died at 7:45 on the morning of August 1, 1714. That event was the dawn of a new political world.

Conclusion:
Augustan Polity, Society,
and Culture, ca. 1714

Imagine a woman, born around 1630 under the government of King Charles I and the Anglican religious ascendancy. Imagine that she still lives in 1714, having grown to the ripe old age of 84. As a child, she might have heard her parents and grandparents (if hers were among the few living grandparents) talk about the Armada, the Gunpowder Plot, and political and religious strife under Queen Elizabeth and King James. She would almost certainly have heard her parents complain about hard economic times. In the 1640s, while she was a teenager, her father and brothers might have gone off to fight in the Civil Wars. At the end of the decade she would have witnessed the dismantling of the national Church and the execution of her king. In her twenties, during the 1650s, she would have been ruled by a series of unstable governments and exposed to a wide variety of political and religious ideas. In 1660, at the age of 30, she would have experienced the restoration of the Stuart monarchy and the Church of England, but thereafter, during her middle age, heard of unsuccessful foreign wars, domestic plots, and increasing tension between king and Parliament over money and religion. Then, in 1688, at the end of her fifties, she would have lived through a second revolution in Church and State. This would be followed in her old age by two decades of almost continuous warfare abroad and bitter party strife at home. Now, at the end of her life, she was to be ruled by a new, foreign king. Had she been a betting woman, would she have wagered that he and his advisers could bring England peace, stability, and prosperity? In fact, had she taken that bet, she would have won, for that is precisely what King George I (reigned 1714–27)[1] and his advisers managed to accomplish.

Hanoverian Political Stability

The Treaty of Utrecht, the death of Queen Anne, and the safe accession of the new king from Hanover were to solve problems that had tormented the

British State and its citizens for over a century. After 1714, and particularly after a Jacobite Rebellion in Scotland fizzled in the following year, the related questions of sovereignty and the succession were settled once and for all: Britain was to be a constitutional monarchy ruled by Parliament's nominee, the nearest Protestant heir, George of Hanover. Protestantism would remain the official religious orientation of the British State, as represented by the Anglican Church in England and Ireland and the Presbyterian Kirk in Scotland. Thanks to Marlborough's victories and the benefits reaped from the Treaty of Utrecht, Britain would continue to be a European and a world power and her economy would prosper as never before. Indeed, the Hanoverian connection would require greater involvement in Europe, just as Britain's expanded colonial empire and economy would necessitate more frequent activity abroad. This would, in turn, continue to require a strong military and naval profile, which meant, further, that Parliament and the government funds would have to continue to keep the Crown well supplied with money. Since King George, his ministers, and his Parliaments would all share Whig sympathies, there was to be little debate on these issues.

As heir designate, Georg Ludwig had taken a keen interest in British politics, and he had concluded that only Whigs could be trusted to support the Hanoverian succession. This conviction was only confirmed when, in the fall of 1715, a small band of Scottish Jacobites led a brief and unsuccessful revolt against Hanoverian rule. Even before the "Fifteen," as it came to be called, King George began to purge Tory officeholders and appoint Whigs at the center and in the localities. This facilitated a Whig landslide in the general election of 1715. The Whigs also won back the leadership of the Lords when George obligingly created 14 new Whig peers. The Whigs' overwhelming parliamentary majority enabled them, in 1716, to pass the Septennial Act. This legislation repealed the Triennial Act and instead required that a new Parliament be elected only every seven years. This guaranteed that the Whigs would have seven years to further establish themselves in power and to ensure that they would be victorious in the next election. It also meant that individual election contests would be less frequent, more important individually, and so more expensive to mount – thus freezing out the middling and minor gentry who formed the backbone of the Tory party. This, combined with the Hanoverian bias against the Tories, would ensure that Whigs dominated the political world through the reign of George's son, George II (1683–1760; reigned 1727–60).

But which Whigs? The leaders of the Junto's generation died off soon after Anne did, leaving younger Whigs to fight a bitter internal struggle for control of the party and government. That struggle was especially significant because, unlike his Stuart predecessors, George was not particularly interested in running the country himself. He was, after all, 54 years old when he ascended the British throne. He spoke little English. And he was far more concerned with the affairs of his tiny German State of Hanover, which he continued to rule as elector. Historians have recently demonstrated that George was more active in British affairs than used to be thought, especially military and foreign policy. Nevertheless, he needed a "premier minister" to whom he could delegate the management of Parliament and the details of both domestic and foreign affairs.

The eventual winner of this competition was Sir Robert Walpole (1676–1745). Knighted in 1725, Walpole was a Whig gentleman from Norfolk. He had served as Anne's secretary at War and treasurer of the Navy from 1708 to 1711 and was the Junto's point man in the Commons during the Oxford ministry. After a period in opposition, Walpole returned as first lord of the Treasury in 1721 following his successful handling of a financial scandal known as the South Sea Bubble which had conveniently brought down his rivals.[2] Sir Robert would retain this position for 21 years. Walpole is usually thought of as the first modern prime minister and he still holds the record for the length of his premiership. More to our purposes, he presided over a quarter-century of political stability which put an end to many of the problems that had racked English public life for most of this book. How did he do it?

He did it, first, by the careful distribution of government patronage. By the second quarter of the eighteenth century, several decades of war and colonial acquisitions had expanded English government tremendously. Besides the pensions, real estate, and honors the Crown had to give away, it also controlled a central bureaucracy numbering over 12,000 offices. King George allowed Walpole free play to distribute the government's patronage so as to increase his following. If a peer or an MP voted as Walpole bid, he might receive a government job; or a good Church living for a younger son in the clergy; or a promotion for a nephew in the army; or similar favors for his provincial friends and neighbors – all of which added to the power and prestige of that peer or MP in his home county. On the other hand, if he voted *against* Walpole's government, he might lose his office, be powerless to assist his family and friends, and acquire the reputation of being "out of the loop." This policy resulted in a cadre of about 75 peers in the House of Lords (including a nucleus of loyal Whig bishops, see below) and about 150 MPs in the House of Commons who always supported the prime minister no matter what their personal feelings. Indeed, they were so reliable that contemporaries began to call them "the Old Corps."

This led the Tories under Bolingbroke and, eventually, dissatisfied country Whigs such as Sir William Pulteney (1684–1764) to charge that Walpole was corrupting Parliament, offering its members the Devil's bargain of selling their votes for offices, lands, and titles. By the late 1720s, opponents accused Walpole of setting a low moral tone for the nation itself. A growing opposition press came up with cant names like "Bob Booty" and "Bribemaster General" for the prime minister. In Jonathan Swift's *Gulliver's Travels* of 1726 he appears as Flimnap, the corrupt and vain premier of Lilliput. In Alexander Pope's (1688–1744) *Dunciad* of 1728, he is "Palinarus," who teaches "kings to fiddle and makes senators dance." In *The Beggar's Opera* also of 1728, John Gay (1685–1732) compares him to the crooked jailer Peachum, who acts as a fence for goods stolen by his loyal band of thieves.

But the Old Corps never amounted to a majority of the membership of either house. That is, while they formed the *core* of Walpole's parliamentary support, they could never, by themselves, ensure majorities. In order to maintain control of both houses for 21 years, Sir Robert had to convince independent members that his policies were the right ones. Like a modern politician who watches the polls, seeking what is popular and avoiding what is controversial, Walpole did so by choosing the majority position on the great issues of the day. That is, on the succession, he was a staunch Hanoverian, who developed a spy system to ferret out Jacobite plots. In fact, the Jacobite alternative was not really much of a threat, for the movement to restore the Stuarts was romantic, wildly impractical, and generally incompetent. But as long as Walpole could convince the king and political nation that all Tories were really Jacobites; that all Jacobites were a clear and present danger to the Hanoverian stability; and that he was their nemesis, his power was secure. In religion, Walpole observed that the vast majority of the country was Anglican: there were perhaps 340,000 Dissenters, amounting to about 6 percent of the population, and a mere handful of Catholics and Jews. Rather than pursue traditional Whig Dissenter aims like repeal of the Test Act, he did everything he could to safeguard the remaining privileges of the Church of England. This earned him the support of the Anglican majority in the countryside and Whig bishops in the House of Lords. On finance and foreign policy, he tried to reduce taxes by staying out of wars. While some Whigs and their mercantile allies wanted to repudiate the Treaty of Utrecht in favor of a more aggressive foreign policy, Walpole realized, as Oxford had done, that France, now led by the teenage Louis XV (1710–74; reigned 1715–74), was effectively broken for the time being as a military power and that Utrecht had secured British trade and colonial supremacy for a generation.

On three of these four issues – religion, foreign policy, and government finance – the prime minister sounds very much like a Tory. By choosing popular Tory positions on these issues, he made himself virtually impregnable on them. The loss of something to fight about, combined with the infrequency and expense of elections as a result of the Septennial Act, lowered the country's political temperature. Indeed, it is tempting to argue that there were no major issues facing the British polity for a generation after 1714. That temptation should be resisted, for the prosperity of the late seventeenth and early eighteenth centuries was working a quiet revolution on British society, wrenching it away from strict hierarchy and toward greater social fluidity and individual opportunity, and, thus, disrupting the inherited mental world of the English people. Nevertheless, speaking politically, the half-century or so following Anne's death was far more stable than what came before – or after. Signs of instability would only appear in the 1730s and become serious in the 1750s. But that is a tale for another book. As this one ends, the English had found political peace at home. This, combined with their ability to wage war successfully abroad, produced a vibrant economy and a society on the verge of modernity.

An *Ancien Régime* or a Polite and Commercial People?

Since the late 1980s historians have advanced two competing views of England at the end of our period. One view, promulgated most memorably by J. C. D. Clark, argues that England was in 1714, and in 1760, and perhaps even in 1815, a fundamentally agricultural, traditional, conservative, Royalist, Anglican polity, still dominated by a privileged landed aristocracy. That is, he sees eighteenth-century England as very much an *ancien régime*, not so very different from other contemporary European monarchies or from the Stuart, Tudor, or even medieval polities with which our account started.[3] Other historians, most notably Paul Langford, have focused not so much on what looked backward but what looked forward in eighteenth-century England. That is, while Langford and others would concede that England was still very much run by the old aristocracy in partnership with the monarchy and the Church, he reminds us that the post-Revolutionary English monarchy was, almost uniquely in Europe, a constitutional one; that the Church had competition from nonconformist Protestant faiths; and that the governing partnership was expanding to include the propertied middling orders.[4] Partisans of this view would argue, further, that the aristocracy's hold on the larger society was loosening; that the new wealth created by the commercial, financial, and industrial revolutions was eroding hierarchy, increasing opportunity, and rendering English society much more fluid. England was becoming, to borrow a phrase from the title of a like-minded book, "the first modern society."[5]

Certainly, and despite the fact that the topmost links of the Great Chain of Being had been severed by the Glorious Revolution, English society remained hierarchical. Examined from the top down, this society also looks remarkably stable. The landed aristocracy seemed to have created for itself an ideal world, having tamed, by means of that revolution, both the king on the one hand and the general populace on the other. During the late seventeenth and early eighteenth centuries the English nobility, in particular, often compared itself to that of ancient Rome and the period is often referred to as Britain's Augustan Age. It was also a period in which novelist Henry Fielding's (1707–54) slightly later definition of the word "nobody" – "[a]ll the people in Great Britain, except about 1200"[6] – might equally apply. But this does not mean that the Augustan aristocracy was a closed society. It was relatively open to upstarts from below, and perfectly willing to ally with members of the middling orders for political or economic advantage. The latter gained a new sense of their own respectability and even, by some definitions, gentility as they reaped the benefits of England's growing prosperity. Both the aristocracy and their middling allies, however, worried that the attitudes and appetites of the lower orders threatened stability, property, and deference. They feared that those attitudes and appetites would result in crime, disorder, riot, even revolution. In short, if England was both ordered and stable at the beginning of the eighteenth century, that order was often thought to be fragile, that stability provisional.

The Demographic and Economic Base

To understand what was happening in English society at the end of the Stuart period, it is necessary to confront the basic facts of demographic and economic change. First, the dizzying population growth which characterized the period 1550–1650 slowed down and, for a few decades, even reversed. That is, the number of people in England and Wales is estimated to have actually fallen from 5.5 million in 1661 to 5.2 million in 1686 before rising to 5.4 million in 1701 and 5.7 million by 1721. The population of the British Isles as a whole in 1714 would be about 9.5 million: 5,600,000 for England and Wales, 1,100,000 for Scotland, and a further 2,800,000 for Ireland.[7] The demographic downturn is hard to explain.[8] During this period agricultural improvements made famine almost a thing of the past in England, if not in the Celtic lands (Scotland experienced famine in 1696–9, Ireland in 1708–10). In fact, England became a net exporter of grain in the eighteenth century. Still, occasional bad harvests, particularly in the 1690s, raised food prices, reducing consumption and, so, resistance to disease. Illness was always a factor: 1665–7 saw the last, but arguably the most devastating, outbreak of plague in English history, killing 70,000–100,000 Londoners. Epidemics of diphtheria, dysentery, influenza, measles, scarlet fever, smallpox, typhoid fever, typhus, and whooping cough also ripped through the populace periodically. All were virulent and often fatal, particularly among children. Professional medical help remained beyond the reach of most English men and women, and would have done them little good in any case: only after about 1750 would new scientific techniques have an impact on the curing, as opposed to the diagnosis, of disease. This left most villagers to rely on the local priest, cunning woman, or midwife for folkloric advice and herbal remedies. Their effectiveness was limited. Average life expectancy sank in the 1680s to under 30 years. The odds improved between 1700 and 1720, when the number of epidemics decreased and the harvests were generally good. As a result, life expectancy rose from about 37 in 1700 to perhaps 42 by the 1750s. But even as the odds improved, the lingering perception of a flooded labor market, combined with political and religious turmoil, led perhaps 300,000 English men and women to emigrate to America between 1650 and 1700.

But the real motor for population stagnation in this period (as for its rise later) was age at marriage. A higher proportion of the population chose either not to marry (some 20–25 percent), or to do so later than their Tudor and early Stuart predecessors. In a sample of 12 parishes, the average age at marriage for males during the last half of the seventeenth century was 28 years, for females 26 years. This meant a later start to childrearing, smaller families, and, ultimately, fewer people. Those families were kept smaller still by infant mortality, which remained high. Fifteen percent of all infants died within the first year of life; a further 10 percent expired before their tenth birthday. While it was still true that anyone who made it to their thirtieth birthday had a good chance of seeing 30 years more, old people remained scarce in this society. Rather, 40 percent of the population was under 20. This helps to explain the contemporary obsession with order and "reformation of manners" (see below): young people always strike their elders as being short on both. Finally, the death rate remained high – 30 per 1,000 per year – which left many broken marriages and families.

The slowdown in population growth was crucial in economic terms.[9] As in the period after the Black Death, the number of agricultural workers fell in relation to the amount of land available. This placed those workers in high demand, allowing them to command good wages and low rents. Combined with generally good harvests in the 1680s and 1700–20, it also meant lower food prices. This was all good news for poor tenant farmers, but bad news for landowners, who, remember, also bore a hefty Land Tax. Nevertheless, agriculture remained the beating heart of the English economy, feeding the whole population, employing most of it, and enriching its most powerful members. At the end of our period, two-thirds of the land in England was still being cultivated and perhaps 80 percent of the population lived in rural villages or hamlets. Most still worked as tenants on the estates of noble or gentle landowners; it has been estimated that 15–20 percent of the land was owned by peers and the wealthier gentry, 45–50 percent by the middling and lesser gentry, 25–35 percent by yeomen or husband-men, and just 5–10 percent by the Crown or the Church.

The proportion of land held by the great magnates was increasing. Low food prices and rents, high wages and taxes annoyed big landowners, but they were rarely fatal. In fact, the period 1660–1730 saw the construction of increasingly magnificent country houses by wealthy aristocrats. Rather, it was the middling and lesser landowners, the smaller gentry and yeomen who were hurt most significantly by the economic situation at the turn of the eighteenth century. This group formed the backbone of the Tory party, embracing Swift's critique of the monied men, military contractors, and officers who seemed to profit from the wars. Often, these smallholders fell into debt and had to sell to the large landowners, sometimes becoming tenants on what was once their own land.

For those who could still afford to farm their land, the age saw a number of agricultural improvements which could lead to big profits. From 1660 on, great landowners increasingly hired full-time stewards to better manage their lands. New fodder crops like turnips and clover meant that animals could be kept year round. This meant more fertilizer (manure), which produced richer soil, which yielded more wheat, rye, oats, and barley, which resulted in surpluses that could be sold to the continent. Where the soil was not so rich, there was always dairy or sheep farming: the 11 million sheep in England estimated by Gregory King in 1688 outnumbered people two to one. The same aristocrats who improved their holdings through enclosure and use of new fodder crops also exploited their mineral rights, becoming proprietors of mines and quarries. Finally, while some poured their profits into conspicuous consumption – say, a new country palace or a London townhouse – many more invested in trading ventures or high finance than had done so a century earlier.

Overseas trade may not have been the anchor of the British economy, but it was the marquee arena that got most of the attention of contemporary writers and government officials. In fact, the desire to expand England's foreign trade figured in every decision to go to war between 1585 and 1763. The Commonwealth and restored Stuart governments had laid important foundations for growth in the Navigation Acts and the acquisition of territory in the West Indies. The former eventually broke the commercial domination of the Dutch; the latter made possible the lucrative sugar trade. Meanwhile, the period 1650–1730 saw another boom in the American colonial population (including the British West Indies and, from 1713, Newfoundland, but excluding slaves) from 55,000 to 538,000. That population supplied about half of Britain's transatlantic imports and absorbed almost a quarter of her exports. In addition, the period after the Revolution of 1688–9 saw the breakup of the old trading company monopolies, such as the Royal Africa, and Russia Companies; the expansion of English trade into new markets; the continued rise of the new draperies; and the expansion of credit facilities with the stock market boom and financial revolution. Against this could be placed the devastation wrought by French privateers on English shipping during the wars. But the eventual harvest from those wars was a bumper crop for trade: above all, the commercial provisions of Utrecht, which expanded British trade in the Mediterranean, Canada, Italy, Spain, and the Spanish colonies.

Overall, British trade expanded in total gross value from £7.9 million in 1663–9 to £14.5 million by 1722–4. Imports passed exports in value, for Britain's most important trade was no longer the export of wool but the importation of sugar from the West Indies and the reexport of sugar, colonial produce, or Asian goods to Europe. Demand for sugar rose steadily, from £26.2 million in the late 1660s, to £42.5 million by the early 1700s, to £92.6 million by the late 1720s. Increasingly, that sugar was harvested by African slaves rather than indentured servants. During the late seventeenth century, the notorious "triangular trade" hit its stride. First, English slavers shipped metal goods and textiles to Africa where they were traded for native people, usually captives in local wars. In the second leg of the triangle, those captives were then transported, under appalling conditions, to the New World at the rate of over 5,000 a year. If they did not die on the voyage (the death rate on the late seventeenth-century "middle passage" across the Atlantic has been estimated at 13–23 percent), they were sold to plantation owners in the Spanish colonies; or in the British West Indies, for whom they harvested sugar; or in Virginia and the Carolinas, where they harvested tobacco. That sugar and tobacco were then sent to American or British ports for refining and distribution to Great Britain and Europe – the third leg of this notorious triangle of greed, demand, and human misery. As for the slaves, wherever they ended up, they were treated like human machinery, forced to work in a sweltering climate and under brutal conditions on vast plantations whose land had been claimed by Europeans as a right, but whose landlords were often resident in the mother country. The Herefordshire squire Ferdinando Gorges (fl. 1630–80) is a prime example: he was known as "king of the Blacks" because he first made his wealth as a Barbados slave trader before investing it in land during the late seventeenth century. In short, much of Britain's prosperity in the Augustan period and beyond was erected on the backs of captive and exploited Africans and at the expense of Native Americans driven slowly from what had once been their land.

Asian goods amounted to just 13 percent of England's total import trade. They were led by imports of cottons, silks, spices, and indigo from India and, by the

1720s, tea from China. Unfortunately, the East India Company still had little but wool to offer in return, though the new draperies were somewhat more attractive than the old heavy woolens. For the most part, therefore, the English paid for Asian goods with bullion (silver and gold), some £537,000 a year by the 1720s.

The English people increasingly wanted and could afford what their empire and trading partners had to offer. As the population slowed down and the labor market shrank, wages rose, providing more disposable income for ordinary men and women. Large landowners, professionals, merchants, and monied men were doing well enough to want luxury items. They demanded madeira and port wine from Portugal; figs, raisins, and oranges from Spain; silks and olive oil from Italy; sugar, tobacco, furs, and salt-fish from America; coffee from the Middle East; and, as we have just seen, the many goods of India and China.[10] The continent wanted these things too; British merchants, British sea captains, and British ports exploited this desire, dominating the reexport trade. Since the Navigation Acts stipulated that every commodity sent to or from a British colony or possession had to ship in an English (after 1707 a British) vessel, the English merchant marine expanded to meet the demand. It rose from 115,000 ships in 1629 to 323,000 in 1702, becoming the largest merchant marine in the world. Since the same legislation required that most of this trade (including all bulk items, like sugar) had to pass through a British port, the yields to the king from Customs grew, as did the wealth of his merchant subjects. Most of this trade flowed to Britain and the continent through London: in 1722–4 the metropolis handled 80 percent of England's imports, 67 percent of its exports, and 87 percent of its reexports. But the trade boom also enriched western ports like Bristol, Liverpool, and, in Scotland, Glasgow. Cities with naval bases and dockyards, like Plymouth and Portsmouth, also grew with the wars. Britain had become the great crossroads of the world's trade.

Later in the century, the British economy would make another leap by becoming the first to industrialize. Some historians have argued that the industrial revolution was partially bankrolled by the profits from trade. But that was in the future in 1714. During the previous half-century English industry grew slowly and steadily, taking the first tentative steps toward the greater use of machines and mass production. Shipbuilding on the coasts, the Midlands and Durham coal industries, tin-mining in Cornwall, and iron-mining in Yorkshire all required many workers in one place. There is also evidence of mass production in the refining of sugar and the making of silk and ribbons. In 1724 John Lombe's silk mill at Derby employed 300 women and children working two 12–hour shifts: the first real factory – accompanied by the exploitation of labor that went with it. The cities that would spearhead the industrial revolution – Birmingham, Leeds, Manchester, and Sheffield – were already notable centers for the production of metal goods in 1714. By the early eighteenth century, Sheffield scissorsmiths, filesmiths, and razormakers were catering to markets in London, Virginia, Jamaica, and elsewhere. Immigrants, many of them war refugees attracted by religious toleration and free trade, were important innovators: French Huguenots and other Protestants driven from the continent by Louis XIV spurred the English porcelain, clock, silk, and paper industries. But most manufacturing still relied either on the small craftsman working in his shop with apprentices and family members, or, in the textile industry especially, the "putting-out" system, whereby a cotton factor, say, would distribute raw materials to individual housewives over a wide geographic area for spinning and weaving.

Such a traditional, decentralized system of manufacture depended, paradoxically, on an increasingly sophisticated system of distribution and communication. A growing service economy facilitated the movement of goods and services throughout England, making possible specialized centers such as Sheffield. A more integrated national transportation grid emerged, often with Parliament's active encouragement. Parliamentary statutes authorized the dredging of rivers and the establishment of turnpikes. Bulky items, like grain and coal, were shipped down the many navigable rivers or along the coasts. But cattle, always shipped to market on the hoof, needed roads. Turnpikes were toll-roads which could be much better maintained over long distances than the patchwork of back-roads maintained by parish authorities. By the mid-1650s there were regular stage services between London and Exeter to the west, Chester to the north-west, and York and Newcastle to the north. Important routes would begin, end, and cross other routes at large inns. These provided not only accommodation but food, drink, entertainment, postal services, stabling, and a place where businessmen, such as drovers who brought cattle to market or corn factors who transported grain, could make deals. Wares could also be displayed and deals made at fairs and in the great market towns. But after 1660 fairs and markets grew less necessary as the transportation network improved and as craftsmen increasingly sold their goods in established shops with a ready stock. According to one estimate, the number of market towns fell from about 800 in 1690 to just under 600 by 1720. Finally, the more remote parts of the countryside also relied on less substantial traders – peddlers, hawkers, chapmen, and tinkers – to distribute books, metalware, ribbons, and other small manufactured goods. These individuals could not afford to stay at something so grand as an inn, often taking shelter in a farmer's barn or hayloft.

If the transportation system was developing, so were the nation's information and credit facilities. The establishment of the London penny post and regular newspapers at the end of the seventeenth century made it possible to keep track of business in far-flung parts of England and to follow the shipping news. At the same time, some of the big goldsmith-banking houses evolved into fully fledged banks. There were 25 of these in London by the 1720s. They received deposits, paid out interest, issued notes of exchange, and made loans. Since the legal rate of interest was, for much of the period, under 6 percent, money was relatively cheap, loans readily accessible, and new ventures easy to start. Thus, by 1714 the wealthy aristocrat or successful merchant had some real choices in what to do with his money: he could deposit it with a bank or he could invest it in government bonds, one of the great trading companies, or one of the new stock companies which proliferated from the 1690s. New companies sold stock in products and ventures as diverse as glass bottles, convex lights, lute strings, sword blades, gunpowder, mines, and fisheries. As this variety implies, there was, at first, no government regulation of the new stock market; nor were professional standards very high. Until the first real London stock exchange was established in 1773, "jobbers" traded stocks in the informal surroundings of Jonathan's or Garroway's coffee-houses. There was as yet nothing to prevent a charlatan from selling stock in a company which did not exist or had no real prospect of producing a profit. The catastrophe of the South Sea Bubble was only the most notable symptom of the "wild West" nature of this side of economic life. Of the 93 joint-stock companies in existence in 1695, only 21 were still around in 1717. Needless to say, stockjobbers and brokers had a very low reputation. Nevertheless, here more than in any other branch of the Augustan economy, a small investment could yield a big profit in very little time. But whole fortunes could be lost just as fast.

The ever-present sense of risk led to some modern solutions. The first insurance companies appeared in London at the end of the seventeenth century. By the 1680s it was possible to purchase fire insurance; marine insurance, against shipping losses, came even earlier. Once again, new requirements led to informal, ad hoc arrangements which were institutionalized only after our period. Thus, Lloyd's of London began life as the coffee-house where merchant investors and captains met; later in the eighteenth century it would evolve into the greatest marine insurance company in the world. Altogether, the initiatives described above were moving early Hanoverian England toward an integrated national economy which was also at the center of world trade.

The Ruling Elite and its Culture

At the beginning of the eighteenth century, the ruling elite was still dominated by the landed aristocracy, divided into the nobility and the gentry. The British nobility (those holding the titles of duke, marquess, earl, viscount, or baron) consisted of about 180 English peers whose titles gave them the right to sit in the House of Lords at Westminster; about 50 Scottish peers, 16 of whom were elected as representatives to the Lords; and about 150 Irish peers, all of whom sat in the upper house of the Irish Parliament. The English peerage had expanded in size under the later Stuarts, partly because successive governments used aristocratic titles to reward powerful supporters and to ensure majorities in the Lords. Despite this expansion in numbers, the titled nobility still comprised but a tiny minority of the British population, not approaching even 1 percent. In fact, because the Whig majority was so secure, the rate of growth slowed after 1714, reducing the openness of the peerage to new blood. Thus, there is a sense of the upper classes "closing ranks" and distancing themselves from their inferiors at the beginning of the eighteenth century. This "withdrawal of the elite" manifested itself physically in the impressive gates and high walls which they increasingly erected around their manor houses. Nevertheless, the English peerage remained far more open to new men than its European counterparts. It also remained paramount in the countryside. While the days of private affinities were long gone, local government, the militia in particular, was still, in effect, at the lord lieuten-ant's beck and call – as James II had found to his cost in 1688.

The nobility remained prosperous, commanding, despite its small size, a very high proportion of the nation's wealth. As we have seen, peers and their greater gentry cousins owned nearly one-fifth of the land in England, and that proportion was rising. The average English peer made perhaps £5,000–6,000 a year, with the greatest magnates (the dukes of Bedford, Beaufort, Marlborough, Newcastle, and Ormond and Lord Brooke) making perhaps £20,000–40,000 by 1714. The annual incomes of Scottish and Irish peers were much smaller, averaging around £500 – a great, if not quite princely, sum. Nearly all peers relied for their wealth primarily on their landed estates, namely, the profits of agriculture and the yield from rents. As indicated above, these profits were often compromised after 1693 by the Land Tax and the depleted labor market, which kept rents and demand for food low. Nevertheless, the big estates not only weathered these difficulties, they profited from them by absorbing the holdings of those who could not do so. Moreover, as we have seen, since the middle of the seventeenth century if not before, enterprising peers had diversified. Some did well from officeholding: a great court or government place could yield anywhere from £1,000 to £5,000 a year in salary, perquisites (like the right to sell subordinate offices), or pensions. Noble families also invested in the new joint-stock companies, trading ventures, canals, mines, turnpikes, and the whole panoply of government financial instru-ments: bonds, lotteries, and the Bank of England. Finally, all great landowning families sought to conserve their holdings by passing them on to a single heir, almost invariably the eldest son, who was usually forbidden, through a legal device called the strict settlement, from alienating any of the family property. At the same time, holdings might be extended through an advantageous marriage – sometimes with another aristocrat, sometimes into mercantile or professional wealth – or the acquisition of such land as did come onto the market. As a result of these initiatives, most noble families in England, at least, were more than able to compensate for the disappointing performance of their landed estates.

Paradoxically, while elder sons consolidated their holdings behind deer parks and high walls, the cold realities of primogeniture forced younger sons into apprenticeships, the professions, and marriage into the middling orders. During the reign of Charles II, an Italian visitor was shocked, thinking that English nobles and gentry apprenticed their sons to "masters of the lowest trades, such as tailors, shoemakers, innkeepers."[11] In fact, while the nobility seemed to close ranks against their inferiors in general, individual families did maintain numerous connections across class lines.

Even more than in previous centuries, their affluence enabled members of the peerage to live lives of ostentation, leisure, and grace, as well as political conse-quence. In fact, the century after 1660 saw the zenith of aristocratic wealth and power in England. During this period the most prominent noble families demonstrated that wealth and power by erecting great baroque palaces. The years 1690–1710 saw the building or rebuilding of, among others, Blenheim Palace in

Oxfordshire (in this one case out of public funds) for the duke of Marlborough, Chatsworth House in Derbyshire for the duke of Devonshire, Petworth House in Sussex for the duke of Somerset, and Castle Howard in Yorkshire for the duke of Norfolk (see plate 26). These palaces were often designed or renovated by the greatest architects of the day, such as Sir John Vanbrugh (1664–1726), Nicholas Hawksmoor (1661–1736), William Talman (fl. 1670–1700), or William Kent (1684–1748). They were decorated by its greatest artists, such as history painter Louis Laguerre (1663–1721), carver Grinling Gibbons, and ironworker Jean Tijou (fl. 1689–1711). They were filled with expensive furnishings, paintings, porcelain, and books, and surrounded by elaborate formal gardens designed by men like Henry Wise (1653–1738), Charles Bridgman (d. 1738), and Kent to demonstrate that even the forces of nature obeyed the commands of their noble proprietors. For an ambitious peer, such a house embodied his wealth and taste and formed the political and social headquarters for networks of friends and followers which extended throughout the county and beyond.

And yet, because their masters played so important a role at court and in London, these houses were only occupied by them for about half the year. From early fall to late spring, with the possible exception of the Christmas holidays, their owners lived in London. By 1714 the landed aristocracy was increasingly "amphibious" between the country and the capital and at home in both. As in

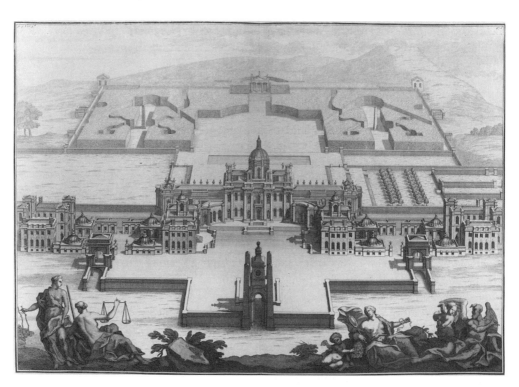

Plate 26 *Castle Howard, engraving. The British Library.*

previous periods, the males attended the House of Lords when Parliament was in session, and some held high office. They and their families enjoyed the pleasures of the season, attending the court, the theater, the opera (newly imported from Italy about 1705), and concerts. Aristocratic men could relax at taverns, coffee-houses, and, increasingly, private clubs (see below). In order to take convenient advantage of these delights and responsibilities, British nobles sometimes built splendid London townhouses, smaller versions of their country houses, also designed and decorated by famous artists. Finally, by the close of the seventeenth century, members of the ruling elite could pursue a second season at the end of the summer at one of the great spas such as Tunbridge Wells in Kent, Epsom in Surrey, and, most importantly, Bath in Somerset. In fact, these long absences from their country seats may have weakened direct noble control of the localities and contributed to the perception of elite withdrawal. As our period closes, that control was increasingly devolving onto the shoulders of the gentry.

Closely allied with the nobility – so that historians often consider them part of the same class – were the gentry (baronets, knights, and plain gentlemen). By the beginning of the eighteenth century the definition of gentility was even vaguer than it had been under the Tudors. The border separating a gentleman from a prosperous (or prosperous-looking) commoner was blurry and permeable, leading to a much more open society than in the rest of Europe. By the same token, it became increasingly difficult, at court, at a London masked ball, or while taking the waters at Bath, to tell who was gentle and who was not. The lead character in Defoe's novel *Moll Flanders* (1722) discovered this difficulty when she sought to marry "this amphibious creature, this land-water thing called a gentleman-tradesman," without realizing that her intended beau might look the part of a gentleman, but his status was all a mirage based on credit. Gentlemen no longer felt it necessary to take out coats of arms or even purchase landed estates. The end of the Stuart period saw the first "urban gentry" or "pseudo-gentry" – often wealthy merchants or professionals – who preferred the amenities of the town to the pleasures of the country.

The seventeenth-century demographer Gregory King (1648–1712) thought that there were about 16,500 gentry families in England in 1688 (see table 1),[12] but modern estimates range as high as 25,000. There was a smaller number of Scottish and Irish gentlemen. Altogether, the English gentry owned over half of the land in England. Only the most prominent sat in the House of Commons: the British Commons after the 1707 Union had 558 members, but not all of these were landed gentlemen. By this time, the average gentleman made perhaps £500 a year, but that "average" disguises wide variations in wealth, power, and status. Historians often distinguish between the "greater gentry" and the "lesser gentry." Members of the greater gentry had incomes averaging over £1,000 a year, and might make as much as £10,000–15,000. As a result, they lived like all but the greatest peers. Like their noble cousins, they often possessed multiple estates; built great country houses; held a parliamentary seat or influence on one; took office, if not at the center then locally as a deputy lieutenant, sheriff, or JP; and split their time between their estates and the London season, Bath Spa, or (horse-)

Table 1 Gregory King's Scheme of the income and expense of the several families of England, calculated for the year 1688

Number of Families	Ranks, Degrees, Titles and Qualifications	Heads per Family	Number of Persons	Yearly income per Family (£ s.)		Yearly income in general (£)	Yearly income per Head (£ s. d.)			Yearly expense per Head (£ s. d.)			Yearly increase per Head (£ s. d.)			Yearly increase in general (£)
160	Temporal Lords	40	6,400	3,200		512,000	80	0	0	70	0	0	10	0	0	64,000
26	Spiritual Lords	20	520	1,300		33,800	65	0	0	45	0	0	20	0	0	10,400
800	Baronets	16	12,800	800		704,000	55	0	0	49	0	0	6	0	0	76,800
600	Knights	13	7,800	650		390,000	50	0	0	45	0	0	5	0	0	39,000
3,000	Esquires	10	30,000	450		1,200,000	45	0	0	41	0	0	4	0	0	120,000
12,000	Gentlemen	8	96,000	280		2,880,000	35	0	0	32	0	0	3	0	0	288,000
5,000	Persons in greater Offices and Places	8	40,000	240		1,200,000	30	0	0	26	0	0	4	0	0	160,000
5,000	Persons in lesser Offices and Places	6	30,000	120		600,000	20	0	0	17	0	0	3	0	0	90,000
2,000	Eminent Merchants and Traders by Sea	8	16,000	400		800,000	50	0	0	37	0	0	13	0	0	208,000
8,000	Lesser Merchants and Traders by Sea	6	48,000	198		1,600,000	33	0	0	27	0	0	6	0	0	288,000
10,000	Persons in the Law	7	70,000	154		1,540,000	22	0	0	18	0	0	4	0	0	280,000
2,000	Eminent Clergy-men	6	12,000	72		144,000	12	0	0	10	0	0	2	0	0	24,000
8,000	Lesser Clergy-men	5	40,000	50		400,000	10	0	0	9	4	0	0	16	0	32,000
40,000	Freeholders of the better sort	7	280,000	91		3,640,000	13	0	0	11	15	0	1	5	0	350,000
120,000	Freeholders of the lesser sort	5½	660,000	55		6,600,000	10	0	0	9	10	0	0	10	0	330,000
150,000	Farmers	5	750,000	42	10	6,375,000	8	10	0	8	5	0	0	5	0	187,500

15,000	Persons in Liberal Arts and Sciences	5	75,000	60	900,000	12 0 0	11 0 0	1 0 0	75,000
50,000	Shopkeepers and Tradesmen	4½	225,000	45	2,250,000	10 0 0	9 0 0	1 0 0	225,000
60,000	Artizans and Handicrafts	4	240,000	38	2,280,000	9 10 0	9 0 0	0 10 0	120,000
5,000	Naval Officers	4	20,000	80	400,000	20 0 0	18 0 0	2 0 0	40,000
4,000	Military Officers	4	16,000	60	240,000	15 0 0	14 0 0	1 0 0	16,000
500,586		5⅓	2,675,520	68 18	34,488,800	12 18 0	11 15 4	1 2 8	3,023,700
								Decrease	*Decrease*
50,000	Common Seamen	3	150,000	20	1,000,000	7 0 0	7 10 0	0 10 0	75,000
364,000	Labouring People and Out Servants	3½	1,275,000	15	5,460,000	4 10 0	4 12 0	0 2 0	127,500
400,000	Cottagers and Paupers	3¼	1,300,000	6 10	2,000,000	2 0 0	2 5 0	0 5 0	325,000
35,000	Common Soldiers	2	70,000	14	490,000	7 0 0	7 10 0	0 10 0	35,000
849,000		3¼	2,795,000	10 10	8,950,000	3 5 0	3 9 0	0 4 0	562,500
	Vagrants; as Gipsies, Thieves, Beggars, &c.		30,000		60,000	2 0 0	4 0 0	2 0 0	60,000
	So the general Account is								
500,586	Increasing the Wealth of the Kingdom	5⅓	2,675,520	68 18	34,488,800	12 18 0	11 15 4	1 2 8	3,023,700
849,000	Decreasing the Wealth of the Kingdom	3¾	2,825,000	10 10	9,010,000	3 3 0	3 7 6	0 4 6	622,500
1,349,586	Neat Totals	4 1/13	5,500,520	32 5	43,491,800	7 18 0	7 9 3	0 8 9	2,401,200

King's estimates of income and expenditure are generally regarded as too low. For figures based upon more recent scholarship, see the text.

race meetings at Newmarket or Epsom. Walpole, with his premiership, his great estate at Houghton in Norfolk, and the splendid art collection which it held (today the core of the famous Hermitage Collection in Russia), is the most glittering example of the type.

In sharp contrast stood the lesser gentry, whose incomes might be as low as £200. Often, they held one poor estate with a few tenants. Their local influence was very limited: they rarely held offices above that of JP or sat in Parliament, for they could not afford the cost of mounting a campaign, especially after passage of the Septennial Act in 1716. While the lesser gentry might be consulted by the real aristocratic leaders of their counties, they would not have a determining influence. Their houses were comfortable, not spectacular; and they rarely left them to go to London. They might, however, take advantage of the growing amenities of the county town, which, in the eighteenth century, was increasingly likely to build assembly rooms where dances, concerts, and even occasional theatrical productions might be held. Political outsiders, they tended to sympathize with the Tories.

In 1714 as in 1485, it was the landed aristocracy who ran the country, determined its relations with other countries, and set the tone of its culture. For most of the period covered by this book, they did so at the royal court. Until at least the 1680s, the court was the epicenter not only of politics but of government finance, religious, social, and cultural life, and royal favor. It was, moreover, the great emporium for acquiring places of all kinds, not only in the household but in the Church, the judiciary, the foreign service, the revenue services (Customs, Excise, Land Tax, etc.), the armed forces, and local government. The court also provided impressive architecture, splendid parks, sumptuous decor and furnishings, dramatic ceremonies, balls, concerts, plays, the royal art collection, free meals, an endless source of gossip, and the greatest marriage market in England. In the Chapel Royal could be heard "excellent Preaching... by the most eminent Bish[ops] & Divines of the Nation,"[13] as well as magnificent choral anthems and organ voluntaries by its greatest composers, Matthew Locke (1622–77), John Blow, and, above all, Henry Purcell. Their music was baroque: contrapuntally complex and heavily ornamented, it was thought to complement the awesome power of absolutist monarchs. The baroque style had its architectural counterpart in the imposing designs of Hugh May (1622–84) and Sir Christopher Wren at Whitehall, Windsor, and Winchester; the elaborate carving of Grinling Gibbons; and the ornate allegorical ceiling painting of Antonio Verrio (1639?–1707). The denizens of this court were painted in the baroque style by Lely and Kneller; their conversation celebrated in the new comedy of manners being written by "court wits" such as Etherege or Wycherley; their politics and their sexual escapades satirized by poets like Rochester or Marvell. Rarely has so much talent been brought together in one place.

But the court's social and cultural lead began to evaporate even before Charles II died. First, continuous money problems and successive retrenchments reduced the attractiveness of the court. In addition, the brief attempt at a Catholic restoration under James II, William III's obsession with business and lack of social graces, Anne's poor health, and George I's desire to be left alone all put a damper on court life. Simultaneously, the "rage of party" followed by the post-1714 Whig ascendancy dictated that at any given time, one half of the political world felt unwelcome at court. Finally, and perhaps above all, the diversion of government revenue to the period's wars left the Crown unable to sustain patronage of the arts and finer pleasures on a grand scale. This is part of the point of the Matthew Prior anecdote told in the previous chapter: while Louis XIV was pouring the treasure of France into both Versailles and a series of losing wars, later Stuart monarchs were neglecting their courts in favor of winning those wars. The destruction by fire of the vast palace of Whitehall in 1698 both sealed and symbolized the court's social and cultural decline; it would be a century before the monarchy once again possessed a great palace in central London.

The decline of court culture did not mean the decline of elite culture. As we have seen, the landed aristocracy took up much of the slack in both town and country. They had always found entertainment and companionship at the public theater, taverns, cock matches, and horse-races. After the Restoration, the concert hall, the pleasure garden, the coffee-house, and the all-male club also competed for their attention. Some of these institutions were open to the general public as well. Taverns, pleasure gardens, sporting events, and, from the 1650s onwards, London's coffee-houses (see plate 25, p. 332) mixed aristocrats with monied men, merchants, and professionals. Rather than cater to a particular social rank, individual coffee-houses tended to attract those with particular interests: overseas merchants congregated at Lloyd's, stockjobbers at Jonathan's and Garroway's, poets at Will's, prose writers at Button's, scholars at the Grecian, Tory politicians at the Cocoa Tree, Whigs at the St. James's.

But other aristocratic pursuits were more exclusive. The Restoration and eighteenth-century theater was more expensive, and so less accessible to the "groundlings," than its Elizabethan forebear. Private clubs were, in part, an aristocratic reaction to the openness of the coffee-house: their membership was more narrowly restricted to the upper classes and their interests more focused. This is not to say that those interests were more elevated: White's catered to gamblers, the Beef-steak Club to gluttons, a series of Hell-fire Clubs to rowdy nobles interested in general mayhem. Political clubs, the Kit-Cat in particular, operated by 1700 like small kingless courts, toasting a roster of beauties who, a few years earlier, might have been painted by Lely or Kneller for a royal patron. Elite women helped shape this new sociability – which in the eighteenth century would establish "gentility," not honor, as the standard for elite social conduct – as balls, musical assemblies, and promenades became an important part of elite culture from 1700. It was increasingly in these venues, and not at court, that art and literature were commissioned, business transacted, political plots laid, and the latest fashions put on display.

Aristocrats also supported artists individually. In 1710 Georg Frideric Handel, the greatest opera composer of the age, came to London to work for Queen Anne; by the end of the decade he was composing anthems for the fabulously wealthy James Brydges, duke of Chandos (1673–1744), whose estate at Cannons, Middlesex, boasted a full orchestra. Lord Somers gave important early support to Swift and his fellow essayists Joseph Addison (1672–1719) and Richard Steele (1672–1729), while Lord Halifax did the same for the playwright William Congreve (1670–1729). Lord Treasurer Oxford employed a stable of writers, including Swift and Defoe, to support his administration. This reminds us that aristocratic patrons had political as well as aesthetic motivations: a talented writer was a valuable asset in the propaganda wars fought between the two parties. Oxford also provided a model for eighteenth-century connoisseurship by assembling a magnificent collection of books and manuscripts which later became part of the nucleus for the British Museum.

The new wealth flooding into later Stuart England enriched not only the landed elite but also merchants and professionals. Some of that money eventually found its way into the hands of artists. The theater was already a "public" venue at the end of the sixteenth century; a little over a century later it was dominated by great entrepreneurial producers, like John James Heidegger (ca. 1659–1749) or Christopher (d. 1714) and John (ca. 1682–1761) Rich, who were adept at appealing to changing aristocratic and popular tastes. For example, after the clergy attacked the comedy of manners as immoral in the 1690s, producers more or less abandoned it in favor of opera and revivals of Shakespeare. In 1708, Heidegger pioneered the first masquerade balls in London, the major attraction to which was that attendees could transcend their own class and personal reputation by hiding behind masks. In other words, a well-dressed army officer or tradesman could hob-nob with a countess.

Sometimes artists banded together to act as their own impresarios. John Banister (1630–79), a royal musician disgruntled at his uncertain pay, organized the first public concerts in Europe in December 1672. They were put on a more regular basis by Thomas Britton (1644–1714), a small coal merchant who presented professional musicians in the room over his London shop from 1678. Conditions were not ideal: the room was "not much bigger than the Bunghole of a Cask."[14] But Britton's concerts featured the best artists of the day, including Handel, and they were supported by the nobility. English Church musicians, who by 1714 were called on less and less to perform at great court ceremonial occasions, used the annual Festivals of the Sons of the Clergy, a glittering charity event, to showcase their talents. By 1714 London boasted a number of regular concert halls as well as Vauxhall Gardens, where music could always be heard by a paying public. The English metropolis was definitely "on the circuit" of great musical capitals that any touring musician had to conquer. Beyond London, the Three Choirs Festival drew singers to the cathedral cities of Gloucester, Hereford, and Worcester from 1713, while music societies were founded in a variety of English provincial cities.

The literary equivalent of a Heidegger or a Britton was the publisher and Kit-Cat Club member Jacob Tonson (1656–1736). He made a fortune (£50,000) selling the works of Addison, Congreve, Dryden, Milton, Prior, Swift, Vanbrugh, and Wycherley, often through subscription lists, whereby sponsors would undertake to support publication collectively. More occasional work – newspapers, essays, almanacs, political broadsides, advice books, travel books, true crime narratives – was churned out by an army of hack writers who congregated in the area around Moorfields, London, known as "Grub Street." The period 1660–1714 saw the rise of the regular newspaper. There had been newspapers during the Civil War, but most had ceased publication after a few issues, and the Cromwellian regime shut down all but pro-government newspapers in the 1650s. The Restoration regime continued this policy of censorship with the Licensing Act of 1662 (see chapter 9). In 1665 it established the *Gazette* as its official mouthpiece; it still publishes today. Licensing lapsed briefly during the Exclusion Crisis and several partisan newspapers flourished. After the Licensing Act expired for good in 1695, *The Post Boy*, *The Post Man*, and *The Flying Post* offered their own slant on the news three times a week. In 1702 the first daily newspaper, *The Daily Courant*, appeared. By the end of George I's reign a number of provincial newspapers would be founded, including *The Worcester Post Man*, *The Newcastle Courant*, and the Norwich *Transactions of the Universe*. Not all periodical publications were strictly news-oriented. Defoe's *Review* (1704–13) and Swift's *Examiner* (1710–11) offered political commentary, while Addison and Steele's *Tatler* (1709–10) and *Spectator* (1711–12 and 1714) delivered social and cultural criticism in brilliant prose essays which did much to perfect the English language and entertain the literate reader. On a less sublime level, John Dunton's *Athenian Mercury* (1690–7) answered questions on any and all subjects, popularizing the latest ideas in science and philosophy. Dunton particularly encouraged questions from women. This period saw the appearance of the first published female authors, including the playwrights Aphra Behn (1640–89) and Susannah Centlivre (1669–1723), the novelist and political satirist Mary Delarivière (better known as Mrs. Manley, 1663–1724), and the social critic Mary Astell (1668–1731). But the biggest sellers were occasional, topical publications: Sacheverell's notorious sermon on *The Perils of False Brethren* (1709) sold 100,000 copies; Defoe's equally topical *True-Born Englishman* (1701), which satirized the xenophobia of those who opposed the Hanoverian succession, sold 80,000.

As this implies, a ready market for literature of all kinds replaced the court as a writer's chief means of support. Alexander Pope, whose poetic career was just getting started as this book ends, is often described as the first writer to be able to ignore royal and aristocratic patronage almost entirely (necessary because he was a Roman Catholic) and rely solely on his sales to an appreciative public. Behn preceded him, however, in having a successful literary career with a minimum of royal and noble encouragement. Perhaps Defoe best represents the changing relationship between writer and reading (paying) public. Today, he is best known for his great novels *Robinson Crusoe* (1719), *Moll Flanders, Journal of the Plague Year* (1722), and *Roxana* (1724). Cheap, abbreviated versions of the first two were stock-in-trade for chapmen to sell to the laboring English poor for decades, but the absence of copyright made it unlikely that Defoe realized much profit. Rather, it was the mercantile boosterism of his *Tour Though the Whole Island of Great Britain* (1724–6) which enriched him by its popularity among readers of the upper and middling orders (seven editions within 50 years).

Increasingly after 1660, members of the merchant and professional classes could afford to imitate their betters and, so, create demand here and in other areas of consumption as well, by having a portrait painted, purchasing maps and prints, or outfitting themselves with clocks and watches.

Nevertheless, the tone was set and the tune called by the ruling elite. If the culture of the Stuart royal court was baroque, then that of the Hanoverian aristocracy was classical. That is, it consciously attempted to hearken back to a classical, especially a Roman, past. For centuries Europeans had looked to ancient Rome in the belief that the Romans had known the secret of good government, enabling them to rule over a Golden Age. The recovery of that secret was especially appropriate for a nation that was building a great empire. British aristocrats saw themselves as the latter-day equivalent of Roman patricians, living in a new Augustan Age, presiding over a hierarchical society held together by patronage, paternalism, and deference. They particularly embraced the idea of *noblesse oblige*; that is, the obligation to their social inferiors to serve them in government, charity, and paternal concern. Given these attitudes, it was perhaps inevitable that the British aristocracy should imitate the Roman in culture and style as well. Members of the ruling elite had always learned Latin in school and often had themselves portrayed on canvas as Roman senators in togas. After about 1714 they would embrace the Palladian style, designing their houses and public buildings to look like Roman temples. It is true that some scholars at the time questioned whether the ancients or the moderns (i.e., their own contemporaries) possessed the greater wisdom, but most aristocrats and educated professionals would have sided with the ancients. It is also true that some modern historians would argue that Augustan *noblesse oblige* cloaked a ruthless combination of snobbery, entitlement, and acquisitiveness which decreed that its members almost always acted out of self-interest, even at their most apparently altruistic. But that is not how they would have seen it.

Closely related to the aristocratic embrace of classical models was a confidence in human reason. The seventeenth century has often been referred to as the Age of Reason, the eighteenth that of the Enlightenment. Reason can be found everywhere in aristocratic life ca. 1700, from the mathematically proportioned symmetry of public buildings, country houses, and gardens to the popularity of the ideas of John Locke. In his *Essay on Human Understanding* (1690), Locke argued for the application of the new scientific method to all aspects of human life, as well as for a more optimistic and liberal view of human nature. Early in the seventeenth century, Francis Bacon, Viscount St. Albans, and others had conceived the scientific method by promoting the necessity of free, untrammeled enquiry; skepticism toward *a priori* assumptions and received ideas; the keen observation of nature; the coordination of a body of such observations with mathematics; and the testing of resultant theories about the world by experimentation. Over the course of the next hundred years, great observers, mathematicians, and experimenters, many of them English, used this new intellectual tool to revolutionize human understanding of nature. For example, the physicist

Robert Boyle (1627–91) discovered the laws of gas and pressure. In *The Skeptycal Chemist* of 1661, he proposed a theory of matter composed of many irreducible elements, thus refuting the old Aristotelian theory of only four. The physicist Robert Hooke (1635–1703) assisted Boyle in his experiments; described the true nature of combustion, elasticity, and the arch; invented the marine barometer and other instruments; and pioneered the telescopic determination of parallax of a fixed star. The astronomer Sir Edmund Halley (1656–1742) learned how to predict accurately such events as solar eclipses and the return of comets.

But perhaps Halley's greatest service to learning was that, as secretary to the Royal Society, he encouraged the most brilliant of all English scientists, Sir Isaac Newton (1642–1726). As an undergraduate at Cambridge, Newton had wondered why, if Galileo was correct that bodies set in motion remain in motion, moving in a straight line, the planets do not fly out of orbit. To explain the simple, observable fact that they do not, Newton postulated an attractive force between heavenly bodies which kept them in their orbits. He argued that this force was the same one that holds our feet to the ground and which impels an apple to fall to earth: gravity. To further explain his observations of the movement of the heavenly bodies, he eventually postulated three laws of motion: that every body at rest or in motion remains so unless some force is exerted upon it; that the change in motion is proportional to the force exerted upon it; and that for every action there is an equal and opposite reaction. In order to measure and predict these forces, Newton developed (in parallel with the German scholar Gottfried Wilhelm von Leibniz [1646–1716]) a whole branch of mathematics, calculus. The result was a series of mathematical formulae, supported by observation and experiment, which explained and could be used to predict the movements of the sun, moon, planets, and other heavenly bodies. In 1687, with the assistance of the Royal Society, Newton published his findings in *Principia Mathematica: or the Mathematical Principles of Natural Philosophy.*

The book quickly caught the imaginations of not only scientists but lay people as well. It did so because it explained, for the first time to widespread satisfaction, how the universe worked. Pope captured the general euphoria:

> Nature and Nature's laws lay hid in night:
> God said, Let Newton be! and all was light.

Newton's *Principia*, and the other discoveries noted above, suggested that the universe ran according to laws that were precise, unvarying, and readily discoverable by human beings using the scientific method. This meant that, if one only knew the applicable law, one could determine what nature would do next. Thus, human beings might one day be able to affect, even control, nature for their own use. It was no accident that the later eighteenth century would see the first vaccination for disease (smallpox) and the popularization of agricultural improvements by landowners anxious to apply the new scientific principles to managing their estates.

Increased human agency implied a diminished role for God in the world. This is not to say that Boyle, Hooke, Halley, and Newton were atheists; far from it. Newton, in particular, wrote commentaries on the Bible. But their embrace of rationality seemed to undermine the legitimacy of faith, while their portrayal of nature as unchanging and predictable suggested that the Supreme Being was not concerned at the fall of every sparrow. In the wake of the scientific revolution, many eighteenth-century Presbyterian clergymen rejected the mysteries of the Trinity and became Unitarians; some eighteenth-century Anglicans became **Deists**. Deists believed that the universe operated not as the moment-to-moment expression of God's will exercised over every occurrence but, rather, according to the laws of nature, which He had established at the beginning of the world, set in motion, and allowed to run unvaryingly. God was a sort of celestial watchmaker; the world a vast mechanism. As humans figured out that mechanism, nature would be understood and, eventually, tamed.

Thus, we find reason even in eighteenth-century religion. Other Whig Anglicans became **Latitudinarians**. Not quite Deists, they nevertheless rejected the superstition of Roman Catholicism, the zealotry of Puritanism, and the rigid dogmatism of more conservative high Anglicans. For them Christianity was something that could be made rational, moderate, and accommodating to human and natural realities. It did not necessarily conflict with science. In fact, the new scientific discoveries were an argument *for* God's existence in that they implied a rational Creator. Nor did their religion require great displays of emotion or encyclopedic knowledge of Scripture. Locke argued in *The Reasonableness of Christianity* (1695) that there was nothing in that belief system which contradicted reason. His self-proclaimed disciple John Toland (1670–1722) went further to assert, in *Christianity not Mysterious* (1696), that there was no need for suspension of reason in faith; that anything in the Bible which did not conform to human reason and scientific possibility was patently untrue. This infuriated traditional high Church Anglicans, leading them to charge all Latitudinarians with heresy and infidelity. But the Latitudinarian philosophy fit beautifully with the eighteenth century's optimism about human nature, its embrace of the Roman virtues of moderation and stoicism, and its rejection of the violent fanaticism of the seventeenth century; in particular, it complemented the aristocrat's need to maintain dignity, self-composure, and aloofness from the emotions and enthusiasms to which ordinary mortals were prone.

The aristocratic desire for control went beyond the world of nature to that of men and women. Hence the rise of political economists who sought to discover the laws of the political and economic world as Boyle, Halley, and Newton had done for the natural world. Sir William Petty (1623–87), John Graunt (1620–74), and Gregory King compiled early population statistics, while Charles Davenant (1656–1714), Bernard de Mandeville (1660–1733), and the versatile Defoe sought to explain and exploit the wider economy. All believed that human behavior, especially political and economic behavior, could be explained naturally (therefore, scientifically), reduced to quantitative data, and predicted with mathematical certainty. These virtuosi seemed wildly ambitious to their critics: Swift, a defender of the ancients, satirized these "projectors" and their relentlessly mathematical understanding of human nature in Book 3 of *Gulliver's Travels* and, even more bitingly, in *A Modest Proposal* (1729). But their confidence tells us a great deal about the mindset and social milieu of their times.

Finally, Augustan art embraced the rationality and confidence noted above. As we have seen, the period's architecture was increasingly classical in inspiration, which meant mathematical symmetry, simplicity, and rationality. Its gardens, laid out by Wise and others, were also regular, proportioned, and geometrical, at least up to 1714. Its music evolved gradually from the heavily ornamented baroque of Purcell and Handel to a more streamlined classicism, although that transition would not take place until the mid-eighteenth century. The poetry of the age was also eminently classical and rational in its models, subject matter, and structure. Its great poets translated classical texts into Augustan English: Dryden translated Plutarch and Virgil; Pope, Homer. All wrote in traditional forms or modifications of traditional forms such as epic, mock epic, and, above all, verse satire. All wrote their poetry in the very strict form of rhymed heroic couplets in iambic pentameter. Take, for example, Pope's *Essay on Man* (1732–4):

> Know then thyself, presume not God to scan,
> The proper study of mankind is man.
> Placed on this isthmus of a middle state,
> A being darkly wise, and rudely great:
> With too much knowledge for the sceptic side,
> With too much weakness for the Stoic's pride,
> He hangs between; in doubt to act, or rest;
> In doubt to deem himself a God, or beast;
> In doubt his mind or body to prefer;
> Born but to die, and reas'ning but to err;
> Alike in ignorance, his reason such,
> Whether he thinks too little or too much:
> Chaos of thought and passion, all confused:
> Still by himself abused or disabused;
> Created half to rise, and half to fall;
> Great lord of all things, yet a prey to all;
> Sole judge of truth, in endless error hurled:
> The glory, jest, and riddle of the world!

The effect of the poem, with its neatly trimmed lines, is not unlike that of a formal garden. But the author seems to be ambivalent about the human race's advances, wary of reason's limitations. He still agrees with the Great Chain in placing humankind between God and the beasts, but worries that, for all their powers of reason, they may incline more to the latter than the former. This uncertainty, combined with the new audiences that artists like Pope and Handel found to support themselves, implies that, despite their veneer of rationality and composure, all was not certain for the governing classes of Augustan England.

The Middling Sort and their Culture

Unlike the landed aristocracy, those in the middle of the social pyramid were not yet conscious of themselves as a separate class, and so not unified in pursuit of common aims. Nevertheless, it could be argued that they were responsible for the most dynamic changes – and tensions – in English life between the Restoration and the first quarter of the eighteenth century. They were the government officials who ran the wars; the military and naval officers who planned and executed them; the "monied men" who financed them; the merchants who created the wealth in trade which supported and grew by them; and the professional men who solved the disputes which arose out of the resulting new wealth. All benefited from the expansion in the English economy which they helped to engineer. Later in the eighteenth century, these groups would demand a greater say in how the country was run; but for now they were content to ape their betters and aspire to be their junior partners in that enterprise.

Of all these groups, the oldest were the merchants. According to Gregory King's estimate for 1688, these numbered about 10,000 families of substantial merchants who only acted as middlemen; and about 110,000 families of manufacturers, artisans, and tradesmen who actually made their goods prior to selling them (see table 1).[15] This group varied enormously in wealth. At the top were the great international merchants who invested in joint-stock companies or, increasingly, established family or partner-based firms sending out voyages on their own. They traded with North America and the West Indies for furs, tobacco, and sugar, in return for manufactured goods – and slaves. They traded with China and India for tea and cloth. They reexported these commodities, adding British wool, to Europe for grain; and to Russia for timber, furs, naval stores, and, of course, cash. Great merchants such as this could reap thousands of pounds a year, rivaling the wealth of middling aristocrats and gentry, whom their daughters might marry. Their sons might inherit the family business outright or be apprenticed to another great merchant house, possibly amassing enough wealth to purchase land and, eventually, get out of trade. Middling domestic merchants, trading within the British Isles for grain from the south, coal or wool from the north, or cheese and butter from the west, earned less, perhaps £200–1,000 a year. These might be substantial men in their localities, well connected with urban oligarchies, but less so with the local gentry.

Turning to those who made the goods which merchants sold, at the top were manufacturers whose trade required large numbers of workers and so could not be done in a shop or at home. These included brewers, ironmasters, glassmakers, paper makers, sugar boilers, and some textile manufacturers. Such men were proto-industrialists, presiding over family firms whose operations required complicated equipment and substantial capital investment; employing platoons (if not yet small armies) of workers; and making hundreds, perhaps thousands, of pounds a year. During the eighteenth century their operations would grow larger, more complicated, and more lucrative.

More numerous, but on the whole less wealthy, were the artisans and crafts-men. They could make anywhere from £3 to £800 a year depending on their trade and location, but their income was most likely to fall into the £40–80 range. This group included, but was certainly not limited to, tailors, haberdashers, shoe-makers, weavers and spinners in the cloth trade, blacksmiths, coopers (barrel makers), candle makers, wheelwrights, carpenters, turners and furniture makers, goldsmiths, silver workers, leather dyers and tanners, and booksellers. They worked or oversaw work in small shops which probably also doubled as their places of residence. Theirs would be a family business, but they might employ several apprentices or additional servants. Increasingly, their shops became show-rooms, with finished goods in the front room, their fashioning taking place in back. It was more difficult for artisans and craftsmen to profit from the wealth flowing into eighteenth-century England. For years, their trades had been regu-lated by guilds and, more recently, the Statute of Artificers of 1563. But by 1700 the power of the guilds and the effectiveness of the statute were both waning, especially in London. This meant more freedom for artisans and new manufac-turers such as the French Huguenot silk weavers in Spitalfields, London. But it also meant less security, as there were fewer safeguards against cut-throat com-petition. Such businesses were, moreover, always subject to the hazards of fire, theft, debt, even laziness or incompetence on the part of their owners, though the new concept of insurance would soften the first of these.

A second longstanding contingent of the middling orders comprised the profes-sions: salaried government officials, attorneys, military and naval officers, med-ical men, clergymen, and specialized private servants. According to King, the professional classes numbered about 55,000 families in 1688 (see table 1).[16] None of these groups was really new during the Augustan period, but several, such as the government and military officers, grew due to the demands of war. The number of civil attorneys, solicitors, notaries, and scriveners also probably increased because the new kinds of financial activities at the end of the period lent themselves to new kinds of disputes, abuses, and frauds. All of these groups benefited to varying degrees from the economic health of later Stuart and early Hanoverian England.

Some of these professions were becoming more "professional" at the beginning of the eighteenth century, regulating their membership and maintaining standards by demanding a higher level of education and competence. One impetus for this was war. England's future depended on the competence of her financial adminis-tration and fighting forces. Thus, government Excise officers underwent a rigor-ous training. A Royal Naval College was established to train naval officers and strict examinations were set (from 1677) for candidates for the lieutenancy. Though most such officers still emerged from the younger sons of the nobility and gentry, promotion according to seniority and merit, as opposed to birth, became the norm in the 1690s. In contrast, the army, a traditional preserve of the aristocracy, remained much less of a meritocracy: throughout the eighteenth century commissions were purchased and commands determined by court pat-ronage. Traditionally, both military and naval officers had inflated their £80–100 salaries by selling commissions; by contracting at advantageous rates for arms, uniforms, and food; and by seizing plunder. As standards tightened, these sources of income began to dry up, though shady opportunities still remained.

Among professionals, the lawyers and physicians did best. A successful barrister (criminal lawyer) might make £3,000–4,000 a year, an attorney £1,500. A prosperous country physician might bring in £500 a year. The average for both groups, however, was closer to £200 a year. In theory, legal professionals continued to be trained at the universities, followed, in the case of barristers, by instruction at the Inns of Court. Doctors were trained at universities both at home and abroad and regulated by the Royal College of Physicians. In fact, by the end of the period, legal education at the Inns of Court and medical education at Oxford and Cambridge were fairly moribund. Increasingly, barristers learned their trade through informal apprenticeships with experienced members of the profession. The best medical training, embracing the scientific method, could be found in European universities, especially Leyden, and, from the 1720s, the medical school of the University of Edinburgh. This did not necessarily mean that eighteenth-century physicians became much more skillful at cure, but they better understood symptoms and hygiene. In any case, most people could not afford the services of physicians, who represented the medical elite. Apothecaries who dispensed drugs and surgeons who set bones and cut for stone were both more numerous and more reasonable in their fees. The former gained business from the availability of new pain-killing drugs from the East. Surgeons also made great strides in the century after 1660: having broken away from their association with barbers, they increasingly benefited from formal training and better instruments, which led to a rise in wealth and prestige.

The clergy also became more professionalized. Successive seventeenth-century purges of, first, Puritans under Laud, then Arminians under the Commonwealth and Protectorate, next Presbyterians and Independents under Charles II, and finally nonjurors under William III had fractured and demoralized this group. But under the able leadership of Archbishops Sheldon (served 1663–77), Sancroft (1677–90), Tillotson (1691–4), and Tenison (1695–1715), the quality and *esprit de corps* of the clergy improved steadily: by 1680 nearly four-fifths of the 12,000 or so parish priests were university graduates. Nevertheless, this group experienced the widest variations in income and status of any profession in Augustan England. Most clergymen were poor: while some benefices yielded £100–150, nearly 42 percent paid less than £50 and 13 percent paid less than £20 according to a survey done in 1704. In the words of one commentator, "[t]here are a vast many poor Wretches, whose Benefices do not bring them in enough to buy them Cloaths."[17] High Tory parsons struggling to make ends meet grew to resent Latitudinarian Whig bishops who were increasingly drawn from the younger sons of the peerage and who reaped anywhere from £300 to £7,000 a year from their episcopal estates. The fact that the Anglican clergy could marry offered some consolation, but it also served to put more pressure on their finances. As a result, despite reform efforts by Tenison and others, pluralism and absenteeism continued, not least because contemporaries still asked clergymen to do so much.

The clergy were often the linchpins of their communities, not only ministering to souls, but also caring for the sick, educating the young, and looking after the poor. In 1704 Queen Anne made some attempt to rectify the general poverty of the clergy by donating back to them First Fruits and Tenths, an ancient tax that had been confiscated by Henry VIII. Despite Queen Anne's Bounty, clerical incomes and workload would remain serious issues well into the nineteenth century and beyond.

Government officials also saw wide variations in income. Ignoring the great offices suitable for peers, there were thousands of middling positions in the Household, Treasury, Customs, and Excise paying anywhere from £100 to £1,000 a year, plus perquisites. The existence of such perks tells us that professionalism came late here: most appointment was through patronage; sale of office was only outlawed in 1702 and probably continued under the table; tenure was virtually for life. Nevertheless, if Augustan government was hardly a model of modern bureaucratic probity, it was well ahead of its continental counterparts, as it proved in successive wars. Finally, one should include in the middling ranks of society the many private servants of the aristocracy who had some particular expertise: estate stewards, clerks, valets, and ladies' maids. These, too, were professionals and might make a few hundred pounds a year for their services.

While the professions were expanding and rising in wealth, this does not mean that a professional career was open to just anyone. All, except service in a noble household, required a "stake," that is, the money for university tuition or to purchase an office or an army commission. Moreover, one of the traditional paths to a career, university education, was becoming less available to talented poor boys during this period, as scholarships heretofore reserved for them began to be monopolized by the sons of the elite and middling orders. In short, despite the new wealth flooding into the country, the middling sort, like the aristocracy, were in some ways less open to new blood than they had been a century earlier. As with their betters, this period saw the consolidation of merchant and professional dynasties. Successive generations of one family would join the family firm or pursue the same profession, often intermarrying into other mercantile or professional families in their circle. Still, this group remained open to movement within its ranks and, sometimes, to those above. The most common way for a middle-ranking family to rise was by the marriage of a wealthy merchant's daughter to a member of the aristocracy. More unusually, the great East India merchant and financial adventurer Thomas "Diamond" Pitt (1653–1726) single-handedly founded a family fortune that bankrolled the political careers of two prime ministers.[18]

Most members of the middling orders did not make this transition. Nonetheless, they were a force for change which alarmed the more traditional minded. Many started off as outsiders, coming from heretofore marginalized groups: Dissenters, Huguenots, or Jews. Many were foreign; they rose quickly to prominence in English life on their wits, not on their birth or connections. Most were Whigs and most lived in cities, beyond the hegemony of the landed aristocracy. By 1714 some 20–25 percent of the English population lived in urban areas and half of these lived in cities of 5,000 or more. London remained, at 500,000 in 1700, the greatest metropolis in the kingdom, the center of government, finance, and trade,

the mighty Rendezvous of Nobility, Gentry, Courtiers, Divines, Lawyers, Physitians, Merchants, Seamen, and all kinds of Excellent Artificers, of the most Refined Wits, and most Excellent Beauties.[19]

The period after the Restoration saw the rise in both population and importance of the West End, which included not only the court and Parliament but the splendid townhouses and lodgings of the elite (see map 10, p. 186). This was a great age for speculation and building by the powerful aristocrats who owned so much of the metropolis: hence the many famous squares and streets named for aristocratic speculators such as the Lords Berkeley of Stratton and the Russells, dukes of Bedford.

And yet, the phenomenal growth experienced by London in the seventeenth century began to slow down in the eighteenth. Henceforth, the big story in England's urban history was the expansion of cities of over 10,000 inhabitants. In 1670 there were five of these; in 1750, 20. Next to London, the greatest urban concentrations continued to be the clothmaking center of Norwich, with 30,000 people; the port of Bristol, with 21,000; and the coal capital, Newcastle, with 16,000 (see map 3, p. 16). As we have seen, much of the new growth came in ports and naval dockyards like Liverpool and Portsmouth, or manufacturing centers like Birmingham and Manchester. Increasingly, these regional centers, along with county towns, market towns, and spas, were establishing their own cultural institutions, such as assembly rooms and theater companies, to entertain their residents and the local aristocracy closer to home. True, some merchants and professional men, particularly military and naval officers, moved out to the country, buying landed estates and seeking to ape the aristocracy. But most opted to stay in their professions and their townhouses, avoiding the Land Tax and unknowingly providing an alternative model, urban and "middle class," for a successful English life. Their increasing wealth and leisure time meant that they could now join with the aristocracy in pursuing "polite sociability": sponsoring art, buying luxury goods (for example, fine china), forming clubs, attending coffee-houses, reading newspapers, going to Bath. The wealthiest continued to dominate their local corporations as mayors and aldermen. Increasing numbers served as MPs: there were 55 merchants and a handful of lawyers in the Parliament of 1641; by 1754 there would be 60 merchants, but also 60 lawyers and 40 military or naval officers, albeit mostly younger sons of the gentry.

These men continued to respect their aristocratic betters but were not the least bit ashamed of making money. Rather, they held an ever-higher esteem for their own contributions to the commonweal and increasingly saw themselves as every bit as gentle, in their own way, as the landed classes. This further blurred the once clear pecking order of the old Great Chain of Being. When, in 1712, Edward and Nathaniel Harley, brothers of the earl of Oxford, wrote to one another, the former addressed the latter, a merchant living in Turkey, with the gentle title "esquire," either as the brother of a peer or out of the now fashionable view that a prosperous man in any field was gentle. Nathaniel balked: "[p]ray Sir inform your clark who superscribes your letters that no merchants are wrote Esqs. but fools, coxcombs, and cuckolds."[20] Was he so traditional as to feel unworthy of the more elevated rank? Or was he sufficiently proud of being plain old "Mr.," customarily borne by all merchants, to spurn the pretensions of the fancier title?

Ordinary People and Popular Culture

Whatever became of the Great Chain of Being, the vast majority of the English people, well over 1 million families, some 90 percent of the population, remained at the bottom of the social pyramid. The most prosperous of these, some 310,000 families according to King, were yeomen farmers and husbandmen (see table 1).[21] As will be recalled, the most successful among this group had, in the sixteenth century, evolved into gentlemen. Those who remained could still live reasonably comfortable lives, making anywhere from £30 to £350 or more a year. While they worked their own farms and rarely left them, they could afford to employ servants and farm laborers and to apprentice a son to a trade. A substantial yeoman might send that son to university and an Inn of Court. But the relative agricultural depression of the late seventeenth and early eighteenth centuries hurt this group more than any other. The Land Tax and falling grain prices rendered them unable to make the agricultural improvements that aristocratic landowners could afford. Many at the lower end of the income scale went into debt and, eventually, lost their land to more prosperous neighbors who could weather the storm. For others, the gradual replacement of long-term **copyhold** tenure for short-term leases meant that they were thrown off their land in any case. Upward movement into the elite nearly disappeared; rather, many yeomen families sank gradually, over several generations, into the ranks of cottagers and even laborers.

Conversely, the nearly 800,000 families of "Labouring People" or "Cottagers and Paupers" (table 1), while significantly poorer than yeomen and husbandmen, benefited from the slowdown in population and fall in grain prices during the second half of the seventeenth century. Because their numbers stayed relatively stable, the labor market ebbed in their favor. Landlords had to charge lower rents and employers pay higher wages to retain tenants and workers who might otherwise go elsewhere. Since they bought more grain than they sold, lower prices meant good news and full bellies. As a result, Defoe could write in 1724 that "[e]ven those we call poor people, journeymen, working and pains-taking people, do thus: they lie warm, live in plenty, work hard and know no want."[22] Admittedly, families at this level of society could expect to labor just as hard as their ancestors for no more than £6–20 a year. Since most of that figure would have to be spent on food, there was relatively little left for other necessaries such as candles, soap, or cloth. For example, in the late seventeenth-century village of Terling, Essex, it took £13 14 shillings to support a family of five, consisting of a husband, wife, and three children. Of this amount, £9 14 shillings went for food, leaving £2 for clothes and £1 each for rent and fuel. It would therefore seem that concepts like "discretionary income" and "conspicuous consumption" would be unknown to members of this social rank. And yet, there is some evidence that the new consumer economy penetrated even to this level. Wills and inventories of agricultural workers during this period often list linen sheets, window curtains, brassware, and books. Only in the second quarter of the eighteenth century, as the population began to grow again, putting upward pressure on rents, downward pressure on wages, would their situation deteriorate. When it did, many would tumble into the ranks of the poor.

According to Gregory King, there were about 30,000 vagrants in England in 1688. But this number might skyrocket between wars as many common seamen and soldiers, representing some 85,000 families, were demobilized (table 1). Moreover, significant numbers of the "working poor" (the cottagers and laborers described above) were periodically thrown out of work when planting, harvesting, or the building season ended. As this implies, poverty was often a seasonal or stage-of-life (widowhood, for example) condition. Widows, orphans, and those disabled in war were often alone in the world, without a familial support network. As we have seen, this led the poor to move about, looking for work or for charity or just to stay one step ahead of the authorities (see chapter 6). As we have also seen, this produced fear and loathing among the more prosperous classes. Vagrants and beggars were a nuisance, and one could never tell who was really deserving, who just too lazy to work. Nor could one easily distinguish them from thieves, pickpockets, pimps, prostitutes, or murderers. In short, the poor, including, but by no means limited to, the criminal element, still represented to their betters a force for disorder, a reminder to respectable English men and women that they might have mastered the French and, perhaps, the natural universe, but that their own world was liable to explode into disturbance, crime, or riot at any moment.

The early modern English polity tried a number of remedies. The traditional one was to urge obedience and deference from the pulpit. The Church of England was still the religion of the vast majority of people, its rituals still the milestones of their lives, its physical plant still the religious and, to some extent, the social center of their communities. But much had changed about the beliefs espoused by the community which celebrated those rites and holidays.

The good news in religion was that the wrenching conflicts of the sixteenth and seventeenth centuries, combined, perhaps, with the new emphasis on empirical demonstration, reason, and moderation, had, by the early eighteenth century, left most English men and women deeply averse to religious zealotry (what they called "enthusiasm") and its corollary, persecution. It is true that Dissenters remained second-class citizens, theoretically banned from office by the Test and Corporation Acts; and that Catholics and Jews really were kept out of many walks of public life, including the universities and Parliament, by the same and other legislation. But the old hatreds which inspired these laws were subsiding in the eighteenth century and one could even hear a few voices for their repeal.

Similarly, old fears and superstitions, such as that inspired by witches, had also died out among the educated classes. While common folk continued to believe in their existence, it was almost impossible by 1700 to find anyone in authority who would treat the complaint seriously. The last execution for witchcraft in England took place in the 1680s; the last trial in 1712; and the statute which made it a felony was finally repealed in 1737. In fact, while the educated classes grew wealthier, spent more time in cities, and embraced rationality and experimental science, most of the population, with little access to this brave new intellectual world, seem to have retained their ancient beliefs in folk custom, herbal remedies, and superstition. Anthony à Wood (1632–95) reported in the 1680s that country people still believed in ghosts and fairies.

Paradoxically – and alarmingly from the point of view of the elite – this credulity did not, apparently, extend to belief in all the tenets of the Anglican faith. Rather, the political and intellectual revolutions of the seventeenth century which had discredited religious zealotry had also weakened popular religiosity. There is conflicting evidence about church attendance in the late seventeenth and early eighteenth centuries, but overall it suggests that fewer people attended Sunday services. The Toleration Act freed not only Dissenters from having to do so but also the skeptical, the lazy, or the just plain sleepy. Church courts, which had traditionally regulated personal behavior (Sabbath breaking, blasphemy and swearing, adultery and fornication, drunkenness, some debt), were clearly in decline in most parts of the country by the 1720s. In short, the Church's ability to coerce obedience and good behavior from its flock was on the wane, while skepticism, excessive materialism (what contemporaries called "luxury"), and general bad behavior were thought to be on the rise.

In response, there arose Societies for the Reformation of Manners which declared their own war on the most objectionable aspects of popular culture. Supported by both Anglicans and Dissenters, members went about identifying drunkards, prostitutes, and blasphemers – and encouraging constables to apprehend them. Clergymen like the nonjuror Jeremy Collier (1650–1726) railed against the licentiousness of the theater. To make up for absenteeism and pluralism, the Society for the Propagation of Christian Knowledge (SPCK) and Society for the Propagation of the Gospel (SPG) were founded. These organizations disseminated religious literature and education at home and in the colonies.

The Church had always played the major role in education. While this period saw a decline in the availability of university and legal education for ordinary people, it continued to witness the growth of grammar schools for the prosperous, private academies (often run by Dissenters) for the offspring of the middling orders, and petty schools to give poorer children some facility in reading and writing. The last two offered education to girls as well as boys. For the very poor, especially in London, manners were to be reformed in charity schools, endowed by a wealthy patron and administered by a Church-licensed teacher, often the pastor himself. Where there was no established school, some rudimentary education could probably be had at the overworked hands of the local parish priest. As a result, by 1715 some 45 percent of the male population and 25 percent of females could sign their names, the best indicator of literacy available to historians.

Perhaps the Church-run institution which had the greatest impact at this level of society was the Poor Law. By the early eighteenth century the poor rates, collected on a parish-by-parish basis, yielded £400,000 a year and supplemented the income of 4 to 5 percent of the general population. The parish vestry distributed this money, but only to the "deserving" poor (widows, orphans, the lame, the sick, the aged) and only to those who could prove that they had been born in the parish. In practice, much depended on the personal generosity of the local JP (who approved or withheld the distribution of charity), the churchwardens (who collected it), and the overseers of the poor (who dispensed it) on site. To fill the gaps in official humanitarianism, many private charitable institutions sprang up in the later Stuart period, including the endowed charity schools noted above as well as hospitals. Admittedly, their existence probably did more to indicate their benefactors' good intentions than they did to solve the problems of ignorance, sickness, and poverty in eighteenth-century England.

One reason that poverty concerned so many contemporaries is that it was thought to lead to crime. As was the case for earlier periods, we do not have valid crime statistics for the century after the Restoration, but there seems to have been a widespread sense that crime was on the rise, especially in the 1690s, and again in the period 1710–25. Grub Street stoked these fears by churning out an endless stream of sensationalist crime literature such as Captain Alexander Smith's *History of the Lives of the Most Noted Highway-men, Foot-pads, House-Breakers, Shoplifters and Cheats* (1714). Famous criminals, like Jack Sheppard (1702–24) or Jonathan Wild (1682–1725), became national celebrities and folk heroes: indeed, Wild was later immortalized in a novel by Fielding. As "boss" of the London criminal underworld he took advantage of the new medium of the daily newspaper to advertise his services in recovering stolen goods – filched by his own gang! Traditional crimes like pickpocketing and shoplifting grew more tempting as trade and wealth increased, while new crimes like fraud, embezzlement, and counterfeiting grew out of the financial and commercial revolutions.

In response, Parliament passed an avalanche of capital legislation: the number of crimes for which one could be put to death rose from about 50 in 1680 to over 200 by 1820. Some of these laws seem draconian by the standards of any society. For example, after 1698 it was a capital crime to steal or assist in stealing goods worth over five shillings (just under a workman's weekly wage) from a shop or warehouse. And yet, "the bloodiest criminal code in Europe" operated more by intimidation and deterrence than by real violence. That is, it actually hanged very few offenders. Many more were never prosecuted to the full extent of the law, or were acquitted, transported to the colonies, or granted a royal pardon. Some historians of crime have argued that the law's real effectiveness stemmed from its theatricality and its constant reminder that it was the upper classes who held all the cards. Others have argued that the lower orders genuinely accepted the hierarchical assumptions of English society and felt protected by the law: after all, they, not the landed aristocracy, were the usual victims of crime. It should also be recalled that the vast majority of people encountered the law not as victims of felonies or through the terrors of criminal prosecution but in its more mundane civil manifestations such as contract, property, debt, libel, or disorderly conduct. Ultimately, we cannot know how most ordinary English men and women felt about the law or whether they were substantially deterred away from criminal behavior and toward a sullen deference by institutions such as the "bloody code."

Certainly, contemporary observers thought the English the most violent people in Europe. In fact, murder was rare and declining. But frequent theft, occasional bread riots, ritualized violence, and political demonstrations suggest that inequalities of status and wealth took their toll. During the period after 1660, in particular, traditional or customary rights (to copyhold, to graze animals in common fields, to gather "waste" wood or grain from the lord's land) were being abolished as part of the rise of a new, more rational, economy. This, too, often led to riots, demonstrations, or industrial disputes. But these demonstrations were neither full-scale rebellions nor unrestrained chaos: as we have seen (see chapter 6), they generally took place around a very specific issue (like the price of bread), had limited aims (like making cheap grain available), specific targets (the miller or the baker), limited violence, and a rationale based upon shared conceptions of customary rights and legal fairness. Generally, the rioters appealed to the local authorities not only for redress of their grievances but for some degree of legitimation or acquiescence in their actions. More often than not, the upper classes, whether out of agreement with the people or fear of the mob, tended to go along, forcing the merchant middlemen to lower their prices, for example, and punishing the demonstration leaders lightly, if at all. Still, the absence of alternative, less dramatic ways to relieve social and economic tensions, combined with the increasing distancing, almost a siege mentality, of the upper classes, suggests that there were deeper problems within English society than the price of grain. Early eighteenth-century England may look stable on the surface; it may actually have been stable in the sense of being unlikely to experience sudden, radical change; but stability is hardly to be enjoyed when much of what maintains it is the constant and mutual threat of violence directed from the have-nots to the haves and back again. English society at the turn of the eighteenth century witnessed increasing opportunity, but also increasing tension and fragmentation.

Let us return to the hypothetical woman with whom we began this chapter and ask how these opportunities and tensions would have shaped her life.[23] If she were a member of the middling orders, she might have been apprenticed as a teenager to learn a craft, possibly in textile manufacture and sale, but she was more likely to have been farmed out as a domestic servant. If she had married and her London-based husband died (during, say, the plague of 1665 or serving in one of the many late seventeenth-century wars), she might well have run his shop or business. Such widow-businesswomen were common in the printing, woolen, and victualing trades, though never in large-scale overseas trade. Lower down the social scale, her life would have been divided between household management and agricultural work or cloth production. If the former, she would have done much of what men did, although less plowing or reaping and more planting, raking, and gathering. In pasture regions, she might have had exclusive control of dairying. If engaged in cloth production, she would almost certainly have been concerned with spinning: our term for an older single woman (spinster) and the symbol of the woman's sphere (the distaff) reveal the close bond between women and this work in the pre-industrial period.

Whatever her work, she would probably have been responsible for "physick," herbal remedies and generally unpaid medical care for her family and, if she were a member of the elite, poorer neighbors. While she might have participated in petitioner marches on Parliament in the 1640s, or been at the forefront of a bread riot for a "just price," she would have had little to do with political demonstrations between 1660 and 1714. While she would probably have been highly involved with the religious and charitable life of her parish, she was unlikely to have embraced the radical ideas of *Women's Speaking Justified* (1667) by the Quaker Margaret Askew Fell Fox (1614–1702). Our particular woman was quite likely a widow by 1714: women were four times more likely to die in the first 10 years of marriage than men, but if they made it to their mid-forties, they tended to survive their husbands. During her marriage, the common law had considered her under the protection of her husband; she had held no freehold, made no will except through him. Some women held substantial property outside of land, and numerous women's wills survive, not simply to take care of the older traditions of the widow's dower or the wife's portion but to settle the goods and property of a myriad of different circumstances – previous marriages, older children, younger children, women's personal property, businesses. Finally, by 1714 our aged widow was probably poor, as age brought poverty below the level of the elite or substantial middling orders. The Hanoverian political future may have been stable, but its socioeconomic realities provided no guarantees for anyone, male or female.

Epilogue

The socioeconomic tensions described above should give us pause and cause us to ask, why should we pay attention to the story just told? If early modern English men and women were not quite certain of how to construct a stable, just, and prosperous society, what could they possibly have to tell us today? Why study their history? The authors would like to conclude this work by offering two reasons to do so.

First, and perhaps the lesser of the two, is that the history of England from 1485 to 1714 is a terrific story. One does not have to be English; one does not have to be an Anglophile; and one certainly does not have to approve of England's actions and policies over this span of time, to be aware of this fact. Ours has been the story of how part of an insignificant island, in 1485 poorer than contemporary Belgium, the military equal of, perhaps, Denmark, rose over the course of 250 years to become the wealthiest, most powerful nation on earth. It is the story of how that nation produced a rich culture, giving the world More's *Utopia*, Shakespeare's plays, Milton's *Paradise Lost*, Purcell's anthems and odes, the buildings of Sir Christopher Wren, the science of Sir Isaac Newton, and, not least, the King James Bible. It is the story of how a people survived repeated epidemics and near famine, one failed invasion and two successful ones, two Civil Wars, a series of violent reformations and counter-reformations in religion, a social and two political revolutions. It is the story of how they faced down, first, Philip II's Spain, then Louis XIV's France, in each instance the most powerful nation in the world. It is the story of how they then stumbled into a constitutional monarchy which would evolve into what was, arguably, the freest, most partici-patory State in Europe, if not yet a democracy. Simultaneously, they originated and eventually tolerated a variety of lasting religious traditions. It is the story of their struggle to assert natural rights and convert them into civil liberties which became the prototypes for many of the same rights and liberties we enjoy today. Along the way, the English story is filled with remarkable personalities: Thomas More dying "the King's good servant, but God's first"; Elizabeth I rallying her troops against the Spanish Empire with "the heart and stomach of a king"; Colonel Rainsborough asserting the civil rights of "the poorest he that is"; or Matthew Prior rating the "monuments of [his] Master's actions" over those of the Sun King. Above all, there are the stories of those countless ordinary people who did not leave us their names, but who struggled to survive and prosper and who, along the way, made of early modern England something greater than it had been.

Admittedly, the quotation of so many authority figures reminds us of a caveat: that the English "story," as most narrative histories tend to be, is *par excellence* a story of rich white men (and a few rich white women) who pursued power and wealth out of ambition and greed. There should be no forgetting that the eco-nomic system which made eighteenth-century England the wealthiest and most powerful nation on earth abducted, sold, and enslaved Africans; displaced Native Americans; destabilized India; reduced the Catholic Irish to near destitution; and exploited the vast majority of its own population – all so that a few landed aristocrats and powerful merchants could live lives of luxury. Nor should we forget the horrors visited on religious minorities in the name of orthodoxy, or that the female half of the population found few or no opportunities to make a career or have a say in the fate of their country. Those who ruled England – those who have, of necessity, received the vast majority of this book's attention – were often guilty of injustice and oppression to their fellow human beings, not only by our own standards but even, sometimes, by those of their own day.

On the other hand, this book has also tried to be about those English people who struggled *against* injustice and oppression. In so doing, they gave every oppressed group the example and the tools with which to seek a more just society. It was, after all, the people of England who, if not always first, then most loudly and successfully among the peoples of Europe taught the modern world that absolute monarchy was not the only viable form of government. It was the people of England who proclaimed that rulers should be answerable to the rule of law, to representative institutions, and, ultimately, to the will of the people. It was the people of England who first stipulated that citizens could not be imprisoned without charge, tried without access to a jury, or taxed without the permission of their representatives. It was the people of England who, more than any of their contemporaries, first extended widely the right to vote, the right to express political opinions in speech or print, and the right to sack a ruler who failed to govern them justly and effectively. It was also the people of England who demonstrated that women could rule every bit as effectively as men: while central Europe would go to war over the question of female rule in 1740, England had already seen the successful reigns of Elizabeth and Anne. Admittedly, the people of England came later than some others – the Dutch, the Poles – to embrace religious toleration, and even then, did so within an exclusively Protestant framework. But it was certainly the people of England, more than any other European society, who demonstrated time and again that social class was not immutable, that one's birth should not solely determine one's future. We saw this with Cardinal Wolsey, Thomas Cromwell, Samuel Pepys, Abigail Masham, "Diamond" Pitt, and all those Whig financiers. Finally, it should never be forgotten that ordinary English people fought and sometimes died fighting for all of these notions. As a result of these choices and sacrifices, England became, in the course of the eighteenth century, if not the first "modern" society, then the European society possessing the greatest number of hallmarks of modernity. No wonder that when the American colonists took up arms against George III (1738–1820; reigned 1760–1820), they claimed to be doing so in order to defend the rights of Englishmen.

As historian Mark Kishlansky has written, "[t]here could be no better measure of [the Stuarts'] accomplishments than the fact that eighteenth-century Frenchmen came to envy the achievements of seventeenth-century Britain."[24] Admittedly, most of those achievements were partial or beneficial to only a small fraction of the English population by 1714, or even by 1760. It would be many years before they would positively affect most people's lives in England, let alone be applied to conditions across the British Empire. Indeed, if the task set by early modern English men and women was to build a just society, it remains, on both sides of the Atlantic, an unfinished one. But this serves to make their experience all the more relevant. It was Sir Winston Churchill (1874–1965) – himself a distinguished historian of Queen Anne's England, descended on his father's side from the duke of Marlborough, but on his mother's side from a citizen of the United States – who famously said to his mother's countrymen: "Give us the tools, and we will finish the job."[25] The tools for which Churchill was asking in 1941 were, of course, material: ships, airplanes, guns. But the job was to defend the political, social, and cultural inheritance of the Atlantic world. As this implies, the idealistic and conceptual tools and traditions necessary to achieve a just society, a democratic government, freedom of worship, and an open intellectual life – the inheritance Churchill sought to perpetuate – had long before been passed across the Atlantic in the opposite direction. They existed, admittedly sometimes only in embryonic form, in but one place in 1714 – thanks to the courage and persistence of the people of early modern England.

Notes

Introduction: England and its People, ca. 1485

1   The authors are keenly aware of the fact that many would object to the inclusion of Ireland under any classification labeled "British." One recent historian has attempted to get around the naming dilemma by referring to the whole archipelago as "the Isles": Norman Davies, *The Isles: A History* (Oxford, 2000). The imprecision of this designation is more indicative of the difficulty of the problem than it is of a solution.

2   There were prehistoric Britons already there of whom little is known who intermingled with the invading Celtic peoples. England was not yet called England. Only after the invasions of the Anglo-Saxons, beginning in the fifth century CE, would "Angle-land" emerge.

3   As this book opens in 1485, the population of Scotland was about 1 million as compared to well over 2 million for England and Wales.

4   Comprising Derbyshire, Leicestershire, Lincolnshire, Northamptonshire, Nottinghamshire, Rutlandshire, Staffordshire, Warwickshire, and Worcestershire. Some would also place Oxfordshire in the Midlands.

5   Comprising Cheshire, Herefordshire, Shropshire, and the anomalous county of Monmouth that was at once both Welsh and English.

6   Comprising Cumberland, Durham, Lancashire, Northumberland, Westmorland, and Yorkshire.

7   It is significant for the study of the early modern period that Europe experienced a "Little Ice Age" from about 1550, and was much cooler than normal for the next hundred years or so. As late as the 1680s, London occasionally was able to set up a temporary winter fair, with booths and streets, on the frozen Thames.

8   Specifically, Jews had been expelled from England in 1290 by Edward I and were not formally readmitted until 1655. However, because the Roman Catholic Church prohibited usury (i.e., lending money at interest), the English Crown and merchant community found it useful to tolerate the existence of small communities of Jewish traders and financiers, as well as artists and musicians, in London. Muslims were unheard of except as occasional visitors on trading voyages. For shades of belief within Christianity, see chapter 2.

9   Toward the end of the fifteenth century, beginning in the southeast and in Devon, more substantial "cruck" houses were being built of stone or wood frame with thatched roofs. See chapter 6.

10 For an accessible selection, see *The Paston Letters: A Selection in Modern Spelling*, ed. N. Davis (Oxford, 1983).

11 The term "Great Chain of Being" was largely an invention of eighteenth-century writers. But the elements of the Chain here laid out can be traced back to the Greeks and were all recognizable to contemporaries.

12 *De Genera* II.

13 Quoted in J. R. Lander, *Government and Community: England, 1450–1509* (Cambridge, Mass., 1980), p. 117.

1 Establishing the Henrician Regime, 1485–1525

1   The term "Wars of the Roses" was coined by the nineteenth-century novelist and poet Sir Walter Scott and so was unknown to Henry's contemporaries. There is a scene in Shakespeare's *Henry VI* in which two prominent characters pluck roses of different colors to show their allegiances. But Shakespeare wrote more than a century after the fact. One of the symbols of the Yorkist side was the white rose. But the red rose was a Tudor symbol; it only became associated with the Lancastrians retrospectively.

2   British Library Add. MS 48031 (A), f. 139, quoted in J. L. Watts, "Ideas, Principles and Politics," in *The Wars of the Roses*, ed. A. J. Pollard (New York, 1995), p. 122.

3   The king's other, inconsistently loyal, brother, Clarence, had been eliminated in 1478 when he was arrested on a charge of witchcraft against Edward, taken to the Tower, and never seen again. Legend and Shakespeare have it that he was there drowned in a butt of Malmsey wine.

4   Along with the murder of Sir Edmondberry Godfrey (see chapter 9), the identity of Jack the Ripper in 1888, and, perhaps, the death of Amy, Lady Dudley (see chapter 4).

5   Quoted in J. R. Lander, *Government and Community: England, 1450–1509* (Cambridge, Mass., 1980), p. 331.

6   Quoted in ibid., p. 340.

7   The payments were intended to reimburse Henry the cost of his campaign as well as to pay arrears due on a previously agreed subsidy negotiated as part of the Treaty of Picquigny of 1475.

8   Sir Thomas Smith, *De Republica Anglorum*, ed. M. Dewar (Cambridge, 1982), p. 88.

9   London had four members. Boroughs were incorporated with a charter from the king granting them the right to send representatives to Parliament. The number of boroughs sending members rose from 222 in 1510 to 251 by 1547 and to 370 in 1603. The number of knights of the shire for Wales increased (although Welsh boroughs and Monmouth returned only one member each to Parliament), raising the number of knights from 74 to 90, for a total of about 460 members at the end of the Tudor period.

10 Quoted in J. A. F. Thomson, *The Transformation of Medieval England, 1370–1529* (London, 1983), p. 235.

11 J. J. Scarisbrick, *Henry VIII* (Berkeley and Los Angeles, 1968), p. 16.

12 Quoted in C. Roberts and D. Roberts, *A History of England*, vol. 1, *Prehistory to 1714*, 2nd ed. (Englewood Cliffs, New Jersey, 1985), p. 233.

13 Pope Adrian IV (ca. 1100–59; reigned 1154–9) was the previous, and so far only, English pontiff.

14 The death of James IV brought the infant James V (1512–42; reigned 1513–42) to the throne. As a consequence, Henry's sister and James IV's widow, Margaret, became regent.

15 The Amicable Grant would have claimed one-sixth of the goods of wealthy lay people, one-third of those of the clergy.

2 (Dis-)Establishing the Henrician Church, 1525–1536

1 Matilda was the only surviving child of Henry I (1068–1135; reigned 1100–35). In 1141, in the midst of a civil war against her cousin, King Stephen (1097?–1154; reigned 1135–54), she briefly controlled the country. A few months' rule allowed no time to prove herself, but sixteenth-century historical opinion held that those months were disastrous for England.

2 For example, Henry Courtney, marquess of Exeter, George Neville, Lord Bergavenny (ca. 1461–1535), Sir Edward Neville (d. 1538), Margaret, countess of Salisbury, Sir Henry Pole, Lord Montague (ca. 1492–1538), Reginald Pole (1500–58), and Sir Geoffrey Pole (ca. 1502–58) were all living descendants of either Edward IV or his brother, George, duke of Clarence.

3 His mother was Elizabeth Blount.

4 Technically, what Henry sought was an annulment (or actually a dispensation and an annulment, because of his previous relations with Anne's older sister!), that is, a categorical statement that his first marriage violated canon law, was therefore invalid in the eyes of the Roman Catholic Church, and had, thus, in effect, never really existed. But contemporaries, perhaps tacitly recognizing that Henry and Catherine had really been married, usually referred to the king's wished-for outcome as a divorce.

5 Brandon had married Anne (d. 1512), the daughter of Sir Anthony Browne (d. 1506), to whom he had been contracted in his youth. This took place after he had married, by papal dispensation, Margaret Mortimer (b. 1466?), whom he abandoned before marrying Anne. In order to wed Mary Tudor, he had to secure an annulment of his marriage to Anne on the grounds that the previous dispensation had been invalid! This example provided some ammunition for Henry's claim.

6 This is disputable. Arthur is supposed to have commented to Henry that he had been in "Spain" on his wedding night.

7 Quoted in J. Guy, *Tudor England* (Oxford, 1988), p. 115.

8 See A. G. Dickens, *The English Reformation* (New York, 1964; 2nd ed., London, 1989); Dickens, *Reformation Studies* (London, 1982); D. MacCulloch, "England," in *The Early Reformation in Europe*, ed. A. Pettegree (Cambridge, 1992), pp. 176–7; MacCulloch, *The Later Reformation in England, 1547–1603*, 2nd ed. (Houndmills, Basingstoke, 2001).

9 C. Haigh, *English Reformations: Religion, Politics, and Society Under the Tudors* (Oxford, 1993), p. 28. See also J. J. Scarisbrick, *The Reformation and the English People* (Oxford, 1984); E. Duffy, *The Stripping of the Altars: Traditional Religion in England, c.1400–c.1580* (New Haven, 1992).

10 Quoted in J. J. Scarisbrick, *Henry VIII* (Berkeley and Los Angeles, 1968), p. 299.

11 Quoted in Guy, *Tudor England*, p. 155.

12 Quoted in R. W. Chambers, *Thomas More* (Ann Arbor, 1958), p. 350.

13 G. R. Elton, *The Tudor Revolution in Government* (Cambridge, 1953).

14 In fact, Cromwell's formulation is somewhat ambiguous on one point: is loyalty owed to the king as a person (Henry VIII himself) or is it owed to his office (the Crown) or perhaps to some even less personal concept like "the State" or "England"? Most contemporaries had not yet thought this through and it is highly doubtful that Cromwell had done so. Later generations would raise the question of precisely who or what was the proper object of those loyalties.

15 Quoted in M. A. R. Graves, *The Tudor Parliaments: Crown, Lords and Commons, 1485–1603* (London, 1985), p. 80.

16 They were the courts of Augmentations, First Fruits and Tenths, General Surveyors, and Wards and Liveries.

17 That is, native Welsh law did not distinguish between legitimate and illegitimate heirs. This led to tensions and violence over disputed lands.

18 The quote is from Guy, *Tudor England*, p. 358.

19 Specifically, this statute, passed in 1536, forbade the bequeathing of land by will and guaranteed that a person having use of a piece of land was its legal owner. This meant that landowners ("users") were now liable for certain fees and taxes which had previously been avoidable thanks to the fiction that the "user" was not the legal owner. Landowners resented the elimination of this legal loophole.

3 Reformations and Counter-Reformations, 1536–1558

1 N. Harpsfield, *A Treatise on the Pretended Divorce Between Henry VIII and Catharine of Aragon* (Camden Society, 1878), p. 297.

2 Throughout the following chapter, the word "Catholic" refers to the doctrine, traditions, and personnel of the Roman Catholic Church. Other Catholic or Orthodox traditions were nonexistent among the native population of sixteenth-century England. "Protestant" will refer to the beliefs or persons of those who advocated reform of Christian doctrine, practice, or structure and rejected the authority of the pope to accomplish it.

3 This had been sanctioned by parliamentary acts in 1536 and 1544.

4 *Calendar of State Papers, Spanish*, 9: 18–21, quoted in P. Williams, *The Later Tudors: England 1547–1603* (Oxford, 1995), p. 36.

5 J. Strype, *Ecclesiastical Memorials, Relating Chiefly to Religion, and the Reformation of It* (1721), 2, pt. ii: 352, quoted in Williams, *The Later Tudors*, p. 48.

6 Lawrence Humphrey, quoted in C. S. L. Davies, *Peace, Print and Protestantism, 1450–1558* (London, 1977), p. 281.

7 She would be known as "Queen Mary" throughout her reign. She only came to be known as "Mary I" upon the accession of Mary II in 1689.

8 Quoted in Williams, *The Later Tudors*, p. 104.

9 Quoted in D. M. Palliser, *The Age of Elizabeth: England Under the Later Tudors, 1547–1603*, 2nd ed. (London, 1992), p. 381.

10 Quoted from the 1563 title-page of *Acts and Monuments*.

11 J. Foxe, *The Acts and Monuments of John Foxe*, ed. S. Reed Cattley (1839), 8: 88–90.

12 Quoted in *The Oxford Book of Royal Anecdotes*, ed. Elizabeth, Lady Longford (Oxford, 1989), p. 231.

4 The Elizabethan Settlement and its Challenges, 1558–1585

1 During her reign she was known simply as "Queen Elizabeth." She only acquired her distinguishing Roman numeral after the accession of Queen Elizabeth II in 1952.

2 Armigal Waad, a former clerk of the Privy Council, quoted in P. Williams, *The Later Tudors: England 1547–1603* (Oxford, 1995), p. 229.

3 "Regiment" here means "government" rather than a crack troop of female fighters.

4 Quoted in C. Haigh, *Elizabeth I*, 2nd ed. (London, 1998), p. 13.

5 Attributed to Elizabeth in ibid., p. 18.

6 Quoted in ibid., p. 24.

7 Quoted in A. G. R. Smith, *The Emergence of a Nation State: The Commonwealth of England, 1529–1660* (London, 1984), p. 121.

8 Francis Bacon, quoted in Haigh, *Elizabeth I*, p. 42.

9 Quoted in ibid., p. 22.

10 The booty was worth twice that amount, but Drake split it with a French privateer who helped in the capture.

11 Her previous husband, the earl of Bothwell, had escaped to the continent and was languishing in a Danish prison. The pope would formalize their divorce in 1570.

5 The Elizabethan Triumph and Unsettlement, 1585–1603

1 "Elizabeth's Tilbury Speech," in *The Norton Anthology of English Literature*, 6th ed. (New York, 1993), 1: 999. In fact, she would fail abysmally to keep the latter promise: see P. Williams, *The Later Tudors: England 1547–1603* (Oxford, 1995), p. 324.

2 Quoted in M. Nicholls, *A History of the Modern British Isles, 1529–1603: The Two Kingdoms* (Oxford, 1999), p. 273.

3 E. Spenser, *A View of the Present State of Ireland* (1596), quoted in Williams, *The Later Tudors*, p. 296.

4 Quoted in Williams, *The Later Tudors*, p. 380.

5 In 1576 the Commons themselves sent Wentworth to the Tower – an indication that most members were far more conservative and respectful of the queen's sensibilities than Mr. Wentworth.

6 Quoted in Williams, *The Later Tudors*, p. 360.

7 Quoted in J. Guy, *Tudor England* (Oxford, 1988), p. 400.

8 Elizabeth's "Golden Speech," November 30, 1601, quoted in J. E. Neale, *Elizabeth I and Her Parliaments 1584–1601* (London, 1953), pp. 388–91.

9 Quotations from Guy, *Tudor England*, pp. 445–6, upon which this paragraph is based.

6 Merrie Olde England?, ca. 1603

1 Below, the terms "aristocracy" and "aristocrat" will refer to the landed nobility and gentry together.
2 See L. Stone, *The Crisis of the Aristocracy 1558–1641* (Oxford, 1965); Stone, "Social Mobility in England, 1500–1700," *Past and Present* 33 (1966): 16–55.
3 R. H. Tawney, "The Rise of the Gentry 1558–1640," *Economic History Review* 11 (1941): 1–38. The debate is well summarized in L. Stone, *Social Change and Revolution in England, 1540–1640* (London, 1965). See, now, F. Heal and C. Holmes, *The Gentry in England and Wales, 1500–1700* (Stanford, 1994), esp. chap. 3.
4 Quoted in D. M. Palliser, *The Age of Elizabeth: England Under the Later Tudors, 1547–1603*, 2nd ed. (London, 1992), p. 82.
5 Stone, "Social Mobility," p. 24. For more conservative estimates, see J. Guy, *Tudor England* (Oxford, 1988), pp. 47–8; P. Williams, *The Later Tudors: England, 1547–1603* (Oxford, 1995), p. 203; and Palliser, *Age of Elizabeth*, pp. 81–3.
6 Quoted in Palliser, *Age of Elizabeth*, p. 77.
7 Heal and Holmes, *Gentry in England and Wales*, p. 255.
8 Arranged marriages of children, as opposed to adolescents, were extremely rare.
9 William Harrison, quoted in K. Wrightson, *English Society, 1580–1680* (New Brunswick, New Jersey, 1982), p. 19.
10 However, if one survived childhood, one stood an excellent chance of living through what we would, today, call middle age: that is, a person who lived to 30 years was likely to live another 30 or more.
11 Quoted in A. Macfarlane, *The Family Life of Ralph Josselin, a Seventeenth-Century Clergyman: An Essay in Historical Anthropology* (New York, 1970), p. 165.
12 See L. Stone, *The Family, Sex and Marriage in England, 1500–1800* (London, 1977); R. A. Houlbrooke, *The English Family, 1450–1700* (London, 1984); L. Pollock, *Forgotten Children: Parent–Child Relations from 1500 to 1900* (Cambridge, 1983); and Wrightson, *English Society*, chap. 4.
13 Quoted in Williams, *The Later Tudors*, p. 507.
14 Such registers record marriage dates and baptismal dates. When a baptism occurred significantly less than eight months after marriage, it is safe to conclude that intimate relations had begun before the date of the ceremony.
15 Quoted in A. Fletcher, *Gender, Sex and Subordination in England, 1500–1800* (New Haven, 1995), p. 194.
16 Quoted in J. A. Sharpe, *Early Modern England: A Social History, 1550–1760*, 2nd ed. (London, 1997), p. 69.
17 This paragraph follows Williams, *The Later Tudors*, pp. 206–7.
18 Quoted in Heal and Holmes, *Gentry in England and Wales*, p. 140.
19 R. Gough, *The History of Myddle*, ed. D. Hey (Harmondsworth, 1981).
20 *The Autobiography of Richard Baxter*, ed. N. H. Keeble (London, 1974), p. 6.
21 Quoted in B. Coward, *The Stuart Age: England, 1603–1714*, 2nd ed. (London, 1994), p. 79 (parishioners sleeping); and D. Underdown, *Fire From Heaven: The Life of an English Town in the Seventeenth Century* (New Haven, 1992), p. 81.
22 Quoted in Palliser, *Age of Elizabeth*, p. 94.
23 Quoted in ibid., p. 92.

24 Quoted in Williams, *The Later Tudors*, p. 513. In popular mythology, horns grew on the heads of cuckolds, i.e., husbands whose wives were committing adultery.

25 This paragraph follows C. Roberts and D. Roberts, *A History of England*, vol. 1, *Prehistory to 1714*, 2nd. ed. (Englewood Cliffs, New Jersey, 1985), p. 304.

26 Surviving but fragmentary court records suggest that prosecutions were rising to about 1620. But this may reflect the increasing amount of criminal legislation and growing responsibilities and competence of JPs, constables, etc., as much as it does a real increase in actual wrongdoing on the part of the English people. See J. A. Sharpe, *Crime in Early Modern England, 1550–1750*, 2nd ed. (London, 1999), esp. chap. 2.

27 Tudor Parliaments imposed the death penalty on rioters, damagers of property, clippers of coins, nocturnal hunters, and witches (whose crimes were against people and property).

28 One could only do this once and anyone who had escaped civil punishment in this way would be branded or, later, transported to the colonies.

29 Quoted in Palliser, *Age of Elizabeth*, p. 365.

30 The following is based on P. Clark, "The Alehouse and the Alternative Society," in *Puritans and Revolutionaries*, ed. D. Pennington and K. Thomas (Oxford, 1978), pp. 47–72; and Clark, *The English Alehouse: A Social History* (London, 1983).

31 Quoted in Clark, "Alehouse," p. 47.

32 Additional legislation followed in 1563 and 1604. All such statutes were repealed in 1736.

33 While only one section of K. Thomas, *Religion and the Decline of Magic* (New York, 1971) was devoted to witchcraft, a 1991 conference and resulting book reevaluated Thomas's work in light of further work on witchcraft: see *Witchcraft in Early Modern Europe: Studies in Culture and Belief*, ed. J. Barry, M. Hester, and G. Roberts (Cambridge, 1996).

34 Figures derived from S. Inwood, *A History of London* (London, 1998), pp. 158–9. Note the discussion of the difficulties in estimating London's population.

35 Quoted in Coward, *Stuart Age*, p. 31.

36 The following paragraphs are based upon E. A. Wrigley, "A Simple Model of London's Importance in Changing English Society and Economy 1650–1750," *Past and Present* 37 (1967): 44–70; amplified by the discussion in Inwood, *History of London*, pp. 157–61; and Williams, *The Later Tudors*, p. 164. Many of the phenomena Wrigley describes clearly began in or applied equally to the period covered by this chapter.

37 Quoted in Inwood, *History of London*, p. 204.

7 The Early Stuarts and the Three Kingdoms, 1603–1642

1 Unlike the first Mary or Elizabeth, James was proclaimed in England as "James the first" to distinguish his English from his Scottish title.

2 L. Stone, *The Causes of the English Revolution, 1529–1642* (New York, 1972), p. 146. Of course, since he wrote, scientists have done just that; perhaps there is hope yet!

3 Quoted in B. Coward, *The Stuart Age: England, 1603–1714*, 2nd ed. (London, 1994), p. 122.

4   Francis Osborne, quoted in E. S. Turner, *The Court of St. James's* (London, 1959), p. 128. See additional contemporary comment in M. B. Young, *King James and the History of Homosexuality* (New York, 2000).

5   *Select Statutes and Other Constitutional Documents Illustrative of the Reigns of Elizabeth and James I*, ed. W. G. Prothero (Oxford, 1913), pp. 293–5.

6   *Form of Apology and Satisfaction* (1604), quoted in *Constitutional Documents of the Reign of James I, 1603–1625*, ed. J. R. Tanner (Cambridge, 1930), p. 222.

7   Quoted in Tanner, ed., *Constitutional Documents*, p. 204.

8   Quoted in ibid., p. 221.

9   Quoted in D. M. Loades, *Politics and Nation: England, 1450–1660*, 5th ed. (Oxford, 1999), p. 306.

10 In D. H. Willson, *James VI and I* (London, 1956), p. 171, quoted in R. Lockyer, *The Early Stuarts: A Political History of England, 1603–1642*, 2nd ed. (London, 1999), p. 31.

11 Quoted in L. L. Peck, *Court Patronage and Corruption in Early Stuart England* (London, 1993), p. 13.

12 Thomas Wentworth, 1608, quoted in D. L. Smith, *The Stuart Parliaments, 1603–1689* (London, 1999), p. 108.

13 Salisbury may not have been a paragon of virtuous retrenchment himself, given that his prodigy house at Hatfield cost £40,000 and that he derived at least £17,000 per annum from the profits of office.

14 Quoted in A. G. R. Smith, *The Emergence of a Nation State: The Commonwealth of England, 1529–1660* (London, 1984), p. 258.

15 Commons Protestation of December 18, 1621, printed in Tanner, ed., *Constitutional Documents*, pp. 288–9.

16 He would become "Charles I" only at the accession of his son, Charles II (see chapters 8–9).

17 Loades, *Politics and Nation*, p. 323.

18 J. Rushworth, *Historical Collections* (1682), 1: 138, quoted in Lockyer, *The Early Stuarts*, p. 50.

19 Quoted in T. G. Barnes, *Somerset, 1625–40: A County's Government During the "Personal Rule"* (Cambridge, Mass., 1961), p. 258.

20 Because he had it printed without a statute number and with his earlier exceptions to it, it is the "Petition" and not the Act of Right.

21 *Letters of King James VI and I*, ed. G. P. V. Akrigg (London, 1984), p. 207, quoted in Lockyer, *The Early Stuarts*, p. 191.

22 February 24, 1629, quoted in Smith, *The Stuart Parliaments*, p. 118.

23 Of course, *all* early modern sovereigns, excepting possibly Edward VI, ruled "personally," by taking an active role in formulating government policy and, often, in executing it. What was thought to be new was the attempt to do so without any parliamentary advice or assistance.

24 *The Parliamentary or Constitutional History of England* (1763), 5: 178, quoted in Coward, *Stuart Age*, p. 137.

25 Quoted in Coward, *Stuart Age*, p. 195.

26 Quoted in A. Hughes, *The Causes of the English Civil War*, 2nd ed. (Houndmills, Basingstoke, 1998), p. 164.

27 Quoted in M. Kishlansky, *A Monarchy Transformed: Britain, 1603–1714* (Harmondsworth, 1996), p. 146.

8 Civil War, Revolution, and the Search for Stability, 1642–1660

1 "Cavaliers" from the Spanish *caballero* or horseman. It was originally a pejorative name for the courtly gallants, often of magnificent appearance but little money, who rallied to the king's side.

2 "Roundheads" was a pejorative reference to the apprentices who protested the king's policies in London in 1641. Apprentices, like all working people in England, tended, for practicality's sake, to cut their hair short – hence "roundheads" – in contrast to courtiers who had the time and assistance of servants to dress long hair.

3 Quoted in J. Morrill, *Revolt in the Provinces: The People of England and the Tragedies of War, 1630–1648*, 2nd ed. (London, 1999), p. 124.

4 Edward Massey (1619–74), March 22, 1645, quoted in ibid., p. 136.

5 Sir William Paston (fl. 1630–40s), quoted in ibid., p. 79.

6 Quoted in ibid., p. 75.

7 And the second bloodiest, after Edward IV's victory at Towton Moor in 1461, ever fought on English soil.

8 Quoted in *Oliver Cromwell: Politics and Religion in the English Revolution, 1640–1658*, ed. D. L. Smith (Cambridge, 1991), p. 51.

9 Quoted in ibid., pp. 17–18.

10 Quoted in G. E. Aylmer, *Rebellion or Revolution? England, 1640–1660* (Oxford, 1986), p. 77.

11 S. R. Gardiner, *The Great Civil War* (1898), 2: 287, quoted in C. Russell, *The Crisis of Parliaments: English History, 1509–1660* (Oxford, 1971), pp. 360–1.

12 *A Declaration, or Representation from His Excellency Sir Thomas Fairfax, and of the army under his command, Humbly tendered to the Parliament ... 14 June 1647*, in *The Stuart Constitution, 1603–1688: Documents and Commentary*, ed. J. P. Kenyon (Cambridge, 1966), p. 296.

13 Quoted in *Divine Right and Democracy: An Anthology of Political Writing in Stuart England*, ed. D. Wootton (Harmondsworth, 1986), pp. 286–90.

14 Act Erecting a High Court of Justice, January 6, 1649, reprinted in *The Trial of Charles I: A Documentary History*, ed. D. Iagomarsino and C. J. Wood (Hanover, New Hampshire, 1989), p. 25.

15 Quoted in ibid., p. 64.

16 The eldest, Princes Charles (1630–85) and James (1633–1701), had been sent out of the country for their protection and to prevent various rebel factions putting either forward as king.

17 Quoted in Iagomarsino and Wood, eds., *Trial of Charles I*, pp. 143–4.

18 He did so silently, omitting the traditional words "Behold the head of a traitor!" This was, presumably, because he did not want to give away his identity by speaking.

19 J. Lilburne, *England's New Chains Discovered* (1649), printed in G. E. Aylmer, *The Levellers in the English Revolution* (Ithaca, 1975), p. 146.

20 *A Fiery Flying Roll* (1649), reprinted (Exeter, 1973), p. 8.

21 L. Clarkson, *A Single Eye all Light*, pp. 8–12, 16, quoted in C. Hill, *The World Turned Upside Down: Radical Ideas During the English Revolution* (London, 1972), p. 215.

22 September 17, 1649, in *Oliver Cromwell's Letters and Speeches*, ed. T. Carlyle (London, 1907), 2: 152.

23   Quoted in C. Hill, *God's Englishman: Oliver Cromwell and the English Revolution* (New York, 1970), pp. 121–2.

24   Quoted in D. Hirst, *England in Conflict, 1603–1660: Kingdom, Community, Commonwealth* (London, 1999), p. 268.

25   Quoted in B. Worden, *The Rump Parliament, 1648–1653* (Cambridge, 1974), p. 1.

26   Quoted in Hill, *God's Englishman*, p. 132.

27   Quoted in ibid., p. 33.

28   J. Evelyn, *The Diary of John Evelyn*, ed. E. S. De Beer (Oxford, 1955), 3: 234.

29   Ibid., 3: 246.

9 Restoration and Revolution, 1660–1689

1   R. A. Beddard, "The Retreat on Toryism: Lionel Ducket, Member for Calne, and the Politics of Conservatism," *Wiltshire Archeological Magazine* 72–3 (1977–8): 84.

2   G. S. Holmes, *The Making of a Great Power: Late Stuart and Early Georgian Britain, 1660–1722* (London, 1993), p. 84.

3   They remained there for 20 years. Eventually, after blowing down in a storm and changing hands several times, Cromwell's head was given to his alma mater, Sidney Sussex College, Cambridge. There, it was respectfully interred, in a location undisclosed – lest some latter-day Royalists seek even now to vent their anger upon it!

4   Gaston-Jean-Baptiste de Cominges to Louis XIV, January 25, 1664, in *A French Ambassador at the Court of Charles II*, ed. J. J. Jusserand (London, 1892), p. 91.

5   S. Pepys, *The Diary of Samuel Pepys*, ed. R. Latham and W. Matthews (Berkeley, 1971), 4: 366.

6   Charles II's mother, Henrietta Maria, was the sister of Louis XIV's father, Louis XIII.

7   The Protestant Netherlands (as opposed to the Spanish Netherlands), also known as the Dutch Republic but more properly known as the United Provinces, was a confederation of individual states. The stadholder served as a sort of chairman of the board, whose powers were minimal in peacetime, extensive in wartime.

8   Henceforward, where the foreign relations and resources of all three Stuart kingdoms were involved, they shall be referred to, collectively, as Britain.

9   For example, in 1671 the Treasury Commission abandoned the farming of the Customs by a group of merchants and the government began to collect these revenues on its own.

10   A. Marvell, *An Account of the Growth of Popery and Arbitrary Government* (1677), quoted in B. Coward, *The Stuart Age: England, 1603–1714*, 2nd ed. (London, 1994), p. 325.

11   Herbert Aubrey (ca. 1635–91), June 27, 1687, British Library, Add. MS. 28,876, fols. 13–14.

12   Quoted in J. R. Western, *Monarchy and Revolution: The English State in the 1680s* (London, 1972), p. 232.

13   Quoted in ibid., p. 280.

14   S. B. Baxter, *William III and the Defense of European Liberty, 1650–1702* (New York, 1966), p. 247.

15   Socinians, i.e., Dissenters who denied the Trinity (Unitarians), were excluded entirely from its protections as were, initially, Quakers.

16   British Library, Add. MS. 5540.

10 War and Politics, 1689–1714

1   As in previous chapters, the terms "Britain" and "British" apply to the combined efforts of England, Scotland, and Ireland when engaged together in war or other foreign policy initiatives.

2   Quoted in M. Zook, "The Propagation of Queen Mary II," in *Women and Sovereignty*, ed. L. O. Fradenburg (Edinburgh, 1992), p. 187.

3   Quoted in J. Hoppit, *A Land of Liberty? England, 1689–1727* (Oxford, 2000), p. 144.

4   From the Spanish *junta*, or council.

5   Quoted in G. Williams and J. Ramsden, *Ruling Britannia: A Political History of Britain, 1688–1988* (London, 1990), p. 32.

6   Admittedly, Pepys was too closely associated with James II's administration to remain in office following the Revolution.

7   J. Swift, *Examiner* 14 (1710).

8   Quoted in W. Durant and A. Durant, *The Age of Louis XIV: A History of European Civilization, 1648–1715* (New York, 1963), p. 702. The Spanish ambassador's words have been retranslated by the authors.

9   Quoted in T. B. Macaulay, *The History of England from the Accession of James II* (London, 1895), 2: 766.

10 G. S. Holmes, *The Making of a Great Power: Late Stuart and Early Georgian Britain, 1660–1722* (London, 1993), p. 325.

11 Quoted in Williams and Ramsden, *Ruling Britannia*, pp. 43–4.

12 *The Parliamentary History of England 1702–1714*, ed. W. Cobbett (London, 1810), 6: 25.

13 The British were still using the Julian calendar. According to the more accurate Gregorian calendar in use on the continent, the date was August 13. The British would not adopt the Gregorian calendar until the middle of the eighteenth century.

14 August 2, 1704, in *The Marlborough–Godolphin Correspondence*, ed. H. L. Snyder (Oxford, 1975), 1: 349.

15 Thomas Coke to Marlborough, June 20, 1704, in *HMC Twelfth Report* (*Cowper MSS.*) (1889), 2: 37–8.

16 Quoted in W. A. Speck, *A Concise History of Britain, 1707–1975* (Cambridge, 1993), p. 22.

17 Quoted in E. Gregg, *Queen Anne* (New Haven, 1980), p. 289.

18 H. Sacheverell, *The Perils of False Brethren in Church and State* (1709).

19 Marlborough to Sir William Cowper, January 18 [1710], quoted in Gregg, *Queen Anne*, p. 302.

20 Quoted in ibid., p. 303.

21 S. Johnson, *Lives of the Poets* (Oxford, 1906), 2: 3.

22 Erasmus Lewis to Jonathan Swift, July 27, 1714, in *The Correspondence of Jonathan Swift*, ed. H. Williams (Oxford, 1963), 2: 86.

23 Quoted in H. L. Snyder, "The Last Days of Queen Anne: The Account of Sir John Evelyn Examined," *Huntington Library Quarterly* 343 (1971): 271.

Conclusion: Augustan Polity, Society, and Culture, ca. 1714

1 As with Mary I, Elizabeth I, and Charles I, he would have been known to his subjects simply as "King George," not "George I," until the accession of his son, George II, in 1727.

2 The previous Whig administration had allowed the South Sea Company to take over three-fifths of the national debt in return for certain trading privileges. The promise of these privileges resulted in a run on South Sea stock, which rose in value by nearly 1,000 percent in the summer of 1720. When it became clear that the Company was not making a profit (having engaged in almost no actual South Sea trade), the stock price collapsed, ruining many holders and discrediting the government, some of whose officials had been bribed to support the scheme. The ministry fell and Walpole persuaded the Bank of England and the East India Company to assume much of the loss, thus saving the government's finances.

3 J. C. D. Clark, *English Society, 1660–1832: Religion, Ideology and Politics During the Ancien Régime*, 2nd ed. (Cambridge, 2000).

4 P. Langford, *A Polite and Commercial People: England, 1727–1783* (Oxford, 1989); and *Public Life and the Propertied Englishman, 1689–1798* (Oxford, 1991).

5 *The First Modern Society: Essays in English History in Honour of Lawrence Stone*, ed. A. L. Beier, D. Cannadine, and J. M. Rosenheim (Cambridge, 1989).

6 H. Fielding, "A Modern Glossary," *The Covent Garden Journal* 4 (January 14, 1752).

7 Estimates derived from G. S. Holmes, *The Making of a Great Power: Late Stuart and Early Georgian Britain, 1660–1722* (London, 1993), tables B.1, p. 403, B.3, p. 408.

8 The following relies heavily on J. A. Sharpe, *Early Modern England: A Social History, 1550–1760*, 2nd ed. (London, 1997), pp. 38–41, 49–53.

9 The following relies heavily on J. Hoppit, *A Land of Liberty? England, 1689–1727* (Oxford, 2000), esp. pp. 242–77, 313–82.

10 This list is based on Holmes, *Making of a Great Power*, p. 67.

11 *Lorenzo Magalotti at the Court of Charles II*, ed. W. E. K. Middleton (Waterloo, Ontario, 1980), p. 114.

12 The estimates of size for various social groups in England are based, roughly, on the figures given by Gregory King in his famous "Scheme of the Income and Expense of the several families of England, calculated for the Year 1688," printed in C. Davenant, *Essay Upon the Probable Methods of Making a People Gainers in the Balance of Trade* (1699). We have added King's categories of baronets, knights, esquires, and gentlemen to arrive at the estimate of the size of the landed gentry. Using Guy Miege's definition of a gentleman as "any one that … has either a liberal or genteel Education, that looks gentleman-like (whether he be so or not)" (G. Miege, *The New State of England Under Our Present Monarch K. William III* [1702], 2: 154), one might possibly include other categories, such as eminent clergymen, persons in greater offices, persons in liberal arts and sciences, and naval and military officers. This would bring the total to nearly 50,000.

13 J. Evelyn, *The Diary of John Evelyn*, ed. E. S. De Beer (Oxford, 1955), 4: 6.

14 Quoted in M. Foss, *The Age of Patronage: The Arts in England, 1660–1750* (Ithaca, 1972), p. 78.

15 Adding, for the substantial merchants, King's categories "Eminent Merchants and Traders by Sea" to "Lesser Merchants and Traders by Sea"; for the manufacturers, artisans, and tradesmen adding "Shopkeepers and Tradesmen" to "Artizans and Handicrafts."

16 This number conflates King's categories of persons in greater and lesser offices, persons in the law, eminent and lesser clergymen, persons in liberal arts and sciences, and naval and military officers.

17 H. Misson, *Memoirs and Observations in His Travels Over England* (1719), p. 36, quoted in Hoppit, *Land of Liberty?*, p. 212.

18 William Pitt the elder (1708–78; prime minister 1756–61; 1766–8), from 1766 earl of Chatham; his son William the younger (1759–1806; prime minister 1783–1801; 1804–6).

19 T. de Laune, *Angliae Metropolis: or, the Present State of London* (1690), p. 298, quoted in Hoppit, *Land of Liberty?*, p. 426.

20 Nathaniel to Edward Harley, September 6, 1712, in *HMC Thirteenth Report, Appendix, Part II (Portland MSS.)* (1893), 2: 254–5.

21 We have conflated King's categories of freeholders, better sort; freeholders, lesser sort; and farmers.

22 Quoted in Holmes, *Making of a Great Power*, p. 391.

23 The next two paragraphs are based on R. B. Shoemaker, *Gender in English Society, 1650–1850: The Emergence of Separate Spheres?* (London, 1998); and A. Laurence, *Women in England, 1500–1760: A Social History* (New York, 1994).

24 M. Kishlansky, *A Monarchy Transformed: Britain, 1603–1714* (Harmondsworth, 1996), p. 342.

25 W. S. Churchill, radio broadcast, February 9, 1941.

Glossary

Cross-references to further definitions in the glossary are given in **bold**.

Advowson   Right of the local landlord to choose the parish priest.

Anabaptists   For England, see **Baptists**.

Anglicans   Conservative or "high Church" members of the Church of England favoring Church government by bishops. Theologically, favorably disposed toward elaborate ritual and ceremony (see **Arminians**). The dominant strain of the Church of England after the Restoration, the term is anachronistic but useful for explaining tendencies before then.

Appeals, Act in Restraint of, 1533   Statute which forbade appeals in legal cases to jurisdictions beyond that of the king of England (such as Rome). It not only made Henry VIII's divorce from Catherine of Aragon possible; some historians believe it established a modern conception of sovereignty in England.

Arminians   Those English and Scottish **Anglicans**, named for Dutch theologian Jacobus Arminius, who believed that good works and efficacious rituals might play a role in salvation (opposed to **Calvinists**). They emphasized "the beauty of holiness" via elaborate church decor and ceremonial. Led by Archbishop Laud, Arminian clergy became influential under Charles I.

Asiento   The right to supply African slaves to the Spanish colonies of the New World, secured for Britain in the Treaty of Utrecht of 1713 (see **Utrecht, Treaty of**).

Assizes   Court held twice a year in a major town as part of a regular circuit of assize judges with jurisdiction over felonies.

Attainder   Statute which declares the party in question "attainted" of treason, without the formal procedure of a trial. Those attainted lost their lives, titles, lands, and goods, ruining whole families.

Babington Plot   Plot engineered by Anthony Babington, page to Mary Queen of Scots, in 1586 to assassinate Elizabeth and place Mary on the throne. Discovered by Secretary

Walsingham's spy system, he waited to see if Mary would incriminate herself. She did so, leading to her trial and execution.

Baptists Protestants who believed in baptism only by adult choice, and, during the seventeenth century, in a Church restricted to the elect (thus vitiating any notion of a national Church).

Calvinists Protestant followers of John Calvin who believed that God has predestined all humans to be saved (elect) or damned (reprobate). Most members of the Church of England prior to 1630, and all **Puritans**, were Calvinists.

Cavaliers Cant name for Royalists during the Civil Wars.

Cavalier Code See **Clarendon Code**.

Chantry A chapel, often a side-chapel in a church, set aside for prayers for the dead in **Purgatory**, often endowed by the deceased. Dissolved by the Crown in 1547.

Clarendon Code Popular name for statutes passed by the Cavalier Parliament to establish the monopoly of the Church of England and outlaw Dissent after the Restoration (see **Conventicle Act, Corporation Act, Five Mile Act, Uniformity, Act of, 1662**). Its effect was to make **Dissenters** second-class citizens.

Conventicle Act 1664 Statute which forbade meetings of more than five people for illegal (i.e., Dissenting) worship on pain of fines and exile for a third offense.

Copyhold Form of land tenure less secure than freehold but more so than leasehold. Copyholders held land at a fixed rent on terms set out in a copy of the manor roll. Prevalent at the beginning of the early modern period, rare at its end; capitalist landlords and market forces hit the generally smallholding copyholders hard in the sixteenth century.

Corporation Act, 1661 Statute which gave Crown-appointed commissioners the right to expel members of town corporations thought to be of questionable loyalty to the Restoration in Church and State, and to replace them.

Corporation The mayor, aldermen, and/or other governors of a city or borough as laid out in its charter, granted by the Crown.

Covenant, National, 1638 and **Covenant, Solemn League and, 1643** Both are at once agreements and oaths to bind together militarily to achieve religious reform. First signed in 1638 by the leaders of Scottish society to defend the Presbyterian Church government and its **Calvinist** theology against the Anglicizing tendencies of Charles I (see **Presbyterians**). The English Parliamentarians in 1643 agreed to a similar Solemn League and Covenant, by which the Scottish Covenanters supplied their army in return for £30,000 a month and a promise to establish Presbyterianism in England. This agreement made possible the crushing parliamentary victory at Marston Moor, 1644.

Declarations of Indulgence, 1672, 1687, 1688 Royal proclamations suspending (see **suspending power**) the laws against both recusants (Catholics) and **Dissenters**. Not supported by many Dissenters because of their fear of Catholics, and fiercely opposed by **Anglicans**.

Deists Those who, in the wake of the scientific revolution and Enlightenment, ceased to believe that God intervenes in worldly occurrences. Rather, they conceived of a "watchmaker God" who set the universe running according to unalterable natural laws. Suspicious of Scripture and dogma as infallible guides for behavior, preferring the exercise of reason.

Demesne   The part of a manor reserved for the landlord's crops and other uses, farmed for him by his tenants.

Diggers   Religious sect emerging out of the toleration following the Civil Wars, who believed that the Bible did not sanction private property. Their brief attempts at communes at St. George's Hill, Surrey, and elsewhere, ca. 1649–50, were broken by government repression and local hostility.

Dispensing power   The customary, but increasingly controversial, right of English kings to dispense with the law in individual cases. Its use died out after the Glorious Revolution of 1688–9.

Dissenters   Protestants, usually theological **Puritans**, who rejected or were expelled from the Church of England after the Restoration (see **Clarendon Code**). Dissenters were persecuted until the passage of the Toleration Act in 1689, after which Dissenters who accepted the Trinity could worship openly if they kept the doors of their meeting houses unlocked.

Enclosure   Process whereby landowners ceased arable (crop) farming and turned their lands over to pastoral, usually sheep, farming. This process was thought to involve not only the enclosing of land by fences but the eviction of the tenant farmers who had worked it. In fact, historical research indicates that its motivations and effects varied considerably from place to place.

Excise   Sales tax, first introduced in 1643, often on necessities – like beer.

Exclusion Crisis   The crisis over the succession which occurred 1678–81 over whether James, duke of York, a Catholic, should be allowed to succeed his brother Charles II. The crisis, which was born of the supposed discovery of a Popish Plot, precipitated three elections and led to the rise of the first two political parties in England. **Whigs** opposed the duke's succession, proposing that Parliament name a Protestant instead; **Tories** favored it.

Five Mile Act, 1665   Statute barring any nonconforming minister from coming within 5 miles of a town in which he had served.

Forced loan   Extraparliamentary levies, occasionally resorted to by the Tudors, but came to be seen as simply extortion under Charles I.

Grammar school   An endowed primary school with a classical curriculum, usually patronized by the middling orders.

Gunpowder Plot   Catholic plot organized in 1605 by Robert Catesby to blow up King James I and both houses of Parliament at the state opening on November 5. The plot was uncovered and one of the conspirators, Guy Fawkes, caught red-handed with the explosives. The conspirators were executed and anti-Catholic legislation toughened.

Heretic   One who publicly denies principal doctrines of the established Church. The Act for Burning Heretics of 1401 decreed burning at the stake in punishment. This was most famously imposed on the Protestant "heretics" under Mary.

Impositions   Additional Customs duties on imported goods "imposed" without parliamentary consent.

Independents   Those who, during and after the Civil Wars, believed that individual congregations should be allowed to decide on forms of worship and discipline within a loose national Church. Many favored a more aggressive war strategy during the Civil Wars and more radical solutions to social problems afterwards. Eventually known as Congregationalists.

Jacobites   Supporters of the exiled King James II and his son, the titular James III, known to his opponents as the Pretender. Jacobite rebellions in 1715 and 1745 failed to restore the Catholic Stuarts.

Junto   From the Spanish *junta*, the group of five Whig politicians who acted in concert to lead the party and, often, the government between 1690 and 1715: Thomas, Lord Wharton, John, Lord Somers, Charles Montagu, later earl of Halifax, Edward Russell, earl of Orford, and Charles Spencer, earl of Sunderland.

Justice of the peace (JP)   An unpaid officer of the Crown in the localities, usually a gentleman, who acted as a magistrate, sitting in judgment over (usually) noncapital felonies; regulating markets and prices; maintaining roads; supervising the Poor Law, among many other responsibilities. The mainstay of county government.

Kett's Rebellion   Rebellion led by Robert Kett in East Anglia in 1549 in response to hard economic times. The rebels demanded lower rents and entry fines, the inviolability of common lands, and a greater say in the selection of local officials. After the duke of Somerset hesitated, its ruthless suppression by the earl of Warwick helped catapult him to power.

Latitudinarians   Late seventeenth-century and, especially, early eighteenth-century Churchmen (many Whig bishops) who sought an inclusive Church of England accommodating a variety of beliefs, including those consistent with reason and the new science.

Legate   A papal representative on a temporary or more permanent mission (e.g., Thomas Wolsey) within a country.

Levellers   Radicals, including members of the army from 1647, who demanded freedom of conscience, near universal manhood suffrage, law reform, and "the sovereignty of the people." A Leveller constitution, *The Agreement of the People*, was debated at Putney in October 1647, but the Commonwealth eventually suppressed the movement.

Lollards   Their name derived from the Dutch for "mumbler," Lollardy was a set of beliefs associated with John Wyclif, an Oxford-based theologian of the fourteenth century. Dismayed at what they saw as the growing corruption of the Church and its distance from ordinary people, Lollards emphasized the importance of Scripture (which they translated into English) and deemphasized that of ritual and hierarchy. Originally encouraged by some in government as a counterweight to papal power, Lollards were persecuted virtually out of existence after an abortive rebellion in 1414. They anticipated, but were not around to contribute to, the Reformation.

Long Parliament   The Parliament summoned in fall 1640, which sat in one form or another to December 1648, at which point a purge of its more moderate members formed the **Rump Parliament** that governed the Commonwealth until 1653 (see

Pride's Purge). First the Rump and then the whole of the Long Parliament were recalled during the period of instability prior to the Restoration, 1659–60.

Lords lieutenant From the late Tudor period on, unpaid government officials, usually the most prominent peer in each county. His duty was to maintain order, keep an eye out for disaffection, and raise the militia when called upon.

Manor The estate of a landlord, usually originally held by feudal tenure.

Mumming Play-acting, usually associated with Church festivals like Christmas, New Year's, etc., in which participants represent religious or mythological figures.

National Covenant See **Covenant, National, 1638**.

Navigation Acts 1651, 1660, 1663 Parliamentary legislation which required that goods shipped to and from the English colonies in America be transported in English vessels through English ports. These measures eventually helped to ensure England's commercial supremacy.

Nonconformists See **Dissenters**.

Nonjurors Anglican clergymen who refused to take the oaths of allegiance to William III and Mary II.

Northern Rebellion Revolt in 1569 that started out as a plot by the duke of Norfolk to marry Mary Queen of Scots and replace William Cecil in Elizabeth's councils. When he hesitated, the earls of Northumberland and Westmorland raised the North for Catholicism and marched south to Durham. The rebellion lost steam and was suppressed brutally.

Occasional conformity The practice by officeholding **Dissenters** of receiving communion at Anglican services in order to qualify under the **Test Act**. The **Tories** attempted legislation to ban the practice repeatedly under Anne. They succeeded in securing a statute in 1711, only to see it repealed in 1719.

Overbury Scandal The scandal which emerged in 1615 when it became apparent that, two years before, Frances Howard, countess of Somerset, had engineered the poisoning of Sir Thomas Overbury in the Tower of London to stop him from revealing embarrassing personal information which might have endangered her marriage to James I's current favorite, the duke of Somerset. Both she and the duke fell from favor and were imprisoned, but later pardoned.

Pale The small area around Dublin in which direct English rule was effective in Ireland.

Petition of Right 1628 Legislation guaranteeing that no subject could be forced to pay a tax not voted by Parliament, imprisoned without charge, have soldiers billeted upon his house, or be subject to martial law. Charles I agreed to it with great reluctance in order to secure five new subsidies (taxes).

Pilgrimage of Grace Uprisings in the North in 1536–7. Ostensibly in reaction to Henry VIII's innovations in religion, they also had economic and social causes. After promising concessions, the Henrician regime crushed the movement, executing its most prominent leader, Robert Aske, and about 180 rebels.

Poor Laws 1536, 1563, 1572, 1598, 1601, 1662 Statutes designed to provide relief for the "deserving" poor, i.e., those who could not work because of gender, age, or illness, out of taxes – the poor rate – collected and distributed on a parish-by-parish basis. Some of these laws also had punitive provisions for "sturdy beggars," i.e., those who would not work. That of 1598 was the basis of poor relief for 200 years. That of 1662 allowed parishes to send itinerant poor back to their parishes of origin.

Poynings's Law 1494   Named for Sir Edward Poynings, lord deputy of Ireland 1494–6, this statute of the Irish Parliament gave the English Privy Council the right to approve the summoning and legislation of the Irish Parliament. Statutes passed by the English Parliament applied to Ireland.

Praemunire, Statutes of 1353, 1365, 1393   Statutes which prohibited English subjects from acknowledging papal jurisdiction in certain cases.

Prerogative   Royal discretionary power.

Presbyterians, parliamentary Presbyterians   Theological **Calvinists** who embraced Church government similar to that established in Scotland in the sixteenth century whereby doctrine and practice were determined by a hierarchy of courts culminating in a general assembly. Parliamentary Presbyterians wanted to apply it to England during and after the Civil Wars (see **Puritans**). They tended to be among the more conservative Puritans, favoring an accommodation with the king prior to 1649, and the restoration of the monarchy in 1660.

Pride's Purge   On December 6, 1648, Colonel Thomas Pride, under orders from the Council of the Army, led troops who purged those remaining members of the Long Parliament who wished to continue negotiations with the king. Their removal paved the way for the trial and execution of Charles I by the remnant, known as the **Rump Parliament**.

Proclamation   Royal decree (similar to the modern presidential executive order) which does not carry quite the same force as statute law.

Prophesyings   Meetings of clergy and some laymen to improve preaching and apply Biblical texts to everyday life. Elizabethan **Puritans** and most bishops approved of them, but the queen did not and suppressed them as potentially disruptive and seditious.

Public school   Original term for an endowed grammar school, has come to be associated with the wealthiest and most exclusive examples, such as Eton, Harrow, and Winchester. Offering a curriculum emphasizing the Latin classics, public schools have long been famous as the training grounds for England's elite.

Purgatory   Roman Catholic belief that, at death, souls who are not damned but not of sufficient perfection to merit Heaven go to this place to become so. Catholics believe that the prayers of the faithful and the indulgences granted by the Church for good deeds in life are efficacious in reducing the amount of time a soul spends there. The sale of indulgences provoked Martin Luther and other Protestant reformers to question whether *any* good works by sinful man could affect salvation (thus questioning the very existence of Purgatory).

Puritans   Protestants who sought the continued reform of the Church of England after its establishment in 1559–63. Puritans tended to be **Calvinists**, favoring plain Church ritual consistent with Scriptural injunction. Many, though not all, favored a **Presbyterian** form of Church government. After a brief moment in the sun following the Civil Wars, most were driven out of the Church of England by the **Clarendon Code** and so are known after the Restoration as **Dissenters**.

Quakers   Large religious sect emerging out of the toleration following the Civil Wars. They believed that each human being possessed God's inner light in equal measure, regardless of gender or social rank. This inclined them, notoriously, to flout gender roles, denounce professional clergy, deny deference to social superiors, refuse to swear oaths, and "quake" with their inner light at services. Harshly suppressed at the Restoration, they became more quietist.

Ranters   Religious radicals emerging out of the toleration following the Civil Wars who believed that those in tune with God, who is pure good, can commit no sin. Many others at the time feared them and blamed them for all manner of debauchery, though their writings suggest mainly a rigorous questioning of then dominant **Calvinist** theology (see **Puritans**).

Regency Act, 1706   Statute of Parliament guaranteeing that that body would continue to sit for six months after the death of Queen Anne, the realm administered by a council of regency to ensure the smooth accession of the elector of Hanover as king of England in keeping with the Act of Settlement. Its implementation in 1714 did precisely that.

Ridolfi Plot   Plot engineered by Robert Ridolfi and supported by Philip II and the pope in 1571 to overthrow Elizabeth and replace her with Mary Queen of Scots. Foiled by the government.

Roundheads   Cant name for Parliamentarians during the Civil Wars.

Rump Parliament   Popular nickname for the radical remnant of the Long Parliament which continued to sit after **Pride's Purge** (see **Long Parliament**) in December 1648. The Rump was the effective legislature of the Commonwealth. It was dissolved by Cromwell in 1653, but briefly revived in 1659–60 during the chaos leading to the Restoration.

Ryswick, Treaty of, 1697   Treaty ending the Nine Years' War, by which Louis XIV recognized William III as the rightful king of England, Scotland, and Ireland, gave back European territory taken since 1678, and agreed to work out with William a partition of the Spanish Empire after the death of Carlos II.

Settlement, Act of, 1701   Statute which established the Hanoverian succession after William III and Queen Anne. It passed over dozens of Catholic claimants in favor of the Protestant descendants of James I's youngest daughter Elizabeth, namely Sophia, electress of Hanover, and her successor, Georg Ludwig. The act also restricted the power of future monarchs.

Sheriff   Originally the shire reeve, an unpaid officer of the Crown in the localities, responsible for collecting taxes, impaneling juries, and, early in the period, raising the militia. Considered onerous and to be avoided if possible.

Ship Money   Tax levied on coastal counties to rid sea channels of pirates and other threats. Charles I's extension to the entire country in the 1630s to pay for the whole Royal Navy was financially lucrative, but highly resented, leading to Hampden's Case, which the king barely won. Abolished by the **Long Parliament**, 1641.

Shrovetide   The three days before Ash Wednesday, which begins the season of Lent in the Church calendar. Prior to the Reformation in England, a time for confession and absolution.

Solemn League and Covenant See **Covenant, Solemn League and, 1643**.

Star Chamber   The council acting as a court of law in matters involving riot and disorder. Its rules were few, its justice quick, which made it popular initially with the Crown and litigants. Its use to enforce Charles I's program of "thorough" in the 1630s led to its abolition in 1641.

Statute   Act of Parliament; that is, legislation passed by the Houses of Commons and Lords and approved by the monarch.

Suspending power   The customary, if always controversial, right of English kings to suspend the operation of the laws in a time of national emergency. Condemned in the Declaration of Rights of 1689 and extinct thereafter.

Test Acts 1673, 1678   Statutes introduced in response to the Declaration of Indulgence requiring all civil officeholders and members of either house of Parliament to take communion in the Church of England and to take oaths of supremacy and allegiance and repudiating transubstantiation annually. These requirements "flushed out" many Catholics in government but were less effective against **Dissenters** because of the practice of **occasional conformity**.

Tories   English political party which arose in response to the **Exclusion Crisis** of the 1680s. The Tories began as a court party defending the hereditary succession in the person of James, duke of York. They favored the rights of the monarch and the Church of England. During the 1690s, as they became associated with Jacobitism and lost power, the Tories became more of a country party.

Uniformity, Acts of 1549, 1552, 1559, 1662   Statutes mandating attendance at church and the use of the English Book of Common Prayer.

Union, Acts of 1536 with Wales, 1707 with Scotland   Statutes uniting the country in question with England as one state with one Parliament and one executive. The 1707 Union created Great Britain.

Utrecht, Treaty of, 1713   Treaty between Great Britain and France ending their hostilities in the War of the Spanish Succession. Britain acquired Gibraltar, Newfoundland, and Nova Scotia, territory in the Caribbean, the *Asiento*, Louis XIV's recognition of the Protestant succession, and the promise that the crowns of France and Spain would never be united.

Visitation   Inspection of ritual, vestments, etc., of a parish or, more usually, a diocese by a bishop or his representative.

Wardship   As feudal lord, the king had the right to administer the estates of underage or female heirs of deceased vassals. Moreover, he often assumed lordship of estates whose previous owners had died without heirs. This allowed him to collect feudal dues through the Court of Wards until the abolition of these rights and this court in 1646.

Whigs   English political party which arose in response to the **Exclusion Crisis** of the 1680s. The Whigs began as a country party demanding the exclusion of the Catholic

James, duke of York, from the throne, emphasizing the rights of Parliament and of **Dissenters,** and championing a Protestant (pro-Dutch) foreign policy. In the 1690s they became a party of government and grew less radical.

Wyatt's Rebellion   Rebellion led in 1554 by Sir Thomas Wyatt against Mary's intended marriage to Philip, king of Naples. Mary's fledgling army beat back the rebels, many of whom were executed.

Select Bibliography

Introduction

Years ago, when the authors were themselves students, textbooks such as C. Hill, *The Century of Revolution, 1603–1714* (London, 1961) and C. Russell, *The Crisis of Parliaments: English History, 1509–1660* (Oxford, 1971) opened their eyes to the excitement and worth of studying early modern England (even if the occasional reference puzzled those of us not actually reared in the United Kingdom). More recently, the authors first began teaching their own students about British history by assigning C. Roberts and D. Roberts, *A History of England*, vol. 1, *Prehistory to 1714* (1st ed., Englewood Cliffs, New Jersey, 1980; 2nd ed., 1985) or L. B. Smith, *This Realm of England, 1399–1688* (1st ed., Lexington, Mass., 1966). Such general surveys remain valuable syntheses of English history and we have learned much from them. Indeed, one of the pleasures of writing history is to return occasionally to older national histories, by, say, Keith Feiling (1950), Lord Macaulay (1848–61), or even David Hume (1754–62), to look for a long-buried fact, quote, argument, or turn of phrase that might (ignoring some biased interpretation here and there) help one construct a clearer view of the past even as it brings into question some currently accepted verity.

But we recognize that those just beginning to study this period will turn to this bibliography to learn the latest word about a person, place, or event mentioned in this text or to prepare a report or paper on a more specific subject. Much recent scholarship in early modern British history is to be found in articles (now in print and online, depending on your library's subscriptions) in journals such as *Albion, Continuity and Change, English Historical Review, History, Journal of British Studies*, and *Past and Present*. Our companion sourcebook includes, in the headnotes to each chapter, references to specific articles and debates found in journals like these. Here, however, we list mainly books published in the last quarter-century. We deploy this somewhat arbitrary cut-off date in order to have room to note the many useful studies prepared recently for graduate and advanced undergraduate students, in place of the array of still excellent monographs from the 1960s and 1970s, many of which are referred to in the endnotes of this book. We cannot list all the works used in preparation of this text; after all, between us we have been reading in the history of this period for over a half-century. But we might single out a half-dozen general studies below which have been consistently valuable and seem particularly reliable, in particular Coward (1994), Guy (1988), Hirst (1999), Holmes (1993), Hoppit (2000), Kishlansky (1996), Lockyer (1985, 1999), Palliser (1992), Sharpe (1997), Williams (1995), and Wrightson (1982, 2000).

For additional works, we recommend consulting *Historical Abstracts* online and the *Royal Historical Society Bibliography: The History of Britain, Ireland, and the British Overseas* (printed annually; and online, http://www.rhs.ac.uk/bibl/). The sampling of collections of printed and online sources from the period is just that: a sampling.

General

Cannon, J., ed. *The Oxford Companion to British History*, rev. ed., Oxford, 2002.

Davies, N. *The Isles: A History.* Oxford, 2000.

Heal, F. and Holmes, C. *The Gentry in England and Wales, 1500–1700.* Stanford, 1994.

Hindle, S. *The State and Social Change in Early Modern England, 1550–1640.* Houndmills, Basingstoke, 2000.

Inwood, S. *A History of London.* London, 1998.

Laurence, A. *Women in England, 1500–1760: A Social History.* New York, 1994.

Loades, D. M. *Politics and Nation: England, 1450–1660*, 5th ed. Oxford, 1999.

Lockyer, R. *Tudor and Stuart Britain, 1471–1714*, 2nd ed. Harlow, 1985.

Morrill, J., ed. *The Oxford Illustrated History of Tudor and Stuart Britain.* Oxford, 1996.

O'Day, R. *The Longman Companion to the Tudor Age.* London, 1995.

Sharpe, J. A. *Early Modern England: A Social History, 1550–1760*, 2nd ed. London, 1997.

Smith, A. G. R. *The Emergence of a Nation State: The Commonwealth of England, 1529–1660.* London, 1984.

Todd, M., ed. *Reformation to Revolution: Politics and Religion in Early Modern England.* London, 1995.

Wall, A. *Power and Protest in England, 1525–1640.* London, 2000.

Worden, B., ed. *Stuart England.* Oxford, 1986.

Wroughton, J. *The Longman Companion to the Stuart Age, 1603–1714.* London, 1997.

Pre-Tudor (1400s–1485)

Britnell, R. *The Closing of the Middle Ages? England, 1471–1529.* Oxford, 1997.

Carpenter, C. *The Wars of the Roses: Politics and the Constitution in England, c.1437–1509.* Cambridge, 1997.

Griffiths, R. A. and Thomas, R. S. *The Making of the Tudor Dynasty.* Gloucester, 1985.

Lander, J. R. *Government and Community: England, 1450–1509.* Cambridge, Mass., 1980.

Pollard, A. J., ed. *The Wars of the Roses.* New York, 1995.

Schama, S. *A History of Britain*, vol. 1, *At the Edge of the World, 3500 B.C.–1603 A.D.* London, 2000.

Thomson, J. A. F. *The Transformation of Medieval England, 1370–1529.* London, 1983.

See also Thurley (1993), below.

Tudor (1485–1603)

Biography

Ackroyd, P. *The Life of Sir Thomas More.* New York, 1999.

Chrimes, S. B. *Henry VII.* London, 1972; reprinted 1977.

Gwyn, P. *The King's Cardinal: The Rise and Fall of Thomas Wolsey.* London, 1990.

Haigh, C. *Elizabeth I*, 2nd ed. London, 1998.

Ives, E. W. *Anne Boleyn.* Oxford, 1986.

Kelsey, H. *Sir Francis Drake: The Queen's Pirate.* New Haven, 2000.

Loades, D. M. *Mary Tudor: A Life.* Oxford, 1989.

Lockyer, R. and Thrush, A. *Henry VII*, 3rd ed. London, 1997.

MacCaffrey, W. *Elizabeth I.* London, 1993.

MacCulloch, D. *Thomas Cranmer.* New Haven, 1996.

MacCulloch, D. *The Boy King: Edward VI and the Protestant Reformation.* New York, 2001.

Marius, R. *Thomas More: A Biography.* Cambridge, Mass., 1984.

Palmer, M. D. *Henry VIII*, 2nd ed. London, 1983.

Scarisbrick, J. J. *Henry VIII.* Berkeley and Los Angeles, 1968.

Starkey, D. *Elizabeth: The Struggle for the Throne.* New York, 2001.

Sugden, J. *Sir Francis Drake.* New York, 1990.

Political and Governmental

Anglo, S. *Images of Tudor Kingship.* London, 1992.

Bernard, G. W. *Power and Politics in Tudor England.* Aldershot, 2000.

Braddick, M. J. *The Nerves of State: Taxation and the Financing of the English State, 1558–1714.* Manchester, 1996.

Brigden, S. *New Worlds, Lost Worlds: The Rule of the Tudors, 1485–1603.* New York, 2000.

Collinson, P., ed. *The Sixteenth Century, 1485–1603.* Oxford, 2002.

Dean, D. M. *Law-Making and Society in Late Elizabethan England: The Parliament of England, 1584–1601.* Cambridge, 1996.

Ellis, S. G. *Tudor Frontiers and Noble Power: The Making of the British State.* Oxford, 1995.

Elton, G. R. *Reform and Reformation: England, 1509–1558.* Cambridge, Mass., 1977.

Elton, G. R. *The Parliament of England, 1559–1581.* Cambridge, 1986.

Fletcher, A. and MacCulloch, D. *Tudor Rebellions*, 4th ed. London, 1997.

Graves, M. A. R. *The Tudor Parliaments: Crown, Lords and Commons, 1485–1603.* London, 1985.

Guy, J. *Tudor England.* Oxford, 1988.

Guy, J., ed. *The Tudor Monarchy.* London, 1997.

Kishlansky, M. *Parliamentary Selection: Social and Political Choice in Early Modern England.* Cambridge, 1986.

Levin, C. *The Heart and Stomach of a King: Elizabeth I and the Politics of Sex and Power.* Philadelphia, 1994.

Loach, J. and Tittler, R., eds. *The Mid-Tudor Polity c.1540–1560*. London, 1980.

Loades, D. M. *The Tudor Court*. London, 1986.

MacCulloch, D. *The Reign of Henry VIII: Politics, Policy, and Piety*. New York, 1995.

McGurk, J. *The Tudor Monarchies, 1485–1603*. Cambridge, 1999.

Nicholls, M. *A History of the Modern British Isles, 1529–1603: The Two Kingdoms*. Oxford, 1999.

Starkey, D. *The Reign of Henry VIII: Personalities and Politics*. London, 1985.

Starkey, D., ed. *The English Court: From the Wars of the Roses to the Civil War*. London, 1987.

Tittler, R. *The Reign of Mary I*, 2nd ed. London, 1991.

Williams, P. *The Tudor Regime*. Oxford, 1979.

Williams, P. *The Later Tudors: England, 1547–1603*. Oxford, 1995.

See also Schama (2000), above.

Religious and Intellectual

Brigden, S. *London and the Reformation*. Oxford, 1989.

Coffey, J. *Persecution and Toleration in Protestant England, 1558–1689*. London, 2000.

Collinson, P. *The Birthpangs of Protestant England: Religious and Cultural Change in the Sixteenth and Seventeenth Centuries*. New York, 1988.

Dickens, A. G. *Reformation Studies*. London, 1982.

Dickens, A. G. *The English Reformation*, 2nd ed. London, 1989.

Doran, S. and Durston, C. *Princes, Pastors and People: The Church and Religion in England, 1529–1689*. London, 1991.

Duffy, E. *The Stripping of the Altars: Traditional Religion in England, c.1400–c.1580*. New Haven, 1992.

Duffy, E. *The Voices of Morebath: Reformation and Rebellion in an English Village*. New Haven, 2000.

Dures, A. *English Catholicism, 1558–1642: Continuity and Change*. Harlow, 1983.

Haigh, C. *English Reformations: Religion, Politics, and Society Under the Tudors*. Oxford, 1993.

Helgerson, R. *Forms of Nationhood: The Elizabethan Writing of England*. Chicago, 1992.

Lake, P. *Moderate Puritans and the Elizabethan Church*. Cambridge, 1982.

Loades, D., ed. *John Foxe: An Historical Perspective*. Aldershot, 1999.

MacCulloch, D. *The Later Reformation in England, 1547–1603*, 2nd ed. Houndmills, Basingstoke, 2001.

O'Day, R. *Education and Society, 1500–1800: The Social Foundations of Education in Early Modern Britain*. London, 1982.

Prall, S. E. *Church and State in Tudor and Stuart England*. Arlington Heights, Ill., 1993.

Scarisbrick, J. J. *The Reformation and the English People*. Oxford, 1984.

Thomas, K. *Religion and the Decline of Magic*. New York, 1971. (See also the reevaluation of Thomas's work in *Witchcraft in Early Modern Europe: Studies in Culture and Belief*, ed. J. Barry, M. Hester, and G. Roberts. Cambridge, 1996.)

Watt, T. *Cheap Print and Popular Piety, 1550–1640*. Cambridge, 1991.

See also Brigden (2000), Collinson (2002), Elton (1977), Fletcher and MacCulloch (1997), Guy (1988, 1997), MacCulloch (1995), Marius (1984), Tittler (1991), Wall (2000), and Williams (1995), above.

Social and Cultural

Amussen, S. D. *An Ordered Society: Gender and Class in Early Modern England.* Oxford, 1988.

Appleby, A. B. *Famine in Tudor and Stuart England.* Liverpool, 1978.

Barry, J., ed. *The Tudor and Stuart Town: A Reader in English Urban History, 1530–1688.* London, 1990.

Beier, A. L. *Masterless Men: The Vagrancy Problem in England, 1560–1640.* London, 1985.

Clark, P. *The English Alehouse: A Social History.* London, 1983.

Clark, P., ed. *Migration and Society in Early Modern England.* Totowa, New Jersey, 1988.

Clay, C. *Economic Expansion and Social Change: England, 1500–1700.* 2 vols. Cambridge, 1984.

Coleman, D. C. *The Economy of England, 1450–1750.* Oxford, 1977.

Coleman, D. C. *Industry in Tudor and Stuart England.* London, 1985.

Coster, W. *Family and Kinship in England, 1450–1800.* London, 2001.

Coward, B. *Social Change and Continuity: England, 1550–1750,* rev. ed. London, 1997.

Cressy, D. *Bonfires and Bells: National Memory and the Protestant Calendar in Elizabethan and Stuart England.* London, 1989.

Cressy, D. *Birth, Marriage and Death: Ritual, Religion, and the Life-Cycle in Tudor and Stuart England.* Oxford, 1997.

Eales, J. *Women in Early Modern England, 1500–1700.* London, 1998.

Fletcher, A. *Gender, Sex and Subordination in England, 1500–1800.* New Haven, 1995.

Gittings, C. *Death, Burial and the Individual in Early Modern England.* London, 1986.

Houlbrooke, R. A. *The English Family, 1450–1700.* London, 1984.

Houston, R. A. *The Population History of Britain and Ireland, 1500–1750.* London, 1992.

Hutton, R. *The Rise and Fall of Merry England: The Ritual Year, 1400–1700.* Oxford, 1994.

Ingram, M. *Church Courts, Sex and Marriage in England, 1570–1640.* Cambridge, 1987.

Kermode, J. and Walker, G., eds. *Women, Crime and the Courts in Early Modern England.* Chapel Hill, 1994.

Levine, D. and Wrightson, K. *The Making of an Industrial Society: Whickham, 1560–1765.* Oxford, 1991.

Manning, R. B. *Village Revolts: Social Protest and Popular Disturbances in England, 1509–1640.* Oxford, 1988.

Palliser, D. M. *The Age of Elizabeth: England Under the Later Tudors, 1547–1603,* 2nd ed. London, 1992.

Pollock, L. *Forgotten Children: Parent–Child Relations from 1500 to 1900.* Cambridge, 1983.

Prest, W., ed. *The Professions in Early Modern England.* London, 1987.

Sacks, D. H. *The Widening Gate: Bristol and the Atlantic Economy, 1450–1700.* Berkeley, 1991.

Sharpe, J. A. *Instruments of Darkness: Witchcraft in Early Modern England.* University Park, Penn., 1997.

Sharpe, J. A. *Crime in Early Modern England, 1550–1750,* 2nd ed. London, 1999.

Shepard, A. and Withington, P., eds. *Communities in Early Modern England*. Manchester, 2000.

Slack, P. *From Reformation to Improvement: Public Welfare in Early Modern England*. New York, 1999.

Smuts, R. M. *Culture and Power in England, 1585–1685*. New York, 1999.

Stone, L. *The Family, Sex and Marriage in England, 1500–1800*. London, 1977. (See also a contrasting perspective in A. Macfarlane, *Marriage and Love in England: Modes of Reproduction, 1300–1840*. Oxford, 1986.)

Thurley, S. *The Royal Palaces of Tudor England: Architecture and Court Life, 1460–1547*. New Haven, 1993.

Wrightson, K. *English Society, 1580–1680*. New Brunswick, New Jersey, 1982.

Wrightson, K. *Earthly Necessities: Economic Lives in Early Modern Britain*. New Haven, 2000.

Wrightson, K. and Levine, D. *Poverty and Piety in an English Village: Terling, 1525–1700*, rev. ed. Oxford, 1995.

Youings, J. A. *Sixteenth-Century England*. Harmondsworth, 1984.

See also Collinson (2002), Fletcher and MacCulloch (1997), Guy (1988), Heal and Holmes (1994), Hindle (2000), Laurence (1994), Sharpe (*Early Modern England*, 1997), Tittler (1991), Wall (2000), and Williams (1995), above.

Stuart (1603–1714)

Biography

Carlton, C. *Charles I: The Personal Monarch*, 2nd ed. London, 1995.

Claydon, T. *William III*. London, 2002.

Coward, B. *Oliver Cromwell*. London, 1991.

Gregg, E. *Queen Anne*, 2nd ed. New Haven, 2001.

Gregg, P. *King Charles I*. London, 1981.

Harris, F. *A Passion for Government: The Life of Sarah, Duchess of Marlborough*. Oxford, 1991.

Hutton, R. *Charles II: King of England, Scotland, and Ireland*. Oxford, 1989.

Jones, J. R. *Marlborough*. London, 1993.

Lockyer, R. *Buckingham, the Life and Political Career of George Villiers, First Duke of Buckingham, 1592–1628*. London, 1981.

Lockyer, R. *James VI and I*. New York, 1998.

Miller, J. *Charles II: A Biography*. London, 1991.

Miller, J. *James II: A Study in Kingship*, 2nd ed. New Haven, 2001.

Political and Governmental

Aylmer, G. E. *Rebellion or Revolution? England, 1640–1660*. Oxford, 1986.

Barnard, T. *The English Republic, 1649–1660*, 2nd ed. London, 1997.

Bennett, M. *The English Civil War, 1640–1649*. London, 1995.

Bucholz, R. O. *The Augustan Court: Queen Anne and the Decline of Court Culture*. Stanford, 1993.

Coward, B. *The Stuart Age: England, 1603–1714*, 2nd ed. London, 1994.

Dickson, P. G. M. *The Financial Revolution in England*. London, 1967.

Gentles, I. J. *The New Model Army in England, Ireland, and Scotland, 1645–1653*. Oxford, 1992.

Glassey, L. K. J., ed. *The Reigns of Charles II and James VII & II*. New York, 1997.

Harris, T. *Politics under the Later Stuarts: Party Conflict in a Divided Society, 1660–1715*. London, 1993.

Hibbard, C. *Charles I and the Popish Plot*. Chapel Hill, 1983.

Hirst, D. *England in Conflict, 1603–1660: Kingdom, Community, Commonwealth*. London, 1999.

Holmes, G. S. *British Politics in the Age of Anne*, rev. ed. London, 1987.

Holmes, G. S. *The Making of a Great Power: Late Stuart and Early Georgian Britain, 1660–1722*. London, 1993.

Hoppit, J. *A Land of Liberty? England, 1689–1727*. Oxford, 2000.

Hughes, A. *The Causes of the English Civil War*, 2nd ed. Houndmills, Basingstoke, 1998.

Hutton, R. *The Restoration: A Political and Religious History of England and Wales, 1658–1667*. Oxford, 1985.

Kenyon, J. and Ohlmeyer, J., eds. *The Civil Wars: A Military History of England, Scotland and Ireland, 1638–1660*. Oxford, 1998.

Kishlansky, M. *A Monarchy Transformed: Britain, 1603–1714*. Harmondsworth, 1996.

Lockyer, R. *The Early Stuarts: A Political History of England, 1603–1642*, 2nd ed. London, 1999.

Marshall, A. *The Age of Faction: Court Politics, 1660–1702*. Manchester, 1999.

Morrill, J. *Revolt in the Provinces: The People of England and the Tragedies of War, 1630–1648*, 2nd ed. London, 1999.

Peck, L. L. *Court Patronage and Corruption in Early Stuart England*. London, 1993.

Prest, W. *Albion Ascendant: English History, 1660–1815*. Oxford, 1998.

Russell, C. *The Causes of the English Civil War*. Oxford, 1990.

Russell, C. *The Fall of the British Monarchies, 1637–1642*. Oxford, 1991.

Schama, S. *A History of Britain*, vol. 2, *The Wars of the British, 1603–1776*. London, 2001.

Schwoerer, L. G., ed. *The Revolution of 1688–1689: Changing Perspectives*. Cambridge, 1992.

Scott, J. *England's Troubles: Seventeenth-Century English Political Instability in European Context*. Cambridge, 2000.

Seaward, P. *The Restoration, 1660–1688*. Houndmills, Basingstoke, 1991.

Sharp, K. *The Personal Rule of Charles I*. New Haven, 1992.

Smith, D. L. *The Stuart Parliaments, 1603–1689*. London, 1999.

Smuts, R. M., ed. *The Stuart Court and Europe: Essays in Politics and Political Culture*. Cambridge, 1996.

Sommerville, J. P. *Royalists and Patriots: Politics and Ideology in England, 1603–1640*, 2nd ed. London, 1999.

Speck, W. A. *Reluctant Revolutionaries: Englishmen and the Revolution of 1688*. Oxford, 1988.

Underdown, D. *Revel, Riot and Rebellion: Popular Politics and Culture in England, 1603–1660*. Oxford, 1985.

Williams, G. and Ramsden, J. *Ruling Britannia: A Political History of Britain, 1688–1988*. London, 1990.

Young, M. B. *King James and the History of Homosexuality*. New York, 2000.

See also Braddick (1996), Kishlansky (1986), Loades (*Politics and Nation*, 1999), Smith (1984), Starkey (1987), and Wall (2000), above; and Black (1993), Brewer (1983), and O'Gorman (1997), below.

Religious and Intellectual

Burgess, G. *The Politics of the Ancient Constitution: An Introduction to English Political Thought, 1603–1642*. University Park, Penn., 1992.

Clark, J. C. D. *English Society, 1660–1832: Religion, Ideology and Politics During the Ancien Régime*, 2nd ed. Cambridge, 2000.

Fincham, K., ed. *The Early Stuart Church, 1603–1642*. Stanford, 1993.

Harris, T., Seaward, P., and Goldie, M. eds. *The Politics of Religion in Restoration England*. Oxford, 1990.

Keeble, N. H. *The Literary Culture of Nonconformity in the Later Seventeenth Century*. Leicester, 1987.

Pocock, J. G. A. *The Ancient Constitution and the Feudal Law: A Study of English Historical Thought in the Seventeenth Century (A Reissue with a Retrospect)*. Cambridge, 1987.

Smith, N. *Literature and Revolution in England, 1640–1660*. New Haven, 1994.

Spurr, J. *The Restoration Church of England, 1646–1689*. New Haven, 1991.

Spurr, J. *English Puritanism, 1603–1689*. New York, 1998.

Tyacke, N. *Anti-Calvinists: The Rise of English Arminianism, ca. 1590–1640*. Oxford, 1989.

Underdown, D. *Fire From Heaven: The Life of an English Town in the Seventeenth Century*. New Haven, 1992.

See also Coffey (2000), Coward (1994), Doran and Durston (1991), Glassey (1997), Hibbard (1983), Hirst (1999), Hoppit (2000), Hughes (1998), Hutton (1985), Kishlansky (1996), Morrill (1999), Prall (1993), Smuts (1996), Sommerville (1999), and Speck (1988), above; and Porter (2000), below.

Social and Cultural

Borsay, P. *The English Urban Renaissance: Culture and Society in the Provincial Town, 1660–1770*. London, 1989.

Bostridge, I. *Witchcraft and its Transformations, c.1650–c.1750*. Oxford, 1997.

Earle, P. *The Making of the English Middle Class: Business, Society and Family Life in London, 1660–1730*. Berkeley, 1989.

Ford, B., ed. *Seventeenth-Century Britain: The Cambridge Cultural History*. Cambridge, 1989.

Harris, T., ed. *Popular Culture in England, c.1500–1850*. New York, 1995.

Holmes, G. S. *Augustan England: Professions, State and Society, 1680–1730*. London, 1982.

Hunt, M. R. *The Middling Sort: Commerce, Gender, and the Family in England, 1680–1780.* Berkeley, 1996.

Reay, B. *Popular Cultures in England, 1550–1750.* London, 1998.

Rosenheim, J. M. *The Emergence of a Ruling Order: English Landed Society, 1650–1750.* London, 1998.

Seaver, P. *Wallington's World: A Puritan Artisan in Seventeenth-Century London.* Stanford, 1985.

Sharpe, J. *The Bewitching of Anne Gunter: A Horrible and True Story of Deception, Witchcraft, Murder, and the King of England.* New York, 2001.

Shoemaker, R. B. *Gender in English Society, 1650–1850: The Emergence of Separate Spheres?* London, 1998.

Thompson, E. P. *Customs in Common: Studies in Traditional Popular Culture.* New York, 1991.

See also Amussen (1988), Appleby (1978), Barry (1990), and Beier (1985), above; Brewer (1983), below; Bucholz (1993), Clark (2000), Clay (1984), Coleman (1977, 1985), Coster (2001), Coward (1994, 1997), Cressy (1989, 1997), Eales (1998), Fletcher (1995), Glassey (1997), Gittings (1986), Heal and Holmes (1994), Hindle (2000), Hirst (1999), Hoppit (2000), Houlbrooke (1984), Houston (1992), Hutton (1994), Ingram (1987), Keeble (1987), Kermode and Walker (1994), Laurence (1994), Levine and Wrightson (1991), Manning (1988), Marshall (1999), O'Day (1982), Peck (1993), Pollock (1983), Prest (1987), Sacks (1991), Sharpe (*Early Modern England*, 1997; 1999), Slack (1999), Smuts (1996, 1999), Stone (1977), Thomas (1971), Underdown (1985, 1992), Wall (2000), Wrightson (1982, 2000), Wrightson and Levine (1995), Young (2000), above.

Hanoverian (1714 to 1730s)

Black, J. *The Politics of Britain, 1688–1800.* Manchester, 1993.

Brewer, J. *The Sinews of Power: War, Money and the English State, 1688–1783.* London, 1983.

Colley, L. *Britons: Forging the Nation, 1707–1837.* New Haven, 1994.

Langford, P. *Public Life and the Propertied Englishman, 1689–1798.* Oxford, 1991.

O'Gorman, F. *The Long Eighteenth Century: British Political and Social History, 1688–1832.* London, 1997.

Porter, R. *The Creation of the Modern World: The Untold Story of the British Enlightenment.* New York, 2000.

See also Clark (2000), Earle (1989), Hoppit (2000), Hunt (1996), Prest (1998), Reay (1998), Rosenheim (1998), Schama (2001), Shoemaker (1998), and Williams and Ramsden (1990), above.

Ireland, Scotland, and Wales

Bradshaw, B. and Morrill, J., eds. *The British Problem, c.1534–1707: State Formation in the Atlantic Archipelago.* New York, 1996.

Brown, K. M. *Kingdom or Province? Scotland and the Regal Union, 1603–1715.* London, 1992.

Canny, N. *Kingdom and Colony: Ireland in the Atlantic World, 1560–1800.* London, 1988.

Canny, N. *Making Ireland British, 1580–1650.* Oxford, 2000.

Devine, T. M. *The Scottish Nation: A History, 1700–2000.* Harmondsworth, 1999.

Dickson, D. *New Foundations: Ireland, 1660–1800,* 2nd ed. Dublin, 2000.

Ellis, S. G. *Ireland in the Age of the Tudors, 1447–1603: English Expansion and the End of Gaelic Rule.* London, 1998.

Ellis, S. G. and Barber, S., eds. *Conquest and Union: Fashioning a British State, 1485–1725.* London, 1995.

Jenkins, G. H. *The Foundations of Modern Wales, 1642–1780.* Oxford, 1993.

Jenkins, P. *A History of Modern Wales, 1536–1990.* London, 1992.

Levack, B. P. *The Formation of the British State: England, Scotland and the Union, 1603–1707.* Oxford, 1987.

Lydon, J. *The Making of Ireland: From Ancient Times to the Present.* London, 1998.

MacInnes, A. I. *Charles I and the Making of the Covenanting Movement, 1625–1641.* Edinburgh, 1991.

Mullan, D. G. *Scottish Puritanism, 1590–1638.* Oxford, 2001.

Williams, G. *Recovery, Reorientation and Reformation: Wales, c.1470–1642.* Oxford, 1987.

Wormald, J. *Court, Kirk, and Community: Scotland, 1470–1625.* Edinburgh, 1981.

See also Kenyon and Ohlmeyer (1998) and Russell (1990, 1991), above.

Europe and Empire

Black, J. *A System of Ambition? British Foreign Policy, 1660–1793.* London, 1991.

Bonney, R. *The European Dynastic States, 1494–1660.* Oxford, 1991.

Cameron, E., ed. *Early Modern Europe: An Oxford History.* Oxford, 1999.

Canny, N., ed. *The Origins of Empire: British Overseas Enterprise to the Close of the Seventeenth Century.* Oxford, 1998.

Doran, S. *England and Europe, 1485–1603,* 2nd ed. London, 1996.

Henshall, N. *The Myth of Absolutism: Change and Continuity in Early Modern European Monarchy.* London, 1992.

Howat, G. M. D. *Stuart and Cromwellian Foreign Policy.* London, 1974.

Jones, J. R. *Britain and the World, 1649–1815.* London, 1980.

Jones, J. R. *The Anglo-Dutch Wars of the Seventeenth Century.* London, 1996.

Lenman, B. *England's Colonial Wars, 1550–1688: Conflicts, Empire and National Identity.* London, 2001.

Loades, D. M. *England's Maritime Empire: Seapower, Commerce and Policy, 1490–1690.* London, 2000.

Macfarlane, A. *The British in the Americas, 1480–1815.* London, 1994.

Monod, P. K. *The Power of Kings: Monarchy and Religion in Europe, 1589–1715.* New Haven, 1999.

Munck, T. *Seventeenth-Century Europe, 1598–1700.* New York, 1990.

Pennington, D. H. *Europe in the Seventeenth Century,* 2nd ed. London, 1989.

Reitan, E. A. *Politics, War, and Empire: The Rise of Britain to a World Power, 1688–1792.* Arlington Heights, Ill., 1994.

Documents and Other Primary Sources

Bowle, J., ed. *The Diary of John Evelyn*. Oxford, 1983. (Selections)

Byrne, M. St. Clare, ed. *The Lisle Letters: An Abridgement*. Chicago, 1983.

Carrier, I. *James VI and I: King of Great Britain*. Cambridge, 1998.

Crawford, P. and Gowing, L., eds. *Women's Worlds in Seventeenth-Century England: A Sourcebook*. London, 2000.

Cressy, D. and Ferrell, L. A., eds. *Religion and Society in Early Modern England: A Sourcebook*. London, 1996.

Elizabeth I: Collected Works, ed. L. S. Marcus, J. Mueller, and M. B. Rose. Chicago, 2000.

Elton, G. R., ed. *The Tudor Constitution: Documents and Commentary*, 2nd ed. Cambridge, 1986.

Iagomarsino, D. and Wood, C. J., eds. *The Trial of Charles I: A Documentary History*. Hanover, New Hampshire, 1989.

Kenyon, J. P., ed. *The Stuart Constitution, 1603–1688: Documents and Commentary*, 2nd ed. Cambridge, 1986.

Key, N. and Bucholz, R., eds. *Sources and Debates in English History, 1485–1714*. Oxford, 2004, forthcoming.

Latham, R., ed. *The Shorter Pepys*. Berkeley, 1985. (Selections)

Lindley, K., ed. *The English Civil War and Revolution: A Sourcebook*. London, 1998.

Malcolm, J. L., ed. *The Struggle for Sovereignty: Seventeenth-Century English Political Tracts*, 2 vols. Indianapolis, 1999.

Raymond, J., ed. *Making the News: An Anthology of the Newsbooks of Revolutionary England, 1641–1660*. New York, 1993.

Smith, D. L., ed. *Oliver Cromwell: Politics and Religion in the English Revolution, 1640–1658*. Cambridge, 1991.

Stroud, A. *Stuart England*. London, 1999.

Tomlinson, H. and Gregg, D., eds. *Politics, Religion and Society in Revolutionary England, 1640–60*. Houndmills, Basingstoke, 1989.

Wootton, D., ed. *Divine Right and Democracy: An Anthology of Political Writing in Stuart England*. Harmondsworth, 1986.

Yeoman, L., ed. *Reportage Scotland: History in the Making*. Edinburgh, 2000.

See also sources printed in Barnard (1997), Bennett (1995), Braddick (1996), Carrier (1998), Coward (1997), Doran (1996), Fletcher and MacCulloch (1997), Lockyer and Thrush (1997), and Tittler (1991), above.

Websites and Online Primary Sources

The American Colonist's Library. http://personal.pitnet.net/primarysources/. (Includes Voyages, Puritans)

The Avalon Project at the Yale Law School: Pre-Eighteenth-Century Documents. http://www.yale.edu/lawweb/avalon/pre18.htm. (Colonial Charters, Treaties, Discourses on Trade, Bill of Rights, etc.)

The Cromwell Association. http://www.cromwell.argonet.co.uk/. (Oliver Cromwell, Civil Wars)

Documents Illustrating Jacobite History. http://members.rogers.com/jacobites/documents/ index.htm. (Exclusion Crisis, Glorious Revolution, Exile)

Early Modern England Source. http://www.quelle.org/emes/emes.html. (Listserv, Research links, Bibliographies)

EuroDocs: History of the United Kingdom. http://library.byu.edu/~rdh/eurodocs/uk.html. (Links to Elizabeth's writings, etc.)

Fire and Ice: Puritan and Reformed Writings. http://www.puritansermons.com/index.htm. (Richard Baxter, John Calvin, etc.)

Internet Archive of Texts and Documents: The Protestant Reformation. http://history. hanover.edu/early/prot.html. (Texts from English and Scottish Reformations)

Internet Modern History Sourcebook: The Early Modern West. http://www.fordham.edu/ halsall/mod/modsbook1.html. (Sources on Reformations, Colonial Conquests, Political Theorists and Revolutions)

Public Record Office. http://www.pro.gov.uk/index.htm. (Pathways to the Past includes Uniting the Kingdoms? 1066–1603; Virtual Museum includes Kings and Queens, Crime and Punishment)

Renascence Editions. http://darkwing.uoregon.edu/%7Erbear/ren.htm. (Shakespeare and other works, 1477–1799)

Richard III Society, American Branch. http://www.r3.org/. (Wars of the Roses, Fifteenth-Century Society and Culture)

Appendix: Genealogies

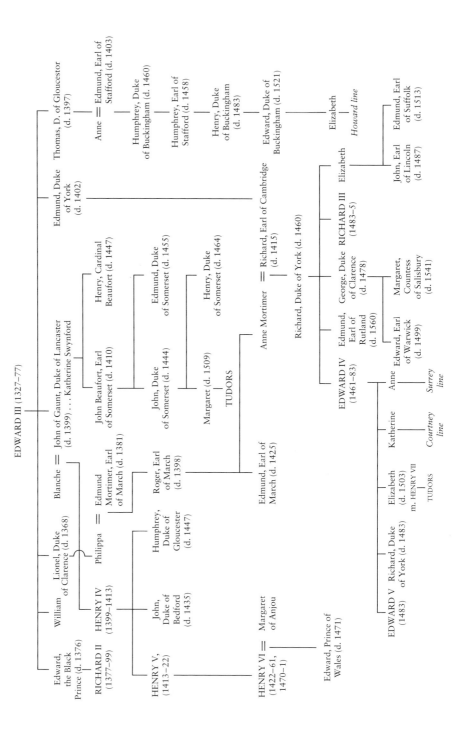

Genealogy 1 The Yorkists and Lancastrians

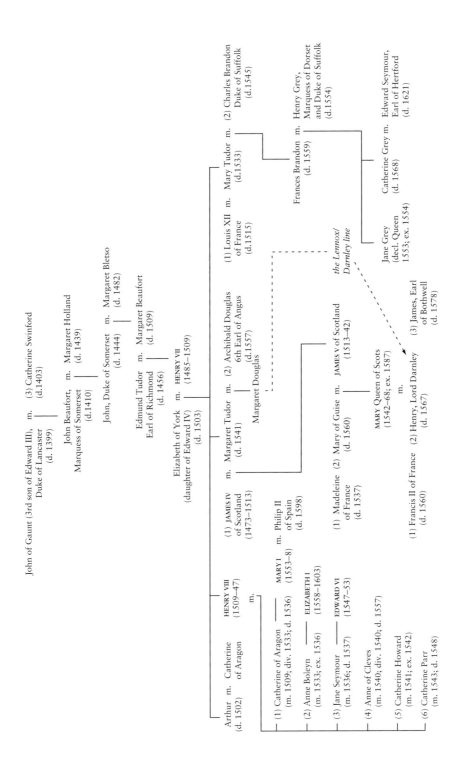

Genealogy 2   The Tudors and Stuarts

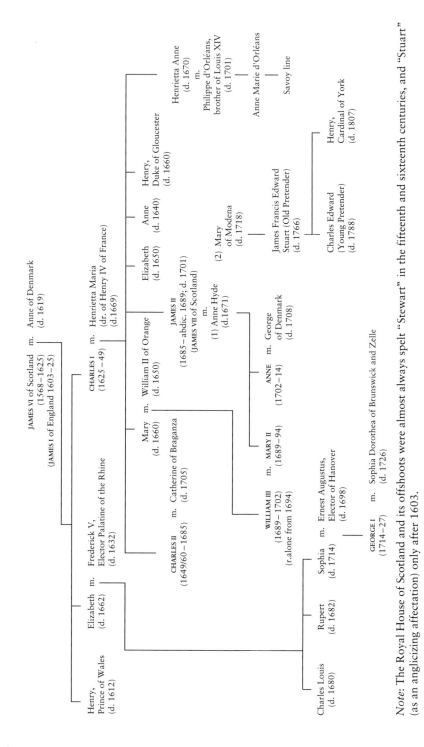

Note: The Royal House of Scotland and its offshoots were almost always spelt "Stewart" in the fifteenth and sixteenth centuries, and "Stuart" (as an anglicizing affectation) only after 1603.

Genealogy 3   The Stuarts and Hanoverians

Index

Note: Peers are listed under the title by which they are most frequently identified in the text. Where other titles are referred to in the text, a cross-reference is provided. Page references in *italic* are to illustrations.

Abhorrers, 285
accidents, 15
acting companies, 197
  see also theater and theaters
Addison, Joseph, 358, 359
administration, *see* government
advowson, 21, 269
agriculture
  18th century, 345, 346, 369
  and climate, 14
  demesne farming, 21
  under Edward VI, 100, 102
  feeding London, 184
  labor force, 19–20, 155–6, 369–70
  late medieval, 20, 21
  wages, 20, 153, 156, 346
Albemarle, Arnold Joost van Keppel, earl
  of, 305
alcohol, 20, 179
aldermen, 29, 50, 183
alehouses, 20, 179
Alençon and Anjou, François, duke of, 131
Alfred the Great, 6
Allen, Fr. William, 129
Almanza, battle of (1707), 327
Alva, Fernando Alvarez de Toledo, duke of,
  128
Amboyna, Dutch massacre of colony at
  (1623), 192
Americas

Spanish possessions in, 126–7, *127*, 132
  see also North American English colonies
Amicable Grant, 62
Anabaptists, 94
Ancient Constitution, 210
angels, 23
Anglicans, 222–3, 224, 235
  see also Arminians and Arminianism
Angus, Archibald Douglas, earl of, 65
animals
  family livestock, 19
  hierarchy of, 23
Anjou, Philippe, duke of (Philip V of Spain),
  316, 327, 330, 334, 336
annates, 27, 74, 75
Anne, queen of Great Britain and Ireland,
  318
  death, 338–9
  favorites, 319, 333
  foreign policy, 322–3, 330, 334–7
  and Glorious Revolution, 295
  government, 319–23, 325–8, 329–34,
    337–8
  health, 317, 333, 338
  marriage, 281
  ministers, choice of, 319–20, 331, 333–4,
    337–8
  and Old Pretender, 292, 321, 327
  personality and appearance, 317–19
  place in succession, 274, 299

Anne, queen of Great Britain and Ireland (*cont'd*)
  reign, 317–38
  and religion, 321–2, 325, 330–1, 337–8, 367
  and Scotland, 328–30
  succession to, 315, 321, 327–8, 338
Anne of Cleves, 94
Anne of Denmark, queen of England,
    Scotland and Ireland, 208
Antwerp, 128, 190
apothecaries, 366
apprentices, behavior, 181
apprenticeships, 164
architecture, 194–5, 273, 351–2, 356, 363
  see also housing
aristocracy, *see* nobility and noble families
Arlington, Henry Bennet, earl of, 277, 278
armies
  army careers, 365–6
  under Charles II, 266–7, 287
  in Civil Wars, 241
  under Elizabeth I, 136, 140
  under James II, 288, 290, 295
  nobles' private, 50
  under William III, 294, 313, 315
  see also New Model Army
Arminians and Arminianism, 225–6
  in Scotland, 231–2
Arminius, Jacobus, 225
Army Plot (1641), 234
art, 194–200, 273, 356, 357–60, 363
  patronage, 194, 197, 273, 357–8
Arthur, prince of Wales (Henry VII's son),
    43, 45, 64, 66
Artificers, Statute of (1563), 365
artisans, 183, 365
Arundel, Henry Fitzalan, earl of, 104, 116
Arundel, Thomas Howard, earl of, 195
Ashley, Anthony Ashley Cooper, Lord, *see*
    Shaftesbury, earl of
Asia, trade with, 347–8
  see also India
Asiento, 334
Aske, Robert, 77–8
assizes, 49, 178
Astell, Mary, 359
Astley, Jacob, Lord, 245
astrology, 26
astronomy, 361
attainder, 28
  Henry VII's use of, 43, 50, 52
  Long Parliament and Strafford, 234
  during Wars of the Roses, 36
"Auld Alliance," 9, 95, 98, 123

Babington, Anthony, 134
Babylonian Captivity (1309–77), 30
Bacon, Sir Francis, Viscount St. Albans,
    161, 217, 360
Bacon, Sir Nicholas, 115
Balliol, John de, 9
Baltimore, George Calvert, Lord, 193
Baltinglass, Lord, 142
Bancroft, Archbishop Richard, 224
Banister, John, 358
Bank of England, 311–12
banks, 349
Bannockburn, battle of (1314), 9
Baptists, 252–3, 257
Barbary pirates, 260
Barebone, Praise-God, 257
Barnet, battle of (1471), 37
baronets, 154, 213
Barton, Elizabeth, 77
Bastwick, John, 226
Bate, John, 213
Bate's case (1606), 213
Bavaria, 323–5
Baxter, Richard, 171
Beachy Head, battle of (1690), 306–7
Beaton, David, Cardinal, 95
Beaufort, Margaret, 40
Bedford, earl of (1593–1641), 233
Bedford, earls of (Russell family), 189
begging, 175–6, 370
Behn, Aphra, 359
beliefs
  Age of Reason, 360–2
  birth mishaps, 64
  Great Chain of Being, 22–30
  superstition, 179–80, 371
  see also religion
Bentinck, Hans William, earl of Portland,
    305
Berwick, Treaty of (1639), 232
Bible
  Catholic and Protestant views of, 89–91
  King James version, 198–9, 224
  and Somerset, 99
  and Thomas Cromwell, 76, 93
Birmingham, 348
births, registration, 258
Bishops' Wars (1639, 1640), 231–2, 242
Black Death, 15, 19
Blair, Tony, 11
Blathwayt, William, 313
Blenheim, battle of (1704), 323–5, 326
Blenheim Palace, 325, 351–2

Bloody Assizes (1685), 288
Blow, John, 273, 356
Bohemia, 217
Boleyn, Anne, Queen of England
   background, 65
   marriage and coronation, 68, 74, 75
   and religion, 88, 92
   trial and execution, 92–3
Boleyn, George, Lord Rochford, 92
Boleyn, Mary, 65
Boleyn, Sir Thomas, 65
Bolingbroke, Henry St. John, Viscount,
   337, 338
Bombay, 273
book ownership, 198
Boston, 193
Bosworth Field, battle of (1485), 31, 40–1
Bothwell, James Hepburn, earl of, 124, 381
Bouchain, battle of (1711), 327
Boyle, Robert, 361
Boyne, battle of the (1690), 307
Bradshaw, John, 249, 272
"Braveheart" (Sir William Wallace), 9
Bray, Sir Reginald, 51
Breda, Declaration of (1660), 262, 268
Bridgman, Charles, 352
Brihuega, battle of (1710), 327
Bristol, 17, 182, 348, 368
British Isles, map, 2
British Museum, 358
Britton, Thomas, 358
Browne, Robert, 121
Bruce, Robert the, 9
Buchanan, George, 224
Buckingham, George Villiers, first duke of
   (1582–1628), *215*
   art collection, 195
   assassination, 222
   and Charles I, 217, 218, 220
   and James I, 208, 214, 216
   and Spanish war, 220–2
Buckingham, George Villiers, second duke
   of (1628–87), 274, 277
Buckingham, Henry Stafford, duke of
   (1455–83), 39, 40
building, 194–5, 273, 356, 363
   churches, 69
   see also housing
Burbage, James, 197
Burbage, Richard, 197
Burghley, Lord, *see* Cecil, William, Lord
   Burghley
Burgundy, 44, 45

Burgundy, Margaret, duchess of, 41, 44
burials, 168–9
Burton, Henry, 226
Byrd, William, 195

Cabal (political group), 277, 280
Cabot, John, 192
Cabot, Sebastian, 192
Cadiz, Drake's attack on (1587), 133–4
Calais, loss of (1558), 110
calendars, 387
Calvin, John, 92
Calvinists, 92, 226
Camden, William, 198, 210
Campeggio, Lorenzo, Cardinal, 66–7
Campion, Edmund, 129
Canada, 334, 336
capital punishment, 178, 372–3
   see also crime and punishment
Caribbean, 260, 334, 336
Carlos II, king of Spain, 278, 316
Cartwright, Thomas, 120
Casket Letters, 124
Castle Howard, 352, *352*
Castlemaine, Barbara *née* Villiers Palmer,
   countess of, 273
castles, 159
Catherine of Aragon, queen of England
   death, 92
   divorce, 62, 63–8, 73–5
   marriage, 45, 55
Catherine of Braganza, queen of England,
   Scotland and Ireland, 273, 283
Catholics and Catholicism
   16th-century beliefs, 89–92
   18th century, 370
   under Anne, 322
   barred from English throne, 299
   under Charles I, 226
   Charles II's beliefs, 268, 276, 278–9, 287
   Charles II's treatment of, 280, 281
   under Elizabeth I, 117–19, 121–2, 128–31
   emigration to America, 192
   and Glorious Revolution, 299–300
   under Henry VIII, 94–5, 96, 97
   Ireland, 10–11, 142, 223, 256, 307
   under James I, 223, 224–5
   James II's beliefs, 276, 289–90
   James II's treatment of, 290–1
   under Mary I, 104, 106–10
   during Protectorate, 259
   see also Roman Catholic Church; Roman
      Catholic Church in England

Cavaliers
  definition, 239
  post-Restoration treatment, 272
  and Tory party, 265
Cecil, Sir Robert, earl of Salisbury
  and Elizabeth I, 139, 146, 149–50
  house, 159, *160*
  and James I, 151, 201, 213
  on kings and money, 212
Cecil, William, Lord Burghley
  background, 115
  as Elizabeth I's adviser, 115–16, 145
  foreign policy, 131, 139
  and government finances, 144, 146
  in old age, 148, 149
  on religion, 108
censorship
  18th century, 359
  under Charles II, 275, 284, 359
  under Commonwealth, 251, 252
  under Elizabeth I, 199
Centlivre, Susannah, 359
Chamber, 47, 48
Chancery, 47, 57, 188, 258
Chandos, James Brydges, duke of, 357
chantries, dissolution of, 85–6, 99, 100
Chantries Act (1547), 99
Chapel Royal, 195–6, 356
charity, *see* Poor Law; social welfare
Charles I, king of England, Scotland, and
    Ireland, *219*
  art collection, 195, 218–20, 229
  Bishops' Wars, 232
  and Civil Wars, 202–3, 237
  Civil Wars, negotiations after, 244–8
  Eikon Basilike, 251
  finances under, 220, 221, 228–30, 232, 233
  foreign policy, 220–2, 229
  government, 229
  marriage, 217, 218, 222, 226–7
  on monarchy, 220, 234
  Personal Rule, 228–30
  personality and appearance, 218–20
  post-Restoration view of, 268
  regicides' punishment, 272
  reign, 219–22, 225–50
  and religion, 225–7, 233, 235
  and Spanish war, 220–2
  trial and execution, 248–50, *250*
  see also Parliament, and Charles I
Charles II, king of England, Scotland, and
    Ireland, *263*, *271*
  death, 287–8

finances under, 266–8, 275, 277, 278–9,
  281–2, 287
foreign policy, 276–9
government, 266–70, 275–7, 280–2, 287
local government, 287
mistresses and children, 273–4
personality, 270–4
plots against, 269, 282–3, 287
powers, 266–8, 270
reign, 266–88
religious beliefs, 268, 276, 278–9, 287
religious policies, 268–70, 280, 281
Restoration, 262–4
succession to, 283–6
and Worcester (1651), 256
see also Parliament, and Charles II
Charles V, king of Spain and Holy Roman
    Emperor
  and Henry VIII, 61, 62, 66, 92, 93
  and Ireland, 83
  marriage, 65
  military campaigns, 67
Charles VI, king of France, 32, 33
Charles VIII, king of France, 44
Charles IX, king of France, 116
Charles, archduke of Austria (would-be
    Carlos III of Spain), 316, 336
Charles, archduke of Styria, 116
Chatsworth House, 352
Chester, county palatinate of, 81
Chichester, Sir Arthur, 143
childbirth, 166, 173
children
  infant mortality, 15, 162–3, 345
  infanticide, 177
  labor, 348
  nobles and gentry, 156–7
  non-elite, 163–4
China, trade with, 348
church ales, 19
Church of England
  18th century, 371–2
  under Anne, 337–8, 367
  under Charles I, 226, 233, 235
  under Charles II, 268–70
  Church courts, 179, 233, 269, 371
  Church music, 195–6, 356, 358
  during Commonwealth, 258
  and Edward VI, 98–9, 102–3
  and Elizabeth I, 117–19, 120–1
  and Glorious Revolution, 296–8
  and Henry VIII, 68, 73–8, 85–6, 93–4,
    94–5, 97

Hooker on, 198
under James I, 222–3, 225
under James II, 291–2
and law and order, 174
and Mary I, 104, 106–10
monasteries, dissolution of, 85–6
and morality, 174
place in daily life, 170, 371–2
pre-Reformation, *see* Roman Catholic
    Church in England
during Protectorate, 259
structure, 118
and Walpole, 343
and Wolsey, 55–6
see also clergy; Reformation; Roman
    Catholic Church in England
churches
    appearance and seating arrangement, 170
    church attendance, 171, 371
    church-building programs, 69
    community role of, 17–19
    Reformation changes, *71*, 93, 102–3,
        170
Churchill, John, Lord, *see* Marlborough,
    John Churchill, duke of
Churchill, Sarah, *see* Marlborough, Sarah
    Churchill, duchess of
Churchill, Winston, 376
cities, *see* towns and cities
Civil Wars (1642–51), 237–56, *242*
    causes, 202–3
    First, 237–44
    lessons, 265–6
    Second, 247–8
City (London), 187
clans, 8
Clarence, George, duke of, 37, 378
Clarendon, Edward Hyde, earl of, 269,
    275, 277
Clarendon Code, 269, 391
Clark, J. C. D., 343–4
Clarkson, Laurence, 253
classes, *see* ranks, social
classical tradition, 18th-century popularity,
    360, 363
Clement VII, Pope, 66–7
clergy
    17th and 18th centuries, 366–7
    and Act of Uniformity (1662), 269
    appointment of, 21, 258, 269
    benefit of, 178
    Catholic and Protestant views of, 89–91
    education, 171, 366

Henry VIII's attacks on, 73–4
income, 171, 366, 367
and marriage, 94, 99
and Mary I, 107
monasteries, dissolution of, 85–6
morality, 70–2
numbers, 70, 170–1
Puritan views of, 120–1
Reformation, reaction to, 76
Clifford, Thomas, Lord, 277, 278
climate, 14
cloth trade, *see* wool trade
clubs, private, 357
coaches, 162
coal-mining, 191, 348, 368
coffee-houses, *332*, 357
Cognac, League of, 62
coinage, 102, 153
Coke, Sir Edward, 209–10, 211
Coke, Thomas, 325
Coleman, Edward, 282
Colet, John, 70
Collier, Jeremy, 371
colonies, English
    Canada, 334, 336
    West Indies, 260, 334, 336
    see also North American English colonies
colonies, Scottish, 328
colonies, Spanish, 126–7, *127*, 132
commissioners of array, 24
Committee of Public Safety, 261
Common Pleas, court of, 48, 188
Commonwealth, 251–8
    government, 256–7, 258
    pacification of Ireland and Scotland,
        255–6
    radicalism and religious sects, 251–5
Commonwealthmen, 84, 100
Company of Scotland, 328
Compton, Bishop Henry, 291, 293–4
concerts, public, 358
Confederation of Kilkenny (1642), 236
Congreve, William, 358
constitution
    Ancient Constitution, 210
    Anne's powers, 321, 331, 338
    Charles I's trial, implications of, 248–50
    Charles II's powers, 266–8, 270
    Declaration of Rights (1689), 296
    after Glorious Revolution, 298–9, 300,
        309
    under Hanoverians, 341
    Henry VIII's changes, 79–80, 87, 97

constitution (*cont'd*)
  monarch's rights and powers, Charles I on, 220, 234
  monarch's rights and powers, Charles II on, 274–5
  monarch's rights and powers, Henry VII on, 42
  monarch's rights and powers, James I on, 208–9
  monarch's rights and powers, James II on, 290
  monarch's rights and powers, medieval, 23
  monarch's rights and powers, Stuart era, 204–5, 210–11, 233
  Parliament and the sovereign, 49, 205, 210–11, 233, 341
  at Restoration, 266–8, 270
  post-Restoration views, 265–6
  and William III, 312–13
consumerism, 348, 351–2, 370
contraception, 166
Conventicle Act (1664), 269
convents, dissolution of, 85–6, 106
Coppe, Abiezer, 253
Cornbury, Edward Hyde, Viscount, 295
Cornish rebellion (1497), 44
Cornwall, 12, 44, 191, 348
Cornyshe, William, 54
Corporation Act (1661), 269
corporations, 50, 183
cottagers, 155–6, 369–70
council, royal, 46
  under Henry VII, 51
  under Henry VIII, 57, 80
  see also Privy Council
Council of the North, 81, 233
Council of Trent (1545–63), 128–9
Counter-Reformation, 128–9
country houses, 159–61, 346, 351–2, 352
  see also manors
countryside, *see* rural life
court, royal
  18th century, 356–7
  under Charles I, 220
  under Charles II, 273, 356
  under Elizabeth I, 149–50, 194, 195–6
  under Henry VIII, 54
  under James I, 212
  under James II, 290
  late medieval, 46–7
  at Whitehall, 188–9
  under William and Mary, 304

courts of law
  assizes, 49, 178
  borough courts, 179
  Chancery, 47, 57, 188, 258
  Common Pleas, 48, 188
  ecclesiastical, 27, 179, 233, 269, 371
  High Commission, 233
  King's Bench, 48, 188
  manorial courts, 179
  petty sessions, 50, 179
  quarter sessions, 50, 179
  Requests, 233
  Star Chamber, 38, 45, 50, 57, 233
Covenanters
  and Charles I, 256
  and Civil Wars, 243, 247
  establishment, 231
Covent Garden, 189
Coverdale, Miles, 93
Cowley, Abraham, 198
craftsmen, 183, 365
Cranmer, Archbishop Thomas
  burning of, 107, 108
  under Edward VI, 99
  under Henry VIII, 68, 74, 88, 96
  Prayer Books, 99, 102
credit, *see* money
crime and punishment, 177–82, 372–3
  see also law and order
Cromwell, Oliver, *259*
  background and personality, 258
  as Civil War soldier, 243, 244, 248
  during Commonwealth, 256–7, 258
  death and funeral, 261
  in Ireland, 255–6
  as lord protector, 254, 258–61
  posthumous hanging, 272
  religious beliefs, 252, 259
  in Scotland, 256
Cromwell, Richard, 261
Cromwell, Thomas
  background, 73
  fall, 94–5
  foreign policy, 92, 93
  and Henry VIII's marriages, 68, 73, 92–3, 94
  and Reformation, 73–6, 85–6, 88, 93–4
  reforms of, 78–87
culture, 194–200, 273, 356, 357–60, 363
Customs duties
  under Charles I, 228, 229
  under Charles II, 267, 287
  under Edward IV, 38

under Henry VII, 52
under James I, 213
under William III, 311
see also taxation

Dacre family, 81
Danby, Thomas Osborne, earl of, 280–2, 283, 293–4
Darcy, Thomas, Lord, 68
Darién, Scottish colony at, 328
Darnley, Henry Stewart, Lord, 124
Davenant, Charles, 362
Davison, William, 134
De facto Act (1495), 43
deaths
    registration, 258
    see also mortality
debt, treatment of creditors, 258
Declaration of Rights (1689), 296
Dee, John, 198
deference, 27–8, 172–3, 301, 343–4, 360
Defoe, Daniel
    on the common people, 369
    and Oxford, 321, 358
    on power of money, 312
    publishing history, 358
    and *Review*, 321, 359
    works, 353, 362
Deists, 362
Dekker, Thomas, 184–5
Delarivière, Mary, 359
demesne farming, 21
demographic statistics
    Gregory King, 346, 353, 354–5, 364, 370
    see also mortality; population
Derbyshire, 191
Dering, Sir Edward, 235
devolution, 8, 9, 10–11
Devonshire, William Cavendish, earl of, 293–4
Dickens, A. G., 68
Diggers, 253
diplomacy, *see* foreign policy
dispensing power, 292
Dissenters, *see* Nonconformists
Divine Right of Kings, *see* monarchs and monarchy
divorce, 165
Donne, John, 198
Dorchester, Catherine Sedley, countess of, 290
Douai seminary, 129
Dover, Treaty of (1670), 278–9

Dowland, John, 196
Drake, Sir Francis, 126–7, 133–4, 139–40
dramatists, *see* plays and playwrights
Drayton, Michael, 198
Drogheda, Cromwell's capture (1649), 255–6
Dryden, John, 273, 286, 358, 363
Dudley, Edmund, 50–1, 55
Dudley, Lord Guildford, 103–4, 106
Duffy, Eamon, 68
Dunbar, battle of (1296), 9
Dunbar, battle of (1650), 256
Dunton, John, 359
Durham, county palatinate of, 80, 81
Dyck, Anthony van, 195, 218–20

East Anglia, geography and trade, 13, 14
East India Company, 191–2, 273, 348
East Stoke, battle of (1487), 44
Easter Rising (1916), *see* Irish Rebellion (1916)
Eastland Company, 191
economics, development of, 362–3
economy
    16th century, 146, 152–6
    18th century, 346–50
    under Edward VI, 99–101, 102
    Halifax's financial revolution, 310–12, 312–14
    under James I, 211
Edgehill, battle of (1642), 240–1
Edinburgh, Treaty of (1328), 9
Edinburgh, Treaty of (1560), 123
Edinburgh, University of, 366
education
    clergy, 171, 366
    nobles and gentry, 157, 158
    Nonconformist, 337
    non-elite, 155, 163–4, 371–2
    professions, 366
    scholarships, 367
Edward I, king of England, 8, 9
Edward III, king of England, 32
Edward IV, king of England (formerly duke of York), 36–8, 39
Edward V, king of England, 38–40, 41
Edward VI, king of England and Ireland
    birth, 93
    finances under, 100, 102
    and Mary Queen of Scots, 95, 98–9
    and Protestantism, 98–9, 102–3
    reign, 97–103
    tutors, 96

Edward, prince of Wales (Henry VI's son), 37
Edwards, Thomas, 251
elections, frequency of general, 49, 233, 320, 341
electoral system, *see* franchise, electoral
Eliot, Sir John, 228
Elizabeth I, queen of England and Ireland, *113*
  birth, 75
  finances under, 139, 144–8, 212
  foreign policy, 115, 122–8, 131–41, 149
  government, 144–8
  and Ireland, 141–4
  and marriage, 116–17, 131
  and Mary I, 106, 110–11
  and money, 212
  Parliamentary address (1601), 147–8
  and patronage of arts, 194, 197
  personality and appearance, 114–15, 117, 118, 147
  and plays, 196–7
  plots against, 128–31
  reign, 112–51
  and religion, 108, 117–19, 120, 121, 122, 130–1
  royal progresses, 160–1
  and Spanish Armada, 133–8
  succession to, 151
  Tilbury speech, 136–7
Elizabeth, queen of Bohemia (the Winter Queen), 216–17
Elizabeth, queen of England (Henry VII's wife), 43, 45
Elton, G. R., 78–9, 80
emigration, 154, 193, 345
Empson, Sir Richard, 51, 55
enclosure, 21
  under Edward VI, 100
  under Henry VIII, 57, 58, 85
enclosure riots, 181–2
Engagers, 247–8
England
  county map, 7
  early history and development, 5–6
  power and relationships within British Isles, 8–11
  regional tensions, 11
English
  ethnicity, 4
  view of foreigners, 3, 5
  view of selves, 1–3
English Channel, roles, 3–4
English language, 4, 197–8

entertainment
  alehouses, 20, 179
  holidays, 19, 27, 196
  nobles and gentry, 161–2, 352–3, 353–6, 357–8
  popular, 19, 196
  sport, 19, 208
  theater and theaters, 185, 196–7, 357, 358
epidemics, 345
  influenza and sweating sickness, 102, 114, 152, 345
  plague, 15, 19, 152, 275, 345
Erasmus, 54, 70
Erik XIV, king of Sweden, 116
esquires, 24
Essex, Robert Devereaux, second earl of (ca. 1566–1601)
  art collection, 195
  on Elizabeth I, 114
  fall, 150–1
  on foreign policy, 139, 149
  houses, 189
  in Ireland, 143, 150
  personality and background, 149
Essex, Robert Devereaux, third earl of (1591–1646)
  and Charles I, 233
  in Civil Wars, 240, 243, 244
  marriage, 214
  on Strafford, 234
Essex House, 189
Étaples, Treaty of (1492), 44–5
Etherege, George, 273, 356
Eugene of Savoy, Prince, 323, 327
Europe, map, *60*
European Union, 11
Evelyn, John, 261, 262, 265
Exchequer, 47–8, 102
Excise duties
  under Charles II, 267, 287
  creation, 241
  during Commonwealth, 258
  during Protectorate, 260
  under William III, 311, 313
Exclusion Crisis, 283–6
Exeter, Henry, marquis of, 41
Exeter, siege of (1549), 99
exploration, 126–7, 192–3
  works on, 198

factories, 348–9
Fairfax, Sir Thomas, 244, 248, 256

families
  family life, 165
  hierarchy within, 25, 28
  non-elite size, 162–3
  see also children; marriage
famine, 15, 146, 345
farming, *see* agriculture; livestock farming;
    sheep farming
Fawkes, Guy, 225
Felipe, *see* Philip
Felton, John, 222
Ferdinand of Aragon, king of Spain, 45, 59
Festivals of the Sons of the Clergy, 358
Field of the Cloth of Gold (1520), 61
Fielding, Henry, 344, 372
Fifth Monarchy Men, 254, 257, 268
Filmer, Sir Robert, 286
finances, government
  Chamber, 47, 48
  under Charles I, 220, 221, 228–30, 232,
    233
  under Charles II, 266–8, 275, 277,
    278–9, 281–2, 287
  under Edward IV, 38
  under Edward VI, 100, 102
  under Elizabeth I, 139, 144–8, 212
  Exchequer, 47–8, 102
  under George I, 343
  under Henry VII, 51–2
  under Henry VIII, 61, 62, 80, 85–6,
    95–6, 97
  under James I, 211–16
  under James II, 288
  Halifax's financial revolution, 310–12,
    312–14
  and Parliament, 49
  during Protectorate, 260
  Treasury, 277, 313
  under William III, 310–12, 312–14
  see also taxation
fine arts, 195, 352
fiscal policy, *see* finances, government
Fish, Simon, 70
Fisher, Bishop John, 67, 77
Five Knights' Case (1626), 221
Five Mile Act (1665), 269
flags, union, 230
Fleetwood, Gen. Charles, 261
Flodden, battle of (1513), 59
food
  average diet, 15, 168
  expenditure on, 370
  famine, 15, 146, 345

London, 184
  prices, 21, 100, 146, 153, 346
food riots, 181–2
foreign policy
  under Anne, 322–3, 330, 334–7
  under Charles I, 220–2, 229
  under Charles II, 276–9
  under Elizabeth I, 115, 122–8, 131–41,
    149
  under George I, 343
  under Henry VII, 43–6
  under Henry VIII, 58–62, 92–4, 95–6, 97
  under James I, 216–21
  under Mary I, 110
  during Protectorate, 260
  under William III, 294, 300, 302, 304
Forest Laws, Charles I's revival, 229, 233
forests, 14
Form of Apology and Satisfaction (1604),
    210–11, 217–18
Forty-Two Articles of Faith (1553), 103
Fox, Margaret Askew Fell, 374
Foxe, John, 74, 108
Foxe's *Book of Martyrs*, 108–10, *109*, 126
France
  16th-century weakness, 125
  18th-century economy and strength, 330,
    336, 343
  absolute monarchy, 274
  Charles I's war, 221, 229
  and Charles II, 277–9, 287
  Dutch Republic, invasion of (1667), 278
  and Edward VI, 102
  and Elizabeth I, 131, 140–1
  and English succession, 316–17, 334–5
  Estates General, 209
  expansionism under Louis XIV, 274,
    277–9, 294, 300, 316
  and Henry VII, 44–5
  and Henry VIII, 59–62, 92, 93, 95–6
  Hundred Years' War (1337–1453), 32–3,
    44
  James II, support for, 305–6, 307
  Lancastrian links, 37
  map, *35*
  and Mary I, 110
  Nine Years' War (1689–97), 302, 308, 312
  and Scotland, 9, 95, 98, 123
  tax administration, 230
  Thirty Years' War (1618–48), 216
  and Treaty of Utrecht (1713), 334–6
  and War of Spanish Succession
    (1702–14), 315–17, 323–5, 327

franchise, electoral, 24, 48–9, 155
    after Glorious Revolution, 320–1
    during Protectorate, 258
    in towns, 48, 183
franchises (independent), 80–1
Francis I, king of France, 61, 93
Francis II, king of France, 122
Frederick V, elector Palatine and king of
    Bohemia (the Winter King), 216–17
Frobisher, Sir Martin, 126
funerals, 168–9

Gamage, Barbara, 159
gardens, 352, 363
Gardiner, Bishop Stephen, 68, 94, 96, 107
Gay, John, 342
gender issues
    contemporary views of female rule, 64
    marital relationships, 165
    sexual morality standards, 158
    women's status, 25, 374
    see also women
gentry
    18th-century position, 344, 346, 350–1,
      353
    childcare, 156–7
    daily life, 156–62, 352–3
    duties owed to, 27, 172–3, 360
    education, 157, 158
    expenditure, 354–5
    and Glorious Revolution, 298
    houses and households, 159–61, 353, 356
    income, 24, 56, 155, 353, 354, 356
    late medieval, 24
    late Tudor–early Stuart period, 154–5,
      156–62
    and law and order, 21, 50
    marriage, 158–9
    mobility, 28–9, 154–5
    moral responsibilities, 27, 172–3, 360
    pastimes, 161–2, 352–3, 353–6, 358
    powers as landlords, 20–2
    and Restoration, 261, 265
    rise in numbers, 154–5
    younger sons, 157, 351
geography, 1–4, 11–14
    works on, 198
George I, king of Great Britain and Ireland
    and elector of Hanover
    involvement in English affairs, 341
    place in succession, 315, 338, 339
    reign, 340–3
George II, king of Great Britain and Ireland
    and elector of Hanover, 341

George of Denmark, Prince, 281, 295, 317,
    331
Gibbons, Grinling, 273, 303, 352, 356
Gibbons, Orlando, 195
Gibraltar, 327, 334, 336
Glasgow, 348
Glencoe Massacre (1692), 328
Glorious Revolution (1688–9), 294–301
Gloucester, Richard, duke of, *see* Richard
    III, king of England (formerly duke of
    Gloucester)
Gloucester, William, duke of, 315
Godfrey, Sir Edmund Berry, 282–3
Godolphin, Sidney, earl of, 319, 323, 330,
    331, 333
Golden Hind, 127
golf, 208
Good Friday Accords (1998), 11
Goodwin, Sir Francis, 210
Goodwin's case (1604), 210–11
Gorges, Ferdinando, 347
Gouge, William, 165
Gough, Richard, 170
government, workings of
    Anglo-Saxon, 6
    under Edward IV, 38
    first prime minister, 341–2
    growth in professionalism, 313, 365, 367
    under Henry VII, 46–52
    under Henry VIII, 56–8, 78–81, 84–7, 97
    under James I, 211
    late medieval, 46–50
    ministers and political parties, 319–20,
      331
    monarch's role, *see* monarchs and
      monarchy
    Parliament's role, *see* Parliament
    patronage, 342, 367
    during Protectorate, 258–60
    royal court's role, 46–7, 356–7
    see also local government
grain prices, *see* food, prices
grain trade, 57, 58
Grand Alliance, War of, *see* Nine Years'
    War (1689–97)
Grand Remonstrance (1641), 235
Grand Tour, 157
Graunt, John, 362
Great Chain of Being, 22–30
    Glorious Revolution's effects, 301
    late Tudor–early Stuart changes, 154–6
Great Contract (1610), 213
Great Fire of London (1666), 275

Great Plague of London (1665), 275, 345
Great Schism (1378–1417), 30
Great Seal of England, 47
Green Ribbon Club, 284, 285
Greene, Henry, 171
Gresham, Sir Thomas, 187
Grey, Lady Jane, 103–4, 106
Grindal, Edmund, 121
Grub Street, 359
Guildhall, London, 187
guilds, 183, 365
Gunpowder Plot (1605), 225
Gwyn, Nell, 273

Haigh, Christopher, 68
Hakewill, William, 147
Hakluyt, Richard, 198
Halifax, Charles Montagu, Lord, 311–12, 331, 358
    financial revolution, 310–12, 312–14
Halley, Sir Edmund, 361
Hampden, John, 229–30, 233
Hampton Court, 56, 303, 305
Hampton Court Conference (1604), 224
Handel, Georg Frideric, 357, 358
Hanover dynasty, succession to throne, 299, 315, 321, 327, 338
Hanseatic League, 189, 190
Harley, Edward, 368–9
Harley, Nathaniel, 368–9
Harley, Robert, *see* Oxford, Robert Harley, earl of
Harpsfield, Nicholas, 88
Harrison, Maj.-Gen. Thomas, 254
Harrison, William, 154–5
Hastings, William, Lord, 37, 39
Hatfield House, 159, *160*
Hatton, Sir Christopher, 115, 146
Hawkins, John, 126, 133, 140
Hawksmoor, Nicholas, 352
health, 15, 168, 345
    see also epidemics; medicine
Hearth Tax (1662), 267
Heidegger, John James, 358
Henrietta Maria, queen of England, Scotland and Ireland, 222, 226–7
Henry IV, king of England, 32
Henry V, king of England, 32–3, 58
Henry VI, king of England, 33, 36, 37
Henry VII, king of England, *42*
    assumption of throne, 31, 40–1
    exploration under, 192
    finances under, 51–2

foreign policy, 43–6
government, 46–52
personality and background, 41–2, 55
reign, 41–52
Henry VIII, king of England, *53*
    and building, 194
    and Church of England, 68, 73–8, 85–6, 93–4, 94–5, 97
    death, 97
    finances under, 61, 62, 80, 85–6, 95–6, 97
    foreign policy, 58–62, 92–4, 95–6, 97
    government, 56–8, 78–81, 84–7, 97
    and Ireland, 81–4, 141
    marriage, to Catherine of Aragon, 45, 62, 63–8, 73–5
    marriage, to other wives, 74, 92–3, 94–5, 96
    personality and appearance, 52–5
    reign, 52–97
    religious beliefs, 72, 88–9, 94–5, 96–7
    and Royal Navy, 93, 133
    and Wales, 81
    and Whitehall, 188
    will and testament, 97–8
    and Wolsey, 55–8
Henry III, king of France, 140
Henry IV, king of France, 140–1
Henry, prince of Wales (James I's son), 211, 216–17, 218
Herbert, George, 198
heretics, treatment of
    under Elizabeth I, 108
    under Henry VII, 42
    under Henry VIII, 67, 108
    under Mary I, 107–10
Hertford, Edward Seymour, earl of, *see* Somerset, Edward Seymour, duke of
hierarchy, social
    18th century, 343–4
    Glorious Revolution's effect, 301
    late medieval, 22–30
    late Tudor–early Stuart period, 154–6
    urban, 182–3
High Commission, court of, 233
Hilliard, Nicholas, 195
history, works on, 198
Holbein, Hans, 53, 54, 94
holidays, 19, 27, 196
Holinshed, Raphael, 198
Holles, Denzil, 228, 233, 243
Holmes, Geoffrey, 321
Holy League, 59

Holy Roman Empire
  extent, 59
  and Henry VII, 44, 45
  and Henry VIII, 61–2, 92, 93, 95
  Thirty Years' War (1618–48), 216
  and War of the Spanish Succession
    (1702–14), 323–5, 334
Home Counties, geography, 11–12
Hooke, Robert, 361
Hooker, Richard, 198
horse-racing, 356
Houlbrooke, Ralph, 163
House of Commons
  composition, 24, 48–9, 353, 368
  election frequency, 49, 233, 320, 341
  selection of MPs, *see* franchise, electoral
  see also Parliament
House of Lords
  abolition by Commonwealth, 250
  composition, 48
  under George I, 341
  size under Elizabeth I, 146
  see also Parliament
housing
  nobles and gentry, 20, 159–61, *160*, 189,
    346, 351–2, *352*
  non-elite, 15, 19, 166–8, *167*
Howard, Catherine, Queen of England, 94–5
Howard of Effingham, Charles, Lord, 133
Hudson, Christopher, 179
Hudson's Bay, 334
Huguenots, 125, 216, 348–9
Hundred Years' War (1337–1453), 32–3
husbandmen, 24, 153, 155–6, 354, 369

Ignatius of Loyola, 129
illegitimacy, 164–5
impositions, 213, 228, 229, 233
income, 354–5
  middling sort, 364–7
  nobility and gentry, 24, 56, 155, 351,
    353, 354–5, 356
  non-elite, 155–6, 354–5, 369
  Wolsey, 56
  see also finances, government; taxation;
    wages
Indemnity and Oblivion, Act of (1660), 272
India, 273, 287, 347–8
  see also East India Company
Indulgence, Declaration of (1672), 280
Indulgence, Declaration of (1687), 290,
  291–2
indulgences, 91

industrial revolution, 13
industrialization, 348–9
industry
  iron, 191, 348
  manufacturers' lifestyle, 364
  publishing, 198, 199, 251, 358–9
  regional, 13, 191
  sea's influence, 4
  silk, 348, 349, 365
  textile, 349
  timber, 14
infanticide, 177
influenza, 102, 114, 152, 345
inheritance
  land, 84
  noble families, 23–4, 157, 351
Injunctions (1536, 1538), 93–4
inns, 349
  see also alehouses
Inns of Court, 189
insurance, 350
Interregnum, *see* Commonwealth;
  Protectorate
Ireland
  during Civil Wars, 241–3
  Cromwell in, 255–6
  and England, 9–11
  and Elizabeth I, 141–4
  flight of the earls, 144
  and Henry VII, 44, 82
  and Henry VIII, 81–4, *83*, 141
  historical overview, 6–8, 9–11
  independence (1937), 10
  population, 18th century, 345
  religion, 10–11, 142, 223, 256, 307
  union with England (1801), 10
  William III's campaigns and aftermath,
    305–8
  see also Northern Ireland
Ireton, Henry, 244, 247, 272
Irish Rebellion (1641–50), 235–7, 255–6
Irish Rebellion (1916), 10
iron industry, 191, 348
Isabella of Castile, queen of Spain, 45
"island mentality," 1–5

Jacobite Rebellion (1715), 341
Jacobites, 302
  under Anne, 321, 338
  under George I, 341, 343
Jamaica, 260
James I and VI, king of England, Scotland,
  and Ireland, 9, *207*

accession to English throne, 151, 201
accession to Scottish throne, 124
and building, 194–5
favorites, 208, 212–13
finances under, 211–16
foreign policy, 216–21
government, 211
King James Bible, 198–9, 224
on London, 184
and Parliament, 209–11, 213, 214, 216,
  217–18, 220–1
personality and appearance, 206–9
reign, 201–18, 222–5
and religion, 206, 222–5
on the Sabbath, 196, 223
sale of titles, 154, 213
sexuality, 208
on smoking, 193
writings, 206, 209
James II and VII, king of England, Scotland,
  and Ireland (formerly duke of York), 289
death, 316–17
Exclusion Crisis, 283–6
in exile, 302, 308
finances under, 288
and Glorious Revolution, 294–301
as heir to throne, 274, 281, 283–6
Irish campaigns (1688–91), 305–7
as lord high admiral, 277, 280
local government, 291
and Parliament, 288, 290
personality, 289–90
reign, 288–95
religious beliefs, 276, 280, 289–90
religious policies, 290, 291–2
son's birth, 292–4, 293
James IV, king of Scotland, 45, 59
James V, king of Scotland, 95
James Francis Edward, the Old Pretender
birth, 292–4, 293
debarment from succession, 299
exile, 295
Jacobite Rebellion (1715), 341
recognition by Louis XIV, 316–17
and Scotland, 328–9
support in England, 321, 338
Jamestown, Virginia, 192–3
Jeffreys, George, Lord ("Hanging Judge"),
  288
Jesuits, English missions, 129
Jews, 259, 370, 377
Johnson, Samuel, 336–7
Jones, Inigo, 189, 194–5, 196, 212

Jonson, Ben, 196
Josselin, Ralph, 163
JPs, *see* justices of the peace
judicial system, *see* courts of law; trials
Julius II, Pope, 64
Junto, 310–14, 327
justices of the peace (JPs), 21, 50, 51, 372
Juxon, Archbishop William, 250

Kensington Palace, 303, 305
Kent, 191
Kent, Henry Grey, marquess of, 333
Kent, William, 352
Keppel, Arnold Joost van, earl of
  Albemarle, 305
Keroualle, Louise de, *see* Portsmouth,
  Louise de Keroualle, duchess of
Kett, Robert, 100–1
Kildare, earls of (Fitzgerald family), 82, 142
Kildare, Gerald Fitzgerald, eighth earl of
  (1456–1513), 44
Kildare, Gerald Fitzgerald, ninth earl of
  (1487–1534), 82
Kildare, Thomas Fitzgerald, tenth earl of
  ("Silken Thomas"), 82–4
Kilkenny, Statutes of (1366), 10
King, Gregory, 346, 353, 354–5, 364, 370
King William's War, *see* Nine Years' War
  (1689–97)
kings and kingship, *see* monarchs and
  monarchy
King's Bench, 48, 188
Kinsale, siege of (1601), 143
kinship, 173
Kishlansky, Mark, 376
Kit-Kat Club, 357
Kneller, Sir Godfrey, 273
knights, 24
  distraint of knighthood, 229, 233
Knollys, Sir Francis, 115
Knox, John, 114

La Hogue, battle of (1692), 310
labor force, rural, 19–20, 155–6, 369–70
  wages, 20, 153, 156, 346
Laguerre, Louis, 352
Land Tax (1693), 310–11, 315, 346
landownership
  18th century, 346, 351
  and dissolution of monasteries, 85–6, 106
  under Henry VII, 52
  under Henry VIII, 84, 85–6
  Ireland, 144

landownership (*cont'd*)
  landlords, powers of, 20–2
  late medieval, 20–1, 22, 23–4, 69
  late Tudor–early Stuart changes, 153, 155
  and litigation, 188
Langford, Paul, 344
Langside, battle of (1568), 124
languages
  Cornish, 12
  English, 4, 197–8
  Welsh, 8
Latimer, Bishop Hugh, 107
Latitudinarians, 362
Laud, Archbishop William, 226
Lauderdale, John Maitland, duke of, 277
law
  commons' attitude to, 373
  passage of, 49
  and the sovereign, 205, 210–11, 266
  see also courts of law
law and order, 177–82, 372–3
  rural, 21, 49–50, 174
  urban, 50
  Wales, 81
  see also courts of law
law schools, 189
lawyers, 366
lead-mining, 191
Leeds, 348
legislation, *see* law
Leibniz, Gottfried Wilhelm von, 361
Leicester, Robert Dudley, earl of
  art collection, 195
  death, 148
  and Dutch rebellion, 131, 132, 140
  and Elizabeth I, 115, 116, 161
  investments, 126
  and Northern Rebellion (1569–70),
    129–30
  and patronage, 197
  personality, 115
  policies, 115–16
Lely, Sir Peter, 273
Lennox, Esmé Stuart, duke of, 208
Levant Company, 191
Levellers, 247, 251–2
Leyden University, 366
liberties, 80–1
Licensing Act (1662), 275
  lapse, 284
life expectancy, 15, 163, 345
  London, 184
Lilburne, John, 252

Limerick, Treaty of (1691), 307
Lincoln, John de la Pole, earl of, 41, 44
literacy, 19, 161, 163–4, 371–2
literature
  crime literature, 372
  Georgian, 356, 358, 359–60, 362–3
  late Tudor and early Stuart, 161, 196–200
Liveries, Statute Against (1487, 1504), 50
Liverpool, 348
livery companies, 183
livestock farming, 19, 100
  see also sheep farming
Lloyd's of London, 350
local government
  under Charles II, 287
  corporations, 50, 183
  after Glorious Revolution, 300–1
  under James II, 291
  late medieval, 49–50
  during Protectorate, 260
Locke, John, 286, 287, 360, 362
Locke, Matthew, 356
Lollards, 30
Lombe, John, 348
London, *186, 187*
  18th century, 368
  and Edward IV, 36
  Great Fire (1666), 275
  Great Plague (1665), 275, 345
  late medieval, 15–17
  layout, 185–9
  life in, 184–9
  livery companies, 183
  population, 17, 29, 184, 368
  "season," 162, 352–3
  and trade, 189–90, 275, 348
London, Treaty of (1518), 61
London, Treaty of (1604), 224
London Bridge, 185, *187*
Longleat House, 159
lord chancellors, 47, 56
lords lieutenant, 49
Louis XI, king of France, 37
Louis XII, king of France, 59, 61, 65
Louis XIII, king of France, 230
Louis XIV, king of France, 274
  and Charles II, 277, 278–9, 287
  economy under, 330, 336–7
  foreign policy, 277–9, 294, 300
  and James II, 300, 305–6, 312, 316–17
  and Nine Years' War (1689–97), 302,
    308, 312
  and Old Pretender, 316–17

religious policies, 348
and War of Spanish Succession
    (1702–14), 316–17, 323, 325, 327,
    330
and William III, 312
Louis XV, king of France, 343
Lowndes, William, 313
Ludford Bridge, battle of (1459), 36
Lumley, Richard, Lord, 293–4
Luther, Martin, 72, 90–1

MacCulloch, Diarmaid, 68
madness, under the law, 258
Magellan, Ferdinand, 127
Malplaquet, battle of (1709), 327, 330
Manchester, 348
Manchester, Edward Montagu, earl of,
    243, 244
Mandeville, Bernard de, 362
Manley, Mrs., 359
manors, *18*
    labor force, 19–20
    and landlords, 20–2
    manorial courts, 179
manufacturers, 364
Marches, Welsh, 8, 11–12, 38, 80, 81
Margaret of Anjou, 33, 36, 37
Margaret Tudor, queen of Scotland (James
    IV's wife), 45, 61, 65
Marlborough, John Churchill, duke of
    fall, 333, 334
    and James II, 288, 295, 308
    and politics, 331
    and War of Spanish Succession
        (1702–14), 319, 323–5, 327, 330
Marlborough, Sarah Churchill, duchess of,
    319, 333
Marlowe, Christopher, 196
marriage
    average age, 158, 162, 345
    nobles and gentry, 158–9
    non-elite, 162, 164–6, 174
    registration, 258
Marston Moor, battle of (1644), 243
Martin V, Pope, 30
Marvell, Andrew, 282, 356
Marxist theory, Civil Wars, 203
Mary I, queen of England and Ireland, *105*
    birth, 63
    death, 110–11, 112
    marriage, 61–2, 105–6, 110–11
    personality, 104
    reign, 103–11

and religion, 106–10
Mary II, queen of England, Scotland, and
    Ireland, *297*
    accession to throne, 296
    death, 304
    during James II's reign, 292
    marriage, 281
    personality and popularity, 303–4
    place in succession, 274
    reign, 303–4
Mary Queen of Scots
    and Edward VI, 95, 98–9
    execution, 134
    personality and appearance, 124
    and plots against Elizabeth I, 129–30, 134
    reign, 123–5
Mary Beatrice of Modena, queen of
    England, Scotland and Ireland, 281,
    292, *293*, 295
Mary of Guise, 123
Mary Tudor, queen of France and duchess
    of Suffolk, 61, 65, 103
Maryland, 193
Masham, Abigail, 333
masquerade balls, 358
masques, 196, 212, 229
Massachusetts Bay Company, 191, 193
mathematics, 361
Matilda, queen of England, 64
Maurice of Nassau, Prince, 140
Maximilian I, Holy Roman Emperor, 59,
    61
Maximilian II, king of Bavaria, 323
May, Hugh, 356
Mayflower, 193
Medici, Catherine de', 125
medicine, 168, 345, 366, 374
Medina del Campo, Treaty of (1489), 45
Medina-Sidonia, Alonso Pérez de Guzmán,
    duke of, 135, 137
menopause, 162
Merchant Adventurers, 100, 189–91
merchant marine, 348
merchants, 364
metals, 14, 191, 348
Methven, Henry Stewart, Lord, 65
Middlesex, Lionel Cranfield, earl of,
    214–16, 220
middling rank, 364–9
Midlands, 12–13, 348
militia
    under Charles II, 266–7
    under Elizabeth I, 136

Militia Acts (1661, 1662), 266
Millenary Petition (1603), 224
mills, 21
Milton, John, 251, 358
mining, 191, 346, 348, 368
Minorca, 334
monarchs and monarchy
    Anne's powers, 321, 331, 338
    Charles I on, 220, 234
    Charles I's trial, implications of, 248–50
    Charles II on, 274–5
    Charles II's powers, 266–8, 270
    contemporary views of female rule, 64
    duties owed to, 27
    eligibility for, 25
    French absolutism, 274
    Glorious Revolution's influence, 298–9,
      309
    Hanoverian powers, 341
    Henry VII on, 42
    Henry VIII's changes, 79–80, 87, 97
    James I on, 208–9
    James II on, 290
    moral responsibilities, 27
    papacy's power, 30, 67
    and Parliament, 49, 205, 210–11, 233,
      341
    Parliament's abolition of office, 250
    post-Restoration beliefs, 265–6
    post-Restoration powers, 266–8, 270
    rights and powers, medieval, 23
    rights and powers, Stuart era, 204–5,
      210–11, 233
    rise of, 5–8
    Tory view, 285, 286
    Whig view, 202, 284, 286
    William III's powers, 312–13
monasteries, dissolution of, 85–6, 106, 184
Monck, Gen. George, 261–2
money
    banks, 349
    coinage, 102, 153
    credit exploitation, growth in, 313–14
    credit facilities, 184
    insurance, 350
    South Sea Bubble, 342
    stock market, 349–50
Monmouth, James Scott, duke of, 284,
    287, 288
Monmouth's Rebellion (1685), 288–9
monopolies, royal, 146–8, 191, 213, 229,
    233
Monteagle, William Parker, Lord, 225

morality
    18th century, 371
    Church's influence, 69, 371
    among clergy, 70–2
    Commonwealth legislation, 257
    legislation, 178–9
    Protectorate's attempted reforms, 260
    sex and marriage, 164–5
    sexual fidelity, 158
Moray, James Stewart, earl of, 123–4
More, Sir Thomas
    life, 54, 67–8, 74, 77
    writings, 21, 39, 70, 159, 161
mortality, 15, 162–3, 345
    London, 184
mountains, 13
Mountjoy, Charles Blount, Lord, 143
Muggleton, Lodowick, 254
Mugletonians, 254
murder, 177, 373
Muscovy Company, 191
music, 195–6, 273, 356, 357, 363
    public concerts, 358

Nantes, Edict of (1598), 141
Naseby, battle of (1645), 244
Nashe, Thomas, 198
National Covenant (1638), 231
    see also Covenanters
national debt, 311, 312–13
natural resources, 14
Navigation Acts (1650–1, 1660), 257,
    276
Nayler, James, 254
neighborliness, 173–4
Netherlands, Dutch Republic (United
    Provinces)
    Charles II's alliances with, 278, 281
    Commonwealth trade war, 257, 260
    Dutch massacre of colony at Amboyna
      (1623), 192
    and Louis XIV, 278
    Nine Years' War (1689–97), 302, 308,
      312
    religion, 276
    Second Anglo-Dutch war (1665–7), 275,
      276–7
    Third Anglo-Dutch war (1672–4), 277,
      280
    and War of Spanish Succession
      (1702–14), 334
Netherlands, Spanish
    French invasion (1667), 278

revolt against Spanish rule, 128, 131–2,
   137, 140
New Model Army
   creation, 244
   in Ireland, 255–6
   paid off, 267
   and Parliament, 246–7, 255, 261
   politicization, 246–7, 251–2
   in Scotland, 256
Newburn, battle of (1640), 232
Newby, Edward, 165
Newcastle, 191, 368
Newfoundland, 334, 336, 347
news distribution, 19
newspapers, 251, 319, 349, 359
Newton, Sir Isaac, 361–2
Nine Years' War (1594–1603), 141–4
Nine Years' War (1689–97), 302, 308, 312
   financing, 310–12
nobility and noble families
   18th-century attitudes, 360
   18th-century position, 344, 346, 350–1
   childcare, 156–7
   daily life, 156–62, 352–3
   duties owed to, 27, 172–3, 360
   education, 157, 158
   expenditure, 354–5
   funerals, 168
   and Glorious Revolution, 298
   growth in numbers, 154
   and Henry VII, 50–1
   and Henry VIII, 58–9
   houses and households, 20, 159–61,
      351–2, 352, 353
   income, 24, 56, 155, 351, 354–5
   and James II, 291
   late medieval, 23–4
   and law and order, 49
   marriage, 158–9
   mobility, 28
   moral responsibilities, 27, 172–3, 360
   in North, 12
   pastimes, 161–2, 352–3, 357–8
   powers as landlords, 20–2
   in remote areas, 80–1
   and Restoration, 261, 265
   sale of titles, 154, 213
   younger sons, 157, 351
Nonconformists
   18th century, 370
   under Anne, 322, 337–8
   under Charles II, 269–70, 280, 281, 287
   under George I, 343

and Glorious Revolution, 296–8,
   299–300
under James II, 290–1
sects during Commonwealth and
   Protectorate, 252–5
and Tories, 285
and Whigs, 285
see also Puritans and Puritanism
nonjurors, 303
Norfolk, Thomas Howard, third duke of
   (1473–1554), 55, 68, 78, 94, 95
Norfolk, Thomas Howard, fourth duke of
   (1536–72), 129–30
North
   famine (1590s), 146
   geography and government, 12–13
   industry, 13
   under Henry VIII, 81
   Northern Rebellion (1569–70), 129–30
   Pilgrimage of Grace (1536–7), 77–8, 81
North, Council of the, 81, 233
North Africa
   English possessions, 273
   pirates, 260
North American English colonies, 192–3
   18th century, 347
   Canada, 334, 336
   emigration to, 345
   trade with, 257
   transportation to, 288
Northampton, battle of (1460), 36
Northampton, Henry Howard, earl of, 224
Northern Ireland, 10–11
Northern Rebellion (1569–70), 129–30
Northumberland, earls of (Percy family),
   12, 81
Northumberland, Henry Percy, earl of, 81
Northumberland, John Dudley, duke of
   (formerly earl of Warwick), 101–4
Northumberland, Thomas Percy, earl of,
   129–30
Norwich
   and Kett's Rebellion (1549), 101
   population, 17, 182, 368
   wool trade, 184
Nottingham, Daniel Finch, earl of, 334
Nottinghamshire, 191
Nova Scotia, 334, 336
novels, 359

Oates, Titus, 282–3
Old Corps, 342
Old Sarum, 48

Orford, Edward Russell, earl of, 310
Orléans, Henrietta Anne, duchess of, 278
Ormond, earls of (Butler family), 82–4, 142
Ormond, James Butler, marquess of (later
    first duke of), 241
Ormond, James Butler, second duke of,
    295, 334
Oudenarde, battle of (1708), 327
outdoor relief, 176
Overbury, Sir Thomas, 214
Oxford, Robert Harley, earl of
    and Anne, 319, 331, 333, 337–8
    as collector, 358
    and development of Tory party, 314, 321,
        358
    and Treaty of Utrecht (1713), 334–6
    and William III, 314
Oxford University, 56

painting, 195, 273, 352, 356
Pale, Irish, 10, 82
pamphlets, political and religious, 251,
    284, 321
Panama, and Drake, 126, 140
papacy
    and Elizabeth I, 122, 128, 130, 135
    and Henry VIII, 62, 66–7
    and Ireland, 83–4
papal authority, 30, 67
    and Elizabeth I, 118
    and Henry VIII, 73–6
    see also Roman Catholic Church
Parliament
    under Anne, 321, 327–8
    Barebones Parliament, 257–8
    buildings, 188
    as cause of Civil Wars, 202–3
    and Charles I, see below
    and Charles II, see below
    during Commonwealth, 250, 251–8
    composition, 24, 48–9, 353, 368
    Convention Parliament (Glorious
        Revolution), 295–6, 297
    and Elizabeth I, 144–8, 205
    and Glorious Revolution, 295–6, 297,
        298–9, 300, 309
    Goodwin's case (1604), 210–11
    Gunpowder Plot (1605), 225
    and Henry VII, 43, 51, 52
    and Henry VIII, 68, 73, 79–80, 86, 87,
        95, 97, 205
    and James I, 209–11, 213, 214, 216,
        217–18, 220–1

and James II, 288, 290
and Mary I, 106
meeting frequency, 49, 233, 275, 313, 341
passage of legislation, 49
during Protectorate, 258, 260, 261
Rump, Cromwell's dissolution, 257
and Scottish union (1707), 329
and the sovereign, 49, 205, 210–11, 233,
    341
Walpole's control, 342–3
and William III, 310, 312–13, 314–15
see also House of Commons; House of
    Lords
Parliament, and Charles I
    adjournment (1629), 228
    Buckingham, attempts to impeach, 221,
        222
    Civil Wars, 238–44
    Long Parliament, 232–7
    Personal Rule, 228
    Petition of Right (1628), 222
    post-Civil War negotiations, 244–6, 248
    Pride's Purge (1648), 248
    Rump, 248, 261, 262
    Short Parliament, 232
    trial and execution of king, 248–50
Parliament, and Charles II
    attempt to rule without, 286–7
    Cavalier Parliament (1661–78), 268–70,
        274, 275, 281–2
    Convention Parliament (Restoration),
        262, 266–7, 268
    Danby's bribery, 281–2
    Exclusion Parliaments, 283, 284–5, 286
    Oxford Parliament, 286
Parma, Alexander de Farnese, duke of, 132,
    137, 140
Parr, Catherine, queen of England and
    Ireland, 96
Parsons, Robert, 129
Partition Treaty (1697), 312, 336–7
party politics
    under Anne, 319–23, 325–8, 329–34,
        337–8
    development, 319–20, 321
    under George I, 341–3
    origins, 265–6, 284–6
    under William III, 305
    see also Tory party; Whig party
The Paston Letters, 21
paternalism, 27, 172–3, 301, 343–4, 360
patronage
    arts, 194, 197, 273, 357–8

government, 342, 367
Pavia, battle of (1525), 61
Peace and War, Act Annent (1703), 328
peers and peerage, *see* nobility and noble
    families
Penal Code (1695–1727), 307
Penry, John, 199
Pepys, Samuel, 313
Petition of Right (1628), 222
Petty, Sir William, 362
petty sessions, 50, 179
Petworth House, 352
pharmacists, *see* apothecaries
Philip II, king of Spain
    and Elizabeth I, 116, 128, 130, 132
    finances, 145
    and French civil wars, 140
    invasion of England (1588), 133–8
    and Mary I, 106, 110
    size of empire, 126
Philip III, king of Spain, 143
Philip V, king of Spain (Philippe, duke of
    Anjou), 316, 327, 330, 334, 336
physicians, 366
Pickering, Sir William, 116
Pilgrimage of Grace (1536–7), 77–8, 81
Pinkie Cleugh, battle of (1547), 98
piracy
    Barbary pirates, 260
    English against Spain, 126–7
Pitt, Thomas "Diamond," 367
Pius V, Pope, 130
plague, 15, 19, 275, 345
plantation, Irish, 10, 141, 144, 235–6, 256
playhouses, 185, 197, 358
plays and playwrights, 196–7, 273, 356,
    358
    female playwrights, 359
    see also masques
pluralism, 70, 366
Plymouth, 348
Plymouth Plantation, 193
pocket boroughs, 48
poetry, 198, 273, 356, 363
Pole, Reginald, Cardinal, 106, 107
political economics, development of, 362–3
political parties, *see* party politics
Pollock, Linda, 163
Poor Law
    16th century, 85, 146, 154, 176–7
    18th century, 372
    Commonwealth reforms, 257
Poor Palatines, 330–1

Pope, Alexander, 342, 359, 361, 363
Popish Plot (1678), 282–3
population
    16th-century expansion, 152
    17th and 18th centuries, 344–5
    under Edward VI, 99
    late medieval, 15
    towns, 15–17, 29
Portland, Hans William Bentinck, earl of,
    305
Portland, Richard, earl of (formerly Lord
    Weston), 228–9
Portsmouth, 348
Portsmouth, Louise de Keroualle, duchess
    of, 273
postal service, 162, 184, 349
pottery industry, 191
poverty, 175–7, 370
    see also Poor Law; social welfare
Poynings, Sir Edward, 82
Poynings's Law (1494), 82
Praemunire, Statutes of (1353, 1365,
    1393), 30, 67
    Henry VIII's charges under, 67, 73
Presbyterian Kirk in Scotland
    establishment, 123, 124
    under James I, 231
    Scots attempt to impose on English,
        243–4, 247
    seizure of power after Glorious
        Revolution, 328
    workings and beliefs, 223
Presbyterianism
    under Charles II, 269–70
    within English Parliament, 243, 245,
        246, 248, 255
press
    newspapers, 251, 319, 349, 359
    pamphlets, political and religious, 251,
        284, 321
    publishing industry, 198, 199, 251,
        358–9
    see also censorship
pretenders to throne, 44, 45
prices, food, 21, 100, 146, 153, 346
Pride, Col. Thomas, 248
Pride's Purge (1648), 248
"princes in the Tower," 39–40
    pretenders, 44, 45
Prior, Matthew, 336–7
Privy Chamber, 47
Privy Council
    under Edward VI, 101, 102

Privy Council (*cont'd*)
  under Elizabeth I, 118, 148–9
  establishment, 46, 80
Privy Seal office, 47
professional classes, 365–7
propaganda
  and Henry VII, 42, 51
  and party politics, 321, 358
prophesyings, 121
Protectorate, 258–61
  finances during, 260
  foreign policy, 260
  government, 259–60
  local government, 260
  and religion, 259
Protestants and Protestantism
  16th-century beliefs, 89–92
  under Edward VI, 98–9, 102–3
  under Elizabeth I, 117–19
  emigration to America, 193
  France, 125, 140–1
  under Henry VIII, 88–9, 93–4, 94, 96, 97
  Ireland, 10–11, 142, 223, 256, 307
  under Mary I, 104, 106–10
  Scotland, 123–4
  see also Huguenots; Nonconformists;
    Presbyterian Kirk in Scotland;
    Presbyterianism; Puritans and
    Puritanism; Reformation
Provisors, Statutes of (1351, 1390), 30
Prynne, William, 226
public houses, 20, 179
publishing industry, 198, 199, 251, 358–9
Pulteney, Sir William, 342
punishment, *see* crime and punishment
Purcell, Henry, 273, 303, 356
Puritans and Puritanism
  beliefs, 120–1, 170, 171, 222–3
  as cause of Civil Wars, 202
  and Charles I, 226, 229
  under Charles II, 266, 268–70
  definition, 120
  under Elizabeth I, 119–21
  emigration to America, 193
  James I on, 224
  under James I, 222–3, 224
  under Mary I, 119
  and morality, 179, 260
  in Protectorate government, 260
  and witchcraft, 180
  see also Nonconformists
Putney Debates (1647), 247
Pym, John, 233, 234–5, 241, 243

Quaker Act (1662), 269
Quakers, 253–4, 268, 269, 270, 287
quarter sessions, 50, 179
Queen Anne's Bounty, 367
Queen Anne's War, *see* Spanish Succession,
    War of the
Queen's House, Greenwich, 212

radicalism, under Commonwealth, 251–5
Rainsborough, Col. Thomas, 247
Ralegh, Sir Walter, 146, 148, 161
Ramillies, battle of (1706), 327
ranks, social
  18th century, 343–4
  18th-century middling, 364–9
  Glorious Revolution's effect, 301
  late medieval, 22–30
  late Tudor–early Stuart period, 154–6
  mobility, 73, 154–5
  urban, 182–3
Ranters, 253
rape, 177
Rastadt, Treaty of (1714), 334
rationality and reason, 360–2
rebellion, medieval view of, 25–6
Reformation
  Catholic vs. Protestant beliefs, 89–92
  causes, 68–73
  church buildings, changes to, 71, 93,
    102–3
  under Edward VI, 98–9, 102–3
  under Elizabeth I, 108, 117–19, 120,
    121, 122, 130–1
  under Henry VIII, 73–8, 85–6, 88–9,
    93–4, 94–5, 97
  and Ireland, 83–4
  under Mary I, 104, 106–10
  Roman Catholic Church's response,
    128–9
  Scotland, 123–4
  and witchcraft, 180
  see also Nonconformists; Presbyterian
    Kirk in Scotland; Presbyterianism;
    Protestants and Protestantism;
    Puritans and Puritanism
Regency Act (1706), 327
religion
  16th-century beliefs, 89–92, 107–8
  18th-century beliefs, 370–2
  and Age of Reason, 362
  under Anne, 321–2, 325, 330–1, 337–8,
    367
  under Charles I, 225–7, 233, 235

under Charles II, 268–70, 280, 281
during Commonwealth, 252–5, 257
in daily life, 169–72
under Edward VI, 98–9, 102–3
under Elizabeth I, 108, 117–19, 120, 121, 122, 130–1
England, pre-Reformation, 9, 18–19, 22–3, 29–30, 68–73
France, 125, 140–1
and Glorious Revolution, 296–8, 299–300
under Henry VIII, 73–8, 85–6, 88–9, 93–4, 94–5
Ireland, 10–11, 83–4, 142, 223
under James I, 206, 222–5
under James II, 290, 291–2
under Mary I, 104, 106–10
place in daily life, 17–19, 30, 68–73, 170, 371–2
during Protectorate, 259
Scotland, 9, 123, 124, 223, 231, 328
Wales, 8
see also Catholics and Catholicism; Nonconformists; Presbyterian Kirk in Scotland; Presbyterianism; Protestants and Protestantism; Puritans and Puritanism; Reformation; Roman Catholic Church; Roman Catholic Church in England
rents, 21, 153, 346
Republicans, Irish, 11
Requests, Court of, 233
Restoration, 261–4, 263
    Settlements, 266–70
Restraint of Annates, Act in (1534), 75
Restraint of Appeals, Act in (1533), 74–5
revenues, government, see finances, government; taxation
Revisionists, 203
Rhode Island, 193
Rhuddlan, Statute of (1284), 8
Riccio, David, 124
Rich, Christopher, 358
Rich, John, 358
Richard II, king of England, 32
Richard III, king of England (formerly duke of Gloucester), 31, 37, 38–41, 42
Richmond, Henry Fitzroy, duke of, 64
Ridley, Bishop Nicholas, 107
Ridolfi, Robert, 130
riots, 180–2, 373
Ripon, Treaty of (1640), 232
rivers, 13, 184, 349

Rivers, Anthony, Earl, 39
Rizzio, David, see Riccio, David
roads, 162, 184, 349
Robsart, Amy, 116
Rochester, John Wilmot, earl of, 273, 356
Rochford, George Boleyn, Lord, 92
Rogers, John, 107
Roman Catholic Church
    Counter-Reformation, 128–9
    and divorce, 65
    and Elizabeth I, 128–9, 130
    England, Jesuit missions to, 128–9, 131
    England's severance from, 63–78
    English adherence to, 68–73
    hierarchy, 29–30
    see also Catholics and Catholicism; papacy; papal authority
Roman Catholic Church in England
    Church courts, 27
    corruption, 56, 91, 129
    income, 27, 74, 75
    place in daily life, 17–19, 30, 68–73
    see also Church of England
Roundheads
    definition, 239
    post-Restoration treatment, 272
    and Whig party, 265–6
Royal Africa Company, 191
Royal Exchange, London, 187
Royal Navy
    under Charles I, 221, 229
    under Charles II, 277
    under Elizabeth I, 131, 133, 135, 137
    under Henry VIII, 93, 133
    professionalization, 365–6
    under William III, 310
Royal Society, 271
Royalists, see Cavaliers
Rubens, Peter Paul, 195, 249
Rupert of the Rhine, Prince, 240, 243, 244, 245
rural life, 17–22, 24
    medicine, 345
    nobles and gentry, 159–61, 351–2
Rye House Plot (1683), 287
Ryswick, Treaty of (1697), 312

Sacheverell, Henry, 331, 332, 333, 359
St. Albans, battle of (1455), 36
St. Bartholomew's Day Massacre (1572), 125
St. John, Oliver, 233, 244

St. Kitts, 334, 336
Salisbury, Margaret, countess of, 41
Salisbury, Robert Cecil, earl of, *see* Cecil,
    Sir Robert, earl of Salisbury
Sancroft, Archbishop William, 292,
    366
satire, 198, 286, 342
Savoy, 323, 327
Saye and Sele, William, Viscount, 233,
    243–4
Scarisbrick, J. J., 68
Schism Act (1714), 337
scholarship, 161
    monarchs as scholars, 54, 114,
      206
scholarships, 367
Schomberg, Frederick Herman, duke of,
    306
schools, *see* education
science, 271, 360–1
Scotland
    Bishops' Wars (1639, 1640), 232
    under Charles I, 231–2, 234
    in Civil Wars, 243, 246, 247, 256
    Covenanters, 231, 243, 247, 256
    early history and development, 6–8,
      8–9
    and Edward VI, 98–9, 102
    and Elizabeth I, 123, 130
    after Glorious Revolution, 328–30
    and Henry VII, 44, 45
    and Henry VIII, 59, 95
    Jacobite Rebellion (1715), 341
    under James VI, 206, 230–1
    under Mary Queen of Scots, 122–5
    population, 18th century, 345
    religion, 9, 123, 124, 223, 231, 328
    today, 9
    Tudor relations with, 9
    union with England (1707), 9, 328–30
    see also Presbyterian Kirk in Scotland
sea, English relationship with, 4–5
Security, Act of (1703), 328
Sedgemoor, battle of (1685), 288
Sedley, Catherine, *see* Dorchester,
    Catherine Sedley, countess of
Seekers, 253
Selden, John, 210
Senegal Adventurers, 191
Septennial Act (1716), 341
serfdom, 19–20
servants, 161, 164, 367
Settlement, Act of (1662), 176

Settlement, Act of (1701), 299, 313, 315,
    327–8
Seymour, Jane, queen of England, 92, 93
Shaftesbury, Anthony Ashley Cooper, earl
    of (formerly Lord Ashley), 277, 282,
    283–4, 285, 287
Shakespeare, William, 197
    plays, 1–3, 25–6, 31, 32, 39
    sonnets, 198
sheep farming
    16th century, 100
    17th century, 346
    late medieval, 13, 14, 21
    see also enclosure
Sheffield, 191, 348
Sheldon, Archbishop Gilbert, 366
Sheppard, Jack, 372
sheriffs, 6, 50, 51
Ship Money, 229–30, 233
shipbuilding, 191, 348
shipping industry, 184
Shrewsbury, Charles Talbot, earl of, 293–4,
    339
Sicily, 334
Sidney, Algernon, 286, 287
Sidney, Henry, 293–4
Sidney, Sir Philip, 161
Sidney, Robert, 159
silk industry, 348, 349, 365
Simnel, Lambert, 44
simony, 56
Six Articles, Act of (1539), 94, 99
Sixtus V, Pope, 135
Skelton, John, 57
skimmington rides, 174
slave trade
    16th century, 126
    17th century, 191, 193
    18th century, 334, 336, 347
Smith, Sir Thomas, 192
social mobility, 73, 182–3
social order
    18th century, 343–4
    Great Chain of Being, 22–30
    Tudor–Stuart changes, 154–6
social welfare
    and the Church, 69, 86, 89,
      106–7
    and guilds, 183
    private and local initiatives, 176
    see also Poor Law
Societies, for the Reformation of Manners,
    371

Society for the Propagation of Christian Knowledge (SPCK), 371
Society for the Propagation of the Gospel (SPG), 371
Solway Marsh, battle of (1542), 95
Somers, John, Lord, 310, 357–8
Somerset, 191
Somerset, dukes of (Beaufort family), 33, 36
Somerset, Edward Beaufort, duke of, 36
Somerset, Edward Seymour, duke of (formerly earl of Hertford)
  and Henry VIII, 95, 96
  houses, 189
  as lord protector, 98–100, 101–2
Somerset, Frances Howard, countess of, 214
Somerset, Robert Carr, earl of, 208, 213–14
Somerset House, 189
Sophia, electress of Hanover, 315, 338
South Sea Bubble, 342
Southwark, 185
sovereignty, *see* monarchs and monarchy
spa towns, 353
Spain
  Charles I's war, 220–1, 229
  Dutch revolt, 128, 131–2, 137, 140
  and Elizabeth I, 116, 125–8, 130, 132
  Elizabeth I's war, 139–41, 216
  and Henry VII, 45
  and Henry VIII, 59, 61, 92, 93
  and Ireland, 143
  and James I, 216, 217, 218
  and Mary I, 110
  Parliament's power, 209
  and Protectorate, 260
  Thirty Years' War (1618–48), 216
Spanish Armada, 133–8, *136*, 201
Spanish Company, 191
Spanish Empire
  English naval attacks on, 126–7
  extent, 126, 132, 278
  Louis XIV's attempts to annex, 278
Spanish Inquisition, 126, 128
Spanish Succession, War of the (1702–14), 315–17, 323–7, *324*, *326*, 330
  Treaty of Utrecht (1713), 334–7
  Whig and Tory views, 322–3
SPCK, *see* Society for the Propagation of Christian Knowledge
Spectator, 359
SPG, *see* Society for the Propagation of the Gospel
Spenser, Edmund, 117, 142, 198
sport, 19, 208

Staffordshire, 191
Stanley family, 40–1
Staple Act (1663), 276
Star Chamber, 38, 45, 50, 57, 233
Steele, Richard, 358, 359
steelworking, 191, 348
Stewart, Henry (later Lord Methven), 65
stock market, 349–50
  Royal Exchange, 187
  South Sea Bubble, 342
Stone, Lawrence, 154, 155, 163, 203
Strafford, Thomas Wentworth, earl of, 232, 233, 234, 236
Strand, 185, 189
Stuart, Frances "La Belle," 274
Succession, Act of (1533), 75
Suckling, Sir John, 198
Suffolk, Charles Brandon, duke of, 65
sugar industry, 336, 347, 348
Sunderland, Charles Spencer, earl of, 310, 333
superstition, 179–80, 371
Supremacy, Act of (1534), 75–6
Supremacy, Act of (1559), 118
surgeons, 366
Surrey, Henry Howard, earl of, 96
suspending power, 229, 292
Sussex, 191
Sussex, Thomas Radcliffe, earl of, 115, 131
sweating sickness, 102, 114, 152
Swift, Jonathan
  and *Examiner*, 359
  on Ireland, 307–8
  on political economists, 362–3
  publishing history, 358
  on social order, 313–14
  on Walpole, 342

Tallard, Marshall Camille de, 323
Tallis, Thomas, 54, 195
Talman, William, 352
Tangier, 273
Tatler, 359
taverns, *see* alehouses; inns; public houses
Tawney, R. H., 154
taxation
  18th century, 343, 346
  Anglo-Saxon, 6
  under Charles I, 221–2, 228, 229–30, 232, 233
  under Charles II, 267, 287
  during Civil Wars, 241
  during Commonwealth, 258

taxation (*cont'd*)
  Cornish rebellion (1497), 44
  under Edward IV, 38
  under Edward VI, 100
  under Elizabeth I, 139, 145–8
  under Henry VII, 51–2
  under Henry VIII, 62, 84
  under James I, 213
  under James II, 288
  and Parliament, 49
  during Protectorate, 260
  under William III, 310–11, 313, 315
  see also Customs duties; Excise duties
Taylor, John, 198
tea, 348
Ten Articles, 93
Tenison, Archbishop, 366
terrorism, Irish, 11
Test Act (1673), 280, 297–8, 322
Tewkesbury, battle of (1471), 37
textile industry, 349
  see also silk industry; wool trade
Thames, River, 13, 185–6, *187*, 191
Thatcher, Margaret, 11, 238
theater and theaters, 185, 196–7, 357, 358
  see also masques; plays and playwrights
theft, 177–8, 372
theology
  16th-century beliefs, 89–92, 107–8
  18th-century beliefs, 370–2
  works on, 198
Thirty Years' War (1618–48), 216, 217
Thirty-Nine Articles of Faith (1563), 118
Thomas, Keith, 180
Thomason, George, 251
"Thorough," 229
Three Choirs Festival, 358
Thynne, Sir John, 159
Throckmorton, Job, 145
Tijou, Jean, 352
Tillotson, Archbishop John, 366
timber industry, 14
tin-mining, 191, 348
tithes, 27, 258
tobacco, 193, 347
Toland, John, 362
Toleration Act (1689), 297, 371
Tonson, Jacob, 358
Torrington, Arthur Herbert, earl of, 306–7
Tory party
  and Anne, 319–20, 325–7, 331, 333–4,
    337–8
  beliefs, 285, 286, 309

  and Charles II, 287
  and Exclusion Crisis, 285–6
  foreign policy, 322–3, 330
  and George I, 341
  and Glorious Revolution, 293–4, 296
  and Hanoverian succession, 321, 338
  and James II, 288, 291
  origins, 265, 285–6
  and religion, 322, 337–8
  and William III, 305, 308, 309, 314–15
Tournai, English capture of (1513), 59–61
Tower of London, 187
towns and cities
  18th century, 367–8
  government, 50, 183, 287
  growth in, 29
  hierarchy, 29
  late medieval, 15–17
  law and order, 50, 179
  life in, 182–5
  market towns, 17, 349
  migration to, 153–4, 182
  population, 15–17, 29
Towton Moor, battle of (1461), 36
trade
  16th and 17th centuries, 189–93
  18th century, 336, 346–8
  American colonies, 257
  under Charles II, 281, 287
  Ireland, 307
  merchants' lifestyle, 364
  under Protectorate, 260
  Scotland, 328
  see also grain trade; slave trade; wool
    trade
transport and transportation (goods), 13,
  162, 184, 349
transportation (people), 154, 288
Treason Act (1534), 75, 99
Treason Act (1563), 118
Treasury, 277, 313
trials, 178
Triennial Act (1642), 233, 275
Triennial Act (1694), 313
Tudor dynasty, background, 40
Tunstall, Bishop Cuthbert, 67, 107
Turkey Company, 191
turnpikes, 349
Tyndale, William, 70, 93
Tyrconnell, Richard Talbot, earl of, 306
Tyrconnell, Rory O'Donnell, earl of, 144
Tyrone, Hugh O'Neill, earl of (the Great
  O'Neill), 142–4

Ulster
  20th century, 10
  plantations, 10, 144, 235–6
  rebellion (1594–1603), 141–4
  and William III, 306, 307
  see also Northern Ireland
unemployment, 100, 370
Uniformity, Act of (1549), 99
Uniformity, Act of (1662), 269
Unionists, 11
universities, scholarships, 367
urban life, *see* towns and cities
Uses, Statute of (1536), 84
Utrecht, Treaty of (1713), 334–7

vagrancy, 175–6, 370
Vagrancy Act (1547), 176
Vanbrugh, Sir John, 352, 358
Vauxhall Gardens, 358
Verrio, Antonio, 356
Versailles, Palace of, 330, 336–7
Verviens, Treaty of (1598), 141
Vestarian Controversy, 120–1
village life, *see* rural life
Villiers, Barbara, *see* Castlemaine, Barbara
    née Villiers Palmer, countess of
Virginia, 192–3
Virginia Company, 191

wages, 20, 153, 156, 346
Wakefield, battle of (1460), 36
Wales
  coal-mining, 191
  county map, 7
  early history and development, 6–8
  geography, 13
  under Henry VIII, 81
  language, 8, 81
  Marches, Welsh, 8, 11–12, 38, 80,
    81
  religion, 8
  today, 8
  union with England (1284), 8
Wales, prince of, creation of title, 8
wall, giving the, 27–8
Wallace, Sir William ("Braveheart"), 9
Walpole, Sir Robert, 342–3, 356
Walsingham, Sir Francis
  death, 148
  and foreign policy, 131
  investments, 126
  as spy-master, 115, 130, 134
Warbeck, Perkin, 44, 45

Wars of the Roses (1455–85), 31, 32–41,
    34
  persistent memory under Henry VIII, 64
Warwick, Edward, earl of, 41, 43, 44
Warwick, John Dudley, earl of, *see*
    Northumberland, John Dudley, duke of
Warwick, Richard Neville, earl of
    ("kingmaker"), 36, 37
Weber, Max, 202
Welsh language, 8, 81
Wentworth, Paul, 145
Wentworth, Peter, 145
West Country
  famine (1590s), 146
  geography, 12
  Monmouth's Rebellion (1685), 288–9
  rebellion (1549), 99, 102
  sheep farming, 14, 191
West Indies, 260, 334, 336, 347
Westminster, 188–9, *188*
Westminster, Act of (1714), 307
Westmorland, Charles Neville, earl of,
    129–30
Westmorland, earls of (Neville family), 12,
    36, 81
Weston, Richard, Lord, *see* Portland,
    Richard, earl of
Wexford, Cromwell's capture (1649),
    255–6
Wharton, Thomas, Lord, 310
Whig party
  and Act of Union (1707), 329
  allegiances, 287
  and Anne, 319–20, 325, 327–8, 330–1,
    333–4, 337–8
  beliefs, 202, 284, 286, 309
  and Charles II, 287
  and Exclusion Crisis, 284–6
  foreign policy, 322–3, 327, 330
  and George I, 341–2
  and Glorious Revolution, 293–4,
    295–6
  and Hanoverian succession, 321, 327–8,
    338
  and James II, 288, 291
  Junto, 310–14, 327, 330–1, 333
  and middling sort, 367
  origins, 265–6, 284
  and religion, 322, 330–1, 337–8
  and Treaty of Utrecht (1713), 334–5
  and William III, 305, 308–14
Whitehall, 188–9, 357
  Banqueting House, 194–5, 212, 249

White's, 357
Whitgift, John, 121
Whittington, Dick, 182–3
Wild, Jonathan, 372
William III, king of England, Scotland, and
    Ireland (1650–1702, William of
    Orange), 297
  accession to throne, 296
  death, 317
  as Dutch stadholder, 278
  favorites, 305
  finances under, 310–12, 312–14
  foreign policy, 294, 300, 302, 304
  as general, 312
  and Glorious Revolution, 294–6
  government, 313
  Irish campaigns, 305–8
  marriage, 281
  on Mary II, 304
  Nine Years' War (1689–97), 302, 308,
    312
  and Parliament, 310, 312–13,
    314–15
  and party politics, 305
  personality, 304–5
  popularity, 303, 304
  reign, 302–17
  religious beliefs, 297
William of Orange (1533–84, "William the
    Silent"), 128, 132
Williams, Roger, 193
Wilson, Thomas, 157
Wine Act (1703), 328
Winstanley, Gerrard, 253
Winthrop, Gov. John, 193
Wise, Henry, 352
witchcraft, 179–80, 371
Wolsey, Thomas, Cardinal
  and Henry VIII's divorce, 65–7
  palaces, 56, 188
  and papal authority, 72–3
  powers and policies, 55–8, 59–62
  and Thomas Cromwell, 73
women
  authors, 359
  contemporary views of female rule, 64
  daily life, 373–4
  education, 158, 163
  and inheritance, 23–4

Knox on, 114
labor, 20, 156, 165, 348, 373–4
literacy, 372
marital relationships, 165
menopause, 162
moral standards expected, 158
rape, 177
and riots, 181, 374
status, 25, 374
widows, 165–6, 370, 373
and witchcraft, 180
wood, *see* timber industry
Wood, Anthony à, 371
woods, *see* forests
Woodville, Elizabeth, 37, 39
Wool Act (1703), 328
wool trade
  15th century, 17
  16th century, 100, 153, 154, 190
  17th century, 153
  18th century, 347–8
  decentralization, 184
  decline in, 190–1
  East Anglia, 13, 14
  and London, 190
Worcester, battle of (1651), 256
workhouses, 176
Wren, Sir Christopher, 273, 289–90, 303,
    356
Wrightson, Keith, 163
Wrigley, E. A., 184
Wyatt, Sir Thomas (1503–42), 161
Wyatt, Sir Thomas, the Younger
    (1520?–54), 106
Wycherley, William, 273, 356, 358

yeomen, 24, 155, 354, 369
Yeomen of the Guard, 47
York, population, 17, 182
York, Anne Hyde, duchess of, 281
York, Edward, duke of, *see* Edward IV, king
    of England (formerly duke of York)
York, James, duke of, *see* James II and VII,
    king of England, Scotland and Ireland
    (formerly duke of York)
York, Richard, duke of (1411–60), 33–6
York, Richard, duke of (1472–83?; "prince
    in Tower"), 39–40, 41, 44
Yorkshire Plot (1663), 269